CUNNINGHAM'S ANCIENT GEOGRAPHY OF INDIA

CUNNINGHAM'S ANCIENT GEOGRAPHY OF INDIA

SURENDRANATH MAJUMDAR SASTRI

GYAN

Published by

Gyan Publishing House
5, Ansari Road
Daryaganj, New Delhi-110002
Phone: 011-47034999, 9811692060
E-mail: books@gyanbooks.com

Distribution Network
gyanbooks.com
India, USA, Canada, UK, Australia

ISBN: 978-93-7169-556-5 (PB)

First Published, 1924

2nd Impression 2025

Printed at: Gyan Press, Delhi.

CUNNINGHAM'S ANCIENT GEOGRAPHY OF INDIA
Author: SURENDRANATH MAJUMDAR SASTRI

SIR ALEXANDER CUNNINGHAM.

FRONTISPIECE.

CUNNINGHAM'S

ANCIENT GEOGRAPHY

OF

INDIA.

CUNNINGHAM'S ANCIENT GEOGRAPHY OF INDIA.

EDITED
WITH INTRODUCTION AND NOTES

BY

SURENDRANATH MAJUMDAR SASTRI, M.A.
Premchand Roychand Scholar,
Reader, Patna University.

CALCUTTA:
CHUCKERVERTTY, CHATTERJEE & Co., LTD.,
15, College Square,
1924.

PREFACE TO THE NEW EDITION.

The late Sir Alexander Cunningham's Ancient Geography of India is the standard treatise on the subject, and is an indispensable hand-book for those who are interested in Indian antiquities. Though it is over fifty years that it was published, and so naturally some portions have become to some extent antiquated in the light of more recent knowledge, it has not yet been superseded, and still remains indispensable. Unfortunately it has long been out of print, and students of Ancient Indian History have thus been put to great difficulties. When therefore the Publishers, after securing the very kind permission of Lt. Col. A. J. C. Cunningham, R.E., son of the late Sir Alexander, to bring out a new edition of this work, invited me to undertake the work of revision, I accepted the offer very gladly, though I knew full well the great difficulty and responsibility of the task.

The text in the present edition is exactly the same as in the original edition. But it has not been found possible to keep the paging identical. For the convenience, however, of those who wish to localise any references to the original edition, the original paging has also been given within brackets, in the table of Contents and Notes.

I have tried, in my Introduction and Notes, to supplement Cunningham's text by the most up-to-date information available to me which could be gleaned from the latest researches on the subject. And I venture to hope that with the help of these supplementary notes, the student will be accurately posted in the subject. As the space at my disposal is very short, I have been compelled to use in these Notes a very concise style, almost reminiscent of the Sûtra literature (अर्द्धमात्रा लाघवेन पुत्रोत्पत्तिः) and to refrain from pointing out mere slips of pen, exploded theories of Chronology (e.g. Imperial Guptas flourishing in the first or second century A.D.), etc. which could be easily detected.

As to the spelling of Classical words, I have followed M'Crindle and Schoff; and in the matter of Chinese names I have followed Watters. In the transliteration of Sanskrit and Pali words, I have to offer an apology. The use of proper diacritical marks to indicate cerebrals, palatals, etc. has had to be abandoned due to the exigencies of the Press; but I have tried to minimise this inconvenience by giving, within brackets, the words in Sanskrit letters, in my Introduction and Notes.

I have tried to indicate as a rule my sources by giving full references; and my thanks are due to all those from whom such help has been obtained. But I think I ought specially to mention my indebtedness to Mr. Pargiter for the majority of my references to Epic and Purânic literature.

I feel I shall be failing in my duty if I do not close this short preface on a more personal note. To the inspiration of two men I owe all the work that

I have been able to do in the domain of Ancient Indian History—Mahâmahopâdhyâya Haraprasâd Sâstri and the late Sir Ashutosh Mukhopâdhyâya. Mahâmahopâdhyâya Sâstri is my *Guru* in the field of Indology; and it was the patronage and encouragement of the late Sir Ashutosh which enabled me to carry on the research-work the results of which are embodied here. My most heart-felt thanks are due to them both. And I am only sorry that Sir Ashutosh has not lived to see the completion of this work.

My own, and also the Publishers' thanks are due to Lt. Col. A. J. C. Cunningham R.E., the worthy son of our author, for his kind permission to the Publishers to bring out an up-to-date and revised edition of this standard treatise of his illustrious father.

S. N. M.

The 10th September, 1924,
CALCUTTA.

CONTENTS.

N.B.—The figures within brackets give the page number of the original edition.

INTRODUCTION

INTRODUCTION

TO THE STUDY OF

THE ANCIENT GEOGRAPHY OF INDIA.

1. Pioneers in this field of research.

1. *Mr. Francis Wilford, Engineer.*—"A learned and laborious, but injudicious writer" (Wilson's *Hindu Theatre,* I.9). His essays—on Egypt and the Nile from the Ancient Books of the Hindus ; the Sacred Islands in the West ; etc. (*Asiatic Researches* III, IX, XIV); the Comparative Geography of India (published posthumously in 1851). His great merit was to point out the existence of Sanskrit sources of geography. His account of the Nile from Sanskrit sources enabled Lieut. J. H. Speke to discover its source. (Speke's *Discovery of the Source of the Nile,* chaps. I, V, X).

2. *H. H. Wilson.*—In 1824 he contributed to the *Oriental Magazine* (Vol. II, p. 180) an article in which he described a Skr. MS. professing to be a section of the *Bhabishya Purâna* which elucidates the local geography of Bengal. In his translation of the *Vishnu Purâna* he commented on the Purânic geography. His *Notes on the Indica of Ctesias* was published in 1836 (Oxford). The geographical portion of his *Ariana Antiqua* (London, 1841)—an account of the coins and antiquities discovered by Mr. Masson during his travels in Afghanistan—is full and valuable.

3. *Christian Lassen*—the encyclopœdic Indologist.—(*a*) *His Pentapotamia Indica* (1827) gives an account of the Punjab from the "classical" sources and from the *Mahâbhârata,* the *Koshas* and other Skr. sources. (*b*) In the geographical section of his *Indische Alterthumskunde*

(Bonn, 1843)—the very learned and exhaustive work on the antiquities of India—he described the physical features of India and gave (especially in the footnotes) whatever information he could collect from classical and Skr. sources. Though "his system of identification is based on a wrong principle" (M'Crindle's *Ptolemy*, Preface, p. vii) and hence many of his identifications are wrong (Pargiter in *J.A.S.B.*, 1895, p. 250), these works of erudition are 'precious mines of materials' utilised by later scholars.

4. *Vivien de Saint-Martin*, the father of the geography of Ancient India.—(*a*) His *Etude sur la géographie et les populations primitives du Nord-ouest de l'Inde d'après les Hymnes Védiques* (Paris, 1860) is the sole work on Vedic geography. Its treatment is masterly in the extreme. But as he relied solely on M. Langlois's French translation of the *Rigveda*—"a version which does not seem altogether to have commended itself to later interpreters" (E. Thomas in J. R. A. S., 1883, p. 358)—and as much Vedic research has been done since that time, it is necessary to revise this *Etude*.

In his (*b*) *Etude sur la géographie Grecque et Latine de l'Inde, et en particulier sur l'Inde de Ptolémie* and (c) *Mémoire Analytique sur la carte de l'Asie centrale et de l'Inde* (appended to Vol. III of M. Julien's translation of Hwen Thsang, 1858), he critically examined the classical and the Chinese sources. "His identifications have been made with so much care and success that few places have escaped his research and most of these have escaped only because the imperfection or want of fulness in the maps of India rendered actual identifications quite impossible" (Cunningham's *A.S.R.*, II, Preface, p. 85).

5. *Sir Alexander Cunningham*, the father of Indian archæology. A son of Allan Cunningham the poet, he came to India as a "Royal Engineer." The influence of

Prinsep—"the decipherer of the early Indian Alphabets" —made him fix his eyes on the antiquities of this country. In 1861 he applied to Lord Canning to sanction an "archæological survey" which he justly showed in his letter to be the only means for the reconstruction of an account of Ancient India. He was appointed the Archæological Surveyor in January 1862; but as after a few years the post was abolished, he went home and produced *The Ancient Geography of India,* Vol. I (1871). In it he gave a summary of the results of V. de St. Martin and Lassen *revised* and corrected in light of his own researches and discoveries due chiefly to his *vast travels* in this country—an advantage which the earlier writers did not possess. Thus he brought to a focus the then accumulated knowledge into a single *English* volume which is still the work to which every student of this subject has to refer to. But it must be borne in mind that—

(*a*) Cunningham (following St. Martin and Julien) gave in most cases the proposed *restorations* of foreign sounds as the Skr. names. Though nothing more than this could have *then* been possible, it is clear that such restoration of a Greek, Latin or Chinese transcript of an Indian proper name could not always be identical with the original one. Hence one ought to search for the original names from Indian sources and there is no doubt that they would eventually be found out. Thus Pânini furnishes *Kâpisî* (IV. 2. 99), *Sânkala* (IV. 2. 75), *Varnu* (IV. 2. 103; IV. 3. 93), *Parvata* (IV. 2. 143), etc.—the Skr. forms of Kapisene, Sangala, Fa-la-na, Po-lo-fo-ta, etc. [*I.A.* Vol. I, p. 21]. Kâsikâ supplies Ayomukhî (A-ye-mu-ka'). Râjataranginî mentions *Udabhândapura.* (Wu-to-ka-han-cha). *Vinaya Texts* (ii, 38) and *Jâtaka* (iv, 30) supply *Kajangala* (Cunningham's *Kajughira*). Inscription No. 14 of *E.I.* VI shows that the Skr. form of Kong-yu-to is *Kongoda* and not Konyodha as given by Cunningham.

(*b*) In utilising the accounts of Fa Hian and Hwen Thsang—undoubtedly his chief sources—he took 6 *li* of Hwen Thsang as one mile and one *yojana* of Fa Hian to be 6·75 miles. But later researches have shed much light on this subject causing a scrutinization of his work.

(*c*) Cunningham usually says that Hwen Thsang made mistakes when his evidence is not in accord with what he (Cunningham) wishes to prove. It is very easy to say that Hwen Thsang meant East when he wrote West, or that instead of a thousand he meant a hundred. But one must not do this without any strong proof.

(*d*) He estimated Ptolemy's geography to be of much value (His Preface, p. vii). But it will be shown to be otherwise.

(*e*) Cunningham himself has, in his voluminous reports (*A.S.R.*) in 23 volumes (the first two only of which were written, though not published, before the publication of his Geography), embodying his researches occupying a period of more than a quarter of a century, abandoned many of the identifications stated in his Geography. And the researches of various other scholars—M'Crindle, Stein, Raverty, Foucher, Fleet, V. Smith, Watters, to name only a few of them)—have shown that not only are many of his identifications doubtful but that some are positively wrong.

6. *H. Yule.*—His annotations on Marco Polo and his map of Ancient India from classical sources in Dr. Smith's *Atlas of Ancient Geography* (1875) are valuable.

7. *Dr. M'Crindle,* the translator of Megasthenes, Arrian, Strabo, Periplus, Ptolemy, and other classical writers on India, gave, in his geographical notes a summary of the conclusions of the above writers.

8. *Mr. Pargiter.*—His *Geography of Râma's Exile*

(*J.R.A.S.*, 1894), *Eastern Indian Nations* (*J.A.S.B.*, 1895). Eng. translation of *Mârkandeya Purâna* (Published by the Asiatic Society, Bengal), *Nations at the time of the Great War* (*J.R.A.S.*, 1908), and Ancient Indian Historical Traditions (Oxford, 1922) have elucidated Epic and Puranic Geography.

9. *Nandalal Dey's Geographical Dictionary of Ancient and Mediæval India.* (A dictionary and not a systematic treatise. Grounds of identifications and references are generally not given). A second edition of it is in course of publication as an appendix to Indian Antiquary.

10. *Prof. F. Pullé's* Cartography of India in the *Studi Italiani di Filologia Indo-Iranica,* Vols. IV & V. is a valuable contribution.

2. Sources of the Geography of Ancient India.

I.—Foreign.*

1. Classical.

Though a few references to India may be gathered from the *Phœnician* and *Persian* sources, they are not of any importance. Hence of the foreign accounts we have first to turn to that of the Greeks. Their *earliest notion of the earth* was that it was a flat and round disc encircled by the mighty river—Ocean. Homer and his contemporaries knew very little beyond Greece, the Archipelago, Asia Minor, Egypt, Sicily and a part of Italy. But the colonizing spirit expanded their knowledge ; and the first introduction of maps, at least in Greece,(for the Egyptians and Babylonians are said to have drawn maps long

* Fleet in *J.A.*, 1901, p. 24 *ff.*; *The Evolution of Geography* by J. Keane, London, 1899; *The Dawn of Modern Geography* by C. R. Beazly. London, 1897; etc.

before—J. Keane, p. 5) and the discovery of an instrument to fix the latitude by Anaximander, a disciple of Thales, helped this expansion.

HECATOEUS (500 B.C.), the first Greek geographer, knew of two continents only—Europe and Asia (a part of which was Africa). His "Survey of the World" is lost.

HERODOTUS (484-431 B.C.), the Father of History, was a traveller. He rejected the flat theory of the earth, but gave none of his own. He knew something of the countries from Scythia to Abyssinia and from India to the Pillars of Hercules. But "his knowledge of India was meagre and most vague. He knew that it was one of the remotest provinces of the Persian Empire towards the East ; but of its extent and exact position he had no proper conception." (M'Crindle's *Ancient India*, p. 1). Hence though his work can be utilised as a source of history for informing us of Skylax's Voyage, etc., it contributes little towards the geography of India.

The *Indika* of KTESIAS (398 B.C.), the royal physician of Persia, is full of old wives' tales not to be trusted.

ALEXANDER THE GREAT'S march through the Punjab and Sindh brought, for the first time, the direct Greek knowledge of India to the banks of the Sutlej. The great invader *caused the whole of India to be described* by men well acquainted with it (M'crindle's *Invasion*, p. 6. f. n.). Some of the eminent men of science and letters who had accompanied him wrote invaluable memoirs which are now totally lost, but they furnished materials to subsequent writers—1. DIODORUS (100 B.C.—A.D. 100) who mixed history with fiction. 2. PLUTARCH, 3. STRABO, (60 B.C.—A.D. 19). 4. CURTIUS, (A.D. 100), who was 'deficient in the knowledge of Geography, Chronology and Astronomy' (M'Crindle's Invasion, p. 11), 5. ARRIAN (A.D. 200)—the best of Alexander's historians, and 6.

JUSTINUS (not later than A.D. 500). As none of these abstractors had even a very slight personal knowledge of India, their works, though based on accounts written by persons who actually visited India, are not so much invaluable for geography as for history. A little vagueness due to want of personal knowledge and a few mutual contradictions diminish not a little of their usefulness as a source of the geography of the North-Western and Western districts of India. Hence it is that "few of the places mentioned in them have been identified with any real approach to certainty" (Fleet in *I.A.*, 1901, p. 24) and a greater number of identifications can only be made from Indian sources and not from them.

MEGASTHENES (305 B.C.). His *long stay in the very heart of India* might probably have given his work great authority in topographical matters also ; but, unluckily for us, it exists only in fragments preserved as quotations. In the existing fragments we can only find out his idea of the shape of India, names of some mountains and an important but doubtful catalogue of Indian races and tribes.

About 240 *B.C.* ERATOSTHENES, who was placed in charge of the great library established by the Ptolemies at Alexandria, brought Mathematics to his aid and laid the first foundation of a really scientific geography. Accepting the theory which is said to have originated from Thales (600 B.C.) but the credit of which ought to go to Pythagoras, he took the *earth* to be *spherical* and as lying in the centre of the universe. Though he had various errors, Sir E. Bunbury has justly pointed out that his geography is not only much nearer to the truth than that adopted by Ptolemy three centuries later, but it is actually a better approximation than was arrived at by modern geographers till about two centuries ago. (*Hist. of Ancient Geography*, Vol. I, p. 635). He described

India on the authority of Alexander's historians, Megasthenes, and the Register of *Stathmi* or Marches.

After the lapse of about two centuries flourished STRABO (60 B.C.—A.D. 19) whose object in writing a new geography was 'to correct the earlier works in light of the increase of knowledge' due to the foundation of the mighty Roman Empire. He "did not carry us much further than Eratosthenes. Indeed in some respects he is even inferior to his predecessor." He distorted the shape of various countries. But he conceived rightly, noticed the difficulty of correctly representing a curved surface on a plane and perceived that a projection must be to some extent erroneous. As for *his account of India*, he himself has admitted that it *cannot be absolutely true*. As an apology he has pointed out the difficulty of getting correct information about India owing to its great distance and to the fact that only a few have ever visited it, that those few have visited only a part of it, and that those again are ignorant men unqualified to write an account of the places they have visited. (Strabo in M'Crindle's *Ancient India,* pp. 17 and 9.)

PLINY, the Naturalist, (A.D. 23-79) dealt with everything under the sun in his long array of books. Having no new theory of his own and having read (as he himself has said) more than 2,000 books, he became an industrious collector from every source. But "his love of the marvellous disposed him to accept far too readily even the most absurd fiction. He is also liable to the charge of occasional carelessness in his citation." (M'Crindle's Ancient India, p. 102). His notices of Asia are fuller and indicate an increasing trade between Europe and the East. And the discovery, made at this time by Hippalus (a navigator who made a study of the winds of the Indian Ocean), of the periodic nature of the monsoons enabling the European navigators to take a direct route to India and not a coasting course, became a valuable aid to the commercial relations with India. The hearsay tales of these rough sailors were mixed by Pliny with the accounts of Alexander's companions and of Megasthenes in his geography of India. (VI Book of his *Natural History*).

The increase of trade with India created the demand of a guide-book which was produced in the form of the "PERIPLUS OF THE ERYTHRÆAN SEA" by an anonymous writer (first century A.D.). Erythræan sea was the whole expanse of the ocean reaching from the coast of Africa to the utmost boundary of ancient knowledge of the East. It was so called from the entrance into it by the straits of the Red Sea—the "Erythra" of the Greeks. This Periplus *contains the best account of the commerce* carried on from the Red Sea and the coast of Africa to the East Indies during the time that Egypt was a Roman province. It mentions river-mouths, ports etc., with distances from one another, exports, imports, and such other details as a merchant would most value. The *author* of the Periplus *evidently sailed in person round the coast of India*. But owing to the occasional shifting of sea-side emporia, we cannot now expect to find every place on the coast mentioned by him. As to inland details, he was not correct. Thus he placed Paithan at a distance of twenty days' journey to the south of Barygaza while it is 200 miles to the south-east of it. Thus we cannot trust it as a geographical source for inland knowledge, though we can take its mention of commercial products to be true.

The greatest figure of this period is PTOLEMY, whose name marks the highest pitch of perfection in early geography. Klaudios Ptolemaios who flourished in Alexandria (*circa* A.D. 150) was a musician, mathematician, astronomer and geographer. His work on geography is a sequel to his great "Almagest." It is not a descriptive geography like that of Strabo, but is exclusively a mathematical or cosmical one. His object was to correct and reform the map of the world. So he explained the geometrical principles of geography and pointed out that the only scientific basis on which a map could be constructed must be made on astronomical observations. Hence in describing places he gives their longitudes (calculated from Ferro in the Canaries) and latitudes (parallel of Rhodes). These scientific features are the causes of his wide celebrity. But *his* system has many *defects* :—

(1) He placed the *equator* at a considerable distance from its true geographical position and vitiated his Eastern longitudes by about seven degrees.

(2) He took *every degree* of latitude and of longitude measured at the equator as equal to 500 stadia *instead of* 600 *stadia* (or 60 geographical miles). And thus if he had arrived at the conclusion that two places were 5000 stadia from each other, he would place them at a distance of ten degrees apart and thus, in fact, separate them by an interval of 6000 stadia.

(3) As only a *few astronomical observations* were made in his time, he had to rely (and specially so in the case of India of which he had not even the slightest personal observation) upon *second-hand information*—reports of travellers, navigators and works of previous writers.

(4) In general shape his countries are narrowed at the north and enormously extended as they approach the south ; so that the eastern parts of Asia are carried a long way beyond their true distance from Europe and Africa.

(5) As the result of the above defects, the *shape of India is utterly distorted in his map*. His results would

place Paithan in the Bay of Bengal, make Ceylon an enormous island, make the Ganges flow into the sea somewhere near Canton, make the Mahânadî river run over Siam and Cambodia, carry Pâtaliputra to the east of a line from Tonquin to Pekin, etc.

Thus we see that unless we have a thorough adjustment of Ptolemy's results for India, it is with but little confidence that we can use it, with only our present means of applying information given in it, towards reconstructing the geography and political divisions of Ancient India.

It is needless to mention the *other classical writers* [translated by M'Crindle in his *Ancient India*], though they supply some historical information, they do little more than mentioning a *few distorted* Indian *geographical names* wihout the specification of any distance or direction. Nor was the old classical culture destined to live long after Ptolemy and the author of PEUTINGER TABLES (A.D. 222.).

2. Early Christian.

The spread of *Christianity ruined the old* "pagan" *culture.* The *Hebrew theory of flat earth* surrounded by the ocean and having massive pillars at the edges on which the heaven rests like a roof banished the Greek spheroidal view. While the old classical structure was undermined, little was done to further any knowledge. The only work of this period in which we have any interest is *The Christian Topography of the Universe* [M'Crindle's translation of the complete work published by the Hakluyt Society, 1897] by the Egyptian monk COSMAS, nicknamed INDICOPLEUSTES (Indian traveller), who travelled from Egypt to India and Ceylon (A.D. 547). Reviling the impious old pagans for their spheroidal view, he depicts the world in his map—the earliest Christian map—as a flat rectangular island surrounded by the sea beyond which are other regions. He had no idea of what geography is and his work contributed little to the historical geography of India. All that we can learn from him is the name of certain western and South Indian places and their trade.

3. Arabic.

As Arabic enterprise extended their commercial relations for beyond the limits of Ptolemy's world, their knowledge was wider than his and far sounder for many regions in the east and south (Eastern Asia, Africa). In geography, as in astronomy, they had worked *on the old Greek lines,* but on them they had built up their own structures by independent researches on mathematical calculations and reports of travellers. But Arabic geography never got beyond a certain point. It never threw up a truly great writer like Strabo or Ptolemy. What they did was *to preserve the Greek tradition* and to improve it, *while Europe was degrading into barbarism* owing to ecclesiastical authority. "Men like MASSOUDY (A. D. 956), ALBERUNI or EDRISI (11th century) had a better and more adequate conception than any Christian before A.D. 1300. The construction of maps and globes reached a considerable proficiency in their hand while the Christian ones are almost ridiculous." Besides the above writers, SULAIMAN (A. D. 851), ABU ZAID (A. D. 916), IBN KURDADBA (A. D. 912), AL ITAKHRI (A. D. 951) and AL KAZWINI (A. D. 1275) have written about India. But the distortion of Indian names in their works perplexes much. ALBERUNI'S knowledge of Sanskrit enabled him to give a transcript as faithful as the use of the Semitic alphabet allowed him. But his geographical account of India is not a new account ; it is mainly a synopsis [chaps. 25, 29] of the Hindu accounts—*Bhuvana-kosa* and *Kûrmavibhâga.* He has only added a few notes on them. His original contribution [chap. 18] is the account of 16 *itineraries* which seem to have been communicated to him by the military and civil officers of Mahmûd. Here he mentions directions and distances in *farsakh* (=3 miles approx.) [IBN BATUTA in Sindh, *J.R.A.S.*, 1887, p. 401 ff. and a map in 1889 ; RASHIDUDDIN'S geographical notices of India—Col. Yule in *J.R.A.S.*, 1869-70, p. 340 ff.].

4. Chinese.

Having discovered the use of the magnet as early as the third century A. D., the Chinese could make extensive sea-voyages. They are even alleged to have discovered what is now known as the North America in A. D. 500 (Beazly's *Dawn of Modern Geography*, pp. 489-90 ; 493). The conversion of this nation into Buddhism which was introduced into their country in A. D. 67 (Takakusu's Itsing, Introduction) caused a series of pilgrims to visit India—the land of Buddha—and write invaluable accounts of it.

As the Greeks and the early Arabs visited India either in the track of some invader or as merchants, their accounts chiefly inform us of the military glories of nations or of kings little known or altogether unknown in Indian literature which is deficient in the historical sense, or of the trades of places which have long ago been deserted or buried in the silts of rivers and are no longer remembered. Hence though these sources give much information, they do not contribute much to the study of geography. Rather it requires much research to elucidate these foreign accounts.

But the case is different with the Chinese. These pilgrims, saturated with Indian ideas, visited their holy land and described the sacred monuments of places which have been immortalized in Sanskrit or Pali literature, some of which still retain their celebrity, while the ruins of some others still exist enabling us to understand their Chinese description. This fact explains the *importance of the Chinese sources.*

Of the various Chinese accounts, those of SUNG-YUN and HWI SENG (A.D. 600 ; translated in Beal's *Records of the Western World,* Vol. I ; and in *Bull. de l'Ecole Fr. d'Extrême-Orient,* Hanoi, 1903) and of O-KUNG (A.D. 800 ; translated in the *Journal Asiatique,* 1895) are very short, describing a few places of North-Western India (Kabul Valley, the Punjab and Kashmir).

ITSING landed at Tâmralipti, the then port on the Bay of Bengal, in A.D. 673 and visited Nâlandâ, Gridhrakûta, Buddhagayâ, Vaisâlî, Kusînagara, Kapilavâstu, Srâvastî, the Deerpark, Cock Mountain, and left India from Tâmralipti. [Translated by Dr. Takakusu, C. P. S. Oxford, 1896]. His account was not accessible to [Sir] Alexander Cunningham.

Still more important are the accounts of FA-HIAN (A.D. 399-414) and HWEN THSANG (A.D. 629-45) or YUAN-CHWANG (as Mr. Watters prefers to spell it). FA-HIAN entered India from the North-West, travelled over the whole of the Aryâvarta and left it at the port of Tâmralipti. His record (*Fo-Kue-Ki*) is truthful, clear and straightforward. Though a devout Buddhist, he was a sensible and not often a hysterical pilgrim-traveller. The earlier part of his work is strictly geographical. But when he reached India, religion had the better of his geography. Still his geographical notices are valuable for their precision, as he generally fixed the position of every place that he visited by its bearing and distance from that which he left.

Yüan Chwang also entered India from the North-West, travelled through the whole of it and left it by the same route. His records—*Si-Yu-Ki*—are fuller than even that of Fa-Hian and it is almost impossible to exaggerate their importance.

In utilising materials from these sources a student should note that :—

I. In giving the direction of a place from another Fa-Hian mentions only the four principal cardinal points. [Hence his E. may mean N.E. or S.E.; and so with the other points.] Yüan Chwang also generally does the same ; and very seldom does he give the direction as due N.E., etc. But still there are other points of the compass beyond these eight.

II. In stating the distance of a place from another, Fa-Hian states it in the *yojana* and Yüan Chwang in the *yojana* and the *li* measure. Dividing the known-distance-in-miles by the number of *yojanas* which the distance covers according to these pilgrims, Cunningham asserted that a *yojana* of Yüan Chwang is 6·75 miles while that of Fa-Hian is 6·71 miles.

Mr. V. Smith takes a *yojana* of Yüan Chwang to be 6·5 miles and one of Fa-Hian to be 7·25 miles.

M. Julien and probably Dr. Stein take 8 miles as equal to one *yojana* of Yüan Chwang, while in the opinion of Mr. Giles a *yojana* of Fa-Hian varies from 5 to 9 miles.

Now Yüan Chwang has himself stated (Watters, Vol. I, p. 141-2) that a *yojana* is a day's march for a Royal army ; that there are three kinds of *yojanas* of 16 *li* (found in Sacred Writings), of 30 *li* (common reckoning in India) and of 40 *li* (old Chinese account). He has also stated that a *yojana* consisted of eight *krosas* (a *krosa* being originally the distance that the lowing of a cow can be heard). He has also given figures to change a *krosa* into "bows", "cubits", "fingers" and "barley-corns." Making calculations from these materials Fleet tried to prove that there were three kinds of *yojanas* :—I. MAGADHA YOJANA (used by the Buddhists) of 16000 *hastas* or 4·54 miles :

II. GENERAL YOJANA of 32000 *hastas* or 9·09 miles: III. A THIRD YOJANA (which was according to Yüan Chwang 1⅓ of the general *yojana*) of 12·12 miles. This third *yojana* was, according to Fleet, the original *yojana* (from *yuj*, to yoke)—the yoking distance—the distance along which a pair of bullocks could draw a fully laden cart. This *yojana* was taken by the Chinese pilgrims as equal to 100 "*li*"s. [*J.R.A.S.*, 1906, p. 1011.]

In making the above calculations Fleet took a *hasta* = ½ yard. But Major Vost has shewn from Medieval and Ancient Chinese and other sources that the *hasta* was formerly taken to be a little larger than is done now. [*J.R.A.S.*, 1903, p 65.] Hence taking his calculations the three *yojanas* will be—I = 5·288 miles or 5·3 miles very nearly; II = 10·6 miles very nearly; III = 14·2 miles very nearly.

Thus 100 "*li*"s or *a yojana* denoted the distance occupied in making *a day's journey*. The said day's journey averaged very closely *about fourteen miles*. But being actually determined in each case by such considerations as the nature of the country traversed and the distance between the villages, *sarais*, *dharmsâlâs* and other convenient halting places, it might easily be anything from twelve to sixteen miles and in exceptional cases might have even a wider range in either direction.

III. Again, as Fa-Hian gives distances in *yojanas* only and not in fractions of it, his one *yojana* may be any distance more than ½ *yojana* and less than 1½ *yojanas*. Yüan Chwang also uses round numbers, such as 500 "*li*"s, 600 "*li*"s, etc. Hence we may allow a certain margin and take his 500 "*li*"s as any distance above 450 and below 550 "*li*"s. Thus the *distances of* both *the Chinese pilgrims* can be taken only as *approximations*.

IV. Yüan Chwang's dimensions of various countries are generally taken to be exaggerations. It became a common practice of Cunningham to take his thousands as hundreds. But as Yüan Chwang has not stated these details in the decimal system of notation, he is not justified to do so. Nor can we condemn his details of this kind in general terms without considering how they can be applied. For as he usually stated these details in thousands of "*li*"s any one of them may be 50 miles too great or too little. Again re-entering angles may increase a perimeter very considerably, while reducing the area inside it. Conventional ideas as to the size of a country may also have caused some errors in his details. [*J. R. A. S.*, 1907, p. 641 ff.]

V. As the names of a country and its capital are sometimes identical [and even when not identical Yüan Chwang has not mentioned them both] and as Yüan Chwang has not always precisely stated whether by a certain place-name he means a capital or a country, the distances and directions given by him cannot precisely be traced on the map, though the best way would be to take them as from each capital to the next one.

VI. The peculiarity of Chinese phonetics caused Yüan Chwang to insert vowels between Skr. conjuncts and to use "*k*" for Skr. *k, kh, g, gh* ; *ch* for Skr. *ch, chh, j, jh* ; *t* (cerebral) for the cerebrals *th, d, dh, ks, str* ; *t* (dental) for the dentals *t, th, d, dh* ; *p* for *p, ph, b, bh* ; *l* for *r, l* ; *f* for *b* and *v*. Hence the difficulty in finding out the true Skr. form.

VII. Again cases of discrepancy between the *Records* (of the Western World written by the pilgrim himself) and the *Life* (of the pilgrim composed by a friend of him) and some apparent mutual contradictions and a few various readings show that the writings of Yüan Chwang have not been correctly transmitted to us.

We thus see that even the very best of the foreign sources are not fully satisfactory and though the results arrived at from them are of great value, they cannot be taken as anything more than mere approximations.

The Chinese source also includes various notes on India—in Chinese histories and specially in the Chinese translations of Indian works. M. Sylvain Lévi and his pupils have drawn the attention of Indologists to these notes.

3. A critical estimate of Indigenous sources.

I.—LITERARY.

Though the ancient Indians did not pay much attention to history, there are ample geographical materials.

Expansion of geographical knowledge is due to (1) military expedition and colonizing spirit, (2) commercial relations, (3) religious activity, and, in the modern age, (4) scientific exploration. Alexander's Historians' and Alberuni's knowledge of India was due to the first cause. Pliny and the author of the Periplus utilized materials accumulated by commercial enterprisers. The Chinese pilgrims' visit to India was actuated by religion. Similar also is the case with the ancient Indians. Their foreign conquest and colonization are made known to us by a series of Sanskrit Inscriptions discovered in Further India and the Indian Archipelago. A fourth century A.D. Pillar Inscription of the Buddhist sea-captain Mahânâvika Buddhagupta of Raktamr(i)ttikâ (mod. Rângâmâti in Murshidabad district, Bengal) has been discovered* in the Wellesley district of the Malay Peninsula. A series of inscriptions† proves clearly that there ruled, in Further India, from the second century A.D. up to the seventh

---

* Kern's *Verspreide Geschriften*, III, (1915), p. 255.

† Bergaigne's *Insc. Sansk. du Campâ et Cambodge* (1893); Bul. Ecole F.E.O., II, p. 185, III, 206-11; IV, p. 918; XI, p. 264; XII, No. 8, pp. 15-16; XV, No. 2, pp. 3-5; Barth's *Insc. Sk. du Cambodge*.

century at least, a line of Saiva Hindu kings (Dharmamahârâjas) claiming descent from Asvatthâman, son of Drona. Four Yûpa inscriptions* of king Mûlavarman, in the fourth or fifth century A.D. Pallava characters, discovered in 1879-80 at Kœtei in East Borneo, show the existence of a powerful Hindu royal dynasty at that place. As for the Brahman colony in Fahien's Ye-po-ti (Java, or perhaps, Sumatra) and the extensive Buddhist ruins in Java, they are too well-known to call for any remark. Recent discoveries in Central Asia exhibit political and diplomatic relations of India with Central Asian states (so often referred to in Indian literature).

As for commercial intercourse, Von Ihering (in his *Prehistoric Indo-Europeans*) and J. Kennedy (in *J.R.A.S.*, 1898, pp. 241-88) have shown the activity of the early Indians in trading with the Persian Gulf tribes. A couple of Kanarese sentences found embodied in the Greek farce in the Papyrus of Oxyrhynchus† of the first or second century A.D. indicates commercial relations of an intimate nature between Egypt and the Kanarese-speaking Dravidians of Southern India. Cornelius Nepos (who died in the reign of Emperor Augustus, 14 B.C.—A.D. 14) had mentioned Indian commercial activity even in Germany.‡ There are clear statements in Tamil literature supporting Fahien's mention of early Indian's voyage to Java, Sumatra and China.§

As for religious activity in this direction, Asoka's sending Buddhist Missionaries to Syria, Egypt and Macedonia is known to all students of History. The

* Dr. Vogel in *Overdruk int de Bijdragen tot de Toalen Volkenkande van Nederlandsch-Indië Deel* 74, Aflevering 1-2, 1918.

† *J.R.A.S.*, 1904, pp. 399-405.

‡ M'Crindle's *Anc. Ind.*, p. 110.

§ Aiyangar's *Beginnings of South Indian Hist.*, pp. 113-4.

recent discoveries in Central Asia exhibit the great influence of Buddhist Missionaries in that region. India's connection with Tibet, China, Japan and Manchuria does not require any comment. Even such a distant place as Lord North's Island in Micronesia,* was indebted to Buddhist Missionaries for its religious instruction.

We thus see that the political, commercial, and religious activities of early Indians made them acquainted with the greater part of the then known countries of the world. And this acquaintance certainly broadened their knowledge of the geography of foreign lands. And though, owing to their so-called want of historical faculty or to their want of vanity, they left no autobiographies or private memoirs, *peripli* or *itineraries* like those of Fahien or Yüan Chwang to perpetuate their names, yet, the stock of knowledge thus accumulated was not completely lost. It has been preserved in a corrupted form in the Epic and Puranic conception of the world as containing seven concentric islands—Jambu, Sâka, Kusa, Sâlmala, Krauncha, Gomeda (Gomanda or Plaksha), and Pushkara†—encircled by seven *Samudras*.‡ Though this conception is childish, we ought not to compare it with

---

* *Journal of the American Oriental Society*, vol. V, 194.

† The order varies in different sources.

‡ The Buddhist system counts eight *dvipas* and has different names for some of the Samudras. (See Pullé's *Studi Italiani di Filologia Indo-Iranica*, vol. IV, pp. 15-16; see also *J.R.A.S.*, 1902, p. 142; 1907, p. 42.) In Jaina tradition we have new names. A chapter entitled *Dîva-samuddâ* inserted incidentally in *Jivâbhigama-sûtra* names the following *dvîpas* :—1. *Jambu*. 2. *Dhâyaî-Khanda*, 3. *Pukkharavara*, 4. *Vârunavara*, 5. *Khîravara*, 6. *Ghatavara*, 7. *Khodavara*, 8. *Nandîsaravara*, 9. *Arunavara*, 10. *Arunavaravâsa*, 11. *Kundala*, 12. *Kundalavara*, 13. *Kundalavaravâsa*, 14. *Ruyaga*, 15. *Ruyagavara*, 16. *Ruyagavaravâsa*, 17. *Hâra*, 18. *Hâravara*, 19. *Hâravaravâsa*. The names of the first two oceans are *Lavana-samudda* and *Kâloya* (Sk. Kâloda); the other names are made by adding *uda* (=water) to the names of the dvîpas. *Bhagavatî-Sûtra*

that of the twentieth century and stigmatize it as ridiculous. If we compare this fourth or third century B.C. conception of the earth with even the tenth or eleventh century Christian conception as depicted in the maps reproduced in Keane's *Evolution of Geography* (Edward Stanford, London, 1899), it would not certainly appear to be more ridiculous. The true conception of the earth is a thing of modern times—it was formed after the first circumnavigation. Ancient nations had strange notions. The conception of the different parts of the earth as so many islands was maintained also by the Greeks, and is referred to by Teopompo in Eliano, by Eratosthenes, and by Strabo.* As for the Indian theory of concentric islands, its origin may be explained thus:—(1) the change of meanings of the words *dvîpa* and *samudra*; *dvîpa* (derived by Pānini as *dvi+ap*; and thus etymologically connected with *doab*) meant, primarily, land having water (and not sea) on two (and not all) of its sides. The original meaning of *samudra* is a collection of water.† These words lost their original meanings and came to mean *island* and *sea* respectively. (2) Now when the Epic and Puranic writers (who had not the slightest personal knowledge of foreign lands) attempted the difficult task of arranging the traditional accounts of the different parts of the then known world handed down from those who actually visited them, they harmonized (?) the different accounts by reducing them to this system. But though their system is wrong and though there is

---

(II, 8, 1-9) states *ayam Jambuddîva savva-dîva-samuddânam savvabbhantare* and that the first three only of the above dvîpas are inhabited by men—the *Trikhanda* (खु) (II, 9, 1-2). (See Pullé's *Studi*, IV, pp. 10-20; *J.B.B.R.A.S.*, II, p. 411.)

* Pullé's *Studi*, vol. IV, p. 20, (giving *Teopompo* and *Eliano* in their Italian forms) quoting Berger's "Geschichte der wiss. Geographie der Griechen," p. 12.

† St. Martin's *Géographie du Véda*, p. 62.

plenty of the fabulous in Hindu Geography, their accounts of the different parts of the world were based on facts. Mr. Wilford collected an account of the River Nile and of its source and reconstructed a map out of the Purânas.* H. H. Wilson called him an "injudicious writer."† Cunningham remarked that his essay is a "wild speculation."‡ St. Martin stated him to be the first victim of the "imposture" geographical literature of the Hindus.§ But Lieut. J. H. Speke, (in his *Discovery of the Source of the Nile,* chaps. I, V, X) unhesitatingly states that when planning his discovery of the source of the Nile, he secured his best information from Wilford's map and testifies to the substantial correctness of the Puranic account.|| Is it not enough to repay the labours of the Purâna-writers that it is they (and not Ptolemy, the great geographer of Greek Egypt) who helped the nineteenth century explorer with their accurate knowledge of that part of the country? As the subject of our study is the ancient geography of India and not the geographical theories of ancient Indians, we dismiss the theory of seven *dvîpas* with these remarks and return to the sources describing India only.

The indigenous geography of India is, like every other Indian Science, chiefly dependent on religion. India is a land of *tîrthas*—her every crag, every spring, every river, and every hoary tree is sacred. As it is a duty of every pious Indian—Hindu, Jaina, or Buddhist—to make pilgrimages, pilgrims travelled far and wide to pay their respects to the objects of their veneration. This expanded their knowledge which has been embalmed in the sacred

* *Asiatick Researches,* vol. III.

† *Hindu Theatre,* vol. I, p. 9.

‡ *A. S. R.,* vol. I, p. ii.

§ St. Martin's *Etat actuel des études sur l' Inde ancienne,* p. xiii.

|| Schoff's *Periplus,* pp. 87 and 230.

literature—Orthodox (Hindu) or Heterodox (Jaina and Buddhist). Thus, though disregard to the historical order of things, owing to their peculiar religious idea that worldly existence is a misery, has caused the want of historical accounts, yet it is that same peculiar religion which did much to preserve the materials of geography. And though there is plenty of the fabulous in Indian geography of outlandish regions, the allusions to purely Indian topography are generally sober. The main features of the country were adequately known in very early times.

Let us now examine the different branches of Indian literature as geographical sources. The VEDAS are our only source of the geography of Vedic India. Vivien de St. Martin first handled the subject. It was also taken up by Zimmer in his *Alt-Indische Leben*. Hillebrandt, Pischel, Roth and other Vedic scholars also have touched on the subject, Brunhofer has attempted, in his *Iran und Turan*, to locate various Vedic rivers in regions outside India.

The *R*(i)*gveda Samhitâ* generally mentions tribes and rivers only. Names of countries occur seldom. In the mention of the following rivers, there is, as Sir A. Stein* has pointed out, a strict geographical order :—Gangâ, Yamunâ, (and the following tributaries of the Indus) Sarasvatî, Sutudrî (Satadru, Satlej), Parushnî (Ravi), Asiknî (असिक्नी Akesines, Chenab), Marudvr(i)ddhâ† Vitastâ (Jhelum), R(i)jikîyâ and Sushomâ (Sohan). As we find in this list (*Rigveda*, X, 75, 5) a strict geographical order in the mention of the eastern tributaries of the Indus, we ought to take the same order to guide us in

---

* *Bhândârkar Commemoration Volume.*

† Stein has identified it with the Maruwardwan which flows from north to south through the Maru valley of the Kashmir Jammu state and joins the Chenab at Kistawar.

identifying the western tributaries mentioned in the next verse—Tristâmâ, Susartu, Svetî (श्वेती), Gomatî (Gomal), Krumu (Kurram), Kubhâ (Kabul) and Mehantu. In the next two verses (X. 75, 7-8) are named some rivers. As *Rigveda* X. 64.8 mentions *trisapta sasrâ nadyah,* thrice seven sister rivers, we ought to find the names of seven rivers in X, 75. 7-8. Sâyana was ignorant of the geography of the North-Western Frontier, and therefore explained these words as adjectives. But these words are to be taken as proper names—Urnâvatî, Sîlamâvatî, R(i)jitî, Enî, Chitrâ, Hiranmayî and Rus(श)atî—seven tributaries of the Indus to be located to the north-west. The last five (and Añjasî, Amsu(शु)matî, Asm(श्म)anmatî, Kulisî (शी) and Vîrapatnî) have not been mentioned in Macdonell and Keith's *Vedic Index of Names and Subjects.* But those five are to be taken as proper names, and geographical order will be a guide in the attempt to locate them.

The Indus and its tributaries are seldom mentioned in the *Yajurveda,* for the Aryans then lived in the territory of Kuru-Pâñchâla (Thaneswar and Rohilkhand), the old capital of which, Kâmpila, is mentioned. The *Satapatha Brâhmana* (I, 4, 1, 10-18) records the Aryan migration to Videha (Tirhut) ; while the *Atharvaveda-Samhitâ* shows that the Aryans were then acquainted with Anga and Magadha (which might have been known in Rigvedic age as Kîkata, (ट) a country of the non-Aryans, whose leader was *Pra-Maganda* whose name might have some connection with Magadha). The *Aitareya Brâhmana* mentions the Aryan Vaidarbhas and the non-Aryan Andhras, Pundras, (पुण्ड्र), S(श)abaras, Pulindas and Mûtibas. The Vangas seem to be mentioned in the *Aitareya Aranyaka* (ii. 1, 1) as a non-Aryan tribe.

This gradual expansion of the Aryans can also be gathered from the *Dharmasûtras* and *Dharmasâstras.* The

Sûtras (*Vasishtha, I, 8* ; *Baudhâyana, I.* 1, 2, 9, etc.) state that the country of the Aryans आर्यावर्तं lies to east of the region where the (Sarasvatî) disappears, to the west of *Black forest* (KAL'AKAVANA*), to the north of Pâripâtra and to the south of the Himâlayas. It is strange to note that this definition of Aryâvarta excludes the greater portion of the land of the R(i)gvedic Aryans. A famous episode (Karna-Salya-samvâda) in the Karnaparvan of the Mahâbhârata also clearly states the impurity of the Punjab tribes during the Epic age. Various explanations may be suggested. (1) Dr. Bühler's† theory was that the reading of Vasishtha presupposes a reading Adarsa (र्श)‡ which was corrupted into Adars(र्श)ana (=disappearance) and was then paraphrased as "Vinas(श)ana" [of the Sarasvatî]. Ingenious as this theory is, it is not a good solution. Though some of the Sûtras and Patañjali's Mahâbhâshya (II, 4, 10) actually give the Western boundary to be Adarsa(र्श), we gain little by this reading. Adarsa cannot be located in the N.-W. Frontier so as to include the whole of the Panjab in this Aryâvarta of the Sûtras. (2) Recent study of the modern Indian Aryan

---

* I propose to identify Kâlakavana, the eastern boundary of Aryâvarta of the Sûtras, with Prayâga, the eastern boundary of Manu's Madhyadesa, which is identical with the Aryâvarta of the Sûtras. As the other three boundaries are the same (Pâripâtra being a portion of the Vindhyas), the eastern limit also ought to be identical. In the later age there flourished a city (Prayâga) and a country there, where the earlier literature locates a forest. Ayodhyâkânda (LIV and LV) of the *Râmâyana* states that Prayâga was then a clearing in a forest.

† *S.B.E.*, vol. XIV, p. 2.

‡ आदर्श the western boundary of the Aryavarta, has not been located by any scholar. As बृहत्संहिता XIV, 25, mentions Adatsa with the sources of the Yamunâ, Trigarta, etc., it is to be placed not far from the ancient kingdom of Srughna and Trigarta (Kangra). Varâhamihira's mention makes it clear that it cannot be located in the N.-W. Frontier.

dialects indicates, in the opinion of Sir George Grierson, at least two waves of Aryan migration into India. There arose a conflict between the Brahmanical later immigrants (now represented by the speakers of Panjabi, Râjasthânî, Gujaratî and Western Hindi) and the anti-Brahmanical earlier immigrants (now represented by the speakers of Kâshmiri, Mârâthi, Bengali and Oriya). This conflict between the two waves of Aryan migrators might have caused the inhabitants of the Middle land to stigmatize the later immigrants as not truly Aryan and their country as outside the pale of Aryan culture. (3) The country to the West of the Sarasvatî was occupied in the later epic age by non-Aryan (Turanian) immigrants—the Takkas. They are now to be found in Jammu, Kistwar and other places.* They claim their descent from Takshaka Nâga.† The biting of King Parikshit by Takshaka Nâga probably symbolizes the destruction of the Aryan power owing to the inroad of the Takkas. Their name seems to have some connection with Takshasilâ ; for in connection with the serpent sacrifice performed by king Janamejaya to chastise the Nâgas, mention is made of his invasion and conquest of Takshasilâ (*M.Bh,* Adi P., III, 683-3 ; 832-4 ; XL— XLIV ; XLIX, 1954 ; L. 1991). As the Panjab was thus occupied by a non-Aryan race or races, it was outside the boundary of Aryâvarta. (4) As for Pargiter's theory that the Aryans migrated to the Panjab from the *Madhyadesa* (Ancient Indian Historical Traditions), that cannot explain the above facts. For, whether the Panjab was the original home or not, Pargiter could not deny the fact that the Aryans lived there during the Vedic age and if it be so, why was it excluded from the Later Aryâvarta?

The *Dharmasâstra* of Manu, however, calls the

---

* *A.S.R.*, vol. II, pp. 6-7.

† Tod's *Rajasthan*, I, p. 9.

Aryâvarta of the Sûtras to be the *Madhyadesa* or "Middle country" (*Himavad-Vindhyayor-madhyam yat prāk vinasanâd*(विनशनाद्) *api, pratyag-eva Prayâgâchcha Madhyadesah...*) and greatly extends the boundaries of its Aryâvarta by defining it as *â Samudrât tu vai Pûrvâd â Samudrâchcha Paschimât* (पश्चिमात्) *tayor-evâ'ntaram giryor-âryâvarttam vidur-budhâh.*

The "*Middle country* of the BUDDHIST LITERATURE" expanded to the East. Its boundaries as mentioned in Mahâvagga, V, 13, 12 [and Divyâvadâna] are :—E., Kajangala* [or Pundra(पुण्ड्र) varddhana acc. to Div.]; S. E., River Salalavati [Sarâvatî]; S., the town of Satakannika (*v. l.* set...); W., the Brahman district (or village) of Thuna† [Sthûna]; N., Usîradhaja‡ [Usira]. "The middle country is in length 300 yojanas, in breadth 250 yojanas, in circuit 900 yojanas."§ The sixteen great countries mentioned in the Pali literature are :—(1) Anga (C. Champâ), (2) Magadha, (3) Kâsi (subject to Kosala), (4) Kosala (C. Sâvatthî), (5) Wajjis, (6) Mallâ of Kusinara

* It is the Ka-chu-wen-ki-lo of Yüan Chwang, who located it at a distance of above 400 *li* E. from Champâ (Bhagalpore). It was thus somewhere in Rajmahal district. It is the Kayangala mentioned in the com. on *Râma[pâla]Charita* (II, 6). The *ya* for *ja* is to be explained as due to Prakrit influence—intervocal explosive elided and *y* inserted to avoid *hiatus*—the य-श्रुति of Jaina Prakrit.

† Thuna has not been identified by any scholar. As Yüan Chwang's account makes Thaneswar the western-most country of the Buddhist Middle country, I propose to identify Thuna (or Sthûna of *Divyâvadâna*) with Sthânvîsvara. Sthûna and Sthânu seem to be different forms of the same word, such metathesis of vowels being found in Pali and Prakrit. *Isvara*, the second part of Sthânvîsvara (Mod. Thaneswar) is redundant, it being identical in meaning with Sthânu (=Siva).

‡ Usîradhaja is probably Usira-giri, a mountain to the North of Kankhal (Hardwar).—Hultzsch in *Ind., Ant.*, 1905, p. 179.

§ Commentary on *Jâtaka* and *Sumangala*. (Rhys Davids in *J.R.A.S.*, 1904, p. 86.)

and Pâwâ, (7) Chedi, (8) Vatsa (C. Kausâmbî), (9) Kuru, (10) Panchâla, (11) Matsya, (12) Surasena (C. Mathurâ). (13) Assaka on the Godâvari, (14) Avanti (capital Ujjayini ; Mâhissatî was the capital of the *southern division of Avanti* or Avanti-dakshinâpatha).* (15) Gandhâra (C. Takkhasilâ), (16) Kamboja in the extreme North-West (C. Dvâraka ?).† The Pâli literature gives important trade-routes also.‡ But it plainly indicates that Southern India was not then Aryanized.

The next stage of the expansion of the Aryans is to be inferred, as Sir R. G. Bhandarkar has shown (Early History of Dekkan pp. 5-6), from PANINI AND HIS COMMENTATORS. Pânini (700 B.C. ?), an inhabitant of the extreme N.-W. of India, has mentioned many place-names of N. India and specially of the Panjab and Afghanistan. But of S. India, he has mentioned only Kachchha (IV. 2. 133), Avanti (IV. 1. 176), Kosala (IV. 1. 171), Karusa and Kalinga (IV. 1. 178).§ Thus it appears that S. India was probably unknown in his time. Kâtyâyana (400 B.C.), however, knows even Chola, Mâhishmat and Nâsikya. In Patanjali's time (150 B.C.) the whole of India was known.

The EPICS. Both the *Râmâyana* and the *Mahâbhârata* have (*i*) chapters (the importance of which has been somewhat impaired by the corruptness of the texts) directly dealing with the geography of India. Kishkindhyâ Kânda, (XL—XLIV) describes the various countries of the four quarters (of India) where the

* Prof. D. R. Bhandarkar in his *Carmichael Lectures*, 1918, pp. 43, 45.

† Rhys Davids in *Buddhist India*, p. 23.

‡ *Ibid*, pp. 103-4.

§ *Asmaka* (अश्मक) has been mentioned by *Pânini*. But as there was another Asmaka in the N.-W., we are not sure which Asmaka (N.-W. or S.) has been mentioned by Pânini.

"Vânara" chiefs were sent in quest of Sîtâ. In the ninth chapter of the Bhîsma Parvan of the *Mahâbhârata, Sañjaya* gives a general description of India—long lists of countries, nations, mountains and rivers. Again there are (*ii*) descriptions of certain routes which are invaluable ; for though the distance is hardly ever mentioned, the direction and the mention of known places enable one to locate approximately the unknown. The *Râmâyana* describes three routes :—(1) Râma's journey, in company of Visvâmitra, from Ayodhyâ to Mithilâ ; (2) Bharata's return from Kekaya to Ayodhyâ ; (3) Râma's exile. [N. Das's *Geography of Asia based on the Râmâyana* and Pargiter's *Geography of Râma's exile in J.R.A.S.*, 1894, p. 231 deal with the subject.] The *Mahâbhârata* mentions (1) [Adiparvan] the twelve years' sojourn of Arjuna ; (2) [Sabhâparvan] the conquest of the four quarters by the four brothers of Yudhishthira ; (3) [Vanaparvan] an account of the "Tîrthas" and Pândavas' pilgrimage ; (perhaps a later interpolation—but the geographical knowledge is certainly based on actual travels of Pilgrims). (4) Karna's digvijaya ; (5) [Asvamedhaparvan] Arjuna's expedition through various countries. The Udyogaparvan and the parvans describing the war mention almost all the Indian nations siding with the one party or the other. [Pargiter, *On the Nations at the time of the Great War* in *J.R.A.S.*, 1908.] There are also (*iii*) numerous incidental references, [Sörensen's *Index of the Mahâbhârata*]. Another important section is the chapters of the Sabhâparvan dealing with the presents made by different kings to Yudhishthira, and as such describing the natural and commercial products of the different districts of India.

The PURANAS reserve (*i*) a section on Geography—*Bhuvanakosha*—giving lists of rivers, mountains, countries and tribes. They also deal with (*ii*) *Topographia sacra* and contain (*iii*) many incidental references. [Bhuvanakosh of *Mârkandeya Purâna* with notes in Pargiter's translation of the Purâna published by the Asiatic Society of Bengal. Geographical names in the Bhâgavata Purâna in *I. A*. XXVIII. p. 1.]

The MAHATMYAS (of various *tîrthas*) also deal with *Topographia sacra*. These works (claiming to be sections or portions extracted from Purânas or Samhitâs) set forth the legendary origin of *tîrthas*, the rites to be performed there, etc. Their importance may be illustrated thus :— A long and laborious but fruitless search was made for the site of Vâtâpî, the capital of the early Châlukyas. Now the Mâhâtmya of Mahâkûta(ट) a *tîrtha* close to Badami (15° 55′ N. Lat. and 75° 41′ E. Long.) in Bijapore district localised there the story of the brothers Vâtâpi and Ilvala vanquished by the sage Agastya. This localisation of the story of Vâtâpi showed that Bâdâmi, close to the *tîrtha*, is the city of Vâtâpi. (*I. A*., VIII, p. 238.) Dr. Bühler, in his *Kâshmir Report*, pointed out the great geographical importance of the Mâhâtmyas and Dr. Stein has discovered many long forgotten sites with their aid. [Stein's *Topography of Kashmir* in his *Chronicles of Kasmîr*, Vol. II.] The Mâhâtmya literature is very vast.

There are also a few WORKS professing to DEAL WITH GEOGRAPHY. Mr. Wilford has long ago pointed out (*Asiatick Researches*, XIV, pp. 374-380), the existence of the following :—(1) Muñjâ-pratidesa (श)-vyavasthâ, (2) Bhoja-pratidesa-vyavasthā (a revised edition of 1), (3) Bhuvana-Sâgara, (4) A Geography written at the command of Bukkarâya, (5) A commentary on the Geography of the Mahâbhârata written by order of the Raja of Paulastya (? Paurastya ?) by a Pandit in the time of Hussein Shah (1489)—a voluminous work. A MS. acquired by Mr. Wilford once formed a part of the Library of Fort William College ; it is now in the Government Sanskrit College

Library, Calcutta. A detailed description,* of this MS. has been given by M. M. H. P. Sâstrî in the *Journal of the Bihar and Orissa Research Society* (1919). Prof. Pullé has mentioned (in pp. 13-15 of his *Studi Italiani di Filologia Indo-Iranica,* vol. IV.) the existence of the following geographical works in the Library of the Nazionale centrale di Firenze (Florence, in Italy):—(5) *Lokaprakâsa*(श) of Kshemendra (the celebrated Kasmirian writer) ; the MS. consists of 782 pages and it is profusely illustrated. Prof. Pullé has reproduced two of its figures in his *Studi*. (6) Three MSS. of *Kshetra Samâsa,* a Jaina work—with two different commentaries. (7) A MS. of *Kshetra Samâsa Prakarana.* (8) Four MSS. of *Samghayanî* of Chandrasûri with two commentaries ; one of the MSS. is illustrated. (9) A *Laghu-Samghayanî.* He has also pointed out the mention of *Kshetra Samâsa* of Jina Bhadra (1457-1517) in Kielhorn's Report (1880-1), of (10) *Laghu Kshetra Samâsa* of Ratnasekhara in Weber's *Cat.* (No. 1942), of (11) *Trailokya dîpikâ* and (12) *Trailokya Darpana* quoted by Wilford. Besides the above, (13) a Jaina *Tittha Kappa,* and (14) *Tristhalîsetu* dealing with the topography of Prayâga are also known.

St. Martin† characterized the works mentioned by Wilford to be "imposture literature" without sufficiently examining them. Be they "imposture" or not, they have not yet been sufficiently examined.

Certain works on POETICS, *e.g.*, Râjasekhara's *Kâvyamîmâmsâ* (Gaekwad Oriental Series) Vâgbhata(ट)'s and Hemchandra's works (printed in the Kâvyamâlâ Series), contain a section on geography, in order to acquaint a poet with the flora and fauna etc., of the various districts, so that his description of them may be faithful. The *Nâtyasâstra* नाट्यशास्त्र of Bharata (Kâvyamâlâ Series) also

* *Gazetteer literature in Sanskrit.*

† *Etat actuel des études sur l' Inde ancienne,* p. xiii.

gives details as to the colours with which to paint actors personifying the various tribes of India and its borders. It thus gives geographical and ethnological data. [*J.A.S.B.*, 1909, pp. 359-60.]

The VATSYAYANA KAMA SUTRA and its commentary by Yasodhara [first edited by the late M.M. Durgâprasâda of Joypur] are also valuable. The Sûtra refers to various countries and the commentary indicates their location.

THE RAJATARANGINI AND THE HISTORICAL POEMS—the CHARITA KAVYAS—Harshacharita, Gauda vaho (गउड़ वहो) Navasâhasânkacharita, Vikramânkadeva-charita, Dvyâsrayakâvya (द्व्याश्रयकाव्य), Kumârapâlacharita, Râma(pâla)-charita, Prithvîrâja-vijaya, Kîrtikaumudî, Vasantavilâsa, Vallâlacharita, Hammîra-mardana, Vemabhûpâla-charita, Achyutarâyâbhyudaya, etc. Though these works have many shortcomings as sources of history, they are "invaluable" (as Sir A. Stein says of the R. T.) "for the study of historical geography."

Even the ORDINARY LITERARY WORKS sometimes incidentally introduce geography. The plots of some of the plays, the classical poems, and the collection of imaginative stories and fables (*e.g.*, Jâtakas, Pañchatantra, Kathâsaritsâgara) were woven round geographical names. And such allusions can, to a certain extent, be put to a practical use. Thus the statement of the Dasakumâra-charita that Tâmralipti (Mod. Tamluk) was in the Suhma country settled the location Suhma (which was formerly identified by H. H. Wilson with Arakan and Tipperah). Similar incidental references are to be met with in every department of literature. The *Arthasâstra* of *Kautilya* and various *Ratna-sâstras* and *medical works* referring to the natural products of the various countries also throw some light on this subject, and it is with their help that I identified Barbaricum, Alexander's Haven and Bettigo of Ptolemy.

ASTRONOMICAL works. Astronomers discarded the theory of a circular earth (Parimandala) with Mt. Meru in the middle, and proved that the earth is an immovable globe suspended in space. They knew the dimensions and indicated the poles and the equator.* They calculated *desântara* देशान्तर (longitude) and prepared globes. The KURMAVIBHAGA of the बृहत्संहिता (chap. XIV) of वराहमिहिर is very important for geographical study. Here *Kûrma* means the earth, because it resembles a tortoise, being round, surrounded by water, and having a globular convexity on its surface (Alberuni.) Its special object is to provide an arrangement from which it may be determined what countries and peoples would suffer calamity when particular *nakshatras* are vexed by planets. The 27 nakshatras are divided into nine groups and so is the earth (*i.e.* India). Dr. Fleet first examined the list (*Ind. Ant*, XXII, p. 169 *ff*). Prof. Mario Longhena† did the same, giving references to passages of the epics which mention the same nations, etc. The com. of Utpala on the बृहत्संहिता (*Vizianagram Sanskrit Series*, Benares) gives quotations from the *Parâsara tantra* on the same subject which has also been treated in chap. LVIII of the *Mârkandeya Purâna*. Comparing these three lists, we find a number of various readings and the original reading can be reconstructed in some cases.

The third chapter of Bhâskarâchârya's work and the 12th chapter of *Sûryasiddhânta* are also important.

The INTRODUCTIONS AND COLOPHONS OF MSS. sometimes incidentally give historical and geographical notices. The place of composition or copying is mentioned in some MSS. with details.

---

* Thibaut in his *Astronomie* (Grundriss), pp. 21, 30, 37.

† Pullé's *Studi Italiani*, vol. IV.

II.—Traditional.

Local traditions, when properly sifted and corroborated by other sources, give some geographical information. Thus Dr. Fleet's identification of Sâkala (शाकल) with Sialkot is due to the local tradition recorded in Cunningham's *A.S.R.*, XIV, pp. 44-46, that it was founded by Salya and that it was originally called Sâkala.

But tradition sometimes turns out to be wrong. Thus Gaibandhâ (Rangpur district, Bengal) claims to be the country of the Matsyas ; Badnagar (Patna district) to be Kundinapura (the capital of Vidarbha) ; but the Epics show otherwise. Hence uncorroborated tradition has little value. The literary sources also sometimes mention names which cannot be located. Again tribes die out and disappear ; towns decay and are deserted ; seaside emporia sometimes shift ; "the names of countries" [cities, etc.] "change" [Utpala's *Commentary* on the *Br(i)hatsamhitâ*] though the places themselves survive. All these facts make identifications of sites mentioned in foreign and indigenous literary sources difficult. Hence we have to turn to

III.—Archæology.

with its three branches (*i*) Monumental, (*ii*) Numismatic, and (*iii*) Epigraphical.

(*i*) The MONUMENTAL remains of a place enable one to compare its present ruins with those described in a foreign or indigenous source. Thus Mahâban was long taken as the site of Aornos ; but Dr. Stein's survey has proved beyond all question that the natural features of that mountain are totally dissimilar from those of Aornos as described by the historians of Alexander. [*Ann. Rep. of A.S.I.*, 1904-5, p. 42.] The existence of a double-chambered cave answering to the description of Sudatta's proves the identification of Po-lu-sha with Shahbazgarhi. (Cunningham's *A.S.R.*, V., 9-15.)

(*ii*) The discovery of COINS sometimes enables one to locate a particular nation or tribe. Thus at Nâgri, a small town 11 miles north of Chitor, have been found seven copper coins (found nowhere else) with the legend "Majhamikâya s(*i*)bijanapadasa" showing that the *Mâdhyamikas* should be located there. (*C.A.S.R.*, VI., pp. 195-205.) But coins pass from one country to another and so identifications based on their places of discovery may be wrong. Monuments themselves cannot enable us to indicate the real site, unless (*a*) an ancient description of the monument is found or (*b*) it speaks through an inscription. Hence for ancient geography, as for everythig else connected with the past of India, we are really dependent on the (*iii*) EPIGRAPHIC RECORDS which regulate everything that we can learn from tradition, literature, coins, architecture or any other source. Thus when we find a pillar *in situ* bearing the inscription that "here was born the Sâkya sage" we make an identification of which there can be no doubt.

Dr. Fleet has classified the epigraphic records thus* :—

(*a*) *According to the material on which they have been recorded.*

A. *Metals ; Iron, Gold* and *Silver* inscriptions are rare. *Brass* and *Bronze* are more numerous. The majority are on sheets of copper—copper-plate, Pattikâ, Tâmra-pattikâ or Sâsana (ताम्रपट्टिका, or शासन)

B. (*i*) crystal, (*ii*) clay, terra-cotta and brick, (*iii*) earthenware written with ink, (*iv*) stone—(1) Rocks, (2) Pillars, (3) relic receptacles, (4) external parts of Stupas,

* Fleet's Article on Epigraphy in Imp Gaz. of India, vol. II.

(5) Caves, (6) Images and statues, (7) moulds for making seals, (8) walls, beams etc. of temples etc.

(*b*) *According to their topics.*

A. Records making a plain statement of events: the Hâthigumpha inscription, the Allahabad Pillar inscription of Samudragupta and a few other are due to an historical instinct.

B. Records due to Religious motives: the Piprawa relic vase; the Rock and Pillar edicts of Asoka, etc.

C. Records of Religious endowment: Barabar cave inscription of Asoka, Bhitari Pillar, etc.

D. Records of Secular donation.

[To these are to be added a new group :—

E. Literary inscriptions (to preserve Kâvyas and Nâtakas) *e.g.*, The Dhar inscriptions preserving two acts of a drama and two Prâkrit poems (E. I. VIII.)]

The DONATIVE RECORDS (C.D.) are by far the most numerous of all. These are title-deeds of real property and of certificates of the right to duties, taxes, fees, and other privileges. The essential part of all these records was the specification of the details of the donor, donee and donation. As donation consisted in most cases of lands, these deeds specified the village, the territory wherein it was located, its boundaries, etc. Hence these records are valuable as a source of geography. "Thus, not with the express object of preserving the history (and geography), but in order to intensify the importance of everything connected with religion and to secure grantees in the possession of properties conveyed to them, there was gradually accumulated almost the whole of the great mass of epigraphic records on which the Indian Archæologists chiefly depend."*

---

* Dr. Fleet *Ibid.*

A

SUMMARY

BIOGRAPHICAL MEMOIR

OF

MAJOR-GENERAL SIR ALEXANDER CUNNINGHAM,

R.E., C.S.I., C.I.E., K.C.I.E.

Second son of Allan Cunningham, the Scotch Poet.

Born 23-1-1814. Educated at "Christ's Hospital," London, and at the M. E. I. Coy's Mily. Seminary of Addiscombe, and at the R. E. Estate at Chatham.

Second Lieut. Bengal Engineers, 1831. Arrived India June 1833.

Col. R.E. 16-6-1860. Bt. Major Genl. Retd. List 30-6-1861.

A. D. C. to Lord Auckland, Gov.-Genl. of India, July. 1836 to January, 1840.

Married, 30-3-1840, Alicia Maria Whish, daughter of Martin Whish B. C. S. Present at Battle of Punniar when he turned the enemy's guns against them.

With Army of Sutlej 1845-6.

Chief of Commission on Ladak-Tibet boundary with Capt. Strachey and Dr. Thomson in 1847, when he visited the Temples of Kashmir and wrote the Works Nos. 1 and 2 in the List below on these Temples and on Ladak.

Present at battles of Chilianwala and Gujarat 1848.

Held various posts in the P. W. D. 1833 to 1861.

In 1851 explored the Buddhist Monuments of Central India along with Lt. Maisey, and wrote the account of them (No. 3 in the List).

Chief Engineer of Burma 1856 to 1858, and of N. W. P. 1858 to 1861.

Archæological Surveyor to Govt. of India, December, 1861 to end of 1865, when he published Vols. I & II of the Archæological Survey.

Left India in February, 1866. Director of Delhi and London Bank in London 1866 to 1870.

Returned to India as Director Genl. of the Archæological Survey 1st January, 1871 for 15 years, during which he wrote eleven of the volumes marked No. 9 in the List below.

Retired on 30th September, 1885 after a service of about 50 years in India.

In retirement in London from October, 1885 to his death on November 28, 1893: in this period the Works Nos. 10 to 14, and some of No. 15 (See List) were written.

Created C. S. I. May 20, 1871, C.I.E., January 1878, K.C.I.E., March 21, 1887.

LIST OF WORKS

BY

MAJOR-GENERAL SIR ALEXANDER CUNNINGHAM.

1. Essay on the Aryan Order of Architecture, as exhibited in the Temples of Kashmir.
—Calcutta, 8vo, 1848.

2. Ladak, Physical, Satistical and Historical.
—London, roy. 8vo, 1854.

3. The Bhilsa Topes, or Buddhist Monuments of Central India. —London, roy. 8vo, 1854.

4. The Ancient Geography of India I. The Buddhist Period. —London, 8vo. 1871.

5. Corpus Inscriptionum Indicarum, Vol. I. Inscriptions of Asoka. —Calcutta, 4to, 1877.

6. The Stupa of Bharhut, a Buddhist Monument.
—London, 4to, 1879.

7. Book of Indian Eras, with Tables for calculating dates.
—Calcutta, roy. 8vo, 1883.

8. Coins of Alexander's Successors in the East.
—London, 8vo, 1884.

9. Archæological Survey of India, Vols. 1, 2, 3, 5, 9, 10, 11, 14, 15, 16, 17, 20, 21, (13 vols.).
—Calcutta, roy. 8vo, 1862-1885.

(The remaining volumes, Nos. 4, 6, 7, 8, 12, 13, 18. 19, 22, 23, 24 were written by Genl. Cunningham's Assistants under his superintendence).

10. Coins of Ancient India from the earliest times down to the 7th century A. D.
—London, 8vo, 1891.

11. Mahabodhi or the Great Buddhist Temple under the Bodhi Tree at Buddha Gaya.
—London, 4to, 1892.
12. Coins of the Indo-scythians, Sakas, and Kushans.
—London, 8vo, 1893.
13. Later Indo-scythians. —London, 8vo, 1893.
14. Coins of Mediæval India.—London, 8vo, 1893.
15. Numerous Papers in the Journals of the Asiatic Society of Bengal, and Royal Asiatic Society, and in the Numismatic Chronicle.
—Calcutta and London, 1834 to 1893.

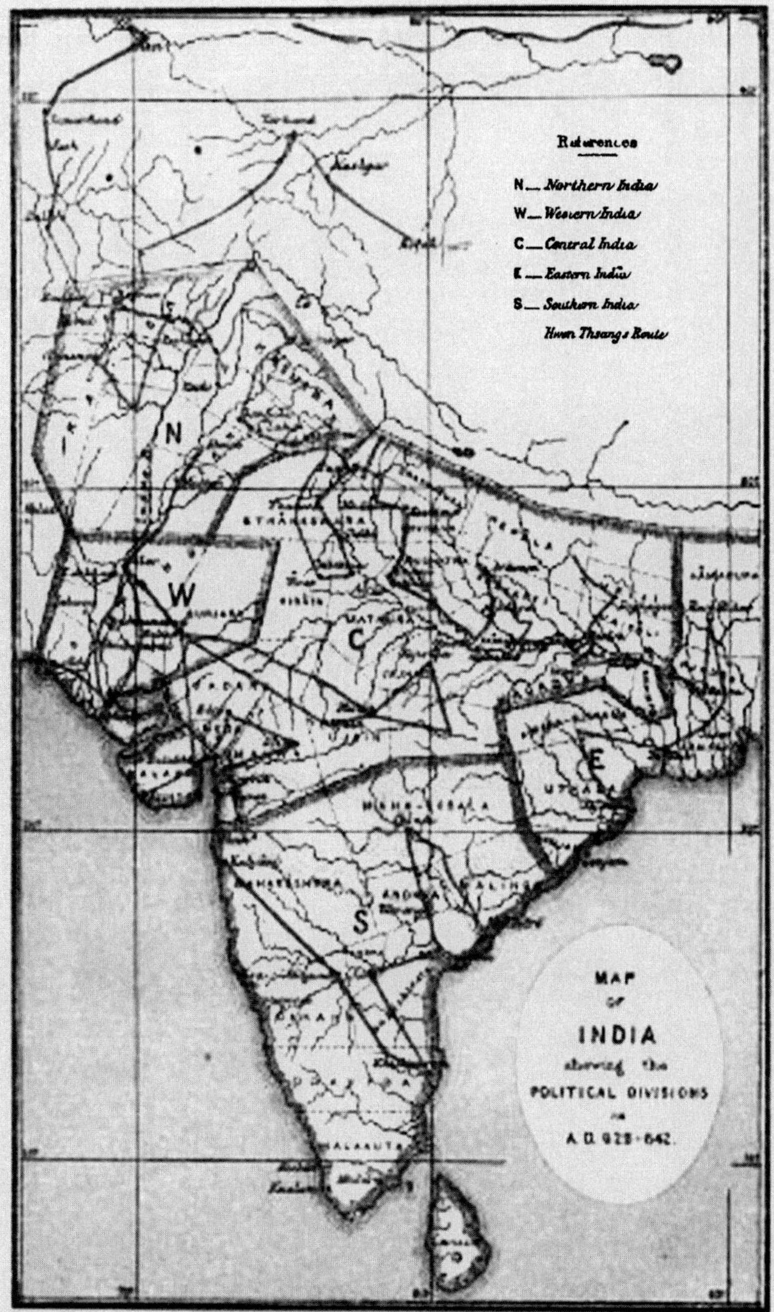
References
N— Northern India
W— Western India
C— Central India
E— Eastern India
S— Southern India
Hwen Thsang's Route
MAP
of
INDIA
showing the
POLITICAL DIVISIONS
in
A.D. 629-642.

THE ANCIENT GEOGRAPHY OF INDIA.

I.

THE BUDDHIST PERIOD,

INCLUDING

THE CAMPAIGNS OF ALEXANDER, AND THE TRAVELS OF HWEN-THSANG.

BY

ALEXANDER CUNNINGHAM,

MAJOR-GENERAL, ROYAL ENGINEERS (BENGAL RETIRED).

"Verum et terrena demonstratio intelligatur,
Alexandri Magni vestigiis insistamus."—*Plinii Hist. Nat.* vi. 17.

WITH THIRTEEN MAPS.

LONDON:
TRÜBNER AND CO., 60, PATERNOSTER ROW.
1871.

TO

MAJOR-GENERAL

SIR H. C. RAWLINSON, K.C.B.

ETC. ETC.,

WHO HAS HIMSELF DONE SO MUCH

TO THROW LIGHT ON

THE ANCIENT GEOGRAPHY OF ASIA,

THIS ATTEMPT

TO ELUCIDATE A PARTICULAR PORTION OF THE SUBJECT

IS DEDICATED

BY HIS FRIEND,

THE AUTHOR.

PRFACE

TO THE ORIGINAL EDITION.

THE Geography of India may be conveniently divided into a few distinct sections, each broadly named after the prevailing religious and political character of the period which it embraces, as the *Brahmanical,* the *Buddhist,* and the *Muhammadan.*

The *Brahmanical* period would trace the gradual extension of the Aryan race over Northern India, from their first occupation of the Panjâb to the rise of Buddhism, and would comprise the whole of the Pre-historic, or earliest section of their history, during which time the religion of the Vedas was the prevailing belief of the country.

The *Buddhist* period, or *Ancient Geography* of India, would embrace the rise, extension, and decline of the Buddhist faith, from the era of Buddha, to the conquests of Mahmud of Ghazni, during the greater part of which time Buddhism was the dominant religion of the country.

The *Muhammadan* period, or Modern Geography of India, would embrace the rise and extension of the Muhammadan power, from the time of Mahmud of Ghazni to the battle of Plassey, or about 750 years, during which time the Musalmâns were the paramount sovereigns of India.

The illustration of the Vedic period has already been made the subject of a separate work by

M. Vivien de Saint-Martin, whose valuable essay* on this early section of Indian Geography shows how much interesting information may be elicited from the Hymns of the Vedas, by an able and careful investigator.

The second, or Ancient period, has been partially illustrated by H. H. Wilson, in his 'Ariana Antiqua,' and by Professor Lassen, in his 'Pentapotamia Indica.' These works, however, refer only to North-west India; but the Geography of the whole country has been ably discussed by Professor Lassen, in his large work on Ancient India,† and still more fully by M. de Saint-Martin, in two special essays,—the one on the Geography of India, as derived from Greek and Latin sources, and the other in an Appendix to M. Julien's translation of the Life and Travels of the Chinese pilgrim Hwen Thsang.‡ His researches have been conducted with so much care and success that few places have escaped identification. But so keen is his critical sagacity, that in some cases where the imperfection of our maps rendered actual identification quite impossible, he has indicated the true positions within a few miles.

For the illustration of the third, or Modern

---

*'Etude sur la Géographie et les populations primitives du Nord-Ouest de l'Inde, d'après les Hymnes Védiques.' Paris, 1859.

† 'Indische Alterthumskunde.' 4 vols. Bonn.

‡ 'Etude sur la Géographie Grecque et Latine de l'Inde,' 1858. M. Julien's 'Hiouen Thsang,' vol. iii. p. 251; "Mémoire Analytique," etc.

period, ample materials exist in the numerous histories of the Muhammadan States of India. No attempt, so far as I am aware, has yet been made to mark the limits of the several independent kingdoms that were established in the fifteenth century, during the troubles which followed the invasion of Timur. The history of this period is very confused, owing to the want of a special map, showing the boundaries of the different Muhammadan kingdoms of Delhi, Jonpur, Bengal, Malwa, Gujarât, Sindh, Multân, and Kulbarga, as well as the different Hindu States, such as Gwalior and others, which became independent about the same time.

I have selected the Buddhist period, or Ancient Geography of India, as the subject of the present inquiry, as I believe that the peculiarly favourable opportunities of local investigation which I enjoyed during a long career in India, will enable me to determine with absolute certainty the sites of many of the most important places in India.

My chief guides for the period which I have undertaken to illustrate, are the campaigns of Alexander in the fourth century before Christ, and the travels of the Chinese pilgrim, Hwen Thsang, in the seventh century after Christ. The pilgrimage of this Chinese priest forms an epoch of as much interest and importance for the Ancient History and Geography of India, as the expedition of Alexander the Great. The actual campaigns of the Macedonian conqueror were confined to the valley of the Indus and its tributaries; but the information collected by himself and his companions, and by the subsequent embassies and expeditions of the Seleukide kings of Syria, embraced the whole valley of the Ganges on the north, the eastern and western coasts of the peninsula, and some scattered notices of the interior of the country. This information was considerably extended by the systematic inquiries of Ptolemy, whose account is the more valuable, as it belongs to a period just midway* between the date of Alexander and that of Hwen Thsang, at which time the greater part of North-west India had been subjected by the Indo-Scythians.

With Ptolemy, we lose the last of our great classical authorities; and, until lately, we were left almost entirely to our own judgment in connecting and arranging the various geographical fragments that lie buried in ancient inscriptions, or half hidden in the vague obscurity of the Purânas. But the fortunate discovery of the travels of several Chinese pilgrims in the fifth, sixth, and seventh centuries of the Christian era, has thrown such a flood of light upon this hitherto dark period, that we are now able to see our way clearly to the general arrangement of most of the scattered fragments of the Ancient Geography of India.

---

* Campaign of Alexander, B.C. 330, and Ptolemy's 'Geography,' A.D. 150, or 480 years later. Beginning of Hwen Thsang's travels in India, A.D. 630, or just 480 years after Ptolemy.

The Chinese pilgrim Fa-Hian was a Buddhist priest, who travelled through India from the banks of the Upper Indus to the mouth of the Ganges, between the years 399 and 413 A.D. Unfortunately his journal is very concise, and is chiefly taken up with the description of the sacred spots and objects of his religion, but as he usually gives the bearings and distances of the chief places in his route, his short notices are very valuable. The travels of the second Chinese pilgrim, Sung-Yun, belong to the year 502 A.D., but as they were confined to the Kabul valley and North-west Panjâb, they are of much less importance, more especially as his journal is particularly meagre in geographical notices.*

The third Chinese pilgrim, Hwen Thsang, was also a Buddhist priest, who spent nearly fifteen years of his life in India in studying the famous books of his religion, and in visiting all the holy places of Buddhism. For the translation of his travels we are wholly indebted to M. Stanislas Julien, who with unwearied resolution devoted his great abilities for no less than twenty years to the acquirement of the Sanskrit and Chinese languages for this special purpose.† The period of Hwen Thsang's travels extended from A.D. 629 to 645.

---

* The travels of both of these pilgrims have been most carefully and ably translated by the Rev. S. Beal.

† Max Müller's 'Buddhism and Buddhist Pilgrims,' p. 30.

During that time he visited most of the great cities throughout the country, from Kabul and Kashmir to the mouths of the Ganges and Indus, and from Nepâl to Kânchipura near Madras. The pilgrim entered Kabul from the north-west, viâ Bamian, about the end of May, A.D. 630, and after many wanderings and several long halts, crossed the Indus at Ohind in April of the following year. He spent several months in Taxila for the purpose of visiting the holy places of Buddhism, and then proceeded to Kashmir, where he stayed for two whole years to study some of the more learned works of his religion. On his journey eastward he visited the ruins of *Sangala,* so famous in the history of Alexander, and after a stay of fourteen months in *Chinapati,* and of four months in *Jâlandhara,* for the further study of his religion he crossed the Satlej in the autumn of A.D. 635. From thence his onward course was more devious, as several times he retraced his steps to visit places which had been left behind in his direct easterly route. Thus, after having reached Mathurâ he returned to the north-west, a distance of 200 miles to *Thâneswar,* from whence he resumed his easterly route viâ *Srughna* on the Jumna, and *Gangâdwâra* on the Ganges to *Ahichhatra,* the capital of Northern *Panchâla,* or Rohilkhand. He next recrossed the Ganges to visit the celebrated cities of *Sankisa, Kanoj,* and *Kosâmbi* in the Doâb, and then turning northward into Oudh he paid his devotions at the holy places of *Ayodhyâ* and *Srâvasti.* From thence he resumed his easterly route to visit the scenes of Buddha's birth and death at *Kapilavastu* and *Kusinagara;* and then once more returned to the westward to the holy city of *Banâras,* where Buddha first began to teach his religion. Again resuming his easterly route he visited the famous city of *Vaisâli* in Tirhût, from whence he made an excursion to Nepâl, and then retracing his steps to Vaisâli he crossed the Ganges to the ancient city of *Pâtaliputra*, or Palibothra. From thence he proceeded to pay his devotions at the numerous holy places around Gaya, from the sacred fig-tree at *Bodh Gaya,* under which Buddha sat for five years in mental abstraction, to the craggy hill of *Giriyek,* where Buddha explained his religious views to the god Indra. He next visited the ancient cities of *Kusâgârapura* and *Râjagriha*, the early capitals of Magadha, and the great monastery of *Nâlanda*, the most famous seat of Buddhist learning throughout India, where he halted for fifteen months to study the Sanskrit language. Towards the end of A.D. 638 he resumed his easterly route, following the course of the Ganges to *Modagiri* and *Champâ*, and then crossing the river to the north he visited *Paundra Varddhana*, or Pubna, and *Kâmarûpa*, or Assam.

Having now reached the most easterly district of India he turned towards the south, and passing through *Samatata*, or Jessore, and *Tâmralipti*, or Tamluk, he reached *Odra*, or Orissa, early in A.D. 639. Continuing his southerly route he visited *Ganjam* and *Kalinga*, and then turning to the north-west he reached *Kosala*, or Berar, in the very heart of the peninsula. Then resuming his southerly course he passed through *Andhra*, or Telingâna to *Dhanakakata*, or Amaravati on the Kistna river, where he spent many months in the study of Buddhist literature. Leaving this place early in A.D. 640 he pursued his southerly course to *Kânchipura*, or Conjeveram, the capital of *Dravida*, where his further progress in that direction was stopped by the intelligence that Ceylon was then in a very troubled state consequent on the recent death of the king. This statement is specially valuable for the purpose of verifying the dates of the pilgrim's arrival at different places, which I have calculated according to the actual distances travelled and the stated duration of his halts.* Now the troubled state of Ceylon followed immediately after the death of Raja *Buna-Mu-galân*, who was defeated and killed in A.D. 639; and it is only reasonable to infer that the Ceylonese monks, whom the pilgrim met at Kânchipura, must have left their country at once, and have reached that place early in A.D. 640, which accords exactly with my calculation of the traveller's movements.

From Drâvida Hwen Thsang turned his steps to the north, and passing through *Konkana* and *Mahârâshtra* arrived at *Bhâroch* on the Narbada, from whence, after visiting Ujain and Balabhi and several smaller states, he reached Sindh and Multân towards the end of A.D. 641. He then suddenly returned to

* See Appendix A for the Chronology of Hwen Thsang's Travels.

Magadha, to the great monasteries of *Nâlanda* and *Tiladhaka,* where he remained for two months for the solution of some religious doubts by a famous Buddhist teacher named Prajnabhadra. He next paid a second visit to *Kâmrûp,* or Assam, where he halted for a month. Early in A.D. 643 he was once more at *Pâtaliputra,* where he joined the camp of the great king Harsha Varddhana, or Silâditya, the paromount sovereign of northern India, who was then attended by eighteen tributary princes, for the purpose of adding dignity to the solemn performance of the rites of the Quinquennial Assembly. The pilgrim marched in the train of this great king from *Pâtaliputra* through *Prayâga* and *Kosâmbi* to *Kanoj.* He gives a minute description of the religious festivals that were held at these places, which is specially interesting for the light which it throws on the public performance of the Buddhist religion at that particular period. At Kanoj he took leave of Harsha Varddhana, and resumed his route to the north-west in company with Raja *Udhita* of Jâlandhara, at whose capital he halted for one month. In this part of his journey his progress was necessarily slow, as he had collected many statues and a large number of religious books, which he carried with him on baggage elephants.* Fifty of his manuscripts were lost on crossing over the Indus at *Utakhanda,* or Ohind. The pilgrim himself forded the river on an elephant, a feat

---

* M. Julien's 'Hiouen Thsang,' i. 262, 263.

which can only be performed during the months of December, January and February, before the stream begins to rise from the melted snows. According to my calculations, he crossed the Indus towards the end of A.D. 643. At *Utakhanda* he halted for fifty days to obtain fresh copies of the manuscripts which had been lost in the Indus, and then proceeded to Lamghân in company with the King of Kapisa. As one month was occupied in this journey, he could not have reached Lamghân until the middle of March, A.D. 644, or about three months before the usual period, when the passes of the Hindu Kush become practicable. This fact is sufficient to account for his sudden journey of fifteen days to the south to the district of *Falana,* or Banu, from whence he reached *Kapisa* viâ Kâbul and Ghazni about the beginning of July. Here he again halted to take part in a religious assembly, so that he could not have left Kapisa until about the middle of July A.D. 644, or just fourteen years after his first entry into India from Bamian. From Kapisa he passed up the Panjshir valley and over the Khâwak Pass to Anderâb, where he must have arrived about the end of July. It was still early for the easy crossing of this snowy pass, and the pilgrim accordingly notices the frozen streams and beds of ice which he encountered on his passage over the mountain. Towards the end of the year he passed through Kâshgâr, Yârkand, and Kotan, and at last, in the spring of A.D. 645, he arrived in safety in the western capital of China.

This rapid survey of Hwen Thsang's route is sufficient to show the great extent and completeness of his Indian travels, which, as far as I am aware, have never been surpassed. Buchanan Hamilton's survey of the country was much more minute, but it was limited to the lower provinces of the Ganges in northern India and to the district of Mysore in southern India. Jacquemont's travels were much less restricted; but as that sagacious Frenchman's observations were chiefly confined to geology and botany and other scientific subjects, his journeyings in India have added but little to our knowledge of its geography. My own travels also have been very extensive throughout the length and breadth of northern India, from Peshawar and Multan near the Indus, to Rangoon and Prome on the Irawadi, and from Kashmir and Ladâk to the mouth of the Indus and the banks of the Narbada. Of southern India I have seen nothing, and of western India I have seen only Bombay, with the celebrated caves of Elephanta and Kanhari. But during a long service of more than thirty years in India, its early history and geography have formed the chief study of my leisure hours; while for the last four years of my residence these subjects were my sole occupation, as I was then employed by the Government of India as Archæological Surveyor, to examine and report upon the antiquities of the country. The favourable opportunity which I thus enjoyed for studying its geography was used to the best of my ability; and although much still remains to be discovered I am glad to be able to say that my researches were signally successful in fixing the sites of many of the most famous cities of ancient India. As all of these will be described in the following account, I will notice here only a few of the more prominent of my discoveries, for the purpose of showing that I have not undertaken the present work without much previous preparation.

1. *Aornos,* the famous rock fort captured by Alexander the Great.

2. *Taxila,* the capital of the north-western Panjab.

3. *Sangala,* the hill fortress in the central Panjab, captured by Alexander.

4. *Srughna,* a famous city on the Jumna.

5. *Ahichhatra,* the capital of northern Pânchâla.

6. *Bairât,* the capital of Matsya, to the south of Delhi.

7. *Sankisa,* near Kanoj, famous as the place of Buddha's descent from heaven.

8. *Srâvasti,* on the Rapti, famous for Buddha's preaching.

9. *Kosâmbi,* on the Jumna, near Allahabad.

10. *Padmâvati,* of the poet Bhavabhuti.

11. *Vaisâli,* to the north of Patna.

12. *Nâlanda,* the most famous Buddhist monastery in all India.

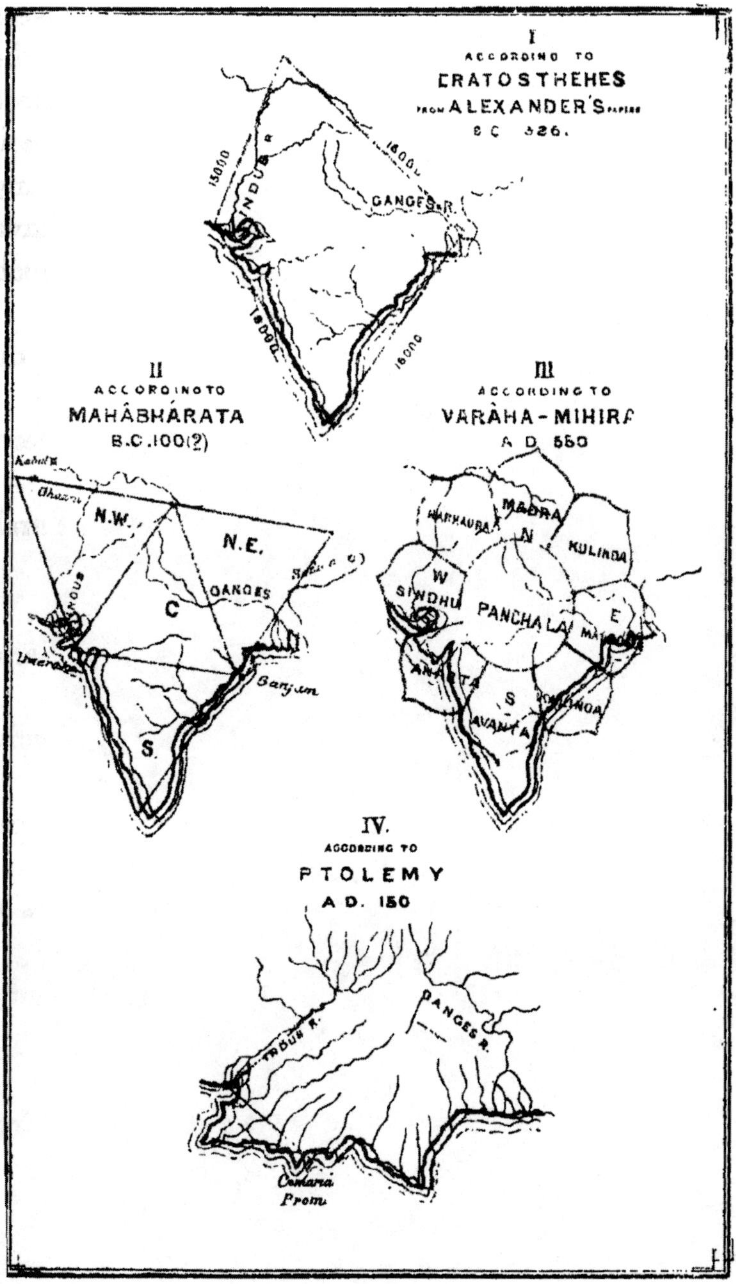
I
ACCORDING TO
ERATOSTHENES
FROM ALEXANDER'S PAPERS
B.C. 326.
15000
16000
18000
16000
INDUS R.
GANGES R.
II
ACCORDING TO
MAHÂBHÁRATA
B.C. 100(?)
Kabul
Ghazni
N.W.
N.E.
C
S.
INDUS
GANGES
Ganjam
III
ACCORDING TO
VARÂHA-MIHIRA
A.D. 550
MADRA
N
KULINDA
W
SINDHU
PANCHALA
E
S
AVANTA
IV.
ACCORDING TO
PTOLEMY
A.D. 150
INDUS R.
GANGES R.
Comara
Prom.

THE
ANCIENT GEOGRAPHY OF INDIA.

FROM the accounts of the Greeks it would appear that the ancient Indians had a very accurate knowledge of the true shape and size of their country. According to Strabo,* Alexander "caused the whole country to be described by men well acquainted with it;" and this account was afterwards lent to Patrokles by Xenokles, the treasurer of the Syrian kings. Patrokles himself held the government of the north-east satrapies of the Syrian empire under Seleukus Nikator and Antiochus Soter, and the information which he collected regarding India and the Eastern provinces, has received the approbation of Eratosthenes and Strabo for its accuracy. Another account of India was derived from the register of the *Stathmi*,† or "Marches" from place to place, which was prepared by the Macedonian Amyntas, and which was confirmed by the testimony of

* Geographia, ii. 1, 6.

† Strabo, x. 1, 11. The name of the author of the 'Stathmi' is preserved by Athenæus, i. 103. The original measurements were most probably made by Diognetus and Baiton, whose duty it was to ascertain the distances and lengths of Alexander's expeditions. See Plin. Hist. Nat., vi. 21.

Megasthenes, who had actually visited Palibothra as the ambassador of Seleukus Nikator. On the authority of these documents, Eratosthenes and other writers have described India as a *rhomboid*, or unequal quadrilateral, in shape, with the Indus on the west, the mountains on the north, and the sea on the east and south.* The shortest side was on the west, which Patrokles estimated at 12,000 stadia, and Eratosthenes at 13,000 stadia.† All the accounts agree that the course of the Indus from Alexander's Bridge to the sea was 10,000 stadia, or 1149 British miles; and they differ only as to the estimated distance of the snowy mountains of Caucasus or Paropamisus above the bridge. The length of the country was reckoned from west to east, of which the part extending from the Indus to Palibothra had been measured by *schœni* along the royal road, and was 10,000 stadia, or 1149 British miles in length. From Palibothra to the sea the distance was estimated at 6000 stadia, or 689 British miles; thus making the whole distance from the Indus to the mouth of the Ganges 16,000 stadia,‡ or 1838 British miles. According to Pliny,§ the distance of Palibothra from the mouth of the

* Strabo, ii. 1, 31, and xv. 1, 11. See, also, Diodorus, Hist., ii. 3, and Dion Perieg. v. 1131. Compare fig. 1 in the accompanying plate of small maps.

† Strabo, xv. 2, 8. Arrian, 'Indica,' iii.

‡ Artemidorus makes it 16,800 stadia, or 2100 Roman miles. See Pliny, vi. 22.

§ Plin. Hist. Nat., vi. 21.

Ganges was only 637.5 Roman miles; but his numbers are so corrupt that very little dependence can be placed upon them. I would, therefore, increase his distance to 737.5 Roman miles, which are equal to 678 British miles. The eastern coast from the mouth of the Ganges to Cape Comorin was reckoned at 16,000 stadia, or 1838 British miles; and the southern (or south-western) coast, from Cape Comorin to the mouth of the Indus at 3,000 stadia more* than the northern side, or 19,000 stadia, equivalent to 2183 British miles.

The close agreement of these dimensions, given by Alexander's informants, with the actual size of the country is very remarkable, and shows that the Indians, even at that early date in their history, had a very accurate knowledge of the form and extent of their native land.

On the west, the course of the Indus from Ohind, above Attok, to the sea is 950 miles by land, or about 1200 miles by water. On the north, the distance from the banks of the Indus to Patna, by our military route books, is 1143 miles, or only 6 miles less than the measurement of the royal road from the Indus to Palibothra, as given by Strabo on the authority of Megasthenes. Beyond this, the distance was estimated by the voyages of vessels on the Ganges at 6000 stadia, or 689 British miles,

* Strabo, xv. 1, 11. "Each of the greater sides exceeding the opposite by 3000 stadia." (Falconer's translation.)

which is only 9 miles in excess of the actual length of the river route. From the mouth of the Ganges to Cape Comorin the distance, measured on the map, is 1600 miles, but taking into account the numerous indentations of the coast-line, the length should probably be increased in the same proportion as road distance by one-sixth. This would make the actual length 1866 miles. From Cape Comorin to the mouth of the Indus there is a considerable discrepancy of about 3000 stadia, or nearly 350 miles, between the stated distance and the actual measurement on the map. It is probable that the difference was caused by including in the estimate the deep indentations of the two great gulfs of Khambay and Kachh, which alone would be sufficient to account for the whole, or at least the greater part, of the discrepancy.

This explanation would seem to be confirmed by the computations of Megasthenes, who "estimated the distance from the southern sea to the Caucasus at 20,000 stadia,"* or 2298 British miles. By direct measurement on the map the distance from Cape Comorin to the Hindu Kush is about 1950 miles,† which, converted into road distance by the addition of one-sixth, is equal to 2275 miles, or within a few

---

* Strabo, xv. 1, 12.

† Elphinstone, Hist. of India, Introd. p. 1, estimates the distance from Kashmir to Cape Comorin at about 1900 miles. The Caucasus is at least 50 miles to the north of Kashmir.

miles of the computation of Megasthenes. But as this distance is only 1000 stadia greater than the length of the coast-line from Cape Comorin to the mouth of the Indus, as stated by Strabo, it seems certain that there must be some mistake in the length assigned to the southern (or south-western) coast. The error would be fully corrected by making the two coast-lines of equal length, as the mouths of the Ganges and Indus are about equidistant from Cape Comorin. According to this view, the whole circuit of India would be 61,000 stadia; and this is, perhaps, what is intended by Diodorus,* who says that "the whole extent of India from east to west is 28,000 stadia, and from north to south 32,000 stadia," or 60,000 stadia altogether.

At a somewhat later date the shape of India is described in the 'Mahâbhârat' as an equilateral triangle, which was divided into four smaller equal triangles.† The apex of the triangle is Cape Comorin, and the base is formed by the line of the Himâlaya mountains. No dimensions are given, and no places are mentioned; but, in fig. 2 of the small maps of India in the accompanying plate, I have drawn a small equilateral triangle on the line between Dwâraka, in Gujarat, and Ganjam on the eastern coast. By repeating this small triangle on

* Diodorus, Hist., ii. 3.

† Journ. Asiat. Soc. Bengal. xx. Wilford, quoting the Bhishma Parva of the 'Mahâbhârata,' as communicated to him by Colebrooke.

each of its three sides, to the north-west, to the north-east, and to the south, we obtain the four divisions of India in one large equilateral triangle. The shape corresponds very well with the general form of the country, if we extend the limits of India to Ghazni on the north-west, and fix the other two points of the triangle at Cape Comorin, and Sadiya in Assam. At the presumed date of the composition of the 'Mahâbhârata,' in the first century A.D., the countries immediately to the west of the Indus belonged to the Indo-Scythians, and therefore may be included very properly within the actual boundaries of India.

Another description of India is that of the *Nava-Khanda*, or Nine-Divisions, which is first described by the astronomers Parâsara and Varâha-Mihira, although it was probably older than their time,* and was afterwards adopted by the authors of several of the Purânas. According to this arrangement, *Panchâla* was the chief district of the central division, *Magadha* of the east, *Kalinga* of the south-east, *Avanta* of the south, *Anarta* of the south-west, *Sindhu-Sauvira* of the west, *Hârahaura* of the north-west, *Madra* of the north, and *Kauninda* of the

---

* Dr. Kern, in preface to the 'Brihat-Sanhitâ' of Varâha-Mihira, p. 32, states that Varâha's chapter on Geography is taken almost intact, but changed in form, from the 'Parâsaratantra,' and must, therefore, be considered as representing the geography of Parâsara, or perhaps yet more ancient works, "and not as the actual map of India in Varâha-Mihira's time."

north-east.* But there is a discrepancy between this epitome of Varâha and his details, as *Sindhu-Sauvira* is there assigned to the south-west, along with Anarta.† This mistake is certainly as old as the eleventh century, as Abu Rihân has preserved the names of Varâha's abstract in the same order as they now stand in the 'Brihat-Sanhitâ.'‡ These details are also supported by the 'Mârkandeya Purâna,' which assigns both *Sindhu-Sauvira* and *Anarta* to the south-west.§

I have compared the detailed lists of the 'Brihat-Sanhitâ' with those of the Brahmânda, Mârkandeya, Vishnu, Vâyu, and Matsya Purânas; and I find that, although there are sundry repetitions and displacements of names, as well as many various readings, yet all the lists are substantially the same.|| Some

---

* 'Brihat-Sanhitâ,' ch. xiv. 32, 33.

† *Ibid.*, xiv. 17,—

Nairrityâm disi desâ
Pahlava Kâmboja Sindhu-Sauvira—

Wilford has given Varâha's list in vol. viii. p. 341, of Bengal Asiat. Researches; but he has made two divisions of *Sindhu-Sauvira*, and omitted *Kauninda*. His details, however, agree with the 'Brihat-Sanhitâ,' in assigning *Sindhu-Sauvira* as well as *Anarta* to the south-west.

‡ The Nine Divisions of Abu Rihân are given in Reinaud's 'Mémoire sur l'Inde,' pp. 116, 117. Compare No. II. Map, fig. 3.

§ Ward's 'Hindus,' iii. 10.

|| The list of the Brahmânda is given by Wilford in Bengal Asiat. Researches, viii. 334,—that of the Vishnu Purâna in Wilson's translation, where, also, will be found

of them, however, are differently arranged. All of the Purânas, for instance, mention the Nine Divisions and give their names, but only the Brahmânda and Mârkandeya state the names of the districts in each of the Nine Divisions; as the Vishnu, Vâyu, and Matsya Purânas agree with the 'Mahâbhârata' in describing only five Divisions in detail, namely, the middle Province and those of the four cardinal points.

The names of the Nine Divisions given in the 'Mahâbhârata' and the Puranas differ entirely from those of Varâha-Mihira; but they agree with those of the famous astronomer Bhâskarâcharya.* They follow the same order in all; namely, *Indra, Kaseru-mat, Tâmraparna, Gabhastimat, Kumârika, Nâga, Saumya Vâruna, Gândharva.* No clue is given to the identification of these names, but they certainly follow a different order from that of Varâha's Nine Divisions, as *Indra* is the east, *Vâruna* the west, and *Kumârika* the middle, while *Kâseru* must be the north, as the name is found in the detailed lists of the Vâyu and Brahmânda Purânas.

The division of India into five great provinces would appear to have been the most popular one during the early centuries of the Christian era, as it was adopted by the Chinese pilgrims, and from them by all Chinese writers. According to the Vishnu

---

the list of the 'Mahabhârata;' that of the Mârkandeya Purana is in Ward's 'Hindus,' iii. 9.

* 'Siddhânta Siromani,' chap. iii. 41.

Purâna,* the centre was occupied by the *Kurus* and *Pânchâlas;* in the east was *Kamarupa,* or Assam; in the south were the *Pundras, Kalingas,* and *Magadhas;* in the west were the *Surâshtras, Suras, Abhîras, Arbudas, Kârushas, Mâlavas, Sauviras,* and *Saindhavas;* and in the north the *Hunas, Sâlwas, Sâkalas, Râmas, Ambashtas,* and *Parâstkas.*

In the Geography of Ptolemy the true shape of India is completely distorted, and its most striking feature, the acute angle formed by the meeting of the two coasts of the Peninsula at Cape Comorin is changed to a single coast-line, running almost straight from the mouth of the Indus to the mouth of the Ganges. The cause of this mistake is partly due to the erroneous value of 500, instead of 600, Olympic stadia, which Ptolemy assigned to an equatorial degree, partly to an over-estimate in converting road-distance into map-measurement, but chiefly to the excess which he allowed for the distances of land journeys over those of sea voyages.†

---

* Wilson's 'Vishnu Purâna,' edited by Hall, vol. ii. b. iii. c. 3. p. 132. The *north* Division is not mentioned in the text; but as the *Hunas* and *Sâkalas* certainly belonged to the north, I presume that the *north* has been accidentally omitted. There is a similar omission of the name of *Kumârika* in this Purâna, which has only eight names for the Nine Divisions.

† The question of Ptolemy's erroneous longitudes is treated at length in Appendix C, where I have given all the data on which Sir Henry Rawlinson has founded his

If the measures of distance by sea had been increased in the same proportion, or had been estimated at the same value, as the measures of distance by land, all the places would have retained the same relative positions. But the consequence of Ptolemy's unequal estimate of the value of land and sea distances was to throw all the places determined by land measurement too far to the east; and as this error went on increasing the further he advanced, his eastern geography is completely vitiated by it. Thus Taxila, which is almost due north of Barygaza, is placed 11° to the east of it; and the mouth of the Ganges, which was fixed by land-measurement from Taxila and Palibothra, is placed 38° to the east of the mouth of the Indus, the true difference being only 20°. In fig. 4 of the accompanying plate of small maps I have given an outline of Ptolemy's 'Geography of India.' By referring to this it will be seen at a glance that, if the distance between the mouths of the Indus and Ganges were reduced from 38° to 20°, the point of Cape Comorin would be thrown far to the south, and would form an acute angle very nearly in its true position. The amount of error in Ptolemy's value of land distances is well shown in the difference of longitude between Taxila and Palibothra. The former he places in 125° and the latter in 143°, the difference being 18°, which is nearly one-third too much, as the actual difference

---

correction of three-tenths of the geographer's distances in easting.

between Shah-Dheri in 72° 53′ and Patna in 85° 17′ is only 12° 24′. By applying the correction of three-tenths, as proposed by Sir Henry Rawlinson, Ptolemy's 18° will be reduced to 12° 36′, which is within 12′ of the true difference of longitude.

India was first known to the Chinese in the time of the Emperor Wuti, of the later Han dynasty, in the second century before Christ.* It was then called *Yuan-tu* or *Yin-tu*, that is *Hindu*, and *Shin-tu*, or *Sindhu*. At a later date it was named *Thian-tu*;† and this is the form which the historian Matwanlin has adopted. In the official records of the Thang dynasty in the seventh century, India is described as consisting of "Five Divisions," called the East, West, North, South, and Central, which are usually styled the "Five Indies." I have not been able to discover when this system of the "Five Divisions" was first adopted; but the earliest notice of it that I can find is in the year 477 A.D.,‡ when the king of Western India sent an ambassador to China, and again only a few years later, in A.D. 503 and 504, when the kings of Northern and Southern India are mentioned as having followed his example.§ No divisions are alluded to in any of the earlier Chinese notices of India; but the different provinces are described by name, and not by posi-

* See M. Pauthier's translations from Chinese in the 'Journal Asiatique,' Oct. 1839, p. 257.

† *Ibid.* Nov. 1839, p. 384.

‡ *Ibid.* Nov. 1839, p. 291.

§ *Ibid.* Nov. 1839, pp. 290-292.

tion. Thus we have mention of *Yue-gai,* king of Kapila, in A.D. 428, and of the king of Gândhâra in A.D. 455.* It would appear also that previous to this time India was sometimes called *Magadha,* after the name of its best known and richest province; and sometimes the "kingdom of *Brahmans,*" after the name of its principal inhabitants.† The first of these names I would refer to the second and third centuries after Christ, when the powerful Guptas of Magadha ruled over the greater part of India.

The same division of five great provinces was adopted by the Chinese pilgrim Hwen Thsang in the seventh century, who names them in the same manner, as North, South, East, West, and Central, according to their relative positions.‡ He compares the shape of the country to a half-moon, with the diameter or broad side to the north, and the narrow end to the south. This is not unlike the configuration of India in Ptolemy's Geography; but a much more accurate description is given by the Chinese author of the *Fah-kai-lih-to,* who says, "this country in shape is narrow towards the south and broad towards the north;" to which he humorously adds,

* Pauthier, in Journ. Asiatique, Oct. 1839, p. 273, and Journ. Asiat. Soc. Bengal, 1837, p. 65.

† M. Julien's 'Hiouen Thsang,' ii. 58; and Pauthier, in Journ. Asiatique, Dec. 1839, p. 447.

‡ M. Julien's 'Hiouen Thsang,' ii. 162, 163; see also Pauthier, in Journ. Asiatique, 1839, p. 384.

that "the people's faces are the same shape as the country."*

Hwen Thsang makes the circumference of India 90,000 *li*,† which is more than double the truth. But in the Chinese official records,‡ the circuit of India is said to be only 30,000 *li;* which is too small, if we reckon 6 *li* to the British mile, according to the usual road distance of the Chinese pilgrims. But if, as was probably the case, the measurement was made on a map, the *li* may be reckoned at the full value of 1079.12 feet which it possessed in the eighth century; then the 30,000 *li* will be equal to 6130 British miles, which is only 764 miles short of the dimensions recorded by Strabo on the authority of Alexander's papers, and the published works of Megasthenes and Patrokles.

The Five Divisions of India, or the "Five Indies," as they are usually called by the Chinese, are as follows (see No. I. Map):—

I. *Northern India* comprised the Panjâb proper, including Kashmir and the adjoining hill states, with the whole of eastern Afghanistan beyond the Indus, and the present Cis-Satlej States to the west of the Saraswati river.

II. *Western India* comprised Sindh and Western Rajputâna, with Kachh and Gujarât, and a portion

---

* 'Fah-Hian's Travels,' translated by the Rev. S. Beal, p. 36, note.

† M. Juien's 'Hiouen Thsang,' ii. 58.

‡ Pauthier, in Journ. Asiatique, Nov. 1839, p. 384.

of the adjoining coast on the lower course of the Narbadâ river.

III. *Central India* comprised the whole of the Gangetic provinces from Thânesar to the head of the Delta, and from the Himâlaya mountains to the banks of the Narbadâ.

IV. *Eastern India* comprised Assam and Bengal proper, including the whole of the Delta of the Ganges, together with Sambhalpur, Orissa, and Ganjam.

V. *Southern India* comprised the whole of the Peninsula from Nâsik on the west and Ganjam on the east, to Cape Kumâri (Comorin) on the south, including the modern districts of Berâr and Telingâna, Mahârâshtra and the Konkan, with the separate states of Haidarabad, Mysore, and Travancore, or very nearly the whole of the peninsula to the south of the Narbadâ and Mahânadi rivers.

Although the Chinese division of India into five great provinces is simpler than the well-known native arrangement of nine divisions, as described by Varâha-Mihira and the Purânas, yet there can be little doubt that they borrowed their system from the Hindus, who likened their native country to the lotus-flower, the middle being Central India, and the eight surrounding petals being the other divisions, which were named after the eight chief points of the compass.* In the Chinese arrangement, the middle

* Wilson's 'Vishnu Purâna,' edited by Hall, vol. ii.

and the four primary divisions only are retained; and as this division is much simpler, and also more easily remembered, I will adopt it in the present description.

At the time of Hwen Thsang's visit, in the seventh century, India was divided into eighty* kingdoms, each of which would appear to have had its separate ruler, although most of them were tributary to a few of the greater states. Thus, in Northern India, the districts of Kabul, Jalâlâbâd, Peshâwar, Ghazni, and Banu were all subject to the ruler of Kapisa, whose capital was most probably at Charikâr, or Alexandria ad Caucasum. In the Panjâb proper the hilly districts of Taxila, Singhapura, Urasa, Punach, and Rajaori, were subject to the Raja of *Kashmir;* while the whole of the plains, including Multan and Shorkot, were dependent on the ruler of Tâki, or Sangala, near Lahor. In Western India the provinces were divided between the kings of *Sindh, Balabhi,* and *Gurjjara.* In Central and Eastern India, the whole of the different states, from the famous city of Sthâneswara to the mouth of the Ganges, and from the Himâlaya mountains to the banks of the Narbadâ and Mahânadi

---

b. ii. c. 12. p. 309; "the lotus-shaped earth." Ward's 'Hindus,' i. 9, and ii. 449.

* 'Hiouen Thsang,' ii. 59. The text has "seventy"; but the number actually described is eighty-two, from which, deducting Persia and Ceylon, the true number of kingdoms is eighty.

rivers, were subject to Harsha Vardhana, the great King of Kanoj. Jâlandhara, the most easterly district of the Panjâb, was also subject to him; and it is highly probable that the ruler of *Tâki*, or the plains of the Panjâb, must likewise have been a dependent of Kanoj, as we are informed by the Chinese pilgrim that Harsha Varddhana advanced through his territory to the foot of the Kashmir hills, for the purpose of coercing the ruler of that country to deliver up to him a much-venerated tooth of Buddha. The Rajput king of Mahârâshtra, in Southern India, was the only sovereign who had successfully resisted the armies of Kanoj. This statement of the Chinese pilgrim is corroborated by several inscriptions of the Châlukya princes of Mahârâshtra, who make a proud boast of their ancestor's discomfiture of the great king Harsha Varddhana.* This powerful prince was the paramount sovereign of thirty-six different States, comprising nearly one-half of India in extent, and including all its richest and most fertile provinces. The substantial reality of his power may be gathered from the fact that no less than eighteen, or just one-half, of these tributary princes attended on their suzerain lord during his great religious procession from Pâtaliputra to Kanoj, in A.D. 643. The extent of his dominions is clearly indicated by the names of the countries against which he directed his latest campaigns, namely, Kashmir in the north-

---

* See copper-plate inscriptions in Journ. Bombay Asiat. Soc. ii. 5, and iii. p. 207.

west, Mahârâshtra in the south-west, and Ganjam in the south-east.* Within these boundaries he was the paramount ruler of the continent of India during the first half of the seventh century of the Christian era.

The dominion of Southern India was nearly equally divided between the nine rulers of the following states:—Mahârâshtra and Kosala, in the north; Kalinga, Andhra, Konkana, and Dhanakakata, in the centre; and Jorya, Drâvida, and Mâlakuta, in the south. These complete the round number of eighty kingdoms into which India was divided in the seventh century of our era.

1. NORTHERN INDIA.

The natural boundaries of India are the Himâlaya mountains, the river Indus and the sea. But on the west, these limits have been so frequently overstepped by powerful kings that most authors, from the time of Alexander down to a very late period, have considered Eastern Ariana, or the greater part of Afghanistan, as forming a portion of the Indian continent. Thus Pliny† says that "most writers do not fix the Indus as the western boundary

---

* Julien's 'Hiouen Thsang,' Kashmir, i. 251; Mahârâshtra, iii. 150; Ganjam, i. 220, 236.

† Plin. Hist. Nat., vi. 23. "Etenim plerique ab occidente non Indo amne determinant, sed adjiciunt quatuor satrapias, Gedrosos, Arachotas, Arios, Paropamisadas, ultimo fine Cophete fluvio."

(of India), but add to it the four satrapies of the Gedrosi, Arachotæ, Arii, and Paropamisadæ,—thus making the river Cophes its extreme boundary." Strabo* also says that "the Indians occupy (in part) some of the countries situated along the Indus, which formerly belonged to the Persians. Alexander deprived the Ariani of them, and established there settlements of his own. But Seleukus Nikator gave them to Sandrokottus, in consequence of a marriage contract, and received in return five hundred elephants." The prince here mentioned is the well-known Chandra Gupta Maurya, whose grandson Asoka dispatched missionaries to the most distant parts of his empire for the propagation of Buddhism. *Alasadda,* or Alexandria ad Caucasum, the capital of the *Yona,* or Greek country, is recorded as one of these distant places; and as the Chinese pilgrim Hwen Thsang notices several *stupas* in that neighbourhood as the work of Asoka, we have the most satisfactory proofs of the Indian occupation of the Kabul valley in the third and fourth centuries before Christ. The completeness of this occupation is well shown by the use of the Indian language on the coins of the Bactrian Greeks and Indo-Scythians, down to

* Geogr., xv. 2, 9. In another place, xv. I, II, he states that at the time of the invasion of Alexander "the Indus was the boundary of India and of Ariana, situated towards the west, and in the possession of the Persians, for *afterwards* the Indians occupied a larger portion of Ariana, which they had received from the Macedonians."

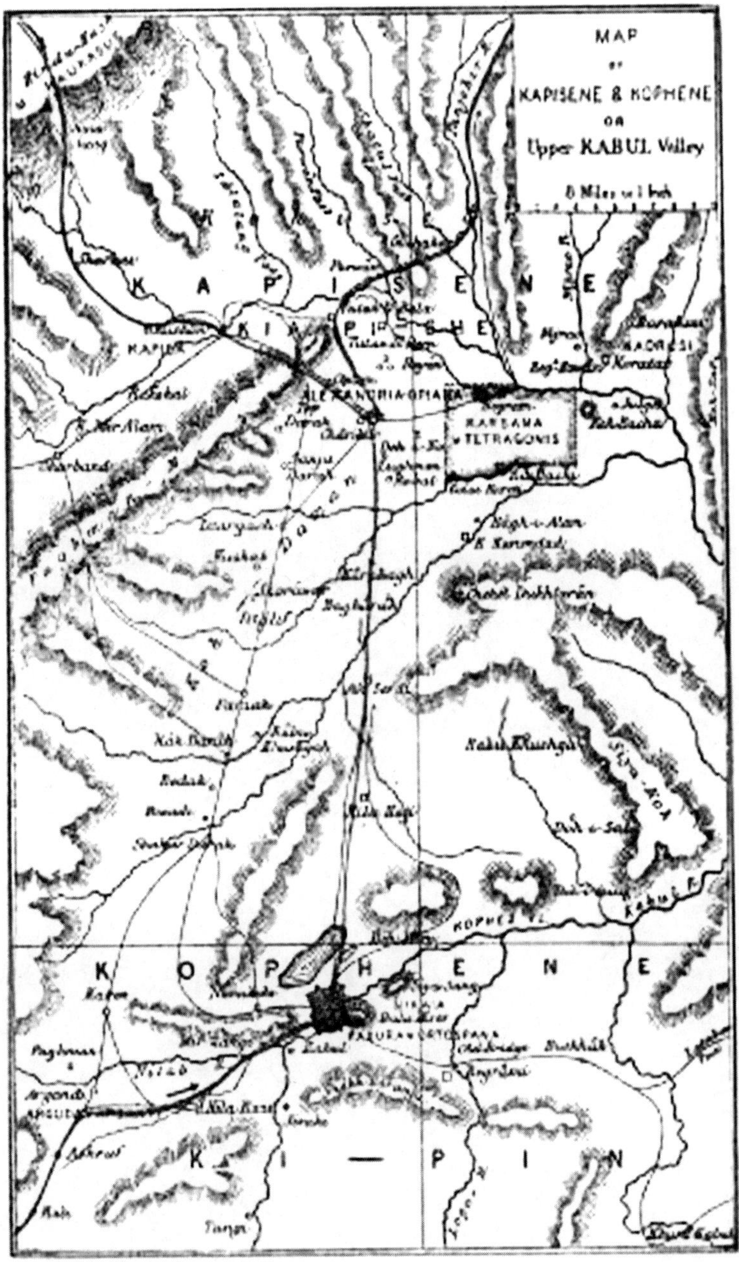
MAP
OF
KAPISENE & KOPHENE
OR
Upper KABUL Valley
K A P I S E N E
ALEXANDRIA OPIANA
KARSANA TETRAGONIS
K O P H E N E
K I — P I N

A.D. 100, or perhaps even later; and although it is lost for the next two or three centuries, it again makes its appearance on the coins of the Abtelites, or White Huns, of the sixth century. In the following century, as we learn from the Chinese pilgrim, the king of Kapisa was a *Kshatriya*, or pure Hindu. During the whole of the tenth century the Kabul valley was held by a dynasty of Brahmans, whose power was not finally extinguished until towards the close of the reign of Mahmud Ghaznavi. Down to this time, therefore, it would appear that a great part of the population of eastern Afghanistan, including the whole of the Kabul valley, must have been of Indian descent, while the religion was pure Buddhism. During the rule of the Ghaznavis, whose late conversion to Muhammadanism had only added bigotry to their native ferocity, the persecution of idol-loving Buddhists was a pleasure as well as a duty. The idolaters were soon driven out, and with them the Indian element, which had subsisted for so many centuries in Eastern Ariana, finally disappeared.

NOTHERN INDIA.

I. KAOFU, OR AFGHANISTAN.

For several centuries, both before and after the Christian era, the provinces of Northern India beyond the Indus, in which the Indian language and religion were predominant, included the whole of Afghanistan from Bamian and Kandahar on the west to the Bholân Pass on the south. This large tract was then divided into ten* separate states or districts, of which Kapisa was the chief. The tributary states were Kabul and Ghazni in the west, Lamghân and Jalâlâbâd in the north, Swât and Peshâwar in the east, Bolor in the north-east, and Banu and Opokien in the south. The general name for the whole would appear to have been *Kao-fu*, which in the second century before Christ is described as being divided between the Parthians, the Indians, and the Su or Sacæ of Kipin. According to this statement, the south-west district of Kandahar would have belonged to the Parthians, the eastern districts of Swât, Peshâwar, and Banu, to the Indians, and the north-western districts of Kabul and Ghazni with Lamghân and Jalâlâbâd to the Sacæ Scythians. *Kaofu* has usually been identified with Kabul on account of its similarity of name and correspondence of position; but this can only be accepted as politically correct, by extending the boundaries of Kabul into Parthia† on the west, and into India on the east. The *Kaofu* of the Chinese would, therefore, have embraced the whole of modern Afghanistan.

* M. Julien's 'Hiouen Thsang,' i. 71.

† That Kandahar then belonged to Persia is proved by the fact, that the begging-pot of Buddha, which Hwen Thsang (ii. 106) mentions as having been removed from Gândhâra to Persia, still exists at Kandahar, where it was seen by Sir H. Rawlinson. The removal must have taken place during the sixth century, after the conquest of Gândhâra by the king of Kipin.

Etymologically, however, it seems quite possible that the two names may be the same, as *Kaofu* was the appellation of one of the five tribes of the *Yuchi* or Tochari, who are said to have given their own name to the town which they occupied, towards the end of the second century before Christ. This statement of the Chinese writers is confirmed by the historians of Alexander, who notice the city of Ortospana, without making any mention of Kabul. The latter name is first given by Ptolemy, who describes *Kabura* or *Ortospana* as the capital of the Paropamisadæ. I conclude, therefore, that Ortospana was most probably the original metropolis of the country, which was supplanted by Alexandria during the Greek domination, and restored by the earlier Indo-Scythian princes. But it would appear to have been again abandoned before the seventh century, when the capital of Kapisene was at Opiân.

1. KAPISENE, OR OPIÂN.

According to the Chinese pilgrim *Kiapishe*, or *Kapisene*, was 4000 *li*, or about 666 miles in circuit. If this measurement be even approximately correct, the district must have included the whole of Kafiristan, as well as the two large valleys of Ghorband and Panjshir, as these last are together not more than 300 miles in circuit. *Kiapishe* is further described as being entirely surrounded by mountains; to the north by snowy mountains, named *Po-lo-si-na*, and by black hills on the other three sides. The name of *Polosina* corresponds exactly with that of Mount *Paresh* or *Aparasin* of the 'Zend Avesta,'* and with the Paropamisus of the Greeks, which included the Indian Caucasus, or Hindu Kush. Hwen Thsang further states, that to the north-west of the capital there was a great snowy mountain, with a lake on its summit, distant only 200 *li,* or about 33 miles. This is the Hindu Kush itself, which is about 35 miles to the north-west of Charikâr and Opiân; but I have not been able to trace any mention of the lake in the few imperfect notices that exist of this part of Afghanistan.

The district of *Capisene* is first mentioned by Pliny, who states that its ancient capital, named Capisa, was destroyed by Cyrus. His copyist, Solinus, mentions the same story, but calls the city *Caphusa,* which the Delphine editors have altered to *Capissa.* Somewhat later, Ptolemy places the town of *Kapisa* amongst the Paropamisadæ 2½ degrees to the north of Kabura or Kabul, which is nearly 2 degrees in excess of the truth. On leaving Bamian, in A.D. 630, the Chinese pilgrim travelled 600 *li,* or about 100 miles, in an easterly direction over snowy mountains and black hills (or the Koh-i-Bâbâ and Paghmân ranges) to the capital of *Kiapishe* or Kapisene. On his return from India, fourteen years later, he reached *Kiapishe* through Ghazni

* 'Zend Avesta,' iii. 365, Boundehesh. "It is said that Aparasin is a great mountain, distinct from Elburj. It is called Mount Paresh."

and Kabul, and left it in a north-east direction by the Panjshir valley towards Anderâb. These statements fix the position of the capital at or near *Opiân*, which is just 100 miles to the east of Bamian by the route of the Hajiak Pass and Ghorband Valley, and on the direct route from Ghazni and Kabul to Anderâb. The same locality is, perhaps, even more decidedly indicated by the fact, that the Chinese pilgrim, on finally leaving the capital of Kapisene, was accompanied by the king as far as the town of *Kiu-lu-sa-pang*, a distance of one *yojana*, or about 7 miles to the north-east, from whence the road turned towards the north. This description agrees exactly with the direction of the route from Opiân to the northern edge of the plain of Begrâm, which lies about 6 or 7 miles to the E. N. E. of Charikâr and Opiân. Begrâm itself I would identify with the *Kiu-lu-sa-pang* or *Karsawana* of the Chinese pilgrim, the *Karsana* of Ptolemy, and the *Cartana* of Pliny. If the capital had then been at Begrâm itself, the king's journey of seven miles to the north-east would have taken him over the united stream of the Panjshir and Ghorband rivers, and as this stream is difficult to cross, on account of its depth and rapidity, it is not likely that the king would have undertaken such a journey for the mere purpose of leave-taking. But by fixing the capital at Opiân, and by identifying Begrâm with the *Kiu-lu-sa-pang* of the Chinese pilgrim, all difficulties disappear. The king accompanied his honoured guest to the bank of the Panjshir river, where he took leave of him, and the pilgrim then crossed the stream, and proceeded on his journey to the north, as described in the account of his life.

From all the evidence above noted it would appear certain that the capital of *Kiapishe*, or *Kapisene*, in the seventh century, must have been situated either at or near *Opiân*. This place was visited by Masson,* who describes it as "distinguished by its huge artificial mounds, from which, at various times, copious antique treasures have been extracted." In another place† he notes that "it possesses many vestiges of antiquity; yet, as they are exclusively of a sepulchral or religious character, the site of the city, to which they refer, may rather be looked for at the actual village of Malik Hupiân on the plain below, and near Charikâr." Masson writes the name Hupiân, following the emperor Baber; but as it is entered in Walker's large map as *Opiyân*, after Lieutenant Leach, and is spelt *Opiân* by Lieutenant Sturt, both of whom made regular surveys of the Koh-dâman, I adopt the unaspirated reading, as it agrees better wih the Greek forms of *Opiai* and *Opiane* of Hekatæus and Stephanus, and with the Latin form of *Opianum* of Pliny. As these names are intimately connected with that of the Paropamisan Alexandria, it will clear the way to further investigation, if we first determine the most probable site of this famous city.

---

* 'Travels,' iii. 126.

† 'Travels,' iii. 161.

The position of the city founded by Alexander at the foot of the Indian Caucasus has long engaged the attention of scholars; but the want of a good map of the Kabul valley has been a serious obstacle to their success, which was rendered almost insurmountable by their injudicious alterations of the only ancient texts that preserved the distinctive name of the Caucasian Alexandria. Thus Stephanus* describes it as being ἐν τῇ 'Οπιανῇ κατὰ τὴν 'Ινδικήν, "in Opiane, near India," for which Salmasius proposed to read Αριανῇ. Again, Pliny† describes it as *Alexandriam Opianes*, which in the Leipsic and other editions is altered to *Alexandri oppidum*. I believe, also, that the same distinctive name may be restored to a corrupt passage of Pliny, where he is speaking of this very part of the country. His words, as given by the Leipsic editor, and as quoted by Cellarius,‡ are "Cartana oppidum sub Caucaso, quod postea Tetragonis dictum. Hæc regio est ex adverso. Bactrianorum deinde cujus oppidum Alexandria, a conditore dictum." Both of the translators whose works I possess, namely Philemon Holland, A.D. 1601, and W. T. Riley, A.D. 1855, agree in reading *ex adverso Bactrianorum*. This makes sense of the words as they stand, but it makes nonsense of the passage, as it refers the city

---

* *In voce* Alexandria.

† Hist. Nat., vi. c. 17 Philemon Holland calls it "the city of Alexandria, in Opianum."

‡ Hist. Nat., vi. 23.

of Alexandria to Bactria, a district which Pliny had fully described in a previous chapter. He is speaking of the country at the foot of the Caucasus or Paropamisus; and as he had already described the Bactrians as being "aversa montis Paropamisi," he now uses almost the same terms to describe the position of the district in which Cartana was situated; I would, therefore, propose to read "hæc regio est ex adverso Bactriæ"; and as *cujus* cannot possibly refer to the Bactrians, I would begin the next sentence by changing the latter half of Bactrianorum in the text to *Opiorum;* the passage would then stand thus, "Opiorum (regio) deinde, cujus oppidum Alexandria a conditore dictum,"—"Next the Opii, whose city, Alexandria, was named after its founder." But whether this emendation be accepted or not, it is quite clear from the other two passages, above quoted, that the city founded by Alexander at the foot of the Indian Caucasus was also named Opiane. This fact being established, I will now proceed to show that the position of Alexandria Opiane agrees as nearly as possible with the site of the present Opiân, near Charikâr.

According to Pliny, the city of Alexandria, in Opianum, was situated at 50 Roman miles, or 45.96 English miles, from Ortospana, and at 237 Roman miles, or 217.8 English miles, from Peucolaitis, or Pukkalaoti, which was a few miles to the north of Peshâwar. As the position of Ortospana will be discussed in my account of the next province,

I will here only state that I have indentified it with the ancient city of Kabul and its citadel, the Bala Hisar. Now Charikâr is 27 miles* to the north of Kabul, which differs by 19 miles from the measurement recorded by Pliny. But as immediately after the mention of this distance he adds that "in some copies different numbers are found,"† I am inclined to read "triginta millia," or 30 miles, instead of "quinquaginta millia," which is found in the text. This would reduce the distance to 27½ English miles, which exactly accords with the measurement between Kabul and Opiân. The distance between these places is not given by the Chinese pilgrim Hwen Thsang; but that between the capital of *Kiapishe* and *Pu-lu-sha-pu-lo*, or Purushapura, the modern Peshâwar, is stated at 600 + 100 + 500 = 1200 *li*, or just 200 miles according to my estimate of 6 *li* to the English mile. The last distance of 500 *li*, between Nagarahâra and Purushâwar, is certainly too short, as the earlier pilgrim, Fa Hian, in the beginning of the fifth century, makes it 16 *yojanas*, or not less than 640 *li*, at 40 *li* to the *yojana*. This would increase the total distance to 1340 *li*, or 223 miles, which differs only by 5 miles from the statement of the Roman author. The actual

* Measured by Lieutenant Sturt with a perambulator. Masson gives the same distance for Begrâm. See No. III. Map from Sturt's Survey.

† Hist. Nat., vi. 21. "In quibusdam exemplaribus diversi numeri reperiuntur."

road distance between Charikâr and Jalâlâbâd has not been ascertained, but as it measures in a direct line on Walker's map about 10 miles more than the distance between Kabul and Jalâlâbâd, which is 115 miles, it may be estimated at 125 miles. This sum added to 103 miles, the length of road between Jalâlâbâd and Peshâwar, makes the whole distance from Charikâr to Peshâwar not less than 228 miles, which agrees very closely with the measurements recorded by the Roman and Chinese authors.

Pliny further describes Alexandria as being situated *sub ipso Caucaso,** "at the very foot of Caucasus," which agrees exactly with the position of Opiân, at the northern end of the plain of *Koh dâman*, or "hill-foot." The same position is noted by Curtius, who places Alexandria *in radicibus montis*,† at the very base of the mountain. The place was chosen by Alexander on account of its favourable site at the τρίοδον,‡ or parting of the "three roads" leading to Bactria. These roads, which still remain unchanged, all separate at Opiân, near Begrâm.

1. The north-east road, by the Panjshir valley, and over the Khâwak Pass to Anderâb.
2. The west road, by the Kushân valley, and over the Hindu Kush Pass to Ghori.

---

* Hist. Nat., vi. s. 21. † Vit. Alex., vii. 3.

‡ Strabo, xv. 2, 8.

3. The south-west road, up the Ghorband valley, and over the Hâjiyak Pass to Bamian.

The first of these roads was followed by Alexander on his march into Bactriana from the territory of the Paropamisadæ. It was also taken by Timur on his invasion of India: and it was crossed by Lieutenant Wood on his return from the sources of the Oxus. The second road must have been followed by Alexander on his return from Bactriana, as Strabo* specially mentions that he took "over the same mountains another and shorter road" than that by which he had advanced. It is certain that his return could not have been by the Bamian route, as that is the longest route of all; besides which, it *turns* the Hindu Kush, and does not cross it, as Alexander is stated to have done. This route was attempted by Dr. Lord and Lieutenant Wood late in the year, but they were driven back by the snow. The third road is the easiest and most frequented. It was taken by Janghez Khan after his capture of Bamian; it was followed by Moorcroft and Burnes on their adventurous journeys to Balkh and Bokhara; it was traversed by Lord and Wood after their failure at the Kushan Pass; and it was surveyed by Sturt in A.D. 1840, after it had been successfully crossed by a troop of horse artillery.

Alexandria is not found in Ptolemy's list of the towns of the Paropamisadæ; but as his *Niphanda*,

* Geogr., xv. 1, 26.

which is placed close to Kapisa, may with a very little alteration be read as *Ophianda,* I think that we may perhaps recognize the Greek capital under this slightly altered form. The name of *Opiân* is certainly as old as the fifth century B.C., as Hekatæus places a people called *Opiai* to the west of the upper course of the Indus. There is, however, no trace of this name in the inscriptions of Darius, but we have instead a nation called *Thatagush,* who are the *Sattagudai* of Herodotus, and perhaps also the people of *Si-pi-to-fa-la-sse* of the Chinese pilgrim Hwen Thsang.* This place was only 40 *li,* or about 7 miles, distant from the capital of Kiapishe, but unfortunately the direction is not stated. As, however, it is noted that there was a mountain named *Aruna* at a distance of 5 miles to the south, it is almost certain that this city must have been on the famous site of Begrâm, from which the north end of the *Siah-koh,* or Black Mountain, called *Chehel Dukhtarân,* or the "Forty Daughters," lies almost due south at a distance of 5 or 6 miles. It is possible, also, that the name of *Tâtarangzâr,* which Masson gives to the south-west corner of the ruins of Begrâm, may be an altered form of the ancient *Thâtagush,* or *Sattagudai.* But whether this be so or not, it is quite certain that the people dwelling on the upper branches of the Kabul river must be the *Thâtagush* of Darius, and the *Sattagudai* of Hero-

---

* Sipitofalasse is probably the Sanskrit *Saptavarsha* or *Sattavasa,* which might easily be changed to Thatagush.

dotus, as all the other surrounding nations are mentioned in both authorities.

Karsana, Kartana or Tetragonis.

The passage of Pliny describing the position of Alexandria is prefaced by a few words regarding the town of *Cartana,* which, while they assign it a similar position at the foot of the Caucasus, seem also to refer it to the immediate vicinity of Alexander's city. I quote the whole passage, with the correction which I have already proposed:*—"Cartana oppidum sub Caucaso, quod postea Tetragonis dictum. Hæc regio est ex adverso Bactriæ. Opiorum (regio) deinde cujus oppidum Alexandria a conditore dictum." "At the foot of the Caucasus stands the town of Cartana, which was afterwards called Tetragonis (or the Square). This district is opposite to Bactria. Next (to it) are the Opii, whose city of Alexandria was named after its founder." Solinus makes no mention of Cartana, but Ptolemy has a town named Karsana, or Karnasa, which he places on the right bank of a nameless river that comes from the vicinity of Kapisa and Niphanda (or Opiân), and joins the river of *Locharna,* or Loh-garh, nearly opposite Nagara. This stream I take to be the united Panjshir and Ghorband river, which joins the Lohgarh river about halfway between Kabul and Jalâlâbâd. This identification is rendered nearly certain by the position assigned to the *Lambatæ,* or people of Lampaka or Lamghan, who are placed to the east of

* Hist. Nat., vi. 23.

the nameless river, which cannot therefore be the Kunar river, as might otherwise have been inferred from its junction with the Lohgarh river opposite Nagara.

This being the case, the *Karsana* of Ptolemy may at once be identified with the *Cartana* of Pliny; and the few facts related by both authors may be combined to aid us in discovering its true position. According to Pliny, it was situated at the foot of the Caucasus, and not far from Alexandria; whilst, according to Ptolemy, it was on the right bank of the Panjshir river. These data point to Begrâm, which is situated on the right bank of the united Panjshir and Ghorband rivers, immediately at the foot of the Kohistan hills, and within 6 miles of Opiân, or Alexandria Opiane. As I know of no other place that answers all these requirements, it seems most probable that Begrâm must be the true locality. Parwân and Kushân are ancient places of some consequence in the neighbourhood of Opiân; but they are both on the left bank of the Ghorband river, while the first is probably the *Baborana* of Ptolemy, and the other his *Kapisa*. Begrâm also answers the description which Pliny gives of Cartana, as *Tetragonis*, or the "Square"; for Masson, in his account of the ruins, specially notices "some mounds of great magnitude, and accurately describing a square of considerable dimensions."*

---

* 'Travels,' iii. 155. For the position of Begrâm see No. III. Map.

If I am right in identifying Begrâm with the *Kiu-lu-sa-pang* of the Chinese pilgrim, the true name of the place must have been *Karsana*, as written by Ptolemy, and not *Cartana*, as noted by Pliny. The same form of the name is also found on a rare coin of Eukratides, with the legend *Karisiye nagara*, or "city of *Karisi*," which I have identified with the *Kalasi* of the Buddhist chronicles, as the birthplace of Raja Milindu. In another passage of the same chronicle,* Milindu is said to have been born at *Alasanda*, or Alexandria, the capital of the *Yona*, or Greek country. Kalasi must therefore have been either Alexandria itself or some place close to it. The latter conclusion agrees exactly with the position of Begrâm, which is only a few miles to the east of Opiân. Originally two distinct places, like Delhi and Shah Jahanabad, or London and Westminster, I suppose *Opiân* and *Karsana* to have gradually approached each other as they increased in size, until at last they virtually became one large city. On the coins of the earlier Greek kings of Ariana,—Euthydemus, Demetrius, and Eukratides,—we find the monograms of both cities; but after the time of Eukratides, that of Opiana disappears altogether, while that of Karsana is common to most of the later princes. The contemporary occurrence of these mint monograms proves that the two cities were existing at the same time; while the sudden disuse

---

* *Milindu-prasna*, quoted by Hardy, in 'Manual of Buddhism,' pp. 440, 516.

of the name of Opian may serve to show that, during the latter period of Greek occupation, the city of Alexandria had been temporarily supplanted by Karsana.

The appellation of Begrâm means, I believe, nothing more than "the city" *par excellence,* as it is also applied to three other ancient sites in the immediate vicinity of great capitals, namely, Kabul, Jalâlâbâd, and Peshâwar. Masson derives the appellation from the Turki *be* or *bi,* "chief," and the Hindi *grâm,* or city,—that is, the capital.* But a more simple derivation would be from the Sanskrit *vi,* implying "certainty," "ascertainment," as in *vijaya,* victory, which is only an emphatic form of *jaya* with the prefix *vi.* *Vigrâma* would therefore mean emphatically "the city"—that is, the capital; and *Bigrâm* would be the Hindi form of the name, just as *Bijay* is the spoken form of *Vijaya.*

The plain of Begrâm is bounded by the Panjshir and the Koh-dâman rivers on the north and south; by the Mahighir canal on the west; and on the east by the lands of Julgha, in the fork of the two rivers. Its length, from Bayân, on the Mahighir canal, to Julgha, is about 8 miles; and its breadth, from Kilah Buland to Yuz Bashi, is 4 miles. Over the whole of this space vast numbers of relics have been discovered, consisting of small images, coins, seals, beads, rings, arrow-heads, fragments of pottery, and

* 'Travels,' iii. 165.

other remains, which prove that this plain was once the site of a great city. According to the traditions of the people, Begrâm was a Greek city, which was overwhelmed by some natural catastrophe.* Masson doubts the tradition, and infers from the vast number of Kufic coins found there, that the city must have existed for some centuries after the Muhammadan invasion. I am inclined to think that Masson is right, and that the decline of the city was caused by the gradual desertion of the people, consequent on the transfer of the seat of government to Ghazni, after the conquest of the country by the Muhammadans. Coins of the last Hindu Rajas of Kabul and of the first Muhammadan kings of Ghazni are found in great numbers; but the money of the later Ghaznavi princes is less plentiful, whilst of the succeeding Ghori dynasty only a few specimens of some of the earlier sovereigns have yet been discovered. From these plain facts, I infer that the city began gradually to decay after the Muhammadan conquest of Kabul by Sabuktugîn, towards the end of the tenth century, and that it was finally deserted about the beginning of the thirteenth century. As the latter period corresponds with the date of Janghez Khan's invasion of these provinces, it is very possible, as Masson has already supposed, that Begrâm may have been finally destroyed by that merciless barbarian.

* Masson, 'Travels,' iii. 159.

Other Cities of Kapisene.

I will close this account of Kapisene with some remarks on the few other cities of the same district that are mentioned by ancient authors. Pliny describes one city as "ad Caucasum Cadrusi, oppidum ab Alexandro conditum," which is slightly altered by Solinus to "Cadrusia oppidum ab Alexandro Magno ad Caucasum constitutum est, ubi et Alexandria."* Both authors place the city close to the Caucasus, to which Solinus adds, that it was also near Alexandria. Following these two distinct indications, I am disposed to identify the city of *Cadrusi* with the old site of *Koratâs,* which Masson discovered under the hills of Kohistan, 6 miles to the north-east of Begrâm, and on the north bank of the Panjshir river.† There are the usual remains of an old city, consisting of mounds covered with fragments of pottery, amongst which old coins are frequently found. There are also remains of masonry works about the hills, which the people call Kâfir-kot, or the Kâfir's fort. The commentators have accused Solinus of misunderstanding Pliny, whose *Cadrusi,* they say, was the name of a people, and whose "oppidum ab Alexandro conditum" was the city of Alexandria.‡ But the passage was differently understood by Philemon Holland, who renders it thus:—"Upon the hill Caucasus standeth

* Plin. Hist. Nat., vi. 25. Solin. lvii.

† 'Travels,' iii. 166.

‡ Cellarius, iii. 22, p. 514, "quod Solinus pervertit."

the town *Cadrusi,* built likewise by the said Alexander." As a general rule, the Greeks would seem to have designated the various peoples whom they encountered by the names of their principal towns. Thus we have Kabura and the Kabolitæ, Drepsa and the Drepsiani, Taxila and the Taxili, Kaspeira and the Kaspeiræi, from which I would infer, that there was most probably also a town named Cadrusia, whose inhabitants were called Cadrusi. This inference is strengthened by the correspondence, both in name and in position of the ruined mound of Koratâs, with the Cadrusi of Pliny.

The names of other peoples and towns are recorded by Ptolemy; but few of them can now be identified, as we have nothing to guide us but the bare names. The *Parsii,* with their towns *Parsia* and *Parsiana,* I take to be the *Pashais,* or people of the Panjhir or Panjshir valley. The true name is probably *Panchir,* as the Arabs always write *j* for the Indian *ch.* The modern spelling of Panjshir adopted by Burnes, Leech, and others, appears to be only an attempt to give the Afghan pronunciation of *ch* as *ts* in *Pantsir.* A town named *Panjhir* is mentioned by the early Arab geographers, and a mountain named *Pashâi* was crossed by Ibn Batuta, on his way from Kunduz to Parwân.*

Other tribes are the *Aristophyli,* a pure Greek name, and the *Ambautæ,* of whom nothing is

---

* 'Travels,' p. 98.

known. The towns not already noticed are *Artoarta* and *Barzaura* in the north, and *Drastoka* and *Naulibis* in the south. The second of these may be Bazârak, a large town in the Panjshir valley, and the last may be Nilâb of Ghorband. The third was most probably a town in one of the *darâs* or valleys of the Koh-dâman.

2. KOPHENE, OR KABUL.

The district of Kabul is first mentioned by Ptolemy, who calls the people *Kabolitœ,* and their capital *Kabura,* which was also named *Ortospana.* The latter name alone is found in Strabo and Pliny, with a record of its distance from the capital of Arachosia, as measured by Alexander's surveyors, Diognetes and Baiton. In some copies of Pliny the name is written *Orthospanum,* which, with a slight alteration to *Orthostana,* as suggested by H. H. Wilson,* is most probably the Sanskrit *Urddhasthâna,* that is, the "high place," or lofty city. The same name is also given to the Kabul district by the Chinese pilgrim Hwen Thsang. But I strongly suspect that there has been some accidental interchange of names between the province and its capital. On leaving Ghazni, the pilgrim travelled to the north for 500 *li,* or 83 miles, to *Fo-li-shi-sa-tang-na,* of which the capital was *Hu-phi-na.* Now by two different measured routes the distance between Ghazni and Kabul was found to be 81 and 88½

* 'Ariana Antiqua,' p. 176.

miles.* There can be no doubt, therefore, that Kabul must be the place that was visited by the pilgrim. In another place the capital is said to be 700 *li*, or 116 miles, from Bamian, which agrees very well with the measured distance of 104 miles† between Bamian and Kabul, along the shortest route.

The name of the capital, as given by the Chinese pilgrim, has been rendered by M. Vivien de St. Martin as *Vardasthâna*, and identified with the district of the Wardak tribe, while the name of the province has been identified with Hupiân or Opiân. But the Wardak valley, which receives its name from the Wardak tribe, lies on the upper course of the Logarh river, at some distance to the south of Kabul, and only 40 miles to the north of Ghazni, while Hupiân or Opiân lies 27 miles to the north of Kabul, or more than 70 miles distant from Wardak. My own researches lead me to conclude that both names refer to the immediate neighbourhood of Kabul itself.

Professor Lassen has already remarked that the name of *Kipin*, which is so frequently mentioned by other Chinese authors, is not once noticed by Hwen Thsang. Remusat first suggested that Kipin was the country on the Kophes or Kabul river; and this suggestion has ever since been accepted by the unanimous consent of all writers on ancient India, by whom the district is now generally called Kophene.

---

* Thornton's 'Gazetteer,' Appendix.

† Lieutenant Sturt, Engineers, by perambulator.

It is this form of the name of *Kipin* that I propose to identify with the *Hu-phi-na* of Hwen Thsang, as it seems to me scarcely possible that this once famous province can have remained altogether unnoticed by him, when we know that he must have passed through it, and that the name was still in use for more than a century after his time.* I have already stated my suspicion that there has been some interchange of names between the province and its capital. This suspicion is strengthened when it is found that all difficulties are removed, and the most complete identification obtained, by the simple interchange of the two names. Thus *Hu-phi-na* will represent *Kophene*, or *Kipin*, the country on the Kabul river, and *Fo-li-shi-sa-tang-na*, or *Urddhasthâna*, will represent *Ortostana*, which, as we know from several classical authorities, was the actual capital of this province. I may remark that *Huphina* is a very exact Chinese transcript of *Kophen*, whereas it would be a very imperfect transcript of *Hupiân*, as one syllable would be altogether unrepresented, and the simple *p* would be replaced by an aspirate. The correct transcript of Hupiân would be *Hu-pi-yan-na*.

M. Vivien de St. Martin has objected† to the name of *Urddhasthâna* that it is a "conjectural etymology without object." I am, however, quite

* Lassen, 'Points in the History of the Greek Kings of Kabul,' p. 102.

† 'Hiouen Thsang,' iii. 416.

satisfied that this reading is the correct one, for the following reasons:—1st. The name of Ortospana is not confined to the Paropamisadæ; but is found also in Karmania and in Persis. It could not, therefore, have had any reference to the Wardak tribe, but must be a generic name descriptive of its situation, a requirement that is most satisfactorily fulfilled by *Urddhasthâna,* which means literally the "high place," and was most probably employed to designate any hill fortress. 2nd. The variation in the reading of the name to *Portospana* confirms the descriptive meaning which I have given to it, as *porta* signifies "high" in Pushtu, and was, no doubt, generally adopted by the common people instead of the Sanskrit *urddha.*

The position of Ortospana I would identify with Kabul itself, with its *Bala Hisâr,* or "high fort," which I take to be only a Persian translation of *Ortospana,* or *Urddhasthâna.* It was the old capital of the country before the Macedonian conquest, and so late as the tenth century it was still believed "that a king was not properly qualified to govern until he had been inaugurated at Kabul."* Hekatæus also describes a "royal town" amongst the *Opiai,*† but we have no data for determining either its name or its position. It seems most probable, however, that Kabul must be intended, as we know of no other

---

* Ouseley, 'Oriental Geography,' p. 226.

† Steph. Byz. in v. *'Ωπίαι. 'Εν δὲ τεῖχος Βασιλήϊον μέχρι τούτου 'Ωπίαι, ἀπὸ τούτων ἐρημίη μέχρι "Ινδων.*

place that could have held this position after the destruction of Kapisa by Cyrus; but in this case Kabul must have been included within the territories of the Opiai.

It is strange that there is no mention of Kabul in the histories of Alexander, as he must certainly have passed through the town on his way from Arachosia to the site of Alexandria. I think, however, that it is most probably the town of *Nikaia,* which was Alexander's first march from his new city on his return from Bactria. *Nikaia* is described by Nonnus as a stone city, situated near a lake. It was also called Astakia, after a nymph whom Bacchus had abused.* The lake is a remarkable feature, which is peculiar in Northern India to Kabul and Kashmir. The city is also said to have been called *Indophôn,* or "Indian-killer," on account of the victory which Bacchus had gained over the Indians on this spot. From this name I infer, that Nonnus had most probably heard of the popular meaning which is attributed to the name of *Hindu-kush,* or "Hindu-killer," and that he adopted it at once as corroborative of the Indian conquests of Dionysius.

---

* 'Dionysiaca,' xvi., last three lines :—

Καὶ πτόλιν εὐλάϊγγα φιλακρήτῳ, παρὰ λίμνῃ,
Τεῦξε θεὸς Νίκαιαν ἐπώνυμον, ἣν ἀπὸ Νύμφης
'Αστακίης ἐκάλεσσε, καὶ 'Ινδοφόνον μετὰ νίκην.

The meaning of which appears to be, that "Bacchus built a stone city, named *Nikaia,* near a lake, which he also called *Astakia,* after the nymph, and *Indophôn,* in remembrance of his victory."

The province is described as being 2000 *li*, or 333 miles, in length from east to west, and 1000 *li*, or 166 miles, in breadth from north to south. It is probable that this statement may refer to the former extent of the province, when its king was the paramount ruler of Western Afghanistan, including Ghazni and Kandahar, as the actual dimensions of the Kabul district are not more than one-half of the numbers here stated. Its extreme length, from the sources of the Helmand river to the Jagdalak Pass, is about 150 miles, and its extreme breadth, from Istâlif to the sources of the Logarh river, is not more than 70 miles.

The name of Kophes is as old as the time of the Vedas, in which the *Kubhâ* river is mentioned as an affluent of the Indus; and as it is not an Arian word, I infer that the name must have been applied to the Kabul river before the Arian occupation, or, at least, as early as B.C. 2500. In the classical writers we find the *Khoes*, *Kophes*, and *Khoaspes* rivers, to the west of the Indus, and at the present day we have the *Kunar*, the *Kuram*, and the *Gomal* rivers to the west, and the *Kunihar* river to the east of the Indus, all of which are derived from the Scythian *ku*, "water." It is the guttural form of the *Assyrian hu* in Euphrates and Eulæus, and of the Turki *su* and the Tibetan *chu*, all of which mean water or river. The district of *Kophene* must, therefore, have received its name from the river which flowed through it, like as Sindh from the Sindhu or Indus, Margiana from the

Margus, Aria from the Arius; Arachosia from the Arachotus, and others. It is not mentioned by Alexander's historians, although the river Kophes is noticed by all of them.

In Ptolemy's 'Geography' the city of *Kabura* and the *Kabolitæ*, with the towns of *Arguda,* or Argandi, and *Locharna,* or Logarh, are all located in the territories of the Paropamisadæ along the Kabul river. Higher up the stream he places the town of *Bagarda,* which corresponds exactly in position, and very closely in name with the valley of *Wardaḳ*. All the letters of the two names are the same; and as the mere transposition of the guttural to the end of the Greek name will make it absolutely identical with the modern name, there is strong evidence in favour of the reading of *Bardaga* instead of *Bagarda*. According to Elphinstone,* the *Wardaḳ* tribe of Afghans occupy the greater part of the Logarh valley. This is confirmed by Masson,† who twice visited the district of Wardak; and by Vigne,‡ who crossed it on his way from Ghazni to Kabul. The only objection to this identification that occurs to me is, the possibility that *Bagarda* may be the Greek form of *Vaeḳereta,* which is the name given in the 'Zend Avesta' to the seventh country that was successively occupied by the Arian race. From its position between Bactria, Aria, and Arachosia, on

---

* 'Kabul,' i. 160.

† 'Travels,' ii. 223.

‡ 'Ghazni,' p. 140.

one side, and India on the other, *Vaekereta* has usually been identified with the province of Kabul. This, also, is the opinion of the Parsis themselves. Vaekereta is further said to be the seat or home of *Duzhâk*, which further tends to confirm its identification with Kabul, as the acknowledged country of Zohâk. If the *Wardaks* had ever been a ruling tribe, I should be disposed to infer that the name of *Vaekereta* might, probably, have been derived from them. But in our present total ignorance of their history, I think that it is sufficient to note the very great similarity of the two names.

In the seventh century the king of Kophene was a Turk, and the language of the country was different from that of the people of Ghazni. Hwen Thsang mentions that the alphabet of Kapisene was that of the Turks, but that the language was not Turki. As the king, however, was an Indian, it may reasonably be inferred that the language was Indian. For a similar reason it may be conjectured that the language of Kophene was some dialect of Turki, because the king of the district was a Turk.

3. ARACHOSIA, OR GHAZNI.

The Chinese pilgrim places the country of *Tsau-ku-ta* at 500 *li*, or 83 miles, to the south of *Huphina*, or Kophene, and to the north-west of *Falana*, or Banu. The valley of the *Lo-mo-in-tu* river, which is mentioned as producing assafoetida, is readily identified with the Helmand by prefixing the syllable *Ho* to the Chinese transcript. The kingdom is said to have been 7000 *li*, or 1166 miles, in circuit, which cannot be far from the truth, as it most probably included the whole of south-western Afghanistan with the exception of Kandahar, which at that time, from the story of the begging-pot of Buddha already noted, would appear to have belonged to Persia.

This district possessed two capitals, called *Ho-si-na* and *Ho-sa-lo*. The first has been identified by M. de St. Martin with *Ghazni*, which is quite satisfactory; but his suggestion that the other may be connected with *Hazâra* is, I think, very doubtful. Hazâra is the name of a district, and not of a town; and its application to this part of the country is said by the people themselves not to be older than the time of Janghez Khan.* I would, therefore, identify it with *Guzar* or *Guzaristan*, which is the chief town on the Helmand at the present day; and with the *Ozola* of Ptolemy, which he places in the north-west of Arachosia, or in the very same position as *Guzaristan*.

The name of *Tsaukuta* still remains to be explained. The identifications just made show that it corresponds exactly with the Arachosia of classical writers, which is the *Arokhaj* and *Rokhaj* of the Arab geographers. The latter form is also found in Arrian's 'Periplus of the Erythræan Sea' as *'Ραχούσοι*. It was, therefore, not unusual both before

* 'Ayin Akbari,' ii. 163.

and after the time of Hwen Thsang to drop the initial syllable of the name. The original form was the Sanskrit *Saraswati*, which in Zend became *Hara-qaïti*, and in Greek Ἀραχωτός, all of which agree in the last two syllables with the Chinese *Tsaukuta*. The first Chinese syllable *Tsau* must, therefore, correspond with the *Ra* of the other forms. This change may, perhaps, be explained by a peculiarity of the Turki language, which frequently changes the letter *r* into a soft *z* or *sh*, as the Turki words *dengiz*, "sea," and *okuz*, "ox," are the same as the Hungarian *tenger* and *okur*.* On the Indo-Scythian coins, also, we find the Turki names of *Kanishka*, *Huvishka*, and *Kushâna* changed to *Kanerke*, *Hoverke*, and *Korano* in Greek. It seems possible, therefore, that the initial syllable *Tsau* of the Chinese transcript may be only the peculiar Turki pronunciation of the Indian *Ra*, which would naturally have come into use with the occupation of the country by the Turki tribe of Tochari, about the beginning of the Christian era.

In the seventh century the king of Ghazni, who was a Buddhist, was descended from a long line of ancestors. Both the alphabet and the language of the people are said to have been different from those of other countries; and as Hwen Thsang was acquainted with both the Indian and Turki languages, I infer that the speech of the people of Ghazni was most probably Pushtu. If so, the people must have

---

* Prichard, 'Physical History of Mankind,' iv. 403.

been Afghans; but, unfortunately, we have no other clue to guide us in settling this very interesting point, unless, indeed, the name of *O-po-ḳien*, a place to the south-east of Ghazni, may be identified with *Afghân*, a point which will be discussed hereafter.

Of Guzaristân, on the Helmand, I am not able to give any further information, as that part of the country has not yet been visited by any European. Ghazni itself is too well known to require any particular description, but I may note that it must have been in a very flourishing condition in the seventh century, as Hwen Thsang estimates its circuit at 30 *li*, or 5 miles. At the present day the circuit of the walled town is not more than one mile and a quarter. Vigne calls it an irregular pentagon, with sides varying from 200 to 400 yards in length, strengthened by numerous towers. He adds,* that "the Afghans boast much of the strength of the walls and fortifications of Ghazni." But Ghazni has always been famous in the East as a place of strength and security; and for this very reason it received its name of *Gaza*, an old Persian term for a "treasury." It is described in some crabbed lines of the 'Dionysiaca' of Nonnus, who lived about A.D. 500, and also in the 'Bassarica' of Dionysius, who lived not later than A.D. 300. Both of them refer pointedly to its impregnability. Dionysius calls it,—

'Αστύφελον δηΐοισι, καὶ εἰ παγχάλκεον ἦεν,
"As stern in war as if 'twas made of brass,"

* 'Ghazni,' p. 122.

and Nonnus says,* "They fortified, with a net-like enclosure of interlacing works, *Gazos*, an immoveable bulwark of Ares, and never has any armed enemy breached its compact foundations." These early notices of this famous place suggest the possibility that the *Gazaka* of Ptolemy may have been misplaced amongst the Paropamisadæ to the north of Kabul, instead of to the south of it. But as Stephanus of Byzantium, who quotes the 'Bassarica' of Dionysius as his authority for this Indian town, πόλις Ἰνδική, takes no notice of the Indian *Gazaka*, I conclude that he must have looked upon it as a different place.

4. LAMGHÂN.

The district of *Lan-po*, or Lamghân, is noted by Hwen Thsang as being 600 *li*, or just 100 miles, to the east of Kapisene. He describes the road as a succession of hills and valleys, some of the hills being of great height. This description agrees with all the recent accounts of the route along the northern bank of the river from Opiân to Lamghân. The bearing and distance also coincide so exactly with

* 'Dionysiaca,' xxvi. 30 :—

καὶ οἳ λινοεργέϊ κύκλῳ
ΓΑΖΟΝ ἐπυργώσαντο λινοπλέκτοισι δομαίοις,
Ἄρεος ἀκλινὲς ἕρμα, καὶ οὔποτε δήϊος ἀνὴρ
Χαλκὸν ἔχων ἔρρηξε ἐϋκλώστοισι θεμέθλοις.

the position of Lamghân that there can be no doubt of the identity of the two districts. Ptolemy, also, places a people called *Lambatœ* in the very same position. From a comparison of this term with the modern appellation of Lamghân, it seems probable that the original form of the name was the Sanskrit *Lampaka*. I would, therefore, correct Ptolemy's *Lambatœ* to *Lambagœ*, by the slight change of Γ for Τ. The modern name is only an abbreviation of *Lampaka*, formed by the elision of the labial. It is also called *Laghmân* by the simple transposition of the middle consonants, which is a common practice in the East. The credulous Muhammadans derive the name from the patriarch Lamech, whose tomb they affirm still exists in Lamghân. It is noticed by Baber and by Abul Fazl.

The district is described by Hwen Thsang as being only 1000 *li*, or 166 miles, in circuit, with snowy mountains on the north, and black hills on the other three sides. From this account it is clear that *Lan-po* corresponds exactly with the present Lamghân, which is only a small tract of country, lying along the northern bank of the Kabul river, bounded on the west and east by the Alingar and Kunar rivers, and on the north by the snowy mountains. This small tract is very nearly a square of 40 miles on each side, or 160 miles in circuit. It had formerly been a separate kingdom; but in the seventh century the royal family was extinct, and the district was a dependency of Kapisene.

5. NAGARAHÂRA. OR JALÂLÂBÂD.

From Lamghân the Chinese pilgrim proceeded for 100 *li*, or nearly 17 miles, to the south-east, and, after crossing a large river, reached the district of *Nagarahâra*. Both the bearing and distance point to the Nagara of Ptolemy, which was to the south of the Kabul river, and in the immediate vicinity of Jalâlâbâd. Hwen Thsang writes the name *Na-ki-lo-ho;* but M. Julien* has found the full transcript of the Sanskrit name in the annals of the Song dynasty, in which it is written *Nang-go-lo-ho-lo*. The Sanskrit name occurs in an inscription which was discovered by Major Kittoe in the ruined mound of *Ghosrâwâ*, in the district of Bihâr.† Nagarahâra is said to be 600 *li*, or 100 miles, in length from east to west, and upwards of 250 *li*, or 42 miles, in breadth from north to south. The natural boundaries of the district are the Jagdalak Pass on the west, and the Khaibar Pass on the east, with the Kabul river to the north, and the *Safed Koh*, or snowy mountains, to the south. Within these limits the direct measurements on the map are about 75 by 30 miles, which in actual road distance would be about the same as the numbers stated by Hwen Thsang.

The position of the capital would appear to have been at Begrâm, about 2 miles to the west of Jalâlâbâd, and 5 or 6 miles to the W.N.W. of Hidda, which by the general consent of every inquirer has

* 'Hiouen Thsang,' ii. 96, *note*.

† Journ. Asiat. Soc. Bengal, 1848, pp. 490, 491.

been identified with the *Hi-lo* of the Chinese pilgrims. The town of *Hilo* was only 4 or 5 *li*, or about three-quarters of a mile, in circuit; but it was celebrated for its possession of the skull-bone of Buddha, which was deposited in a *stupa,* or solid round tower, and was only exhibited to pilgrims on payment of a piece of gold. Hidda is a small village, 5 miles to the south of Jalâlâbâd; but it is well known for its large collection of Buddhist stupas, tumuli, and caves, which were so successfully explored by Masson. The presence of these important Buddhist remains, in the very position indicated by the Chinese pilgrims, affords the most satisfactory proof of the identity of Hidda with their *Hilo*. This is further confirmed by the absolute agreement of name, as *Hi-lo* is the closest approximation that could be made in Chinese syllables to the original *Hira* or *Hida*. The capital must, therefore, have been situated on the plain of Begrâm, which is described by Masson* as "literally covered with tumuli and mounds." "These," he adds, "are truly sepulchral monuments; but, with the topes, sanction the inference that a very considerable city existed here, or that it was a place of renown for sanctity. It may have been both." I think it is just possible that *Hidda* may be only a transposition of *Haddi,* a bone, as the stupa of the skull-bone of Buddha is said in one passage† to have been in the town of *Hilo,* while in another passage it is located in the town of *Fo-ting-ko-ching,* which is only a

* 'Travels,' ii. 164. † 'Hiouen Thsang,' i. 77.

Chinese translation of "Buddha's skull-bone town." During the course of this disquisition I shall have to notice the frequent occurrence of short descriptive names of places which were famous in the history of Buddha. I am, therefore, led to think that the place which contained the skull-bone of Buddha would most probably have been known by the familiar name of *Asthipura* amongst the learned, and of *Haddipura*, or "Bone-town" amongst the common people. Similarly the skull-necklace of Siva is called simply the *asthimâlâ*, or 'bone-necklace.'

Nagarahâra was long ago identified by Professor Lassen with the *Nagara* or *Dionysopolis* of Ptolemy, which was situated midway between Kabura and the Indus. The second name suggests the probability that it may be the same place as the *Nysa* of Arrian and Curtius. This name is perhaps also preserved in the *Dinus* or *Dinuz* of Abu Rihân,* as he places it about midway between Kabul and Parashâwar. According to the tradition of the people, the old city was called *Ajûna*,† in which I think it possible to recognize the Greek *Διον*, as the river Yamuna or Jumna is rendered *Diamuna* by Ptolemy, and the Sanskrit *yamas* or *jamas*, the south, is rendered *Diamasa* by Pliny.‡ It is, however, much more likely that *Ajûna*, by transposition of the vowels

---

* Reinaud's 'Fragments,' p. 114.

† Masson's 'Travels,' ii. 164.

‡ Hist. Nat., vi. c. 22.

may be only a corrupt form of the Pali *Ujjâna,* and Sanskrit *Udyâna,* "a garden," as M. Vivien de St. Martin states that *Udyânapura* was an old name of Nagarahâra.* If this identification be correct the position of the capital must certainly have been at Begrâm, as I have already suggested. The name of Dionysopolis was no doubt the most usual appellation during the whole period of Greek dominion, as one of the commonest mint-monograms on the coins of the Greek kings of Ariana forms the letters *ΔΙΟΝ*, which will not suit the name of any Indian city recorded by ancient authors, save that of Dionysopolis. In the beginning of the fifth century it is called simply *Na-kie* or *Nagara,* by Fa Hian, who adds that it was then an independent State governed by its own king. In A.D. 630, at the time of Hwen Thsang's visit, it was without a king, and subject to Kapisene. After this it most probably followed the fortunes of the sovereign State, and became successively a part of the Brahman kingdom of Kabul and of the Mahommedan empire of Ghazni.

6. GÂNDHÂRA, OR PARASHÂWAR.

The district of Gândhâra is not mentioned by Alexander's professed historians; but it is correctly described by Strabo, under the name of *Gandaritis,* as lying along the river Kophes, between the Choaspes and the Indus. In the same position

* 'Hiouen Thsang,' iii. 305.

IV.

MAP
of GANDHARA or
Lower KABUL Valley
16 Miles to 1 Inch
Alexander's Route
SUASTUS FL.
Suat R.
SUASTENE
Charbagh
Manglora
MASSAGA
Buner
Pranguruh
Lundkhwar
Jamalgarhi
Takht-i-Bahi
1859
Tangi
Shirpao
Hashtnagar
Pushkalavati
PEUKELAOTIS
Amarzai
Utmanzai
Rajar
Charsada
Nisata
GANDHARA
Hoti
Toru
Yar Husen
Ambela
Sura
Bazar
Palo Dheri
HAZARIA
3480
Karamar
Kapurdigiri
AORNOS
Kograw
Mahaban M.
Amb
Kabul R.
KOPHES FL.
Peshawar
Akora
Lahor
Salatura
Zedao
Ambar
Ohand
EMBOLIMA
2140
Panjpir
Torbela
Indus
INDUS FL.
Attak

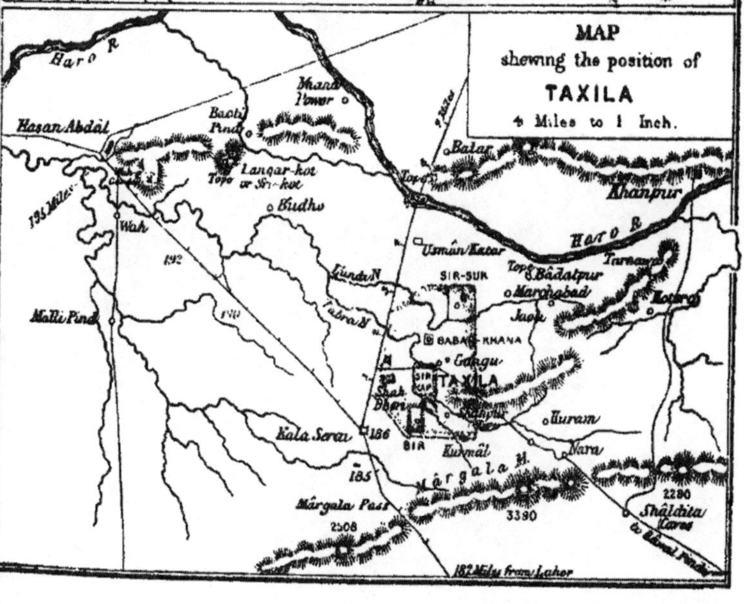
MAP
shewing the position of
TAXILA
4 Miles to 1 Inch.
Haro R.
Hasan Abdal
Baoti Pind
Langar-kot
or Sri-kot
Budho
Wah
192
Malli Pind
Balar
Khanpur
Usman Katar
SIR-SUK
Badalpur
Marchabad
Jaoli
BABAR-KHANA
Gangu
TAXILA
Shah Dheri
SIR KAP
SIR
Kala Serai
186
185
Kurmal
Nara
Huram
Margala M.
Margala Pass
2508
3380
2290
Shaldita Caves
182 Miles from Lahor

Ptolemy places the *Gandaræ*, whose country included both banks of the Kophes immediately above its junction with the Indus. This is the *Kien-to-lo*, or Gândhâra of all the Chinese pilgrims, who are unanimous in placing it to the west of the Indus. The capital, which they call *Pu-lu-sha-pulo* or *Parashapura* is stated to be three or four days' journey from the Indus, and near the south bank of a large river. This is an exact description of the position of Peshâwar, which down to the time of Akbar still bore its old name of *Parashâwar*, under which form it is mentioned by Abul Fazl and Baber, and still earlier by Abu Rihân and the Arab geographers of the tenth century. According to Fa Hian, who calls it simply *Fo-lu-shâ* or *Parashâ*, the capital was 16 *yojans*, or about 112 miles, distant from Nagarahâra. Hwen Thsang, however, makes the distance only 500 *li*, or 83 miles, which is certainly a mistake, as the measurement by perambulator between Jalâlâbâd and Peshâwar is 103 miles, to which must be added 2 miles more for the position of Begrâm to the west of Jalâlâbâd.

The actual boundaries of the district are not described, but its size is given as 1000 *li*, or 166 miles, from east to west, and 800 *li*, or 133 miles, from north to south. This is, perhaps, nearly correct, as the extreme length, whether taken from the source of the Bara river to Torbela, or from the Kunar river to Torbela, is 120 miles, measured on the map direct, or about 150 miles by road. The extreme breadth, measured in the same way, from

Bâzâr, on the border of the Bunir hills, to the southern boundary of Kohât, is 100 miles direct, or about 125 miles by road. The boundaries of Gândhâra, as deduced from these measurements, may be described as Lamghân and Jalâlâbâd on the west, the hills of Swât and Bunir on the north, the Indus on the east, and the hills of Kâlabâgh on the south. Within these limits stood several of the most renowned places of ancient India; some celebrated in the stirring history of Alexander's exploits, and others famous in the miraculous legends of Buddha, and in the subsequent history of Buddhism under the Indo-Scythian prince Kanishka.

The only towns of the Gandaræ named by Ptolemy are Naulibe, Embolima, and the capital called Proklaïs. All of these were to the north of the Kophes; and so also were Ora, Bazaria, and Aornos, which are mentioned by Alexander's historians. Parashâwar alone was to the south of the Kophes. Of Naulibe and Ora I am not able to offer any account, as they have not yet been identified. It is probable, however, that *Naulibe* is *Nilâb*, an important town, which gave its name to the Indus river; but if so, it is wrongly placed by Ptolemy, as *Nilâb* is to the south of the Kophes. The positions of the other towns I will now proceed to investigate, including with them some minor places visited by the Chinese pilgrims.

Pushkalavati, or Peukelaotis.

The ancient capital of Gândhâra was *Pushkalavati,* which is said to have been founded by

Pushkara, the son of Bharata, and the nephew of Rama.* Its antiquity is undoubted, as it was the capital of the province at the time of Alexander's expedition. The Greek name of *Peukelaotis*, or *Peucolaïtis*, was immediately derived from *Pukka·laoti*, which is the Pali, or spoken form of the Sanskrit Pushkalavati. It is also called *Peukelas* by Arrian, and the people are named *Peukalei* by Dionysius Periegetes, which are both close transcripts of the Pali *Pukkala*. The form of Proklaïs, which is found in Arrian's 'Periplus of the Erythræan Sea,' and also in Ptolemy's 'Geography,' is perhaps only an attempt to give the Hindi name of *Pokhar* instead of the Sanskrit Pushkara.

According to Arrian, Peukelas was a very large and populous city, seated not far from the river Indus.† It was the capital of a chief named Astes,‡ perhaps *Hasti*, who was killed in the defence of one of his strongholds, after a siege of thirty days, by Hephæstion. Upon the death of Astes the city of Peukelaotis was delivered up to Alexander on his march towards the Indus. Its position is vaguely described by Strabo and Arrian as "near the Indus." But the geographer Ptolemy is more exact, as he fixes it on the eastern bank of the river of Suastene, that is, the Panjkora or Swât river, which is the very locality indicated by Hwen Thsang. On leaving Parashâwar the Chinese pilgrim travelled towards

* Wilson's 'Vishnu Purâna,' edited by Hall, b. iv. c.4.

† Arrian, 'Indica,' i. ‡ Arrian, 'Anabasis,' iv. 22.

the north-east for 100 *li,* or nearly 17 miles; and, crossing a great river, reached *Pu-se-ḳia-lo-fa-ti,* or Pushkalavati. The river here mentioned is the Kophes, or river of Kabul; and the bearing and distance from Peshâwar point to the two large towns of Parang and Chârsada, which form part of the well-known *Hashtnagar,* or "Eight Cities," that are seated close together on the eastern bank of the lower Swât river. These towns are Tangi, Shirpao, Umrzai, Turangzai, Usmânzai, Rajur, Chârsada, and Parang. They extend over a distance of fifteen miles; but the last two are seated close together in a bend of the river, and might originally have been portions of one large town. The fort of Hisâr stands on a mound above the ruins of the old town of Hashtnagar, which General Court places on an island, nearly opposite Rajur.* "All the suburbs," he says, "are scattered over with vast ruins."† The eight cities are shown in No. IV Map.

It seems to me not improbable that the modern name of Hashtnagar may be only a slight alteration of the old name of *Hastinagara,* or "city of Hasti," which might have been applied to the capital of Astes, the Prince of Peukelaotis. It was a common practice of the Greeks to call the Indian rulers by the names of their cities, as Taxiles, Assakanus, and others. It was also a prevailing custom amongst

---

* Journ. Asiat. Soc. Bengal, 1836, p. 479.

† *Ibid.,* 1836, p. 394.

Indian princes to designate any additions or alterations made to their capitals by their own names. Of this last custom we have a notable instance in the famous city of Delhi; which, besides its ancient appellations of *Indraprastha* and *Dillı,* was also known by the names of its successive aggrandizers as Kot-Pithora, Kila-Alai, Tughlakâbâd, Firuzâbâd, and Shahjahânâbâd. It is true that the people themselves refer the name of Hashtnagar to the "eight towns" which are now seated close together along the lower course of the Swât river; but it seems to me very probable that in this case the wish was father to the thought, and that the original name of Hastinagar, or whatever it may have been, was slightly twisted to Hashtnagar, to give it a plausible meaning amongst a Persianized Muhammadan population, to whom the Sanskrit Hastinagara was unintelligible. To the same cause I would attribute the slight change made in the name of *Nagarahâra,* which the people now call *Nang-nihâr,** or the "Nine Streams."

In later times Pushkalavati was famous for a large *stupa,* or solid tower, which was erected on the spot where Buddha was said to have made an alms-offering of his eyes. In the period of Hwen Thsang's visit, it was asserted that the "eyes gift"

* Baber's 'Memoirs,' p. 141.—Wood's 'Journey to the Source of the Oxus,' p. 167.—Macgregor's 'Geography of Jalalabad,' in Journ. Asiat. Soc. Bengal, xi. 117, and xiii. 867.

had been made one thousand different times, in as many previous existences: but only a single gift is mentioned by the two earlier pilgrims, Fa-Hian in the fifth century, and Sung-Yun in the sixth century.

Varusha, or *Palodheri.*

Hwen Thsang next visited a town called *Po-lu-sha,* which, I think, may be identified with *Palodheri,* or the village of *Pali,* which is situated on a *dheri,* or "mound of ruins," the remains of some early town. To the north-east of the town, at 20 *li,* or 3⅓ miles, rose the hill of *Dantaloka,* with a cave, in which Prince Sudâna and his wife had taken refuge. The position of *Palodheri,* which is the *Pelley* of General Court, agrees with Hwen Thsang's distance of about 40 miles from Pushkalavati;* and this identification is supported by the existence of the great cave of *Kashmiri-Ghâr,* in the hill to the east-north-east, and within 3 or 4 miles of Palodheri. Mount *Dantalok* I take to be the *Montes Dædali,* of Justin,† as in the spoken dialects the nasal of the word *danta* is assimilated with the following letter, which thus becomes doubled, as in the well-known *datton,* a "tooth-brush," or twig used for cleaning the teeth.

* See No. IV. Map.

† 'Historiæ,' xii. 7.

Utakhanda, or Ohind, or Embolima.

From *Polusha* Hwen Thsang travelled 200 *li*, or 33 miles, to the south-east to *U-to-kia-han-cha*, which M. Julien transcribes as *Udakhanda*, and M. Vivien de St. Martin identifies with Ohind on the Indus. The pilgrim describes *Udakhanda* as having its south side resting on the river, which tallies exactly with the position of Ohind, on the north bank of the Indus, about 15 miles above Attok. General Court and Burnes call this place *Hund*, and so does Mr. Loewenthal, who styles *Ohind* a mistaken pronunciation. But the name was written ويهند *Waihand* or *Oaihand*, by Abu Rihân in A.D. 1030, and *Ohind* by Mirza Mogal Beg in 1790. To my ear the name sounded something like *Wahand*, and this would appear to have been the pronunciation which Rashid-ud-din obtained in A.D. 1310, as he names the place *Wehand*.* According to all these authors *Waihand* was the capital of Gândhâra, and Rashid-ud-din adds that the Mogals called it *Kârajâng*. The only native writer who uses the abbreviated form of the name is Nizâm-ud-din, who in his 'Tabakât-i-Akbari' says that Mahmud besieged Jaipal in the fort of *Hind* in A.D. 1002. But this place is differently named by Ferishta, who calls it the fort of *Bithanda*, بتهندہ In this last name we have a very near approach to the old form of *Utakhanda*, which is given by Hwen Thsang.

---

* There is a place of the same name on the Jhelam, which Moorcroft spells *Oïn*.

From all these examples, I infer that the original name of *Utakhanda*, or *Ut-khand*, was first softened to *Uthand* or *Bithanda*, and then shortened to *Uhand* or *Ohind*. The other form of *Wehand* I look upon as a simple misreading of *Uthand*, as the two words only differ in the position of the diacritical points of the second letter. General James Abbott, in his 'Gradus ad Aornon,' calls the place *Oond*, and says that it was formerly called *Oora*, from which he thinks it probable that it may be identified with the Ora, *Ὦρα*, of Alexander's historians.

I have entered into this long detail out of respect for the acknowledged learning of the late lamented Isidor Loewenthal. His opinion as to the name of Ohind was most probably, although quite unconsciously, biassed by his belief that Utakhanda was to be found in the modern Attak. But this place is unfortunately on the wrong side of the Indus, besides which its name, as far as I am aware, is not to be found in any author prior to the reign of Akbar. Abul Fazl calls the fort *Atak-Banâras*, and states that it was built in the reign of his Majesty. Baber never mentions the place, although he frequently speaks of Nilâb. Rashid-ud-din, however, states that the Parashâwar river joins the Indus near *Tankur*, which most probably refers to the strong position of Khairabad. I have a suspicion that the name of *Attak*, the "forbidden," may have been derived by Akbar from a mistaken reading of *Tankur*, with the Arabic article prefixed, as *Et-tankur*. The name of *Banâras* was undoubtedly derived from *Banâr*, the old name of the district in which the fort is situated. The name of Banâr suggested Banâras, and as *Kâsi-Baânras* was the city which all Hindus would wish to visit, so we may guess that this fact suggested to the playful mind of Akbar the exactly opposite idea of *Attak Banâras*, or the "forbidden" Banâras, which all good Hindus should avoid. Or the existence of *Katak Banâras** (or Cuttack) in Orissa, on the extreme eastern limit of his kingdom, may have suggested an alteration of the existing names of Attak and Banâr to *Attak-Banâras* as an antithesis for the extreme west.

Wehand, or *Uhand* as I believe it should be written, was the capital of the Brahman kings of Kabul, whose dynasty was extinguished by Mahmud of Ghazni in A.D. 1026. Masudi, who visited India in A.D. 915, states that "the king of El-kandahar (or Gândhâra), who is one of the kings of Es-Sind ruling over this country, is called *Jahaj;* this name is common to all sovereigns of that country."† Now, *Chach* is the name of the great plain to the east of the Indus, immediately opposite to Ohind; and as the plain of *Banâr* is said to have been named after Raja *Banâr*, it seems probable that the plain of *Chach* may have been named after the Brahman

* 'Ayin Akbari,' ii. 194, and Stirling's 'Orissa,' in Bengal Asiat Researches, xv. 189.

† Sir Henry Elliot's 'Muhammadan Historians of India,' i. 57. In the new edition by Professor Dowson, i. 22, the name is altered to *Hahaj*.

dynasty of Ohind. It is curious that the Brahman dynasty of Sindh was also established by a *Chach* in A.D. 641; but it is still more remarkable that this date corresponds with the period of the expulsion of the Brahman dynasty from *Chichito*, or *Jajhoti*, by the Chandels of Khajurâ. I think, therefore, that there may have been some connection between these events, and that the expelled Jajhotiya Brahmans of Khajurâ may have found their way to the Indus, where they succeeded in establishing themselves at first in Sindh and afterwards in Ohind and Kabul.

In the time of Hwen Thsang the city was 20 *li*, or upwards of 3 miles, in circuit, and we may reasonably suppose that it must have increased in size during the sway of the Brahman dynasty. It would seem also to have been still a place of importance under the successors of Changiz Khan, as the Mogals had changed its name to Kârajâng. But the building of Attak, and the permanent diversion of the high-road, must seriously have affected its prosperity, and its gradual decay since then has been hastened by the constant encroachments of the Indus, which has now carried away at least one-half of the old town.* In the sands at the foot of the cliff, which are mixed with the *débris* of the ruined houses, the gold-washers find numerous coins and trinkets, which offer the best evidence of the former prosperity of the city. In a few hours' washing I

* See No. IV. Map for its position.

obtained a bronze buckle, apparently belonging to a bridle, a female neck ornament, several flat needles for applying antimony to the eyes, and a considerable number of coins of the Indo-Scythian and Brahman princes of Kabul. The continual discovery of Indo-Scythian coins is a sufficient proof that the city was already in existence at the beginning of the Christian era, which may perhaps induce us to put some faith in the tradition, mentioned by Abul Feda, that *Wehand*, or *Ohind*, was one of the cities founded by Alexander the Great.

After the surrender of Peukelaotis, Arrian* relates that Alexander captured other small towns on the river Kophenes, and "arrived at last at *Embolima*, a city seated not far from the rock Aornos," where he left Kraterus to collect provisions, in case the siege should be protracted. Before he left Bazaria, Alexander, with his usual foresight, had despatched Hephæstion and Perdikkas straight to the Indus with orders to "prepare everything for throwing a bridge over the river." Unfortunately, not one of the historians has mentioned the name of the place where the bridge was made; but as the great depôt of provisions and other necessaries was formed at Embolima, I conclude that the bridge must have been at the same place. General Abbott has fixed Embolima at *Amb-Balima* on the Indus, 8 miles to the east of Mahâban; and certainly if Mahâban was Aornos the identity of the other places

* 'Anabasis,' iv. 28.

would be incontestable. But as the identification of Mahâban seems to me to be altogether untenable, I would suggest that *Ohind* or *Ambar-Ohind* is the most probable site of Embolima. Ambar is a village two miles to the north of Ohind, and it is in accordance with Indian custom to join the names of two neighbouring places together, as in the case of *Attak-Banâras*, for the sake of distinction, as there is another *Ohin* on the Jhelam. It must be remembered, however, that *Embolima* or *Ekbolima* may be only a pure Greek name, descriptive of the position of the place, at the junction of the Kabul river with the Indus, where it is placed by Ptolemy. In this case the claim of Ohind would be even stronger than before. That the bridge over the Indus was at, or near, Embolima, seems almost certain from the statement of Curtius, that when Alexander had finished his campaign to the west of the Indus by the capture of Aornos, "he proceeded towards *Ecbolima;*"* that is, as I conclude, to the place where his bridge had been prepared by Hephæstion and Perdikkas, and where his provisions had been stored by Kraterus. I infer that the depôt of provisions must have been close to the bridge, because one guard would have sufficed for the security of both bridge and stores.

Sâlâtura, or Lahor.

Hwen Thsang next visited *So-lo-tu-lo*, or Sâlâtura, the birthplace of the celebrated grammarian

* Vit. Alex., viii. 12,—"inde processit Ecbolima."

Pânini, which he says was 20 *li*, or 3⅓ miles, to the north-west of Ohind. In January, 1848, during a day's halt at the village of *Lahor*, which is exactly four miles to the north-east of Ohind, I procured several Greek and Indo-Scythian coins, from which it may be inferred, with some certainty, that the place is at least as old as the time of Pânini himself, or about B.C. 350. I have, therefore, no hesitation in identifying Sâlâtura with *Lahor*. The loss of the first syllable of the name is satisfactorily accounted for by the change of the palatal sibilant to the aspirate, according to the well-known usage of the people of western India, by whom the *Sindhu* river was called *Hendhu* and *Indus*, and the people on its banks *Hindus* or Indians; Sâlâtura would, therefore, have become *Hâlâtura* and *Alâtur*, which might easily have been corrupted to *Lahor*; or, as General Court writes the name, to *Lavor*.

Aornos.

In describing the countries to the west of the Indus I must say a few words on the much vexed question of the position of Aornos. In 1836 General Court wrote as follows :—"As relates to Aornos, it is probably the castle which was opposite Attak, and the vestiges of which we see upon the summit of the mountain. Its foundation is attributed to Raja *Hodi*."* In 1848 I suggested that the "vast hill fortress of *Râni-gat*, situated immediately above the

* Journ. Asiat. Soc. Bengal, 1836, p. 395.

small village of Nogrâm, about 16 miles north by west from Ohind, corresponded in all essential particulars with the description of Aornos, as given by Arrian, Strabo, and Diodorus; excepting in its elevation, the height of *Râni-gat* not being more than 1000 feet, which is, however, a very great elevation for so large a fortress."* In 1854 General James Abbott took up the subject in a very full and elaborate article, in which the various authorities are ably and critically discussed. His conclusion is that the *Mahâban* hill is the most probable site of Aornos.† This opinion was combated early in 1863 by Mr. Loewenthal, who again brought forward the claims of Raja Hodi's fort, opposite Attak, which had first been suggested by General Court.‡ Towards the end of the year General Abbott replied to Mr. Loewenthal's objections, and reiterated his conviction that "the *Mahâban* is the Aornos of history," although he thinks that the question is still "open to discussion."§

In reopening this discussion, I believe that I am able to clear away some of the difficulties with which the subject has confessedly been obstructed by the vague and contradictory accounts of Alexander's historians; but I can scarcely venture to hope that my identification of Aornos will be received as satisfac-

---

* Journ. Asiat. Soc. Bengal, 1848, p. 103.

† *Ibid.*, 1854, p. 309.

‡ *Ibid.*, 1863, p. 14.

§ *Ibid.*, 1863, p. 409.

tory, when I am constrained to own that I am not perfectly satisfied with it myself. But if I do not succeed in convincing others, I feel that my failure will be shared in common with two such able writers as General James Abbott and the lamented missionary, Loewenthal.

I will begin with the name *Aornos,* which, though a Greek word, can hardly, as Mr. Loewenthal observes, be an invention of the Greeks. It must, therefore, be the transcription, either more or less altered, of some native name. Mr. Loewenthal thinks that it was derived from Banâras in its Sanskrit form of *Varânasi,* which a Greek of Alexander's time could only have pronounced by prefixing a vowel. He would thus have got *Avaranas* or *Aornos*. But this is, perhaps, proving too much, as the final letter in *Aornos* is almost certainly the Greek termination, which need not, therefore, have formed part of the original native name. It is also suspicious that the literal transcription of the native name should form a pure Greek word. If *Banâras* or *Varânasi* was the original form of the name, then we ought to find another Banâras to the north of the Caucasus, as Arrian relates that after passing *Drapsaka,* or Andarâb, Alexander "moved against *Aornos* and *Bactra,* the two chief cities of the Bactrians, which being immediately surrendered to him, he placed a garrison in the castle of Aornos."* On comparing Arrian's names with Ptolemy's map,

* 'Anabasis,' iii. 29.

it seems evident that his *Bactra* and *Aornos* are the same as Ptolemy's *Zariaspa* and *Bactra regia*, and as the latter is placed in the country of the *Varni*, or Οὔαρνοι, I conclude that the name *Aornos*, Ἄορνος, is only a natural and slight alteration of Οὔαρνος or *Varnos*, made by the followers of Alexander for the sake of obtaining a significant name in Greek. Similarly I would refer the second *Aornos* to *Raja Vara*, whose name is still attached to all the ruined strongholds between Hashtnagar and Ohind. Thus the old hill fort and city of *Takht-i-Bahai*, 15 miles to the north-east of Hashtnagar, is said to have been the residence of Raja *Vara*. But his name is more particularly attached to the grand hill-fort of *Râni-gat* above Nogrâm. *Râni-gat*, or the *Queen's rock*, is a huge upright block on the north edge of the fort, on which Raja Vara's *Rani* is said to have seated herself daily. The fort itself is attributed to Raja *Vara*, and some ruins at the foot of the hill are called Raja *Vara's* stables. Some people call him Raja *Virât*, but as they connect him with the story of the five Pândus, I conclude that the name has been altered to suit the story. Th position of the true *Virât* was in *Matsya* or *Mâcheri*, to the south of Delhi: all others are spurious. I think, therefore, that the hill fort of *Aornos* most probably derived its name from Raja *Vara*, and that the ruined fortress of *Râni-gat* has a better claim to be identified with the Aornos of Alexander than either the *Mahâban* hill of General Abbott, or the castle of

Raja Hodi proposed by General Court and Mr. Loewenthal.

My chief objections to the Mahâban hill as the representative of Aornos are the following :—1. It is a vast mountain of comparatively easy access, and of which no spur presents a very steep face towards the Indus. 2. The Mahâban hill is not less than 50 miles in circuit, whereas Aornos was not more than 200 stadia, or about 22 miles, according to Arrian, or 100 stadia or 11 miles, according to Diodorus. 3. The *Mahâvana* hill was visited by Hwen Thsang in A.D. 630, and he describes it simply as a great mountain, which derived its name from the *Mahâvana* monastery, in which Buddha had dwelt in a former existence under the name of *Sarvvada* Raja.* That the monastery was on the top of the mountain we know from the subsequent statement, that he descended the mountain towards the north-west for about 30 or 40 *li* to the *Masura* Monastery. This place may, I believe, be identified with the large village of *Sura* in the Chumla valley, which is just 10 miles to the north-west of the highest peak of *Mahâban*. If any fort had then existed on the top of the mountain, it is almost certain that the pilgrim would have mentioned its name, with his usual statement of its size, and of any special point of noteworthiness, such as its inaccessibility, etc. His total silence I look upon as decisive against the

* Julien's 'Hiouen Thsang,' ii. 136.

existence of any fort on the top of Mahâban, whether occupied or in ruins.

Mr. Loewenthal's objection, based on the opinion of a high military authority, that the Mahâban hill "commands nothing," only shows how readily even a very learned man will accept an utterly false argument when it tells in his own favour. General Abbott has noticed this subject in his reply to Mr. Loewenthal; but some months previous to the publication of his reply, I had already given a similar refutation to this objection, both in conversation with different friends and in writing to Mr. Loewenthal himself. It is objected that Mahâban "commands nothing;" I reply that it commands the very thing that the people of an invaded country wanted, it commands safety for those who seek its shelter. It is said to be "so much out of the way" that none would have sought it as a place of refuge, and that Alexander would not have wasted time in its reduction, as it did not impede his passage to the Indus.* This objection supposes that Alexander's chief object was the passage of the Indus, whereas it is clear, both from his previous and subsequent career, that his invariable plan was never to leave an enemy behind him. For this he had given up the pursuit of Bessus, to conquer Aria, Drangiana, and Arachosia; for this he had spent two years in Sogdiana and Bactriana, until the death of Spitamenes left no enemy remaining: for this he now

* Journ. Asiat. Soc. Bengal, 1863, p. 17.

turned aside from the passage of the Indus to subdue the people who had refused their submission by taking refuge in Aornos; and for this he afterwards recrossed the Hydraotes to attack Sangala, an isolated rock, which commanded nothing but the jangal around it.

Mr. Loewenthal rests his arguments in favour of the castle of Raja Hodi being the Aornos of Alexander, chiefly on the great similarity of the name of *Banâras*, and partly on Sir Neville Chamberlain's opinion "that the hill above Khairabad is not only a most conspicuous point for friend and foe, but also one that must be taken before a passage of the Indus at Attok would be attempted by an invading force." The first argument has already been disposed of in my discussion on the name of Aornos. The second argument takes two things for granted; first, that Alexander crossed the Indus at Attak, and, therefore, that he must have reduced the castle of Raja Hodi before he attempted the passage of the river; and next, that the people of the country had thrown themselves into Aornos to *oppose* his passage. The latter was certainly not the case, as we are told by Arrian that the people of Bazaria, "distrusting their strength, fled out of the city in the dead of night, and betook themselves to a rock, called *Aornos*, for safety.* Here we see clearly that the people of Bazaria were desirous of avoiding instead of opposing Alexander; from which we may

* 'Anabasis,' iv. 28.

infer that Aornos did not command that passage of the Indus which Alexander had chosen for his bridge of boats. But as all the accounts agree in placing the scene of Alexander's campaign before crossing the Indus in the country to the north of the *Kophes*, or Kabul river, it appears quite certain that neither Aornos itself nor the bridge of boats could have been in the neighbourhood of Attak. For these reasons I conclude that the ruined castle of Raja Hodi cannot possibly be identified with the Aornos of Alexander. Indeed, its name alone seems sufficient to forbid the identification, as the people are unanimous in calling it Raja *Hodi-da-garhi*, or *Hodi-garhi*, an appellation which has not even one syllable in common with Aornos.

After a careful consideration of all the points that have been just discussed, I am satisfied that we must look for Aornos in the direction of the hills somewhere in the north-east corner of the Yusufzai plain. It is there that the people still seek for refuge on the approach of an invader; it is there only that we can expect to find a hill fort that will tally even approximately with the exaggerated descriptions of Alexander's historians, and it is there also that we ought to look for Aornos, according to the almost unanimous opinion of all those who have studied the subject.

The accounts of Alexander's historians are often vague and sometimes conflicting, but we are generally able to correct or explain the statements of one by those of the others. Where they agree, we can follow them with confidence, as it may be presumed that the original authors from whom they copied were not at variance. The last is fortunately the case with their accounts of Alexander's movements shortly before his approach to Aornos. According to Arrian, immediately after crossing the Guræus river Alexander marched straight to *Massaga,* the capital of the Assakeni, and after its capture he dispatched Koinos against Bazaria. Curtius calls the river Choes, and makes Koinos proceed straight to Bazaria, whilst Alexander advanced against *Mazagœ.* Arrian then states that as Bazaria still held out, the king determined to march thither, but hearing that many Indian soldiers had thrown themselves into *Ora,* he changed his plan, and moved against that city, which was captured at the first assault. According to Curtius, the siege of Ora was entrusted to Polysperchon, while the king himself took many small towns, whose inhabitants had sought refuge in Aornos. Arrian makes the people of Bazaria fly to Aornos for safety, but he agrees with Curtius in stating that the inhabitants of many of the neighbouring villages followed their example. From these accounts it is evident that *Aornos* was beyond Bazaria, and from the subsequent narratives of Arrian and Curtius, it is equally clear that *Embolima* was beyond Aornos, and on the Indus, where Ptolemy has placed it. Taking all these points into consideration, I believe that *Bazaria, Aornos* and *Embolima* may be best identified with *Bâzâr, Râni-gat* and *Ohind.**

Bâzâr is a large village situated on the bank of the *Kalpan,* or *Kâli-pâni* river, and quite close to the town of *Rustam,* which is built on a very extensive old mound attributed to the time of the *Kafirs* or Hindus. According to tradition, this was the site of the original town of *Bâzâr.* The position is an important one, as it stands just midway between the Swât and Indus rivers, and has, therefore, been from time immemorial the *entrepôt* of trade between the rich valley of Swât and the large towns on the Indus and Kabul rivers. Indeed, its name of *Bâzâr,* or "Mart," is sufficient to show that it has always been a place of consequence. Judging, therefore, by the importance of the place alone, I should be induced to select *Bâzâr* as the most probable representative of *Bazaria;* but this probability is turned almost to certainty by its exact correspondence, both in name and in position, with the ancient town that was besieged by Alexander. This identification is much strengthened by the proximity of Mount *Dantalok,* which is most probably the same range of hills as the *Montes Dœdali* of the Greeks. In the spoken dialects of the present day, as well as in the ancient Pali, the nasal of the word *danta* is assimilated with

* It would appear also from Arrian, iv. 28, that Aornos was only one day's march from Embolima, which agrees with the distance of Rânigat from Ohind of 16 miles. See No. IV. Map.

the following letter, which thus becomes doubled, as in *datton*, a "tooth brush," or twig used for cleaning the teeth. Hence the Greek *Daidalos* is a very fair rendering of the Pali *Dattalok*. The *Dœdalian* mountains are mentioned by Justin* as adjoining the kingdom of Queen Cleofis, or Cleophes, who, according to Curtius, was the mother (a mistake for wife) of Assacanus, king of Massaga. I have already identified the cave of Prince *Sudâna* in Mount *Dantalok*, as described by Hwen Thsang, with the great cave of *Kashmiri-Ghâr*, which is just eight miles to the north-west of Bâzâr. The *Dantalok* range would, therefore, have been on the right-hand of the Greeks on their march over the hills from Massaga in the Swât valley to Bazaria. From all these concurring circumstances, I conclude that Bâzâr is almost certainly the same place as Alexander's Bazaria, and that Ohind was Embolima, as I have previously endeavoured to show.

In proposing the ruined fortress of *Râni-gat* as the most probable representative of the famous *Aornos*, I must confess that the identification is incomplete. In 1848, I estimated the perpendicular height of Rânigat as about one thousand feet above the plain, and Mr. Loewenthal has since confirmed my estimate. But this height is so insignificant when compared with the 11 stadia, or 6674 feet of

---

* Hist., xii. 7. "Inde montes Dædalos, regnaque Cleofidis reginæ petit."

Arrian,* that I should hesitate to attempt the identification, did I not believe that the height has been very much exaggerated. Philostratus† calls it 15 stadia; and Diodorus‡ makes it even greater, or 16 stadia, equivalent to 9708 feet; but as he gives the circuit of the base at only 100 stadia, or just one-half of that of Arrian, I think it probable that his height may have been originally in the same proportion which we may obtain by simply reading 6 stadia instead of 16, or 3640 feet instead of 9708 feet. It is certain at least that one of the numbers of Diodorus must be erroneous, for as a circuit of 100 stadia, or 60,675 feet, would give a base diameter of 19,200 feet, or just twice the recorded height of 9708 feet, the slope would have been exactly 45°, and the hill would have terminated in a mere point, instead of a large platform with arable land, as described by Arrian. Where the difference between the two authorities is so great, and the exaggeration so apparent, it is difficult to suggest any possible alteration that would reconcile the discrepant measurements, and at the same time bring them within the range of probability. I believe, however, that we are quite safe not only in preferring the lesser numbers, but also in applying the altitude to the slant height instead of to the perpendicular height. But even with these lesser measurements, the Indian Aornos would still be twice the size, and more than twice the height of

* 'Anabasis,' iv. 28.

† Vit. Apollonii, ii. 10.

‡ Hist., xvii. 44.

the famous rock of Gibraltar, which is 7 miles in circuit at base, and only 1600 feet in height.

In the similar case of the great fortress of Gwalior, we find the usually accurate English traveller, William Finch, describing it as a castle situated on a steep craggy cliff, "6 *kos* in circuit, or, as some say, 11 *kos*." As Finch generally adopts the short imperial kos of 1⅓ mile, his estimate of the circuit of Gwalior will be 9 miles, or nearly twice the actual measurement of 5 miles, while the popular estimate will be nearly four times greater than the truth. It is possible, however, to reconcile these different numbers by supposing that the larger refers to the imperial kos, and the smaller to the greater kos of Akbar, which is just double the former. But in this case the estimate of the circuit of the fort of Gwalior would be from 14 to 15 miles, or just three times too great. Finch does not mention the height of Gwalior, but he notes that the "steep ascent" to the castle of *Narwar* was "rather more than a mile" in length, which is just double the truth. Here the traveller was led to exaggerate the height by the mere steepness of the ascent. But in the case of Aornos, the Greeks had an additional motive for exaggeration in the natural wish to enhance their own glory. For this reason I would suggest, as a possible explanation of the discrepancy between the 16 stadia of Diodorus and the 11 stadia of Arrian, that the original authority of the former may have quadrupled or trebled the true measurement, while that of the latter only trebled or doubled it. Under this explanation the two numbers would become either 4 and 3⅓ stadia, or 5⅓ and 5½ stadia, or from 2300 to 3400 feet, which might be accepted as a very probable measure of the slant height; similarly the circuit might be reduced to 50 stadia, which are equivalent to 5¾ miles or 30,300 feet, or rather more than the circuit of the road around the base of the Gwalior hill. A slant height of 2300 feet, with a base of 1900 feet, would give a perpendicular height of 1250 feet, or an ascent of 2 feet in every 3 feet. I do not propose this mode of reduction as a probable explanation of the discrepancies in the recorded measurements, but I venture to suggest it only as a possible means of accounting for the evident exaggeration of the numbers in both of the authorities.

All the accounts of Aornos agree in describing it as a rocky hill of great height and steepness. Justin calls it *saxum miræ asperitatis et altitudinis*, "an exceedingly rugged and lofty rock."* Diodorus, Strabo, Arrian, Curtius, and Philostratus, all call it *petra*, or a "rock fort." Its rocky ruggedness was, therefore, a special feature of *Aornos*. According to Arrian, it was "only accessible by one difficult path, cut out by hand, and it possessed a fine spring of pure water on the very summit, besides wood and sufficient arable soil for the cultivation of one thousand men." The last expression is still in common use in India, under the form of ploughs of

* Hist., xii. 7.

land, and means simply as much land as one man can plough in a day. The same thing was expressed by the Greeks and Romans by *yokes*, each being as much as one yoke of oxen could plough in a single day. Now the smallest plough of land would not be less than 100 feet square, or 10,000 square feet, which would give 10,000,000 square feet for 1000 men. This would show an area of 4000 feet in length by 2500 feet in breadth, or, making allowance for buildings, of one mile in length by half a mile in breadth, or 2 miles in length by a quarter of a mile in breadth, which is just the size of Gwalior. But if such a vast fortress as Gwalior had ever existed on the western frontier of India, it would certainly not have escaped the notice of the early Muhammadan conquerors, and it could scarcely have eluded the searching inquiries of General Court and General Abbott. I, therefore, look upon the thousand ploughs of land as another gross exaggeration of Alexander's followers for the sake of ministering to their master's vanity. I accept the one difficult path of access and the spring of pure water, as two of the necessary possessions of a strong military post, but I unhesitatingly reject the 100 ploughs of arable land, for if such an extensive tract as half a square mile of irrigable land had ever existed on the top of a hill in this arid district, I cannot believe that such an important and valuable site ever would have been abandoned.

In searching for a position that will answer the general description of Aornos. it is unfortunate that our range is limited to the few points which have been visited by Europeans. The claims of the Mahâban hill have already been discussed; and the only other possible positions that I know of are the following :—

1. The ruined city of *Takht-i-Bahai.*
2. The lofty isolated hill of *Kâramâr.*
3. The hill of *Panjpir.*
4. The ruined fortress of *Rânigat.*

The first of these places stands on an isolated hill, about halfway between Bâzâr and Hashtnagar; Mr. Loewenthal describes it as a barren hill of no great height, which forms three sides of a square, with the open side towards the north-west.* By the trigonometrical survey maps, *Takht-i-Bahai* is only 1859 feet above the sea, or 650 feet above the Yusufzai plain. Mr. Loewenthal also describes the ascent as easy; and as the place is situated not less than 35 miles from the nearest point of the Indus, I think it may be rejected at once as not answering the description of lofty and difficult access, and as being too far from the probable position of Embolima. The position of the lofty isolated hill of *Kâramâr,* which is situated 6 miles to the south of Bâzâr, and only 18 miles to the north-north-west of Ohind, added to its height, which is 3480 feet above the sea, or 2280 feet above the Yusufzai plain, would give it a most prominent claim to notice if it possessed any remains of former occupation. But

* Journ. Asiat. Soc. Bengal, 1863, p. 2.

the *Kâramâr* hill is a mere bluff ridge, without ruins and without a name in the traditions of the people. The *Panjpir* hill is a similar but smaller ridge, which rises to the height of 2140 feet above the sea, or 940 feet above the Yusufzai plain. It is a mere sharp ridge crowned with a single building, which is now dedicated to the Panjpir, or five Great Saints of the Muhammadans, of whom the earliest is *Baha-ud-din Zakariya* of Multan, commonly called *Bahâwal Hakk*. But the Hindus affirm that the place was originally dedicated to the *Panch-Pandu*, or Five Pandu brothers of the 'Mahâbhârata.'

The last probable position that I know of is the ruined fortress of *Rânigat*. I visited this place in January, 1848, and I had intended revisiting it during my tour in 1863, but the war on the Buner frontier most unfortunately prevented me from carrying out my intentions. I can, therefore, add but little to the information which I collected in 1848; but as that has not been made public, and as no one but Mr. Loewenthal would appear to have visited the place since then, my account will still possess all the advantage of novelty.

Rânigat is situated on a lofty hill above the village of Nogram, which is just 12 miles to the south-east of Bâzâr, and 16 miles to the north of Ohind. Its position, therefore, is strongly in favour of its identification with Aornos. The hill itself is the last point of one of the long spurs of the Mahâban range. Its base is rather more than two miles in length from north to south by about half a mile in width, but the top of the hill is not more than 1200 feet in length by 800 feet in breadth. In 1848, I estimated its height at 1000 feet; but from the unanimous assertions of the people that it is higher than Panjpir, I think that it is probably not less than 1200 feet. The sides of the hill are covered with massive blocks of stone, which make it exceedingly rugged and inaccessible. There is only one road, cut in the rock, leading to the top, although there are two, if not more, rather difficult pathways. This, we know, was also the case with Aornos, as Ptolemy succeeded in reaching the top by a "rugged and dangerous path,* whilst Alexander himself attacked the place by one regular path which was cut out by the hand.† *Rânigat* may be described as consisting of a castle, 500 feet long by 400 feet broad, surrounded on all sides except the east, where it springs up from the low spur of Mahâban, by a rocky ridge, which on the north side rises to an equal height. On all sides the castle rock is scarped; and on two sides it is separated from the surrounding ridge by deep ravines, that to the north being 100 feet deep, and that to the west from 50 to 150 feet. At the north-west angle of the castle two dykes have been thrown across the ravine, which would appear to have been intended to arrest the flow of water, and thus to form a great reservoir in the west hollow. In the north ravine, between the castle and the great isolated block called *Rânigat*, there are three square

* Arrian, 'Anabasis,' iv. 29.

† *Ibid.*, iv. 28.

wells; and to the north-east lower down, I thought that I could trace another dyke, which was most probably only the remains of part of the outer line of defences. The entire circuit of this outer line is about 4,500 feet, or somwhat less than a mile.

The castle itself is thus described by Mr. Loewenthal* :—"The summit of the hill offers a flat plateau of some size, which had been very strongly fortified by buildings all round the brow. These buildings are constructed of large blocks of stone (conglomerate found on the spot) neatly hewn, and carefully fitted, disposed with very great regularity, and laid in a cement of extraordinary excellence. Unavoidable interestices between the large blocks are filled up by layers of thin small stone tablets, this latter practice being an invariable feature in all the so-called Kafir buildings which I have seen in the Trans-Indus country." To this description I may add that all the stone blocks are laid most carefully as headers and stretchers, that is alternately lengthwise and breadthwise, which gives a very pleasing and varied appearance to the massive walls. All the buildings are now much ruined, but the external walls are traceable nearly all round, and on the south and west sides are still standing to a considerable height, and in very good order. The main entrance, which is at the south-west corner, is formed in the usual ancient manner by overlapping stones. The passage is not perpendicular to the

* Journ. Asiat. Soc. Bengal, 1863, p. 5.

face of the wall, but considerably inclined to the right for a short distance. It then turns to the left to a small chamber, and then again to the right till it reaches what must have been an open courtyard. The whole of this passage was originally roofed in by courses of stone with chamfered ends overlapping each other so as to form the two sides of a pointed arch, but the ends of the upper course of stones being left straight, the apex of the arch has the appearance of a rectangular cusp. This peculiarity was also noticed by Mr. Loewenthal, who says that "the arch would be pointed, but the centre line is taken up by a narrow rectangular groove." On the west face I observed a smaller passage of a similar kind, but it was so blocked up with rubbish that I was quite unable to trace its course.

This central castle or citadel, with its open courtyard surrounded by costly buildings, I take to have been the palace of the king, with the usual temples for private worship. At the north end I traced a wide flight of steps leading down to a second plateau, which I presume to have been the outer court of the palace or citadel. The upper courtyard is 270 feet long and 100 feet broad; and the lower courtyard, including the steps, is just half the size, or 130 feet by 100 feet. These open areas were covered with broken statues of all sizes, and in all positions. Many of them were figures of Buddha the Teacher, either seated or standing; some were of Buddha the Ascetic, sitting under the holy Pipal tree; and a few represented Mâyâ, the mother of

Buddha, standing under the sâl tree. But there were fragments of other figures, which apparently were not connected with religion, such as a life-size male figure in chain armour, a naked body of a man with the Macedonian *chlamys*, or short cloak, thrown over the shoulders and fastened in front in the usual manner, and a human breast partly covered with the *chlamys* and adorned with a necklace of which the clasps are formed by two human-headed, winged, and four-footed animals, something like centaurs. All these figures are carved in a soft, dark-blue clay slate, which is easily worked with a knife. It is exceedingly brittle, and was therefore easily broken by the idol-hating Musalmans. But as the surface was capable of receiving a good polish, many of the fragments are still in very fine preservation. The best piece that I have seen was a head of Buddha, with the hair massed on the top of the head, and worked in a peculiar manner in wavy lines, instead of the usual formal curls. It was found at Jamâl Garhi, and is by far the best piece of Indian sculpture that I have seen. The calm repose of the finely chiselled features is not unworthy of Grecian art, but the striking beauty of the face is somewhat marred by the round projecting Indian chin.

I have already noticed that the Rânigat hill is covered on all sides with massive blocks of stone, which make the approach very rugged and difficult. Numbers of these stones are of very large size, and some of those on the top of the hill have been hollowed out to form cells. Mr. Loewenthal notices this as "one of the most marked features" amongst these remains. Many of the cells are quite plain inside, whilst others have the simple ornament of a niche or two. The most notable of these excavated blocks is on the ridge to the south of the castle. It is called *Katri-kar*, or the "Grain Merchant's house," by the people; but I observed nothing about the rock that would give any clue to its original purpose, save the smallness of the entrance, which was certainly better suited for the cell of a monk than for the shop of a dealer. Mr. Loewenthal notices that "the vegetation on the hill is principally olive and myrtle"; but in 1848 there was a considerable number of good-sized trees scattered over the summit.

I do not insist upon the identification, but if we admit that the accounts of the historians are very much exaggerated, I think that the ruins of Rânigat tally much better with the vague descriptions of Aornos that have come down to us, than any other position with which I am acquainted. In all essential points, save that of size, the agreement is wonderfully close. Its position between Bâzâr and Ohind, or Bazaria and Embolima, is quite unobjectionable. Its attribution to Raja *Vara* renders it probable that the place may have been named after him, which would give a very near approach to the Aornos of the Greeks. Its great height, its ruggedness, and difficulty of access, its one path cut in the rock, its spring of water and level ground, and its deep ravine separating the outer works from the castle, are so many close and striking points of resemblance, that, were it not for the great difference in size, I should be very much disposed to accept the identification as complete. But though in this point it does not come up to the boastful descriptions of the Greeks, yet we must not forget the opinion of Strabo that the capture of Aornos was exaggerated by Alexander's flatterers. It must also be remembered that as the campaign against Assakanus took place "during the winter,"* and the Macedonians entered Taxila "at the beginning of spring," the siege of Aornos must have been carried on during the very depth of winter, when the Mahâban hill, 7,471 feet above the sea, and every other hill of the same height, is usually covered with snow. It is almost certain, therefore, that even the lesser height of 11 stadia, or 6,674 feet above the Yusufzai plain, equivalent to 7,874 feet above the sea, must be grossly exaggerated. In this part of the country the snow falls annually as low as 4,000 feet above the sea, or 2,800 above the Yusufzai plain, and as no snow is said to have fallen on Aornos, although the Greeks mention that they saw snow during the winter, I think that their silence on this point is absolutely conclusive against the recorded height of Aornos, and therefore also against the claims of Mahâban, and of any other hill exceeding 4,000 feet in height. All the ancient authorities agree in describing Aornos as a πέτρα, or 'rock,' with rugged

* Strabo, Geogr., xv. 1, 17.

and precipitous sides, and with only a single path cut by hand. The Mahâban hill does not, therefore, fulfil any one condition of the ancient description. It is a huge mountain of comparatively easy access, and is more than twice the size of the most exaggerated estimate of Alexander's flatterers. Its name also has no resemblance to Aornos; whilst the traditions of Raja *Vara*, attached to Rânigat, would seem to connect that place directly with Aornos.

Parashâwara, or Peshâwar.

The great city now called Peshâwar is first mentioned by Fa-Hian, in A.D. 400, under the name of *Fo-leu-sha.** It is next noticed by Sung-Yun in A.D. 502, at which time the king of Gândhâra was at war with the king of Kipin, or Kophene, that is Kabul and Ghazni, and the surrounding districts. Sung-Yun does not name the city, but he calls it the capital, and his description of its great *stupa* of king *Kia-ni-sse-kia*, or Kanishka, is quite sufficient to establish its identity.† At the period of Hwen Thsang's visit, in A.D. 630, the royal family had become extinct, and the kingdom of Gândhâra was a dependency of Kapisa or Kabul. But the capital which Hwen Thsang calls *Pu-lu-sha-pu-lo*, or *Parashâwara*, was still a great city of 40 *li*, or 6⅔ miles, in extent.‡ It is next mentioned by Masudi and Abu Rihân, in the tenth and eleventh centuries,

* Beal's translation of 'Fah-Hian,' p. 34.

† Beal's translation of 'Sung-Yun,' p. 202.

‡ Julien's 'Hiouen Thsang,' ii. 104.

under the name of *Parashâwar,* and again by Baber, in the sixteenth century, it is always called by the same name throughout his commentaries. Its present name we owe to Akbar, whose fondness for innovation led him to change the ancient *Parashâwar,* of which he did not know the meaning, to *Peshâwar,* or the "frontier town." Abul Fazl gives both names.*

The great object of veneration at Parashâwar, in the first centuries of the Christian era, was the begging pot of Buddha, which has already been noticed. Another famous site was the holy Pipal tree, at 8 or 9 *li,* or 1½ mile, to the south-east of the city. The tree was about 100 feet in height, with wide spreading branches, which, according to the tradition, had formerly given shade to Sakya Buddha when he predicted the future appearance of the great king Kanishka. The tree is not noticed by Fa-Hian, but it is mentioned by Sun-Yung as the *Pho-thi,* or *Bodhi* tree, whose "branches spread out on all sides, and whose foliage shuts out the sight of the sky." Beneath it there were four seated statues of the four previous Buddhas. Sung-Yun further states that the tree was planted by Kanishka over the spot where he had buried a copper vase containing the pearl tissue lattice of the great *stupa,* which he was afraid might be abstracted from the tope after his death. This same tree would appear to have been seen by the Emperor Baber in A.D.

* 'Ayin Akbari,' ii. 341.

1505, who describes it as the "stupendous tree" of Begrâm, which he "immediately rode out to see."* It must then have been not less than 1500 years old, and as it is not mentioned in A.D. 1594 by Abul Fazl,† in his accout of the *Gor-Katri* at Peshâwar, I conclude that it had previously disappeared through simple old age and decay.

The enormous *stupa* of Kanishka, which stood close to the holy tree on its south side, is described by all the pilgrims. In A.D. 500 Fa-Hian says that it was about 400 feet high, and "adorned with all manner of precious things," and that fame reported it as superior to all other topes in India. One hundred years later, Sung-Yun declares that "amongst the topes of western countries this is the first." Lastly, in A.D. 630, Hwen Thsang describes it as upwards of 400 feet in height and 1½ *li,* or just one quarter of a mile, in circumference. It contained a large quantity of the relics of Buddha. No remains of this great *stupa* now exist.

To the west of the *stupa* there was an old monastery, also built by Kanishka, which had become celebrated amongst the Buddhists through the fame of *Arya-Pârswika, Manorhita,* and *Vasubandhu,* three of the great leaders and teachers of Buddhism about the beginning of the Christian era. The towers and pavilions of the monastery were two stories in height, but the building was already much

---

*'Memoirs, translated by Leyden and Erskine,' p. 157.

†'Ayin Akbari,' ii. 165.

ruined at the time of Hwen Thsang's visit. It was, however, inhabited by a small number of monks, who professed the "Lesser Vehicle" or exoteric doctrines of Buddhism. It was still flourishing as a place of Buddhist education in the ninth or tenth century* when Vira Deva of Magadha was sent to the "great Vihâra of Kanishka where the best of teachers were to be found, and which was famous for the quietism of its frequenters." I believe that this great monastery was still existing in the times of *Baber* and *Akbar* under the name of *Gor-Kotri*, or the Baniya's house.

The former says, "I had heard of the fame of *Gurh-Katri*, which is one of the holy places of the Jogis of the Hindus, who come from great distances to cut off their hair and shave their beards at this *Gurh-Katri*." Abul Fazl's account is still more brief. Speaking of Peshawur he says, "here is a temple, called *Gor-Katri*, a place of religious resort, particularly for Jogis." According to Erskine, the grand caravansara of Peshawur was built on the site of the *Gor-Katri*.

7. UDYÂNA, OR SWÂT.

On leaving Utakhanda Hwen Thsang travelled about 600 *li*, or 100 miles, towards the north, to *U-chang-na*, or *Udyâna*, which was situated on the river *Su-po-fa-su-tu*, the *Subhavastu* and *Suvastu* of Sanskrit, the *Suastus* of Arrian, and the *Swât* or *Süât*

---

* Jour. As. Soc. Bengal, 1849, i. 494.

river of the present day. It is called *U-chang* by the earlier pilgrims Fa-Hian and Sung-yun, which is a close transcript of *Ujjâna,* the Pali form of Udyâna. The country is described as highly irrigated, and very fertile. This agrees with all the native accounts, according to which Swât is second only to the far-famed valley of Kashmir. Hwen Thsang makes it 5000 *li*, or 833 miles, in circuit, which must be very near the truth, if, as was most probably the case, it included all the tributaries of the Swât river. *Udyâna* would thus have embraced the four modern districts of Panjkora, Bijâwar, Swât, and Bunîr, which have a circuit of only 500 miles, if measured on the map direct, but of not less than 800 miles by road measurement. Fa-Hian mentions *Su-ho-to* as a small district to the south of Udyâna. This has generally been identified with the name of Swât; but from its position to the south of Udyâna, and to the north of Parashâwar, it cannot have been the large valley of the Swât river itself, but must have been limited to the smaller valley of Bunîr. This is confirmed by the legend told by Fa-Hian of the hawk and pigeon; in which Buddha, to save the pigeon, tears his own flesh and offers it to the hawk. The very same legend is related by Hwen Thsang, but he places the scene at the north-west foot of the *Mahâban* mountain, that is, in the actual valley of Bunîr. He adds that Buddha was then a king, named *Shi-pi-ḳia,* or *Siviḳa,* which may, perhaps, be the true form of Fa-Hian's *Suhoto*.

The capital of Udyâna was called *Mung-ḳie-li,*

or *Mangala,* which is probably the *Mangora* of Wilford's surveyor, Mogal Beg, and the *Manglora* of General Court's map. It was 16 or 17 *li,* about 2¾ miles, in circuit, and very populous. At 250 or 260 *li,* about 42 miles, to the north-east of the capital the pilgrim reached the source of the *Subhavastu* river, in the fountain of the Nâga king *Apalâla;* and at 750 *li,* or 125 miles, further in the same direction, after crossing a mountain range and ascending the Indus, he arrived at *Tha-li-lo,* or *Dârel,* which had been the ancient capital of Udyâna. *Dârel* is a valley on the right or western bank of the Indus, now occupied by *Dârdus,* or *Dârds,* from whom it received its name. It is called *To-li* by Fa-Hian, who makes it a separate kingdom. The Dârds are now usually divided into three separate tribes, according to the dialects which they speak. Those who use the *Arniya* dialect occupy the north-western districts of *Yasan* and *Chitrâl;* those who speak the Khajunah dialect occupy the north-east districts of Hunza and Nager; and those who speak the Shinâ dialect occupy the valleys of Gilgit, Chilâs, Dârel, Kohli, and Pâlas, along the banks of the Indus. In this district there was a celebrated wooden statue of the future Buddha Maitreya, which is mentioned by both of the pilgrims. According to Fa-Hian it was erected 300 years after the *Nirvâna* of Buddha, or about B.C. 243, that is, in the reign of Asoka, when the Buddhist religion was actively disseminated over India by missionaries. Hwen Thsang describes the statue as 100 feet in height, and states that it was erected by *Madhyântika.** The name and the date mutually support each other, as *Madhyântika*, or *Majjhima* in Pali, was the name of the Buddhist teacher, who, after the assembly of the Third Synod in Asoka's reign, was sent to spread the Buddhist faith in Kashmir and the whole Himavanta country.† This is most probably the period alluded to by Hwen Thsang when *Dârel* was the capital of Udyâna.

8. BOLOR, OR BALTI.

From Dârel Hwen Thsang travelled 500 *li*, or 83 miles, over a mountain range, and up the valley of the Indus to *Po-lu-lo*, or *Bolor*. This district was 4000 *li*, or 666 miles, in circuit; its greatest length being from east to west. It was surrounded by snowy mountains, and produced a large quantity of gold. This account of the route, compared with the bearing and distance, show that *Po-lu-lo* must be the modern *Balti*, or Little Tibet, which is undoubtedly correct, as the people of the neighbouring Dârdu districts on the Indus know Balti only by the name of *Palolo*.‡ Balti also is still famous for its gold washings. The name, too, is an old one, as Ptolemy calls the people Βύλται, or *Byltœ*. Lastly,

* Julien's 'Hiouen Thsang,' ii. 168. But he fixes the date at only 50 years after Buddha, for which we should most probably read 250 years.

† Turnour's 'Mahâwanso,' p. 71 ; see also my 'Bhilsa Topes,' p. 120.

‡ 'Hiouen Thsang' ii. 150 ; and my 'Ladak,' p. 34.

both in size and position Balti corresponds exactly with the account of the Chinese pilgrim, as the length of the province is along the course of the Indus from east to west for 150 miles, and the breadth about 80 miles from the mountains of Deoseh to the Karakoram range, or altogether 460 miles in circuit, as measured direct on the map, or about 600 miles by road measurement.

9. FALANA, OR BANU.

The name of *Fa-la-na* is mentioned only by Hwen Thsang, who places the country to the south-east of Ghazni, and at fifteen days' journey to the south of Lamghân.* It was 4000 *li*, or 666 miles, in circuit, and was chiefly composed of mountains and forests. It was subject to Kapisene, and the language of the people had a slight resemblance to that of Central India. From the bearing and distance, there is no doubt that *Banu* was the district visited by Hwen Thsang, from which it may be inferred that its original name was *Varana*, or *Barna*. This is confirmed by Fa-Hian, who calls the country by the shorter vernacular name of *Po-na*, or *Bana*, which he reached in thirteen days from Nagarahâra in going towards the south. *Pona* also is said to be three days' journey to the west of the Indus, which completes the proof of its identity with Banu, or the lower half of the valley of the Kuram river. In the time of Fa-Hian the kingdom of Banu was limited to this small tract, as he makes the upper part of the

* H. Th., i. 265.

Kuram valley a separate district, called *Lo-i,* or *Roh.** But in the time of Hwen Thsang, when it had a circuit of more than 600 miles, its boundaries must have included the whole of the two large valleys of the Kuram and Gomal rivers, extending from the Safed Koh, or "Little Snowy Mountains" of Fa-Hian, to Sivastan on the south, and from the frontiers of Ghazni and Kandahar on the west to the Indus on the east.

I think it not improbable that the full name of this district, *Falana* or *Barana,* may have some connection with that of the great division of the Ghilji tribe named *Burân,* as the upper valleys of both the Kuram and Gomal rivers, between Ghazni and the Sulimâni mountains, are now occupied by the numerous clans of the Sulimâni Khel, or eldest branch of the Burâns. *Iryûb,* the elder son of Burân, and the father of Sulimân, is said to have given his name to the district of *Haryûb* or *Iryâb,* which is the upper valley of the Kuram river.

M. Vivien de St. Martin† identifies *Falana* with *Vâneh,* or *Wanneh,* or Elphinstone.‡ But *Vâna,* or *Wâna,* as the Afghans call it, is only a petty little tract with a small population, whereas *Banu* is one of the largest, richest, and most populous districts to the west of the Indus. Vâna lies to the south-south-east, and Banu to the east-south-east of Ghazni, so that

* Beal's Translation, c. 14, p. 50.

† 'Hiouen Thsang,' appendice iii.

‡ Elphinstone's 'Kabul,' ii. 156, 158.

either of them will tally very well with the south-east direction noted by Hwen Thsang; but Vâna is from 20 to 25 days' journey to the south of Lamghân, while Banu is just 15 days' journey as noted by the pilgrim. As Fa-Hian's notice of Banu dates as high as the beginning of the fifth century, I think that it may be identified with the *Banagara* of Ptolemy, which he places in the extreme north of Indo-Scythia, and to the south-south-east of *Nagara*, or Jalâlâbâd. A second town in the same direction, which he names *Andrapana*, is probably *Drâband* or *Derâband*, near Dera Ismaïl Khan.

Hwen Thsang mentions a district on the western frontier of Falana, named *Ki-ḳiang-na*, the position of which has not yet been fixed. M. Vivien de St. Martin and Sir H. Elliot have identified it with the *Kaiḳânân*, or *Kiḳân*, of the Arab historians of Sindh;* but unfortunately the position of *Kaiḳânân* itself is still undetermined. It is, however, described as lying to the north or north-east of Kachh Gandâva, and as *Kiḳiangna* was to the west of *Falana* or *Banu*, it appears probable that the district intended must be somewhere in the vicinity of *Pishin* and *Kwetta;* and as Hwen Thsang describes it as situated in a valley under a high mountain, I am inclined to identify it with the valley of Pishin itself, which lies between the Khoja Amrân hills on the north, and the lofty Mount Takatu on the south.

---

* 'Hiouen Thsang,' iii. 185; Dowson's edition of Sir H. Elliot's 'Muhammadan Historians,' i. 381.

This position agrees with that of *Kaikân*, قيقان given by Biladûri,* who says that it formed part of Sindh in the direction of Khorasan. This is further confirmed by the statement that *Kaikân* was on the road from Multan to Kabul, as the usual route between these places lies over the Sakhi Sarwar Pass in the Sulimâni mountains, and across the Pishin valley to Kandahar. A shorter, but more difficult, route is by the valley of the Gomal river to Ghazni. But as the valley of the Gomal belonged to *Falana*, it follows that the district of *Kikiangna* must have been somewhere in the neighbourhood of *Pishin;* and as this valley is now inhabited by the tribe of *Khakas*, it is not improbable that the name of *Kikân*, or *Kaikân*, may have been derived from them.

10. OPOKIEN, OR AFGHANISTAN?

O-po-kien is mentioned only once by Hwen Thsang in a brief paragraph, which places it between Falana and Ghazni, to the north-west of the former, and to the south-east of the latter. From this description it would appear to be the same as the *Lo-i* of Fa-Hian, and the *Roh* of the Indian historians. Perhaps the name of *Opokien* may have some connection with *Vorgun* or *Verghin*, which Wilford's surveyor, Mogal Beg, places near the source of the *Tunchí*, or *Tochi* branch of the Kuram river. In the map attached to Burnes's Travels by Arrowsmith the name is written *Borghoon*. I am, however,

* Reinaud's 'Fragments Arabes, etc.,' p. 184.

inclined to identify *Opokien*, or *Avakan*, as it is rendered by M. Julien, with the name of *Afghan*, as I find that the Chinese syllable *kien* represents *ghan* in the word *Ghanta*. From the cursory notice of the district by Hwen Thsang, I infer that it must have formed part of the province of Falana. It was certainly a part of the mountainous district called *Roh* by Abul Fazl and Ferishta,* or south-eastern Afghanistan, which would appear to have been one of the original seats of the Afghan people. Major Raverty† describes Roh as "the mountainous district of Afghanistan and part of Biluchistan," or "the country between Ghazni and Kandahar and the Indus." The people of this province are called *Rohilas*, or *Rohila Afghans*, to distinguish them from other Afghans, such as the *Ghori Afghans* of Ghor, between Balkh and Merv. There is, however, a slight chronological difficulty about this identification, as the Afghans of Khilij, Ghor, and Kabul are stated by Ferishta to have subdued the province of Roh so late as A.H. 63, or A.D. 682, that is about thirty years later than the period of Hwen Thsang's visit. But I think that there are good grounds for doubting the accuracy of this statement, as Hwen Thsang describes the language of Falana as having but little resemblance to that of Central India. The inhabitants of Roh could not, therefore, have been Indians; and if not Indians,

---

* Briggs's 'Ferishta,' i. p. 8.

† Pushtu Dictionary, *in voce*.

they must almost certainly have been Afghans. Ferishta* begins his account by saying that the Muhammadan Afghans of the mountains "invaded and laid waste the inhabited countries, such as Kirmân, Shivarân, and Peshâwar"; and that several battles took place between the Indians and Afghans "on a plain between Kirmân and Peshâwar." The *Kirmân* here mentioned is not the great province of Kirman, or Karmania, on the shore of the Indian Ocean, but the *Kirmân,* or *Kirmâsh,* of Timur's historians, which is the valley of the Kuram river. The difficulty may be explained if we limit the part of Kirmân that was invaded to the lower valley, or plains of the Kuarm river, and extend the limits of the Afghan country beyond Ghazni and Kabul, so as to embrace the upper valley, or mountain region of the Kuram river. Politically the ruler of Peshâwar has always been the ruler of Kohât and Banu, and the ruler of Kabul has been the lord of the upper Kuram valley. This latter district is now called *Khost;* but it is the *Iryâb* of Timur's historians, and of Wilford's surveyor, Mogul Beg, and the *Haryûb* of Elphinstone. Now the *Sulimân-Khel* of the *Burân* division of the Ghiljis number about three-fourths of the whole horde. I infer, therefore, that the original seat of the Ghiljis must have included the upper valleys of the Kuram and Gomal rivers on the east, with Ghazni and Kelât-i-Ghilji on the west. Haryûb would thus have formed part

* Briggs's Translation, i. 7.

of the Afghan district of *Khilij*, or *Ghilji*, from which the southern territories of Peshâwar were easily accessible.

But whether this explanation of Ferishta's statement be correct or not, I feel almost certain that Hwen Thsang's *O-po-kien* must be intended for *Afghân*. Its exact equivalent would be *Avaghan*, which is the nearest transcript of *Afghan* that the Chinese syllables are capable of making. If this rendering is correct, it is the earliest mention of the Afghans that I am aware of under that name.

II. Kingdom of Kashmir.

In the seventh century, according to the Chinese pilgrim, the kingdom of Kashmir comprised not only the valley of Kashmir itself, but also the whole of the hilly country between the Indus and the Chenâb to the foot of the Salt range in the south. The different states visited by Hwen Thsang were *Urasa*, to the west of Kashmir; *Taxila* and *Sinhapura*, to the south-west; and *Punach* and *Rajaori* to the south. The other hill-states to the east and south-east are not mentioned; but there is good reason for believing that they also were tributary, and that the dominions of Kashmir in the seventh century extended from the Indus to the Râvi. The petty independent state of *Kullu*, in the upper valley of the Biâs river, was saved by its remoteness and inaccessibility; and the rich state of *Jâlandhar*, on the lower Biâs, was then subject to Harsha Vardhana, the great king of Kanoj. But towards the end of the ninth century the Kangra valley was conquered by Sankara Varmma, and the sovereign power of Kashmir was extended over the whole of the Alpine Panjab from the Indus to the Satlej.*

Hwen Thsang describes Kashmir as surrounded on all sides by lofty mountains, which is a correct description of the valley itself; but when he goes on to say that its circuit is 7,000 *li,* or 1,166 miles, he must refer to the extended kingdom of Kashmir, and not to the valley, which is only 300 miles in circuit. But the extent of its political boundary, from the Indus on the north to the Salt range on the south, and from the Indus on the west to the Râvi on the east, cannot be estimated at less than 900 miles, and may very probably have reached the amount stated by the pilgrim.

1. KASHMIR.

Hwen Thsang entered the valley of Kashmir from the west in September, A.D. 631. At the entrance there was a stone gate, where he was met by the younger brother of the king's mother; and after paying his devotions at the sacred monuments, he went to lodge for the night in the monastery of *Hu-se-kia-lo,* or *Hushkara.*† This place is mentioned by Abu Rihân,‡ who makes *Ushkara* the same as *Barâmula,* which occupied both sides of the

* 'Raja Tarangini,' v. 144.
† 'Hiouen Thsang,' i. 90.
‡ Reinaud, 'Fragments Arabes,' p. 116.

river. In the 'Raja Tarangini'* also *Hushkapura* is said to be near *Varâha*, or *Varâhamula*, which is the Sanskrit form of *Barâmula*. Hushkara or Uskar still exists as a village on the left or eastern bank of the Behat, two miles to the south-east of Barâmula. The Kashmiri Brahmans say that this is the Hushkapura of the 'Raja Tarangini,' which was founded by the Turushka king Hushka, about the beginning of the Christian era.

According to the chronology of the 'Raja Tarangini,' the king of Kashmir in A.D. 631 was Pratâpâditya; but the mention of his maternal uncle† shows that there must be some error in the native history, as that king's father came to the throne in right of his wife, who had no brother. Pratâpâditya's accession must, therefore, have taken place after Hwen Thsang's departure from Kashmir in A.D. 633, which makes an error of three years in the received chronology. But a much greater difference is shown in the reigns of his sons *Chandrapida* and *Muktapida*, who applied to the Chinese emperor for aid against the Arabs.‡ The date of the first application is A.D. 713, while, according to the native chronology, Chandrapida reigned from A.D. 680 to 688, which shows an error of not less than twenty-five years. But as the Chinese annals also record that about A.D. 720 the emperor granted the title of

* B. vii. 1310 and 1312.

† 'Hiouen Thsang,' ii. 90.

‡ Rémusat, 'Nouveaux Mélanges Asiatiques,' i. 197.

king to Chandrapida, he must have been living as late as the previous year A.D. 719, which makes the erorr in the Kashmirian chronology amount to exactly thirty-one years. By applying this correction to the dates of his predecessors, the reign of his grandfather, *Durlabha*, will extend from A.D. 625 to 661. He, therefore, must have been the king who was reigning at the time of Hwen Thsang's arrival in Kashmir in A.D. 631. Durlabha, who was the son-in-law of his predecessor, is said to have been the son of a *Nâga*, or Dragon; and the dynasty which he founded is called the *Nâga*, or *Karkota* dynasty. By this appellation I understand that his family was given to ophiolatry, or serpent-worship, which had been the prevailing religion of Kashmir from time immemorial. Hwen Thsang designates this race as *Ki-li-to*, which Professor Lassen and M. Stanislas Julien render by *Kritya* and *Kritiya*. They were extremely hostile to the Buddhists, who had frequently deprived them of power, and abolished their rights; on which account, says the pilgrim, the king, who was then reigning, had but little faith in Buddha, and cared only for heretics and temples of the Brahmanical gods. This statement is confirmed by the native chronicle, which records that the queen, *Ananga-lekha*, built a *Vihâra*, or Buddhist monastery, named after herself, *Anangabhavana;* while the king built a temple to Vishnu, called after himself, *Durlabha-swâmina*.* I infer from this

* 'Raja Tarangini,' iv. 3 and 5.

that the queen still adhered to the Buddhist faith of her family, and that the king was, in reality, a Brahmanist, although he may have professed a lukewarm attachment to Buddhism.

The people of Kashmir are described as good looking, easy and fickle in manner, effeminate and cowardly in disposition, and naturally prone to artifice and deceit. This character they still bear; and to it I may add that they are the dirtiest and most immoral race in India. Hwen Thsang states that the neighbouring kings held the base Kashmiris in such scorn that they refused all alliance with them, and gave them the name of *Ki-li-to* or *Krityas*, which would appear to be a term of contempt applied to evil-minded and mischievous persons, as enemies, traitors, assassins, etc. The term which I have heard used is *Kîr-Mlechchhas*, or the "Barbarian *Kîras*," and Wilson gives *Kîra* as a name of the valley of Kashmir, and *Kîrâh* as the name of the people.

In the seventh century the capital of the country was on the eastern bank of the river, and about 10 *li*, or less than 2 miles, to the north-west of the ancient capital. Abu Rihân* calls the capital *Adishtân*, which is the Sanskrit *Adhisthâna*, or "chief town." This is the present city of *Srinagar*, which was built by Raja Pravarasena about the beginning of the sixth century, and was, therefore, a new place at the time of Hwen Thsang's visit. The "old capital" I have

* Reinaud, 'Fragments Arabes, etc.', p. 116.

already identified with an old site, 2 miles to the south-east of the Takht-i-Sulimân, called *Pân-drethân,* which is the corrupt Kashmirian form of *Purânâdhisthâna,* or "the old chief city." *Pân* is the usual Kashmiri term for "old," as in *Pân Drâs,* or "old Dras," to distinguish it from the new village of Drâs, which is lower down the river.* Near the old capital there was a famous *stupa,* which in A.D. 631 enshrined a tooth of Buddha; but before Hwen Thsang's return to the Panjâb in A.D. 643 the sacred tooth had been given up by the Raja to Harsha Vardhana, the powerful king of Kanoj, who made his demand at the head of an army on the frontier of Kashmir.† As Raja Durlabha was a Brahmanist, the sacrifice of the Buddhist tooth was a real gain to his religion.

From the earliest times Kashmir has been divided into the two large districts of *Kamrâj* and *Merâj,* the former being the northern half of the valley, below the junction of the Sindh river with the Behat, and the latter the southern half above that junction. The smaller divisions it is unnecessary to mention. But I may note the curious anomaly which a change of religious belief has produced in the use of two of the most distinctive Hindu terms. By the Hindu who worships the sun, the cardinal

---

* Wilson altered this spelling to *Payin Drâs,* which in Persian signifies "Lower Drâs," in spite of the fact that *Pân Drâs* is higher up the river.

† Compare 'Hiouen Thsang,' ii. 180 with i. 251.

points are named with reference to the east, as *para*, the "front," or the "east," to which he turns in his daily morning worship; *apara*, "behind," or the "west;" *vâma*, the "left" hand, or the "north;" and *dakshina*, the "right" hand, or the "south." By the Muhammadan, who turns his face to the west, towards Mecca, these terms are exactly reversed, and *dachin*, which still means the "right" hand in Kashmiri, is now used to denote the "north," and *kâwar*, or the "left" hand to denote the "south." Thus, on the Lidar river there is the subdivision of *Dachinpâra* to the north of the stream, and *Kâwarpâra* to the south of it. On the Behat river also, below Barâhmula, the subdivision of *Dachin* lies to the north, and that of *Kâwar* to the south of the stream. This change in the meaning of *Dachin* from "south" to "north" must have taken place before the time of Akbar, as Abul Fazl* describes *Dachinpâra* as "situated at the foot of a mountain, on the side of Great Tibet," that is to the north of the river Lidar.

The principal ancient cities of Kashmir are the old capital of *Srinagari*, the new capital called *Pravarasenapura*; *Khâgendra-pura* and *Khunamusha*, built before the time of Asoka; *Vijipâra and Pântasok*, which are referred to Asoka himself; *Surapura*, a restoration of the ancient *Kâmbuva*; *Kanishkapura*, *Hushkapura*, and *Jushkapura*, named after the three Indo-Scythian Princes by whom they

* 'Ayin Akbari,' ii. 130.

were founded; *Parihâsapura,* built by Lalitâditya; *Padmapura,* named after Padma, the minister of Raja Vrihaspati; and *Avantipura,* named after Raja Avanti Varmma.

Srinagari, the old capital of Kashmir prior to the erection of Pravarasenapura, is stated to have been founded by the great Asoka,* who reigned from B.C. 263 to 226. It stood on the site of the present *Pândrethân,* and is said to have extended along the bank of the river from the foot of the *Takht-i-Sulimân* to *Pântasok,* a distance of more than three miles. The oldest temple in Kashmir, on the top of the Takht-i-Sulimân, is identified by the unanimous consent of all the Brahmans of the valley with the temple of *Jyeshta Rudra,* which was built by Jaloka, the son of Asoka, in Srinagari.† This identification is based on the fact that the hill was originally called *Jyeshteswara.* The old bridge abutments at the village of Pântasok are also attributed to Asoka; and the other ruins at the same place are said to be the remains of the two *Asokeswara* temples which are noted in the native chronicle of Kashmir. Srinagari was still the capital of the valley in the reign of Pravarasena I., towards the end of the fifth century, when the King erected a famous symbol of the god Siva, named after himself *Pravareswara.* This city still existed in A.D. 631, when the Chinese pilgrim arrived in Kashmir,

* 'Raja Tarangini,' i. 104.

† 'Raja Tarangini, i. 124.

although it was no longer the capital of the valley. He speaks of the capital of his time as the "new city," and states that the "old city" was situated to the south-east of it, at a distance of ten *li*, or nearly two miles, and to the south of a high mountain. This account describes the relative positions of Pândrethân and the present capital with the lofty hill of Takht-i-Sulimân so exactly, that there can be no hesitation in accepting them as the representatives of the ancient places. The old city was still inhabited between A.D. 913 and 921, when Meru, the minister of Raja Pârtha, erected in *Purânadhisthâna,* that is in the "old capital," a temple named after himself *Meru-Varddhana-swâmi*. This building I have identified with the existing temple of *Pândrethân*, as Kalhan Pandit relates* that, when Raja Abhimanyu set fire to his capital, all the noble buildings "from the temple of *Varddhana Swâmi,* as far as *Bhikshukipâraka*" (or the asylum of mendicants) were destroyed. I attribute the escape of the limestone temple to its fortunate situation in the midst of a tank of water. To this catastrophe I would assign the final desertion of the old capital, as the humble dwellings of the people could not possibly have escaped the destructive fire which consumed all the "noble edifices" of the city.

Pravarasenapura, or the new capital, was built by Raja Pravarasena II. in the beginning of the sixth

---

* See my 'Temples of Kashmir,' p. 44; and 'Raja Tarangini,' vi. 191.

century. Its site, as already noted, was that of the present capital of Srinagar. This is determined beyond all possibility of doubt by the very clear and distinct data furnished by the Chinese pilgrim Hwen Thsang, and by the Hindu historian *Kalhan Pandit*. The statements of the first have already been quoted in my account of the old capital; but I may add that Hwen Thsang resided for two whole years in Kashmir in the *Jayendra Vihâra,** or Buddhist monastery, built by Jayendra, the maternal uncle of Pravarasena. The Hindu author describes the city as situated at the confluence of two rivers, and with a hill in the midst of it. This is an exact description of the present Srinagar, in the midst of which stands the hill of *Hari Parbat*, and through which flows the river *Hara*, or *Ara*, to join the Behat at the northern end of the city.†

The question now arises, how did the new city of *Pravarasenapura* lose its own name, and assume that of the old city of Srinagari? I think that this difficulty may perhaps be explained by the simple fact that the two cities were actually contiguous, and, as they existed together side by side for upwards of five centuries, the old name, as in the case of Delhi, would naturally have remained in common use with the people, in preference to the new name, as the customary designation of the capital. The old name

---

* 'Hiouen Thsang,' i. 96.

† 'Moorcroft's Travels,' ii. 276. I speak also from personal knowledge, as I have twice visited Kashmir.

of Delhi is exactly a case in point. There, new city after new city was built by successive kings, each with the distinctive name of its founder; but as they were all in the immediate vicinity of Delhi itself, the old familiar name still clung to the capital, and each new appellation eventually became absorbed in the one general name of "Delhi." In the same way I believe that the old familiar name of *Srinagar* eventually swamped the name of the new city of *Pravarasenapura*.

The names of *Khâgipura* and *Khunamusha* are referred by Kalhan Pandit* to Raja *Khâgendra*, who, as the sixth predecessor of Asoka, must have reigned about 400 B.C. Wilson and Troyer have identified these two places with *Kâkapur* and *Gaumoha* of Muhammadan writers. The first is certain, as *Kâkapur* still exists on the left bank of the Behat, at 10 miles to the south of the Takht-i-Sulimân, and 5 miles to the south of Pâmpur. But the identification of *Gaumoha*, wherever that may be, is undoubtedly wrong, as *Khunamusha* is now represented by the large village of *Khunamoh*, which is situated under the hills at 4 miles to the north-east of Pâmpur.

The old town of *Bij Biâra*, or *Vijipâra*, is situated on both banks of the Behat, at 25 miles to the south-east of the capital. The original name was *Vijayapâra*, so called after the ancient temple of *Vijayesa*, which still exists, although its floor is 14

* 'Raja Tarangini,' i. 90.

feet below the present level of the surrounding ground. This difference of level shows the accumulation of ruins since the date of its foundation. The people refer its erection to Asoka, B.C. 250, who is stated by Kalhan Pandit* to have pulled down the old brick temple of *Vijayesa*, and to have rebuilt it of stone. This is apparently the same temple that is mentioned in the reign of Arya Raja, some centuries after Christ.†

Sûrapura, the modern *Sûpur* or *Sopur*, is situated on both banks of the Behat, immediately to the west of the Great Wular Lake. It was originally called *Kâmbuva*, and under this name it is mentioned in the chronicles of Kashmir as early as the beginning of the fifth century.‡ It was rebuilt by *Sura*, the minister of Avanti Varmma, between A.D. 854 and 883, after whom it was called *Sûrapura*. From its favourable position at the outlet of the Wular Lake, I think it probable that it is one of the oldest places in Kashmir.

Kanishkapura was built by the Indo-Scythian prince Kanishka,§ just before the beginning of the Christian era. In the spoken dialects of India it is called *Kanikhpur*, which in Kashmir has been still further corrupted to *Kâmpur*. It is situated 10 miles to the south of Srinagar, on the high-road leading to the Pir Panchâl Pass. It is a small village with a *sarai* for travellers, and is now generally known as

---

* 'Raja Tarangini,' i. 105.
† *Ibid.*, ii. 123.
‡ *Ibid.*, iii. 227.
§ *Ibid.*, i. 168.

Kâmpur Sarai. In the large map of Kashmir by Captain Montgomerie the name is erroneously given as *Khanpoor.*

Hushkapura, which was founded by the Indo-Scythian prince *Hushka,* or *Huvishka,* the brother of Kanishka, would appear to have been the same place as the well-known *Varâhamula,* or *Barâhmula,* on the Behat. Abu Rihân* calls it "*Ushkar,* which is the town of *Barâmula* built on both banks of the river." It is noted under the same name by the Chinese pilgrim Hwen Thsang, who entered the valley from the west by a stone gate, and halted at the monastery of *Hu.se.kia-lo,* or *Hushkara.* The name of *Barâhmula* has now eclipsed the more ancient appellation, which, however, still exists in the village of *Uskara,* 2 miles to the south-east of the present town, and immediately under the hills. The place has been visited, at my request, by the Rev. G. W. Cowie, who found there a Buddhist *stupa* still intact. This is probably the same monument that is recorded to have been erected by Raja Lalitâditya† between A.D. 723 and 760. It is again mentioned in the native chronicle‡ as the residence of the Queen Sugandhâ in A.D. 913. From all these notices, it is certain that the town still bore its original name down to the beginning of the eleventh century, when Abu Rihân mentions both names. But after this time the name of *Varâhamula* alone is found in

* Reinaud, "Fragments Arabes, etc." p. 116.

† 'Raja Tarangini,' iv. 188. ‡ *Ibid.*, v. 258.

the native chronicles, in which it is mentioned during the reigns of Harsha and Sussala, early in the twelfth century. I think it probable that the main portion of the town of Hushkapura was on the left, or south bank of the river, and that Varâhamula was originally a small suburb on the right bank. On the decline of Buddhism, when the monastic establishment at Hushkapura was abandoned, the old town also must have been partially deserted, and most probably it continued to decrease until it was supplanted by the Brahmanical suburb of Varâhamula.

Jushkapura was founded by the Indo-Scythian prince Jushka, a brother of Kanishka and Hushka. The Brahmans of Kashmir identify the place with *Zukru*, or *Zukur*, which is still a considerable village. 4 miles to the north of the capital. This is evidently the "*Schecroh*, ville assez considérable," which Troyer and Wilson* have identified with Hushkapura. I visited the place in November, 1847, but the only traces of antiquity that I could discover were a considerable number of stone pillars and mouldings of the style of architecture peculiar to Kashmir, all of which had been trimmed and adapted to Muhammadan tombs and Masjids. *Parihâsapura* was built by the great Raja Lalitâditya,† who reigned from A.D. 723 to 760. It was situated on the right, or eastern bank of the Behat, near the present village of Sumbal. There are still many traces of walls and broken

* 'Raja Tarangini,' i. 370 ; Asiat. Res. xv. 23.

† 'Raja Tarangini,' iv. 194.

stones on the neighbouring mounds, which show that a city must once have existed on this spot; but the only considerable remains are a bridge which spans the Behat, and a canal which leads direct towards Sûpur, to avoid the tedious passage by the river through the Wular Lake. As *Parihâsapura* is not mentioned again in the native chronicle, it must have been neglected very soon after its founder's death. His own grandson, *Jayapida,* built a new capital named *Jayapura,* in the midst of a lake, with a citadel, which he named *Sri-dwâravati,* but which the people always called the "Inner Fort."* The position of this place is not known,but I believe that it stood on the left bank of the Behat, immediately opposite to *Parihâsapura,* where a village named *Antar-kot,* or the "Inner Fort," exists to this day. The final destruction of this city is attributed by the people to Sangkara Varmma, who reigned from A.D. 883 to 901. He is said to have removed the stones to his own new city of *Sangkarapura,* which still exists as *Pathan,* 7 miles to the south-west of the Sumbal bridge. The great temple at *Parihâsa* was destroyed by the bigoted Sikandar, who reigned from 1389 to 1413, A.D. Of this temple a curious story is told by the Muhammadan historians. Speaking of *Pârispur,* Abul Fazl† says, "here stood a lofty idolatrous temple which was destroyed by Sikandar. In the ruins was found a plate of copper with an inscription in the Indian language purporting that

* 'Raja Tarangini,' iv. 505, 510.

† 'Ayin Akbari,' ii. 135.

after the expiration of 1100 years the temple would be destroyed by a person named Sikandar." The same story is told by Ferishta,* with the addition of the name of the Raja, whom the translator calls *Balnat*, which is probably a mistake for *Laldit*, the usual contracted form of Lalitâditya among the Kashmiris. As the difference of time between this prince and Sikandar is barely 700 years, it is strange that the tradition should preserve a date which is so much at variance with the chronology of their own native chronicles.

Padmapura, now called *Pâmpur*, was founded by Padma, the minister of Raja Vrihaspati, who reigned from A.D. 832 to 844.† It is situated on the right bank of the Behat, 8 miles to the south-east of the capital, and about midway on the road to Avantipura. The place is still well inhabited, and its fields of saffron are the most productive in the whole valley.

Avantipura was founded by Raja *Avanti-Varmma*,‡ who reigned from A.D. 854 to 833. It is situated on the right bank of the Behat, 17 miles to the south-east of the present capital. There is now only a small village called *Wantipur*; but the remains of two magnificent temples, and the traces of walls on all sides, show that it must have been once an extensive city. The name of *No-nagar*, or the "New Town," which is now attached to the high tract of alluvial table-land on the opposite side of the river,

* Briggs's 'Ferishta,' iv. 465.

† 'Raja Tarangini,' iv. 694.

‡ 'Raja Tarangini,' v. 44.

is universally allowed by the people to refer to *Avantipura* itself, which is said to have occupied both banks of the river originally.

2. URASA.

Between Taxila and Kashmir Hwen Thsang places the district of *U-la-shi*, or *Urasa*, which, from its position, may at once be identified with the *Varsa Regio* of Ptolemy, and with the modern district of *Rash*, in Dhantâwar, to the west of Muzafarâbâd. It is mentioned in the native chronicle of Kashmir* as a mountainous district in the vicinity of the valley, where Raja *Sangkara Varmma* received his death wound in A.D. 901. It corresponds exactly with the Pakhali of Abul Fazl, which included all the hilly country between the Indus and Kashmir, as far south as the boundary of Attak. At the present day the principal towns of the district are *Mânsera*, in the north-east; *Noshahra*, in the middle; and *Kishangarh*, or *Haripur*, in the south-west. In Hwen Thsang's time the capital is said to have been either 300 or 500 *li*, that is, 50 or 83 miles, distant from Taxila. This difference in the distance makes it impossible to identify the actual position of the capital in the seventh century; but it seems probable that it must have been at *Mângali*, which is said by the people to have been the ancient capital of the district. This place stands midway between Noshahra and Mânsera, and about 50 miles to the north-east of Taxila.

---

* 'Raja Tarangini,' v. 216.

According to Hwen Thsang, Urasa was 2000 *li*, or 333 miles, in circuit, which is probably correct, as its length from the source of the Kunihâr river to the Gandgarh mountain is not less than 100 miles, and its breadth from the Indus to the Behat, or Jhelam, is 55 miles in its narrowest part. Its distance from Kashmir is stated at 1000 *li*, or 167 miles, which would place the capital somewhere in the neighbourhood of Noshahra, and within a few miles of Mângala, which was the ancient capital according to the traditions of the people.

3. TAXILA, OR TAKSHASILA.

The position of the celebrated city of Taxila has hitherto remained unknown, partly owing to the erroneous distance recorded by Pliny, and partly to the want of information regarding the vast ruins which still exist in the vicinity of Shah-dheri. All the copies of Pliny agree in stating that Taxila was only 60 Roman, or 55 English, miles from Peucolaïtis, or Hashtnagar, which would fix its site somewhere on the Haro river, to the west of Hasan Abdâl, or just two days' march from the Indus. But the itineraries of the Chinese pilgrims agree in placing it at three days' journey to the east of the Indus,* or in the im-

* 'Fa-Hian,' c. xi., Beal's translation, makes it seven days' journey from Peshâwar, that is, four days to the Indus plus three days to Taxila. Sun-yun (Beal's translation, p. 200) places it three days to the east of the Indus. Hiouen Thsang makes it three days' journey to the south-east of the Indus (Julien's translation, i. 263). See Maps

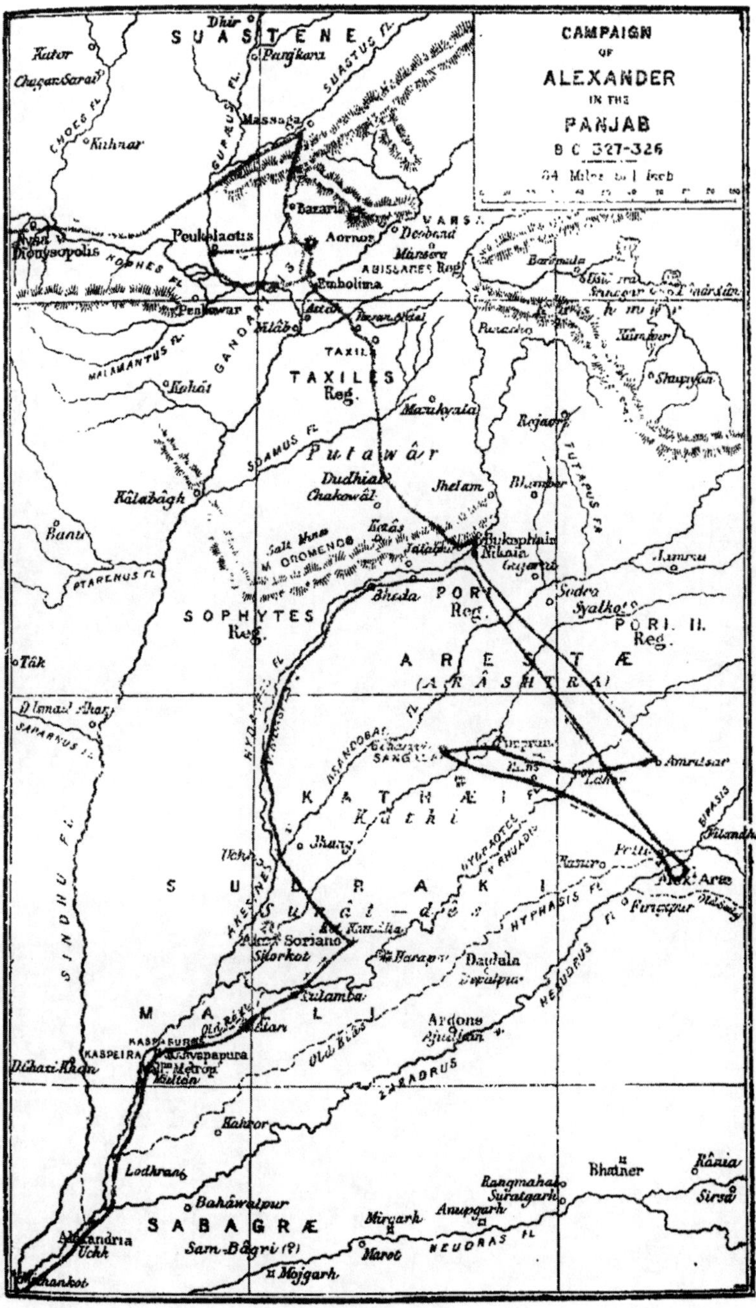
CAMPAIGN
OF
ALEXANDER
IN THE
PANJAB
B C 327-326
SUASTENE
Dhir
Massaga
Bazaria
Aornos
Peukelaotis
Dionysopolis
Embolima
Peshawar
TAXILA
TAXILES
Reg.
Putawâr
Kohât
Kâlabâgh
Banu
Dudhial
Chakowâl
Jhelam
Bukephala
Nikaia
Gujarat
PORI
Reg.
PORI. II.
Reg.
SOPHYTES
Reg.
Tâk
ARESTÆ
(ARÂSHTRA)
Amritsar
Lahor
SANGALA
KATHÆI
Kathi
Jhang
SUDRAKI
Soriano
Tulamba
MALLI
Ardons
Multan
Dera Ghazi Khan
Kahror
Lodhran
Bahâwalpur
SABAGRÆ
Sam-Bâgri (?)
Alexandria
Uchh
Mithankot
Mojgarh
Marot
Mirgarh
Anupgarh
Suratgarh
Bhatner
Rânia
Sirsa
Jalandhar
Firozpur
Alex. Aræ
Jamu
Syalkot
Mânsera
Barâmula
Srinagar
Kashmir
Punch
Rajaori
Bhimber
SINDHU FL.
KOPHES FL.
SOAMUS FL.
HYDASPES FL.
AKESINES
HYPHASIS FL.
HESUDRUS FL.
ZARADRUS
NEUDRAS FL.
HYDRAOTES
TUTAPUS FL.
SUASTUS FL.
GURAEUS FL.
CHOES FL.
MALAMANTUS FL.
PTARENUS FL.
SAPARNUS FL.
ABISSARES Reg.
M. OROMENOS
Salt Mines

VI.

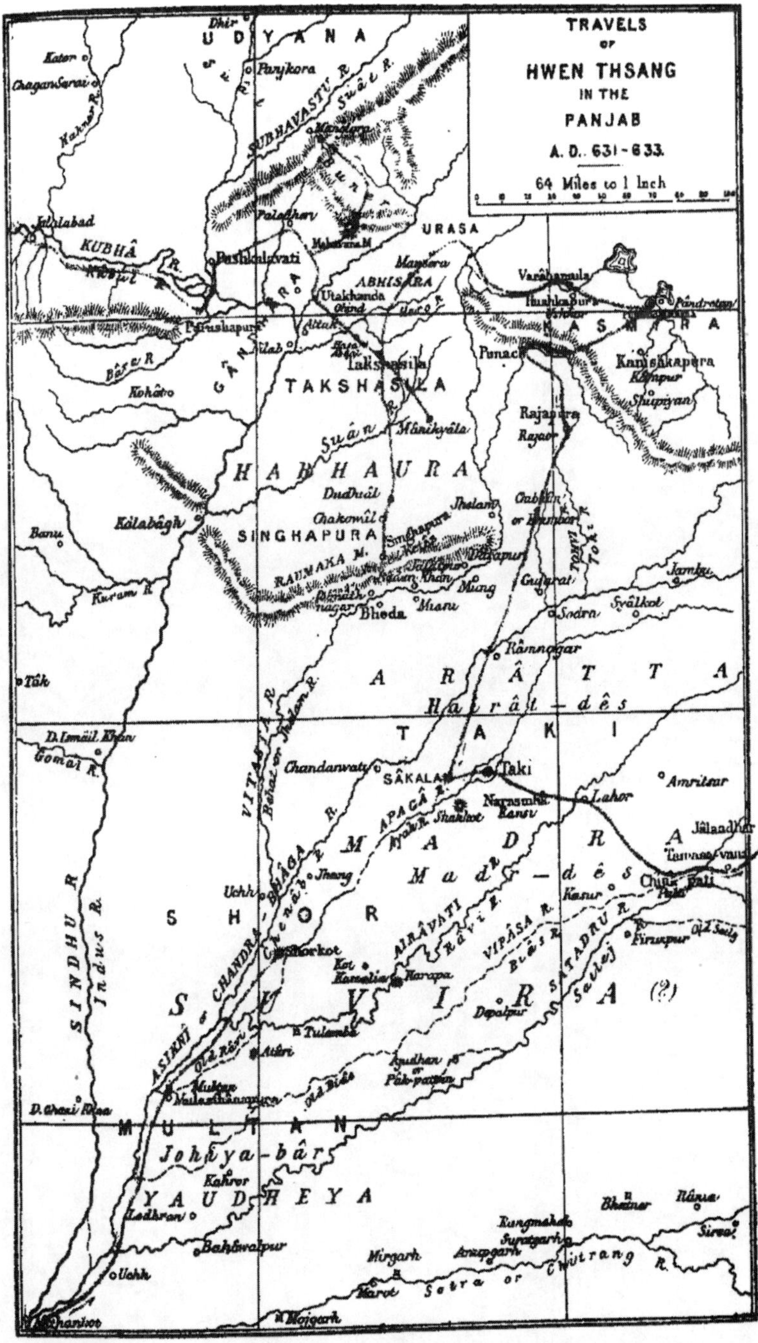
TRAVELS
OF
HWEN THSANG
IN THE
PANJAB
A. D. 631-633.
64 Miles to 1 Inch
UDYANA
URASA
ABHISARA
KASMIRA
TAKSHASILA
HABHAURA
SINGHAPURA
ARÂTTA
TAKI
MADRA
SHORKOT
SAUVIRA (?)
MULTAN
YAUDHEYA
Jalalabad
Purushapura
Utakhanda
Takshasila
Mânikyâla
Punach
Rajapura
Jhelam
Gujarat
Sialkot
Râmnagar
Chandanwati
SÂKALA
Taki
Lahor
Amritsar
Jâlandhar
Jhang
Shorkot
Harapa
Tulamba
Multan
Pâk-pattan
Depalpur
Firuzpur
Kasur
Bahâwalpur
Uchh
D. Ismail Khan
D. Ghazi Khan
Kohât
Kâlabâgh
Banu
SINDHU R.
Indus R.
VITASTA R.
CHANDRA-BHÂGA R.
AIRÂVATI
VIPÂSA R.
SATADRU R.

mediate neighbourhood of Kâla-ka-sarâi, which was the third halting-place of the Mogul emperors, and which is still the third stage from the Indus, both for troops and baggage. Now as Hwen Thsang, on his return to China, was accompanied by laden elephants, his three days' journey from *Takhshasila* to the Indus at *Utakhanda*, or Ohind, must necessarily have been of the same length as those of modern days, and, consequently, the site of the city must be looked for somewhere in the neighbourhood of *Kâla-ka-sarâi*. This site is found near *Shah-dheri,* just one mile to the north-east of Kâla-ka-sarâi, in the extensive ruins of a fortified city, around which I was able to trace no less than 55 stupas, of which two are as large as the great Mânikyâla tope, twenty eight monasteries, and nine temples. Now the distance from Shah-dheri to Ohind is 36 miles, and from Ohind to Hashtnagar is 38 more, or altogether 74 miles, which is 19 in excess of the distance recorded by Pliny between Taxila and Peukelaotis. To reconcile these discrepant numbers I would suggest that Pliny's 60 miles, or LX., should be read as 80 miles, or LXXX., which are equivalent to 73/1/2 English miles, or within half a mile of the actual distance between the two places.

The classical writers are unanimous in their accounts of the size and wealth of Taxila. Arrian describes it as "a large and wealthy city, and the most

---

Nos. IV., V., and VI. for the position of Shah-dheri or Taxila.

populous between the Indus and Hydaspes."* Strabo also declares it to be a large city, and adds, that the neighbouring country was "crowded with inhabitants, and very fertile."† Pliny calls it "a famous city, situated on a low but level plain, in a district called *Amanda*."‡ These accounts agree exactly with the position and size of the ancient city near *Shah-dheri*, the ruins of which are spread over several square miles.

About fifty years after Alexander's visit, the people of Taxila rebelled against *Bindusâra*, king of Magadha, who sent his eldest son *Susima* to besiege the place. On his failure, the siege was entrusted to his younger son, the celebrated Asoka; but the people came out 2½ *yojanas*, or 17½ miles, to meet the young prince and offer their submission.§ At the time of Asoka's accession the wealth of Taxila is said to have amounted to 36 *kotis*, or 360 millions of some unnamed coin, which, even if it was the silver *tangka*, or sixpence, would have amounted to nine *karors* of rupees, or £9,000,000. It is probable, however, that the coin intended by the Indian writer was a gold one, in which case the wealth of this city would have amounted to about 90 or 100 millions of pounds. I quote this statement as a

* 'Anabasis,' v. 8: πόλιν μεγάλην καὶ εὐδαίμονα.

† Geogr. xv. i. 17; xv. i. 28.

‡ Hist. Nat., vi. 23. "Taxillæ, cum urbe celebri, jam in plana demisso tractu, cui universo nomen Anandæ."

§ Burnouf, 'Introduction à l'Histoire du Buddhisme Indien,' p. 361.

proof of the great reputed wealth of Taxila within fifty years after Alexander's expedition. It was here that Asoka himself had resided as Viceroy of the Panjab during his father's lifetime; and here also resided his own son *Kunâla*, or the "fine-eyed," who is the hero of a very curious Buddhist legend, which will be described hereafter.

Just before the end of the third century B.C. the descendants of the Maurya kings must have come in contact with the Bactrian Greeks under Demetrius, the son of Enthydemus, and in the early part of the following century Taxila must have formed part of the Indian dominions of Eukratides. In 126 B.C. it was wrested from the Greeks by the Indo-Scythian *Sus* or *Abars*, with whom it remained for about three-quarters of a century, when it was conquered by the later Indo-Scythians of the *Kushân* tribe, under the great Kanishka. During this period Parshâwar would appear to have been the capital of the Indo-Scythian dominions, while Taxila was governed by satraps. Several coins and inscriptions of these local governors have been found at Shah-dheri and Mânikyâla. Of these the most interesting is the copper plate obtained by Mr. Roberts, containing the name of *Takhasila*, the Pali form of *Takshasila*, from which the Greeks obtained their Taxila.*

* See translation by Professor J. Dowson in Journ. Royal Asiat. Soc., xx. 221; see also notes on the same inscription by the author, Journ. Asiat. Soc. Bengal, 1863, p. 139.

During the reign of the Parthian Bardanes, A.D. 42 to 45, Taxila was visited by Apollonius of Tyana and his companion, the Assyrian Damis, whose narrative of the journey Philostratus professes to have followed in his life of Apollonius. His account is manifestly exaggerated in many particulars regarding the acts and sayings of the philosopher, but the descriptions of places seem to be generally moderate and truthful. If they were not found in the narrative of Damis, they must have been taken from the journals of some of Alexander's followers: and in either case they are valuable, as they supply many little points of information that are wanting in the regular histories. According to Philostratus, Taxila was "not unlike the ancient *Ninus*, and was walled in the manner of other Greek towns."* For *Ninus*, or *Nineveh*, we must read Babylon, as we have no description of the great Assyrian city, which was destroyed nearly two centuries before the time of Herodotus. Now we know from Curtius that it was the "symmetry as well as the antiquity" of Babylon that struck Alexander and all who beheld it for the first time.† I conclude, therefore, that Taxila must have reminded the Greeks of Babylon by its *symmetry*, as Philostratus goes on to say, that the city was "divided into narrow streets with great regularity." He mentions also a temple of the sun, which stood outside the walls, and a

* Vita Apollon., ii. 20.

† Vita Alex., v. 1: "Pulchritudo ac vetustas."

palace in which the usurper was besieged. He speaks also of a garden, one stadium in length, with a tank in the midst, which was filled by "cool and refreshing streams." All these points will be noticed in a separate work when I come to describe the existing ruins of this ancient city.

We now lose sight of Taxila until A.D. 400, when it was visited by the Chinese pilgrim *Fa-Hian*, who calls it *Chu-sha-shi-lo*, or the "severed head;" and adds, that "Buddha bestowed his head in alms at this place, and hence they gave this name to the country."* The translation shows that the original Sanskrit name must have been *Chutyasira*, or the "fallen head," which is a synonym of *Takṣha-sîra*, or the "severed head," the usual name by which Taxila was known to the Buddhists of India. In A.D. 502, "the place where Buddha made an alms-gift of his head" was visited by *Sung-yun*, who describes it as being three days' journey to the east of the river *Sin-tu*, or *Indus*.†

We now come to Hwen Thsang, the last and best of the Chinese pilgrims, who first visited *Ta-cha-shi-lo*, or *Takṣhasila*, in A.D. 630, and again in A.D. 643, on his return to China. He describes the city as about 10 *li*, or 1⅔ mile, in circuit. The royal family was extinct, and the province, which had previously been subject to Kapisa, was then a dependency of Kashmir. The land, irrigated by

---

* Beal's Translation, c. xi.

† Beal's Translation, p. 200.

numbers of springs and watercourses, was famous for its fertility. The monasteries were numerous, but mostly in ruins; and there were only a few monks who studied the *Mahâyâna*, or esoteric doctrines of Buddhism. At 12 or 13 *li*, or 2 miles, to the north of the city there was a stupa of King Asoka, built on the spot where Buddha in a former existence had made an alms-gift of his head; or, as some said, of one thousand heads in as many previous existences. This was one of the four great stupas that were famous all over north-west India;* and accordingly on his return journey Hwen Thsang specially notes that he had paid his adorations, for the second time, to the "stupa of the alms-gift of one thousand heads."† The present name of the district is *Chach-Hazâra*, which I take to be a corruption of *Sîrsha-sahasra*, or the "thousand heads." In the Taxila copper-plate of the Satrap Liako Kujuluka, the name is written *Chhahara-Chukhsa*, which appears to me to be only another form of the same appellation.

From these accounts of the Chinese pilgrims, we see that Taxila was specially interesting to all Buddhists as the legendary scene of one of Buddha's most meritorious acts of alms-giving, when he bestowed his head in charity. The origin of this legend I think may be certainly traced to the name, which as *Takshasila* means simply the "cut rock;"

---

* 'Fah-Hian,' (Beal's translation) c. xi.

† Julien's 'Hiouen Thsang,' i. 262.

but with a slight alteration, as *Takṣha-sîra* means the "severed head." "*Aut ex re nomen, aut ex vocabulo fabula,** either the name sprang from the legend, or the legend was invented to account for the name." In this case we may be almost certain that the latter was the process, as the Greeks have preserved the spelling of the original name before Buddhism had covered the land with its endless legends of Sakya's meritorious acts in previous births. It is nowhere stated to whom Buddha presented his head, but I believe that it was offered to the hungry tiger whose seven cubs were saved from starvation by a similar offering of his *blood*.† I am led to this belief by the fact that the land immediately to the north of the ruined city is still called *Babar Khâna*, or the "Tiger's House," a name which is as old as the time of Mahmud, as Abu Rihân speaks of *Babarkân* as being halfway between the Indus and the Jhelam,‡ a description which is equally applicable to the Babarkhâna of the ancient Taxila. The name is a Turki one, and is, therefore, probably as old as the time of Kanishka. From the continued existence of this name, I infer that, in the immediate neighbourhood of the great stupa of the "head-gift," there was most probably a temple enshrining a group in which Buddha was

* Pomponius Mela, iii. 7.

† Sun-yun mentions that the head was offered "for the sake of a man;" that is, Buddha offered his own life to save that of another man. (Beal's translation, p. 200).

‡ Reinaud's 'Fragments Arabes, etc.,' p. 116.

represented offering his head to the tiger. This temple the *Turks* would naturally have called the *Babar-Khâna,* or "Tigers'-house;" and as Taxila itself decayed, the name of the temple would gradually have superseded that of the city. The remembrance of this particular act of Buddha's extreme charity is, I believe, preserved in the name of *Mârgala,* or the "beheaded," which is applied to the range of hills lying only two miles to the south of Shah-dheri. *Mârgala* means literally "decollated," from *gala-mârna,* which is the idiomatic expression for "cutting the neck," or beheading.

The ruins of the ancient city near Shah-dheri, which I propose to identify with Taxila, are scattered over a wide space extending about 3 miles from north to south, and 2 miles from east to west. The remains of many stupas and monasteries extend for several miles further on all sides, but the actual ruins of the city are confined within the limits abovementioned. These ruins consist of several distinct portions, which are called by separate names even in the present day.* The general direction of these different works is from south-south-west to north-north-east, in which order I will describe them. Beginning at the south, their names are:—

1. *Bir* or *Pher.*
2. *Hatiâl.*
3. *Sir-Kap-ka-kot.*

---

* See Map No. IV.

4. *Kacha-kot.*
5. *Babar Khâna.*
6. *Sir-Suk-ka-kot.*

The most ancient part of these ruins, according to the belief of the people, is the great mound on which stands the small village of *Bir* or *Pher*. The mound itself is 4000 feet in length from north to south, and 2600 feet in breadth, with a circuit of 10,800 feet, or rather more than two miles. On the west side towards the rock-seated village of Shah-dheri, the Bir mound has an elevation of from 15 to 25 above the fields close by; but as the ground continues to slope towards Shah-dheri, the general elevation is not less than from 25 to 35 feet. On the east side, immediately above the *Tabrâ*, or *Tamrâ Nala*, it rises 40 feet above the fields, and 68 feet above the bed of the stream. The remains of the walls can be traced only in a few places both on the east and west sides; but the whole surface is covered with broken stones and fragments of bricks and pottery. Here the old coins are found in greater numbers than in any other part of the ruins; and here, also, a single man collected for me, in about two hours, a double handful of bits of lapis lazuli, which are not to be seen elsewhere. Judging from the size of the place, I take it to be the site of the inhabited part of the city in the time of Hwen Thsang, who describes it as being only 10 *li*, or 1⅔ mile, in circuit. This conclusion is confirmed by the position of the great ruined stupa in the midst of the *Babarkhâna* land, which is 8000 feet north-north-east from the near end of the Bir mound, and 10,000 feet, or just 2 miles, from the main entrance to the middle of the old city. As Hwen Thsang describes the position of the stupa of the "Head Gift" as being 12 or 13 *li*, or rather more than 2 miles, to the north of the city,* I think that there can be little doubt that the city of his time was situated on the mound of Bir. I traced the remains of three small topes on the north and east sides of the mound, all of which had been opened previously by the villagers, who, however, stoutly denied the fact, and attributed the explorations to General Abbott and Major Pearse.

Hatiâl is a strong fortified position on the west end of a spur of the *Mârgala* range, and immediately to the north-east of the *Bir* mound, from which it is separated by the *Tabrâ Nala*. About half a mile from Bir the spur is divided into two nearly parallel ridges, about 1500 feet apart, which run almost due west to the bank of the Tabrâ, where they are joined by a high earthen rampart. The clear space thus enclosed is not more than 2000 feet by 1000 feet, but the whole circuit of the defences, along the hill-ridges and the artificial ramparts, is about 8400 feet, or upwards of 1½ mile. At the east end the two parallel ridges are joined by stone walls, 15 feet 4 inches thick, with square towers at intervals, all of which are still in very good order. The crest of the south or main ridge is 291 feet above the general level of the fields, but the north ridge has an elevation of

* Julien's 'Hiouen Thsang,' ii. 153.

only 163 feet. Between these two there is a small rocky ridge, 206 feet in height, crowned by a large bastion or tower, which the people look upon as a stupa or tope. There is a similar tower on the crest of the north ridge, which I was induced to excavate by the report of a villager named *Nûr*, who informed me that he had found a copper coin at each of the four corners of the basement, which he considered as a certain sign that the building was a tope. I knew also that it was the custom in Barma to erect a stupa in each of the corner bastions of their square fortified cities. But my excavation, which was carried down to the bare rock, a depth of 26 feet, showed only regular courses of large rough blocks, which were extracted with much difficulty. Close to the west of this tower I traced the remains of a large enclosure, 163 feet long by 151½ feet broad, divided into rooms on all four sides, from which I at first thought that the building was a monastery. But the subsequent discovery of a large quantity of burnt clay pellets of a size well adapted for slingers led me to the conclusion that the place was most probably only a guard-house for soldiers. The two ridges fall rapidly towards the west for about 1200 feet, till they meet the general slope of the intervening ground, and at these points are the two gateways of the fort, the one being due north of the other. The north ridge then rises again, and running to the west-south-west for 2000 feet, terminates in a square-topped mound, 130 feet high. This part of the ridge is entirely covered with the remains of buildings, and near its east end the villager Nûr discovered some copper coins in a ruined tope. Of the name of *Hatiâl* I could obtain no information whatever: but it is probably old, as I think it may possibly be identified with *Hattiâr-Lank,* which Abul Fazl places in the Sindh-Sâgar Doab. The spelling of the name would refer it to *Hatti,* a shop, and *Hatti-âla* would then be the market-place or bazaar. But the *Hatiâl* fort is so evidently the stronghold or citadel of this ancient place that I look upon this derivation as very doubtful.

The fortified city of *Sir-kap* is situated on a large level mound immediately at the north foot of Hatiâl, of which it really forms a part, as its walls are joined to those of the citadel. It is half a mile in length from north to south, with a breadth of 2000 feet at the south end, but of only 1400 feet at the north end. The circuit of Sirkap is 8300 feet, or upwards of 1½ mile. The walls, which are built entirely of squared stone, are 14 feet 9 inches thick, with square towers of 30 feet face, separated by curtains of 140 feet. The east and north walls are straight, but the line of west wall is broken by a deep recess. There are two large gaps in each of these walls, all of which are said to be the sites of the ancient gates. One of these in the north face is undoubted, as it lies due north of the two gateways of the *Hatiâl* citadel, and due south of the three ruined mounds in the *Babar-khâna.* A second in the east face is equally undoubted, as parts of the walls of the gateway still remain, with portions of paved roadway leading directly up to it. A third opening in the west face, immediately opposite the last, is almost equally certain, as all the old foundations inside the city are carefully laid out at right angles due north and south. The position of Sirkap is naturally very strong, as it is well defended on all sides,—by the lofty citadel of Hatiâl on the south, by the *Tabrâ Nala* on the west, and by the *Gau Nala* on the east and north sides. The entire circuit of the walls of the two places is 14,200 feet, or nearly 2¾ miles.

Kacha-ḳot, or the "mud fort," lies to the north of Sirkap, in a strong isolated position formed by the doubling round of the Tabrâ Nala below the junction of the Gau Nala, which together surround the place on all sides except the east. The ramparts of Kacha-kot, as the name imports, are formed entirely of earth, and rise to a height of from 30 to 50 feet above the stream. On the east side there are no traces of any defences, and inside there are no traces of any buildings. It is difficult therefore to say for what purpose it was intended; but as the Gau Nala runs through it, I think it probable that Kacha-kot was meant as a place of safety for elephants and other cattle during a time of siege. It is 6700 feet, or upwards of 1¼ mile in circuit. The people usually called it Kot, and this name is also applied to Sir-kap, but when they wish to distinguish it from the latter they call it *Kacha-ḳot*. Now this name is found both in Baber's 'Memoirs,' and in the 'Ayin Akbari.' In the former the Haro river is called the river of Kacha-kot, which therefore must have been some large place near the banks of that stream, but I suspect that it ought rather to be looked for near Hasan Abdâl, or even lower down.

Babar Khâna is the name of the tract of land lying between the Lundi Nala on the north and the Tabrâ and Gau Nalas on the south. It includes Kacha-kot, and extends about one mile on each side of it to the east and west, embracing the great mound of *Seri-ḳi-Pind* on the north-west, and the Gângu group of topes and other ruins on the east. In the very middle of this tract, where the Lundi and Tabrâ Nalas approach one another within one thousand feet, stands a lofty mound, 45 feet in height, called *Jhandiâla Pind*, after a small hamlet close by. To the west of the *Pind*, or mound, there is another mass of ruins of greater breadth, but only 29 feet in height, which is evidently the remains of a large monastery. It is remarkable that the road which runs through the two gateways of the *Hatiâl* citadel, and through the north gateway of *Sirḳap*, passes in a direct line due north between these two mounds until it meets the ruins of a large stupa, on the bank of the Lundi river, 1200 feet beyond the Jhandiâla Pind. This last I believe to be the famous "Headgift *Stupa*" which was said to have been erected by Asoka in the third century before Christ. I have already alluded to its position as answering almost exactly to that described by Hwen Thsang; and I may now add as a confirmation of this opinion that the main road of the city of Taxila was laid in a direct line running due north upon the Jhandiâla stupa, a fact which proves incontestably the very high estimation in which this particular monument must have been held. This is further confirmed by the vicinity of another mound, 3600 feet to the north-west, called *Seri-ki-pind*, or *Siri-ki-pind*, which would appear to refer directly to the "Head Gift," as the *Sîrshâ-dânam*, or *Sir-dân* of Buddha. Taking all these points into consideration, I think that there are very strong grounds for identifying the great ruined tope of *Babar-khâna* with the famous stupa of the "Head Gift" of Buddha.

The large fortified enclosure called *Sir-Suk* is situated at the north-east corner of the Babar-khâna, beyond the Lundi Nala. In shape it is very nearly square, the north and south sides being each 4500 feet in length, the west side 3300 feet, and the east side 3000 feet. The whole circuit, therefore, is 15,300 feet, or nearly 3 miles. The south face, which is protected by the Lundi Nala, is similar in its construction to the defences of *Sir-kap*. The walls are built of spared stones, smoothed on the outer face only, and are 18 feet thick, with square towers at intervals of 120 feet. The towers of this face have been very carefully built with splayed foundations, all the stones being nicely bevelled to form a smooth slope. The tower at the south-east corner, which is the highest part now standing, is 10 feet above the interior ground, and 25 feet above the low ground on the bank of the stream. Towards the west end, where the stones have been removed, the south wall is not more than 2 or 3 feet in height, about the interior ground. Of the east and west faces, about one-half of the walls can still be traced, but of the north face there is but little left except some mounds at the two corners. Inside there are three villages named Mirpur, Tupkia, and Pind, with a large ruined mound, called Pindora, which is 600 square feet at base. To the south of Pindora, and close to the village of Tupkia, there is a *Khângâh,* or shrine of a Muhammadan saint, on a small mound. As this is built of squared stones, I presume that the Khângâh represents the position of a stupa or tope which must have given its name to the village of Tupkia, and that the great Pindora mound is the remains of a very large monastery. I found two massive channelled stones, or spouts, which, from their size, could only have been used for conveying the rain-water from a courtyard to the outside of the walls. At half a mile to the west there is an outer line of high earthen mounds running due north and south for upwards of 2000 feet, when it bends to the east-north-east. Beyond this the line is only traceable by a broad belt of broken stones, extending for 3500 feet, when it turns to the south-east for about 1200 feet and joins the north face of *Sir-Suk*. These external lines would appear to be the remains of a large outwork which once rested its north-west angle on the Lundi Nala. The entire circuit of Sir-Suk and its outwork is about 20,300 feet, or nearly 5 miles.

I have now described all the different parts of this great city, the ruins of which, covering an area of six square miles, are more extensive, more interesting, and in much better preservation than those of any other ancient place in the Panjab. The city of *Sirkap,* with its citadel of *Hatiâl,* and its detached works of *Bir* and *Kacha-kot*, has a circuit of 4¾ miles; and the large fort of *Sir-Suk,* with its outwork, is of the same size, each of them being nearly as large as Shah Jahan's imperial city of Delhi. But the number and size of the stupas, monasteries, and other religious buildings are even more wonderful than the great extent of the city. Here both coins and antiquities are found in far greater numbers than in any other place between the Indus and Jhelam. This then must be the site of Taxila, which, according to the unanimous testimony of ancient writers, was the largest city between the Indus and Hydaspes. Strabo and Hwen Thsang both speak of the fertility of its lands, and the latter specially notices the numbers of its springs and water-courses. As this description is applicable only to the rich lands lying to the north of the Tabrâ Nala, which are amply irrigated by numerous channels drawn from the Haro river, the proof of my identification is complete. Burnes crossed this tract in 1832, when he encamped at Usmân Khatar, 3 miles to the north of Shah-dheri, and about 1 mile to the south of the Haro river. He describes the village as standing "on a plain at the mouth of a valley close to the base of the outlying hills."* This agrees most exactly with the accounts

* 'Travels,' ii. 61.

of Strabo and Pliny, who describe Taxila as situated in a level country where the hills unite with the plains. Of Usmân, Burnes goes on to say that "its meadows are watered by the most beautiful and crystal rivulets that flow from the mountains." In the first part of this statement he is quite correct; but in the latter part he is undoubtedly wrong, as every rill of water that passes through Usmân is drawn by artificial means from the Haro river. Two miles to the south, towards the ruins of the old city, the irrigation is carried on by cuts from the Lundi Nala, but as the main body of water in this stream is artificially obtained from the Haro, the whole of the irrigation may be truly said to be derived from that river.

The district of Taxila is described by Hwen Thsang as being 2000 *li*, or 333 miles, in circuit. It was bounded by the Indus on the west, by the district of Urasa on the north, by the Jhelam or Behat river on the east, and by the district of Sinhapura on the south. As the capital of the last was in the Salt range of mountains, either at or near Ketâs, the boundary of Taxila on that side was most probably defined by the Suhân river to the south-west, and by the Bakrâla range of hills to the south-east. Accepting these limits as nearly correct, the frontier lines of the Indus and Jhelam will be respectively 80 miles and 50 miles in length, and those of the northern and southern boundaries 60 and 120 miles, or, all together, 310 miles, which accords very nearly with the measurement given by Hwen Thsang.

Mânikyâla.

The great stupa or Buddhist monument of Mânikyâla, was first made known by the journey of Elphinstone,* and has since been explored by Generals Ventura and Court. The name is said to have been derived from Raja *Mân*, or *Mânik*,† who erected the great stupa. This tradition is probably correct, as I discovered a coin and relic deposit of the Satrap *Jihoniya*, or *Zeionises*, the son of *Manigal*, in a small tope to the east of the village. The old town, which is usually called *Mânikpur*, or *Mânik-nagar*, is the scene of the curious legend of Râsâlu, who expelled the *Râkshasas*, or Demons, and delivered the people from the tyranny of *Sir-kap*, the "decapitator," and his brothers.

The name of Mânikyâla is not mentioned by any of the Chinese pilgrims, although every one of them has described the situation of the place. Fa-Hian merely states that at two days' journey to the east of Taxila is the spot where Buddha "gave his

---

* 'Cabul,' i. 106. *Stûpa* is the Sanskrit term for a mound or barrow, either of masonry or of earth ; see Colebroke, 'Amara Kosha,' *in voce*. The Pâli form is *Thûpo* ; see Turnour 'Mahâwanso,' and also *Thûpa*, or *Thûva*, in the early Arian inscriptions from the Punjâb. The term now used is *Thûp* for a tolerably perfect building, and *Thûpi* for a ruined mound. It is, therefore, very much to be regretted that we should have adopted the word *Tope*, which preserves neither the spelling nor the pronunciation of the native word.

† Moorcroft, 'Travels.' ii. 311.

body to feed a starving tiger."* But Sung-yun fixes the scene of this exploit at eight days' journey to the south-east of the capital of Gândhâra,† which is a very exact description of the bearing and distance of Mânikyâla, either from Peshâwar or from Hashtnagar. Lastly, Hwen Thsang places the site of the "Body-offering" at 200 *li*, or nearly 34 miles, to the south-east of Taxila,‡ which are the exact bearing and distance of Mânikyâla from Shah-dheri; but his statement that he crossed the *Sin-tu*, or Indus, is a simple mistake for the *Suhân* or *Süân* river, which flows between the two places.§

The great stupa of the "Body-offering" I have identified with the monument that was opened by General Court,|| which, according to the inscription found inside, was built in the year 20, during the reign of the great Indo-Scythian prince Kanishka, shortly before the beginning of the Christian era. Mânikyâla was, therefore, one of the most famous places in the Panjâb at a very early period; but I think that it must have been the site of a number of large religious establishments rather than that of a great city. General Abbott, when he examined the ruins around the Mânikyâla tope in 1853, could "not see any evidence of the existence of a city. The area occupied by submerged ruins would not

* Beal's translation of 'Fa-Hian,' c. xi. p. 32.

† Beal's translation of 'Sung-yun,' p. 193.

‡ Julien's 'Hiouen Thsang,' ii. 164.

§ See Maps Nos. V. and VI.

|| Journ. Asiat. Soc. Bengal, 1834, p. 562.

have comprised a very considerable village, while the comparatively large number of wrought stones denotes some costly structure which might have occupied the entire site."* In 1834, General Court described "the ruins of the town itself as of very considerable extent, massive walls of stone and lime being met with everywhere, besides a great number of wells." After a careful examination of the site, I have come to the same conclusion as General Abbott, that there are no traces of a large city; and I am quite satisfied that all the massive walls of cut stone, which General Court truly describes as being met with everywhere, must have belonged to costly monasteries and other large religious edifices. Doubtless, a few private houses might be built of squared stones even in a village, but these massive edifices, with their thickly gilded roofs, which still repay the labour of disinterment, are, I think, too numerous, too large, and too scattered to be the remains of private buildings even of a great city. The people point to the high ground immediately to the west of the great tope, as the site of the Raja Mân's palace, because pieces of plaster are found there only, and not in other parts of the ruins. Here it is probable that the satraps of Taxila may have taken up their residence when they came to pay their respects at the famous shrine of the "Body-gift" of Buddha. Here, also, there may have been a small town of about 1500 or 2000 houses, which

* Journ. Asiat. Soc. Bengal, 1853, p. 570.

extended to the northward, and occupied the whole of the rising ground on which the village of Mânikyâla now stands. I estimate the entire circuit of the space that may have been occupied by the town as about one mile and a half, which, at 500 square feet per man, would give a population of 12,500 persons, or just six persons to each house.

The people are unanimous in their statements that the city was destroyed by fire; and this belief, whether based on tradition or conviction, is corroborated by the quantities of charcoal and ashes which are found amongst all the ruined buildings. It was also amply confirmed by the excavations which I made in the great monastery to the north of General Court's Tope. I found the plaster of the walls blackened by fire, and the wrought blocks of kankar limestone turned into quicklime. The pine timbers of the roofs also were easily recognized by their charred fragments and ashes. Unfortunately, I discovered nothing during my researches that offered any clue to the probable period of the destruction of these buildings, but as this part of the country had fallen into the power of the Kashmirian kings, even before the time of Hwen Thsang, I am inclined to attribute their destruction rather to Brahmanical malignity than to Muhammadan intolerance.

4. SINGHAPURA, OR KETÂS.

According to Hwen Thsang, the capital of the kingdom of *Seng-ho-pu-lo*, or *Singhapura*, was situated at 700 *li*, or 117 miles, to the south-east of Taxila. The bearing points to Jhelam, near which is the town of *Sangohi*, which has been noted by M. Vivien de St. Martin as the possible representative of Singhapura. But Sangohi stands on an open plain, instead of on a high mountain of difficult access, as described by the pilgrim. The vicinity of ten pools of limpid water, with surrounding temples and sculptures, points to the holy tanks of *Ketâksh*, or *Khetâs*, which are still visited by crowds of pilgrims from all parts of India. I think also that the name of *Ketâs* is only a slightly altered form of the Sanskrit *Swetavâsa*, or the "White Robes," which Hwen Thsang mentions as the title of the chief religious sect then resident near Singhapura. In the western countries, where the compound *sw* is changed to *kh*, the name would have been pronounced *Khetavâsa*, or by a slight contraction, *Khetâs*.* The Brahmans of course refer the name to their own religion, and say that the place was called *Katâksha*, or the "Raining Eyes," because the tears literally rained from Siva's eyes when he heard of the death of his wife Sati. But as their own spelling of the name *Ketâksh*, which I received from themselves, is at variance with the meaning which they give to it, I am inclined to adopt the etymology that I have already suggested as *Swetavâsa*, or the "White Robes." This sect would

* Thus the Sanskrit *Saraswati* became the Zend *Harakhaiti*, and the Greek *Arakhôtos*.

appear to have belonged to the *Swetâmbara*, or "White-robed" division of the Jains, while another sect at the same place, who are described by Hwen Thsang as going naked, must be the *Digâmbara*, or "unclothed" (literally "sky-clad") division of the Jains. Their books also are stated to have been chiefly copied from the Buddhist literature, while the statue of their god resembled that of Buddha himself. From these curious details it seems almost certain that this heretical sect must have been Jains, whose religion has much in common with Buddhism, while their statues are frequently mistaken for those of Buddha.

Ketâs is situated on the north side of the Salt Range, at 16 miles from Pind Dâdan Khan, and 18 miles from Chakowâl, but not more than 85 miles from Shah-dheri, or Taxila. Now the distance of Singhapura from Taxila is given at 700 *li*, or 117 miles, which is certainly too great, as it would place the capital about 30 miles beyond the most distant point of the hills in any direction between the south and east. *Singhapura* is described as situated on the top of a high hill of difficult access; and as the climate is said to be very cold, it is certain that the place must have occupied one of the isolated peaks either of the Salt Range on the south-south-east, or of the Bâlnâth Range on the east-south-east.* But as there are no clear pools swarming with fish in the Bâlnâth Range, I have little hesitation in

---

* See Maps Nos. V. and VI.

identifying the place described by Hwen Thsang with the beautiful limpid pool of *Ketâs*, which has been esteemed holy from time immemorial.

The capital of *Singhapura* was situated at from 40 to 50 *li*, or 7 to 8 miles, to the north-west of the sacred tanks; but I know of no place that corresponds with this bearing and distance. *Malot* was the capital of the *Janjuhas* at a very early period; but its bearing is south-east, and its distance 12 miles. If we might read 4 to 5 *li*, instead of 40 to 50, the capital might at once be identified with the ruined fort of *Kotera*, which is situated on a steep hill to the west, about 200 feet in height, that overhangs the town and holy pools of *Ketâs*. This is called the ancient town. It consists of an upper fort, 1200 feet long, by 300 broad, and of a lower fort, 800 feet long, by 450 broad, the circuit of the two being about 3500 feet, or less than three-quarters of a mile. But the whole circuit of *Ketâs*, including the modern town on both banks of the stream, both above and below the fort, is about 2 miles. This is rather smaller than the capital described by Hwen Thsang, which was 14 or 15 *li*, 2¼ to 2½ miles, in circuit. But as it corresponds in all other material particulars, I think that *Ketâs* has a very good claim to be identified with the capital of Singhapura.

According to Hwen Thsang,* the district was 3600 *li*, or 600 miles, in circuit. On the west it was bounded by the Indus, on the north by the

---

* Julien's 'Hiouen Thsang,' ii. 162.

southern frontier of Taxila, 120 miles in length, and on the south by the Jhelam and the northern frontier of *Tâḳi*, or the plains of the Panjâb. It cannot therefore have extended much beyond the foot of the Salt Range. This limit would make the Indus frontier about 60 miles in length, the Jhelam frontier about 50 miles, and the northern and southern frontiers each 120 miles, or altogether 350 miles. The only explanation that occurs to me of the difference between this number and that of Hwen Thsang, is the probability that the ancient *ḳos* of the Panjâb was the same as the modern one, that is, a short kos of $1\frac{9}{32}$ mile, or 1 mile and 2¼ furlongs, and that the Chinese pilgrim, ignorant of the difference, made his calculations in the common Indian kos of about two miles. This would reduce his numbers by very nearly one-third, and at the same time bring them into close accordance with the actual measurements of our maps. Thus, Hwen Thsang's 3600 *li*, or 600 miles, for the circuit of Singhapura, would become 400 miles, which is within 50 miles of the actual measurement already given. Great accuracy cannot be expected in these estimates of frontier distances, as the pilgrim had no means of checking the numbers of his informants. With the road distances which he had himself travelled it was different, as he could test them by his own knowledge of the time occupied, as well as by the number of journeys between any two points. In the present instance of Singhapura it is quite certain that the frontier distance is exaggerated, as the boundary of

Tsekia, or Tâki, is also said to have extended to the Indus, which could not have been the case if the frontier of Singhapura had stretched further to the south than I have placed it.

5. PUNACHA, OR PUNACH.

The district of *Puan-nu-tso,* or *Punacha,* is placed by Hwen Thsang at 700 *li,* or 117 miles, to the south-west of Kashmir.* It is called *Punats* by the Kashmiris, who have adopted a soft pronunciation of the *ch,* as in *Pir Pantsal* for *Panchâl* of the Panjâbis. Moorcroft† spells the name *Prunch,* or *Pruntz,* according to the Kashmiris. General Court also has *Prunch;* but it is called *Punje* by Wilford's surveyor, Mirza Mogal Beg, and *Punch* by Vigne, both of whom actually visited the place. Its distance from Kashmir, as measured on the map *viâ* Barâhmula and Uri is 75 miles, which is equal to about 100 miles of actual road distance.‡

Hwen Thsang describes Punach as 2000 *li,* or 333 miles, in circuit, which is just about twice its actual size. On the west it is bounded by the Jhelam, on the north by the Pir Panchâl range, and on the east and south-east by the small state of Rajaori. But these limits, which include the petty state of Kotali, are not more than 170 miles in circuit; and even if the tract at the source of the Punach river

---

* Julien's 'Hiouen Thsang,' ii. 187.

† 'Travels,' ii. 298.

‡ See Maps Nos. V. and VI.

be included, the frontier will not be more than 200 miles in circuit. But as the distances in the mountain districts were most probably estimated by the lengths of the roads, the circuit of the frontier line may be taken as equivalent to about 300 miles in road distance.

In the seventh century Punach was without a king, and subject to Kashmir; but in later times it had a chief of its own, whose descendants, Shir Jang Khan and Shams Khan, were put to death by Gulâb Singh, of Jammu, and this petty sovereignty once more forms part of the kingdom of Kashmir.

6. RAJAPURA, OR RAJAORI.

From Punach, Hwen Thsang proceeded to the south-east for 400 *li*, or 67 miles, to *Ko-lo-she-pu-lo*, or *Râjapura*,* which I long ago identified with the petty chiefship of Rajaori, to the south of Kashmir. The circuit of the district is described as 4000 *li*, or 667 miles, which is about double the true amount, unless, as is not improbable, the whole of the hill-states as far as the Râvi be included within its boundaries. From the native chronicle of Kashmir we learn that the petty chiefships of the hills to the south and south-east of the valley were generally subject to Kashmir; and there is no reason to suppose that they were independent at the time of Hwen Thsang's visit.

* Julien's 'Hiouen Thsang,' ii. 188.

The district of Rajaori proper is nearly a square of about 40 miles each side, bounded on the north by the Pir Panchâl, on the west by Punach, on the south by Bhimbar, and on the east by Rihâsi and Aknur.* By extending its boundary on the east to the Chenab, and on the south to the plains, it would include all these petty places; even then its frontier would not be more than 240 miles, or by road about 320 miles. But if the frontier of these hill-states subject to Kashmir be extended to the Râvi on the east, the circuit would be about 420 miles measured on the map, or not less than 560 miles by road.

Râjapuri is frequently mentioned during the medieval period of Kashmirian history, but chiefly in the eleventh and twelfth centuries, when it was an independent state under its own rajas. In the fifteenth century the Hindu family was dispossessed in favour of a son of the Muhammadan king of Kashmir; and his descendant was so reduced by Gulâb Singh that in 1846 he was glad to accept an estate in the British district of Kângra in exchange for his petty chiefship of Rajaori.

HILL-STATES OF THE PANJÂB.

As the Chinese pilgrim has noticed so few of the many hill-states of the Panjâb, I will here add a brief outline of the information which I have myself been able to collect regarding them.

According to popular opinion the petty states of the Alpine Panjâb, at the present time, consist of

* See Maps Nos. V. and VI.

twenty-two Muhammadan and twenty-two Hindu chiefships, the former lying to the west, and the latter to the east of the Chenâb river. An older classification divides them into three groups, each named after the most powerful state which formed the head of the confederation. These were Kashmir, Dogra, and Trigartta. The first consisted of the rich valley of Kashmir, and all the petty states between the Indus and Jehlam; the second included Jammu, and the other petty states between the Jhelam and the Râvi; the third comprised Jâlandhar, and the various small states between the Râvi and the Satlej.

This division into three groups most probably existed prior to the seventh century, as we find that the states to the east of the Râvi were quite independent of Kashmir, while those of Urasa, Punach, and Rajapuri are spoken of in such a way as to show that they had kings of their own previous to their subjection by Kashmir. Trigartta is repeatedly mentioned in the chronicles of Kashmir as an independent kingdom; and its own history shows that one-half of the present petty states of the Jâlandhar hills have sprung from the division of the possessions of a single family.

The following list gives the names and possessions of the various states attached to Kashmir, or the western division of the Alpine Panjâb:—

	1. Kashmir.
Khâka Bambas .	2. Gingal, on the Behat R.
	3. Muzafarabad ,,
	4. Khâgân, on the Kunihâr R.
	5. Garhi, ,,

Afghâns . .	6. Rash, on Pakhli R.
	7. Dhantâwar on Dor R.
	8. Gandgarh, ,,
	9. Darband, on the Indus R.
	10. Torbela, ,,
Gakars	11. Pharwâla, near Behat R.
	12. Sultânpur, on Behat R.
	13. Khânpur, on Haro R.

The *Khâka-Bamba* chiefs hold the valley of the Behat river below Barâhmula, and the whole course of the Kunihâr river to the north-west of Kashmir. They are all Muhammadans, and are most probably the descendants of the early inhabitants of the country, who retired to their present position on the advance of the Afghân invaders.

The *Afghân* chiefs hold the valleys of the Pakhli and Dor rivers, to the south-west of Kashmir. They are all Muhammadans. and their settlement in this part of the country is of recent date. Abul Fazl mentions that before the time of Akbar, the raja of Pakhli was a tributary of Kashmir. He also states that Timur left a small body of troops in this district, whose descendants were still there in his time.*

The Gakar chiefs hold the lower valley of the Jhelam, and the upper course of the Haro river to the south-west of Kashmir. They are all Muhammadans; but their conversion is comparatively recent, as their names were Indian down to the invasion of Timur. Their occupation of these districts is of very

* 'Ayin Akbari,' ii. 155.

early date; but they are *Turanians*, and not *Arians*, as none but a Gakar will intermarry with a Gakar, a practice that is utterly repugnant to Hinduism, which permits no man to marry one of his own tribe. The Gakars also occupy several portions of the eastern Doab, as Guliâna, near Gujar Khan, and Bugiâl, under the lofty hill of Bâlnâth. But these districts do not properly belong to the hills, although they were subject to Kashmir at the time of Hwen Thsang's visit in the seventh century.

The following list gives the names and positions of the various states attached to the central, or Jammu division of the Alpine Panjâb :—

Hindus . . .	1. Jammu, to east of Chenâb R. 2. Bhao, ,,
Muhammadans.	3. Rihâsi, on Chenâb R. 4. Aknûr, ,, 5. Punach, on Punach R. 6. Rajaori, on Tohi R. 7. Kotali, on Punach R. 8. Bhimbar, at foot of hills. 9. Khariâli, near Bhimbar. 10. Kâshtwâr, on upper Chenâb R. 11. Bhadrwâr, to south of Kastwar.
Hindus . . .	12. Chaneni, to west of Bhadrwâr 13. Bandrâlta, to south of Chaneni. 14. Sâmba, to S.W. of Bandrâlta.

Hindus . . .	15. Jasrota, to south of Bandrâlta. 16. Tirikot, near Jasrota. 17. Mânkot, to south of Bandrâlta 18. Badwâl, or Vaddiwâsa. 19. Ballâwar, or Bisohli.

The towns of Jammu and Bhao, which were founded by two brothers, are situated on opposite banks of the Tohi, a small stream that joins the Chenab at the foot of the hills. Jammu is mentioned several times in Muhammadan history, from the time when Timur forcibly converted the Raja down to the end of the last century. The three famous brothers of Ranjit Singh's court—Gulâb Singh, Dhyân Singh, and Suchet Singh, belonged to a younger branch of this family, and the son of Gulâb Singh now rules over Kashmir and the whole of the states in the western and central divisions of the Alpine Panjâb.

The petty chiefs of *Rihâsi* and *Aknur* were branches of the Jammu family, on which they were generally dependent. Punach was sometimes independent; but its proximity to Kashmir placed it at the mercy of its more powerful neighbour. *Rajaori* and *Kotali* were held in later times by two branches of the royal family of Kashmir, to which they were usually tributary. But in the middle ages, under the Hindu rulers, Kotali formed part of Punach, to which it naturally belonged as part of the same valley. *Bhimbar* and *Khariâli* were divisions of the Chibh, or Chibhân, branch of the Somvansi Rajas of Kângra and Jâlandhar. In early times the name of Bhimbar was little used, the common appellation being *Chibhân,* which is found in Sharifuddin's history of Timur, under the form of *Jibhâl.* The conversion of the family to Muhammadanism is probably of late date, as Ferishta mentions *Howns* Raja of Bhimbar in A.H. 891, or A.D. 1486.* But so many of these hill chiefs retained their Hindu names after they became Muhammadans, that the Hindu name alone cannot be taken as a decisive proof of his being unconverted. *Kâshtwâr* and *Bhadrwâr* are situated on opposite banks of the upper Chenâb river, to the south-east of Kashmir, to which they were generally subject. These nine chief-ships of the central division, added to the thirteen of the western division, form the twenty-two Muhammadan states which the popular belief assigns to the western half of the Alpine Panjâb.

Of the eight remaining chiefships of this division I am not able to give much information, as many of them became extinct during the early period of Sikh rule, and all of them are now absorbed by the Jammu family in the great kingdom of Kashmir. *Jasrota,* in the outer range of hills, was once of some importance, and its chiefs intermarried with the other Rajput families of the Alpine Panjâb; but I can find no mention of it in any of the histories. *Ballâwar* and *Badwâl* were certainly at one time under a single chief, as Kalasa, the son of Tukka, who is twice mentioned in the 'Raja Tarangini'† as lord of *Vallâ-*

* Briggs, 'Ferishta,' iv. 483.

† 'Raja Tarangini, vii. 220, 589.

pura between 1028 and 1801, is found in the genealogical lists of both families. It is true that *Vaddivâsa* is noticed in the same chronicle* as a separate district at an earlier date, but as there is no mention of any chief, it may be inferred that it formed part of the small kingdom of Vallâpura. As the names in the two genealogical lists differ from *Kalasa* downwards, it seems probable that the state may have been dismembered after his death. It is certain that he was mixed up with Kashmirian politics; and as the contemporary Raja of the neighbouring state of Chamba was put to death by Ananta of Kashmir, I conclude that Ballâwar must have been subjected at the same time.

I may remark that all the chiefs of the Central Division, whose genealogies I possess, trace their origin to the *Surajvansi,* or Solar Race, with the single exception of the intrusive *Chibhân* of Bhimbar. The chiefs of Jammu, Jasrota, and Ballâwar, with their offshoots, amounting together to eight of these petty states, all assert their descent from the Sun, a claim which is admitted by their Rajput neighbours.

The following list gives the names and positions of the various states attached to the eastern, or Jâlandhar division of the Alpine Panjâb.

Somvansi . . {
1. Kângra, or Kâtoch.
2. Guler, to S. W. of Kângra.
3. Jaswâl, on Suhan R.
4. Datârpur, on lower Biâs R.
5. Siba, do.

* 'Raja Tarangini', vi. 318, Nandigupta.

Surajvansi . .	6. Chamba, on Râvi R. 7. Kullu, on upper Biâs R.
Pundir, or Pândayas . .	8. Mandi, on middle Biâs R. 9. Sukhet, to south of Mandi. 10. Nûrpur, between Râvi and Biâs R. 11. Kotila, to E. of Nûrpur.
	12. Kotlehar.

Of these twelve states no less than five are mere subdivisions of the once rich kingdom of Jâlandhar, which embraced the whole of the Doâb, or plain country, between the Biâs and Satlej, and all the hill country lying between the Râvi and the frontiers of Mandi and Sukket, to the south of the Dhaola-dhâr mountains. This included Nûrpûr, Kotila, and Kotlehar; and as Mandi and Sukhet were at first under one rule, there were originally only four chiefships in the eastern division of the Alpine Panjâb, namely, Jâlandhar, Chamba, Kullu, and Mandi.

Jâlandhara.

Since the occupation of the plains by the Muhammadans, the ancient kingdom of Jâlandhara has been confined almost entirely to its hill territories, which were generally known by the name of *Kângra,* after its most celebrated fortress. The district is also called *Kâtoch*, the meaning of which is unknown, and *Trigartta,** wihch is the usual

* 'Hema-Kosha.' *Jâlandharâs Trigarttâsyuh*—"Jâlandhara, that is Trigartta."

Sanskrit name found in the Purânas, and in the native chronicle of Kashmir.

In the seventh century *Jâlandhara* is described by the Chinese pilgrim* as about 1000 *li*, or 167 miles in length from east to west, and 800 *li*, or 133 miles in breadth from north to south. If these dimensions are even approximately correct, Jâlandhar must then have included the state of Chamba on the north, with Mandi and Sukhet on the east, and Satadru on the south-east. As the last is the only district to the east of the Satlej, which is included in N. India, I infer that it must have belonged to the kingdom of *Jâlandhar*. With the addition of these districts the size of the province will agree very well with the dimensions assigned to it by the Chinese pilgrim.

At the time of Hwen Thsang's visit, Jâlandhar itself was the capital, which he describes as from 12 to 13 *li*, or upwards of 2 miles in circuit. Its antiquity is undoubted, as it is mentioned by Ptolemy as *Kulindrine*, or *Ktulindrine*, which should probably be corrected to *Sulindrine*, as the *K* and *Σ* are frequently interchanged in Greek manuscripts. According to the Padma Purâna,† the city of *Jâlandhara* was the capital of the great Daitya king *Jalandhara*, who became so powerful by virtue of his austerities as to be invincible. At last,

* Julien's 'Hiouen Thsang,' ii. 202.

† Uttara Khanda of the Padma Purâna. Kennedy's 'Hindu Mythology,' p. 456.

however, he was overcome by Siva, through a disgraceful fraud, and his body was devoured by the *yoginis*, or female demons. But the conclusion of the legend is differently given in the local Purâna,* which states that he was overwhelmed and crushed to death by a mass of mountains which Siva placed upon him. Flames then sprang out of his mouth, which was under *Jwâla-mukhi;* his back was under the upper part of the Doâb, which is still called *Jâlandhara-pitha,* or *Jâlandhar-pith*, by the people; and his feet were under the lower part of the Doâb at Multân. Akbar partially adopted this version of the legend when he named the different Doâbs after the enclosing rivers, by calling the land between the Satlej and Bïâs the *Doâb-i-Bist Jâlandhar*, or *Bit Jâlandhar*, instead of the *Sab Doab*, which it should have been if he had placed the initial of the eastern river first, as he did in the names of the Bâri and Chaj Doâbs.

The royal family of Jâlandhara and Kângra is one of the oldest in India, and their genealogy from the time of the founder, *Susarma Chandra*, appears to me to have a much stronger claim to our belief than any one of the long strings of names now shown by the more powerful families of Rajputana. All the different scions of this house claim to be of *Somavansi* descent; and they assert that their ancestors held the district of Multân and fought in the Great War on the side of Duryodhan against

* Jâlandhara Purâna.

the five Pându brothers. After the war they lost their country, and retired under the leadership of Susarma Chandra to the Jâlandhar Doâb where they established themselves, and built the stronghold of Kangra. The expedition of Alexander terminated on the banks of the Hyphasis, or Bïâs; but he received the submission of *Phegelas** or *Phegœus*, the king of the district, beyond the river, that is of the Jâlandhar Doâb. Towards the end the fifth century, the kingdom of Trigartta was presented to Pravaresa by the Raja of Kashmir.† In the seventh century, the Chinese pilgrim, Hwen Thsang, was courteously entertained for a whole month by Raja *U-ti-to*, or *Udita*,‡ whom I would identify with *Adima* of the genealogical lists. One hundred and sixty years later, in an inscription dated A.D. 804, the Raja of Jâlandhara is named Jaya Chandra, who is the Jaya Malla Chandra of the lists, the seventh in descent from Adima. Lastly, Avanta, king of Kashmir, from A.D. 1028 to 1081, married two daughters of Indu Chandra,§ Raja of Jâlandhara, who is the Indra Chandra of the genealogical lists of Kângra. These instances are sufficient to show that *Jâlandhara* existed as an independent State for many centuries before the Muhammadan conquest.

* Diodorus, xvii. 51, "Phegæus." Curtius, ix. I. 2, "Phegelas erat gentis proximæ rex."

† 'Rajâ Tarangini,' iii. 100.

‡ Julien's 'Hiouen Thsang,' i. 261.

§ 'Raja Tarangini, vii. 150.

The smaller chiefships of Guler, Jaswâl, Datârpur, and Siba, are offshoots from the parent stem of Kângra. The independence of *Guler*, or *Haripur*, was established by Hari Chandra, about A.D. 1400, when he yielded Kângra to his younger brother, Karmma Chandra. The date of the foundation of the other principalities is unknown, but I believe that they were always tributary to the parent state until the time of the Muhammadans, when the capture of Kângra by Mahmud of Ghazni afforded them an opportunity of asserting their independence.

The French traveller Thevenot,* in his account of the dominions of the Emperor of Delhi, mentions that "there are many Rajas who own not the authority of the Great Mogul." But the territories of these Rajas must have been far in the interior of the hills, as we know that the chiefs of all the outer hills were subjected by the Mogul emperors. Thevenot specially mentions the province of "*Ayoud*, or *Haoud*," as containing "the most northern countries that belong to the Great Mogul, as *Caucares*, *Bankish*, *Nagarcut*, *Siba*, and others." The Caucares must be the Gakars who hold the lower hills to the west of the Jhelam. Terry† calls them *Kakares*, and their principal cities *Dekalee* and *Purhola* (or Dângali and Pharwâla). The *Bankish* are the *Banchish* of Terry‡ whose "chief

* 'Travels,' part iii. c. 37.

† 'Voyage to East India,' p. 88.

‡ *Ibid.*, p. 81 : London, 1655.

city called *Bishur* (Peshâwar) lyeth east (read west) somewhat southerly from Chishmere, from which it is divided by the river Indus." *Nagarcut* is Kângra or Nagarkot, which is mentioned under the same name by Abu Rihân,* who was present at its capture by Mahmud of Ghazni. *Siba* is not as we might suppose, the small state in the neighbourhood of Kângra, but a district on the Ganges, of which the chief city, according to Terry, was "*Hardware* (or Haridwâra), where the river Ganges, passing through or amongst large rocks, makes presently after a pretty full current." From these accounts it is clear that the whole of the states in the lower hills, from Peshâwar on the west to the Ganges on the east, were subject to the emperor of Delhi. Regarding the general name of *Ayoud*, or *Haoud*, which Thevenot applies to them, I can only conjecture that it may be some corrupt form of *Himavat*, or *Himwat*, one of the well-known names of the *Himâlaya* mountains, which the Greeks have preserved under the two different forms of *Emôdos* and *Imäus*.

Champa, or Chamba.

Chamba is a large district, which includes the valleys of all the sources of the Râvi, and a portion of the upper valley of the Chenâb, between Lâhul and Kâshtwâr. It is not mentioned by Hwen Thsang, and was, therefore, probably included by

* 'Fragments Arabes, etc.,' 149.

him within the limits of Kashmir. The ancient capital was *Varmmapura*, or Barmâwar, on the Budhil river, where many fine temples, and a brazen bull, of life size, still exist to attest the wealth and piety of its early rulers. According to the inscriptions these works belong to the ninth and tenth centuries. The country is frequently mentioned in the native chronicle of Kashmir, under the name of *Champa*, and each notice is confirmed by the local genealogies. Between A.D. 1028 and 1031 the district was invaded by Ananta of Kashmir,* when the native Raja, named *Sâla*, was defeated and put to death. His son founded a new capital, *Champapura*, called after the goddess *Champâvati Devi;* which, under the name of *Chamba*, is still the chief place in the district. The Rajas of Kashmir afterwards intermarried with the Chamba family;† and during the troubles that followed the Muhammadan invasions this petty state became independent, and remained so until reduced by Gulâb Singh, early in the present century.‡

Kullu.

The kingdom of *Kiu-lu-to* is placed by Hwen Thsang at 700 *li*, or 117 miles, to the north-east of

---

* Briggs's 'Ferishta,' i. 283. The Gakars inhabited the banks of the Nilâb (or Indus) up to the foot of the mountains of Siwâlik.

† 'Raja Tarangini,' vii. 218.

‡ *Ibid.*, vii. 589, 1520; viii. 1092.

Jâlandhar,* which corresponds exactly with the position of the district of *Kullu*, in the upper valley of the Byâs river. The Vishnu Purâna† mentions a people called *Ulûta*, or *Kulûta*, who are most probably the same as the *Kaulutas* of the 'Râmâyana' and the 'Brihat Sanhitâ.'‡ As this form of the word agrees precisely with the Chinese *Kiuluto*, I conclude that the modern *Kullu* must be only an abbreviation of the ancient name. The district is stated to be 3000 *li*, or 500 miles, in circuit, and entirely surrounded by mountains. The size is very much exaggerated for the present restricted limits of Kullu; but as the ancient kingdom is said by the people themselves to have included Mandi and Sukhet on the west, and a large tract of territory to the south of the Satlej, it is probable that the frontier measurement of 500 miles may be very near the truth if taken in road distance.

The present capital of the valley is Sultânpur; but the old capital of Makarsa is still called Nagar, or the city, by which name it is most generally known. Hwen Thsang states that gold, silver, and copper are all found in the district, which is only partially true, as the amount of gold to be obtained by washing is very small, and the silver and copper mines have long been abandoned.

---

* Julien's 'Hiouen Thsang,' ii. 203.

† Wilson's 'Vishnu Purâna,' edited by Hall, ii. 3, vol. ii. p. 174.

‡ Kern's 'Brihat Sanhita,' xiv. 29.

To the north-east of Kullu Hwen Thsang places the district of *Lo-hu-lo,* which is clearly the *Lho-yal* of the Tibetans, and the *Lâhul* of the people of Kullu and other neighbouring states. Still further to the north he places the district of *Mo-lo-so,* which, from his position, must certainly be Ladâk. I would, therefore, alter the Chinese name to *Mo-lo-po,* which is an exact transcript of *Mar-po,* the actual name of the province of Ladâk, as *Mar-po-yul,* or the "Red district," in allusion to the general appearance of its soil and mountains. The Chinese syllables *so* and *po* are so much alike that they are frequently interchanged, as in the well-known name of Salatura, the birth-place of Pânini, which is given in the original Chinese of Hwen Thsang's travels as *Po-lo-tu-lo,* or *Palatura.*

Mandi and Sukhet.

The petty chiefships of *Mandi* and *Sukhet* were originally a single state, bounded by Kângra on the west and Kullu on the east, and by the Dhaoladhâr mountains on the north and the Satlej on the south. *Mandi* means the "market;" and its favourable position on the Bïâs river, at the junction of the two roads from the west and south, must have ensured its early occupation, which was rendered prosperous and lasting by the existence of valuable mines of iron and black salt in its immediate vicinity.

Nûrpûr, or Pathâniya.

The town of Nûrpûr derives its name from the celebrated Nûr Jahân, the wife of the emperor

Jahânjîr. Its original name was *Dahmari*, or *Dahmâla;* or as Abul Fazl writes, *Dahmahri*, although he mentions no fort. The people pronounce the name as if written *Dahmeri*. In the 'Târikh-i-Alfi' it is called *Damâl*, and is described as "situated on the summit of a high hill, on the borders of Hindustan." The fort was taken after a long siege by Ibrahim Ghaznavi. The name of the district is *Pathâwat*, and the old capital in the plains was called *Pathiân*, or *Pathiânkot*, which is now slightly altered to *Pathânkot*. But the name is derived from the Pathân tribe of Hindu Rajpûts, and not from the well-known Muhammadan Pathâns, or Afghâns. The Raja was imprisoned in 1815 by Ranjit Singh, who took possession of his country.

The petty chief of Kotila, to the east of Nûrpûr, who was a scion of the Pathâniya family, was seized about the same time, and his estate incorporated with the Sikh dominions.

Kotlehar is a petty state in the Jaswâl Dûn, to the south-east of Jwâla-Mukhi. It was generally a dependency of Kangra.

Satadru.

The district of *She-to-tu-lo*, or *Satadru*, is described by the Chinese pilgrim* as 2000 *li*, or 333 miles in circuit, with a large river forming its western boundary. The capital is placed at 700 *li*, or 117 miles, to the south of Kullu, and 800 *li*, or 133 miles,

* Julien's 'Hiouen Thsang,' ii 205.

to the north-east of Bairât. But there is a mistake in one of these numbers, as the distance between the capital of Kullu and Bairât is 336 miles, measured direct on the map, or not less than 360 miles, by road. There is a deficiency, therefore, in one of the distances of about 110 miles, or nearly 700 *li*, in a direct line between the two places, or of about 150 miles, or nearly 1000 *li*, in the detour, as shown by his bearings. Now it is remarkable that there is a deficiency of about the same amount in the return journey along a parallel line of road, from Mathura to Thanesar, which the pilgrim makes only 500 *li*, or 83 miles,* instead of 1200 *li*, or 200 miles, the actual distance being 199 miles. As it would seem that both routes, for some unknown reason, had been subjected to the same amount of curtailment, it is probable that the deficiency in the western line will lie in the southern portion between Satadru and Bairât, which is contiguous to the parallel line between Mathura and Thanesar. I would, therefore, increase the distance between the two former places by 150 miles, or in round numbers 1000 *li*, which would make the total distance 283 miles, or nearly 1800 *li*, instead of 800 *li*. Taking this corrected distance from Bairât, and the recorded distance of 117 miles south from Kullu, the position of Satadru will correspond almost exactly with the large city of Sarhind, which both history

* Julien's 'Hiouen Thsang,' i. 104, and ii. 211.

and tradition affirm to be the oldest place in this part of the country.

The present ruins of Sarhind consist almost entirely of Muhammadan buildings of a late period; but it must have been a place of some consequence in the time of the Hindus, as it was besieged and captured by Muhammad Ghori, the first Mussuliman king of Delhi.* The name of *Sarhind*, or "frontier of Hind" is popularly said to have been given to the city at an earlier period, when it was the boundarv town between the Hindus and the later Muhammadan kingdom of Ghazni and Lahor. But the name is probably much older, as the astronomer Varâha Mihira mentions the *Sairindhas*† immediately after the *Kulûtas,* or people of Kullu, and just before *Brahmapura,* which, as we learn from the Chinese pilgrim, was the capital of the hill country to the north of Haridwâr. The *Sairindhas*, or people of *Sirindha*, must, therefore, have occupied the very tract of country in which the present Sarhind is situated, and there can be little doubt that the two names are the same. But the geographical list of Varâha Mihira is copied almost *verbatim* from that of the still earlier astronomer Parâsara, who is believed to have flourished not later than the first century after Christ.‡

* Dowson's edition of Sir H. Elliot's 'Muhammadan Historians of India,' ii. 295.

† Dr. Kern's edition of the 'Brihat Sanhitâ,' b. xiv. 29, 30.

‡ Kern's Preface to the 'Brihat Sanhitâ,' p. 32.

If we apply the correction of 110 miles, or about 700 *li*, to the northern half of the line between Kullu and Satadru, the position of the latter will be brought down to Hânsi, which is an ancient fortified city of even greater strength and reputation than Sarhind. But as Hwen Thsang specially notes that the territory of Satadru was only 2000 *li*, or 333 miles, in circuit, and that it was bounded on the west by a great river, which can only be the Satlej or Satadru, it is quite impossible that Hânsi could be the place intended, as it is upwards of 130 miles distant from the nearest point of that river.

The position of the celebrated fortress of Bhatner would suit the description of a small district bounded on the west by the Satlej, and would also agree with the corrected distance from Kullu : but the direction is south-west instead of south, and the distance from Bairât is upwards of 200 miles, instead of 800 *li*, or 133 miles, as stated by the pilgrim. The bearing of Bairât is, however, in favour of Bhatner, as the pilgrim's south-west is certainly a mistake for south-east, otherwise the distance of Bairât from Mathura would be nearly 1500 *li*, or 250 miles, instead of 500 *li*, or 83 miles, as recorded. If we might read 1500 *li* instead of 500 *li*, the relative positions of Bhatner and Bairât would correspond very well with the pilgrim's account, as the road distance between the two places, *viâ* Hânsi, is about 250 miles. It is quite possible also that there may be a mistake in the initial Chinese character, *She* or *Sa*, which is very much like *Po* or *Bha;* and if so, the Chinese syllables

Po.to-tu-lo would represent *Bhatasthala*, or Bhatner. The latter name means the "fortress of the Bhatis," but the town itself was called *Band*, or *Bando*, which was probably the contracted form of *Bhatasthala*, just as *Mâru* is now the common contracted form of *Marusthala*. But in spite of these plausible agreements both in name and in position, I am inclined to think that Sarhind must be the place indicated by the pilgrim as the capital of the ancient district of *Satadru*. This conclusion is strengthened by the pilgrim's statement that the country produced gold, which, so far as I know, can only apply to the lower hills lying to the north of Sarhind, where gold is still found in some of the smaller affluents of the Satlej.

Accepting Sarhind as the capital of Satadru, the boundaries of the district may be determined approximately from its size. On the west and north it was bounded by the Satlej for upwards of 100 miles from the neighbourhood of Simla to Tihâra, below Lûdiâna. On the south the boundary extended for about 100 miles from Tihâra to Ambâla, and on the east for about the same distance, from Ambâla to Simla. The circuit thus described embraces a considerable portion of the hill states to the west and south of Simla, together with the districts of Sarhind proper and Lûdiâna in the plains. As it is the only district lying to east of the Satlej that is included within the limits of Northern India, I infer that it must have been a dependency of the neighbouring state of Jâlandhar.

TÂKI, OR PANJÂB.

The kingdom which Hwen Thsang calls *Tse-ḳia*, or *Tâḳi*, embraced the whole of the plains of the Panjâb from the Indus to the Biâs, and from the foot of the mountains to the junction of the five rivers below Multân.* The Chinese syllable *tse* is used by Hwen Thsang to represent the cerebral *t* of the Sanskrit in the name of *Danaḳaḳata*, which is found in no less than five of the western cave inscriptions at Kanhari and Kârli.† In Hwen Thsang's travels this name is written *To.no.ḳia-tse.ḳia*, in which the last two syllables are transposed. It is the *Danaḳa* of Abu Rihân, which, as will be shown hereafter, is most probably the same as the old town of *Dhârani-ḳotta*, on the Kistna river, adjoining the modern city of Amaravati. *Tse-ḳia*, therefore, represents *Tâḳi*, which would appear to have been the name of the capital as well as of the kingdom of the Panjâb in the seventh century, just as *Lahor* has since been used to describe both the kingdom and the capital of Ranjit Singh. The position of the capital will be discussed hereafter. It will be sufficient at present to note that it was within a few miles of the more ancient capital of *She-ḳie-lo*, which was long ago identified by Professor Lassen with the

---

* See Maps Nos. V. and VI.

† Dr. Stevenson read this name as the Pali form of the Greek *Xenoḳrates*, but in all the inscriptions at Kanhari and *Kârli* it is clearly the name of a town or country.

Sâkala of the Mahâbhârata, and with the *Sangala* of Arrian. Now the people of *Sâkala* are called *Madras, Arattas, Jârttikas,* and *Bâhîkas,** in the *Mahâbhârata;* and in the Lexicon of Hemachandra the *Bâhîkas* are said to be the same as the *Takkas.*† Again, in the 'Raja Tarangini,' the district of *Takkadesa* is mentioned as a part of the kingdom of *Gurjjara* (or Gujarât, near the Chenâb), which Raja Alakhâna was obliged to cede to Kashmir between A.D. 883 and 901.‡ From these statements it is clear that *Sakala* was the old capital of the powerful tribe of *Takkas,* whose country was named after themselves *Takka-desa.*§ The name of the new capital is not actually stated by Hwen Thsang, but I believe it to have been *Taki,* or *Takkâwar,* which I would identify with the *Tahora* of the Pentingerian Tables by the mere softening of the guttural *k* to the aspirate *h.* In the latter authority *Tahora* is placed at 70 Roman miles, or 64⅓ English miles from *Spatura,* opposite *Alexandria Bucefalos.*

I will now turn to the early Muhammadan

---

* In the Mahâbhârata and Vishnu Purâna the name is written *Bâlhîka;* but as they follow the *Kulûtus,* it seems certain that the true reading is *Bâhîka,* as proposed by Lassen.

† Lassen, 'Pentapot Indica,' p. 21. *Bâhîkâshtakkanâmâno.*

‡ 'Raja Tarangini,' v. 150, Troyer; *v.* 155, Calcutta edit.

§ For the position of Sâkala, or Taki, see Maps, Nos. V. and VI.

writers who have noticed Kashmir and Sindh, and who, therefore can scarcely have omitted all mention of so important a country as the Panjâb, which lies immediately between them. In A.D. 915, Masudi thus describes the Indus, according to Sir Henry Elliot's translation :* "The *Mihrân* of es-Sind comes "from the well-known sources of the high land of "es-Sind, from the country belonging to Kinnauj in "the kingdom of Budah, and of Kashmir, el "Kandahâr, and *et-Tâkin*. The tributaries which "rise in these countries run to el Multân, and from "thence the united river receives the name of "*Mihrân*." In this passage *Tâkin* must certainly be intended for the hills of the Panjâb. The Kabul river and the Indus both flow through *Gândhâra*, or el Kandahâr; the Jhelam comes from Kashmir; and the Biâs and Satlej flow through Jâlandhar and Kahlur, which in the time of Hwen Thsang were subject to Kanoj. The only other tributaries of the Indus are the Chenâb and the Râvi, which must therefore have flowed through the kingdom of *Tâkin*. The mention of Gândhâra and Kanoj shows that Masudi does not refer to the actual sources of the rivers, but to the points in the lower ranges of hills, where they enter the plains. *Tâkin*, therefore, in the time of Masudi, represented the lower hills and

---

* Sir H. M. Elliot's 'Muhammadan Historians of India,' p. 56 ; and Prof. Dowson's edition, i. 21, where the name is read as *Tâfan*. But Sprenger, in his translation of 'Masudi,' p. 193, gives *Tâfi*, with *Tâkan* and *Tâfan* as variants, and at p. 390, *Tâkin*.

plains of the Panjâb to the north of Multân, which was then in the possession of the Brahman kings of Kabul.

The name is read *Tâkin*, طاقين, by Sir Henry Elliot, and *Tâfan*, طافن, by Gildemeister,* in his extracts from Masudi. The first reading is supported by the strong authority of Abu Rihân and Rashid-ud-din, who agree in stating that the great snowy mountain of *Kelârjik* (or Lârjk), which resembled Demavend by its cupola form, could be seen from the boundaries of *Tâkishar* and Lohâwar.† Elliot, in one passage, corrects *Tâkishar* to *Kashmir;* but this alteration is quite inadmissible, as the mountain is specially noted to have been only 2 farsangs, or about 8 miles, distant from Kashmir. One might as well say that St. Paul's Cathedral is visible from Ludgate Hill and Windsor. The mountain here referred to is the great *Dayamur*, or *Nanga Parbat*, to the west of Kashmir, which is 26,629 feet in height; and which I have myself seen repeatedly from Râmnagar, on the Chenâb, a distance of 200 miles. In a second passage of the same author, Sir Henry calls the mountain *Kalârchal*,‡ and the two places from

* 'De Rebus Indicis,' p. 161.

† Reinaud, 'Fragments Arabes,' p. 118. In Sir H. M. Elliot, p. 41, and in Dowson's edition of Elliot, i. 65, Tâkishar is altered to Kashmir.

‡ Sir H. M. Elliot, p. 30; and Dowson's edition, i. 46. If this is the same as Ibn Batuta's *Karâchal*, or "Black Mountain," the identification with *Nanga Parbat*,

which it can be seen he names *Tâkas* and Lohâwar. This *Tâkas,* or *Tâkishar,* I take to be the same place as the *Tsekia,* or *Tâki* of Hwen Thsang, and the *Tâkin* of Masudi.

The earliest Muhammadan author who mentions *Tâki* is the merchant Sulimân, who visited the east before A.D. 851, when his account was written. He describes *Tâfak,* طافك, as not of very great extent, and its king as weak, and subject to the neighbouring princes; but he adds that he possessed "the finest white women in all the Indies."* As *Tâfak* and *Tâkin* are almost the same in unpointed Persian characters, I have no hesitation in identifying *Tâfak* with the Panjâb, where the women, and especially those of the lower hills, are the "fairest," as well as the "finest," in India.

Ibn Khurdâdba, who died in A.D. 912, mentions the king of *Taffa*† as next in eminence to the Balha Râ. Lastly, Kazwini describes *Taifand,* طيفند, which was taken by Mahmud of Ghazni in A.D. 1023, as a strong Indian fort, on the top of an inaccessible mountain.‡ This account agrees with the actual hill of *Sangala,* which is almost inaccessible on three

---

or the "Bare Mountain" is nearly certain, as "bareness" means "blackness," from want of snow.

* Sir Henry Elliot, p. 49; and Dowson's edition, i. 4.

† Sir Henry Elliot, 'Muhammadan Historians of India,' p. 53. In Dowson's edition, i. 13, this name is written *Tâfan.*

‡ Gildemeister, 'De Rebus Indicis,' p. 208.

sides, and on the fourth is protected by a sheet of water.

All these slightly different names of *Tâkin, Tâfan, Tâfak, Tâffa, Tâkas,* and *Tâkishar,* I take to be only various readings of the one original form of *Tâki,* or *Tâkin,* which, when written without the diacritical points, may be read in several different ways. M. Reinaud gives another spelling as *Tâban,* طابن, which, without the points, may be read in as many different ways as the other form of *Tâfan.* I conclude, therefore, that the true form of the name of the country was *Tâki,* or *Tâka,* as recorded by Hwen Thsang. The name of the capital was probably either *Tâkin* or *Takkâwar,* of which the former agrees exactly with Kazwini's *Taifand* طيفند, and the latter with the *Tahora* of the Pentingerian Tables. I consider it almost certain that the name must have been derived from the tribe of *Tâks* or *Takkas,* who were once the undisputed lords of the Panjâb, and who still exist as a numerous agricultural race in the lower hills between the Jhelam and the Râvi.

The former importance of this race is perhaps best shown by the fact that the old *Nâgari* characters, which are still in use throughout the whole country from Bamiyan to the banks of the Jumna, are named *Tâkari,* most probably because this particular form was brought into use by the *Tâks* or *Takkas.* I have found these characters in common use under the same name amongst the grain dealers to the west of the Indus, and to the east of the Satlej, as well as amongst the Brâhmans of Kashmir and Kangra. It is used in the inscriptions, as well as upon the coins of Kashmir and Kangra; it is seen on the *Sati* monuments of Mandi, and in the inscriptions of Pinjor; and lastly, the only copy of the 'Raja Tarangini' of Kashmir was preserved in the *Tâkari* characters. I have obtained copies of this alphabet from twenty-six different places between Peshâwar and Simla. In several of these places the *Tâkari* is also called *Mundé* and *Lundé*, but the meaning of these terms is unknown. The chief peculiarity of this alphabet is, that the vowels are never attached to the consonants, but are always written separately, with, of course, the single exception of the inherent short *a*. It is remarkable also that in this alphabet the initial letters of the cardinal numbers have almost exactly the same forms as the nine unit figures in present use.

In the seventh century the kingdom of *Tâki* was divided into three provinces, namely, *Tâki* in the north and west, *Shorkot* in the east, and *Multân* in the south. The province of *Tâki* comprised the plains of the Panjâb, lying between the Indus and the Biâs, to the north of the Multân district, or the whole of the *Chaj* Doâb, together with the upper portions of the three Doâbs of Sindh-Sâgar, Richna, and Bâri. The province of *Shorkot* comprised the middle portions of these Doâbs, and the province of *Multân* their lower portions. It is probable, also, that the possessions of Multân may have extended some distance to the west of the Indus as well as to the east of the Satlej, as was the case in the time of Akbar.

1. TÂKI, OR NORTHERN PANJÂB.

The province of Tâki contained several of the most celebrated places of ancient India; some renowned in the wars of Alexander, some famous in Buddhist history, and others known only in the widely-spread traditions of the people. The following is a list of the most important of the ancient places, arranged according to their relative geographical positions from west to east. The names of the Doâbs were invented by Akbar by combining the names of the including rivers. Thus, *Chaj* is an abbreviation of Chenâb and Jhelam; *Richna* of Râvi and Chenâb; and *Bâri* of Biâs and Ravi.

Sindh-Sâgar Doâb	1. Jobnâthnagar, or Bhira. 2. Bukephala, or Dilâwar.
Chaj Doâb	3. Nikæa, or Mong. 4. Gujarât.
Richna Doâb	5. Sâkala, or Sangala. 6. Tâki, or Asarur. 7. Narsingha, or Ransi. 8. Ammakatis, or Ambakapi.
Bâri Doâb	9. Lohâwar, or Lahor. 10. Kusâwar, or Kasur. 11. Chinapati, or Patti.

Jobnâthnagar, or Bhira.

The modern town of *Bhira*, or Bheda, is situated on the left, or eastern bank, of the Jhelam; but on the opposite bank of the river, near Ahmedabad, there is a very extensive mound of ruins, called *Old Bhira*, or *Jobnâthnagar*, the city of Raja *Jobnâth*, or *Chobnâth*. At this point the two great routes of the salt caravans diverge to Lahor and Multân; and here, accordingly, was the capital of the country in ancient times; and here also, as I believe, was the capital of Sophites, or Sopeithes, the contemporary of Alexander the Great. According to Arrian, the capital of Sopeithes was fixed by Alexander as the point where the camps of Kraterus and Hephæstion were to be pitched on opposite banks of the river, there to await the arrival of the fleet of boats under his own command, and of the main body of the army under Philip.* As Alexander reached the appointed place on the third day, we know that the capital of Sophites was on the Hydaspes, at three days' sail from Nikæa for laden boats. Now Bhira is just three days' boat distance from *Mong*, which, as I will presently show, was almost certainly the position of Nikæa, where Alexander defeated Porus. Bhira also, until it was supplanted by Pind Dâdan Khan, has always been the principal city in this part of the country. At *Bhira*† the Chinese pilgrim, Fa-Hian, crossed the Jhelam in A.D. 400; and against Bhira, eleven centuries later, the enterprising Baber conducted his first Indian expedition.

---

* 'Anabasis,' vi. 3.

† Beal's translation, chap. xv.; Fa-Hian calls it *Pi-cha* or *Bhi-da*—the Chinese *ch* being the usual representative of the cerebral *d*.

The classical notices of the country over which Sophites ruled are very conflicting. Thus Strabo* records:—"Some writers place *Kathœa* and the country of Sopeithes, one of the monarchs, in the tract between the rivers (Hydaspes and Akesines); some on the other side of the Akesines and of the Hyarotes, on the confines of the territory of the other Porus,—the nephew of Porus, who was taken prisoner by Alexander, and call the country subject to him *Gandaris*." This name may, I believe, be identified with the present district of *Gundalbâr*, or *Gundar-bâr*. *Bâr* is a term applied only to the central portion of each Doâb, comprising the high lands beyond the reach of irrigation from the two including rivers. Thus *Sandal*, or *Sandar-bâr*, is the name of the central tract of the Doâb between the Jhelam and the Chenâb. The upper portion of the *Gundal Bâr* Doâb, which now forms the district of Gujarât, belonged to the famous Porus, the antagonist of Alexander, and the upper part of the *Sandar-Bâr* Doâb belonged to his nephew, the other Porus, who is said to have sought refuge among the Gandaridæ. The commentators have altered this name to *Gangaridœ*, or inhabitants of the Ganges; but it seems to me that the text of Diodorus† is most probably correct, and that the name of *Gandaridœ* must refer to the people of the neighbouring district of *Gandaris*, who were the subjects of Sophites.

The rule of the Indian prince was not, however,

---

* Geogr., xv. 1, 30. † Hist., xix. 47.

confined to the Doâb between the Hydaspes and Akesines; for Strabo* relates that "in the territory of Sopeithes there is a mountain composed of fossil salt sufficient for the whole of India." As this notice can only refer to the well-known mines of rock salt in the Salt Range, the whole of the upper portion of the Sindh Sâgar Doâb must have been included in the territories of Sopeithes. His sway, therefore, would have extended from the Indus on the west to the Akesines on the east, thus comprising the whole of the present district of Pind Dâdan and Shâhpur. This assignment of the valuable salt mines to Sopeithes, or Sophites, may also be deduced from a passage in Pliny by the simple transposition of two letters in the name of a country, which has hitherto puzzled all the commentators. Pliny says, "when Alexander the Great was on his Indian expedition, he was presented by the king of *Albania* with a dog of unusual size," which successfully attacked both a lion and an elephant in his presence.† The same story is repeated by his copyist, Solinus,‡ without any change in the name of the country. Now, we know from the united testimony of Strabo, Diodorus,

---

* Geogr., xv. 1-30. This notice was most probably derived from Kleitarchos, one of the companions of Alexander, as Strabo quotes him in another place (v. 2-6) as having mentioned the salt mines of India, *καὶ τοὺς ἐν Ἴνδοις ἅλας*.

† Hist. Nat., viii. 61.

‡ *Ibid.*, xxxi. 39. "Sunt et montes nativi salis, ut in Indis Oromenus."

and Curtius, that the Indian king who presented Alexander with these fighting dogs was *Sophites*, and *he*, therefore, must have been the king of *Albania*. For this name I propose to read *Labania*, by the simple transposition of the first two letters. *ΑΛΒΑΝ* would, therefore, become *ΛΑΒΑΝ* which at once suggests the Sanskrit word *lavana*, or 'salt,' as the original of this hitherto puzzling name. The mountain itself is named *Oromenus* by Pliny,* who notes that the kings of the country derived a greater revenue from the rock salt than from either gold or pearls. This name is probably intended for the Sanskrit *Raumaḳa*, which, according to the Pandits, is the name of the salt brought from the hill country of *Ruma*. H. H. Wilson, however, identifies *Ruma* with *Sâmbhar*;† and as *rauma* means "salt," it is probable that the term may have been applied to the *Sâmbhar* lake in Rajputana, as well as to the Salt Range of hills in the Panjâb.‡

The historians of Alexander have preserved several curious particulars regarding Sophites and the country and people over which he ruled. Of the king himself, Curtius§ records that he was preeminent amongst the barbarians for beauty; and Diodorus|| adds, that he was six feet in height. I possess a coin of fine Greek workmanship, bearing

---

* Hist. Nat., xxxi. 39. "Sunt et montes nativi salis, ut in Indis Oromenus."

† See his Sanskrit Dictionary *in voce. Ruma, Rauma, Raumaḳa*.

‡ See Maps Nos. V. and VI. § Vita Alex., ix. 1.

|| Hist., xvii. 49.

a helmeted head on one side, and on the reverse a cock standing, with the legend *ΣΩΦΥΤΟΥ*, which, there seems good reason to believe, must have belonged to this Indian prince. The face is remarkable for its very striking and peculiar features. The subjects of Sophites also were distinguished by personal beauty, which, according to Diodorus, they endeavoured to preserve, by destroying all their children who were not well formed. Strabo relates the same thing of the *Kathœi*, but, as he adds, that they elected the handsomest person for their king,* his account must be referred to the subjects of Sophites, as the *Kathœi* of Sangala had no king. There is, however, so much confusion between all the authorities in their accounts of the *Kathœi* and of the subjects of Sophites, that it seems highly probable that they were one and the same people. They were certainly neighbours; and as both of them would appear to have had the same peculiar customs, and to have been equally remarkable for personal beauty, I conclude that they must have been only different tribes of the same race of people.

2. BUKEPHALA, OR DILÀWAR.

The scene of Alexander's battle with Porus has long engaged the attention, and exercised the ingenuity, of the learned. The judicious Elphinstone† placed it opposite to Jalâlpur; but Burnes‡ con-

* Geogr., xv. 1, 30.
† Elphinstone's 'Kabul,' i. 109.
‡ 'Travels in Panjab, Bokhara, etc.,' ii. 49.

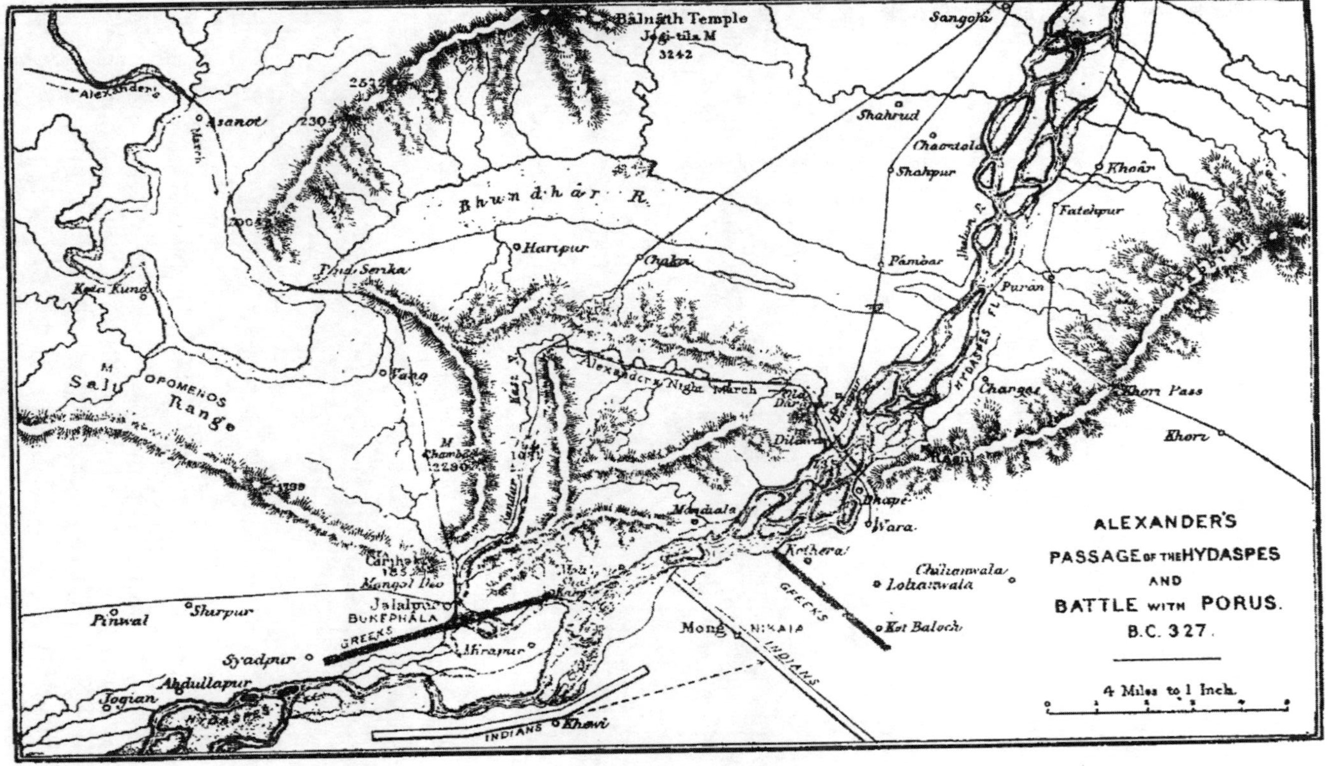
ALEXANDER'S
PASSAGE OF THE HYDASPES
AND
BATTLE WITH PORUS.
B.C. 327.
4 Miles to 1 Inch.
Bâlnâth Temple
Jogi-tila M
3242
Sangohi
Shahrud
Shahpur
Khoâr
Fatehpur
Bhundhâr R.
Haripur
Chaki
Pâmbar
Puran
HYDASPES FL.
Asanot
Alexander's
March
2532
2304
Kota Kung
Vang
OPOMENOS
Range
Sal
Alexander's Night March
Changar
Khori Pass
Khori
Dilawar
Rasul
Bhape
Wara
Mandiala
Kothera
Chilianwala
Lohanwala
Kot Baloch
GREEKS
Mong
NIKAIA
INDIANS
Jalalpur
BUKEPHALA
Mangol Deo
Pinwal
Shrpur
Syadpur
Mirapur
Abdullapur
Jogian
HYDASPES
Khewi

cluded that it must have been near Jhelam, because that place is on the great road from Tartary, which appears to have been followed by Alexander. In 1836 the subject was discussed by General Court,* whose early military training, and unequalled opportunities for observation during a long residence in the Panjâb, gave him the best possible means of forming a sound opinion. General Court fixed the site of Alexander's camp at Jhelam, his passage of the river at Khilipatam, 3 kos, or 6 miles, above Jhelam, the scene of his battle with Porus at Patti-koti on the Jaba Nadi, 8 miles to the east of Jhelam, and the position of Nikæa at *Vessa*, or *Bhesa*, which is 3 miles to the south-east of *Pathi* or *Patti-koti*. The late Lord Hardinge took great interest in the subject, and twice conversed with me about it in 1846 and 1847. His opinion agreed with mine that the camp of Alexander was most probably near Jalâlpur. In the following year, General Abbott† published an elaborate disquisition on the battle-field of Alexander and Porus, in which he placed the camp of the former at Jhelam, and of the latter on the opposite bank near Norangabad. The passage of the river he fixed at *Bhuna*, about 10 miles above Jhelam, and the field of battle near Pakrâl, about 3 miles to the north of Sukchenpur. In this state

* 'Journal of the Asiatic Society,' Bengal, 1836, pp. 472, 473.

† *Ibid.*, 1848, part ii. p. 619.

the question remained until the end of 1863, when my tour through the Panjâb gave me an opportunity of examining at leisure the banks of the Hydaspes from Jalâlpur to Jhelam.

Before discussing Alexander's movements, I think it best to describe the different places on the line of the river, between Jhelam and Jalâlpur, with the approaches to them from the westward. When we have thus ascertained the site that will best agree with the recorded descriptions of Bukephala, we shall then be in a better position for deciding the rival claims of Jhelam and Jalâlpur as the site of Alexander's camp. The distances that I shall make use of in this discussion are all taken from actual measurements.*

The town of Jhelam is situated on the west bank of the river, 30 miles to the north-east of Jalâlpur, and exactly 100 miles to the north-north-west of Lahor. The remains of the old town consist of a large ruined mound, to the west of the present city, about 1300 feet square and 30 feet high, which is surrounded by fields covered with broken bricks and pottery. The square mound I take to be the ruins of the citadel, which is said to have been called *Puta*. Numbers of old coins are still discovered in the mound after rain; but those which I was able to collect were limited to the mintages of the later Indo-Scythians, the Kabul-Brahmans, and the princes of

* See No. VII. Map of 'Alexander's Passage of the Hydaspes.'

Kashmir. As similar and even earlier coins are described by Court and Abbott to have been found in great numbers in previous years, it is certain that the city must have been in existence as early as the first century before Christ. But the advantages of its situation, on one of the two principal lines of road across the North Panjâb, are so great that it must, I think, have been occupied at a very early date. This opinion is confirmed by the numbers of large bricks that have been dug out of the old mound.

The ruined city near Dârâpur, which has been described by Burnes* and Court,† is situated on the west bank of the river, 20 miles below Jhelam, and 10 miles above Jalâlpur. In their time, the old mound was unoccupied, but about 1832 A.D. the people of Dilâwar abandoned their village on a hill to the west, and settled on the site of the ruined city. Before that time, the place was usually called *Pind*, or "the mound," although its true name is said to have been Udamnagar, or Udinagar. The same name is also given by Burnes, but Court, who twice alludes to these ruins, mentions no name, unless he includes them under that of *Gagirakhi*, the ruins of which he describes as extending along the banks "of the Hydaspes from near Jalâlpur to Dârâpur." According to this account, the ruins would not be less than 6 or 7 miles in length. I think it probable that there has been some confusion between two

* 'Travels in Panjâb, Bokhara, etc.,' ii. 51.

† Journ. Asiat. Soc. Bengal, 1836, 472, 473

different places, which have here been joined together as one continuous extent of ruins. *Girjhâk*, which I take to be the original of Court's *Gagirakhi,* is an old ruined fort on the top of the hill to the north of Jalâlpur, to which the people assign a fabulous extent; but it is at least 8 miles from *Dârâpur,* and is, besides, separated from it by the deep Kandar ravine, and by the precipitous range of hills at whose west foot Dilâwar is situated. Burnes also describes the old city as extending "for three or four miles." But this is certainly an exaggeration, as I was unable to trace the ruins for more than one mile in length by half a mile in breadth. The ruins consist of two large mounds just half a mile apart, with two smaller mounds about midway between them. The south mound on which Dilâwar is situated, is about 500 feet square at top, and 1100 or 1200 feet at base, with a height of 50 or 60 feet. The north mound, on which old Dârâpur stands, is 600 feet square, and from 20 to 30 feet in height. Between these mounds the fields are covered with broken bricks and pottery, and the whole place is said to be the ruins of a single city. The walls of the Dilâwar houses are built of the large old bricks dug out of this mound, which are of two sizes, one of 11½ by 8¼ by 3 inches, and the other of only half this thickness. Old coins are found in great numbers in the Dilâwar mound, from which the Jalâlpur bazar is said to be supplied, just as Pind Dâdan is supplied from the ruins of Jobnâthnagar. The coins which I obtained belonged to the first Indo-Scythians, the Kabul-Brahmans, the kings of Kashmir, and the *Karlûki Hazâra* chiefs, Hasan and his son Muhammad. The site, therefore, must have been occupied certainly as early as the second century before the Christian era. Its foundation is attributed to Raja Bharati, whose age is not known. I conclude, however, that the dominating position of Dilâwar, which commands the passage of the Jhelam at the point where the lower road from the west leaves the hills, just below the mouth of the Bunhâr river, must have led to its occupation at a very early period.

The town of Jalâlpur is situated on the west bank of the Jhelam at the point where the Kandar ravine joins the old bed of the river. The stream is now 2 miles distant, but the intervening ground, though partially covered with small trees, is still very sandy. The town is said to have been named in honour of Akbar, in whose time it was most probably a very flourishing place. But since the desertion of the river, and more especially since the foundation of Pind Dâdan, the place has been gradually decaying, until it now contains only 738 houses, with about 4000 inhabitants. From the appearance of the site, I estimated that the town might formerly have been about three or four times its present size. The houses are built on the last slope at the extreme east end of the salt range, which rises gradually to a height of 150 feet above the road. Its old Hindu name is said to have been *Girjhâk,* and as this name is found in Abul Fazl's 'Ayin Akbari'* as *Kerchak* (read *Girjak*) of Sindh Sâgar, we have a proof that it was in use until the time of Akbar, when it was changed to Jalâlpur. But the people still apply the name of *Girjhâk* to the remains of walls on the top of the Mangal-De hill, which rises 1100 feet above Jalâlpur. According to tradition, *Girjhâk* extended to the west-north-west as far as the old temple of Bâghanwâla, a distance of 11 miles. But this is only the usual exaggeration of ignorance that is told of all ancient sites. There is no doubt that the city did once extend to the westward for some considerable distance, as the ground on that side is thickly strewn with broken pottery for about half a mile. Its antiquity is undoubted, as the coins which it yields reach back to the times of Alexander's successors. But I believe that it is much older, as its favourable position at the south-east end of the lower road would certainly have led to its occupation at a very early period. I think, therefore, that it may be identified with the *Girivraja* of the Râmâyana. Tradition has preserved the name of only one king, named *Kâmkamârath*, who is said to have been the sister's son of *Moga*, the founder of Mong. Mogal Beg† writes the name *Ghir-Jehâk*, and it is so written by some of the people of the place, as if it was derived from *Giri-Zohâk*, or "Zohâk's Hill."

---

* Gladwyn's Translation, ii. 263.

† Manuscript Map of the Panjâb and Kabul Valley, by Wilford, from the surveys of Mirza Mogal Beg, in my possession.

But the usual spelling, which accords with the pronunciation, is Jhâk.

From Jhelam to Jalâlpur the course of the river is from north-east to south-west, between two nearly parallel ranges of mountains, which are generally known as the Tila and Pabhi Hills. The Tila range, which is about thirty miles in length, occupies the west bank from the great east bend of the river below Mangala, to the bed of the Bunhâr river, 12 miles to the north of Jalâlpur. *Tila* means simply a "peak or hill," and the full name is *Gorakhnâth-ka-Tila.* The more ancient name was *Bâlnâth-ka-Tila.* Both of these are derived from the temple on the summit, which was formerly dedicated to the sun, as *Bâlnâth*, but is now devoted to the worship of *Gorakhnâth*, a form of Siva. The latter name, however, is very recent, as Mogal Beg, who surveyed the country between A.D. 1784 and 1794, calls the hill "*Jogion-di-Tibi,* or tower of the Jogis, whose chief is called *Bilnât.*" Abul Fazl* also mentions the "Cell of Balnât," and the attendant *Jogis*, or devotees, from whom the hill is still sometimes called *Jogi-tila.* But the name of Bâlnâth is most probably even older than the time of Alexander, as Plutarch† relates that, when Porus was assembling his troops to oppose Alexander, the royal elephant rushed up a hill sacred to the Sun, and in human accents exclaimed, "O great king, who art

* 'Ayin Akbari,' ii. 110.

† 'De Fluviis,' in voce "Hydaspes." Gegasios must be *Yayâti* or *Jajâti* in a Greek form.

descended from *Gegasios*, forbear all opposition to Alexander, for *Gegasios* himself was also of the race of Jove."

The "Hill of the Sun" is only a literal translation of *Bâlnâth-ka-Tila*, but Plutarch goes on to say that it was afterwards called the "Hill of the Elephant," which I take to be another proof of its identity with Bâlnâth, for as this name is commonly pronounced *Bilnât* by the people, and is so written by Mogal Beg, the Macedonians, who had just come through Persia, would almost certainly have mistaken it for *Fil-nath*, or *Pil-nath*, the "Elephant." But wherever Alexander's camp may have been, whether at Jhelam or Jalâlpur, this remarkable hill, which is the most commanding object within fifty miles of the Hydaspes, must certainly have attracted the attention of the Macedonians. Its highest peak is 3242 feet above the sea, or about 2500 feet above the level of the river.

The *Pabhi* range of hills, on the east bank of the river, stretches from the neighbourhood of Bhimbar to Rasûl, a length of 30 miles. This range is a very low one, as the highest point is not more than 1400 feet above the sea, and is less than 500 feet above the river; but the broken and difficult ground on both flanks of the hill presents a barrier quite as impassable as a much loftier range. Until the British occupation of the Panjâb, the Pabhi hills were crossed by only one carriage-road through the Khori Pass, 5 miles to the north-east of Rasûl, and bv one foot-path through the Khârian Pass, 10 miles to the south-east of Jhelam. But though the main road has since been carried through the latter pass, it is still liable to interruption after heavy rain.

In approaching the Hydaspes from the westward, Alexander had the choice of two different lines, which are distinguished by Baber as the upper and lower roads. From the Indus to Hasan Abdâl, or Shahdheri, the two lines were the same. From the latter place, the upper road proceeded by the Mârgala Pass through Râwal Pindi and Mânikyâla to Dhamâk and Bakrâla, from which place it descended by the bed of the Kâhan river, through a gap in the Tila range, to Rohtâs, and from thence over an open plain to Jhelam. From Bakrâla there was also a foot-path to Jhelam, which crossed the Tila range about 6 miles to the north-east of Rohtâs, but this pass was always a dangerous one for horses and camels, and was difficult even for foot passengers. The length of this upper road from Shah-dheri, viâ Rohtâs, to Jhelam, was 94 miles; but this has since been shortened to 87 miles by the new road, which avoids the two long *détours* by Rohtâs and Dhamâk.

From Taxila, or Shah-dheri, the lower road proceeds viâ the Mârgala Pass to Jangi, from whence it strikes off viâ Chaontra to Dudhiâl. From this point the road branches into two lines, that to the south proceeding by Chakowâl and the salt mines to Pind Dâdan and Ahmadabad, and that to the east proceeding viâ Asanot and the Bunhâr river to Dilâwar, opposite Rasûl, or viâ Asanot and Vang to Jalâlpur. From Shah-dheri to Dudhiâl the distance is 55 miles, from thence to Asanot 33 miles, and thence to Dilâwar, or Jalâlpur, each 21 miles, the whole distance by this route being 118 miles. But this distance would be shortened to 114 miles by the traveller proceeding direct from the foot of the Salt Range to Jalâlpur. There is also a third line, which branches off from the upper road at Mandra, 6 miles to the south of the Mânikyâla tope, and proceeds viâ Chakowâl and Pind Dâdan to Jalâlpur. By this route the whole distance from Shah-dheri to Jalâlpur is 116¾ miles, or only 112¾ by leaving the line at the foot of the Salt Range and proceeding direct to Jalâlpur. The respective distances by these three different routes are 109, 114, and 112¾ miles, the mean distance being 112¼ miles.

Now, the distance from Taxila to the Hydaspes is given by Pliny,* from the measurement by Alexander's surveyors, Diognetes and Beiton, at 120 Roman miles, which are equal to 110⅓ English miles, at the value of 0.9193 each, as fixed in Smith's 'Dictionary of Antiquities.' As all the copies of Pliny give the same number, we must accept it as the actual measurement of the route that was followed by Alexander from Taxila to his camp on the Hydaspes. In comparing this distance with those already given from Shah-dheri to Jhelam and Jalâlpur, we must unhesitatingly reject Jhelam,

---

* Hist. Nat., vi. 21, "Ad Hydaspen fluvium clarum, cxx. mill."

which is no less than 16 miles short of the recorded distance, while Jalâlpur differs from it by less than 2 miles. But there is another objection which is equally fatal to the claims of Jhelam. According to Strabo,* "the direction of Alexander's march, as far as the Hydaspes, was, for the most part, towards the *south;* after that, to the Hypanis, it was more towards the *east.*" Now, if a line drawn on the map from Ohind on the Indus, through Taxila to Jhelam, be continued onwards, it will pass through Gujarat and Sodhra to Jâlandhar and Sarhind. As this is the most northerly road to the Ganges that Alexander could possibly have taken, his route by Jhelam would have been in *one continuous straight line*, which is in direct opposition to the explicit statement of Strabo. But if we adopt Jalâlpur this difficulty will be obviated, as the change in the direction would have been as much as 25° more easterly.† There is also a third objection to Jhelam, which, though not entitled to the same weight as either of the preceding, is still valuable as an additional testimony on the same side. According to Arrian, the fleet, on descending the Hydaspes from Nikæa, reached the capital of Sopeithes on the third day. Now, I have already shown that the residence of Sopeithes must have been at *Jobnâthnagar*, or Ahmedabad, which is just three days' distance for a laden boat from Jalâlpur, but is six days from Jhelam. As the

* Geogr., xv. 1, 32.
† See Map No. V.

evidence in each of these three separate tests is as directly in favour of Jalâlpur as it is strongly opposed to Jhelam, I think that we are fully justified in accepting the latter as the most probable site of Alexander's camp.

We have now to examine how the river and the country about Jalâlpur will agree with the recorded accounts of Alexander's operations in his passage of the Hydaspes and subsequent battle with Porus. According to Arrian* "there was a high wooded promontory on the bank of the river, 150 stadia, or just 17¼ miles above the camp, and immediately opposite to it there was a thickly-wooded island." Curtius† also mentions the wooded island as "well fitted for masking his operations." "There was also," he adds, "not far from the spot where he was encamped, a very deep ravine (*fossa prœalla*), which not only screened the infantry but the cavalry too." We learn from Arrian‡ that this ravine was not near the river because "Alexander marched at *some distance from the bank*, lest the enemy should discern that he was hastening towards the promontory and island." Now, there is a ravine—to the north of Jalâlpur which exactly suits the descriptions of both historians. This ravine is the bed of the Kandar Nala, which has a course of 6 miles from

---

* 'Anabasis,' v. 11. *Ἀπέχει δὲ ἥ τε ἄκρα καὶ ἡ νῆσος τοῦ μεγάλου στρατοπέδου ἐς πεντήκοντα καὶ ἑκατὸν σταδίους.*

† Vita Alex., viii. 13, "tegendis insidiis apta."

‡ 'Anabasis,' v. 12, *ἀπέχων τῆς ὄχθης.*

its source down to Jalâlpur, where it is lost in a waste of sand. Up this ravine there has always been a passable but difficult road towards Jhelam. From the head of the Kandar, which is 1080 feet above the sea, and 345 above the river, this road proceeds for 3 miles in a northerly direction down another ravine called the Kasi, which then turns suddenly to the east for 6½ miles, and then again 1½ mile to the south, where it joins the Jhelam immediately below Dilâwar, the whole distance from Jalâlpur being exactly 17 miles. I marched along this ravine road myself, for the purpose of testing the possibility of Alexander's march; and I satisfied myself that there was no difficulty in it except the fatigue of making many little ascents and descents in the first half, and of wading through much heavy sand in the latter half. The ravine lies "at some distance from the bank" as described by Arrian, as the bend in the Kasi is 7 miles from the Jhelam. It is also "a very deep ravine," as described by Curtius, as the hills on each hand rise from 100 to 250 and 300 feet in height. Therefore, in the three leading particulars which are recorded of it, this ravine agrees most precisely with the accounts of the ancient historians.*

Amongst the minor particulars, there is one which seems to me to be applicable only to that part of the river immediately above Jalâlpur. Arrian†

* See Map No. VII.

† 'Anabasis,' v. ii. *Παρὰ πᾶσαν δὲ τὴν ὄχθην φυλακα τε αὐτῷ καθεστηκυῖαι ἦσαν, διαλείπουσαι ὅσον ξύμμετρον ἐς τὸ*

records that Alexander placed running sentries along the bank of the river, at such distances that they could see each other, and communicate his orders. Now, I believe that this operation could not be carried out in the face of an observant enemy along any part of the river bank, excepting only that one part which lies between Jalâlpur and Dilâwar. In all other parts, the west bank is open and exposed, but in this part alone the wooded and rocky hills slope down to the river, and offer sufficient cover for the concealment of single sentries. As the distance along the river bank is less than 10 miles, and was probably not more than 7 miles from the east end of the camp, it is easy to understand why Alexander placed them along this line instead of leaving them on the much longer route, which he was to march himself. Another minor particular is the presence of a rock in the channel by the river, on which, according to Curtius, one of the boats was dashed by the stream. Now, rocks are still to be found in the river only at Kotera, Meriâla, Malikpur, and Shah Kubir, all of which places are between Dilâwar and Jalâlpur. The village of Kotera is situated at the end of a long wooded spur, which juts out upon the river just one mile below Dilâwar. This wooded jutting spur, with its adjacent rock, I would identify with the *ἄκρα*, or promontory of Arrian, and the *petra* of Curtius.* Beyond the rock there was a large

---

ξυνορᾷν τε ἀλλήλους καὶ καταχοὺειν εὐπετῶς ὁπόθεν τι παραγγέλλοιτο.

* Arrian, 'Anabasis,' v. ii., *ἆκρα ἦν ἀνέχουσα τῆς ὄχθης*

wooded island which screened the foot of the promontory from the observation of the opposite bank. There are many islands in this part of the Jhelam, but when a single year is sufficient to destroy any one of these rapidly formed sandbanks, we cannot, after the lapse of more than 2000 years, reasonably expect to find the island of Alexander. But in 1849, opposite Kotera, there was such an island, 2½ miles in length and half a mile in breadth, which still exists as a large sandbank. As the passage was made in the height of the rainy season, the island, or large sandbank, would naturally have been covered with tamarisk bushes, which would have been sufficiently high to screen the movements of infantry and dismounted cavalry.

The position of the two camps I believe to have been as follows:*—Alexander, with about 50,000 men, including 5000 Indian auxiliaries under Mophis of Taxila, had his head-quarters at Jalâlpur, and his camp probably extended for about 6 miles along the bank of the river, from Shah Kabir, 2 miles to the north-east of Jalâlpur, down to Syadpur, 4 miles to the west-south-west. The head-quarters of Porus must have been about Muhâbatpur, 4 miles to the west-south-west of Mong, and 3 miles to the south-east of Jalâlpur. His army of nearly 50,000 men,

---

τοῦ 'Υδάσπου. Curtius, Vita Alex., viii. 11, "Unâ ergo navi, quam petrae fluctus illiserat, hærente cæteræ evadunt."

* See Map No. VII.

including elephant-riders, archers, and charioteers, must have occupied about the same extent as the Macedonian army, and would, therefore, have extended about 2 miles above, and 4 miles below Muhâbatpur. In these positions, the left flank of Alexander's camp would have been only 6 miles from the wooded promontory of Kotera, where he intended to steal his passage across the river, and the right flank of the Indian camp would have been 2 miles from Mong, and 6 miles from the point opposite Kotera.

As my present object is to identify the scene of Alexander's battle with Porus, and not to describe the fluctuations of the conflict, it will be sufficient to quote the concise account of the operation which is given by Plutarch from Alexander's own letters: —"He took advantage of a dark and stormy night, with part of his infantry and a select body of cavalry, to gain a little island in the river, at some distance from the Indians ; when he was there, he and his troops were attacked with a most violent wind and rain, accompanied with dreadful thunder and lightning." But in spite of the storm and rain, they pushed on, and wading through the water breast-high reached the opposite bank of the river in safety. "When they were landed," says Plutarch,* who is

---

* 'Life of Alexander.' Sir W. Napier has paid a just tribute to the skill of both generals. Speaking of Alexander's passage of the Granicus, he says that it cannot "be compared for soldierly skill with his after

still quoting Alexander's letters, "he advanced with the horse 20 stadia before the foot, concluding, that if the enemy attacked him with their cavalry he should be greatly their superior, and that if they made a movement with their infantry his own would come up in time enough to receive them." From Arrian* we learn that, as soon as the army had begun fording the channel, between the island and the main land, they were seen by the Indian scouts, who at once dashed off to inform Porus. When the ford was passed with some difficulty, Alexander halted to form his little army of 6000 infantry and about 10,000 cavalry. He then "marched swiftly forward with 5000 horse, leaving the infantry to follow him leisurely and in order." While this was going on, Porus had detached his son with two or three thousand horse and one hundred and twenty chariots to oppose Alexander. The two forces met at 20 stadia, or 2¼ miles, from the place of crossing, or about two miles to the north-east of Mong. Here the chariots proved useless on the wet and slippery clay, and were nearly all captured. The conflict, however, must have been a sharp one, as Alexander's favourite charger, Bukephalus, was mortally wounded by the young prince, who was himself slain, together with 400 of his men. When Porus heard of the death of his son, he marched

---

passage of the Hydaspes, and defeat of Porus. Before that great man he could not play the same daring game." ('London and Westminster Review,' 1838, p. 377).

* 'Anabasis,' v. 13.

at once against Alexander with the greater part of his army; but when he came to a plain, where the ground was not difficult and slippery, but firm and sandy, and fitted for the evolutions of his chariots, he halted and arrayed his troops ready for battle. His 200 elephants were drawn up in front of the infantry about one plethron, or 100 feet apart, and the chariots and cavalry were placed on the flanks. By this arrangement, the front of the army facing north-east must have occupied an extent of about 4 miles, from the bank of the river to near Lakhnawâli, the centre of the line being, as nearly as possible, on the site of the present town of Mong. Around this place the soil is "firm and sound;" but towards the north-east, where Alexander encountered the young Indian prince, the surface is covered with a hard red clay, which becomes both heavy and slippery after rain.*

When Alexander saw the Indian army drawn up in battle array, he halted to wait for his infantry, and to reconnoitre the enemy's position. As he was much superior to Porus in cavalry, he resolved not to attack the centre, where the formidable line of elephants were supported by masses of infantry, but to fall upon both flanks and throw the Indians into disorder. The right wing, led by Alexander him-

* I speak from actual observation of the field of Chilianwâla for some days after the battle, when the country had been deluged with rain. Both battles were fought on the same ground, between the town of Mong and the southern end of the Pabhi hills.

self, drove back the enemy's horse upon the line of elephants, which then advanced and kept the Macedonians in check for some time. "Wherever Porus saw cavalry advancing, he opposed elephants, but these slow and unwieldy animals could not keep pace with the rapid evolutions of the horse."* At length the elephants, wounded and frightened, rushed madly about, trampling down friends as well as foes. Then the small body of Indian horse being surrounded, was overpowered by the Macedonians, and nearly all slain; and the large mass of Indian infantry, which still held out, being vigorously attacked on all sides by the victorious horse, broke their ranks and fled. Then, says Arrian,† "Kraterus, and the captains who were with him on the other side of the river, no sooner perceived the victory to incline to the Macedonians, than they passed over, and made a dreadful slaughter of the Indians in pursuit."

From the last statement which I have quoted, it is clear that the battle-field was within sight of Alexander's camp. Now, this is especially true of the plain about Mong, which is within easy ken of the east of Alexander's camp at Shah-Kabîr, the nearest point being only 2 miles distant. With this last strong evidence in favour of Jalâlpur as the site of Alexander's camp, I close my discussion of this interesting question. But as some readers, like Mr.

---

* Curtius, Vita Alex., viii. 14, 27.

† 'Anabasis,' v. 18.

Grote,* the historian of Greece, may still think that General Abbott has shown "highly plausible reasons" in support of his opinion that Alexander's camp was at Jhelam, I may here point out that the village of Pabrâl, which he has selected as the battle-field, is not less than 14 miles from Jhelam, and therefore quite beyond the ken of Alexander's camp. I may quote also Abbott's own admission that the bed of the *Sukhetr* river, a level plain of sand one mile in width, "is a torrent after heavy rain, and is so full of quicksands as to be unsuited to military operations." Now, this very *Sukhetr* river actually lies between Pabrâl and the site of the Indian camp opposite Jhelam, and as we know that a heavy storm of rain had fallen during the preceding night, the Sukhetr would have been an impossible torrent at the time of the battle. And so also would have been the Jada river, which joins the Jhelam just below the Sukhetr. With these two intervening rivers, which, whether wet or dry, would have been obstacles equally great to the march of the Indian army, and more specially to the passage of the Indian army, and more specially to the passage of the war-chariots, I am quite satisfied that the battle-field could not have been to the north of the Sukhetr river.

The position of Bukephala still remains to be discussed. According to Strabo,† the city of Buke-

* 'History of Greece,' xii. 308, note.

† Geogr., xv. 1, 29.

phala was built on the west bank of the river, where Alexander had crossed it; but Plutarch* says that it was near the Hydaspes, in the place where Bukephalus was buried. Arrian,† however, states that it was built on the site of his camp, and was named Bukephala in memory of his horse. Diodorus, Curtius, and Justin leave the exact position undecided; but they all agree that it was on the opposite bank of the river to Nikæa, which was certainly built on the field of battle. With these conflicting statements alone to guide us, it is difficult to arrive at any positive conclusion. According as we follow Strabo or Arrian, we must place *Bukephala* at Dilâwar, or at Jalâlpur. Both places are equidistant from the battle-field of Mong, which I take without much hesitation to be the site of Nikæa. If the two cities were built on the same plan, which is not improbable, then Dilâwar would have the preferable claim to represent Bukephala, as its ruined mound is of the same size and height as that of Mong. I have already noticed in another place the possibility that Bugiâd, or Bugiâl, the name of the district in which Dilâwar is situated, may be only an abbreviation of Bukephâlia by the easy elision of the *ph*. But this is only a guess, and I have nothing else to offer on the subject, save the fact that the ancient name of Jalâlpur was certainly *Girjâk*, while that of Dilâwar is quite uncertain, as *Udinagar* is applied to at least three different places. The claims of

* 'Life of Alexander.'

† 'Anabasis,' v. 19.

Dilâwar and Jalâlpur are perhaps equally balanced, excepting in the one important point of position, in which the latter has a most decided advantage; and as this superiority would not have escaped the keen observation of the founder of Alexandria, I think that Jalâlpur must be the site of the famous city of Bukephala.

Nikœa, or Mong.

The position of Mong has already been described, but I may repeat that it is 6 miles to the east of Jalâlpur, and the same distance to the south of Dilâwar. The name is usually pronounced *Mong*, or *Mung*, but it is written without the nasal, and is said to have been founded by Raja *Moga* or *Muga*. He is also called Raja *Sankhâr*, which I take to mean king of the *Sakas*, or *Sacœ*. His brother Râma founded Râmpur, or Râmnagar, the modern Rasul, which is 6 miles to the north-east of Mong, and exactly opposite Dilâwar. His sister's son, named Kâmkamârath, was Raja of Girjâk or Jalâlpur. The old ruined mound on which Mong is situated, is 600 feet long by 400 feet broad and 50 feet high, and is visible for many miles on all sides. It contains 975 houses built of large old bricks and 5000 inhabitants, who are chiefly Jâts. The old wells are very numerous, their exact number, according to my informant, being 175.

I have already stated that I take Mong to be the site of Nikæa, the city which Alexander built on the scene of his battle with Porus. The evidence on this point is, I think, as complete as could be wished; but I have still to explain how the name of Nikæa could have been changed to Mong. The tradition that the town was founded by Raja Moga is strongly corroborated by the fact that *Maharaja Moga* is mentioned in Mr. Roberts's Taxila inscription. Now, *Moga* is the same name as *Moa*, and the coins of *Moa*, or Mauas are still found in Mong. But the commonest Greek monogram on these coins forms the letters NIK, which I take to be the abbreviation of *Nikœa,* the place of mintage. If this inference be correct, as I believe it is, then *Nikœa* must have been the principal mint-city of the great king *Moga,* and therefore a place of considerable importance. As the town of Mong is traditionally attributed to Raja Moga as the founder, we may reasonably conclude that he must have rebuilt or increased the place under the new name of *Moga-grama,* which in the spoken dialects, would be shortened to *Mogaon* and *Mong.* Coins of all the Indo-Scythian princes are found at Mong in considerable numbers, and I see no reason to doubt that the place is as old as the time of Alexander. The copper coins of the Nameless Indo-Scythian king especially are found in such numbers at Mong that they are now commonly known in the neighbourhood as *Monga-sâhis.*

Gujarât.

The city of Gujarât is situated 9 miles to the west of the Chenâb river, on the high-road from Jhelam to Lahor. The city is said to have been first called *Hairât*, and the district *Hairât-des.** Its original foundation is ascribed to a Surajbansi Rajput named *Bachan Pâl*, of whom nothing more is known; and its restoration is attributed to *Ali Khân*, a *Gujar*, whose name is strangely like that of *Alakhâna*, the Raja of Gurjjara, who was defeateed by Sangkara Varmma between A.D. 883 and 901. Following up these traditions, Gujarât is said to have been destroyed in A.D. 1303, and to have been rebuilt by the Gujars in A.H. 996, or A.D. 1588, during the reign of Akbar.

Sâkala, or Sangala.

The *Sangala* of Alexander has long ago been recognized in the *Sâkala* of the Brahmans and the *Sâgal* of the Buddhists; but its position would still perhaps have remained undetermined, had it not fortunately been visited by the Chinese pilgrim Hwen Thsang in A.D. 630. Both Arrian and Curtius place Sangala to the east of the Hydraotes, or Râvi; but the itinerary of Hwen Thsang shows that it was to the west of the Râvi, and as nearly as possible in the position of the present *Sangla-wala-Tiba*, or "Sangala Hill." I first became acquainted with this place in 1839, when I obtained a copy of Mogal Beg's manuscript map, compiled by Wilford, who has three times described its position in the 'Asiatic Researches.'† But I was

---

* I take *Hairât* to be only an aspirated form of *Arâtta*.

† Vols. v. 282; vi. 520; ix. 53.

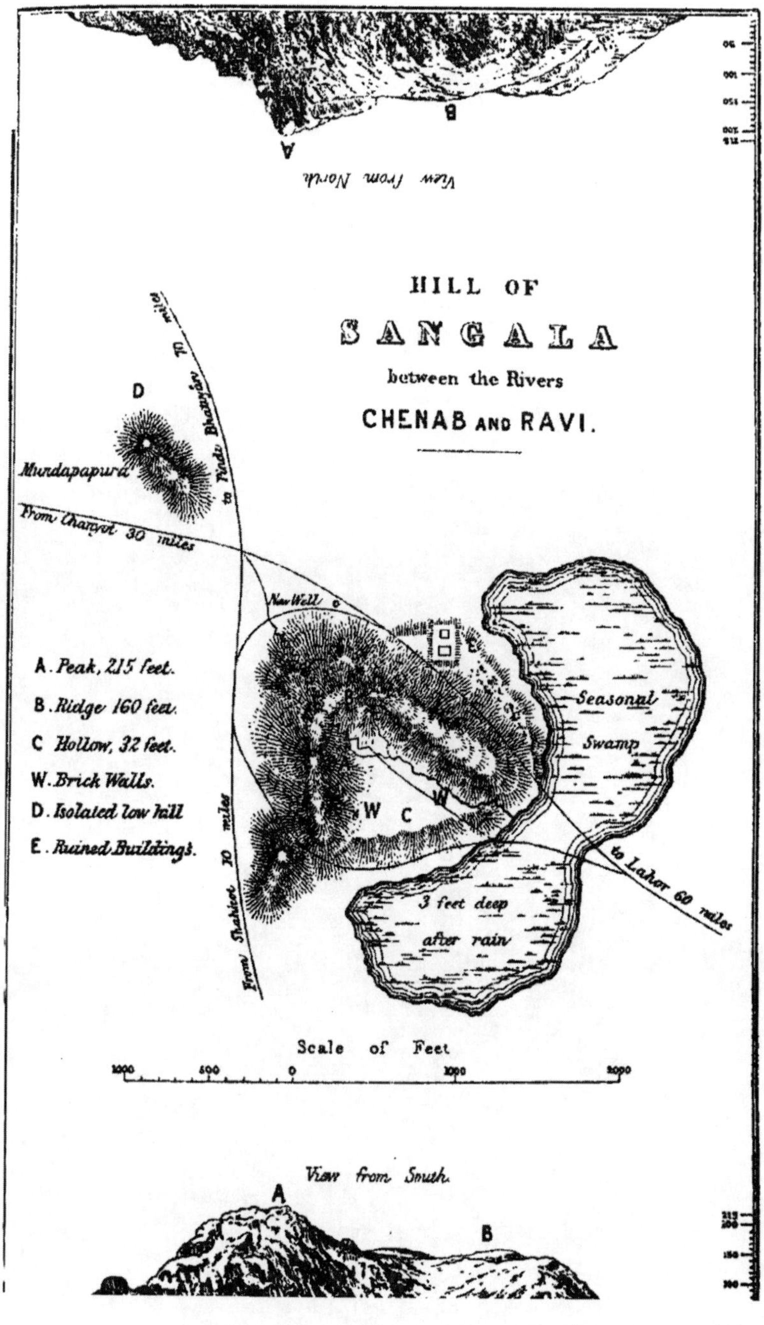
View from North
A
B
HILL OF
SANGALA
between the Rivers
CHENAB AND RAVI.
D
Mundapapura
to Pindi Bhattyân 70 miles
From Chaniot 30 miles
New Well
E
Seasonal
Swamp
A. Peak, 215 feet.
B. Ridge 160 feet.
C Hollow, 32 feet.
W. Brick Walls.
D. Isolated low hill
E. Ruined Buildings.
W
C
to Lahor 60 miles
From Shahkot 70 miles
3 feet deep
after rain
Scale of Feet
1000
500
0
1000
2000
View from South.
A
B

not able to obtain any account of the place until 1854, when I heard from Colonel G. Hamilton, who had visited it, and from Captain Blagrave, who had surveyed it, that Sangala was a real hill with traces of buildings, and with a sheet of water on one side of it. During my tour through the Panjâb, I was able to visit the hill myself, and I am now satisfied that it must be the Sangala of Alexander, although the position does not agree with that which his historians have assigned to it.

In the time of Hwen Thsang *She-ḳie-lo*, or *Sâḳala*, was in ruins, and the chief town of the district was *Tse-ḳia*, or *Cheḳia*, which may also be read as *Dhaḳa* or Taka. The pilgrim places this new town at 15 *li*, or 2½ miles, to the north-east of *Sâḳala;* but as all the country within that range is open and flat, it is certain that no *town* could ever have existed in the position indicated. In the same direction, however, but at 19 miles, or 115 *li*, I found the ruins of a large town, called *Asarur*, which accord almost exactly with the pilgrim's description of the new town of *Tse-ḳia*. It is necessary to fix the position of this place, because Hwen Thsang's measurements, both coming and going, are referred to it and not to Sâkala. From Kashmir the pilgrim proceeded by Punach to Rajapura, a small town in the lower hills, which is now called Rajaori. From thence he travelled to the south-east over a mountain, and across a river called *Chen-ta-lo-po-ḳia*, which is the *Chandrabhâga*, or modern Chenâb, to *She-ye-pu-lo*, or *Jayapura* (probably Hâfizâbâd), where he slept for the night, and on the next day he reached *Tse-kia*, the whole distance being 700 *li*, or 116 miles. As a south-east direction would have taken the pilgrim to the east of the Râvi, we must look for some known point in his subsequent route as the best means of checking this erroneous bearing. This fixed point we find in *She-lan-to-lo*, the well-known *Jâlandhara*, which the pilgrim places at 500, plus 50, plus 140 or 150 *li*, or altogether between 690 and 700 *li* to the east of *Tse-kia*. This place was, therefore, as nearly as possible, equidistant from Rajaori and Jâlandhar. Now, Asarur is exactly 112 miles distant from each of these places in a direct line drawn on the map, and as it is undoubtedly a very old place of considerable size, I am satisfied that it must be the town of *Tse-kia* described by Hwen Thsang.

In A.D. 630 the pilgrim found the walls of *Sâkala* completely ruined, but their foundations still remained, showing a circuit of about 20 *li*, or 3⅓ miles. In the midst of the ruins there was still a small portion of the old city inhabited, which was only 6 or 7 *li*, or just one mile, in circuit. Inside the city there was a monastery of one hundred monks who studied the Hinayâna, or exoteric doctrines of Buddhism, and beside it there was a stupa, 200 feet in height, where the four previous Buddhas had left their footprints. At 5 or 6 *li*, or less than 1 mile, to the north-west, there was a second stupa, also about 200 feet high, which was built by King

Asoka on the spot where the four previous Buddhas had explained the law.

Sânglawâla Tiba is a small rocky hill forming two sides of a triangle, with the open side towards the south-east. The north side of the hill rises to a height of 215 feet, but the north-east side is only 160 feet. The interior area of the triangle slopes gradually down to the south-east till it ends abruptly in a steep bank 32 feet above the ground. This bank was once crowned with a brick wall, which I was able to trace only at the east end, where it joined the rock. The whole area is covered with brick ruins, amongst which I found two square foundations. The bricks are of a very large size, 15 by 9 by 3 inches. During the last fifteen years these bricks have been removed in great numbers. Nearly 4000 were carried to the large village of Marh, 6 miles to the north, and about the same number must have been taken to the top of the hill to form a tower for the survey operations. The base of the hill is from 1700 to 1800 feet on each side, or just 1 mile in circuit. On the east and south sides the approach to the hill is covered by a large swamp, half a mile in length, and nearly a quarter of a mile in breadth, which dries up annually in the summer, but during the seasonal rains has a general depth of about 3 feet. In the time of Alexander this must have been a fine sheet of water, which has been gradually lessened in depth by the annual washings of silt from the hill above. On the north-eastern side of the hill there are the remains of two large buildings, from which I obtained old bricks of the enormous size of 17½ by 11 by 3 inches. Close by there is an old well which was lately cleared out by some of the wandering tribes. On the north-western side, 1000 feet distant, there is a low ridge of rock called *Munda-ḳapura,* from 25 to 30 feet in height, and about 500 feet in length, which has formerly been covered with brick buildings. At 1¾ mile to the south, there is another ridge of three small hills, called *Arna* and little *Sângala.* All these hills are formed of the same dark grey rock as that of Chanyot and of the Karâna hills to the west of the Chenâb, which contains much iron, but is not worked on account of the want of fuel. The production of iron is noticed by Hwen Thsang.

In comparing this account with the description of the Chinese pilgrim, I only find two places that can be indentified. The first is the site of the modern town, which was about a mile in circuit, and was situated in the midst of the ruins. This I take to be the hill itself, which accords exactly with the description, and which would certainly have been occupied in preference to any part of the open plain below, on account of its security. The second is the stupa of Asoka, which was situated at rather less than 1 mile to the north-west of the monastery inside the town. This I would identify with the low ridge of rock on the north-west called *Mundapapura,* of which the highest point at the north-western end is 4000 feet, or more than three-quarters of a mile distant from the central point of the triangular area of the town. The plain on the north and west sides of the hill is strewn with broken pottery and fragments of brick for a considerable distance, showing that the town must once have extended in both of those directions. But the whole circuit of these remains did not appear to be more than 1½ or 1¼ miles, or about one-half of HwenThsang's measurement.

The Brahmanical accounts of Sâkala have been collected from the Mahâbhârata by Professor Lassen in his 'Pentapotamia Indica.'* According to that poem, Sâkala, the capital of the Madras, who are also called Jârtikas and Bâhîkas, was situated on the *Apagâ* rivulet to the west of the *Irâvati,* or Râvi river. It was approached from the east side by pleasant paths through the *Pilu* forest,

"Sami-*pilu* Kâriranâm vaneshu sukhavartmasu."

which Professor Lassen translates "per amœnas *sylvarum* tramites ambulantes." But the *Pilu,* or *Salvadora Persica*, is the commonest wood in this part of the Panjâb, and is specially abundant in the Rechna Doâb. In these "Pleasant paths" of the *Pilu* forest, the traveller was unfortunately liable to be despoiled of his clothes by robbers. This description by the author of the Mahâbhârata was fully verified by Hwen Thsang in A.D. 630, and again by myself in 1863. On leaving Sâkala, the Chinese pilgrim travelled eastward into a forest of *Po-lo-she* trees, where his party encountered fifty brigands,

* Pentapot. Ind., pp. 73, 74.

who robbed them of their clothes.* In November, 1863, I approached Sâkala from the east through a continuous wood of *Pilu* trees, and pitched my tent at the foot of the hill. During the night the tent was three times approached by parties of robbers who were detected by the vigilance of my watch dog. M. Julien has properly rendered Hwen Thsang *Po-lo-she* by *Palâsa,* the *Butea frondosa,* or *Dhâk* tree; but as the forest consisted of *Pilu* trees, both before and after the time of Hwen Thsang, I would suggest the propriety of correcting *Pi-lo-she* to *Pilo;* I conjecture that the Chinese editor of the pilgrim's life, who was most probably ignorant of the *Pilu,* substituted the well-known *Palâsa,* which is frequently mentioned by Hwen Thsang, under the belief that he was making an important and necessary correction.

The country is still well known as *Madr-des,* or the district of the *Madras,* which is said by some to extend from the Biâs to the Jhelam, but by others only to the Chenâb. Regarding the *Apagâ* rivulet, I believe that it may be recognized in the *Ayak Nadî,* a small stream which has its rise in the Jammu hills to the north-east of Syâlkot. After passing Syâlkot the Ayak runs westerly near Sodhra, where in the rainy season it throws off its superfluous water in the Chenâb. It then turns to the south-south-west past Banka and Nandanwâ to Bhutâla, and continues this same course till within a few miles of

* 'Hiouen Thsang,' i. 97.

Asarur. There it divides into two branches, which, after passing to the east and west of Asarur, rejoin at 2½ miles to the south of *Sângalawâla Tîba*. Its course is marked in the revenue survey maps for 15 miles to the south-west of Sângala, where it is called the Nananwâ canal. An intelligent man of Asarur informed me that he had seen the bed of the Nananwâ 20 kos to the south-west, and that he had always heard that it fell into the Râvi a long way off. This, then, must be Arrian's "small rivulet" near which Alexander pitched his camp, at 100 stadia, or 11½ miles, to the east of the Akesines, below its junction with the Hydaspes.* At that time, therefore, the water of the Ayak must have flowed for a long distance below Sângala, and most probably fell into the Râvi, as stated by my informant. Near Asarur and Sângala, the Ayak is now quite dry at all seasons; but there must have been water in it at Dhakawala only 24 miles above Asarur, even so late as the reign of Shâh Jahân, when his son Dârâ Shekoh drew a canal from that place to his hunting seat at Shekohpura, which is also called the Ayak, or Jhilri canal.

The Buddhist notices of Sâkala refer chiefly to its history in connection with Buddhism. There is the legend of the seven kings who went towards *Sâgal* to carry off Prabhâvati, the wife of king Kusa.† But the king, mounting an elephant, met

---

* 'Anabasis,' vi. 6.

† Hardy, 'Manual of Buddhism,' 263, note.

them outside the city, and cried out with so loud a voice, "I am Kusa," that the exclamation was heard over the whole world, and the seven kings fled away in terror. This legend may have some reference to the seven brothers and sisters of Amba-Kâpa, which is only 40 miles to the east of Sângala. Before the beginning of the Christian era *Sâgal* was the capital of Raja *Milinda*, whose name is still famous in all Buddhist countries as the skilful opponent of the holy Nagasena.* The territory was then called *Yona*, or *Yavana*, which might refer either to the Greek conquerors, or to their Indo-Scythian successors; but as Nagasena is said to have lived either 400 or 500 years after Buddha, the date of Milinda is uncertain. Milinda himself states that he was born at Alasadda, which was 200 *yojans*, or about 1400 miles, distant from Sâgal. He was therefore undoubtedly a foreigner; and, in spite of the exaggerated distance, I would identify his birthplace with Alexandria Opiane, at the foot of the Indian Caucasus, about 40 miles to the north of Kabul. At a somewhat *later* period, *Sâkala* was subject to *Mahirkul*, or *Mihirkul*, who lost his kingdom by an unsuccessful campaign against Balâditya, king of Magadha. But being afterwards set at liberty by the conqueror, he obtained possession of Kashmir by treachery. I know of no other mention of Sâkala until A.D. 633, when it was visited by Hwen Thsang, who describes the

* Hardy, Manual of Buddhism, 513.

neighbouring town of *Tse-kia* as the capital of a large kingdom, which extended from the Indus to the Byâs, and from the foot of the hills to the confluence of the five rivers.

The classical notices of Sângala are confined to the two historical accounts of Arrian and Curtius, and a passing mention by Diodorus. Curtius simply calls it "a great city defended not only by a wall, but by a swamp (*palus*)."* But the swamp was a deep one, as some of the inhabitants afterwards escaped by swimming across it (*paludem transnavere*). Arrian calls it a lake, λίμνη, but adds that it was not deep, that it was near the city wall, and that one of the gates opened upon it. He describes the city itself as strong both by art and nature, being defended by brick walls and covered by the lake. Outside the city there was a low hill, γήλοφος, which the Kathæans had surrounded with a triple line of carts for the protection of their camp.† This little hill I would identify with the low ridge to the north-west, called *Mundapapura*, which would certainly appear to have been outside the city walls, as the broken bricks and pottery do not extend so far.‡ I conclude that the camp on the hill was formed chiefly by the fugitives from other

---

* Vita Alex., ix. 1: "Ad magnam deinde urbem pervenit, non muro solum, sed etiam palude munitam."

† 'Anabasis,' v. 22: Κύκλῳ δὲ τοῦ γηλόφου ἁμάξας περιστήσαντες, ἐντός αὐτῶν ἐστρατοπέδευον, ὡς τριπλοῦν χάρακα προβεβλῆσθαι των ἁμαξῶν.

‡ See Map No. VIII.

places, for whom there was no room in the already crowded city. The hill must have been close to the city walls, because the Kathæans, after the second line of carts had been broken by the Greeks, fled into the city and shut the gates. It is clear, therefore, that the triple row of carts could only have surrounded the hill on three sides, and that the fourth side was open to the city. The hill was thus connected with the city as a temporary out-work, from which the defenders, if overpowered, could make their escape behind the walls. As the number of carts captured by Alexander was only 300, the hill must have been a very small one; for if we allow 100 carts to each line, the innermost line, where they were closely packed, at 10 feet per cart, could not have been more than 1000 feet in length round the three sides at the hase. Placing the middle row 50 feet beyond the inner one, its length would have been 1200 feet, and that of the outer row, at the same distance, would have been 1400 feet, or little more than a quarter of a mile. Now this accords so well with the size of the *Mundapapura* hill, that I feel considerable confidence in the accuracy of my identification. As these carts were afterwards used by Ptolemy to form a single line of barrier outside the lake, we obtain a limit to its size, as 300 carts would not have extended more than 5000 feet, or about 17 feet per cart, if placed end to end; but as there may have been numerous trees on the bank of the lake, the length of the barrier may be extended to about 6000 feet. Now it is remarkable that this is the exact length of this outer line according to my survey, which shows the utmost extent of the lake in the rainy season. I could find no trace of the rampart and ditch with which Alexander surrounded the town, but I was not disappointed, as the rains of two thousand years must have obliterated them long ago.

The Kathæans made an unsuccessful attempt to escape across the lake during the night, but they were checked by the barrier of carts, and driven back into the city. The walls were then breached by undermining, and the place was taken by assault, in which the Kathæans, according to Arrian, lost 17,000 slain, and 70,000 prisoners. Curtius, however, gives the loss of the Kathæans at 8000 killed. I am satisfied that Arrian's numbers are erroneous, either through error or exaggeration, as the city was a small one, and could not, at the ordinary rate of 400 or 500 square feet to each person, have contained more than 12,000 people. If we double or triple this for the influx of fugitives, the whole number would be about 30,000 persons. I should like, therefore, to read Arrian's numbers as 7000 slain and 17,000 prisoners. This would bring his number of slain into accord with Curtius, and his total number into accord with probability.

Both Curtius and Arrian agree in stating that Alexander had crossed the Hydraotes before he advanced against Sangala, which should therefore be to the east of that river. But the detailed measurements of Hwen Thsang are too precise, the statement of the Mahâbhârata is too clear, and the coincidence of name is too exact to be set aside lightly. Now, the accounts of both Arrian and Curtius show that Alexander was in full march for the Ganges when he heard "that certain free Indians and Kathæans were resolved to give him battle if he attempted to lead his army thither." Alexander no sooner heard this than he immediately directed his march against the Kathæans, that is, he changed the previous direction of his march, and proceeded towards Sangala. This was the uniform plan on which he acted during his campaign in Asia, to leave no enemy behind him. When he was in full march for Persia, he turned aside to besiege Tyre; when he was in hot pursuit of Bessus, the murderer of Darius, he turned to the south to subdue Drangiana and Arachosia; and when he was longing to enter India, he deviated from his direct march to besiege Aornos. With the Kathæans the provocation was the same. Like the Tyrians, the Drangians, and the Bazarians of Aornos, they wished to avoid rather than to oppose Alexander; but if attacked they were resolved to resist. Alexander was then on the eastern bank of the Hydraotes, or Râvi, and on the day after his departure from the river he came to the city of *Pimprama*, where he halted to refresh his soldiers, and on the third day reached Sangala. As he was obliged to halt after his first two marches, they must have been forced ones, of not less than 25 miles each, and his last may have been a common march of 12 or 15 miles. Sangala, therefore, must have been about 60 or 65 miles from the camp on the bank of the Hydraotes. Now this is the exact distance of the Sangala hill from Lahor which was most probably the position of Alexander's camp when he heard of the recusancy of the Kathæi. I believe, therefore, that Alexander at once gave up his march to the Ganges, and recrossed the Râvi to punish the people of Sangala for daring to withhold their submission.

Taki, or Asarur.

I have already mentioned Asarur as the probable position of Hwen Thsang's *Tse-kia,* which was the capital of the Panjâb in A.D. 633. It is situated about 2 miles to the south of the high-road between Lahor and Pindi Bhatiyân, being 45 miles from the former, and 24 from the latter place.* It is 19 miles distant from Sangala by the road, but not more than 16 miles in a direct line across the country. Nothing whatever is known of its ancient history, but the people say that it was originally called *Udamnagar,* or *Uda-Nagari,* and that it was deserted for many centuries, until Akbar's time, when Ugar Shah, a Dogar, built the Masjid, which still exists, on the top of the mound. The antiquity claimed for the place is confirmed by the large size of the bricks, 18 by 10 by 3 inches, which are found all over the ruins, and by the great number of Indo-Scythian coins that are discovered annually after heavy rain. It therefore reaches back to the first century before the Christian

* See Map No. VI.

era, and from its position I believe it to be the *Pimprama* of Alexander.

The ruins of Asarur consist of an extensive mound 15,600 feet, or nearly 3 miles in circuit. The highest point is in the north-west quarter, where the mound rises to 59 feet above the fields. This part, which I take to be the ancient palace, is 600 feet long and 400 feet broad, and quite regular in shape. It contains an old well 21 feet in diameter, which has not been used for many years, and is now dry. The palace is completely surrounded by a line of large mounds about 25 feet in height, and 8100 feet, or 1½ miles in circuit, which was evidently the stronghold or citadel of the place. The mounds are rounded and prominent, like the ruins of large towers or bastions. On the east and south sides of the citadel the mass of ruins sinks to 10 and 15 feet in height, but it is twice the size of the citadel, and is, no doubt, the remains of the old city. I could find no trace of any ancient buildings, as all the surface bricks have been long ago carried off to the neighbouring shrine of Ugar Shah at *Khângâh* Masrur; but amongst the old bricks forming the surrounding wall of the Masjid I found three moulded in different patterns, which could only have belonged to buildings of some importance. I found also a wedgeshaped brick 15 inches long and 3 inches thick, with a breadth of 10 inhes at the narrow end, and nearly 10½ inches at the broad end. This could only have been made for a stupa, or a well, but most probably for the latter, as the existing well is 21 feet in diameter. *Asarur* is now a small village of only 45 houses.

Hwen Thsang places *Tse-ḳia* at 14 or 15 *li*, or 2½ miles, to the north-east of *Sâḳala;* but as there are no traces of any former town in this position, I think it very probable that the true numbers should be 114 or 115 *li*, or 19 miles, which is just the distance between Sangala and Asarur by the road, although in a direct line it is not more than 16 miles. The circuit of *Tse-ḳia* was about 20 *li*, or upwards of three miles, which agrees sufficiently well with my measurement of the ruins of Asarur at 15,600 feet, or just three miles. At the time of Hwen Thsang's visit there were ten monasteries, but very few Buddhists, and the mass of the people worshipped the Brahmanical gods. To the north-east of the town at 10 *li*, or nearly 2 miles, there was a stupa of Asoka, 200 feet in height, which marked the spot where Buddha had halted, and which was said to contain a large quantity of his relics. This stupa may, I think, be identified with the little mound of *Sâlâr*, near Thata Syadon, just two miles to the north of Asarur.

Ran-si, or Nara-Sinha.

On leaving *Tse-ḳia*, Hwen Thsang travelled eastward to *Na-lo-Seng-ho*, or *Nâra-Sinha*, beyond which place he entered the forest of *Po-lo-she*, or *Pilu* trees (*Salvadora Persica*), where he encountered the brigands, as already related. This town of *Nara-Sinha* is, I believe, represented by the large ruined mound of *Ran-Si,* which is situated 9 miles to the south of Shekohpura, and 25 miles to the east-south-east of Asarur, and about the same distance to the west of Lahor.* *Si,* or *Sih,* is the usual Indian contraction for *Sinh,* and *Ran* is a well-known interchange of pronunciation with *Nar,* as in *Ranod* for *Narod,* a large town in the Gwalior territory, about 35 miles to the south of Narwar, and in *Nakhlor* for *Lakhnor,* the capital of *Katehar,* or *Rohilkhand.* In *Ransi,* therefore, we have not only an exact correspondence of position, but also the most precise agreement of name, with the long-sought-for *Nara-Sinha* of the Chinese pilgrim. This identification is the more valuable, as it furnishes the most conclusive evidence that could be desired of the accuracy of Hwen Thsang's emplacement of Sangala to the westward of the Râvi, instead of to the eastward, as indicated by the classical authorities.

The remains of *Ran-si* consist of a large ruined mound, 600 feet in length from north to south, and 500 feet from east to west, with a general height of from 20 to 25 feet. It is thickly covered with broken bricks of large size, and coins are occasionally found by the saltpetre manufacturers. All the old ruined mounds in the Punjâb, as Shorkot, Multân, Harapa, etc., abound in saltpetre, which has been derived from man's occupation, and which, therefore, affords a certain proof that the mound of

---

* See Map No. VI.

Ransi is not a natural elevation, but an artificial accumulation of rubbish, the result of many centuries. Ransi also possesses a tomb of a *Nao-gaja*, or giant of "nine yards," which I believe to be only the remains of a recumbent statue of Buddha, after his attainment of *Nirvâna*, or death. Similar gigantic statues of bricks and mud are still made in Barma, which, when in ruins, present exactly the same appearance as these *Nao-gaja* tombs. As Buddha was believed to have died with his face to the east, all the *Nirvâna* statues would, of course, be placed in a direction from north to south; and as Muhammadan tombs in India are placed in the same direction, I believe that the early Musalmans took advantage of these Buddhist statues to form ready-made tombs for their leaders who fell in battle. I shall have more to say on this subject hereafter, and I only mention it here as another proof of the antiquity of *Ransi*.

Ambakapi, or Amakatis.

Amba and *Kâpi* are the names of two ruined mounds, the remains of ancient cities, which are said to have been called after a brother and sister, whose story has already been referred to in my account of Mânikyâla. According to the legend, the family consisted of three brothers, named *Sir-kap*, *Sir-suk*, and *Amba*. and of four sisters, named *Kâpi*, *Kalpi*, *Mundê*, and *Mândehi*, each of whom is said to have founded a city to the south of Shekohpura, and in the immediate vicinity of

Ran-si. The ruins of these cities are pointed out at the following places:

1st. *Sir-kap* is a mound of ruins near the village of Balarh, 6 miles to the south of Shekohpura. It is remarkable that the name of Balarh is also connected with Sirkap in the legends of the Sindh Sâgar Doâb, which assign the Balarh Tope as the seat of this Raja.

2nd. *Sir-suk* is a ruined mound, near the village of Murâd, 3½ miles to the south of Shekohpura, and 2½ miles to the north of this Sir-kap mound.

3rd. *Amba* is a large ruined mound and village, upwards of 9 miles to the south of Shekohpura, and one mile to the east of *Ran-si*.

4th. *Kâpi*, or *Kânpi*, as it is also written and pronounced, is a small mound 2½ miles to the east of Amba, on the old high-road to Lahor.

5th. *Kalpi* is another small ruined mound near the village of Bhuipur, about midway between the mounds of Sri-kap and Amba.

6th. *Mundê* is a ruined mound and village on the west bank of the *Bâgh-bachha* river, 8 miles to the south of Ransi and Amba.

7th. *Mândehi* is a ruined mound and village to the south-east of Amba and Kapi, from which it is equidistant 3½ miles.

All of these mounds are on the western bank of the *Bâgh-bachha* river, and at a mean distance of about 25 miles to the westward of Lahor. The whole of the villages just mentioned will be found in the district map of Lahor, but the mounds themselves are shown only in the large map of the *Sarakpur* Parganah. I have already remarked that the name of the *Bâgh-bachha* river is most probably connected with the legend of the "Seven hungry Tiger Cubs" (*Bâgh-bachhas*), whose names are preserved in those of the seven mounds above noted. The same story is told here that is so common in the Sindh Sâgar Doâb. Râsâlu, the Raja of Syâlkot, plays at *Chopar* with *Sir-kap* for a hman head, and having won it accepts his daughter *Kokilâ* instead of the stake. The people have the most undoubting faith in the truth of this legend, and they quoted, with evident satisfaction, the following couplet in support of their belief :—

> "*Amba-Kapa pai larai,*
> *Kalpi bahin chhurâwan ai.*"
> When strife arose 'tween Amb and Kâp
> Their sister Kalpi made it up.

As they could give no explanation of the nature of this quarrel, the couplet adds but little to our information regarding the seven brothers and sisters. I may observe, however, that the junction of the two names of *Amba* and *Kapi* is most probably as old as the time of Ptolemy, who places a town named *Amakatis*, or *Amakapis*, to the west of Râvi, and in the immediate neighbourhood of *Labokla*, or Lahor.*

---

* The identification of Ptolemy's *Labokla* with Lahor was first made in Kiepert's Map of India, according to

The mound of Amba is 900 feet square, and from 25 to 30 feet in height; but as the whole of the surrounding fields, for a breadth of about 600 feet, are covered with broken pottery, the full extent of the ancient town may be taken at not less than 8000 feet, or upwards of 3 miles in circuit. The mound itself is covered with broken bricks of large size, amongst which I discovered several pieces of carved brick. I found also one piece of grey sandstone, and a piece of speckled iron ore, similar to that of Sangala, and of the Karâna hills. According to the statements of the people, the place was founded by Raja Amba 1800 or 1900 years ago, or just about the beginning of the Christian era. This date would make the three brothers contemporary with Hushka, Jushka, and Kanishka, the three great kings of the *Yuchi*, or *Kushân* race of Indo-Scythians, with whom I am, on other grounds, inclined to identify them. At present, however, I am not prepared to enter upon the long discussion which would be necessary to establish their identity.

Lohâwar, or Lâhor.

The gerat city of Lahor, which has been the capital of the Panjâb for nearly nine hundred years, is said to have been founded by *Lava*, or *Lo*, the son of Râma, after whom it was named *Lohâwar*.

Ptolemy, which accompanied Lassen's 'Indische Alterthumskunde.' It has since been confirmed by the researches of Mr. T. H. Thornton, the author of the 'History and Antiquities of Lahor.'

Under this form it is mentioned by Abu Rihân; but the present form of the name, *Lâhor,* which was soon adopted by the Muhammadans, has now become universal. Its history has been described by Mr. Thornton in a very full and able account, replete with interesting information. He has identified Lâhor with the *Labokla* of Ptolemy, which I believe to be correct, taking the first two syllables *Labo* to represent the name of *Lava.* But I would alter the termination of *kla* to *lka,* or *laka,* thus making the whole name *Labolaka* for *Lavâlaka,* or the "abode of *Lava.*"

Hwen Thsang makes no mention of Lahor, although it is almost certain that he must have passed through it on his way from Tâki to Jâlandhar. He notes* that he halted for a whole month at a large city on the eastern frontier of Tâki; but as this kingdom extendd to the Byâs river on the east, the great city on its eastern frontier should be looked for on the line of the Biâs, and not on the Râvi. It was most probably Kasur. The first distinct mention of Lahor occurs in the campaigns of Mahmûd of Ghazni, when the Brâhman kings of the Kabul valley, being driven from Peshâwar and Ohind, established their new capital first at *Bhira* on the Jhelam, and afterwards at Lahor. Thus both *Jay Pâl,* and his son *Anand Pâl,* the successive antagonists of Mahmûd, are called Rajas of Lahor by Ferishta. This Hindu dynasty was subverted

* Julien's 'Hiouen Thsang,' i. 99.

in A.D. 1031, when Lahor became the residence of a Muhammadan governor under the king of Ghazni.* Upwards of a century later, in A.D. 1152, when Bahrâm was driven from Ghazni by the Afghans of Ghor, his son Kushru established himself at Lahor. But this new kingdom lasted for only two generations, until A.D. 1186, when the sovereignty of the Ghaznavis was finally extinguished by the capture and imprisonment of Khusru Malik, the last of his race.

Kusâwar, or Kasûr.

According to the traditions of the people *Kasûr* was founded by *Kusa*, the son of *Râma*, after whom it was named *Kusâwar*, which, like the contemporary city of Lohâwar, has been slightly altered in pronunciation by the transposition of the vowels. The town stands on the high bank of the old bed of the Biâs river, 32 miles to the south-south-east of Lahor,† and is popularly said to have once possessed *bâra kilah*, or "twelve forts," of which seven only are now standing. Its antiquity is undoubted. There are, however, no buildings or remains of any consequence; but the extent of the

---

* This date is derived from Ferishta ; but there are coins of Mahmûd with Arabic and Sanskrit inscriptions, struck at Mahmûdpur in A.H. 1019. Mr. Thomas has identified this city with Lahor. It is found in Abu Rihân, and other Muhammadan historians, under the corrupt form of *Mandhukur*, the capital of Lahor.

† See Map No. VI.

ruins is very great;* and the situation on the high-road between Lahor and the old point of junction of the Biâs and Satlej, opposite Firuzpur, is so favourable that it must have been occupied at a very early date. The position also is a strong one, as it is covered by the Biâs river on he south, and by ravines on the other sides. It is quite impossible to define the limits of the ancient city, as the suburbs of the present town are entirely covered with the ruins of tombs and masjids, and other massive buildings; but it could not, I think, have occupied less than one square mile, which would give a circuit of about four miles for the walled town. Several of the tombs are fully a mile distant from the present town; and at least one-half of the intervening space, which is thickly covered with ruins, would appear to have belonged to the ancient city. It seems probable, therefore, that this must be the "great town" on the eastern frontier of *Tâḳi*, that is, on the Biâs river, at which Hwen Thsang halted for a month on his way from the capital of *Tâḳi* to *Chinapati*. Unfortunately, he has omitted the usual details, and we have only the one bare fact, that it was situated somewhere on the right bank of the Biâs opposite Lahor, to guide us in determining its position.

---

* I speak from personal survey and examination; but I can also refer to Lieutenant Barr's 'Kabul and the Panjâb,' p. 409,—"Kasur, a large and ancient town, that in former days must have covered an extensive area, as its ruins are interminable."

Chinapati, or Pati.

Hwen Thsang places the town of Chinapati at 500 *li*, or 83 miles, to the east of *Tâki*, a position which corresponds almost exactly with *Patti*, a large and very old town, situated 27 miles to the north-east of Kasûr, and 10 miles to the west of the Biâs river.* Unfortunately there is a discrepancy in the recorded distance of the next place visited by the pilgrim, otherwise the site of *Chinapati* might have been fixed absolutely with reference to its bearing and distance from the well-known city of Jâlandhar. In the Life† of Hwen Thsang, Chinapati is said to be 50 *li*, or 8 miles, to the north-west of the *Tâmasa-vana* monastery, which was 150 *li*, or 25 miles, to the south-west of Jâlandhar. But in the Travels‡ of Hwen Thsang the distance of the monastery is stated at 500 *li*, or 83 miles, from *Chinapati*. This last distance is quite impossible, as it would place *Chinapati* about 30 miles to the north of *Tâki*, instead of 83 miles to the east of it, as specified by the pilgrim in his journal. On the other hand, the shorter distance of eight miles would place it in the midst of the sandy bed of Biâs river, where no town has ever existed. I would, therefore, propose to read 150 *li*, or 25 miles, which would fix *Chinapati* at the town of *Patti*, in the

---

* See Map No. VI.

† Julien's 'Hiouen Thsang,' i. 102.

‡ *Ibid.*, ii. 198.

very position that has already been determined by the bearing and distance from *Tâḳi*.

Patti is a large brick town of considerable antiquity. According to Burnes,* it was built in the reign of Akbar; but he is undoubtedly wrong, as the town was already the head of a *Parganah* in the time of Humâyun, who assigned it to his servant Jaohar.† It is called Patti-Haibatpur by Abul Fazl,‡ and it is still known as Haibatpur-Patti. According to the people, the town received its Muhammadan name from Haibat Khân, whose date is not known, but I think it probable that he may be indentified with Haibat Khân Shirwâni, who was a leading noble in the time of Sikandar Ludi, and who commanded the army of the Afghan king against Humâyun on his return from Persia. The antiquity of *Patti* is proved by the numbers of burnt bricks and old wells which are found about the town. The old dry wells were noted more than three hundred years ago by Jaohar,§ the attendant of the Emperor Humâyun; and the profusion of bricks struck Burnes,|| who remarks that "the houses are constructed of bricks, and the streets are even laid with them. Some workmen digging a well in this neighbourhood lately hit upon a former well on which was a Hindu inscription.

* 'Travels in Panjâb and Bokhara,' ii. 9.

† 'Memoirs of Humâyun,' 112.

‡ 'Ayin Akbari,' ii. 260.

§ 'Memoirs of Humâyun,' p. 113.

|| 'Panjâb and Bokhara,' ii. 9.

It set forth that it had been built by one *Agurtuta*, of whom tradition gives no account." I visited the place in 1838, only a few years after Burnes, but I failed to recover the inscription.

Another proof of antiquity is the presence of one of the long graves or tombs, which the people call *No-gaja*, or "Nine-yards," that is the Giant. The Patti *No-gaja* is said by Barr* to have lived in the time of Akbar; but these tombs, which are common in the north-west of India, are more usually referred to the *Ghâzis*, who fell in fight against the infidels in the early ages of Muhammadanism. I would therefore assign the *grave* to the time of Mahmûd of Ghazni, and the brick tomb which has been erected over it to the time of Akbar.

According to Hwen Thsang, the district of *Chinapata* was about 2000 *li*, or 333 miles, in circuit. With these dimensions, it must have comprised the whole of the upper Bâri Doâb, between the Biâs and the Râvi, from the foot of the hills to the old junction of the Biâs and Satlej, near Firuzpur. The name of *Chi-na-po-ti*, or *Chinapati*, is referred to the time of the great Indo-Scythian king Kanishka, who fixed this place as the residence of his Chinese hostages. The pilgrim adds, that previous to their residence, India had possessed neither pears nor peaches, both of which were introduced by the Chinese hostages. The pears were called *Chi-na-ni*, or *Chinâni*, that is, "brought from China," and the peaches *Chi-na-lo-*

* 'Cabul and the Panjâb,' p. 62.

she-fo-ta-lo, or *China-râja-putra,* that is, the "China King's sons." This is not quite correct, as both pears and peaches are found growing wild in the neighbouring hills. But there are now two kinds of cultivated peaches, the one round and juicy, the other flat and sweet. The first, which is called *ârû* in Hindi, and *Shaftâlû* in Persian, is certainly indigenous; but the other, which is called *Chini-shaftâlû,* is most probably that which Hwen Thsang refers to as having been introduced from China.

3. SHORKOT.

Hwen Thsang calls the central district of the Panjâb *Po-fa-to,* or *Po-la-fa-to,* for which M. Stanislas Julien proposes to read *Parvata.* But to this it may be objected that *parvata,* which means a "hill," could not be, and in fact never is, applied as a name to any place in the plains. The capital was situated at 700 *li,* or 117 miles, to the north-east of Multân, a position which agrees almost exactly with the site of *Jhang,* on the Chenâb. But as this place lies at some distance above the junction of the Jhelam and Chenâb, it is most probable that it belonged to the northern division of *Tâki.* In this case the distance recorded by Hwen Thsang would be too great, which might be due to his overlooking the shortness of the *kos* in this part of the country, as I have already explained in my account of Singhapura. This *kos* is only 1 mile and 2½ furlongs, or just $\frac{21}{32}$ of the common *kos.* At this valuation Hwen Thsang's distance would be only 76 miles, which is within a few miles of the position of *Shorkot*, or *Shûr*, as it is called in the 'Ayin Akbari.' Now the initial syllable *po* of the Chinese name is frequently interchanged with the syllable *so*, of which we have a notable instance in *Po-lo-tu-lo* for *So-lo-tu-lo*, or *Salâtura*, the well-known birthplace of the famous grammarian Pânini. It is quite possible, therefore, that the same interchange may have occurred in the name of *Po-lo-fa-to*, for *So-lo-fa-to*, or *Soravati*, which would be a synonym for *Shorkot*. This is a mere suggestion to account for the Chinese name of the capital, which does not affect the identification of the province, as it is quite certain, from its position to the north-east of Multân, that it must correspond with the *parganah*, or district of Shorkot. The people I take to be the *Sudrakæ*, or *Oxudrakæ* of the classical writers, a point which will be fully examined in my account of Ajudhan.

The province is described by Hwen Thsang as being 5000 *li*, or 833 miles, in circuit, which must be greatly exaggerated. On the east the boundary was limited by the Satlej, which for 100 miles formed the frontier line of the kingdom of Gurjjara; on the north it was bounded by the province of *Tâki* for a distance of 200 miles from the Indus to the old junction of the Byâs and Satlej, near Firuzpur; on the south it was bounded by Multân for a distance of 150 miles from the Indus, near *Dera Din-panâh*, to the Satlej, below *Pâkpatan;* on the west it was bounded by the Indus itself for about 50 miles. The total length of frontier is therefore not more than 520 miles, which is considerably less than the circuit recorded by Hwen Thsang. The discrepancy may perhaps be explained, as before, by the use of the short *kos*, which would reduce the circuit of 833 miles to 531, which agrees very closely with the actual measurements.

Within these limits there are several important towns, and many ruined mounds, the remains of ancient cities, which once played an important part in the history of the Panjâb. These are:—

Richna Doâb	1. Shorkot. 2. Kot Kamâlia.
Bâri Doâb	3. Harapa. 4. Akbar. 5. Satgarha.
Doâb Jâlandhar Pith	6. Depâlpur. 7. Ajudhan.

Shorkot.

Shorkot is a huge mound of ruins, which gives its name to the *parganah*, or division of *Shor*, or the lower half of the Richna Doâb.* It was visited by Burnes,† who describes the place as "a mound of earth, surrounded by a brick wall, and so high as to be seen for a circuit of six or eight miles." He adds that it is much larger than Sehwân, which, following the measurement of De la Hoste, is 1200 feet long, by 750 feet broad.‡ According to my information,

* See Map No. VI.
† 'Bokhara and Panjâb,' i. 113.
‡ 'Journ. Asiat. Soc. Bengal,' 1840, p. 913.

Shorkot is much smaller than Harapa, and about the size of Akbar, that is, 2000 feet by 1000 feet, but loftier than either of them. The mound is surrounded by a wall of large-sized bricks, which is an undoubted sign of antiquity. Burnes was informed by the people that their town had been destroyed by some king from the westward, about 1300 years ago. The locality leads him to fix on it as the place where Alexander was wounded, and to assign its downfall to Alexander himself. I received the same tradition about its destruction, which I would attribute to the White Huns, who must have entered the Panjâb from the westward during the sixth century, or about the very time specified in the tradition.

The foundation of the city is attributed to a fabulous Raja *Shor*, of whom nothing is known but the name. I think it probable that *Shorkot* may be the Alexandria Soriane, Σωριάνη, of Stephanus Byzantinus, who gives no clue to its position save the bare fact that it was in India. The names agree so exactly that I feel tempted to suggest that Shorkot may have been enlarged and strengthened by Philip, whom Alexander left behind as governor of the *Oxudrakæ* and *Malli*. This suggestion seems the more probable when we remember that Shorkot was in the direct line of Alexander's route, from the junction of the Hydaspes and Akesines to the capital of the Malli. I would, therefore, identify it with the city of the Malli, which, according to Diodorus and Curtius, surrendered after a short blockade.*

* 'Diodorus,' xvii. 52 ; Curtius, "coronâ cepit."

Curtius* places it at 250 stadia, or 28¾ miles, from the junction of the rivers, a position which corresponds exactly with that of Shorkot. The account of Arrian differs from that of the other two historians in several very important particulars. He states that the first city taken by Alexander after leaving the confluence of the rivers was inland 400 stadia, or 46 miles,† distant from the Akesines, and that it was captured by assault. I infer that this city was *Kot Kamâlia,* and I would explain the discrepancy in the two narratives by a reference to the details of this campaign which are given by Arrian. Alexander divided his army into three great bodies, of which the advanced division, commanded by Hephæstion, marched five days ahead; the centre was commanded by himself, and the rear division, which was commanded by Ptolemy, followed three days behind. As the campaign was directed against the Malli, I conclude that the army marched by the direct route, *viâ* Shorkot towards Multân, which was certainly the capital of the Malli. Shorkot would thus have fallen to Hephæstion, who commanded the advanced division of the army. Alexander's own route will be described presently, when I come to speak of Kot Kamâlia.

The antiquity of Shorkot may be ascertained approximately by the coins which are found in its ruins. These consist chiefly of Indo-Scythian copper

---

* Vita Alex., ix. 4, 10.

† 'Anabasis,' vi. 7.

pieces of all ages, with a few Hindu specimens, and a large number of Muhammadan coins. A single copper piece of Apollodotus was obtained by Burnes. From these data I would infer that the town was certainly occupied as early as the time of the Greek kings of Ariana and the Panjâb, and that it was in a flourishing state during the sway of the Indo-Scythians, or from B.C. 126 down to A.D. 250, or perhaps later. But as the Hindu coins which I obtained from Shorkot were entirely confined to the Brahman kings of the Kabul valley and the Panjâb, I conclude that the place was either deserted, or, at least, in a very decayed state, during the middle ages; and that it was either re-occupied or restored in the tenth century by one of these Brahman kings.

Kot Kamâlia.

Kot Kamâlia is a small but ancient town situated on an isolated mound on the right or northern bank of the Râvi, which marks the extreme limit of the river's fluctuations on that side.* It is 44 miles to the south-east of the junction of the Hydaspes and Akesines, and 35 miles to the east-south-east of Shorkot. It possesses an ancient mound of burnt-brick ruins, and is said to have been overthrown by a king from the West at the same time as Shorkot and Harapa. Its present name, according to some people, was derived from a Muhammadan governor, named Kamâl-ud-din. But this is not certain; and

* See Maps Nos. V. and VI.

I think it is quite possible that it may owe its origin to the *Malli* tribe, which still exists in this part of the country; but whether the name be old or not, it is quite certain that the site is very ancient; and I am, therefore, led to believe that it may be identified with the first city captured by Alexander in his campaign against the Malli.

Arrian's account of the capture is so clear and concise that I will quote it in his own words.* On leaving the junction of the rivers Alexander "marched through a desert country against the Malii, and the first day pitched his tents on the banks of a small rivulet, about one hundred stadia distant from the river Akesines. Having there allowed his troops a little time for refreshment and rest, he ordered every one to fill all his vessels with water, which done, he continued his march the remaining part of that day and all night, and early the next morning arrived at a city, whither many of the Malii had fled for refuge, and this was about 400 stadia distant from the Akesines." The small rivulet here mentioned I believe to be the lower course of the *Ayek* river, which rises in the outer range of hills, and flows past Syâlkot towards Sangala, below which the bed is still traceable for some distance. It appears again 18 miles to the east of *Jhang*, and is finally lost about 12 miles to the east of Shorkot.† Now somewhere between these two points Alexander must have

* 'Anabasis,' vi. 7.

† See Maps Nos. V. and VI.

crossed the *Ayek*, as the desert country, which he afterwards traversed, lies immediately beyond it. If he had marched to the south he would have arrived at Shorkot, but he would not have encountered any desert, as his route would have been over the *Khâdar*, or low-lying lands in the valley of the Chenâb. A march of 46 miles in a southerly direction would have carried him also right up to the bank of the Hydraotes, or Râvi, a point which Alexander only reached, according to Arrian's narrative, after another night's march.* As this march lasted from the first watch of the night until daylight, it cannot have been less than 18 or 20 miles, which agrees exactly with the distance of the Râvi opposite Tulamba from Kot Kamâlia. The direction of Alexander's march must, therefore, have been to the south-east; first to the *Ayek* river, where he halted to refresh his soldiers, and to fill their water vessels, and thence across the hard clayey and waterless tract called *Sandar-bâr*, that is, the *bâr*, a desert of the *Sandar*, or *Chandra* river. Thus the position of the rivulet, the description of the desolate country, and the distance of the city from the confluence of the rivers, all agree in fixing the site of the fortress assaulted by Alexander with *Kot Kamâlia*.

Arrian describes the place as a walled city with a castle seated on an eminence of difficult access, which the Indians held for a long time. At last it

* 'Anabasis,' vi. 7.

was carried by storm, and the whole of the garrison, to the number of 2000, were put to the sword.

Harapa.

Whilst Alexander was engaged in the assault of the city just described, Arrian relates that he had dispatched Perdikkas with the cavalry against "another city of the Malii, into which a great body of Indians had fled for safety."* His instructions were to blockade the city until Alexander arrived; but the inhabitants deserted the place on his approach, and took refuge in the neighbouring marshes. This city I believe to be Harapa. The mention of marshes shows that it must have been near the Râvi, and as Perdikkas was sent in advance of Alexander, it must also have been *beyond* Kot Kamâlia, that is, to the east or south-east of it. Now this is exactly the position of Harapa, which is situated 16 miles to the east-south-east of Kot Kamâlia, and on the opposite high bank of the Râvi.† There are also several marshes in the low ground in its immediate vicinity.

Harapa has been described by two well-known travellers, Burnes and Masson, and to their descriptions I am not able to add much, although I have been encamped at the place on three different occasions. Burnes‡ estimated the extent of the

* 'Anabasis,' vi. 6.

† See Maps Nos. V. and VI.

‡ 'Bokhara,' i. 117.

ruins as "about three miles in circumference, which is one-half too much, as the actual ruined mound forms an irregular square of only half a mile on each side, or two miles in circuit." But this comprises only the remains of the walled town, to which we may fairly add the suburbs, or fields now covered with broken bricks and other remains, which would bring the size of the old town quite up to Burnes's estimate. Masson* notices a tradition that Harapa once extended on the west as far as Chichawatni, a distance of 12 miles, which serves, at least, to show the belief of the people as to the former size and importance of their town.

The great mass of ruins is on the western side, where the mound rises to 60 feet in height in the centre. At this point there are several massive walls built of large bricks, which are, no doubt, the remains of some extensive building. The other portions of the mound vary from 30 to 50 feet in height, the mass being formed almost entirely of broken bricks. Tradition assigns its foundation to Raja Harapa, of unknown date, and its destruction to the same western king, of the sixth century, who overthrew Shorkot, and whom I believe to have the leader of the White Huns. The crimes of its ruler, who claimed the husband's privilege on every marriage, are said to have drawn down the vengeance of Heaven, and Harapa remained uninhabited for

---

* 'Travels,' i. 453, and Journ. Asiat. Soc. Bengal, vi. 57.

several centuries. As the coins that are found in its ruins are similar to those discovered at Shorkot, I think that the two places must have experienced the same fortunes; I would, therefore, assign its downfall to the Arabs, who overran the whole of the lower Panjâb immediately after the capture and occupation of Multân in A.D. 713.

Akbar.

The village of Akbar is situated on the high-road leading from Lahor to Multân, at 6 miles to the south-west of Gugera, and 80 miles from Lahor. The ruins of the old town, which stand close to the village, consist of a large mound 1000 feet square, with a small castle 200 feet square, and 75 feet high at its northern end; and a second low mound 800 feet long, and 400 feet broad at the southern end. It must be a place of great antiquity, as I found many bricks of very large size, 20 by 10 by 3½ inches, such as have not been manufactured for many centuries past. The place was deserted until about A.D. 1823, when Gulâb Singh Povindia established the present village of Akbar. The old name is now utterly lost, which is much to be regretted, as the number of moulded bricks found amongst the ruins show that the place must have contained buildings of some architectural consequence.

Satgarha.

Satgarha is situated 13 miles to the east of Gugera, on one of the projecting points of the high bank which marks the limit of the windings of the Râvi on the east. The name means the "seven castles," but these no longer exist. There is an old brick fort on a mound, and several isolated mounds, covered with broken bricks and other remains, which mark the site of an ancient city. Old coins are found in considerable numbers, from the time of the Indo-Scythians downwards. It has, therefore, most probably been continuously occupied from the beginning of the Christian era down to the present time.

Depâlpur.

During the rule of the Pathân emperors of Delhi, Depâlpur was the capital of the northern Panjâb. It was a favourite residence of Firuz Shah, who erected a large masjid outside the city, and drew a canal from the Satlej for the irrigation of its lands. At the time of Timur's invasion it was second only to Multân in size and importance, and was popularly said to possess 84 towers, 84 masjids, and 84 wells. At present it is very nearly deserted, there being only one inhabited street running between the two gates. In shape it is a square of nearly 1600 feet, with a projection 500 feet square at the south-east quarter. To the south-west there is a high ruined mound, which is said to be the remains of a citadel. It was connected with the town by a bridge of three arches, which is still standing; and from its high and commanding position I conclude that it must have been the citadel. To the south and east there are also long mounds of ruins, which are, no doubt, the remains of the suburbs. The actual ruins of Depâlpur, including the citadel and suburbs, occupy a space three-quarters of a mile in length by half a mile in breadth or 2½ miles in circuit. But in its flourishing days it must have been much larger, as the fields to the east are strewn with bricks right up to the banks of the canal, near which Firuz Shah's masjid was situated. This extension of the city beyond the walls may also be inferred from the fact that the people of Depâlpur, on Timur's invasion, sought refuge in Bhatner, which they would not have done if their own city had been defensible.

The foundation of the place is assigned to Raja Deva Pâla, whose date is unknown. Its antiquity, however, is undoubted, as the interior surface on which the houses are now built is on a level with the terreplein of the ramparts. The old coins, also, which are found there in great numbers, show that Depâlpur was in existence as early as the time of the Indo-Scythians. I am inclined, therefore, to identify it with the *Daidala* of Ptolemy, which was on the Satlej to the south of *Labokla* and *Amakatis*, or Lahor and Ambakâpi.

Ajudhan, or Pâkpatan.

The ancient town of Ajudhan is situated on the high bank of the old Satlej, 28 miles to the south-west of Depâlpur, and 10 miles from the present course of the river. Its foundation is assigned to a Hindu saint, or raja, of the same name, of whom nothing else is recorded. This part of the Doâb is still known as *Surâtdes*, a name which recalls the *Surakousæ* of Diodorus, and the *Sudrakæ* and *Oxudrakæ* of other Greek writers. Now, the *Sudrakæ* are always coupled with the *Malli* by classical authors, just as Ajudhan and Multân are joined together by the Muhammadan historians. I think, therefore, that we may look upon Ajudhan and its neighbour Depâlpur as two of the chief cities of the *Sudrakas*, or *Surakas*, who, in the time of Alexander, were one of the free nations of India. Dionysius and Nonnus use the form of *Hudarkæ*, Pliny has *Sydracæ*, which agrees with Strabo's *Sudrakæ;* and Diodorus has *Surakousæ*. Arrian and Curtius alone give *Oxudrakæ*. Strabo adds that they were said to be descendants of Bacchus;* and as Chares of Mytilene states that the name of the Indian god Σοροάδειος meant οἰνοποιός, or the "Wine-bibber," I infer that the people who boastd a descent from Bacchus may have called themselves *Surâkas*, or Bacchidæ. The *d* in *Sudrakæ* I look upon as a redundant addition of the Greeks, which is also found in the *Adraistæ* of Arrian and the *Andrestæ* of Diodorus. The Sanskrit name of this people was *Arâshtraka*, or "the Kingless," which is well preserved in Justin's *Arestæ*. *Surakai*, or the descendants of *Sura*, must therefore be the true Greek form. This is confirmed by the longer form of the name given by Diodorus as Συρακούσαι, which is most

* Geogr., xiv. 1, 8, and 33.

probably derived from the Sanskrit *surâ*, "wine," and *kusa*, "mad, or inebriated." It would thus mean simply the "drunkards," a nickname which was no doubt given by their Arian neighbours, who were very liberal in their abuse of the Turanian population of the Panjâb. Thus the Kathæi of Sangala are stigmatized in the Mahâbhârata as "thieving *Bâhikas*," as well as "wine-bibbers" and beef eaters."* They are also called by a variety of names, as *Madra*, *Bâhika*, *Aratta*, and *Jârttikka*, and not even once by their own proper name, which, as we know from Alexander's historians, was *Kathœi*, which is still preserved in the *Kathi* of the present day. I confess, therefore, that I look upon many of the ethnic appellations which the Greeks have handed down to us as mere nicknames, or abusive epithets applied by the Brahmanical Arians to their Turanian neighbours. For instance, the name of *Kambistholi*, which Arrian† gives to a people on the Hydraotes, or Râvi, is most probably derived from the Sanskrit *Kapisasthala*, that is, "Wine-land, or the Tavern," which would be a natural epithet for the country of the *Surâkusas*, or "wine-bibbers." Similarly I would explain *Oxudrakœ* as *Asuraka*, or the "Demons."

The doubt now arises whether *Surâka*, or "the drinkers," can have been the true name of this people. Arrian‡ places the *Oxudrakœ* at the junc-

---

* *Stenâ-Bâhikâ dhânâgaudasavam-pîtwa gomânsam.*

† 'Indica,' iv.

‡ *Ibid.*

tion of the Hydaspes and Akesines, where Curtius locates the *Sobii*, Diodorus the *Ibœ*, and Strabo the *Sibœ*. The only explanation of this discrepancy that I can suggest is, the probable confusion between the name of *Sobii*, or *Chobiya*, of Ferishta,* and that of *Sorii*, or *Suraka*. The former was the name of the subjects of Sopeithes, or Sophytes, whose rule extended over the Salt Range of mountains above the junction of the Hydaspes and Akesines. The latter name I would refer to *Shorkot*, which I have already identified with *Alexandria Sôriane*. It is still the capital of the district of *Shor*, which lies just below the junction of the Hydaspes and Akesines. The *Sobii*, therefore, were the immediate neighbours of the *Sorii*, the former people occupying the country above the confluence of the rivers, and the latter the country just below it.

This location of the *Sorii*, or *Surâkas*, explains the statement of Arrian† that the *Kathœi* were allies of the *Oxudrakœ* and *Malii*. They were neighbouring nations, who were generally at war with each other, but were always ready to join against a common enemy.

Pliny places the limit of Alexander's career in the territory of the Sudrakas, "in Sudracis expeditio Alexandri termino,"‡ and the altars on the opposite bank of the Hyphasis, or Biâs river. From this point

---

* Briggs's 'Ferishta,' Introduction, i. lxxii.

† 'Anabasis,' vi. 22.

‡ Hist. Nat., xii. 12.

to the river *Sydrus*, that is the *Hesidrus*, or Satlej, he makes the distance 168 Roman, or 154 British miles; and from the *Sydrus* to the *Jomanes*, or Jumna, exactly the same. But as the whole distance from the Biâs to the Jumna varies from 150 to 160 miles, from the foot of the hills down to Kasûr on the former river, and down to Karnâl on the latter river, I presume that only one distance, namely, that from the Biâs to the Jumna, was stated in Pliny's original authority. The famous spot on the eastern bank of the Hyphasis, where "Alexander halted and wept,"* must have been somewhere in the low ground between the Satlej and the Biâs, at a short distance above the old junction opposite Kasûr and Bazidpur. For 20 miles above this point the courses of the two rivers ran almost parallel, and within a few miles of each other, from the earliest times down to A.D. 1796, when the Satlej suddenly changed its course, and joined the Biâs above *Hari-ḳi-patan*. Within this range of 20 miles the space between the two rivers was so small that it might easily have been overlooked in stating the distance from Alexander's camp to the Jumna. I believe, however, that it was actually noted by Alexander's contemporaries, for Pliny, after stating the distance to the Jumna, says, "some copies add five miles

---

* Gibbon, 'Decline and Fall of the Roman Empire:' "On the eastern bank of the Hyphasis, on the verge of the desert, the Macedonian hero halted and wept."

more."* Now these five Roman miles are the exact distance of the old bed of the Satlej from the eastern bank of the Biâs, a measurement which some of the ancient writers may have omitted to note as a matter of little importance. On a general review of all the data, I think that the site of Alexander's altars must be looked for along the line of the present course of the Satlej, at a few miles below *Hari-ki-patan*, and not far from the well-known field of Sobraon, which is barely five miles distant from several bends of the old bed of the Satlej. To this point, therefore, the territory of the *Sudrakœ*, or *Surâkas*, must have extended in the time of Alexander.

For many centuries Ajudhan was the principal ferry on the Satlej. Here met the two great western roads from Dera Ghazi Khan and Dera Ismaïl Khan; the first viâ Mânkera, Shorkot, and Harapa; the second viâ Multân. At this point the great conquerors Mahmud and Timur, and the great traveller Ibn Batuta, crossed the Satlej. The fort is said to have been captured by Sabuktugin in A.H. 367, or A.D. 977-78, during his plundering expedition in the Panjâb; and again by Ibrâhim Ghaznavi, in A.H. 472, or A.D. 1079-80. On the invasion of Timur, the mass of the population fled to Bhatner, and the few people that remained were spared by that ruthless barbarian out of respect for the famous saint Farid-ud-din Shakar-ganj, whose shrine is in

* Hist. Nat., vi. 21: "Exemplaria aliqua adjiciunt quinque millia passuum."

Ajudhan. From this saint the place derives its modern name of *Pâk-pattan*, or the "Ferry of the Pure One," that is, of Farid, whose latter days were spent at Ajudhan. By continued fasting his body is said to have become so pure that whatever he put into his mouth to allay the cravings of hunger, even earth and stones, was immediately turned into sugar, whence his name of *Shakar-ganj* or "Sugar-store." This miraculous power is recorded in a well-known Persian couplet:—

"Sang dar dast o guhar gardad,
Zaher dar kâm o shakar gardad :"

which may be freely rendered:—

"Stones in his hand are changed to money (jewels),
And poison in his mouth to honey (sugar)."

From another memorial couplet we learn that he died in A.H. 664, or A.D. 1265-66, when he was 95 lunar years of age. But as the old name of *Ajudhan* is the only one noted by Ibn Batuta in A.D. 1334, and by Timur's historian in A.D. 1397, it seems probable that the present name of *Pâk-pattan* is of comparatively recent date. It is, perhaps, not older than the reign of Akbar, when the saint's descendant, *Nûr-ud-din*, revived the former reputation of the family by the success of his prayers for an heir to the throne.

4. MULTÂN PROVINCE.

The southern province of the Panjâb is Multân. According to Hwen Thsang it was 4000 *li*, or 667 miles, in circuit, which is so much greater than the tract actually included between the rivers, that it is almost certain the frontier must have extended beyond them. In the time of Akbar no less than seventeen districts, or separate *parganahs,* were attached to the province of Multân, of which all those that I can identify, namely, *Uch, Dirâwal, Moj,* and *Marot,* are to the east of the Satlej. These names are sufficient to show that the eastern frontier of Multân formerly extended beyond the old bed of the Ghagar river, to the verge of the Bikaner desert. This tract, which now forms the territory of Bahâwalpur, is most effectually separated from the richer provinces on the east by the natural barrier of the Great Desert. Under a strong government it has always formed a portion of Multân; and it was only on the decay of the Muhammadan empire of Delhi that it was made into a separate petty state by Bahâwal Khân. I infer, therefore, that in the seventh century the province of Multân must have included the northern half of the present territory of Bahâwalpur, in addition to the tract lying between the rivers. The northern frontier has already been defined as extending from *Dera Din-panâh,* on the Indus, to *Pâk-pattan* on the Satlej, a distance of 150 miles. On the west the frontier line of the Indus, down to Khânpur, is 160 miles. On the east, the line from Pâk-pattan to the old bed of the Ghagar river, is 80 miles; and on the south, from Khânpur to the Ghagar, the distance is 220 miles. Altogether, this frontier line is 610 miles. If Hwen

Thsang's estimate was based on the short *kos* of the Panjâb, the circuit will be only $\frac{21}{32}$ of 667 miles, or 437 miles, in which case the province could not have extended beyond Mithankot on the south.

In describing the geography of Multân it is necessary to bear in mind the great changes that have taken place in the courses of all the large rivers that flow through the province. In the time of Timur and Akbar the junction of the Chenâb and Indus took place opposite *Uchh,* 60 miles above the present confluence at Mithankot. It was unchanged when Rennell wrote his 'Geography of India,' in A.D. 1788, and still later, in 1796, when visited by Wilford's surveyor, Mirza Mogal Beg. But early in the present century the Indus gradually changed its course, and leaving the old channel at 20 miles above *Uchh,* continued its course to the south-south-west, until it rejoined the old channel at Mithankot.

The present junction of the Râvi and Chenâb takes place near *Diwâna Sanand*, more than 30 miles above Multân; but in the time of Alexander the confluence of the Hydraotes and Akesines was at a short distance below the capital of the Malli, which I have identified with Multân. The old channel still exists, and is duly entered in the large maps of the Multân division. It leaves the present bed at Sarai Siddhû, and follows a winding course for 30 miles to the south-south-west, when it suddenly turns to the west for 18 miles, as far as Multân, and, after completely encircling the fortress, continues its westerly course for 5 miles below Multân. It then suddenly turns to the south-south-west for 10 miles, and is finally lost in the low-lying lands of the bed of the Chenâb. Even to this day the Râvi clings to its ancient channel, and at all high floods the waters of the river still find their way to Multân by the old bed, as I myself have witnessed on two different occasions. The date of the change is unknown; but it was certainly subsequent to the capture of Multân by Muhammed bin Kâsim in A.D. 713; and from the very numerous existing remains of canals drawn from the old channel, I infer that the main river must have continued to flow down it within a comparatively recent period, perhaps even as late as the time of Timur. The change, however, must have taken place before the reign of Akbar, as Abul Fazl* describes the distance from the confluence of the Chenâb and Jhelam to that of the Chenâb and Râvi as 27 kos, and the distance of the latter from the confluence of the Chenâb and Indus as 60 kos, both of which measuremnts agree with the later state of these rivers.

The present confluence of the Biâs and Satlej dates only from about A.D. 1790, when the Satlej finally deserted its old course by Dharmkot, and joined the Biâs at Hariki-pattan. For many centuries previously the point of junction had remained constant just above the ferry of Bhao-ki-pattan, between Kasûr and Firuzpur. This junction is

* 'Ayin Akbari,' ii. 3.

mentioned by Jauhar in A.D. 1555,* and by Abul Fazl in 1596.† But though the confluence of the two rivers near Firuzpur had been long established, yet even at the latter date the waters of the Biâs still continued to flow down their old channel, as described by Abul Fazl:—"For the distance of 12 kos near Firuzpur the rivers Biâs and Sutlej unite, and these again, as they pass on, divide into four streams, the *Hûr, Harê, Dand,* and *Nûrni,* all of which rejoin near the city of Multân." These former beds of the Biâs and Satlej still exists, and form a most complicated network of dry channels, covering the whole of the Doâb between the Satlej and the high bank of the old Biâs. None of the names given in Gladwyn's translation of the 'Ayin Akbari' are now to be found; but I am inclined to attribute this solely to the imperfection of the Persian alphabet, which is a constant source of error in the reading of proper names. The *Har* I would identify with the *Para,* the *Hari* with the *Raghi,* and the *Nurni* with the *Sûk-Nai,* all dry beds of the Biâs river to the south of Harapa. The *Dand* is probably the *Dhamak,* or *Dank,* an old channel of the Satlej, which in its lower course takes the name of Bhatiyâri, and passing by Mailsi, Kahror, and Lodhran, joins the present channel just above its confluence with the Chenâb. In most of our maps the Old Biâs is

---

* 'Memoirs of Humâyun,' p. 113.

† 'Ayin Akbari,' ii. 108.

conducted into the lower course of the Bhatiyâri, whereas its still existing and well-defined channel joins the Chenâb 20 miles below Shujâhabad, and its most southerly point is 10 miles distant from the nearest bend of the Bhatiyâri.

The changes just described are only the most prominent fluctuations of the Panjâb rivers, which are constantly shifting their channels. The change in the Biâs is the most striking, as that river has altogether lost its independent course, and is now a mere tributary of the Satlej. But the fluctuations of the other rivers have been very remarkable. Thus, the valley of the Chenâb below Kalowal is nearly 30 miles broad, and that of the Râvi, near Gugera, is 20 miles, the extreme limits of both rivers being marked by well-defined high banks, on which are situated many of the most ancient cities of the Panjâb. In the Multân division these old sites are very numerous, but they are now mostly deserted and nameless, and were probably abandoned by their inhabitants as the rivers receded from them. This was certainly the case with the old town of Tulamba, which is said to have been deserted so late as 150 years ago, in consequence of a change in the course of the Râvi, by which the water supply of the town was entirely cut off. The same cause, but at a much earlier date, led to the desertion of Aṭâri, a ruined town 20 miles to the west-south-west of Tulamba, which was supplied by a canal from the old bed of the Râvi. The only places which I think it necessary to notice in the present account are the following :—

Bâri Doâb	1. Tulamba. 2. Atâri. 3. Mutân.
Jâlandhar Pith . .	4. Kahror.
At junction . . .	5. Uchh.

Four of these places are celebrated in the history of India, and the second, named Atâri, I have added on account of its size and position, which would certainly have attracted the notice of Alexander and other conquerors of the Panjâb.

Tulamba.

The town of Tulamba is situated on the left bank of the Râvi, at 52 miles to the north-east of Multân. It is surrounded with a brick wall, and the houses are built chiefly of burnt bricks, brought from the old fort of Tulamba, which is situated one mile to the south of the present town. According to Masson,* this "must have been in the ancient time a remarkably strong fortress," which it undoubtedly was, as Timur left it untouched, because its siege would have delayed his progress.†It is curious that it escaped the notice of Burnes, as its lofty walls, which can be seen from a great distance, generally attract the attention of travellers. I have visited the place twice. It consisted of an open city, protected

* 'Travels,' i. 456.

† Briggs's 'Ferishta,' i. 487.

on the south by a lofty fortress 1000 feet square. The outer rampart is of earth, 200 feet thick, and 20 feet high on the outer face, or *faussebraie*, with a second rampart of the same height on the top of it. Both of these were originally faced with large bricks, 12 by 8 by 2½ inches. Inside the rampart there is a clear space, or ditch, 100 feet in breadth, surrounding an inner fort 400 feet square, with walls 40 feet in height, and in the middle of this there is a square tower or castle, 70 feet in height, which commands the whole place. The numerous fragments of bricks lying about, and the still existing marks of the courses of bricks in many places on the outer faces of the ramparts, confirm the statements of the people that the walls were formerly faced with brick. I have already mentioned that this old fort is said to have been abandoned by the inhabitants about 300 years ago, in consequence of the change in the course of the Râvi, which entirely cut off their supply of water. The removal is attributed to Shujâwal Khan, who was the son-in-law and minister of Mahmud Langa of Multân, and the brother-in-law of his successor, from about A.D. 1510 to A.D. 1525.

The antiquity of Tulamba is vouched for by tradition, and by the large size of the bricks, which are similar to the oldest in the walls and ruins of Multân. The old *town* was plundered and burnt by Timur, and its inhabitants massacred; but the fortress escaped his fury, partly owing to its own strength and partly to the invader's impatience to continue his march towards Delhi. There is a tradition that Tulamba was taken by Mahmud of Ghazni, which is very probably true, as it would have been only a few miles out of his direct route to Multân. For the same reason I am led to believe that it must have been one of the cities captured by Alexander. Masson* has already suggested that it represents "the capital of the Malli," or perhaps "the fort held by Brahmans, whose defence was so obstinate and so fatal to themselves, and which was evidently contiguous to the capital of the Malli." But as I do not agree with either of these suggestions, I will now examine and compare the different accounts of this part of Alexander's route.

In my account of Kot Kamâlia I adduced some strong reasons for identifying that place with the first city captured by Alexander on his march from the junction of the Hydaspes and Akesines against the Malli. Arrian† then relates that "Alexander, having allowed his soldiers some time for refreshment and rest, about the first watch of the night set forward, and marching hard all that night came to the river Hydraotes about daylight, and understanding that some parties of the Malii were just passing the river, he immediately attacked them and slew many, and having passed the river himself with his forces in pursuit of those who had gained the further side, he killed vast numbers of them and took many

* 'Travels,' i. 456.

† 'Anabasis,' vi. 3.

prisoners. However, some of them escaped, and betook themselves to a certain town well fortified both by art and nature." A whole night's march of eight or nine hours could not have been less than twenty-five miles, which is the exact distance of the Râvi opposite Tulamba from Kot Kamâlia. Here then I infer that Alexander must have crossed the Râvi; and I would identify Tulamba itself with the "town well fortified both by art and nature," the art being the brick walls, and the nature, the enormous mounds of earthen ramparts. The account of Curtius* agrees with that of Arrian, "on the bank of a river another nation mustering forty thousand infantry opposed him. Crossing the river he put them to flight, and stormed the fort in which they took refuge." Diodorus relates the same story of a people named Agalassæ, who opposed Alexander with forty thousand infantry and three thousand cavalry. All these accounts evidently refer to the same place, which was a strong fort near the left bank of the Râvi. This description would apply also to Harapa; but I have already shown that Harapa was most probably the city against which Perdikkas was detached; besides which it is not more than 16 miles distant from Kot Kamâlia. Tulamba, on the contrary, fulfils all the conditions; and is also

---

* Vita Alex., ix. 4, 10. The text has *in ripâ fluminum*, which is an obvious mistake for *fluminis*, as is proved by the use of *amne* immediately following.

on the high-road to Multân, the capital of the Malli, against which Alexander was then proceeding.

The name of *Agalassæ* or *Agalessensæ* is puzzling. According to Arrian the people of the town were the Malii, but it may be remarked that neither the Oxudrakæ nor the Malli are mentioned by Diodorus and Curtius until later. Justin couples a people called *Gesteani* with the Arestæ or Kathæi, who should therefore be the same as the Malli or Oxudrakæ, but they are not mentioned by any other author. *Agala* or *Agalassa* might be the name of the town itself, but unfortunately it has no similarity with Tulamba, or with any other place in the neighbourhood.

Atâri.

The third city captured by Alexander in his campaign against the Malli is described in similar terms by all the historians. According to Arrian* "Alexander then led his army against a certain city of the Brachmani, where he heard another body of the Malii had fled." The garrison "abandoned the city and fled to the castle," which being stormed they set fire to their houses, and perished in the flames. "About 5000 of them fell during the siege, and so great was their valour that few came alive into the enemy's hands." Both Curtius† and Diodorus‡ mention the fire, and the stout defence

* 'Anabasis,' vi. 7.

† Vita Alex., ix. 4, 10.

‡ Hist., xvii. 52.

made by the garrison, which the latter author numbers at 20,000 men, of whom 3000 only escaped by taking refuge in the citadel, where they capitulated. Curtius also states that the citadel was uninjured, and that Alexander left a garrison in it.*

All these accounts agree very well with the position and size of the old ruined town and fort of Atâri, which is situated 20 miles to the west-south-west of Tulamba, and on the high-road to Multân. The remains consist of a strong citadel 750 feet square and 35 feet high, with a ditch all round it, and a tower in the centre 50 feet high. On two sides are the remains of the town forming a mound 20 feet high, and 1200 feet square, the whole being a mass of ruin 1800 feet in length, and 1200 feet in breadth. Of its history there is not even a tradition, but the large size of the bricks is sufficient to show that it must be a place of considerable antiquity. The name of the old city is quite unknown. *Atâri* is simply that of the adjacent village, which is of recent origin, having been established by a member of the Atâriwâla family of Sikhs. But judging from its size and strength, and its very favourable position between Tulamba and Multân, I think that the ruined mound of Atâri has a very good claim to be indentified with the strong city of

---

* Vita Alex., ix. 4. "Arx erat oppidi intacta, in quâ præsidium dereliquit."

the Brahmans which made so stout a defence against Alexander.

Curtius adds some particulars about this city, which are not even alluded to by either Arrian or Diodorus; but they are still deserving of consideration, as they may perhaps be founded on the statements of one of the companions. He states that Alexander "went completely round the citadel in a boat," which is probable enough, as its ditch was no doubt capable of being filled at pleasure with water from the Râvi, as was actually the case with the ditch of Multân. Now the old citadel of Atâri is still surrounded by a ditch which could easily have been filled from some one of the old canals that pass close by the place. The number of these canal beds is most remarkable; I counted no less than twelve of them in close parallel lines immediately to the west of Atâri, all of them drawn from the old bed of the Râvi to the south of Sarai Siddhu. I am therefore quite prepared to admit the probability that the city of the Brahmans was surrounded by a wet ditch on which Alexander embarked to inspect the fortifications. But when Curtius adds that the three greatest rivers in India, except the Ganges, namely the Indus, the Hydaspes, and the Akesines, joined their waters to form a ditch round the castle,* I can

* Vita Alex., ix. 4. "Ipse navigio circumvectus est arcem; quippe tria flumina, totâ Indiâ præter Gangem maxima, munimento arcis applicant undas. A septentrione Indus alluit; a meridie Acesines Hydaspi confunditur."

only suppose either that the passage has been accidentally transferred from the account of some later siege of a city situated below the confluence of the Five Rivers, or that the author has mixed up into one account two and perfectly distinct statements concerning the ditches of the fort and the confluence of the rivers. Diodorus also describes the junction of the rivers, but as he makes no allusion to their waters forming a ditch about the fort, it is quite possible that this account of three rivers may be due to the inflated imagination of Curtius.

Multân.

The famous metropolis of Multân was originally situated on two islands in the Râvi, but the river has long ago deserted its old channel, and its nearest point is now more than 30 miles distant. But during high floods the waters of the Râvi still flow down their old bed, and I have twice seen the ditches of Multân filled by the natural overflow of the river.* Multân consists of a walled city and a strong fortress, situated on opposite banks of an old bed of the Râvi,

* Burnes, 'Travels in the Punjab, Bokhara,' etc. i. 97, erroneously attributes the inundation of the country around Multân to the "Chenab and its canals." If he had travelled by land instead of by the river, he would have seen that the inundation is due to the flood waters of the Râvi resuming their ancient course from Sarai Siddhu direct upon Multân. I travelled over this line in the end of August, 1856, and saw the old bed of the Râvi in full flood.

which once flowed between them as well as around them. The original site consisted of two low mounds not more than 8 or 10 feet high above the general level of the country. The present height varies from 45 to 50 feet, the difference of 35 to 40 feet being simply the accumulation of rubbish during the lapse of many centuries. This fact I ascertained personally by sinking several wells down to the level of the natural soil, that is, of soil unmixed with bricks, ashes, and other evidences of man's occupation.

The citadel may be described as an irregular semicircle, with a diameter, or straight side of 2500 feet facing the north-west, and a curved front of 4100 feet towards the city, making a circuit of 6600 feet, or just one mile and a quarter. It had 46 towers or bastions, including the two flanking towers at each of the four gates. The walled city, which envelopes the citadel for more than two-thirds of the curve, is 4200 feet in length, and 2400 feet in breadth , with the long straight side facing the south-west. Altogether the walled circuit of Multân, including both city and citadel, is 15,000 feet, or very nearly 3 miles, and the whole circuit of the place, including its suburbs, is 4½ miles. This last measurement agrees very nearly with the estimate of Hwen Thsang, who makes the circuit of Multân 30 *li*, or just 5 miles.* It agrees even more exactly with the estimate of Elphinstone, who, with his usual

* Julien's 'Hiouen Thsang,' iii. 173.

accuracy, describes Multân as "above four miles and a half in circumference."* The fortress had no ditch when seen by Elphinstone and Burnes, as it was originally surrounded by the waters of the Râvi. But shortly after Burnes's visit, a ditch was added by Sâwan Mall, the energetic governor of Ranjit Singh. The walls are said to have been built by Murâd Baksh, the youngest son of Shah Jahân; but when I dismantled the defences of Multân in 1854, I found that the walls were generally double, the outer wall being about 4 feet thick, and the inner wall 3½ feet to 4 feet.† I conclude, therefore, that only the outer wall, or facing, was the work of Murâd Baksh. The whole was built of burnt bricks and mud, excepting the outer courses, which were laid in lime-mortar to a depth of 9 inches.

Multân is known by several different names, but all of them refer either to Vishnu or to the Sun, the latter being the great object of worship in the famous temple that once crowned the citadel. Abu Rihân mentions the names of *Kasyapa-pura, Hansa-pura, Bhâgapura*, and *Sambapura*, to which I may

---

* 'Kabul,' i. 27.

† It may be interesting to note that on dismantling the wall near the *Sikhi Darwâza*, or "Spiked Gate," I found the only two shot that were fired from the great one hundred-pounder gun, which the *Bhangi Misal* of Sikhs brought against Multân in the beginning of this century. The two shot had completely penetrated through the brick wall of 7 feet, and were within three feet of each other.

add, *Prahlâdapura* and *Adyasthâna*. According to the traditions of the people, *Kasyapa-pura* was founded by *Kasyapa*, who was the father of the twelve *Adityas*, or Sun-gods, by *Aditi*, and of the *Daityas*, or Titans, by *Diti*. He was succeeded by his eldest son, the *Daitya*, named *Hiranya-Kasipu*, who is famous throughout India for his denial of the omnipresence of Vishnu, which led to the manifestation of the *Narasinha*, or "Man-lion" *avatâr*. He was followed by his still more famous son *Prahlâda*, the ardent worshipper of Vishnu, after whom the city was named *Prahlâdapura*. His great-grandson, *Bâna* commonly called *Bâna* the *Asur*, was the unsuccessful antagonist of Krishna, who took possession of the kingdom of Multân. Here *Sâmba*, the son of Krishna, established himself in the grove of *Mitra-vana*, and by assiduous devotion to *Mitra*, or the "Sun," was cured of his leprosy. He then erected a golden statue of *Mitra*, in a temple named *Adyasthâna*, or the "First Shrine," and the worship of the Sun thus began by *Sâmba*, has continued at Multân down to the present day.

The story of *Sâmba*, the son of Krishna, is told in the *Bhâvishya Purâna*,* but as it places the *Mitra-vana*, or "Sun-grove," on the bank of the Chandrabhâga, or Chenâb river, its composition must be assigned to a comparatively late period, when all remembrance of the old course of the Râvi

---

* Wilford, 'Asiatic Researches,' xi. 69 ; and H. H. Wilson, in Reinaud, 'Mémoire sur l'Inde,' p. 392.

flowing past Multân had died away. We know, however, from other sources, that the Sun-worship at Multân must be very ancient. In the seventh century Hwen Thsang found a magnificent temple with a golden statue of the god most richly adorned, to which the kings of all parts of India sent offerings. Hence the place became commonly known amongst the early Arab conquerors as "The Golden Temple;" and Masudi even affirms that *el Multân* means "meadows of gold."* Hwen Thsang calls it *Meu-lo-san-pu-lo,* which, according to M. Vivien de St. Martin, is a transcription of *Mûlasthânipura.* The people themselves refer the name to *Mûla-sthâna,* which agrees with the form of *Mûla-tâna,* quoted by Abu Rihân from a Kashmirian writer. *Mûla* means "root, or origin," and *sthâna,* or *thân,* in the spoken dialects, means "place, or shrine." Hence, *Mûla-sthâna* is the "Temple of *Mûla,*" which I take to be an appellation of the Sun. In the *Amarakosha* one of the names of the Sun is *Vradhna,* which is also given as a synonym of *Mûla*; hence *vradhna* must be connected with the Latin *radix* and *radius,* and also with the Greek ῥάβδος. But as *radix* signifies not only origin, or root, in general, but also a particular root, the radish, so also does *mûla*

* Masudi, 'Gildemeister,' p. 134: "domum auream:" so also Sir H. M. Elliot, 'Muhammadan Historians,' p. 56; but at p. 57 he translates "golden temple." Prof. Dowson, i. 23, has "boundary of the house of gold," translating Masudi; and at i. 81, "the house of gold," translating Idrisi.

signify origin, or root, and *mûlaka*, or *mûli*, a radish. The connection between a sunbeam and a radish obviously lies in their similarity of shape, and hence the terms *radius* and *mûla* are both applied to the spoke of a wheel. *Mûla-sthâna* is said by Wilson to mean "heaven, ether, space, atmosphere, God," any one of which names would be applicable to the Sun as the lord of the ethereal space. For these reasons I infer that *mûla* is only an epithet of the Sun, as the God of rays, and that *Mûla-sthâna-pura* means simply the "city of the Temple of the Sun." *Bhâga* and *Hansa* are well-known names of the Sun; and therefore *Bhâgapura* and *Hansapura* are only synonyms of the name of Multân. The earliest name is said to have been *Kasyapapura*, or as it is usually pronounced, *Kasappur*, which I take to be the *Kaspapuros* of Hekatæus, and the *Kaspaturos* of Herodotus, as well as the *Kaspeira* of Ptolemy. The last town is placed at a bend on the lower course of the *Rhuadis*, or Râvi, just above its junction with the *Sandobâg*, or *Chandrabhâga*. The position of Kaspeira therefore agrees most exactly with that of Kasyapapura or Multân, which is situated on the old bank of the Râvi, just at the point where the channel changes its course from south-east to east. This identification is most important, as it establishes the fact that Multân or Kaspeira, in the territory of the Kaspeirei, whose dominion extended from Kashmir to Mathura, must have been the principal city in the Panjâb towards the middle of the second century of the Christian era. But in the seventh century it had already acquired the name of *Mulasthânapura*, or Multân, which was the only name known to the Arab authors down to the time of Abu Rihân, whose acquirement of Sanskrit gave him access to the native literature, from which he drew some of the other names already quoted. The name of *Adyasthâna*, or "First Shrine," is applied in the *Bhâvishya Purâna* to the original temple of the Sun, which is said to have been built by Sâmba, the son of Krishna; but *adya* is perhaps only a corruption of *Aditya*, or the Sun, which is usually shortened to *adit*, and even *ait*, as in *aditwâr* and *aitwâr* for *Adityawâra*, or Sunday. Bilâduri calls the idol a representation of the prophet Job, or *Ayub*, which is an easy misreading of ايوب for اديت, *adit*. *Prahladâpura*, or *Pahlâdpur*, refers to the temple of the *Narsingh Avatâr*, which is still called *Pahlâdpuri*. When Burnes was at Multân, this temple was the principal shrine in the place, but the roof was thrown down by the explosion of the powder magazine during the siege in January, 1849, and it has not since been repaired. It stands at the north-eastern angle of the citadel, close to the tomb of Bahâwal Hak. The great temple of the Sun stood in the very middle of the citadel, but it was destroyed during the reign of Aurangzib, and the Jamai Masjid was erected on its site. This masjid was the powder magazine of the Sikhs, which was blown up in 1849.

By the identification of *Kasyapapura* with the *Kaspeira* of Ptolemy I have shown that Multân was situated on the bank of the Râvi in the first half of the second century of the Christian era. Hwen Thsang unfortunately makes no mention of the river; but a few years after his visit the Brahman Rajah of Sindh, named Chach, invaded and captured Multân, and the details of his campaign show that the Râvi still continued to flow under its walls in the middle of the seventh century. They show also that the Biâs then flowed in an independent channel to the east and south of Multân. According to the native chronicles of Sindh, Chach advanced tc *Pâbiya*, or *Bahiya** on the south bank of the Biâs, from whencc he advanced to Sukah or Sikkah on the bank of the Râvi, at a short distance to the eastward of Multân. This place was soon deserted by its defenders, who retired towards Multân, and joined Raja *Bajhra* in opposing Chach on the banks of the Râvi. After a stout fight the Multânis were defeated by Chach, and retired into their fortress, which after a long siege surrendered on terms.†

This brief notice of the campaign of Chach will now enable us to understand more clearly the campaign of Alexander against the capital of the Malli. My last notice left him at the strong Brahman city, which I have identified with *Atâri*, 34 miles to the north-east of Multân, and on the

---

* Sir Henry Elliot reads *Pâbiya*. (Prof. Dowson's edition, i. 141.) Lieut. Postans reads *Bâhiya*. (Journ. Asiat. Soc. Bengal, 1841, p. 195.)

† Lieut. Postans in Journ. Asiat. Soc. Bengal, 1838, p. 94. Sir H. W. Elliot, 'History of India,' edited by Prof. Dowson, i. 143.

high-road from Tulamba. Here I will resume the narrative of Arrian.* "Having tarried there one day to refresh his army, he then directed his march against others of the same nation, who, he was informed, had abandoned their cities and retired into the deserts; and taking another day's rest, on the next he commanded Python, and Demetrius the captain of a troop of horse, with the forces they then had, and a party of light armed foot, to return immediately to the river, etc. In the meanwhile he led his forces to the capital city of the Malii, whither, he was informed, many of the inhabitants of other cities had fled for their better security." Here we see that Alexander made just two marches from the Brahman city to the capital, which agrees very well with the distance of 34 miles between Atâri and Multân. In searching for the chief city of the *Malli* or *Malii,* we must remember that Multân has always been the capital of the Lower Panjâb, that it is four times the size of any other place, and is undeniably the strongest fort in this part of the country. All these properties belonged also to the chief city of the Malli. It was the capital of the country; it had the greatest number of defenders, 50,000 according to Arrian, and was therefore the largest place; and lastly, it must have been the strongest place, as Arrian relates that the inhabitants of other cities had fled to it "for better security." For these reasons I am quite satisfied that the capital city of the Malli

* 'Anabsis,' vi. 8.

was the modern Multân; but the identification will be still further confirmed as we proceed with Arrian's narrative.

On Alexander's approach the Indians came out of their city, and "crossing the river Hydraotes, drew up their forces upon the bank thereof, which was steep and difficult of ascent, as though they would have obstructed his passage. . . when he arrived there, and saw the enemy's army posted on the opposite bank, he made no delay, but instantly entered the river with the troops of horse he had brought with him." The Indians at first retired; "but when they perceived that their pursuers were only a party of horse, they faced about and resolved to give him battle, being about 50,000 in number." From this account I infer that Alexander must have advanced upon Multân from the east, his march, like that of Chach, being determined by the natural features of the country. Now the course of the old bed of the Râvi for 18 miles above Multân is almost due west, and consequently Alexander's march must have brought him to the fort of *Sukah* or *Sikkah*, which was on the bank of the Râvi at a short distance to the east of Multân. From this point the same narrative will describe the progress of both conquerors. The town on the east bank of the Râvi was deserted by its garrison, who retired across the river, where they halted and fought, and being beaten took refuge in the citadel. The fort of Sukah must have been somewhat near the present Mâri *Sital*, which is on the bank of the old bed of the Râvi, 2½ miles to the east of Multân.

At the assault of the capital Alexander was dangerously wounded, and his enraged troops spared neither the aged, nor the women, nor the children, and every soul was put to the sword. Diodorus and Curtius assign this city to the Oxudrakæ; but Arrian distinctly refutes this opinion,* "for the city," he says "belonged to the Malii, and from that people he received the wound. The Malii indeed designed to have joined their forces with the Oxudrakæ, and so to have given him battle; but Alexander's hasty and unexpected march through the dry and barren waste prevented their union, so that they could not give any assistance to each other." Strabo also says that Alexander received his wound at the capture of a city of the Malli.†

When Alexander opened his campaign against the Malli, he dispatched Hephæstion with the main body of the army five days in advance, with orders to await his arrival at the confluence of the Akesines and Hydraotes.‡ Accordingly after the capture of the Mallian capital, "as soon as his health would admit, he ordered himself to be conveyed to the banks of the river Hydraotes, and from thence down the stream to the camp, which was near the

* 'Anabasis,' vi. 11.

† Geogr., xv. 1, 33.

‡ 'Anabasis,' vi. 5.

confluence of the Hydraotes and Akesines, where Hephæstion had the command of the army and Nearchus of the navy." Here he received the ambassadors from the Oxudrakæ and Malii tendering their allegiance. He then sailed down the Akesines to its confluence with the Indus, where he "tarried with his fleet till Perdikkas arrived with the army under his command, having subdued the *Abastani*, one of the free nations of India, on his way."

At the capture of Multân by Chach, in the middle of the seventh century, the waters of the Râvi were still flowing under the walls of the fortress, but in A.D. 713, when the citadel was besieged by Muhammad bin Kasim, it is stated by Biladuri* that "the city was supplied with water by a stream flowing from the river (name left blank by M. Reinaud); Muhammad cut off the water, and the inhabitants, pressed by thirst, surrendered at discretion. All the men capable of bearing arms were put to death, and the women and children, with 6000 priests of the temple, were made slaves." The canal is said to have been shown to Muhammad by a traitor. I am willing to accept this account as a proof that the main stream of the Râvi had already deserted its old channel; but it is quite impossible that Multân could have been forced to surrender from want of water. I have already explained that one branch of the Râvi formerly flowed between the city and fortress of Multân, and that the old bed still

* Reinaud, 'Fragments Arabes,' p. 199.

exists as a deep hollow, in which water can be reached at most times by merely scratching the surface, and at all times by a few minutes' easy digging. Even in the time of Edrisi* the environs of the town are said to have been watered by a small river, and I conclude that some branch of the Râvi must still have flowed down to Multân. But though the narrative of Biladuri is undoubtedly erroneous as to the immediate cause of surrender, I am yet inclined to believe that all the other circumstances may be quite true. Thus, when the main stream of the Râvi deserted Multân, the city, which is still unwalled on the side towards the citadel, must have been protected by continuing its defences right across the old bed of the river to connect them with those of the fortress. In these new walls, openings must have been left for the passage of the waters of the canal or branch of the Râvi, whichever it may have been, similar to those which existed in modern times. Edrisi specially notes that Multân was commanded by a citadel, which had four gates, and was surrounded by a ditch. I infer, therefore, that Muhammad Kasim may have captured Multân in the same way that Cyrus captured Babylon, by the diversion of the waters which flowed through the city into another channel. In this way he could have entered the city by the dry bed of the river, after which it is quite possible that the garrison of the citadel may have been forced to surrender from want of water. At the present day there are several

* Geogr., Jaubert's translation, i. 168.

wells in the fortress, but only one of them is said to be ancient; and one well would be quite insufficient for the supply even of a small garrison of 5000 men.

Kahror.

The ancient town of Kahror is situated on the southern bank of the old Biâs river, 50 miles to the south-east of Multân, and 20 miles to the north-east of Bahâwalpur. It is mentioned as one of the towns which submitted to Chach* after the capture of Multân in the middle of the seventh century. But the interest attached to Kahror rests on its fame as the scene of the great battle between Vikramâditya and the Sakas, in A.D. 79. Abu Rihân describes its position as situated between Multân and the castle of Loni. The latter place is most probably intended for *Ludhan*, an ancient town situated near the old bed of the Satlej river, 44 miles to the east-north-east of Kahror, and 70 miles to the east-south-east of Multân. Its position is therefore very nearly halfway between Multân and Ludhan, as described by Abu Rihân.

Uchh.

The old town of *Uchh* is situated on the eastern bank of the *Panjnad*, 70 miles to the south-south-west of Multân, and 45 miles to the north-east of the

---

* Lieut. Postans, Journ. Asiat. Soc., Bengal, 1838, p. 95, where the translator reads *Karud*, کرود, instead of کرور, *Karor*.

present confluence with the Indus at Mithunkot. The change in the course of the Indus has taken place since the time of Wilford's surveyor, Mirza Mogal Beg, who surveyed the Panjâb and Kabul between the years 1786 and 1796, and this part in 1787-88. The former channel still exists under the name of *Nala Purân,* or the "Old Stream." *Uchcha* means "high, lofty," both in Sanskrit and in Hindi; and *Uchchanagar* is therefore a common name for any place situated on a height. Thus we have *Uchcha-gaon* or *Bulandshahr,* as the Muhammadans call it, on the high bank of the Kâli Nadi, 40 miles to the south-east of Delhi. We have another *Uchh* on a mound to the west of the confluence of the Chenâb and Jhelam; and a third *Uchh,* which is also situated on a mound, is the subject of the present description. According to Burnes,* Uchh is formed of three distinct towns, a few hundred yards apart from each other, and each encompassed by a brick wall, now in ruins. Masson† mentions only two separate towns; but the people themselves say that there were once seven different towns namd *Uchchanagar.* In Mogal Beg's map Uchh is entered with the remark, "consisting of seven distinct villages." According to Masson, Uchh is chiefly "distinguished by the ruins of the former towns, which are very extensive, and attest the pristine prosperity of the locality." Accordng to Burnes, the town of Uchh stands on a

---

* 'Bokhara,' i. 79.

†. 'Travels,' i. 22.

mound, which he judged, from a section exposed by an inundation of the Chenâb, to be formed of the ruins of houses. This opinion is doubtless correct, as the place has been repeatedly destroyed and rebuilt. After the last great siege, in A.H. 931, or A.D. 1524-25, by Husen Shah Arghun, the walls of Uchh were levelled to the ground, and the gates and other materials were carried off to Bakar in boats.* Its favourable position at the old confluence of the Panjâb rivers must have made it a place of importance from the earliest times. Accordingly, we learn from Arrian that Alexander "ordered a city to be built at the confluence of the two rivers, imagining that by the advantage of such a situation it would become rich and populous."† It is probably this city which is mentioned by Rashid ud din‡ as the capital of one of the four principalities of Sindh under *Ayand*, the son of *Kafand*, who reigned after Alexander. He calls the place *Askaland-usah*, which would be an easy corruption of *Alexandria Uchcha*, or *Ussa*, as the Greeks must have written it. I think, also, that Uchh must be the *Iskandar*, or *Alexandria*, of the Chach-nâmah, which was captured by Chach on his expedition against Multân.‡ After the Muhammadan conquest the place is mentioned only by its native name of Uchh. It was captured by Mahmud of Ghazni, and Muhammad

* Postans, Journ. Asiat. Soc. Bengal, 1841, p. 275.
† 'Anabasis,' vi. 15.
‡ Postans, Journ. Asiat. Soc. Bengal, 1838, p. 94.

Ghori, and it was the chief city of Upper Sindh under Nâser ud din Kubâchah. At a later period it formed part of the independent kingdom of Multân, which was established shortly after the troubles that followed the invasion of Timur.* In A.D. 1524 it was taken by storm by Shah Husen or Hasan Arghun of Sindh, when its walls were dismantled, as I have already noticed. But after the capture of Multân, Husen ordered the fort of Uchh to be rebuilt, in which he left a large garrison to secure the possession of his recent conquests. In the reign of Akbar, Uchh was permanently annexed to the Mogal empire, and is included by Abul Fazl amongst the separate districts of the Subah of Multân.

The country at the confluence of the Panjâb rivers is assigned by Curtius to the *Sambracœ* or *Sabracœ*, and by Diodorus to the *Sambastœ*. They are not mentioned by Arrian, at least under this name; but I think that the *Ossadii*, who tendered their allegiance to Alexander at the confluence of the rivers, were the same people. It is probable also that the *Abastani*, who were subdued by Perdikkas, belonged to the same class. Perdikkas had been dispatched by Alexander to the east of the Râvi, where he captured a town which I have identified with Harapa. I infer that his campaign must have been an extended one, as Alexander, whose own movements had been delayed by his wound, was still obliged to halt for him at the confluence of the

* Briggs's 'Ferishta,' iv. 380.

rivers. It seems highly probable therefore that he may have carried the Greek arms to *Ajudhan* on the banks of the Satlej, from which his march would have been along the course of that river by Ludhan, Mailsi, Kahror, and Lodhran, to Alexander's camp at Uchh. In this route he must have encountered the *Johiya* Rajputs, who have occupied both banks of the Satlej from Ajudhan to Uchh from time immemorial. I think therefore that the *Abastani,* whom Perdikkas subdued have a strong claim to be identified with the *Johiya* Rajputs. The country about Multân is still called *Johiya-bâr* or *Yaudheya-wâra*.

The Johiyas are divided into three tribes, named *Langavira* or *Lakvira, Mâdhovira* or *Mâdhera,* and *Adamvira* or *Admera*. The *Sambracæ* would appear to have been divided into three clans, as being a free people without kings they chose *three* generals to lead them against the Greeks. Now Johiya is an abbreviation of *Jodhiya*, which is the Sanskrit *Yaudheya,* and there are coins of this clan of as early a date as the first century of the Christian era, which show that the *Yaudheyas* were even then divided into three tribes. These coins are of three classes, of which the first bears the simple inscription *Jaya-Yaudheya-ganasya,* that is (money) "of the victorious Yaudheya tribe." The second class has *dwi* at the end of the legend, and the third has *tri,* which I take to be contractions for *dwitiyasya* and *tritiyasya,* or second and third, as the money of the second and third tribes of the *Yaudheyas*. As the coins are found to the west of the Satlej, in Depâlpur, Satgarha, Ajudhan, Kahror, and Multân, and to the eastward in Bhatner, Abhor, Sirsa, Hânsi, Pânipat, and Sonpat, it is almost certain that they belong to the Johiyas, who now occupy the line of the Satlej, and who were still to be found in Sirsa as late as the time of Akbar. The *Yaudheyas* are mentioned in the Allahabad inscription of Samudra Gupta, and at a still earlier date by Pânini in the Junagarh inscription of Rudra Dâma.* Now the great grammarian was certainly anterior to Chandra Gupta Maurya, and his mention of the Yaudheyas proves that they must have been a recognized clan before the time of Alexander. The inscription of Rudra Dâma, in which he boasts of having "rooted out the *Yaudheyas*, shows that this powerful clan must have extended their arms very far to the south, otherwise they would not have come into collision with the princes of Surashtra. From these facts I am led to infer that the possessions of the *Johiyas* in the time of Alexander most probably extended from Bhatner and Pâkpatan to Subzalkot, about halfway between Uchh and Bhakar.

I will now examine the different names of the people who made their submission to Alexander during his halt at the confluence of the Panjâb rivers. According to Curtius they were called *Sambracœ* or *Sabracœ*;† according to Crosius *Sabagrœ;* and

* Dr. Bhau Dâji in 'Bombay Journal,' vii. 120.

† Vita Alex., ix. 8. "Inde *Sabracas* adiit, validam Indiæ gentem, quæ populi, non regum, imperio regebatur."

according to Diodorus, who placed them to the east of the river, *Sambastæ.** They were a powerful nation, second to none in India for courage and numbers. Their forces consisted of 60,000 foot, 6000 horse, and 500 chariots. The military reputation of the clan suggests the probability that the Greek name may be descriptive of their warlike character, just as *Yaudheya* means "warrior or soldier." I think, therefore, that the true Greek name may have been *Sambagræ,* for the Sanskrit *Samvâgri,* that is, the "united warriors," or *Σύμμαχοι,* which, as they were formed of three allied tribes, would have been an appropriate appellation. In confirmation of this suggestion, I may note the fact that the country of which Bikaner is now the capital was originally called *Bâgar-des,* or the land of the *Bâgri,* or "Warriors," whose leader was Bâgri Rao.† *Bhati* also means "warrior or soldier." We thus find three tribes at the present day, all calling themselves "warriors," who form a large proportion of the population in the countries to the east of the Satlej; namely, *Johiyas* or *Yaudheyas* along the river, *Bâgris* in Bikaner, and *Bhatis* in Jesalmer. All three are of acknowledged Lunar descent; and if my suggested interpretation of *Sambâgri* be correct, it is

---

* Hist., xvii. 10.

† This information I obtained at the famous fortress of Bhatner in the Bikaner territory. The name is certainly as old as the time of Jahângîr, as Chaplain Terry describes 'Bikaneer' as the chief city of '*Bakar.*' See 'A Voyage to East India,' p. 86.

possible that the name might have been applied to these three clans, and not to the three tribes of the Yaudheyas. I think, however, that the Yaudheyas have a superior claim, both on account of their position along the banks of the Satlej, and of their undoubted antiquity. To them I would attribute the foundation of the town of *Ajudhan*, or *Ayodhanam*, the "battle-field," which is evidently connected with their own name of *Yaudheya*, or *Ajudhiya*, the "warriors." The latter form of the name is most probably preserved in the *Ossadii* of Arrian, a free people, who tendered their allegiance to Alexander at the confluence of the Panjâb rivers. The *Ossadii* of Arrian would therefore correspond with the Sambastæ of Diodorus and the Sambracæ of Curtius, who made their submission to Alexander at the same place. Now *Ossadioi* or *Assodioi* is as close a rendering of *Ajudhiya* as could be made in Greek characters. We have thus a double correspondence both of name and position in favour of my identification of the Sabagræ or Sambracæ with the Johiyas of the present day.

WESTERN INDIA.

Western India, according to Hwen Thsang, was divided into three great states, named *Sindh, Gurjjara*, and *Balabhi*. The first comprised the whole valley of the Indus from the *Panjâb* to the sea, including the Delta and the island of Kachh; the second comprised Western Rajputâna and the Indian

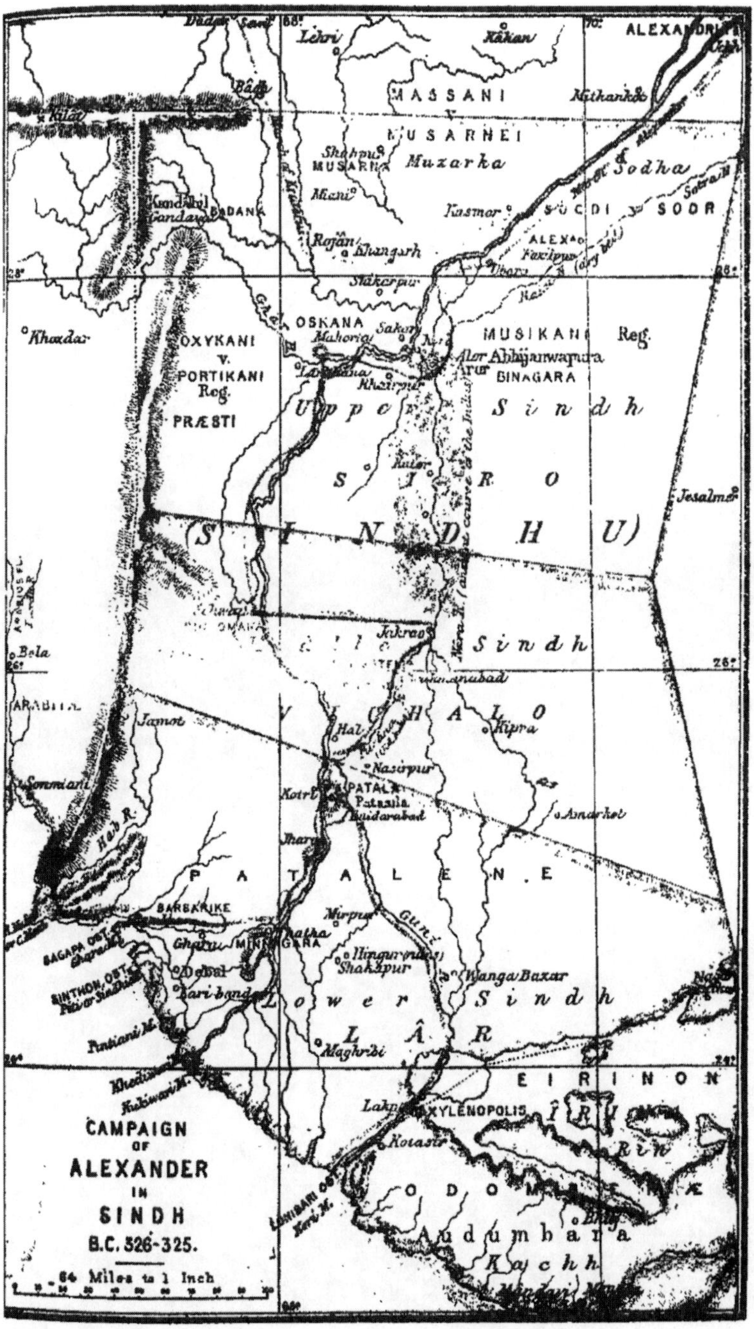
CAMPAIGN
OF
ALEXANDER
IN
SINDH
B.C. 326-325.
64 Miles to 1 Inch
ALEXANDRIA
MASSANI
v.
MUSARNEI
Muzarka
Sodha
SOGDI
SOOR
OXYKANI
v.
PORTIKANI
Reg.
PRÆSTI
OSKANA
MUSIKANI
Reg.
Alor
BINAGARA
Upper Sindh
SINDHU
PATALENE
Lower Sindh
LÂR
EIRINON
XYLENOPOLIS
ODOMBÆ
Audumbara
Kachh
BARSARIKE
MINNAGARA
Khozdar
Bela
ARABITÆ
Sonmiani
Hab R.
Jamot
Hala
Kipra
Nasirpur
Kotri
Haidarabad
Amarkot
Mirpur
Thatha
Shahapur
Maghribi
Lakpat
Kotasir
Bhuj
Jesalmer
Kakan
Lehri
Mithankot
Kasmor
Khangarh
Rojan
Mahorta
Khairpur
Rohri
Gandava
Mani
Wanga Bazar
Debal
Piti or Sia Dhor
Pintiani M.
Kori M.
Guni

Desert, and the third comprised the peninsula of Gujarât, with a small portion of the adjacent coast.

I. SINDH.

In the seventh century Sindh was divided into four principalities, which, for the sake of greater distinctness, I will describe by their geographical positions, as Upper Sindh, Middle Sindh, Lower Sindh, and Kachh.* The whole formed one kingdom under the Raja of Upper Sindh, who, at the time of Hwen Thsang's visit in A.D. 641, was a *Siu-to-lo* or *Sudra*. So also in the time of Chach, only a few years later, the minister Budhimân informs the king that the country had been formerly divided into four districts, each under its own ruler, who acknowledged the supremacy of Chach's predecessors.† At a still earlier date Sindh is said to have been divided into four principalities by *Ayand*, the son of *Kafand*,‡ who reigned some time after Alexander the Great. These four principalities are named *Zor*, *Askalandusa*, *Sâmid*, and *Lohâna*, all of which will be discussed presently, as they would appear to correspond with the divisions noted by Hwen Thsang.

Upper Sindh.

The single principality of Upper Sindh, which is now generally known as *Sîro*, that is the "Head

---

* See Map No. IX.

† Postans in Journ. Asiat. Soc. Bengal, 1838, p. 93.

‡ Rashid ud din, in Reinaud's 'Fragments Arabes', p. 47.

or Upper" division, is described as being 7000 *li*, or 1167 miles, in circuit, which is too great, unless, as is very probable, it comprised the whole of Kachh Gandâva on the west. This was, no doubt, always the case under a strong government, which that of Chach's predecessor is known to have been. Under this view Upper Sindh would have comprised the present districts of Kachh-Gandâva, Kâhan, Shikârpur, and Larkâna to the west of the Indus, and to the east those of Sabzalkot and Khairpur. The lengths of the frontier lines would, therefore, have been as follows:—on the north 340 miles; on the west 250 miles; on the east 280 miles, and on the south 260 miles; or altogether 1030 miles, which is a very near approximation to the estimate of Hwen Thsang.

In the seventh century the capital of the province was named *Pi-chen-po-pu-lo*, which M. Julien transcribes as *Vichava-pura*. M. Vivien de St. Martin, however, suggests that it may be the Sanskrit *Vichâlapura*, or city of "Middle Sindh," which is called *Vicholo* by the people. But the Sindhi and Panjâbi *Vich* and the Hindi *Bîch*, or "middle," are not derived from the Sanskrit, which has a radical word of its own, *Madhya*, to express the same thing. If Hwen Thsang had used the vernacular terms, his name might have been rendered exactly by the Hindi *Bichwâ-pur*, or "Middle City," but as he invariably uses the Sanskrit forms, I think that we must rather look to some pure Sanskrit word for the original of his *Pi-chen-po-pu-lo*. Now we know from tradition, as well as from the native historians, that Alor was the capital of Sindh both before and after the period of Hwen Thsang's visit; this new name, therefore, must be only some variant appellation of the old city, and not that of a second capital. During the Hindu period it was the custom to give several names to all the larger cities,—as we have already seen in the case of Multân. Some of these were only poetical epithets; as *Kusumapura*, or "Flower City" applied to Pâtaliputra, and *Padmavati*, or, "Lotus Town" applied to Narwar; others were descriptive epithets as *Varanâsi*, or Banáras, applied to the city of Kâsi, to show that it was situated between the *Varana* and *Asi* rivulets; and *Kányakubja*, the "hump-backed maiden," applied to Kanoj, as the scene of a well-known legend. The difference of name does not, therefore, imply a new capital, as it may be only a new appellation of the old city, or perhaps even the restoration of an old name which had been temporarily supplanted. It is true that no second name of Alor is mentioned by the historians of Sindh; but as Alor was actually the capital in the time of Hwen Thsang, it would seem to be quite certain that his name of *Pi-chen-po-pu-lo* is only another name for that city.

It is of importance that this identification should be clearly established, as the pilgrim places the capital to the west of the Indus, whereas the present ruins of Alor or Aror are to the east of the river. But this very difference confirms the accuracy of the identification, for the Indus formerly flowed to the east of Alor, down the old channel, now called *Nâra*, and the change in its course did not take place until the reign of Raja Dâhir,* or about fifty years after Hwen Thsang's visit. The native histories attribute the desertion of Alor by the Indus to the wickedness of Raja Dâhir; but the gradual *westing* of all the Panjâb rivers which flow from north to south, is only the natural result of the earth's continued revolution from west to east, which gives their waters a permanent bias towards the western banks.† The original course of the Indus was to the east of the Alor range of hills; but as the waters gradually worked their way to the westward, they at last turned the northern end of the range at Rori, and cut a passage for themselves through the gap in the limestone rocks between Rori and Bhakar. As the change is assigned to the beginning of Dâhir's reign, it must have taken place shortly after his accession in A.D. 680;—and as Muhammad Kasim, just thirty years later, was obliged to cross the Indus to reach Alor, it is certain that the river was permanently fixed in its present channel before A.D. 711.

The old bed of the Indus still exists under the name of Nâra, and its course has been surveyed from the ruins of Alor to the Ran of Kachh. From Alor

* Postans, Journ. Asiat. Soc. Bengal, 1838, p. 103.

† All streams that flow from the poles towards the equator work gradually to the westward, while those that flow from the equator towards the poles work gradually to the eastward. These opposite effects are caused by the same difference of the earth's polar and equatorial velocities which gives rise to the trade winds.

to Jakrao, a distance of 100 miles, its direction is nearly due south. It there divides into several channels, each bearing a separate name. The most easterly channel, which retains the name of *Nâra,* runs to the south-east by Kipra and Umrkot, near which it turns to the south-west by Wanga Bazar and Romaka Bazar, and is there lost in the great Ran of Kachh. The most westerly channel, which is named *Purâna,* or the "Old River," flows to the south-south-west, past the ruins of Brahmanabad and Nasirpur to Haidarabad, below which it divides into two branches. Of these, one turns to the south-west and falls into the present river 15 miles below Haidarabad and 12 miles above Jarak. The other, called the Guni, turns to the south-east and joins the Nâra above Romaka Bazar. There are at least two other channels between the Purâna and the Nâra, which branch off just below Jakrao, but their courses are only partially known. The upper half of the old Nâra, from Alor to Jakrao, is a dry sandy bed, which is occasionally filled by the flood waters of the Indus. From its head down to Jâmiji it is bounded on the west by a continuation of the Alor hills, and is generally from 200 feet to 300 feet wide and 20 feet deep. From Jâmiji to Jakrao, where the channel widens to 600 feet with the depth of 12 feet, the Nâra is bounded on both sides by broad ranges of low sand-hills. Below Jakrao the sand-hills on the western bank suddenly terminate, and the Nâra, spreading over the alluvial plains, is divided into two main branches, which grow wider and shallower as they advance, until the western channels are lost in the hard plain, and the eastern channels in a succession of marshes. But they reappear once more below the parallel of Hala and Kipra, and continue their courses as already described above.*

In Upper Sindh the only places of ancient note are *Alor*, *Rori-Bhakar*, and *Mahorta*, near *Larkâna*. Several other places are mentioned in the campaigns of Alexander, Chach, Muhammad bin Kâsim, and Husen Shah Arghun; but as the distances are rarely given, it is difficult to identify the positions where names are so constantly changed. In the campaign of Alexander we have the names of the *Massanæ*, the *Sogdi*, the *Musikani*, and the *Præsti*, all of which must certainly be looked for in Upper Sindh, and which I will now attempt to identify.

Massanæ and Sodræ, or Sogdi.

On leaving the confluence of the Panjâb rivers, Alexander sailed down the Indus to the realm of the Sogdi, Σόγδοι, where, according to Arrian,† "he built another city." Diodorus‡ describes the same people, but under a different name:—"Continuing his descent of the river, he received the submission of the *Sodræ* and the *Massanæ*, nations on opposite banks of the stream, and founded another Alexan-

* See Map No. IX.

† 'Anabasis,' vi. 15.

‡ Hist. Univers. xvii. 56.

dria, in which he placed 10,000 inhabitants." The same people are described by Curtius,* although he does not mention their names :—"On the fourth day he came to other nations, where he built a town called Alexandria." From these accounts it is evident that the *Sogdi* of Arrian and the *Sodræ* of Diodorus are the same people, although the former have been identified with the *Sodha* Rajputs by Tod and M'Murdo, the latter with the servile *Sudras* by Mr. Vaux. The *Sodhas*, who are a branch of the Pramâras, now occupy the south-eastern district of Sindh, about Umarkot, but according to M'Murdo,† who is generally a most trustworthy guide, there is good reason to believe that they once held large possessions on the banks of the Indus, to the northward of Alor. In adopting this extension of the territory formerly held by the Sodha Rajputs, I am partly influenced by the statement of Abul Fazl, that the country from Bhakar to Umarkot was peopled by the *Sodas* and *Jharejas* in the time of Akbar,‡ and partly by the belief that the *Massanæ* of Diodorus are the *Musarnei* of Ptolemy, whose name still exists in the district of *Muzarka*, to the west of the Indus below Mithankot. Ptolemy also gives a town called *Musarna*, which he places on a small affluent of the Indus, to the north of the *Askana* rivulet. The

* Vita Alex., 8.

† Journ. Royal Asiat. Soc. i. 33.

‡ 'Ayin Akbari,' ii. 117.

Musarna affluent may therefore be the rivulet of Kâhan, which flows past Pulaji and Shahpur, towards Khângarha or Jacobabad, and Musarna may be the town of Shahpur, which was a place of some consequence before the rise of Shikârpur. "The neighbouring country, now nearly desolate, has traces of cultivation to a considerable extent."* The *Sogdi*, or *Sodræ*, I would identify with the people of *Seorai*, which was captured by Husen Shah Arghun on his way from Bhakar to Multân.† In his time, A.D. 1525, it is described as "the strongest fort in that country." It was, however, deserted by the garrison, and the conqueror ordered its walls to be razed to the ground. Its actual position is unknown, but it was probably close to Fâzilpur, halfway between Sabzalkot and Chota Ahmedpur, where Masson‡ heard that there was formerly a considerable town, and that "the wells belonging to it, 360 in number, were still to be seen in the jangals." Now in this very position, that is about 8 miles to the north-east of Sabzalkot, the old maps insert a village named *Sirwahi*, which may possibly represent the *Seorai* of Sindhian history. It is 96 miles in a direct line below Uchh, and 85 miles above Alor, or very nearly midway between them. By water the distance from Uchh would be at least one-third greater, or not less than 120 miles, which

* Thornton, 'Gazetteer,' *in voce*.

† Erskine's Hist. of India, i. 388. Postans, Journ. Asiat. Soc. Bengal, 1841, 275.

‡ 'Travels,' i. 382.

would agree with the statement of Curtius that Alexander reached the place on the fourth day. It is admitted that these identifications are not altogether satisfactory; but they are perhaps as precise as can now be made, when we consider the numerous fluctuations of the Indus, and the repeated changes of the names of places on its banks. One fact, preserved by Arrian, is strongly in favour of the indentification of the old site near Fâzilpur with the town of the *Sogdi*, namely, that from this point Alexander dispatched Kraterus* with the main body of the army, and all the elephants, through the confines of the Arachoti and Drangi. Now the most frequented Ghât for the crossing of the Indus towards the west, viâ the Gandâva and Bolân Pass, lies between Fâzilpur on the left bank, and Kasmor on the right bank. And as the ghâts, or points of passage of the rivers, always determine the roads, I infer that Kraterus must have begun his long march towards Arachosia and Drangiana from this place, which is the most northern position on the Indus for the departure of a large army to the westward. It seems probable, however, that Kraterus was detained for some time by the revolt of Musikanus, as his departure is again mentioned by Arrian,† after Alexander's capture of the Brahman city near Sindomana.

Between Multân and Alor the native historians, as well as the early Arab geographers, place a

* 'Anabasis,' vi. 15.

† 'Anabasis,' vi. 17.

strong fort named *Bhâtia*, which, from its position, has a good claim to be identified with the city which Alexander built amongst the Sogdi, as it is not likely that there were many advantageous sites in this level tract of country. Unfortunately, the name is variously written by the different authorities. Thus, Postans gives *Pâya*, *Bâhiya*, and *Pâhiya;* Sir Henry Elliot gives *Pâbiya*, *Bâtia*, and *Bhâtiya*, while Price gives *Bahâtia*.* It seems probable that it is the same place as *Talhâti*,† where Jâm Janar crossed the Indus; and perhaps also the same as *Mâtila*, or *Mahâtila*,‡ which was one of the six great forts of Sindh in the seventh century.

Bhâtia is described by Ferishta as a very strong place, defended by a lofty wall and a deep broad ditch.§ It was taken by assault in A.H. 393, or A.D. 1003, by Mahmud of Ghazni, after an obstinate defence, in which the Raja, named *Bajjar*, or *Bijé Rai*, was killed. Amongst the plunder Mahmud obtained no less than 280 elephants, a most substantial proof of the wealth and power of the Hindu prince.

Musikani—Alor.

From the territory of the *Sogdi* or *Sodræ*, Alexander continued his voyage down the Indus to-

---

* Dowson's edition of Sir H. Elliot, i. 138.

† Journ. Asiat. Soc. Bengal, 1845, p. 171.

‡ *Ibid.*, 1845, p. 79.

§ Briggs's 'Ferishta,' i. 39 ; and Tabakât. i. Akbari, in Sir Henry Elliot, p. 186.

the capital of a king named *Musikanus*, according to Strabo, Diodorus, and Arrian,* or of a people named Musicani, according to Curtius.† From Arrian we learn that this kingdom had been described to Alexander as "the richest and most populous throughout all India;" and from Strabo we get the account of Onesikritus that "the country produced everything in abundance;" which shows that the Greeks themselves must have been struck with its fertility. Now these statements can apply only to the rich and powerful kingdom of Upper Sindh, of which Alor is known to have been the capital for many ages. Where distances are not given, and names disagree, it is difficult to determine the position of any place from a general description, unless there are some peculiarities of site or construction, or other properties which may serve to fix its identity. In the present instance we have nothing to guide us but the general description that the kingdom of Musikanus was "the richest and most populous throughout all India." But as the native histories and traditions of Sindh agree in stating that Alor was the ancient metropolis of the country, it seems almost certain that it must be the capital of Musikanus, otherwise this famous city would be altogether unnoticed by Alexander's historians, which is highly improbable, if not quite impossible. That the

---

* Strabo, Geogr., xv. i. 22-34 and 54. Diodorus, xvii. 10. Arrian, 'Anabasis,' vi. 15.

† Vita Alex., ix. 8.

territory of Alor was rich and fertile we know from the early Arab geographers, who are unanimous in its praise.

The ruins of Alor are situated to the south of a gap in the low range of limestone-hills, which stretches from Bhakar towards the south for about 20 miles, until it is lost in the broad belt of sand-hills which bound the Nâra, or old bed of the Indus, on the west. Through this gap a branch of the Indus once flowed, which protected the city on the north-west. To the north-east it was covered by a second branch of the river, which flowed nearly at right angles to the other, at a distance of 3 miles. At the accession of Raja Dâhir, in A.D. 680, the latter was probably the main stream of the Indus, which had been gradually working to the westward from its original bed in the old Nâra.* According to the native histories, the final change was hastened by the excavation of a channel through the northern end of the range of hills between Bhakar and Rori.

The true name of Alor is not quite certain. The common pronunciation at present is *Aror,* but it seems probable that the original name was *Rora,* and that the initial vowel was derived from the Arabic prefix *Al,* as it is written *Alror* in Biladûri, Edrisi, and other Arab authors. This derivation is countenanced by the name of the neighbouring town of *Rori,* as it is a common practice in India thus to duplicate names. So *Rora* and *Rori* would mean

---

* See Map No. IX.

Great and Little *Rora*. This word has no meaning in Sanskrit, but in Hindi it signifies "noise, clamour, *roar*," and also "fame." It is just possible, therefore, that the full name of the city may have been *Rora-pura*, or *Rora-nagar*, the "Famous City." This signification suggested itself to me on seeing the name of *Abhijanu* applied to a neighbouring village at the foot of the hill, 2 miles to the south-west of the ruins of Alor. *Abhijan* is a Sanskrit term for "fame," and is not improbably connected with Hwen Thsang's *Pi-chen-po-pu-lo*, which, by adding an initial syllable *o*, might be read as *Abhijanwapura*. I think it probable that Alor may be the *Binagara* of Ptolemy, as it is placed on the Indus to the eastward of *Oskana*, which appears to be the *Oxykanus* of Arrian and Curtius. Ptolemy's name of Binagara is perhaps only a variant reading of the Chinese form, as *pulo*, or *pura*, is the same as *nagara*, and *Pichenpo* may be the full form of the initial syllable *Bi*.

The city of Musikanus was evidently a position of some consequence, as Arrian relates that Alexander "ordered Kraterus to build a castle in the city, and himself tarried there to see it finished. This done, he left a strong garrison therein, because this fort seemed extremely commodious for bridling the neighbouring nations and keeping them in subjection." It was no doubt for this very reason that Alor was originally founded, and that it continued to be occupied until deserted by the river, when it was supplanted by the strong fort of Bhakar.

Præsti—Portikanus, or Oxykanus.

From the capital of Musikanus Alexander allowed his fleet of boats to continue their course down the Indus, while he himself, according to Arrian,* marched against a neighbouring prince named Oxykanus, and took two of his chief cities at the first assault. Curtius makes *Oxycanus* the king of a people named *Præsti*† and states that Alexander captured his chief city after a siege of three days. Diodorus and Strabo call the king *Portikanus*. Now, these various readings at once suggest the probability that the name was that of the city, which, either as *Uchcha-gâm*, or *Porta-gâm*, means simply the "Lofty town," in allusion to its height. The description of Curtius of the "tremendous crash" made by the fall of two towers of its citadel shows that the place must have been more than usually lofty. I would therefore identify it with the great mound of *Mahorta* on the bank of the Ghâr river, 10 miles from Larkâna. Masson describes it as "the remains of an ancient fortress, on a huge mound, named *Maihota*."‡ *Mahorta*, which is the spelling adopted by the surveyors, is probably *Mahorddha*, for *mahâ* + *urddha* + *grâma*, or "the great lofty city," which, as pure Sanskrit, is not

---

* 'Anabasis,' vi. 16.

† Vita Alex., ix. 8, 26.

‡ 'Travels,' i. 461.

likely to be a modern name. This identification appears to me to be very probable, not only on account of the exact correspondence of name, but also on account of the relative positions of Alor and Mahorta with reference to the old course of the Indus. At present Mahorta is within a few miles of the river; but in the time of Alexander, when the Indus flowed down the bed of the Nâra, the nearest point of the stream was at Alor, from which Mahorta was distant 45 miles to the south of west. Hence Alexander was obliged to leave his fleet, and to *march* against Oxykanus.

The site of Mahorta must always have been a position of great importance, both commercially and politically, as it commanded the high-road from Sindh, viâ Kachh-Gandâva, to Kandahar. Since its desertion, the same advantages have made Larkâna, which is situated on the same small stream, 10 miles to the west of Mahorta, one of the most flourishing places in Sindh. The rivulet called the Ghâr rises near Kelât, and traverses the whole length of the *Mula*, or *Gandâva* Pass, below which it is now lost in the desert. But the channel is still traceable, and the stream reappears on the frontier of Sindh, and flows past Larkâna and Mahorta into the Indus. Under a strong and judicious ruler, who could enforce an economical distribution of the available waters, the banks of the Ghâr rivulet must formerly have been one of the most fertile districts of Sindh.

The name of *Prœsti* given by Curtius* might,

* Vita Alex., ix. 8.

according to Wilson, be applied to a people occupying the *thals*, or "oases," of the desert. He refers to *Prastha*, or *Prasthala*, as derived from *sthala*, the Sanskrit form of the vernacular *thal*, which is the term generally used to designate any oasis in Western India. But as the name is simply *Prœsti*, I think that it may rather be referred to *prastha*, which means any clear piece of level ground, and might therefore be applied to the plain country about Larkâna, in contradistinction to the neighbouring hilly districts of Sehwân and Gandâva. It seems possible, however, that it may be connected with the *Piska* of Ptolemy, which he places on the lower course of the small stream that flows past *Oskana* into the Indus. Now Oskana is almost certainly the *Oxykanus* of Arrian and Curtius, for not only are the two names absolutely identical, but the inland position of Oskana, on a small stream to the west of the Indus, agrees exactly with that of Mahorta, which I have identified with Oxykanus. I think also that Ptolemy's *Badana*, which lies immediately to the north of the rivulet, must be the present Gandâva, as the letters B and G are constantly interchanged. In the books of the early Arab writers it is always called *Kandâbil*.

2. MIDDLE SINDH.

The principality of Middle Sindh, which is generally known as *Vichalo*, or the "Midland," is described by Hwen Thsang as only 2500 *li*, or 417 miles, in circuit. With these small dimensions the province must have been limited to the modern district of Sehwân, with the northern parts of Haidarâbâd and Umarkot. Within these limits the north and south frontiers are each about 160 miles in length, and the east and west frontiers about 45 miles each, or altogether not more than 410 miles in circuit. The chief city, named *O.fan.cha,* was situated at 700 *li,* or 117 miles, from the capital of Upper Sindh, and 50 miles from *Pitasila*, the capital of Lower Sindh. As the former was *Alor,* and the latter was almost certainly the *Pattala* of the Greeks, or Haidarâbâd, the recorded distances fix the position of *O-fan-cha* in the immediate vicinity of the ruins of an ancient city called *Bambhra-ka-Tul,* or the "Ruined Tower," or simply *Banbhar,* which, according to tradition, was the site of the once famous city of Brahmanwâs, or Brahmanâbâd. Hwen Thsang's kingdom of *Ofancha,* or *Avanda,* therefore, corresponds as nearly as possible with the province of middle Sindh, which is now called *Vichalo.*

At the present day the principal places in this division of Sindh are Sehwân, Hâla, Haidarâbâd, and Umarkot. In the middle ages, under Hindu rule, the great cities were *Sadusân, Brâhmana,* or *Bâhmanwâ,* and *Nirunkot.* But as I shall presently attempt to show that Nirunkot was most probably the modern Haidarâbâd and the ancient *Pattala,* it will more properly be included in the province of Lower Sindh, or *Lâr.* Close to *Bâhmanwâ* the early Muhammadans founded *Mansura,* which, as the residence of their governors, was the actual capital of the province, and soon became the largest city in all Sindh. In the time of Alexander, the only places mentioned are *Sindomâna,* and a city of *Brahmans,* named *Harmatelia* by Diodorus. I will now describe these places in detail, beginning with the most northerly.

Sindomâna, or Sehwân.

From the city of Oxykanus, Alexander "led his forces against *Sambus,* whom he had before declared governor of the Indian mountaineers." The Raja abandoned his capital, named Sindomana, which, according to Arrian,* was delivered up to Alexander by the friends and domestics of Sambus, who came forth to meet him with presents of money and elephants. Curtius† calls the raja *Sabus,* but does not name his capital. He simply states that Alexander, having received the "submission of several towns, captured the strongest by mining." The narrative of Diodorus‡ also omits the name of the capital, but states that Sambus retired to a great distance with thirty elephants. Strabo§ merely mentions Raja Sabus, and Sindomana his capital, without adding any particulars. Curtius|| alone notes that Alexander returned to his fleet after the capture

* 'Anabasis,' vi. 16.

† Vita Alex., ix. 8.

‡ Hist. Univers., xvii. 56.

§ Geogr., xv. 1, 32.

|| Vita Alex., ix. 8: "Rursus amnem, in quo classem expectare se jusserat, repetit."

of the raja's strongest city, which must therefore have been at some distance from the Indus.

I agree with all previous writers on the ancient geography of this part of India in identifying *Sindomana* with *Sehwân;* partly from its similarity of name, and partly from its vicinity to the Lakki mountains. Of its antiquity there can be no doubt, as the great mound, which was once the citadel, is formed chiefly of ruined buildings, the accumulation of ages, on a scarped rock, at the end of the Lakki range of hills. De La Hoste* describes it as an oval, 1200 feet long, 750 feet broad, and 80 feet high; but when I saw it in 1855, it appeared to me to be almost square in shape, and I judged it to be somewhat larger and rather more lofty above the river bed than Burnes's estimate.† It was then on the main stream of the Indus; but the river is constantly changing its channel, and in all the old maps it is placed on a western branch of the Indus. In ancient times, however, when the river flowed down the eastern channel of the *Nâra,* Sehwân was not less than 65 miles distant from its nearest point at Jakrao, where it leaves the sand-hills. At present its water supply is entirely derived from the Indus, which not only flows under the eastern front of the town, but also along its northern front, by a channel called the Aral river, from the great Manchur lake,

---

* Journ. Asiat. Soc. Bengal, 1840, p. 913.

† Westmacott, in Journ. Asiat. Soc. Bengal for 1840, p. 1209, says about 100 feet above the *Arrul* river, or *Arol,* which in his time was a branch of the Indus.

which is supplied by the other Nâra, or great western branch of the Indus. But as the site could not have been occupied unless well supplied with water, it is certain that the Manchur lake must have existed long previous to the change in the course of the Indus. Judging by its great depth in the middle,* it must be a natural depression; and as it is still fed by two small streams, which take their rise in the Hâla Lakki mountains, to the south, it seems probable that the lake may have extended even up to the walls of Sehwân, before the floods of the western Nâra cut a channel into the Indus, and thus permanently lowered the level of its waters. The lake abounds in fish, from which it would appear to derive its name, as *Manchur* is but a slight alteration of the Sanskrit *Matsya,* and the Hindi *machh,* or *machhi,* "fish." I think, therefore, that *Manchar* may be only a familiar contraction of *machhi-wâla Tâl,* or Fish Lake.

The favourable position of Sehwân, on a lofty isolated rock, near a large lake, with food and water in abundance, would certainly have attracted the notice of the first inhabitants of Sindh. We find, accordingly, that its early occupation is admitted by all inquirers. Thus, M'Murdo† says, "Sehwân is undoubtedly a place of vast antiquity; perhaps more so than either Alor or Bâhmana." The present

* Westmacott, Journ. Asiat. Soc. Bengal, 1840, p. 1207.

† Journ. Royal Asiat. Soc., i. 30.

name is said to be a contraction of *Sewistân*, which was so called after its inhabitants, the *Sewis*, or Sabis. But in all the early Arab geographers the name is somewhat differently written, as *Sadustân*, or *Sadusân*, or *Shârusan*, of which the first two syllables agree with the Greek *Sindomana*. I therefore reject the reading of *Sewistân* as a modern innovation of the Hindus, to connect the place with the name of their god *Siva*. The *Sindo* of the Greek, and the *Sadu* of the early Muhammadans, point to the Sanskrit name of the country, *Sindhu*, or to that of its inhabitants, *Saindhava*, or *Saindhu*, as it is usually pronounced. Their stronghold, or capital, would therefore have been called *Saindhava-sthâna*, or *Saindhu-sthân*, which, by the elision of the nasal, becomes the *Sadustân* of the Arab geographers. In a similar manner Wilson derives the Greek *Sindomana* from "a very allowable Sanskrit compound, *Sindu-mân*," the "possessor of Sindh." I am inclined, however to refer the Greek name to *Saindhava-vanam*, or *Saindhuwân*, as the "abode of the Saindhavas."

It seems strange that a notable place like Sehwân should not be mentioned by Ptolemy under any recognizable name. If we take Haidarâbâd as the most probable head of the Delta in ancient times, then Ptolemy's *Sydros*, which is on the eastern bank of the Indus, may perhaps be identified with the old site of Mattali, 12 miles above Haidarâbâd, and his *Pasipeda* with Sehwân. The identification of Ptolemy's *Oskana* with the *Oxykanus*, or *Portikanus*, of Alexander, and with the great mound of Mahorta of the present day, is, I think, almost certain. If so, either Piska or Pasipeda must be Sehwân.

Hwen Thsang takes no notice of Sehwân, but it is mentioned in the native histories of Sindh as one of the towns captured by Muhammad bin Kasim in A. D. 711. It was again captured by Mahmud of Ghazni in the beginning of the eleventh century; and under the Muhammadan rule it would appear to have become one of the most flourishing places in Sindh. It is now very much decayed, but its position is so favourable that it is not likely ever to be deserted.

Brâhmana, or Brâhmanâbâd.

From Sindomana Alexander "marched back to the river, where he had ordered his fleet to wait for him. Thence, descending the stream, he came on the fourth day to a town through which was a road to the kingdom of Sabus."* When Alexander quitted his fleet at Alor (the capital of Musikanus) to march against Oxykanus, he had no intention of going to Sindomana, as Raja Sambus, having tendered his submission, had been appointed satrap of the hilly districts on the Indus.† He must therefore have ordered his fleet to wait for him at some

---

* Curtius, Vita Alex., ix. 8. "Alexander . . . rursus amnem, in quo classem exspectare se jusserat, repetit. Quarto deinde die, secundo amne, pervenit ad oppidum, quâ iter in regnum erat Sabi."

† Arrian, 'Anabasis,' vi. 16: τῶν ὀρίων Ινδων σατράπην.

point on the river not far from the capital of Oxykanus. This point I would fix somewhere about *Marija Dand*, on the old *Nâra*, below Kator and Tajal, as Mahorta, which I have identified with the chief city of Oxykanus, is about equidistant from Alor and Kator. Thence, descending the stream, he came on the fourth day to a town, through which there was a road to the kingdom of Sambus. From Marija Dand, the point where I suppose that Alexander rejoined his fleet, the distance to the ruined city of Brâhmana, or Brâhmanâbâd, is 60 miles in a direct line by land, or 90 miles by water. As this distance could have been accomplished with ease in four days, I conclude that *Brâhmana* was the actual city of Brahmans which is described by Alexander's historians. The king of this city had previously submitted, but the citizens withheld their allegiance, and shut their gates. By a stratagem they were induced to come out, and a conflict ensued, in which Ptolemy was seriously wounded in the shoulder by a poisoned sword.* The mention of Ptolemy's wound enables us to identify this city with that of *Harmatelia*, which Diodorus describes as the "last town of the Brâhmans on the river."† Now, Harmatelia is only a softer pronunciation of *Brâhma-thala*, or *Brahmana-sthala*, just as Hermes, the phallic god of the Greeks, is the same as Brahmâ, the original phallic god of the Indians. But

* Curtius, Vita Alex., ix. 8.

† Hist. Univers., xvii. 56.

Brâhmana was the old Hindu name of the city which the Muhammadans called Brâhmanâbâd; hence I conclude that the town of Brahmans captured by Alexander corresponds both in name and position with the great city of Brâhmanâbâd.

The narrative of Arrian after the capitulation of Sindomana is unfortunately very brief. His words are "he attacked and won a city which had revolted from him, and put to death as many of the Brahmans as fell into his hands, having charged them with being the authors of the rebellion."* This agrees with the statement of Diodorus, who mentions that Alexander "was satisfied with punishing those who advised the resistance, and pardoned all the others." From a comparison of the three narratives, I infer that *Harmatelia*, or *Brâhmana*, was in the dominions of Musikanus; for Curtius states that the king of this city had previously submitted to Alexander, while Arrian says that he had revolted, and Diodorus adds† that Alexander punished the advisers of the rebellion. Now, all these facts apply to Musikanus, who had at first submitted, and then revolted, and was at last crucified, "and with him as many of the Brahmans as had instigated him to revolt." This identification is of some importance, as it shows that the dominions

---

* 'Anabasis,' vi. 16. *Ὁ δὲ καὶ ἄλλην πόλιν ἐν τούτῳ ἀποστᾶσαν εἷλε, καὶ τῶν Βραχμάνων . . . ὅσοι αἴτιοι τῆς ἀποστάσεως ἐγένοντο, ἀπέκτεινεν.*

† Hist. Univers., xvii. 56.

of Musikanus must have embraced the whole of the valley of the Indus down to the head of the Delta, with the exception of the two outlying districts of Oxykanus and Sambus, under the western mountains. This extension of his dominions explains the report which Alexander had previously received from the people, that the kingdom of Musikanus "was the richest and most populous throughout all India." It also explains how Sambus was at enmity with Musikanus, as the southern territories of the latter were bounded on the west by those of the former. The king of this city, where Ptolemy was wounded by a poisoned arrow, is called *Ambiger* by Justin,* which was probably the true name of Musikanus, the chief of the Musikani, in whose territory Brahmana was situated.

It is much to be regretted that none of the names preserved by Ptolemy can be certainly identified with this city of the Brahmans. *Parabali* corresponds with it in position, and partly also in name, as the first two syllables, *Parab,* are not very different from *Baram,* and the termination, *ali,* may represent *thala* of *Brahmathala,* or *Harmatelia.* After Ptolemy's time we know nothing of Brâhmana until the Muhammadan conquest, a period of nearly six centuries. From the native histories, however, we learn that Brahmana was the chief city of one of the four governments† into which Sindh was divided

* Justin, Hist., xii. 10.

† Postans, Journ. Asiat. Soc. Bengal, 1838, pp. 93-96.

during the rule of the *Rais* dynasty, or from A.D. 507 to 642, and that it continued to be so until the accession of Dâhir in A.D. 680, who made it the capital of the kingdom, after the destruction of Alor by the Indus. In A.D. 641 Sindh was visited by Hwen Thsang, whose account has already been noticed. He found the kingdom divided into the four districts, which for greater distinctness I have named Upper Sindh, Middle Sindh, Lower Sindh, and Kachh. The first has already been described in my account of Alor. The second, *O-fan-cha*, I have just identified with *Brâhmanâbâd*. M. Stanislas Julien transcribes the Chinese syllables as *Avanda*, for which it is difficult to find an exact equivalent. But I have a strong suspicion that it is only a variation of the name of *Brâhmana*, which was pronounced in many different ways, as Bâhmana, Bahmana, Bâbhana, Babhana, Bambhana.* Speaking of Mansura, which we know was quite close to Brâhmanâbâd, Ibn Haukal adds that the Sindhians call it *Bâmiwân*,† which Edrisi alters to *Mirmân*.‡ But in his list of places in Sindh, Edrisi adds after Mansura the name of *Wândân*, or *Kândân*,§ which I take to be only a various reading of Bâmanwâ, or,

* See Dhauli inscription of Asoka for Bâbhano, Babhana, and Bambhana: edicts iii. iv. viii. ix., in Journ. Royal Asiat. Soc., vol. xii.

† Sir Henry Elliot 'Muhammadan Historians of India,' p. 63.

‡ Jaubert's 'Edrisi,' i. 162.

§ Jaubert's 'Edrisi,' i. 160.

as the Sindhians would have pronounced it, *Vâmanwâ*, and *Vânwâ*. The Chinese syllable *fan*, which is the well-known transcript of *Brahma*, is a notable example of this very contraction, and tends to confirm the opinion that *Avanda* is but a slight variation of *Bâhmanwâ*, or *Brâhmanâbád*.

Shortly after the Muhammadan conquest *Brâhmana* was supplanted by *Mansura*, which, according to Biladuri, was founded by Amru, the son of Muhammad bin Kâsim, the conqueror of Sindh,* and named after the second Abasside Khalif Al *Mansûr*, who reigned from A.D. 753 to 774. But according to Masudi,† it was founded by Jamhur, the governor of Sindh, under the last Omnicad Khalif, A.D. 744 to 749, who named it after his own father *Mansûr*. The new city was built so close to Brâhmanâbâd that Ibn Haukal, Abu Rihân, and Edrisi, all describe it as the same place. Ibn Haukal's words are, "Mansura, which in the Sind language is called Bâmiwân."‡ Abu Rihân states that it was originally called *Bamanhwâ*, and after-

* Reinaud, 'Fragments Arabes;' and Jaubert's 'Edrisi,' i. 162.

† Sir Henry Elliot's 'Muhammadan Historians of India,' p. 57.

‡ Sir Henry Elliot's 'Muhammadan Historians of India,' Dowson's edition, p. 34; and Jaubert's 'Edrisi,' i. 162. "Le nom de la ville (Mansura est Indien *Mirimân*." In Gildemeister's 'Ibn Haukal,' this name is *Tâmirman*, which is an obvious mistake for *Bâmiwân*, or Bâmanwâs.

wards *Hamanâbâd*, for which we may read *Bahmanabad*, by simply adding an initial B, which must have been accidentally dropped. It was situated on the eastern branch of the Mihrân, or Indus, and was 1 mile in length, and the same in breadth, or just 4 miles in circuit. Its position is approximately fixed in the neighbourhood of Hâla, by the number of days' journey in the routes to different places. It was 12 days from Multan, 8 from Kandâbil, viâ Sehwân, and 6 days from Debal, viâ Manhâbari, which was itself 4 days from Mansura. It was therefore at two-thirds of the distance from Multan to the mouth of the Indus, or very nearly in the same parallel as Hâla.

Now in this very position the ruins of a large city have been discovered by Mr. Bellasis, to whose zeal and energy we are indebted for our knowledge of this interesting place. The ruins are situated near an old bed of the Indus, at 47 miles to the north-east of Haidarâbâd, 28 miles to the east or east-north-east of Hâla, and 20 miles to the west of the eastern Nâra.* The place is known as *Bambhra-ḳa-thûl*, or "the Ruined Tower," from a broken brick tower which is the only building now standing. The present appearance of the site, as described by its discoverer, is "one vast mass of ruins, varying in size according to the size of the original houses."

---

* Journ. Asiat. Soc., Bombay, v. 413; and Thomas's Prinsep, ii. 119. Eastwick's 'Handbook for Bombay,' p. 490.

Its circumference, measured by a perambulator, is within a few yards of 4 miles. But besides the great mound of *Bambhra-ka-thûl,* there is, at a distance of about 1½ mile, "the distinct and ruined city of *Dolora,* the residence of its last king, and 5 miles in another direction is the ruined city of *Depur,* the residence of his Prime Minister, and between these cities are the ruins of suburbs extending for miles far and wide into the open country." The great mound of *Bambhraka-thûl* is "entirely surrounded with a rampart, mounted with numerous turrets and bastions." In the time of Akbar there were "considerable vestiges of this fortification," which Abul Fazl* says "had 140 bastions, one *tanâb* distant from each other." The *tanâb* was a measuring rope, which the emperor Akbar ordered to be changed for bambus joined by iron links. Its length was 60 *Ilâhi gaz,* which, at 30 inches each, give 150 feet for the *tanâb;* and this multiplied by 140, makes the circuit of the city 21,000 feet, or very nearly 4 miles. Now it will be remembered that Ibn Haukal describes Mansura as being 1 mile square, or 4 miles in circuit, and that Mr. Bellasis's measure of the circumference of the ruined mound

* 'Ayin Akbari,' ii. 115. Gladwyn's translation has 1400 bastions, which would give to the city a circuit of 40 miles ; the MSS. have 140. The Ilâhi *gaz* contained 41½ Sikandari *tangkas,* and as the average breadth of 62 Sikandaris in my collection is ·7234 inches, the length of the Ilâhi gaz will be 30·0211 inches. Mr. Thomas, ii. 123, found exactly 30 inches.

of *Bambhraka thûl* was within a few yards of 4 miles. From this absolute correspondence of size, coupled with the close agreement of position, which has already been pointed out, I conclude that the great mound of *Bambhra ka thûl* represents the ruined city of *Mansura*, the capital of the Arab governors of Sindh. The Hindu city of Brâhmana, or Brâhmanâbad, must therefore be looked for in the neighbouring mound of ruins now called *Dilura*, which is only 1½ mile distant from the larger mound.

Mr. Bellasis, the discoverer of these ruins, has identified the great mound with Brâhmanâbâd itself; but to this it has been justly objected by Mr. Thomas* that amongst the multitudes of mediæval coins found during the excavations, "the number of Hindu pieces was very limited, and that even these seem to be casual contributions from other provinces, of no very marked uniformity or striking age." The local coins consist exclusively of specimens of the Arab governors of Sindh, with the name of Mansura in the margin; and so far as I am aware, there is not a single piece that can be attributed to any of the Hindu rajas of Sindh. It is therefore to be regretted that Mr. Bellasis did not make more extensive excavations in the smaller mound of Dilura, which would probably have yielded some satisfactory evidence of its superior antiquity.

---

* Prinsep's 'Essays,' vol. ii. p. 121, where all the local coins are most carefully described and attributed.

According to the native histories and traditions of the people, Brâhmanâbâd was destroyed by an earthquake, in consequence of the wickedness of its ruler, named *Dilu Rai.* The date of this prince is doubtful. M'Murdo has assigned A.H. 140, or A.D. 757,* as the year in which *Chota,* the brother of *Dilu,* returned from his pilgrimage to Mekka; but as Mansura was still a flourishing city in the beginning of the tenth century, when visited by Masudi and Ibn Haukal, it is clear that the earthquake cannot have happened earlier than A.D. 950. Dilu and Chota are said to have been the sons of *Amir,* the *Rai* or ruler of Brâhmanâbâd. But it is difficult to believe that there were any Hindu chiefs in Brâhmana during the rule of the Arabs in Mansura. The fact is that the same stereotyped legend is told of all the old cities in the Panjâb, as well as of those in Sindh. Shorkot, Harapa, and Atâri, are all said to have been destroyed on account of the sins of their rulers, as well as Alor, Brâhmana, and Bambhura. But the same story is also told of *Tulamba,* which we know to be false, as I have been able to trace its downfall to its desertion by the Râvi, at a very recent date. The excavations of Mr. Bellasis have shown conclusively that Brâhmana was overwhelmed by an earthquake. The human bones "were chiefly found in doorways, as if the people were attempting to escape; others in the corners of the rooms; some upright, some

* Journ. Royal Asiat. Soc., i. 28.

recumbent, with their faces down, and some crouched in a sitting posture."* The city was certainly not destroyed by fire, as Mr. Richardson notes that he found no remains of charcoal or burnt wood, and that the old walls bore no traces of fire. On the contrary, he also found the human remains crushed in the corners of the rooms, as if the terror-stricken inhabitants, finding their houses falling about them, had crouched in the corners and been buried by the falling material.† Mr. Richardson also picked up a brick which had "entered cornerways into a skull, and which, when taken out, had a portion of the bone adhering to it." His conclusion is the same as that of Mr. Bellasis, "that the city was destroyed by some terrible convulsion of nature."

The local coins found in the ruins of *Bambhra ka-tul* belong to the Arab governors of Mansura, from the time of *Jamhur*, son of *Mansûr*, the reputed founder of the city, down to *Umar*, the contemporary of Masudi.‡ It was therefore in existence during the whole of that time, or from A.D. 750 to 940, or even later.

This agrees exactly with what I have already noted, that the city was still flourishing when visited by Masudi and Ibn Haukal in the first half of the tenth century; and I would therefore assign its destruction to the latter half of that century, and not

---

* Journ. Asiat. Soc. Bombay, v. 417.

† *Ibid.*, v. 423.

‡ Thomas in Prinsep's 'Essays,' ii. 113.

earlier than A.D. 970. It is true that Mansura is mentioned by Abu Rihân in the beginning of the next century, and at a still later period by Edrisi, Kazvini, and Rashid-ud-din; but the last three were mere compilers, and their statements accordingly belong to an earlier age. Abu Rihân, however, is entirely original, and as his knowledge of the Indian language gave him special facilities for obtaining accurate information, his evidence is sufficient to prove that Mansura was still existing in his time. In speaking of the itinerary of Sindh, he says,* "From Aror to Bâhmanwâ, also named el Mansura, is reckoned 20 parasangs; from thence to Loharâni, at the mouth of the river, 30 parasangs." Mansura therefore still existed when Abu Rihân wrote his work, about A.D. 1031; but as it is mentioned by only one author in the campaigns of Mahmud of Ghazni, it is almost certain that it no longer existed as a great fortress, the capital of the country, otherwise its wealth would have attracted the cupidity of that rapacious conqueror. I conclude, therefore, that Mansura was already very much decayed before the accession of Mahmud, and that the earthquake which levelled its walls and overthrew its houses, must have happened some time before the beginning of the eleventh century. It is probable that most of the inhabitants who escaped the great catastrophe would have returned to the ruined city to look after their buried property, and that many of them again reared

* Reinaud, 'Fragments Arabes,' etc. p. 113.

their houses on the old sites. But the walls of the city were fallen, and ther weas no security; the river was gradually failing, and there was a scarcity of water; and the place was altogether so much decayed, that even in A.H. 416, or A.D. 1025, when the conqueror of Somnâth returned through Sindh, the plunder of Mansura was not sufficient to tempt him out of his direct march; so he passed on by Sehwân to Ghazni, leaving the old capital unvisited, and even unnoticed, unless we accept the solitary statement of Ibn Athir, that Mahmud on this occasion appointed a Muhammadan governor to Mansura.

3. LOWER SINDH, OR LAR.

The district of *Pitasila,* or Lower Sindh, is described by Hwen Thsang as being 3000 *li,* or 500 miles, in circuit, which agrees almost exactly with the dimensions of the Delta of the Indus from Haidarâbâd to the sea, including a small tract of country on both sides, extending towards the desert of Umarkot on the east, and to the mountains of Cape Monz on the west. Within these limits the dimensions of Lower Sindh are as follows. From the western mountains to the neighbourhood of Umarkot, 160 miles; from the same point to Cape Monz, 85 miles; from Cape Monz to the Kori mouth of the Indus, 135 miles; and from the Kori mouth to Umarkot, 140 miles; or altogether 520 miles. The soil, which is described as sandy and salt, produced plenty of corn and vegetables, but very few fruits and flowers, which is true of the Delta to the present day.

In the time of Alexander, the only place of note in the Delta was Patala; but he is said to have founded several towns himself* during his long stay in Lower Sindh, waiting for the Etesian winds to start his fleet. Unfortunately the historians have omitted to give the names of these places. Justin alone notes that on his return up the Indus he built the city of *Barce*,† to which I shall hereafter refer. Ptolemy has preserved the names of several places, as *Barbara, Sousikana, Bonis*, and *Kolaka*, of which the first is most probably the same as the *Barbariké emporium* of the 'Periplus,' and perhaps also the same as the *Barce* of Justin. In the time of the author of the 'Periplus,' the capital of Lower Sindh was *Minnagara*, which the foreign merchants reached by ascending the river from Barbarike. In the middle of the seventh century, Hwen Thsang mentions only *Pitasila*, or *Patala*. But in the beginning of the eighth century, the historians of Muhammad bin Kâsim's expedition add the names of *Debal* and *Nirankot* to our scanty list, which is still further increased by the Arab geographers of the tenth century, who place *Manhâtara*, or *Manhâbari*, or *Manjâbari*,‡ to the west of the Indus, and

---

* Curtius, Vita Alex., ix. 10: "Interim et urbes plerasque condidit."

† Hist., xii. 10.

‡ Sir Henry Elliot, 'Muhammadan Historians of India,' Dowson's edition, i. 35, quoting Ibn Haukal.

two days' journey from Debal, at the point where the road from Debal crosses the river. The position of these places I will now investigate in their order from north to south, beginning with Patala, at the head of the Delta.

Patala, or Nirankot.

The position of *Nirankot* is fixed at Haidarâbâd by the concurrent testimony of M'Murdo, Masson, Burton, and Eastwick.* Sir Henry Elliot alone places it as Jarak, as he thinks that that locality agrees better with the descriptions of the native historians. But as Haidarâbâd is the modern name of the city, which the people still know as *Nirankot*, there would seem to be no doubt of its identity with the *Nirun*, or *Nirunkot*, of the Arab historians and geographers. Its position is described by Abulfeda as 25 parasangs from Debal, and 15 parasangs from Mansura, which accords with the less definite statements of Istakhri and Ibn Haukal, who simply say that it was between Debal and Mansura, but nearer to the latter. It was situated on the western bank of the river, and is described as a well-fortified but small town, with few trees. Now, Haidarâbâd is 47 miles from the ruined city of Brâhmanâbâd, or Mansura, and 85 miles from Lâri-bandar, which I will presently show to have been the most probable

* M'Murdo in Journ. Royal Asiat. Soc., i. 30 ; Masson, 'Travels,' i. 463 ; Burton, 'Sindh,' pp. 131, 376 ; and Eastwick, 'Handbook for Bombay,' p. 483. See Map No. IX.

position of the ancient Debal; while Jarak is 74 miles from Brâhmanâbâd, and only 60 miles from Lâri-bandar. The position of Haidarâbâd, therefore, corresponds much better with the recorded distances than that of Jarak. At present the main channel of the Indus runs to the west of Haidarâbâd, but we know that the Phuleli, or eastern branch, was formerly the principal stream. According to M'Murdo,* the change of the main stream to the westward of Haidarâbâd took place prior to A.H. 1000, or A.D. 1592, and was coincident with the decay of Nasirpur, which was only founded in A.H. 751, or A.D. 1350. As Nasirpur is mentioned by Abul Fazl† as the head of one of the subdivisions of the province of Thatha, the main channel of the Indus must have flowed to the eastward of Nirunkot or Haidarâbâd at as late a date as the beginning of the reign of Akbar.

Nirunkot was situated on a hill, and there was a lake in its neighbourhood of sufficient size to receive the fleet of Muhammad Kâsim. Sir Henry Elliot identifies the former with the hill of Jarak, to the west of the Indus, and the latter with the Kinjur lake, near Helai, to the south of Jarak. But the Kinjur lake has no communication with the Indus, and therefore could not have been used for the reception of the fleet, which at once disposes of the only special advantage that Jarak was supposed to possess

* Journ. Royal Asiat. Soc., i. 236.

† 'Ayin Akbari,' ii. 272.

over Haidarâbâd as the representative of Nirunkot. Sir Henry* admits "that the establishment of its locality depends chiefly upon the sites which are assigned to other disputed cities, more especially to Debal and Mansura." The former he identifies with Karâchi, and the latter wth Haidarâbâd, and consistently with these emplacements he is obliged to fix Nirunkot at Jarak. But since he wrote his 'Appendix to the Arabs in Sindh,' the ancient city of *Bambhra-ka-Thûl* has been found by Mr. Bellasis in the very position that was long ago pointed out by M'Murdo as the site of Brâhmanâbâd. Its identification as the site of the famous cities of Mansura and Brâhmanâbâd leaves Haidarâbad, or the ancient Nirankot, available as the true representative of the Nirunkot of Biladuri and the Chach-nâma. Its distance of 47 miles from Bambhra-ka-tul, and of 85 miles from Lâri-bandar, agree almost exactly with the 15 and 25 parasangs of Abulfeda. It is also situated on a hill, so that it corresponds in position, as well as in name, with Nirunkot. The hill, called Ganja, is 1½ mile long, and 700 yards broad, with a height of 80 feet.† The present fort was built by Mir Ghulâm Shâh in A.H. 1182, or A.D. 1768.‡ About one-third of the hill, at the southern end, is occupied by the fort, the middle

* Sir H. Elliot's 'Muhammadan Historians of India,' Dowson's edition, i. 400.

† Wood, 'Journey to the Source of the Oxus,' p. 30.

‡ M'Murdo, Journ. Royal Asiat. Soc., i. 234.

portion by the main street and straggling houses of the city, and the northern end by tombs.

In A.D. 641, when the Chinese pilgrim Hwen Thsang visited Sindh, he travelled from *Koteswara*, the capital of Kachh, a distance of 700 *li*, or 117 miles, due north to *Pi-to-shi-lo*,* from whence he proceeded 300 *li*, or 50 miles, to the north-east, to *O.fan. cha*, which I have already identified with Brâhmanâbâd. M. Julien renders the Chinese syllables by *Pitasilâ*, but I should prefer *Pâtasila*, or the "flat rock," which is an accurate description of the long flat-topped hill on which Haidarâbâd is situated. This name recalls that of *Pâtalpur*, which, according to Burton,† was an old appellation of Haidarâbâd, or Nirankot; and as this city is exactly 120 miles to the north of *Kotesar*, in Kachh, and 47 miles to the south-west of Brâhmanâbâd, I have no hesitation in identifying it with the *Pitasila* of the Chinese pilgrim. The size of the hill also, which is 1½ mile in length, by 700 yards in breadth, or upwards of 3 miles in circumference, corresponds very closely with the dimensions of Pitasila, which, according to Hwen Thsang, was 20 *li*, or 3⅓ miles, in circuit.

The names of *Pâtalpur* and *Pâtasila* further suggest the probability that Haidarâbâd may be the *Pattala* of Alexander's historians, which they are unanimous in placing near the head of the Delta.

---

* 'Hiouen Thsang,' iii. 180.

† 'Sindh,' chap. i. note 7.

Now, the present head of the Delta is at the old town of Mattâri, 12 miles above Haidarâbâd, where the *Phuleli* separates from the main channel of the Indus. But in ancient times, when the main stream, which is now called *Purâna,* or the "Old River," flowed past Alor and Brâhmanâbâd to Nirunkot, the first point of separation of its waters was either at Haidarâbâd itself, past which a branch is said to have flowed by Miâni to Trikal, or 15 miles to the south-east of it where the *Phuleli* now throws off the *Guni* branch to the south, and then proceeds westerly to join the present stream of the Indus at Trikal. The true head of the old Delta was therefore either at Haidarâbâd itself, or 15 miles to the south-east of it, where the Guni, or eastern branch of the Indus, separated from the Phuleli, or western branch.

Now, the position of Patala can be determined by several independent data :—

1st. According to Ptolemy, the head of the Delta was exacly midway between *Oskana* and the eastern mouth of the Indus, called *Lonibare ostium.* This fixes Patala at Haidarâbâd, which is equidistant from the capital of *Oxykanus,* that is, from Mahorta near Larkâna, and the *Kori,* or eastern mouth of the Indus, which is also the mouth of the *Loni river,* or *Lonibare ostium.*

2nd. The base of the Delta was reckoned by Aristobulus at 1000 *stadia,* or 115 miles; by Nearchus at 1800 *stadia,* and by Onesikritus at

2000 *stadia*.* But as the actual coast line, from the Ghâra mouth on the west, to the Kori mouth on the east, is not more than 125 miles, we may adopt the estimate of Aristobulus in preference to the larger numbers of the other authorities. And as Onesikritus states that all three sides of the Delta were of the same length, the distance of *Patala* from the sea may be taken at from 1000 *stadia*, or 115 miles, up to 125 miles. Now, the distance of Haidarâbâd from the *Ghâra*, or western mouth of the Indus, is 110 miles, and from the *Kori*, or eastern mouth, 135 miles, both of which agree sufficiently near to the base measuremnt to warrant the descriptions of Onesikritus that the Delta formed an equilateral triangle. Consequently, the city of *Patala*, which was either at or near the head of the Delta, may be almost certainly indentified with the present Haidarâbâd.

3rd. From a comparison of the narratives of Arrian and Curtius, it appears that the Raja of Patala, having made his submission to Alexander at *Brâhmana*, or the city of Brahmans, the conqueror sailed leisurely down the river for three days, when he heard that the Indian prince had suddenly abandoned his country and fled o the desert.† Alexander at once pushed on to Patala. Now, the distance from Brâhmanâbâd to Haidarâbâd is only

* Strabo, Geogr., xv. i. 33.

† Arrian, 'Anabasis,' vi. 17 ; Curtius, Vita Alex., ix. 8, 28, says that he fled to the mountains.

47 miles by the direct land route; but as the old bed of the Indus makes a wide sweep round by Nasirpur, the route along the river bank, which was doubtless followed by the army, is not less than 55 miles, while the distance by water must be fully 80 miles. His progress during the first three days, estimated at the usual rate of 10 or 12 miles by land, and 18 or 20 miles by water, would have brought him within 19 miles of Haidarâbâd by land, and 26 miles by water, which distance he would have easily accomplished on the fourth day by a forced march. From Patala he proceeded down the western branch of the river for a distance of 400 *stadia*, or 46 miles, when his naval commanders first perceived the sea breeze. This point I believe to have been Jarak, which is 30 miles below Haidarâbâd by land, and 45 miles, or nearly 400 *stadia*, by water. There Alexander procured guides, and, pressing on with still greater eagerness, on the third day he became aware of his vicinity to the sea by meeting the tide.* As the tides in the Indus are not felt more than 60 miles from the sea, I conclude that Alexander must then have reached as far as Bambhra, on the Ghâra, or western branch of the river, which is only 35 miles from the sea by land, and about 50 miles by water. Its distance from Jarak by land is 50 miles, and by water 75 miles, which the fleet might have easily accomplished by the third day. From these details it

* Curtius, Vita Alex., ix. 9, 29.

is clear that Patala must have been at a considerable distance from the sea, that is, not less than the length of the tidal reach, plus three days' sail on the river, plus 400 *stadia*. These distances by land are respectively 33 miles, 50 miles, and 30 miles, or altogether 113 miles, which corresponds almost exactly with the measurement of Aristobulus of 1000 *stadia*, or 115 miles.

As these three independent investigations all point to the same place as the most probable representative of Patala, and as that place is called *Patasila* by Hwen Thsang in the seventh century, and is still known as *Pâtalpur*, I think that we have very strong grounds for identifying Haidarâbâd with the ancient *Patala*.

In his account of the Indus, Arrian* says, "this river also forms a delta by its two mouths, no way inferior to that of Egypt, which, in the Indian language, is called *Pattala*." As this statement is given on the authority of Nearchus, who had ample opportunities during his long detention in Sindh of intercourse with the people, we may accept it as the general belief of the Sindhians at that time. I would therefore suggest that the name may have been derived from *Pâtala*, the "trumpet-flower" (*Bignonia suaveolens*), in allusion to the "trumpet" shape of the province included between the eastern and western branches of the mouth of the Indus, as the

* 'Indica,' p. 2.

two branches, as they approach the sea, curve outwards like the mouth of a trumpet.

I cannot close the discussion on the site of this ancient city without noticing another name of which the conflicting accounts appear to me to have a confused reference to Nirunkot. This name is the *Piruz* of Istakhri, the *Kannazbur* of Ibn Haukal, and the *Firabuz* of Edrisi. According to Istakhri, *Piruz* was 4 days' journey from Debal, and 2 days from *Mehâbari,* which was itself on the western bank of the Indus, at 2 days' journey from Debal. Ibn Haukal and Edrisi agree that the road to *Kannazbur*, or *Firabuz,* lay through *Manhâbari,* or *Manjâbari,* which was on the western bank of the Indus, at 2 days from Debal; but they make the whole distance beyond Debal 14 days instead of 4. Now, Ibn Haukal and Edrisi place their city in Mekrân, a position which they were almost forced to adopt by their long distance of 14 days, although the first two days' journey lie exactly in the opposite direction from Mekran. But if we take the shorter distance of 4 days from Debal, which is found in Istakhri, the earliest of the three geographers, the position of their unknown city will then accord exactly with that of *Nirankot. Debal* I will hereafter identify with an old city near *Lâri-bandar* and *Manhâbari* with *Thatha,* which is just mid-way between Lâri-bandar and Haidarâbâd. Now, Ibn Haukal specially notes that *Manjâbari* was situated "to the west of the Mihrân, and *there* any one who proceeds from Debal to Mansura will have to pass the river, the latter place being opposite to

Manjâbari."* This extract shows that Manjâbari was on the western branch of the Indus, and therefore on the high-road to Nirankot as well as to *Piruz,* or *Kannezbur,* or *Firabuz.* I would therefore suggest that the first of these names, which is thus mentioned in conjunction with Manhâbari might possibly be intended for *Nirun,* and the other two for *Nirunkot,* as the alterations in the original Arabic characters required for these two readings are very slight. But there was certainly a place of somewhat similar name in Mekrân, as Bilâduri records that *Kizbun* in Mekrân submitted to Muhammad Kâsim on his march against Debâl. Comparing this name with Ibn Haukal's *Kannazbur,*† and Edrisi's *Firabuz,* I think it probable that they may be intended for *Panjgûr,* as suggested by M. Reinaud. The 14 day's journey would agree very well with the position of this place.

Jarak.

The little town of Jarak is situated on an eminence overhanging the western bank of the Indus, about midway between Haidarâbâd and

* Prof. Dowson's edition of Sir H. Elliot's Hist. of India, i. 37.

† Prof. Dowson's edition of Sir Henry Elliot's Hist. of India, i. 40. Ibn Haukal: *Kannazbur.* At page 29 he gives Istakhri's name as *Kannazbûn,* which Mordtmann reads *Firiun.* The most probable explanation of these differences is some confusion in the Arabic characters between the name of *Nirun* and that of the capital of Mekrân.

Thatha. Jarak is the present boundary between *Vichalo*, or Middle Sindh, and *Lâr*, or Lower Sindh, which latter I have been obliged to extend to Haidarâbâd, so as to include the *Patala* of the Greeks and the *Pitasila* of the Chinese pilgrim, within the limits of the ancient Delta. This is perhaps the same place as *Khor*, or *Alkhor*, a small but populous town, which Edrisi places between Manhâbari and *Firabuz*, that is, between Thatha and Nirunkot. Three miles below Jarak there is another low hill covered with ruins, which the people call *Kâfir kot*, and attribute to Raja *Manjhira*.* The principal ruin is a square basement ornamented with flat pilasters at regular distances. This is supposed to be the remains of a temple. Amongst the ruins were found some fragments of Buddhist statues; and, at a short distance from the hill, an inscription in early Indian characters, of which I can read only the words *putrasa* and *Bhagavatasa*, and a few letters in different parts; but these are sufficient to show that the inscription is Buddhist, as well as the other remains.

Minnagar, Manhâbari, or Thatha.

The city of *Thatha* is situated in a low swampy valley, 3 miles from the western bank of the Indus, and 4 miles above the separation of the *Bâgar*, or western branch, from the *Satâ*, or main stream of the river. Littlewood remarks that "the mounds of

* 'Bombay Journal,' v. 356.

rubbish upon which the houses are piled slightly raise its site above the level of the valley."* The place was visited by Captain Hamilton in A.D. 1699, who describes it,† as situated on a spacious plain about 2 miles from the Indus. It is highly probable, therefore, that the town originally stood on the bank of the river, which has been gradually receding from it. Its name also would seem to point to the same conclusion, as *thattha* means a "shore or bank," so that *Nagar-Thatha*, which is the common name of the place, would mean the "city on the river bank." Its date is not certainly known; but M'Murdo, who is generally very accurate, states that it was founded in the year A.H. 900, or A.D. 1495, by Nizâm-ud-din Nanda, the *Jâm*, or ruler of Sindh. Before his time, the chief city of Lower Sindh was *Sâminagar*, the capital of the *Sammâ* tribe, which stood on a rising ground, 3 miles to the north-west of the site of Thatha. M'Murdo refers its foundation to the time of Ala-ud-din of Delhi, who reigned from A.H. 695—715, or A.D. 1295 to 1315. Of a still earlier date is the great fort of *Kalyân-ḳot*, or Tughlakâbâd, which stands on the limestone hill, 4 miles to the south-west of *Thatha*. Its second name was derived from Ghazi Beg *Tughlaḳ*, who was the governor of Multân and Sindh, during the latter part of Ala-ud-din's reign, in the beginning of the fourteenth century.

---

* 'Journey to the Source of the Oxus,' p. 17.

† 'New Account of the East Indies,' i. 123.

The site of Thatha itself is admitted to be modern, but those of Sâminagar and Kalyân-kot are said to be of great antiquity. This belief of the people is no doubt true, as the position at the head of the inferior Delta commanded the whole traffic of the river, while the hill-fort gave security. Lieut. Wood remarks* that the site of Thatha is so advantageous for commercial purposes that it is probable that a mart has existed in its neighbourhood from the earliest times. "But," he judiciously adds, "as the apex of the Delta is not a fixed point, the site of this city must have varied as the river changed." This change of site would naturally have entailed a change of names; and I am therefore led to believe that Thatha was the actual position of the *Manhâbari* of the Arab geographers, and of the *Minnagara* of the author of the 'Periplus.'†

Manhâbari is described by all the authorities as situated on the western bank of the Indus, at 2 days' journey from Debal. Now, this is the very position of Thatha, which is on the western bank of the Indus, at 40 miles, or 2 days' journey, from Lâri-bandar, which, as I will presently show, was almost certainly within a few miles of the famous city of Debal. The name of *Manhâbari* is variously written as *Mehâbari,* and *Manjâbari,* for which I would suggest that we might perhaps read *Mandâbari,* or *Mandâwari,* the "city of the *Mand*" tribe, just as

* 'Oxus,' p. 20.

† See Map No. IX.

Sâminagar was the "city of the Sammâ" tribe. This derivation of the name is supported by the fact that the *Mand* tribe have occupied Lower Sindh in great numbers from the beginning of the Christian era. Edrisi* describes the *Mand* as a numerous and brave tribe, who occupied the desert on the borders of Sindh and India, and extended their wanderings as far as *Alor* on the north, *Mekran* on the west, and *Mamehel* (or Umarkot) on the east. Ibn Haukal† records that "the *Mands* dwell on the banks of the Mihrân, from the boundary of Multân to the sea, and in the desert between Mekrân and Famhal (or Umarkot). They have many cattle-sheds and pasturages, and form a large population." Rashid-ud-din‡ locates them in Sindh at a still earlier period. According to his account, *Med* and *Zat*, two descendants of Ham, the son of Noah, were the progenitors of the people of Sindh prior to the Mahâbhârata. The name is variously written as *Mer*, *Med*, *Mand*, in all of which forms it is found even at the present day. To these I would add *Mind*, which is the form of the name given by Masudi.§ I have alredy identified this people with the *Medi* and *Mandrueni* of the classical writers; and as their name

* Geogr., i. 163.

† In Elliot, 'Muhammadan Historians of India,' i. 67; and in Gildemeister, 'De Rebus Indicis,' p. 172 where he gives *Kamuhal* as the eastern limit of their wanderings.

‡ Reinaud, 'Fragments Arabes,' etc., p. 25.

§ Sir H. M. Elliot, 'Muhammadan Historians of India,' Dowson's edition, i. 57.

is found in northern India from the beginning of the Christian era downwards, and not before that time, I conclude that the *Mandrueni* and *Iatii* of the Oxus, who are coupled together by Pliny, must be the Sacæ Indo-Scythians, who occupied the Panjâb and Sindh, and who under the name of *Mands* and *Zats* of the early Muhammadan authors, were in full possession of the valley of the Indus towards the end of the seventh century.

To show that the various spellings of the name are but natural modes of pronunciation, I can refer to the two large maps of the *Shâhpur* and *Jhelam* districts, which have been published within the last few years by the Surveyor-General of India. In the latter the name of a village on the Jhelam, 6 miles above Jalâlpur, is spelt *Meriâla,* and in the former *Mandiâli.* Abul Fazl calls the same place *Merali,* while Ferishta names it *Meriâla.* Lastly, Wilford's surveyor, Mogal Beg, writes *Mandyâla,* which is also the form that I received from two different persons, while in General Court's map it is spelt *Mâmriala.*

To this people I refer the name of *Minnagar,* or "city of the *Min,*" which was the capital of Lower Sindh in the second century of the Christian era. That *Min* was a Scythian name we know from its occurrence in the list of Isidor of Kharax as one of the cities of Sakastene, or Sejistan. The appearance of the name in Sindh would alone be sufficient to suggest the presence of Scythians; but its connection with them is placed beyond all doubt by the mention that the rulers of *Minnagara* were rival *Parthians*, who were mutually expelling each other.* These Parthians were Dahæ Scythians from the Oxus, who gave the name of Indo-Scythia to the valley of the Indus, and whose mutual rivalry points to their identity with the rival Meds and Jats of the Muhammadan authors.

The actual position of Minnagar is unknown, and we have but few data to guide us in attempting to fix its site. As it is not found in Ptolemy, who wrote in the first half of the second century, I infer either that the new name had not then been imposed on the capital, or what is more probable, that Ptolemy has inserted only the old name. If I am right in identifying *Min-nagara* or the "city of the *Min*," with *Mand-âbari*, or the "place of the *Mand*," there can be little doubt that the great Indo-Scythian capital was at Thatha. Edrisi† describes Manhâbar as situated on a low plain, and surrounded with gardens and running water. Captain Hamilton‡ gives the same description of Thatha, which, he says, "stands in a spacious plain, and they have canals cut from the river, that bring water to the city, and some for the use of their gardens." According to the author§ of the 'Periplus,' the merchant vessels anchored at the emporium of Barbarike, where the

* Peripl. Mar. Eryth. ; in Hudson's Geogr. Vet., i. 22.

† Geogr., i. 164.

‡ 'New Account of the East Indies,' i. 123.

§ Hudson, Geogr. Vet., i. 22.

goods were unloaded, and conveyed to the capital by the river. Just so in modern times the ships anchored at Lâribandar, while the merchants carried their goods to Thatha either by land or by water. The position of Minnagar is too vaguely described as "inland,"* to be of any use in its determination. If it was, as I suppose, at *Thatha,* then it may perhaps be identified with Ptolemy's *Sousikana,* which I would interpret as *Susi-gâma,* or the "town of the *Su* tribe," an etymology which is supported by the fact that the *Mands,* or *Meds,* were a branch of the great horde of *Sus,* or *Abars,* who gave one name to *Susiana,* at the mouth of the Euphrates, and the other to *Abiria,* at the mouth of the Indus. I should mention, however, that according to M'Murdo,† "*Minagar* was one of the cities dependent on Multân in the twelfth century, and was the possession of a chief by caste an *Agri,* and descended from Alexander. It was situated on the *Lohâna Daryâ,* not far from Bâhmana, in the *parganah* now called *Shehdâdpur.*" It is a suspicious circumstance that this passage has not been verified either by Postans or by Elliot. The latter, who constantly refers to his own MS. of the 'Tohfat-ul-Kirâm,' quotes‡ this notice of Minagar at second-hand from

* The words are, κατὰ νώτου μεσόγειος, which can only mean "inland and beyond" Barbarike.

† Journ. Royal Asiat. Soc., i. 31 ; and again at p. 233, quoting the *Tohfat-ul Girâm.*

‡ 'Muhammadan Historians of India,' Dowson's edition, i. 66.

M'Murdo. I may add that the *Agari* is a well-known caste, of low degree, who are employed in the manufacture of salt. I am therefore not inclined to admit that this petty place could have any connection with the geat capital of Indo-Scythia. On the contrary, I am disposed to look upon this name of *Min-nagara* as meaning simply the city of Min.

Barbarike-Emporium, or Bhambûra.

The ruined town of *Bambhora*, or *Bhambûra*, is situated at the head of the *Ghâra* creek, which is "supposed by the natives to be the site of the most ancient seaport in Sindh."* "Nothing now remains but the foundations of houses, bastions, and walls," but about the tenth century Bhambhûra was the capital of a chief named Bhambo Raja. According to the traditions of the people, the most westerly branch of the Indus once flowed past Bhambûra. It is said to have separated from the main river just above Thatha, and M'Murdo† quotes the 'Tabakât-i-Akbari' for the fact that in the reign of Akbar it ran to the westward of Thatha. To the same effect Sir Henry Elliot‡ quotes Mr. N. Crow, who was for many years the British Resident at Thatha. Writing in A.D. 1800, Crow says, "By a strange turn that the river has taken within these five-and-twenty years just above Tatta, that city is flung out of the angle of the inferior Delta, in which it formerly

---

* Eastwick, 'Handbook of Bombay,' p. 481.

† Journ. Royal Asiat. Soc., i. 25. See Map No. IX.

‡ Muhamm. Hist. of India, Dowson's edition, i. 399.

stood, on the main land towards the hills of Biluchistan." From these statements it would appear that the Ghâra river was the most westerly branch of the Indus down to the latter half of the last century. But long before that time, according to M'Murdo, it had ceased to be a navigable stream, as both Bhambur and Debal were deserted about A.D. 1250, on account of the failure of the river.* My own inquiries give the same date, as Debal was still occupied when Jalâladdin of Khwârazm invaded Sindh in A.D. 1221,† and was in ruins in A.D. 1333, when Ibn Batuta visited *Lâhari Bandar*, which had succeeded Debal as the great port of the Indus.

M'Murdo quotes native authors to show that this western branch of the Indus was called the *Sâgâra* river, which, he thinks, may be identified with the *Sagapa Ostium* of Ptolemy, which was also the most westerly branch of the Indus in his time. It is therefore quite possible, as supposed by M'Murdo, that this was the very branch of the Indus that was navigated by Alexander. From the latest maps, however, it appears that about midway between Thatha and Ghâra this channel threw off a large branch on its left, which flowed parallel to the other for about 20 miles, when it turned to the south and joined the main channel just below Lâri-bandar. Now this channel passes about 2 or 3 miles to the south of Bhambûra, so that the town was also accessible from the *Piti*, the *Phundi*, the *Kyâr*, and

* Journ. Royal Asiat. Soc., i. 25 and 232.

† Rashid-ud-din in Elliot, Dowson's edition, i. 26.

the *Pintiani* mouths of the river. I am therefore inclined to identify Bhambûra not only with the town of *Barke*, which Alexander built on his return up the river, as stated by Justin, but also with the *Barbari* of Ptolemy, and the *Barbarike Emporium* of the author of the 'Periplus.' The last authority describes the middle branch of the Indus as the only navigable channel in his time up to *Barbarike*,* all the other six channels being narrow and full of shoals. This statement shows that the Ghâra river had already begun to fail before A.D. 200. The middle mouth of the river, which was then the only navigable entrance, is called *Khariphon Ostium* by Ptolemy. This name I would identify with the *Kyâr* river of the present day, which leads right up to the point where the southern branch of the Ghâra joins the main river near Lâri-bandar.

From this discussion I conclude that the northern channel of the Ghâra was the western branch of the Indus, which was navigated by Alexander and Nearchus; and that before A.D. 200, its waters found another channel more to the south, in the southern Ghâra, which joins the main stream of the Indus just below Lâri-bandar. By this channel, in the time of the author of the 'Periplus,' the merchant vessels navigated the Indus up to *Barbarike*, where the goods were unloaded, and conveyed in boats to *Minnagar*, the capital of the country. But after some time this channel also

---

* Hudson, Geogr. Vet., i. 22.

failed, and in the beginning of the eighth century, when the Arabs invaded Sindh, *Debal* had become the chief port of the Indus, and altogether supplanted *Bhambûra,* or the ancient *Barbarike.* But though the Ghâra river was no longer a navigable channel, its waters still contiuned to flow past the old town down to the thirteenth century, about which time it would appear to have been finally deserted.

Debal Sindhi, or Debal.

The position of the celebrated port of Debal, the emporium of the Indus during the middle ages, is still unsettled. By Abul Fazl and the later Muhammadan writers, Debal has been confounded with Thatha; but as Debal was no longer in existence when they wrote, I conclude that they were misled by the name of *Debal Thatha,* which is frequently applied to Thatha itself. Similarly, *Brâhmana,* or *Brâhmanâbâd,* was called *Debal Kângra,* and the famous seaport of Debal was named *Debal Sindhi.* But *Diwal,* or *Debal,* means simply a temple, and therefore *Debal Sindhi* means the temple at, or near, the town of Sindhi. Major Burton says that the shawls of *Thatha* are still called *Shâl-i-Debali,* but this only proves that *Debal* was the place where the merchants procured the Thatha shawls. Just so the name of *Multâni-matti,* that is Multan clay, or Armenian bole, is derived from the place where the merchants otbain the article, as the clay is actually found in the hills to the west of the Indus, beyond Dera Ghâzi Khân. So also

Indian-ink is named from India, where the merchants first obtained it, although, as is now well known, it is all manufactured in China. Sir Henry Elliot, who is the last inquirer into the geography of Sindh, places Debal at Karâchi; but admits that Lâri-bandar "is the next most probable site after Karâchi."* But I incline to the opinion of Mr. Crow, who was for many years the British resident in Sindh, that Debal occupied a site between Karâchi and Thatha. His opinion is entitled to special weight, as he is admitted by M'Murdo and Elliot to have "combined much discrimination with ample opportunities of local inquiry." Sir Henry quotes the *Chach-nâma* for the fact that "the Serandip vessels were in their distress driven to the shore of Debal," to show that the port must have been close to the sea. There they were attacked by pirates of the *Tangâmara* tribe, who occupied the seacoast from Karâchi to Lâri-bandar. This statement shows that if Debal cannot be identified either with Karâchi or with Lâri-bandar, it must be looked for somewhere between them.

In favour of Karâchi Sir Henry quotes Biladuri, who records that in the year A.H. 15, or A.D. 636, Hâkim dispatched his brother Mughira on an expeditoin to the Bay of Debal. But as the city of Lyons is not on the shore of the Gulf of Lyons, so it does not necessarily follow that Debal was on the shore of the Bay of Debal. In fact it is described

* 'Sindh,' pp. 222 and 224.

by Ibn Khordâdbeh as being 2 farsangs from the mouth of the Mihran, which is still further extended to 2 days' journey by Masudi.* But as Debal was situated on the Indus, it cannot be indentified with Karâchi, which is on the seacoast beyond the mouth of the river. All our authorities agree in stating that it was on the west side of the Mihran,† that is of the main stream of the river, or Baghâr, which flows past Lâri-bandar, and discharges itself into the sea by several different mouths named the Piti, the Phundi, the Kyâr, and the Pintiani. But M'Murdo also quotes the native authorities to show that it was on the *Sâgâra* branch of the Indus, which flowed past Bhambûra. According to these accounts, Debal must have been situated on the western bank of the Baghâr river, below the junction of the southern branch of the Ghâra, or Sâgâra branch. Its position may therefore be fixed approximately at the point of junction, which is 5 miles to the north of Lâri-bandar, 17 miles to the south-west of Bhambûra, and about 30 miles from the Piti and Pintiani mouths of the river. This position also fulfils the other condition quoted by Sir Henry Elliot, that Debal was between Karâchi and Lâri-bandar, in the territory of the Tangâmara tribe of pirates. It

* Elliot, Muhamm. Hist. of India, Dowson's edition, i. 53-57.

† These will be found in Elliot's Muhamm. Hist., by Dowson, i. 61 ; 'Istakhri,' i. 65 ; 'Ashkâl-ul-Bilâd,' i. 65, note Ibn Haukal. See also Gildemeister, 'De Rebus Indicis,' p. 205, for Kazvini.

further agrees with the position assigned to it by Mr. Crow, who places it between Karâchi and Thatha, which is an exact description of the locality following the course of the river, which is the only course that can be taken, as Debal was situated amongst the intersecting streams of the Delta.

Unfortunately, this part of the Delta has not yet been minutely explored; and to this cause I would attribute our ignorance of the remains of an ancient city, which were noticed by Ibn Batuta in A.D. 1333 in the very position which I have assigned to Debal.* As his statement is of great importance, I will quote the passage at full length:—"I then proceeded by the Sind to the city of *Lâhari*, which is situated upon the shores of the Indian Sea, where the Sind joins it. It has a large harbour, into which ships from Persia, Yemen, and other places put. At a *few miles* from this city are the ruins of another, in which stones in the shape of men and beasts almost innumerable are to be found. The people of this place think that it is the opinion of their historians that there was a city formerly in this place, the greater part of the inhabitants of which were so base that God transformed them, their beasts, their herbs, even to the very seeds, into stones; and indeed stones in the shape of seeds are here almost innumerable." This large ruined city, with its stones in the shape of men and beasts, I take to be the remains of the once great emporium

* 'Travels,' by Dr. Lee, p. 102.

of Debal. According to M'Murdo, the people of Debal moved to Lâri-bandar,* and according to Captain Hamilton, Lâri-bandar possessed "a large *stone* fort," for the protection of merchants against the Biluchis and Makrânis. It is, I think, a very fair and legitimate deduction that the people who deserted Debal removed the materials of their old city for the construction of the new one, and therefore that the stones of the fort of Lâri-bandar were brought from the deserted city of Debal, the remains of which excited the curiosity of Ibn Batuta in A.D. 1333.

This statement of Ibn Batuta I would connect with the curious account of an Indian city in the 'Arabian Nights,' which is found in the story of Zobeide. According to the common edition, this lady sailed from the port of Bassora, and after twenty days anchored in the harbour of a large city in India, where on landing she found that the king and queen and all the people had been turned into stone. One person only had escaped the general transformation, and he was the king's son, who had been brought up as a Muhammadan by his nurse, who was a Musalmâni slave. Now this legend appears to be the same as that of Raja Dilu and his brother Chota of the native histories of Sindh,† according to which Chota had become a Muhammadan, and when the city of Brâhmana was

* Journ. Royal Asiat. Soc., i. 29 and 233.

† M'Murdo, Journ. Royal Asiat. Soc. i. 28; and Postans, Journ. Asiat. Soc. Bengal, vii. 193.

destroyed by an earthquake, on account of the wickedness of the king, Chota alone escaped. As a similar story is told of the ruin of all the chief cities in the Panjâb as well as in Sindh, the scene of the story in the 'Arabian Nights' may be fairly placed in Sindh; and as Debal was the only large city on the coast, and was besides the chief mart to which the Muhammadan merchants traded, it seems to me almost certain that it must be the Indian city in which Zobeide found all the people turned into stone.

According to M'Murdo, the destruction of Brâhmana took place in A.H. 140, or A.D. 757, and as the story of Zobeide is laid in the time of the Khalif Harûn-ul-Rashid, who reigned from A.D. 786 to 809, there are no difficulties of chronology to interfere with the identification of the two legends.

The position of Debal may also be fixed on the Baghâr river, or main channel of the Indus, by its name of *Dibal Sindhi*, or Dibal on the Indus. That it was near Lâri-bandar we learn incidentally from Captain Hamilton,* who says that the river of Sindhi "is only a small branch of the Indus, which appellation is now lost in this country which it so plentifully waters, and is called *Divellee*, or Seven mouths." This statement shows that the branch of the Indus leading up to Lâri-bandar was called *Dibali*, or the river of Dibal, so late as A.D 1699,

* 'New Account of East Indies,' i. 130.

when visited by Hamilton. That this was the *Piti* branch of the Indus I infer from its other name of *Sindhi*, which I take to be the same as the *Sinthon Ostium* of Ptolemy, or the second mouth of the river, reckoning from the west. As the Piti is one of the mouths of the Baghâr river, this position agrees with that which I have already assigned to Dibal, on the concurring testimony of all the previous authorities.

Since Hamilton wrote, Lâri-bandar itself has been deserted, and the present port of the western half of the Delta is Dhârâja, which is only a few miles to the east of Lâri-bandar.

IV. KACHH.

The fourth province of Sindh, in the seventh century, was *Kachh*, and it was still attached to Sindh in the time of Akbar. It is described by Hwen Thsang as situated at 1600 *li*, or 267 miles, to the south-west of the capital of Sindh,* which at that time was *Alor*, near Bhakar, on the Indus. This agrees with the details given elsewhere,† which make the route as follows: from Alor to Brahmana, 700 *li* to the south, then to Pitasila 300 *li* to the south-west, and then to Kachh 700 *li* to the south; the whole distance being 1650 *li*. But the general dirction is south, instead of south-west, which agrees with the actual position of Kachh.

* M. Julien's 'Hiouen Thsang,' i. 207, 208. See Map No. IX.

† *Ibid.*, iii. 175.

The province is named *'O-tien-po-chi-lo*, which M. Julien renders as *Adhyavakila*, or *Atyanvakela*, but for which no Sanskrit equivalent is offered either by himself or by M. Vivien de St. Martin. I think, however, that it may be intended for *Audumbatira*, or *Audumbara*, which Professor Lassen gives as the name of the people of Kachh. They are the *Odomboeræ* of Pliny,* but there is no trace of this name at the present day.

The province is described as being 5000 *li*, or 833 miles, in circuit, which is much too great, unless the whole of the Nagar Pârkar district to the north of the Ran was included, which is most probable, as this tract has always been considered as a part of Kachh, and is still attached to it. Taking its northern boundary as stretching from Umarkot to the neighbourhood of Mount Abu, the whole length of frontier will be upwards of 700 miles. The capital, named *Kie-tsi-shi-fa-lo*, was 30 *li*, or 5 miles, in circuit. This name is rendered as *Khajiswara* by M. Julien, and as *Kachchheswara* by Professor Lassen. But as the Chinese syllable *tse* represents the cerebral *t*, I think that *tsi* must have the same value; and I would therefore read the whole as *Kotiswara*, which is the name of a celebrated place of pilgrimage on the western shore of Kachh. That this is the place actually intended is rendered certain by the pilgrim's description of its position, which is said to be on the western frontier of the country

* Hist. Nat., vi. 23.

close to the river Indus, and to the great ocean.* This is a most exact description of the position of the holy *Kotesar*, which is situated on the western frontier of Kachh, on the bank of the Kori branch of the Indus, and close to the great Indian Ocean. This identification is further supported by the statement that in the middle of the city there was a famous temple of Siva. The name of the place is derived from *Koti* + *iswara*, or the "ten million Iswaras," and refers to the small *lingam* stones that are found there in great numbers. Iswara is the well-known name of Siva, and the lingam is his symbol.

M. Vivien de St. Martin has identified this capital with Karâchi; but the distance from Alor is not more than 1300 *li*, or 217 miles, while only the initial syllable of the name corresponds with the Chinese transcript. The country is described by Hwen Thsang as low and wet, and the soil impregnated with salt. This is an exact description of the lowlands of *Kachh*, which means a "morass" (*Kachchha*), and of the salt desert, or *Ran* (in Sanskrit *Irina*), which forms about one-half of the province. But it is quite inaccurate if applied to the dry sandy soil of Karâchi. There is also a large swamp extending for many miles, immediately to the south of Kotesar.

* M. Julien's 'Hiouen Thsang,' iii. 175: "Elle est située, à l'écart, sur les frontières de l'ouest: elle est voisine du fleuve *Sin-tu* (Sindh), et à proximité d'une grande mer."

Districts to the West of the Indus.

To the west of the Lower Indus all the classical writers agree in placing two barbarous races called *Arabii*, or *Arabitæ*, and *Oritæ* or *Horitæ*, both of whom appear to be of Indian origin. The country of the Arabii is said by Arrian to be the "last part of India" towards the west, and Strabo also calls it a "Part of India,"* but both exclude the Oritæ. Curtius, however, includes the Horitæ in India,† while Diodorus states that generally they resemble the Indians; and Arrian admits that the Oritæ, who "inhabited the inland parts, were clothed in the same manner as the Indians, and used the same weapons, but their language and customs were different." In the seventh century, however, both their language and customs were considered to be like those of the Indians by a much more competent observer, the Chinese pilgrim, Hwen Thsang. According to him, the customs of the inhabitans of *Lang-kie-lo*, which was 2000 *li*, or 333 miles, to the west of Kotesar, in Kachh, were like those of the people of Kachh, and their written characters closely resembled those of India, while their language was only slightly different.‡ For these reasons I think that the Oritæ, as well as the Arabitæ, may fairly be included within the geo-

* Arrian, 'Indica,' 22; Strabo, Geogr., xv. 2, 1.

† Curtius, Vita Alex., ix. 10, 33.

‡ M. Julien's 'Hiouen Thsang,' iii. 177.

graphical limits of India, although they have always been beyond its political boundary during the historical period. As early as the sixth century B.C. they were tributary to Darius Hystaspes, and they were still subject to Persia nearly twelve centuries later, when visited by Hwen Thsang. But their Indian origin is beyond all doubt, as will be shown when I come to speak of the Oritæ.

Arabii, or Arabitæ.

The *Arabii* of Arrian are the *Arabitæ* of Curtius, the *Arbiti* of Ptolemy, the *Ambritæ* of Diodorus, and the *Arbies* of Strabo. They are said to have derived their name from the river *Arabis*, or *Arbis*, or *Arabius*, which flowed along their confines, and divided their territory from that of the Oritæ* From a comparison of the details of Alexander's marches with the diary of Nearchus, it is certain that this boundary river was the Purâli, which flows through the present district of Las into the bay of Sonmiâni. According to Curtius,† Alexander reached the eastern boundary of the Arabitæ in nine days from Patala, and their western boundary in five days more. Now, from Haidarâbâd to Karâchi, the distance is 114 miles, and from Karâchi to Sonmiâni 50 miles,‡ the former being usually performed by troops in nine marches, and the latter

* Arrian, 'Indica,' 21; Strabo, Geogr., xv. 2. 1; Pliny, Hist. Nat., vii. 2.

† Vita Alex., ix. 10, 33.

‡ Eastwick, 'Handbook of Bombay,' pp. 474 and 477.

either in four or five. Karâchi, therefore, must have been on the eastern frontier of the Arabitæ, a deduction which is admitted by the common consent of all inquirers, who have agreed in identifying the Kolaka of Ptolemy and the sandy island of *Krokola*, where Nearchus tarried with his fleet for one day, with a small island in the Bay of Karâchi. *Krokola* is further described as lying off the mainland of the Arabii. It was 150 stadia, or 17¼ miles, from the western mouth of the Indus, which agrees exactly with the relative positions of Karâchi and the mouth of the Ghâra river, if, as we may fairly assume, the present coast-line has advanced 5 or 6 miles during the twenty-one centuries that have elapsed since the time of Alexander. The identification is confirmed by the fact that "the district in which Karâchi is situated is called *Karkalla* to this day."*

On leaving Krokola, Nearchus had Mount Eiros (Manora) on his right-hand, and a low flat island on his left, which is a very accurate description of the entrance to Karâchi harbour, and after stopping at several small places, reached *Morontobara,* which was called the "Women's Haven" by the people of the country.† From this place he made two courses of 70 stadia and 120 stadia, or altogether not more than 22 miles, to the mouth of the river Arabius, which was the boundary between the country of the Arabii and the Oritæ. The name of *Morontobara*

* East wick 'Handbook of Bombay, p. 476 ; Burnes, 'Bokhara,' i. 10, writes the name Crocola.

† Arrian, 'Indica,' p. 22.

I would identify with *Müâri,* which is now applied to the headland of *Râs Muâri,* or Cape Monz, the last point of the Pabb range of mountains. *Bâra,* or *bâri,* means a roadstead or haven, and *moronta* is evidently connected with the Persian *mard,* a man, of which the feminine is still preserved in Kashmiri, as *mahrin,* a woman. The haven itself may be looked for between Cape Monz and Sonmiâni, but its exact position cannot be determined. From the distances given by Arrian in his account of the voyage of Nearchus, I am inclined to fix it at the mouth of the *Bahar* rivulet, a small stream which falls into the sea about midway between Cape Monz and Sonmiâni. If I am right in considering Müâri as an abbreviation of Morontobâra, the cape must have received its name from the neighbouring haven. At the mouth of the Arabius Nearchus found a large and safe harbour, corresponding with the present Bay of Sonmiâni, at the mouth of the Purâli, which is described by Pottinger* as "a very noble sheet of water, capable of affording anchorage to the largest fleet."

Oritæ, or Horitæ.

On crossing the river Arabius, Alexander marched for a whole night through a desert, and in the morning entered a well-inhabited country. Then coming to a small river, he pitched his tents, and waited for the main body of the army under

* 'Biluchistan,' p. 9.

phæstion. On its arrival, says Arrian, Alexander "penetrated further into the country, and coming to a small village which served the Oritæ instead of a capital city, and was named *Rambakia*, he was pleased with its situation, and imagining that it would rise to be a rich and populous city, if a colony were drawn thither, he committed the care thereof to Hephæstion."* On the approach of Alexander, the Oritæ made their submission to the conqueror, who appointed Apollophanes their governor, and deputed Leonatus with a large force to await the arrival of Nearchus with the fleet, and to look after the peopling of the new city. Shortly after Alexander's departure, the Oritæ rose against the Greeks, and Apollophanes, the new governor, was slain, but they were signally defeated by Leonatus, and all their leaders killed.* Nearchus places the scene of this defeat at *Kokala*, on the coast, about halfway between the rivers Arabius and Tomerus. Pliny calls the latter river the *Tonberos*,† and states that the country in its neighbourhood was well cultivated.

From these details I would identify the Oritæ, or *Horitæ* or *Neoteritæ*, as they are called by Diodorus, with the people on the Aghor river, whom the Greeks would have named *Agoritæ*, or *Aoritæ*, by the suppression of the guttural, of which a trace

---

* Arrian, Anab., vi. 21, 22; and 'Indica,' 23; Curtius, ix. 10, 34.

† Hist. Nat., vi. 25.

still remains in the initial aspirate of *Horitæ*. In the bed of this river there are several jets of liquid mud, which, from time immemorial, have been known as *Râm-Chandar-ki-kûp*, or "Râm Chandar's wells." There are also two natural caves, one dedicated to *Kâli*, and the other to *Hingulâj*, or *Hingulâ Devi*, that is, the "Red Goddess," who is only another form of *Kâli*. But the principal objects of pilgrimage in the Aghor valley are connected with the history of Râma. The pilgrims assemble at the *Râmbâgh*, because Râma and Sita are said to have started from this point, and proceed to the Gorakh Tank, where Râma halted; and thence to *Tongabhera*, and on to the point where Râma was obliged to turn back in his attempt to reach Hingulâj with an army. *Râmbâgh* I would identify with the *Rambakia* of Arrian, and *Tongabhera* with the river *Tonberos* of Pliny, and the *Tomerus* of Arrian. At Rambakia, therfore, we must look for the site of the city founded by Alexander, which Leonatus was left behind to complete. It seems probable that this is the city which is described by Stephanus of Byzantium as the "sixteenth Alexandria, near the bay of *Melane*."* Nearchus places the western boundary of the Oritæ at a place called *Malana*, which I take to be the bay of *Malan*, to the east of *Râs Mâlân*, or Cape *Mâlân* of the present day, about twenty miles to the west of the Aghor river. Both Curtius and

---

* In voce Alexandria, *κατά τὸν Μέλανα κόλπον*.

Diodorus* mention the foundation of this city, but they do not give its name. Diodorus, however, adds that it was built on a very favourable site near the sea, but above the reach of the highest tides.

The occurrence of the name of *Râmbâgh* at so great a distance to the west of the Indus, and at so early a period as the time of Alexander, is very interesting and important, as it shows not only the wide extension of Hindu influence in ancient times, but also the great antiquity of the story of Râma. It is highly improbable that such a name, with its attendant pilgrimages, could have been imposed on the place after the decay of Hindu influence.† During the flourishing period of Buddhism many of the provinces to the west of the Indus adopted the Indian religion, which must have had a powerful influence on the manners and language of the people. But the expedition of Alexander preceded the extension of Buddhism, and I can therefore only attribute the old name of *Rambakia* to a period anterior to Darius Hystaspes.

These districts are described by Hwen Thsang under the general name of *Lang-kie-lo,* which M. Julien renders by Langala. M. de St. Martin, however, refers it to the tribe of *Langa,* but it is ex-

---

* Curtius, Vita Alex., ix. 10:—"In hac quoque regione urbem condidit." Diodorus, Hist. xvii.

† Hingulaj (Khingalatchi) is mentioned by the Tibetan Taranath, see 'Vassilief,' French translation, p. 45, as a Rakshasa in the west of India, beyond Barukacha, or Baroch.

tremely doubtful whether this is an ancient name. The other name of *Langalas*, quoted from the Vishnu Purâna, is only a variant reading of *Jângalas*, which is almost certainly the correct form, as it is immediately followed by *Kuru-Jângalas*. Hwen Thsang fixes the capital of *Lang-kie-lo* at 2000 *li*, or 333 miles, to the west of *Kotesar* in Kachh. But as this bearing would place it in the middle of the Indian Ocean, the true direction must be north-west. Now this latter bearing and distance correspond with the position of the great ruined city of *Lâkoriân*, which Masson* found between Khozdar and Kilât. In older maps the name is written simply *Lakûra*, which appears to me to be very fairly represented by the Chinese *Lang-kie-lo*, or *Lânkara*.† Masson describes the ruined fortifications as "remarkable for their magnitude, as well as for the solidity and the skill evident in their construction." From the size and importance of these ruins, I conclude that they are the remains of a large city, which has at some former period been the capital of the country. The Chinese pilgrim describes the province as being many thousands of *li* in breadth as well as in length. It is clear, therefore, that it corresponded, as nearly as possible, with the modern district of Biluchistan, of which the present capital, Kilât, is only 60 miles to the north of *Lâkura*. In the seventh century,

* 'Kilât,' p. 63; and 'Biluchistan,' ii. 46.

† The same Chinese character, *lang*, is found in the transcript of Baghalân, where the vowel of the final syllable is long.

the capital was called *Su-neu-li-shi-fa-lo,* and was 30 *li,* or 5 miles, in circuit. The Chinese syllables are rendered by M. Julien as *Sunuriswara,* of which he offers no translation. But as Hwen Thsang describes a magnificent temple of Siva in the middle of the city, I infer that the Chinese transcript may be intended for *Sambhuriswara,* which is a well-known title of Siva as the "lord of divine beings," or the "god of gods." By assuming that this name belongs properly to the temple, the other name of *Lang-kie-lo,* or *Lâkara,* may be applied to the capital as well as to the province.

II. GURJJARA.

Hwen Thsang places the second kingdom of Western India, named *Kiu-che-lo* or *Gurjjara,* at about 1800 *li,* or 300 miles, to the north of Balabhi, and 2800 *li,* or 467 miles, to the north-west of Ujain. The capital was named *Pi-lo-mi-lo* or *Bâlmer,* which is exactly 300 miles to the north of the ruins of Balabhi. From Ujain in a straight line it is not more than 350 miles; but the actual road distance is between 400 and 500 miles, as the traveller has to turn the Aravali mountains, either by Ajmer on the north, or by Analwâra on the south. The kingdom was 5000 *li,* or 833 miles, in circuit. It must, therefore, have comprised the greater part of the present chiefships of Bikaner, Jesalmer, and Jodhpur. Its boundaries can only be described approximately, as extending about 130 miles on the north from Balar or Sirdarkot to Junjhnu; 250 miles on the east from Junjhnu to near Mount Abu; 170 miles on the south from Abu to near Umarkot; and 310 miles on the west from Umarkot to Balar. These figures give a total circuit of 860 miles, which is as close an approximation to the measurement of Hwen Thsang as can be reasonably expected.

All the early Arab geographers speak of a kingdom named *Jurz* or *Juzr,* which from its position would appear to be the same as the *Kiu-che-lo* of Hwen Thsang. The name of the country is somewhat doubtful, as the unpointed Arabic characters may be read as *Haraz* or *Hazar,* and *Kharaz* or *Khazar,* as well as *Jurz* or *Juzr.* But fortunately there is no uncertainty about its position, which is determined to be Râjputâna by several concurring circumstances. Thus the merchant Sulimân, in A.D. 851,* states that *Haraz* was bounded on one side by *Tâfeḳ* or *Tâḳin,* which, as I have already shown, was the old name of the Panjâb. It possessed silver mines, and could muster a larger force of cavalry than any other kingdom of India. All these details point unmistakably to Râjputâna, which lies to the south-east of the Panjâb, possesses the only silver mines known in India, and has always been famous for its large bodies of cavalry.

According to Ibn Khordâdbeh,† who died about A.D. 912, the *Tâtariya* dirhems were current

* Dowson's Sir Henry Elliot, i. 4.

† Dowson's edition of Sir Henry Elliot's Muhamm. Hist., i. 13.

in the country of Hazar; and according to Ibn Haukal, who wrote about A.D. 977,* these dirhems were also current in the kingdom of Gândhâra, which at that time included the Panjâb. Sulimân says the same thing of the kingdom of the Balhara, or the present Gujarât; and we learn incidentally that the same dirhems were also current in Sindh, as in A.H. 107, or A.D. 725, the public treasury contained no less than eighteen millions of Tâtariya dirhems.† The value of these coins is variously stated at from 1⅛ dirhem to 1½, or from 54 to 72 grains in weight. From these data I conclude that the Tâtariya dirhems are the rude silver pieces generally known as Indo-Sassanian, because they combine Indian letters with Sassanian types. They would appear to have been first introduced by the Scythic or Tâtâr princes, who ruled in Kabul and north-western India, as they are now found throughout the Kabul valley and Panjâb, as well as in Sindh, Râjputâna, and Gujarât. Colonel Stacy's specimens were chiefly obtained from the last two countries, while my own specimens have been procured in all of them. In weight they vary from 50 to 68 grains; and in age they range from the fifth or sixth century down to the period of Mahmud of Ghazni. They are frequently found in company with the silver pieces of the Brahman kings of

* Dowson's edition of Sir Henry Elliot's Muhamm, Hist., i. 35.

† Sir Henry Elliot, 'Arabs in Sindh,' p. 36. Dowson's edit. i. 3.

Kabul, which agrees with the statement of Masudi that the Tâtariya dirhems were current along with other pieces which were stamped at Gândhâra.* The latter I take to be the silver coins of the Brahman kings of Kabul, whose dynasty began to reign about A.D. 850, or shortly before the time of Masudi, who flourished from A.D. 915 to 956. I have also found some of the Indo-Sassanian or Tâtâr dirhems in central India to the east of the Aravali range, as well as in the Upper Gangetic Doâb; but in these provinces they are extremely scarce, as the common coin of Northern India in the mediæval period was the *Varâha,* with the figure of the Boar incarnation of Vishnu, varying from 55 to 65 grains in weight. From this examination of the coins I conclude that the kingdom named *Hazar* or *Juzr* by the early Arab geographers, is represented as nearly as possible by Western Râjputâna.

Edrisi,† quoting Ibn Khordâdbeh, states that *Juzr* or *Huzr* was the hereditary title of the king, as well as the name of the country. This statement confirms my identification of *Juzr* with *Guzr* or *Gujar,* which is a very numerous tribe, whose name is attached to many important places in north-west India and the Panjâb, and more especially to the great peninsula of Gujarât. It is not known when

---

* Dowson's edition of Sir Henry Elliot's Muhamm. Hist., i. 24.

† Geogr., i. 175, Jaubert's translation.

this name was first applied to the peninsula. In early times it was called *Saurashtra,* which is the *Surastrene* of Ptolemy; and it continued to bear this name as late as A.D. 812, as we learn from a copper-plate inscription found at Baroda.* In this record of the Saurashtra kings, *Gurjjara* is twice mentioned as an independent kingdom. About A.D. 770 the king of Gurjjara was conquered by Indra Raja of Saurashtra, but was afterwards reinstated; and about A.D. 800 Indra's son Karka assisted the ruler of Malwa against the king of Gurjjara. These statements show most clearly that Gurjjara still existed as a powerful kingdom, quite distinct from Saurashtra, nearly two centuries after Hwen Thsang's visit in A.D. 640. They show also that Gurjjara must have been adjacent to Malwa, as well as to Saurashtra, a position which clearly identifies it with Râjputâna, as I have already determined from Hwen Thsang's narrative.

In the seventh century the king is said to have been a *Tsa-ti-li* or Kshatriya; but two centuries earlier a dynasty of *Gurjjara* or *Gujar* Rajas was certainly reigning to the north of Mahârâshtra, as we have contemporaneous inscriptions† of a Châlukya prince of Paithan, and of a Gurjjara prince of an unnamed territory, which record grants of land to the same persons. These inscriptions have been translated by Professor Dowson, who

---

* Journ. Asiat. Soc. Bengal, viii. 300.

† Journ. Royal Asiat. Soc., new series, i. 270,277.

refers the dates to the era of Vikramaditya, but in the total absence of any authentic example of the use of this era before the sixth century A.D., I must demur to its adoption in these early records. The Saka era, on the contrary, is found in the early inscriptions of the Châlukya Raja Pulakesi, and in the writings of the astronomers Arya Bhatta and Varâha Mihira. The inscription of Pulakesi is dated in the *Saka* year 411, or A.D. 489, from which I conclude that the record of the earlier Châlukya Prince Vijaya, which is dated in the year 394, must refer to the same era. The contemporary records of the Gurjjara prince, which are dated in S. 380 and 385 must therefore belong to the middle of the fifth century A.D. All these copper-plate inscriptions were found together at *Khaidra*, near Ahmedabad. The first inscription of the Gurjjara Raja records the grant of lands to certain Brahmans "who having left the town of *Jambusara*, dwell in the village of *Sirishapadraka*, included in the district of Akrureswara." Five years later the same Brahman grantees are described as those "who are to dwell in the town of Jambusara;" and accordingly in the Châlukya inscription, which is dated nine years subsequent to the latter, they are described as actually dwelling in the town of Jambusara. This town is no doubt *Jambosir*, between Khambay and Baroch, and as it belonged to the Châlukya princes, who ruled over Maharashtra, the kingdom of Gurjjara must have been situated to the north of Khambay, that is, in Râjputâna, where I have already placed it on the authority of Hwen Thsang, and other independent evidence.

III. VALABHADRA, OR BALABHI.

The ruins of the famous city of Balabhi were discovered by Tod near Bhaonagar, on the eastern side of the peninsula of Gujarât. In an inscription of the fifth century the country is called "the beautiful kingdom of *Valabhadra*,"* but in the local histories and traditions of the people, it is generally known as Balabhi. This also was the name in the time of Hwen Thsang, who calls the kingdom *Fa-la-pi*, or *Balabhi*. In ancient times, however, the peninsula of Gujarât was only known as *Surashtra*, and under this name it is mentioned in the Mahâbhârata and in the Purânas. It is called *Surashtrene* by Ptolemy and the author of the 'Periplus;' and its people are most probably intended by Pliny under the corrupt name of *Suaratаratœ*, or *Varetatœ*, for which I would propose to read *Suratœ*. The change in the name of the country is alluded to in an inscription, dated in the *Saka* year 734, or A.D. 812, of Raja *Karka*, whose remote ancestor Govinda is said to have been the ornament of the *Saurâshtra* kingdom, "which lost its appellation of *Sau-rajya* from the ruin that had fallen upon it."† Karka's father is called Raja of *Lâteswara*, which at once identifies his kingdom with Balabhi, as

* Journ. Asiat. Soc. Bengal, 1838, p. 976.

† *Ibid.*, 1839, p. 300. Inscription from Baroda.

Hwen Thsang notes that Balabhi was also called *Pe-Lo-lo,* or northern *Lâra,* which is the common pronunciation of the Sanskrit *Lâta.* As Karka was only the fifth in descent from Govinda, the name of *Saurâjya* or *Saurashtra* could not have been restored by these representatives of the old family before the middle of the seventh century. From a comparison of all the data I conclude that the old name of Saurashtra was lost in A.D. 319, when the successors of the *Sâh* kings were supplanted by the *Vallabhas,* and the capital changed from *Junagurh* to *Valabhi.* The establishment of the Balabhi era, which dates from A.D. 319, is said by Abu Rihân to mark the period of the extinction of the *Gupta* race, whose coins are found in considerable numbers in Gujarât. This date may therefore be accepted with some certainty as that of the establishment of the Balabhi dynasty, and most probably also as that of the foundation of their city of Balabhi.

According to the native histories and local traditions Balabhi was attacked and destroyed in the Samvat year 580, which is equivalent to A.D. 523, if in the Vikrama era, or A.D. 658, if in the Saka era. Colonel Tod has adopted the former; but as Hwen Thsang visited Balabhi in A.D. 640, the date must clearly be referred to the later era of Saka. If the statement is correct, we may refer the capture of Balabhi to Raja Govinda of the Baroda copper-plate inscription, who is recorded to have re-established the old family, as well as the old name of the former kingdom of Saurashtra. As he was the great-grandfather of the grandfather of Karka Raja, who was reigning in A.D. 812, his own accession must have taken place in the third quarter of the seventh century, that is, between A.D. 650 and 675, which agrees with the actual date of A.D. 658, assigned by the native historians for the destruction of Balabhi, and the extinction of the Balabhi sovereignty in the peninsula of Gujarât.

About a century after their expulsion from Balabhi the representative of the Balabhis, named *Bappa* or *Vappaka*, founded a new kingdom at Chitor, and his son *Guhila*, or *Guhâditya*, gave to his tribe the new name of *Guhilâwat*, or *Gahilot*, by which they are still known. About the same time* a chief of the *Chaura* tribe, named *Ban Raja*, or the "Jangal Lord," founded a city on the bank of the Saraswati, about seventy miles to the south-west of Mount Abu, called *Analwâra Pattan*, which soon became the most famous place in Western India. Somewhat earlier, or about A.D. 720, Krishna, the Pahlava prince of the peninsula, built the fort of *Elâpura*, the beauty of which, according to the inscription, astonished the immortals. In it he established an image of Siva adorned with the crescent. Following this clue I incline to identify *Elâpura* with the famous city of *Somnâth*, which, as the capital of the peninsula, was usually called Pattan Somnâth. According to Postans† the old

* 'Ayin Akbari,' ii. 73. Abul Fazl gives Samvat 802, or A.D. 745, if referred to the era of Vukramaditya.

† Journ. Asiat. Soc. Bengal, 1838, p. 866.

"city of Pattan" is built upon a projection of the "mainland, forming the southern point of the small port and bay of *Verâwal*." This name I take to be the same as *Elâpura* or *Elâwar*, which, by a transposition that is very common in India, would become *Erâwal*. Thus *Nar-sinh* has become *Ran-si*, and *Ranod* is used indifferently with *Narod*, but we have a still more striking instance in the change from the ancient *Vârul* to the modern *Elur* or *Elora*. Now Patan Somnâth was famous for a temple of Siva, which enshrined a figure of the god bearing a crescent on his head as *Somnâth*, or the "lord of the moon." This appellation was therefore the proper name of the temple, and not of the city, which I conclude must have been *Elâpura* or *Erawal*, the modern *Verâwal*.

The earliest notice that we possess of Somnâth is contained in the brief account of the successful campaign of Mahmûd of Ghazni. According to Ferishta* the fortified city of Somnâth was situated "on a narrow peninsula, washed on three sides by the sea." It was the residence of the Raja, and *Naharwâla* (a transposition of Analwâra) was then only "a frontier city of Gujarât." This agrees with the native histories, which place the close of the *Chaura* dynasty of *Analwâra* in S. 998, or A.D. 941, when the sovereignty passed into the hands of the Châlukya prince *Mula Raja*, who became the paramount ruler of Somnâth and Analwâra.

* Briggs's translation, i. 69.

After the time of Mahmûd, Somnath would appear to have been abandoned by its rulers in favour of *Analwâra*, which is mentioned as the capital of Gujarât in the time of Muhammad Ghori and his successor Aibeg.* It was still the capital of the kingdom in A.H. 697, or A.D. 1297, when the country was invaded by the army of Ala-ud-din Muhammad Khilji, which occupied *Nahrwâla*, or *Analwâra*, and annexed the province to the empire of Delhi.

During all these transactions Ferishta invariably designates the peninsula, as well as the country to the north of it, by the modern name of Gujarât. The name is not mentioned by Abu Rihân, although he notices both Analwâra and Somnâth. It occurs first in the Mojmal-ut-tawârikh of Rashid-ud-din, who wrote in A.D. 1310, just thirteen years after the conquest of the country by the Muhammadan king of Delhi. Now I have already shown that the name of *Gurjjara* was confined to Western Râjputâna in the time of Hwen Thsang, and that it was still a distinct country from *Saurashtra* in A.D. 812, when Karka Raja of *Lâteswara* recorded his grant of land. Between this date and A.D. 1310, there is a gap of five centuries, during which period we have no mention of Gurjjara in any contemporary records. I have a strong suspicion, however, that the movement of the Gujars towards the peninsula must have been connected with the permanent conquest of

* Briggs's translation, i. 179, 194.

Delhi, Kanoj and Ajmer by the Muhammadans, which ejected the Chohâns and Râthors from Northern Rajputâna and the Upper Ganges, and thrust them towards the south. We know that the Râthors occupied *Pâli* to the east of Bâlmer in the Samvat year 1283, or A.D. 1226. This settlement of the Râthors must have driven the great body of the Gujars from their ancient seats and forced them to the south towards Analwâra Pattan and Eder. This was actually the case of the Gohils, who, being expelled from Mârwâr by the Râthors, settled in the eastern side of the peninsula, which was named after them Gohilwara. In the time of Akbar the Gujars had certainly not penetrated into the peninsula, as Abul Fazl does not name them in his notice of the different tribes which then occupied the Sirkar of *Surât*. But even at the present day there is no large community of Gujars in the peninsula, so that we must look for some other cause for the imposition of their name on a large province which they have never completely occupied.

In my account of the province of *Gurjjara* I have already noticed an old inscription of the kings of the Gurjjara tribe. From this record we learn that in s. 380, or A.D. 458 the Gujars had pushed their conquests as far south as the banks of the Narbadâ. In that year, and subsequently in A.D. 463, their king Sri Datta Kusali* made several

* Professor Dowson in Journ. Royal Asiat. Soc., new series, i. 280.

grants of land to certain Brahmans in the district of *Akrûreswara*, near Jambusara, which I take to be *Aklesar*, on the south bank of the Narbadâ, opposite Bhâroch. But before s. 394, or A.D. 472, the Gujars must have been driven back to the north, as far at least as Khambay, as the Châlukya prince Vijaya made several grants of land to the same Brahmans in the town of Jambusara, which lies between Bhâroch and Khambay. It is certain, therefore, that the Gujars had occupied the country to the north of the peninsula as early as the fifth century of the Christian era. But two centuries later they had already lost their power, as Hwen Thsang found a *Kshatriya* prince on the throne of *Gurjjara*. They must still, however, have continued to form the bulk of the population of the countries to the west and south of Mount Abu; and as Alaf Khan, the first Muhammadan conqueror, under Ala-ud-din Khilji, fixed his head-quarters at *Nahrwâra*, or *Analwâra*, in the very heart of the Gujar country, I think it probable that the name of Gujarât was then first applied to this new province of the Delhi empire; and as the peninsula of Saurashtra formed a part of the province, it was also included under the same general appellation. I therefore look upon the extension of the name of Gujarât to the peninsula as a political convenience rather than an ethnographical application. Hamilton* notes that the greater part of Malwa and Khandes was

* Gazetteer, *in voce* "Gujerât," i. 60.

formerly called Gujarât; and this is borne out by Marco Polo, who distinguishes between the peninsula, which he calls *Sumenat* (Somnâth) and the kingdom of *Gozurat*, which he places on the coast to the north of Tana; that is, about Bhâroch and Surat. Even at the present day the name of Gujarât is not known to the natives of the peninsula itself, who continue to call their country *Surath* and *Kathiâwar*;* the latter name having been a recent adoption of the Mahrattas.

The capital of Balabhi is described by Hwen Thsang as 30 *li*, or 5 miles, in circuit. Its ruins were first discovered by Tod, although he did not actually visit them.† But they have since been visited by Dr. Nicholson,‡ according to whom they are situated at 18 miles to the west-north-west of Bhaonagar, near the village of *Wale*. The ruins are still known by the name of *Vamilapura*, which is only a slight transposition of *Valami*, or *Valabhipura*. The remains are scattered over a wide extent, but there is nothing remarkable about them, except the unusually large size of the bricks. In the time of Akbar, however, these remains would appear to have been much more considerable, as Abul Fazl§ was informed that "at the foot of the mountains of Sirouj is a large city, now out of

---

* Elphinstone, 'India,' i. 550.

† 'Travels in Western India,' p. 268.

‡ Journ. Royal Asiat. Soc., xiii. 146.

§ 'Ayin Akbari,' ii. 69.

repair, although the situation is very desirable. Mâbidchin and the port of Ghoga are dependent upon it." The vicinity of *Ghoga* is a sufficient indication to enable us to identify this ruined city with the present remains of Balabhi, which are only about 20 miles distant from Ghoga.

In the seventh century Hwen Thsang describes the kingdom of Balabhi as 6000 *li*, or 1000 miles, in circuit, which is very near the truth, if we include the districts of Bhâroch and Surat, on the neighbouring coast, as well as the whole of the peninsula of Surashtra. But in this part of the pilgrim's travels the narrative is frequently imperfect and erroneous, and we must therefore trust to our own sagacity, both to supply his omissions and to correct his mistakes. Thus, in his description of *Bhâroch*, Hwen Thsang omits to tell us whether it was a separate and independent chiefship, or only a tributary of one of its powerful neighbours, Balabhi, Malwa, or Maharashtra. But as it has generally been attached to the peninsula, I infer that it most probably belonged to the great kingdom of Balabhi in the seventh century. In the second century, according to Ptolemy, *Barygaza* formed part of the kingdom of *Larike*, which, in Hwen Thsang's time, was only another name for Balabhi. In the tenth century, according to Ibn Haukal,* it belonged to the kingdom of the Balharâ, whose capital was Analwarâ; but as this city was not founded for more than a

* Elliot, 'Muhammadan Historians of India,' i. 63.

hundred years after Hwen Thsang's visit, I conclude that in the seventh century Bhâroch must have formed part of the famous kingdom of Balabhi. With this addition to its territories, the frontier circuit of Balabhi would have been as nearly as possible 1000 miles.

1. SURǍSHTRA.

According to Hwen Thsang, the province of *Su-la-cha,* or *Surâtha,* was a dependant of Balabhi. Its capital was situated at 500 *li,* or 83 miles, to the west of Balabhi, at the foot of Mount *Yeu-chen-ta,* or *Ujjanta.* This is the Pali form of the Sanskrit *Ujjayanta,* which is only another name for the *Girinar* hill that rises above the old city of *Junagarh.* The name of *Ujjayanta* is mentioned in both of the Girinar inscriptions of Rudra Dâma and Skanda Gupta, although this important fact escaped the notice of the translators.* The mention of this famous hill fixes the position of the capital of Surashtra at *Junagarh,* or *Yavana-gadh,* which is 87 miles to the west of Balabhi, or very nearly the same as stated by Hwen Thsang. The pilgrim notices that the mountain was covered with thick forests, and that its scarped sides contained numerous chambers and galleries. This description agrees with the account of Postans,† who, in 1838, found

---

* Journ. Asiat. Soc. Bombay, vii. 119, "the *Urjayata* hill;" p. 123, "*Urjayat;*" and p. 124, "the Jayanta mountain," should all be rendered *Ujâyanta.*

† Journ. Royal Asiat. Soc. Bengal, 1838, pp. 874,876.

the hill covered with "a thick jungul of the custard-apple tree," and a number of excavations at the base, consisting of "small flat roofed rooms, supported by square pillars without ornament."

The name of *Surath* is still known in this part of the peninsula; but it is confined to a comparatively small tract, which forms one of the ten divisions of Gujarât.* In the time of Akbar, however, it was applied to the southern or larger half of the peninsula, which, according to Abul Fazl, extended from the port of Ghoga to the port of Aramroy, and from Sirdhar to the port of Diu.† The name of the district is also preserved by Terry,‡ whose information was obtained at the Court of Jahângir. According to his account, the chief city of *Soret* was called *Janagar*, that is, *Javanagarh*, or *Jonagarh*. The province was small, but very rich, and had the ocean to the *south*. At that time also it would appear not to have been included in Gujarât, as Terry describes it as *lying upon Gujarat*.

In the seventh century Hwen Thsang states that *Surath*, or *Surashtra*, was 4000 *li*, or 667 miles, in circuit, and touched the river *Mo-hi* on the west. This river has always been identified with the *Mahi* of Malwa, which falls into the Gulf of Khambay.§ Accepting this identification as

---

* Eastwick, 'Handbook of Bombay,' p. 424.

† 'Ayin Akbari,' ii. 66.

‡ 'Voyage to East India,' p. 80.

§ As the *Mahi* river lies to the *north-east* of Gujarât,

correct, the province of *Surath* in the time of Hwen Thsang must have comprised the whole of the peninsula, including the city of Balabhi itself. This is confirmed by the measurement of the frontier given by the pilgrim, which agrees exactly with that of the entire peninsula to the south-west of a line drawn from the Lesser Ran of Kachh to Khambay. In spite of the fame of Balabhi, the old name of *Surath* was still applied to the whole peninsula so late as A.D. 640.

2. BHÂROCH, OR BARYGAZA.

In the seventh century the district of *Po-lu-kie-che-po*, or *Barukachwa*, was from 2400 to 2500 *li*, or from 400 to 417 miles, in circuit; and its chief city was on the bank of the *Nai-mo-tho*, or *Narmadâ* river, and close to the sea. With these data it is easy to identify the capital with the well-known seaport town of *Bhâroch*, under its Sanskrit name of *Bhrigu-Kachha*, as written by the Brahmans, or *Bhârukachha*, as found in the old inscriptions. The latter was no doubt the more usual form, as it is almost literally preserved in the Βαρύγαζα of Ptolemy, and the 'Periplus.' From Hwen Thsang's measurement of its circuit, the limits of the district may be determined approximately as extending from the *Mâhi** river on the north, to Dâmân on the

---

we must either read *east*, or suppose that the pilgrim referred to the western bank of the stream.

* The *Maïs* river of Ptolemy.

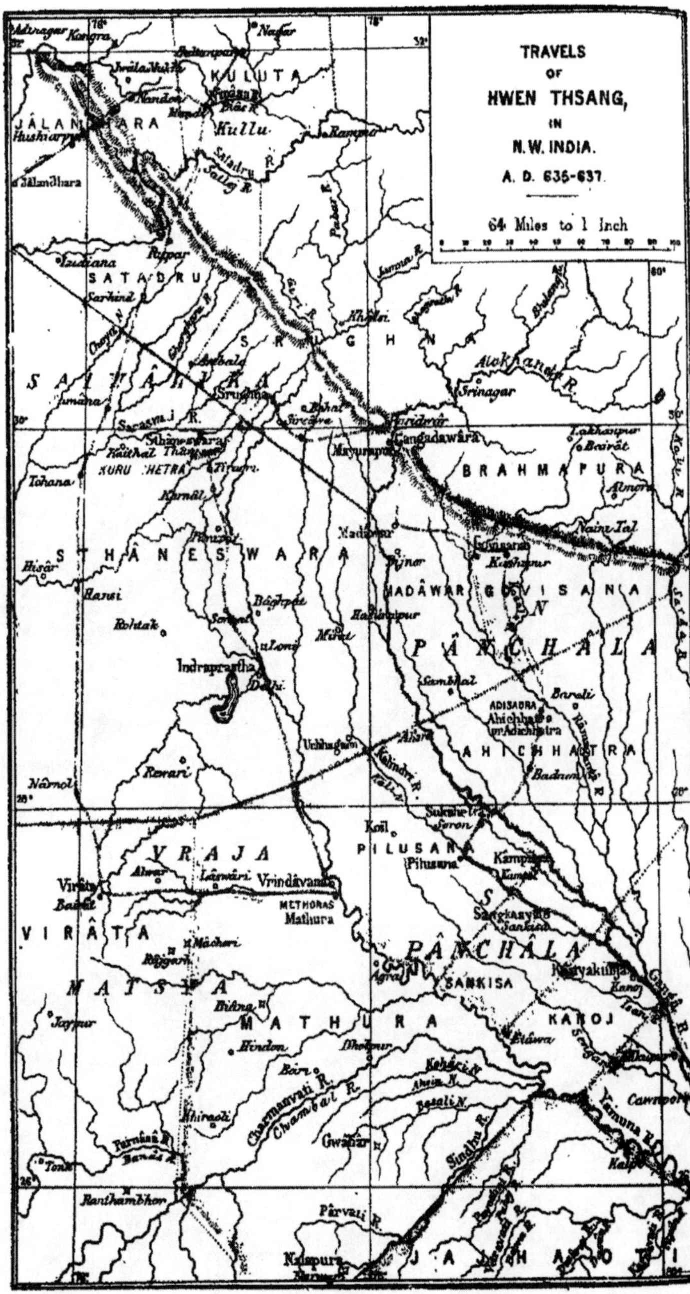
TRAVELS
OF
HWEN THSANG,
IN
N.W. INDIA.
A. D. 636-637.
64 Miles to 1 Inch
KULUTA
JÂLANDHARA
SATADRU
SRUGHNA
SATADRU
STHÂNESWARA
BRAHMAPURA
MADÂWAR
GOVISANA
PÂNCHALA
AHICHHATRA
VRAJA
PILUSANA
VIRÂTA
MATSYA
MATHURA
SANKISA
KANOJ
Indraprastha
Delhi
Mathura
Vrindâvana
Gangadawâra
Srinagar
Mayurapura
Kanyakubja

south, and from the Gulf of Khambay on the west to the *Sahyâdri* mountains on the east.

According to the text of Hwen Thsang, Bhâroch and Balabhi were in Southern India, and Surashtra in Western India; but as he places Malwa in Southern India, and Ujain in Central India, I look upon these assignments as so many additional proofs of the confusion which I have already noticed in the narrative of his travels in Western India. I would therefore assign both Balabhi and Bhâroch to Western India, as they formed part of the great province of Surashtra. The correctness of this assignment is confirmed by the author of the 'Periplus,' who notes that below *Barygaza* the coast turns to the south, whence that region is named *Dakhinabades*, as the natives call the south *Dakhanos*.*

CENTRAL INDIA.

According to the Chinese pilgrim, the great division of Central India extended from the Satlej to the head of the Gangetic Delta, and from the Himalâya mountains to the Narbadâ and Mahânadi rivers. It comprised all the richest and most populous districts of India, with the single exception of the Gangetic Delta, or Bengal proper.† Of the seventy separate states of India that existed in the

---

* Peripl. Mar. Erythr., in Hudson's Geogr. Vet., i. 29.

† See Map No. I.

seventh century, no less than thirty-seven, or rather more than one-half, belonged to Central India. The whole of these districts were visited by Hwen Thsang, whose footsteps I will now attend in describing the different principalities from west to east in the following order:—

1. Sthâneswara.
2. Bairât.
3. Srughna.
4. Madâwar.
5. Brahmapura.
6. Govisana.
7. Ahichhatra.
8. Pilosana.
9. Sankisa.
10. Mathura.
11. Kanoj.
12. Ayuto.
13. Hayamukha.
14. Prayâga.
15. Kosâmbi.
16. Kusapura.
17. Vaisâkha.
18. Srâvasti.
19. Kapila.
20. Kusinagara.
21. Varânasi.
22. Yodhapatipura.
23. Vaisâla.
24. Vriji.
25. Nepâla.
26. Magadha.
27. Hiranya Parvata.
28. Champa.
29. Kânkjol.
30. Paundra Vardhana.
31. Jajhoti.
32. Maheswarapura.
33. Ujain.
34. Malwa.
35. Kheda, or Khaira.
36. Anandapura.
37. Vadari, or Eder.

1. STHÂNESWARA.

In the seventh century *Sa-ta-ni-shi-fa-lo*, or *Sthâneswara,* was the capital of a separate kingdom, which is described as being 7000 *li*, or 1167 miles, in circuit. No king is mentioned, but the state was tributary to Harsha Varddhana of Kanoj, who was the paramount sovereign of Central India. From the large dimensions given by Hwen Thsang, I infer that the district must have extended from the Satlej to the Ganges.* Its northern boundary may be approximately described as a straight line drawn from Hari-ki-patan, on the Satlej, to Muzafarnagar, near the Ganges; and its southern boundary as an irregular line drawn from near Pâk-patan, on the Satlej, viâ Bhatner and Nârnol, to Anupshahar on the Ganges. These limits give a boundary of about 900 miles, which is nearly one-fourth less than is stated by the pilgrim. But it is certain that many of these boundary measurements must be exaggerated, as the distances could only have been estimated, and the natural tendency of most persons is rather to overstate the actual size of their native districts. Another source of error lies in the deficient information of Hwen Thsang's own narrative, which describes each of the 37 districts as a distinct and separate state, whereas it is almost certain that several of the minor states should be included within the boundaries of the larger ones. Thus I believe that the petty districts of *Govisana* and *Ahichhatra* must have formed part of the state of *Madâwar;* that *Vaisâkha* and *Kusapura,* and the other small districts of the Gangetic Doab, *Ayuto, Hayamukha, Kosâmbi,* and *Prayâga,* were included in Kanoj;

* See Map No. X.

that *Kusinagara* belonged to *Kapila;* and that *Vadarī* and *Kheda* were integral parts of *Malwa.* In some instances also, I believe that thousands have been inserted in the text instead of hundreds. I refer specially to the petty districts in the lower Gangetic Doab. Thus, *Prayâga*. or Allahabad, is said to be 5000 *li*, or 833 miles, in circuit, and *Kosâmbi,* which is only 30 miles from Allahabad, is said to be 6000 *li,* or 1000 miles, in circuit! In both of these instances I would read the smaller numbers of 500 *li*, or 83 miles, and 600 *li,* or 100 miles, which would then agree with the actual dimensions of these petty divisions. It is quite certain that they could not have been larger, as they were completely surrounded by other well-known districts. By making due allowance for one or other of these sources of error, I think it will be found that Hwen Thsang's measurements are in general not very far from the truth.

The town of *Sthâneswara,* or Thânesar, consists of an old ruined fort, about 1200 feet square at top, with the modern town on a mound to the east, and a suburb called *Bâhari,* or "without," on another mound to the west. Altogether, the three old mounds occupy a space nearly one mile in length from east to west, and about 2000 feet in average breadth. These dimensions give a circuit of 14,000 feet, or less than 2¾ miles, which is somewhat under the 20 *li*, or 3⅓ miles, of Hwen Thsang. But before the inroads of the Muhammadans, it is certain, from the number of brick ruins still existing, as well as from the statements of the people themselves, that the whole of the intervening space between the present town and the lake, which is now called *Darrâ*, must have formed part of the old city. Taking in this space, the original city would have been, as nearly as possible, an exact square of one mile on each side, which would give a circuit of 4 miles, or a little more than the measurement of the Chinese pilgrim. According to tradition, the fort was built by Raja *Dilipa*, a descendant of Kuru, five generations anterior to the Pândus. It is said to have had 52 towers or bastions, of which some remains still exist. On the west side the earthen ramparts rise to a height of 60 feet above the road; but the mass of the interior is not more than 40 feet high. The whole mound is thickly covered with large broken bricks, but with exception of three old wells, there are no remains of any antiquity.

The name of *Thânesar*, or *Sthâneswara*, is said to be derived either from the *Sthâna* or abode of *Iswara*, or Mahâdeva, or from the junction of his names of *Sthânu* and *Iswara*, or from *Sthânu* and *sar*, a "lake." The town is one of the oldest and most celebrated places in India, but the earliest certain notice of it under this name is by the Chinese pilgrim Hwen Thsang, in A.D. 634, although it is most probably mentioned by Ptolemy as *Batan-Kaisara*, for which we should, perhaps, read *Satan-aisara*, for the Sanskrit *Sthâneswara*. But the place was more famous for its connection with the history of the Pândus, than for its possession of a temple of Mahâdeva, whose worship, in India at least, must be of much later date than the heroes of the Mahâbhârata. All the country immediately around Thânesar, between the *Saraswati* and *Drishadwati* rivers, is known by the name of *Kuru-Kshetra,* that is, the "field or land of *Kuru,*" who is said to have become an ascetic on the bank of the great holy lake to the south of the town. This lake is called by various names, as *Brahmâ-Sar, Râma-hrad, Vâyu,* or *Vâyava-Sar,* and *Pavana-Sar.* The first name is attributed to Brahma, because he performed a sacrifice on its banks. The second name is derived from *Parasu-Rama,* who is said to have spilt the blood of the *Kshatriyas* in this place. The last two titles are derived from the names of the god of Wind, on account of the pleasant breezes which blew over the waters of lake during Kuru's period of asceticism. This lake is the centre of attraction for most pilgrims; but all around it for many miles is holy ground, and the number of holy places connected with the *Kauravas* and *Pândavas,* and with other heroes of antiquity, is very great indeed. According to popular belief, the exact number is 360, but the list given in the *Kuru-kshetra Mahâtmya* is limited to 180 places, of which one-half, or 91, are to the north along the line of the venerated Saraswati river. There are, however, in this list so many omissions of places of acknowledged importance, such as the *Nâgahrada* at *Pundri,* the *Vyâsasthala* at Basthali, the *Parâsara-*

tirath at Bâlu, and the *Vishnu-tirath* at Sagga, near *Narâna,* that I feel inclined to believe that the popular number of 360 may not be exaggerated.

The *Chakra,* or district of *Kuru-Kshetra,* is also called *Dharma-Kshetra,* or the "holy land," which is evidently the original of Hwen Thsang's "*champ du bonheur.*" In his time the circle of pilgrimage was limited to 200 *li,** which, at his valuation of 40 *li* to the Indian *yojana* of 4 kos, is equivalent to 20 kos. In the time of Akbar, however, the circle had already been increased to 40 kos,† and at the time of my visit it had been extended to 48 kos, although the 40 kos circuit was also well known, and is, indeed, noted by Mr. Bowring. The circuit stated by the Chinese pilgrim could not have been *more* than 35 or 40 miles, at 7 or 8 miles to the yojana, but the circle mentioned by Abul Fazl could not be less than 53 miles, at the usual valuation of the Padshahi kos at 1⅓ miles, and might, at Sir H. Elliot's valuation of Akbar's kos at more than 2½ miles, be extended to upwards of 100 miles. It is possible, indeed, to make these different statements agree very closely by changing the pilgrim's number to 400 *li,* or 10 yojanas, which are equivalent to 40 kos, or 80 miles, and by estimating Abul Fazl's 40 kos at the usual Indian rate of about 2 miles each. I am myself quite satisfied of the necessity for making this correction in the pilgrim's

---

* Julien's 'Hiouen Thsang,' ii. 213.

† 'Ayin Akbari,' ii. 517.

number, as the narrow extent of his circle would not only shut out the equally famous shrines at *Prithudaka*, or *Pehoa* on the Saraswati, and at the *Kausiki-Sangam*, or junction of the Kausiki and *Drishadwati* rivers, but would actually exclude the Drishadwati itself, which in the *Vâmana Purâna* is specially mentioned as being within the limits of the holy land,—

Dirgh-Kshetre Kurukshetre dirgha Satranta yire
Nudyâstire Drishadvatyâh punyayâh Suchirodhasah.

"They were making the great sacrifice of *Satranta* in the wide region of *Kurukshetra* on the banks of the *Drishadwati*, esteemed holy on account of its virtues." This river is also specially mentioned in the *Vana Parva* of the *Mahâbhârata* as being the southern boundary of the holy land.*

Dakshinena Sarasvatyâ Drishadvatyuttarena-cha
Ye vasanti Kurukshetre te vasanti trivishtape.

"South from *Saraswati*, and north from *Drishadwati*, they who dwell in *Kurukshetra* live in paradise." From these texts it is certain that the holy land of *Kurukshetra* must have extended to the *Drishadwati* in the time of Hwen Thsang, and therefore that his limitation of its circuit to 200 *li*, or 20 kos, must be erroneous.

In another passage of the *Mahâbhârata*, the boundaries of the holy land are even more explicitly detailed,—†

---

* Chap. 83, v. 4.

† 'Vana Parva,' chap. 83, last verse.

Tad Ratnukâratnukyor yadantaram Râmâhradânân-cha Bhachaknukasya-cha
Etat Kurukshetra, Samanta—panchakam, Pitamahâ-syottara Vediruchyate.

"The tract between *Ratnuka, Aratnuka, Râmâhrada* and *Bhachaknuka*, is called *Kurukshetra, Samanta-panchaka*, and the northern *Vedi* of *Pita-maha* (or Brahmâ)." As this last name of *Brahmâ-vedi* is equivalent to *Brahmâvartta*, we have another testimony in the Code of Manu for extending the holy land to the banks of the Drishadwati.*

Sarasvati Drishadvatyordeva nudyor yadantaram
Tandeva nirmitam-desan Brahmâvarttan prachakshate.

"That region, made by the Gods, which is between the *Saraswati* and *Drishadwati* rivers, is called *Brahmâvartta*."

The great lake of *Kurukshetra* is an oblong sheet of water 3546 feet in length from east to west, and 1900 feet in breadth. It is mentioned by Abu Rihân,† who records, on the authority of Varâha Mihira, that during eclipses of the moon the waters of all other tanks visit the tank at Thânesar, so that the bather in this tank at the moment of eclipse obtains the additional merit of bathing in all the other tanks at the same time.

This notice by Varâha Mîhira carries us back at once to A.D. 500, when the holy tank at Thânesar was in full repute. But the Pauranic legends attribute to it an antiquity long anterior even to

---

* Houghton's 'Institutes of Menu,' ii. 17.

† Reinaud, 'Mémoire sur l'Inde,' p. 287.

the Pândus themselves. On its banks *Kuru*, the common ancestor of the *Kauravas* and *Pândavas*, sat in ascetic abstraction; here Parasu-Râma slew the Kshatriyas, and here Pururavas having lost the nymph *Urvasi*, at length met his celestial bride at Kurukshetra "sporting with four other nymphs of heaven in a lake beautiful with lotuses." But the story of the horse-headed *Dadhyanch*, or *Dadhîcha*, is perhaps even older than the legend of Pururavas, as it is alluded to in the Rig Veda.* "With his bones Indra slew ninety times nine *Vritras*." The scholiast explains this by saying that the thunderbolt of Indra was formed of the horse's head with which the Aswins had supplied the headless Dadhyanch, that he might teach his science to them. According to the legend, Dadhyanch during his lifetime had been the terror of the Asuras, who, after his death, multiplied and overspread the whole earth. Then "Indra inquiring what had become of him, and whether nothing of him had been left behind, was told that the horse's head was still in existence, but no one knew where. Search was made for it, and it was found in the lake *Saryanâvat* on the skirts of Kurukshetra." I infer that this is only another name for the great tank of Kurukshetra, and consequently that the sacred pool is at least as old as the Rig Veda itself. I think it also probable that the *Chakra-tirath*, or spot where Vishnu is said to have taken up his *Chakra*, or discus, to kill Bhishma,

* Wilson's translation, i. 216.

may have been the original spot where Indra slew the Vritras, and that the bones, which were afterwards assigned to the Pândus, may have been those of the Vritras of the older legend. In support of this suggestion, I may mention that the *Chakratirath* is close to *Asthipur,* or the "place of bones." In A.D. 634 these bones were shown to the Chinese pilgrim, Hwen Thsang, who records that they were of very large size.* All my inquiries for them were fruitless, but the site of *Asthipur,* or "Bone-town," is still pointed out in the plain to the west of the city, near *Aujas-ghât.*

Pehoa, or Prithudaka.

The old town of *Pehoa* is situated on the south bank of the Sarasuti, 14 miles to the west of Thânesar. The place derives its name from the famous *Prithu Chakra-vartti,* who is said to have been the first person that obtained the title of Raja. At his birth, according to the Vishnu Purâna,† "all living creatures rejoiced," because he was born to put an end to the anarchy which then prevailed over the whole earth. The story of the cure of Raja Vena's leprosy, by bathing in the Saraswati is told in the same Purâna. On his death, his son Prithu performed the usual *Srâddha,* or funeral ceremonies, and for twelve days after the cremation he sat on the bank of the Saraswati offering water to all comers. The place was therefore named *Prithu-*

* Julien's 'Hiouen Thsang,' ii. 214.

† Book 1-13, Hall's edition of Wilson's translation, i. 183.

daka or Prithu's pool, from *daka* or *udaka* water; and the city which he afterwards built on the spot was called by the same name. The shrine of *Prithudaka* has a place in the *Kurukshetra Mahâtmya*, and is still visited.

Amîn.

Five miles to the south-south-east of Thânesar there is a large and lofty mound called *Amîn*, which is said by the Brahmans to be a contraction of *Abhimanyu Khera*, or the mound of Abbimanyu, the son of Arjun. The place is also named *Chakrabhyu*, or the "Arrayed army," because the Pândus here assembled their troops before their last battle with the Kauravas. Here Abbimanyu was killed by Jayadratha, who was himself killed the next day by Arjun. Here Aditi is said to have seated herself in ascetic abstraction to obtain a son, and here accordingly she gave birth to *Suryya*, or the Sun. The mound is about 2000 feet in length from north to south, and 800 feet in breadth, with a height of from 25 to 30 feet. On the top there is a small village called Amin, inhabited by Gaur Brahmans, with a temple to *Aditi*, and a *Suryya Kund* on the east, and a temple to *Suryya* on the west. The *Suryya Kund* is said to represent the spot where the Sun was born, and accordingly all women who wish for male children pay their devotions at the temple of Aditi on Sunday, and afterwards bathe in the *Suraj Kund*.

2. BAIRÂT.

According to Hwen Thsang the capital of the kingdom of *Po-li-ye-to-lo,* which M. Reinaud has identified with *Pâryâtra* or *Bairât,* was situated at 500 *li,* or 83⅔ miles, to the west of Mathura, and about 800 *li,* 133⅔ miles, to the south-west of the kingdom of *She-to-tu-lo,** that is, of *Satadru,* or the Satlej. The bearing and distance from Mathura point unequivocally to *Bairât,* the ancient capital of *Matsya* as the city of Hwen Thsang's narrative, although it is upwards of 100 miles further to the south of Kullu than is recorded by the pilgrim. But I have already given an explanation of this discrepancy in my account of the intermediate position of Satadru in Northern India.

Abu Rihân, the contemporary of Mahmud, places *Narâna,* the capital of *Karzât,* at 28 parasangs to the west of Mathura,† which, taking the parasang at 3½ miles, would make the distance 98 miles, or 14 miles in excess of the measurement of Hwen Thsang. But as the narratives of the different Muhammadan historians leave no doubt of the identity of *Narâna* the capital of *Karzât,* with *Narâyana* the capital of *Bairât,* this difference in the recorded distance from Mathura, is of

---

* Julien's 'Hiouen Thsang,' pp. 206-207. See Map No. X.

† Reinaud, 'Fragments Arabes et Persans,' p. 107. The translator gives *Bazâna,* but this has been corrected by Sir H. M. Elliot to Narâna.

little moment. According to Abu Rihân, *Narâna*, or *Bazâna*, was called *Narayan*, ناراین by the Musalmans, a name which still exists in *Nârâyanpur*, a town situated at 10 miles to the north-east of Bairât itself. From Kanoj to Narâna, Abu Rihân gives two distinct routes; the first direct viâ Mathura being 56 parasangs, or 196 miles, and the other to the south of the Jumna being 88 parasangs, or 308 miles.* The intermediate stages of the later route are, 1st, *Asi*, 18 parasangs, or 63 miles; 2nd, *Sakina*, 17 parasangs, or 59½ miles; 3rd, *Jandara*, 18 parasangs, or 63 miles; 4th, *Rajauri*, either 15 or 17 parasangs, 54 or 59½ miles, and 5th, *Bazana*, or *Narâna*, 20 parasangs, or 70 miles. As the direction of the first stage is specially recorded to have been to the south-west of Kanoj, it may be at once identified with the *Assai Ghât* on the Jumna, 6 miles to the south of Etawa, and about 60 miles to the south-west of Kanoj. The name of the second stage is written سهینا *Sahina*, for which by the simple shifting of the diacritical points, I propose to read سهنیا *Suhania*, which is the name of a very large and famous ruined town situated 25 miles to the north of Gwalior. Its distance from the Assai Ghât is about 56 miles. The third stage named *Jandara* by M. Reinaud, and Chandra by Sir Henry Elliot, I take to be *Hindon*, reading هندون for چندرا

* Reinaud, 'Fragments,' p. 106; Dowson's edit. of Sir H. Elliot, i. 58.

Its distance from *Suhaniya* by the Khetri Ghât on the Chambal river is about 70 miles. The fourth stage, named Rajori, still exists under the same name, 12 miles to the south-west of *Mâcheri,* and about 50 miles to the north-west of Hindon. From thence to Narainpur and Bairât, the road lies altogether through the hills of Alwar or Mâcheri, which makes it difficult to ascertain the exact distance. By measurements on the lithographed map of eight miles to the inch, I make the distance to be about 60 miles, which is sufficiently near the 20 parasangs, or 70 miles, of Abu Rihân's account.

According to the other itineraries of Abu Rihân, *Narâna* was 25 parasangs to the north of Chitor in Mewar, 50 parasangs to the east of Multan, and 60 parasangs to the north-east of Anhalwâra.* The bearings of these places from Bairât are all sufficiently exact, but the measurements are more than one-half too short. For the first distance of 25 parasangs to Chitor, I would propose to read 65 parasangs, or 227 miles, the actual distance by the measured routes of the quartermaster-general being 217¾ miles. As the distance of Chitor is omitted in the extract from Abu Rihân which is given by Rashid-ud-din, it is probable that there may have been some omission or confusion in the original of the Târikh-i-Hind from which he copied. The erroneous measurement of 50 parasangs to Multan is perhaps excusable, on the ground that the direct

* Reinaud, 'Fragments,' pp. 108-112.

route through the desert being quite impassable for an army, the distance must have been estimated. The error in the distance of Anhalwâra I would explain by referring the measurement of 60 parasangs to Chitor, which lies about midway between Bairât and Anhalwâra. From a comparison of all these different itineraries, I have no hesitation whatever in identifying *Bazâna* or *Narâna*, the capital of *Karzât* or *Guzrât*, with *Nârâyanapura*, the capital of *Bairât* or *Vairât*. In Ferishta the latter name is written either *Kibrât* قيرات as in Dow, or *Kairât* قبرات as in Briggs, both of which names are an easy misreading of ويرت *Wairât* or *Virât*, as it would have been written by the Muhammadans.

Virât, the capital of *Matsya*, is celebrated in Hindu Legends as the abode of the Five Pandus during their exile of 12 years from Dilli or Indraprastha. The country was also famous for the valour of its people, as Manu directs that the van of an army should be composed of "men born in Kurukshetra near Indraprastha, in *Matsya* or *Virâta*, in Panchâla or Kânya Kubja, and in Surasena of the district of Mathura."* The residence of Bhim Pandu is still shown on the top of a long low rocky hill about one mile to the north of the town. The hill is formed of enormous blocks of coarse gritty quartz, which are much weather-worn and rounded on all the exposed sides. Some of these blocks have a single straight face sloping inwards, the

* Haughton's translation, vii. 193.

result of a natural split, of which advantage has been taken to form small dwellings by the addition of rough stone walls plastered with mud. Such is the *Bhim-gupha* or Bhim's cave, which is formed by rough walls added to the overhanging face of a huge rock about 60 feet in diameter and 15 feet in height. Similar rooms, but of smaller size, are said to have been the dwellings of Bhim's brothers. The place is still occupied by a few Brahmans, who profess to derive only a scanty subsistence from the offerings of pilgrims, a statement which is rather belied by their flourishing appearance. Just below Bhim's cave, a wall has been built across a small hollow to retain the rain water, and the fragments of rock have been removed from a fissure to form a tank, about 15 feet long by 5 feet broad and 10 feet deep; but at the time of my visit, on the 10th of November, it was quite dry.

The present town of Bairât is situated in the midst of a circular valley surrounded by low bare red hills, which have long been famous for their copper mines. It is 105 miles to the south-west of Delhi, and 41 miles to the north of Jaypur. The main entrance to the valley is on the north-west along the bank of a small stream which drains the basin, and forms one of the principal feeders of the *Bân Gangâ*. The valley is about 2½ miles in diameter, and from 7½ to 8 miles in circuit. The soil is generally good, and the trees, and more especially the tamarinds, are very fine and abundant. Bairât is situated on a mound of ruins, about one mile in length by half a mile in breadth, or upwards of 2½ miles in circuit, of which the present town does not occupy more than one-fourth. The surrounding fields are covered with broken pottery and fragments of slag from the ancient copper-works, and the general aspect of the valley is of a coppery red colour. The old city, called *Bairâtnagar*, is said to have been quite deserted for several centuries until it was repeopled about 300 years ago, most probably during the long and prosperous reign of Akbar. The town was certainly in existence in Akbar's time, as it is mentioned by Abul Fazl in the 'Ayin Akbari,' as possessing very profitable copper mines. A number of large mounds about half a mile to the east, and immediately under the hill, are said to have formed part of the old city; but, both from their position and appearance, I am inclined to think that they must be the remains of some large religious establishment. At present the surface remains consist of rough stone foundations only, as the whole of the squared stones have been used in building the houses of the modern town.

The number of houses in Bairât is popularly reckoned at 1400, of which 600 are said to belong to Gaur Brahmans, 400 to Agarwâl Baniyas, 200 to Minas, and the remaining 200 to various other races. Allowing the usual average of 5 persons to each house, the population of Bairât will amount to 7000 persons.

The earliest historical notice of Bairât is that of

the Chinese pilgrim Hwen Thsang in A.D. 634.* According to him, the capital was 14 or 15 *li*, or just 2½ miles, in circuit, which corresponds almost exactly with the size of the ancient mound on which the present town is built. The people were brave and bold, and their king, who was of the race of *Fei-she,* either a *Vaisya* or a *Bais Rajput,* was famous for his courage and skill in war. The place still possessed eight Buddhist monasteries, but they were much ruined, and the number of monks was small. The Brahmans of different sects, about 1000 in number, possessed 12 temples, but their followers were numerous, as the bulk of the population is described as heretical. Judging from the size of the town as noted by Hwen Thsang, the population could not have been less than four times the present number, or about 30,000, of whom the followers of Buddha may have amounted to one-fourth. I have deduced this number from the fact that the Buddhist monasteries would appear to have held about 100 monks each, and as those of Bairât are said to have been much ruined, the number of monks in Hwen Thsang's time could not have exceeded 50 per monastery, or 400 altogether. As each Buddhist monk begged his bread, the number of Buddhist families could not have been less than 1200, allowing three families for the support of each monk, or altogether about 6000 lay Buddhists in addition to the 400 monks.

* Julien's 'Hiouen Thsang,' ii. 206.

The next historical notice of Bairât occurs during the reign of Mahmud of Ghazni, who invaded the country in A.H. 400, or A.D. 1009, when the Raja submitted. But his submission was of little avail, as his country was again invaded in the spring A.H. 404, or A.D. 1014, when the Hindus were defeated after a bloody conflict. According to Abu Rihân the town was destroyed, and the people retired far into the interior.* By Ferishta this invasion is assigned to the year A.H. 413, or A.D. 1022, when the king hearing that the inhabitants of two hilly tracts named *Kairât* and *Nârdin* (*or Bairât* and *Nârâyan*) still continued the worship of idols (or lions in some manuscripts) resolved to compel them to embrace the Muhammadan faith.† The place was taken and plundered by Amir-Ali, who found an ancient stone inscription at Nârâyan, which was said to record that the temple of Nârâyan had been built 40,000 years previously. As this inscription is also mentioned by the contemporary historian Otbi, we may accept the fact of the discovery of a stone record in characters so ancient that the Brahmans of that day were unable to read them. I think it highly probable that this is the famous inscription of Asoka that was afterwards discovered by Major Burt on the top of a hill at Bairât, and which now graces the museum of the Asiatic Society in Calcutta.

* Dowson's edition of Sir H. Elliot's Muhamm. Hist., i. 59.

† Briggs's 'Ferishta,' i. 64.

In the seventh century the kingdom of Bairât was 3000 *li*, or 500 miles, in circuit. It was famous for its sheep and oxen, but produced few fruits or flowers. This is still the case with Jaypur to the south of Bairât, which furnishes most of the sheep required for the great Muhammadan cities of Delhi and Agra, and their English garrisons. Bairât, therefore, may have included the greater part of the present state of Jaypur. Its precise boundaries cannot be determined; but they may be fixed approximately as extending on the north from Jhunjnu to Kot Kâsim, 70 miles; on the west from Jhunjnu to Ajmer, 120 miles; on the south from Ajmer to the junction of the Banâs and Chambal, 150 miles; and on the east from the junction to Kot Kâsim, 150 miles; or altogether 490 miles.

3. SRUGHNA.

On leaving Thânesar, Hwen Thsang at first proceeded to the south for about 100 *li*, or 16⅔ miles, to the *Kiu-hoen-cha*, or *Goḳantha* monastery, which has not yet been identified, but it is probably *Gunâna*, between Vyasthali and Nisang, 17 miles to the south-south-west of Thânesar. I am obliged to notice this monastery as it is the starting-point from which Hwen Thsang measures his next journey of 400 *li*, or 66⅔ miles, to *Su-luḳin-na* or *Srughna*, which makes the distance between Thânesar and Srughna just 50 miles.* Now *Sugh*, the place

* Julien's 'Hiouen Thsang,' ii. 215. See Map. No.X.

which I propose to identify with the capital of *Srughna,* is only 38 or 40 miles from Thânesar; but as it agrees exactly in name, and corresponds generally in other particulars, I am quite satisfied that Hwen Thsang's recorded distance must be erroneous, although I am unable to suggest any probable rectification of his figures. The true distance is about 300 *li,* or 50 miles, from the Gokantha monastery.

The Sanskrit name of the country is *Srughna,* which in the spoken dialects becomes *Sughan* and *Sugh,* as it is called at the present day. The village of *Sugh* occupies one of the most remarkable positions that I met with during the whole course of my researches. It is situated on a projecting triangular spur of high land, and is surrounded on three sides by the bed of the old Jumna, which is now the western Jumna canal. On the north and west faces it is further protected by two deep ravines, so that the position is a ready-made stronghold, which is covered on all sides, except the west, by natural defences. In shape it is almost triangular, with a large projecting fort or citadel at each of the angles. The site of the north fort is now occupied by the castle and village of Dyâlgarh. The village of Mândalpur stands on the site of the south-east fort, and that of the south-west is unoccupied. Each of these forts is 1500 feet long, and 1000 feet broad, and each face of the triangle which connects them together is upwards of half a mile in length, that to the east being 4000, and those to the north-west and south-west 3000 feet each. The whole circuit of the position is therefore 22,000 feet, or upwards of 4 miles, which is considerably more than the 3½ miles of Hwen Thsang's measurement. But as the north fort is separated from the main position by a deep sandy ravine called the *Rohara Nala,* it is possible that it may have been unoccupied at the time of the pilgrim's visit. This would reduce the circuit of the position to 19,000 feet, or upwards of 3½ miles, and bring it into accord with the pilgrim's measurement. The small village of Sugh occupied the west side of the position, and the small town of Buriya lies immediately to the north of Dyâlgarh. The occupied houses, at the time of my visit, were as follows:—Mândalpur 100, Sugh 125, Dyâlgarh 150, and Buriya 3500, or altogether 3875 houses, containing a population of about 20,000 souls.

Of *Sugh* itself the people have no special traditions, but of *Mândar,* or *Mândalpur,* they say that it formerly covered an extent of 12 kos, and included Jagâdri and Chaneti on the west, with Buriya and Dyâlgarh to the north. As Jagâdri lies 3 miles to the west, it is not possible that the city could have extended so far; but we may reasonably admit that the gardens and summer-houses of the wealthier inhabitants may once possibly have extended to that distance. At Chaneti, which lies 2 miles to the north-west, old coins are found in considerable numbers; but it is now entirely separated from Buriya and Dyâlgarh by a long space of open country. The same coins are found in Sugh, Mândalpur, and

Buriya. They are of all ages, from the small *Diliâls* of the Chohân and Tomar Rajas of Delhi to the square punch-marked pieces of silver and copper, which are certainly as old as the rise of Buddhism in 500 B.C., and which were probably the common currency of Northern India as early as 1000 B.C. With this undoubted evidence in favour of the antiquity of the place, I have no hesitation in identifying Sugh with the ancient Srughna. The importance of the position is shown by the fact that it stands on the high-road leading from the Gangetic Doâb, viâ *Mirat, Sahâranpur,* and *Ambâla,* to the Upper Panjâb, and commands the passage of the Jumna. By this route Mahmud of Ghazni returned from his expedition to Kanoj; by this route Timûr returned from his plundering campaign at Haridwâr; and by this route Bâber advanced to the conquest of Delhi.

According to Hwen Thsang, the kingdom of *Srughna* was 6000 *li,* or 1000, miles in circuit. On the east it extended to the Ganges, and on the north to a range of lofty mountains, while the Jumna flowed through the midst of it. From these data it would appear that *Srughna* must have comprised the hill states of Sirmor and Garhwâl, lying between the Giri river and the Ganges, with portions of the districts of Ambâla and Sahâranpur in the plains. But the circuit of this tract does not exceed 500 miles, which is only one half of Hwen Thsang's estimate. His excess I would attribute chiefly to the difference between direct measurements on the map, and the actual road distances in a mountainous country.

This would increase the boundary line by about one-half, and make the whole circuit 750 miles, which is still far short of the pilgrim's estimate. But there is an undoubted error in his distance between the Jumna and the Ganges, which he makes 800 *li*, or 133 miles, instead of 300 *li*, or 50 miles, which is the actual distance between the two rivers from the foot of the hills down to the parallel of Delhi. As it is probable that this mistake was doubled by applying the same exaggerated distance to the northern frontier also, its correction is of imporance, as the double excess amounts to 167 miles. Deducting this excess, the circuit of *Srughna* will be only 833 miles according to Hwen Thsang's estimate, or within 83 miles of the probable measurement.

4. MADÂWAR.

From Srughna the Chinese pilgrim proceeded to *Mo-ti-pu-lo*, or *Madipura*, which M. Vivien de St. Martin has identified with *Mandâwar*, a large town in Western Rohilkhand, near Bijnor. I had previously made the same identification myself, and I have since been able to confirm it by a personal examination of the site.* The name of the town is written मडावर *Madâwar*, the Mundore of the maps. According to Johari Lâl, *Chaodri* and *Kanungo* of the place, Madâwar was a deserted site in Samvat 1171, or A.D. 1114, when his ancestor Dwârka Dâs,

* See Map No. X.

an Agarwâla Baniya, accompanied by Katâr Mall, came from Morâri in the Mirat district, and occupied the old mound. The present town of Madâwar contains 7000 inhabitants, and is rather more than three-quarters of a mile in length by half a mile in breadth. But the old mound, which represents the former town, is not more than half a mile square. It has an average height of 10 feet above the rest of the town, and it abounds with large bricks, which are a sure sign of antiquity. In the middle of the mound there is a ruined fort 300 feet square, with an elevation of 6 or 7 feet above the rest of the city. To the north-east, distant about one mile from the fort there is a large village on another mound called *Madiya;* and between the two there is a large tank called *Kûnda Tâl*, surrounded by numerous small mounds which are said to be the remains of buildings. Originally these two places would appear to have formed one large town, about 1¼ mile in length, by a mile in breadth or just 3½ miles in circuit, which agrees very well with Hwen Thsang's measurement of 20 *li*, or 3⅓ miles.

It seems probable that the people of *Madâwar*, as pointed out by M. Vivien de St. Martin, may be the *Mathæ* of Megasthenes, who dwelt on the banks of the Erineses. If so, that river must be the *Mâlini*. It is true that this is but a small stream; but it was in a sacred grove on the bank of the Mâlini that *Sakuntala* was brought up, and along its course lay her route to the court of Dushmanta at Hastinapur. While the lotus floats on its waters, and while the Chakwâ calls to its mate on the bank, so long will the little Mâlini live in the verse of Kâlidâs.

According to Hwen Thsang, the kingdom of *Madipura* was 6000 *li*, or 1000 miles, in circuit; but this estimate, as I have already pointed out, must certainly include the two neighbouring states of *Govisana* and *Ahichhatra*, as they are also in Rohilkhand, and at so short a distance that *Madipur* alone must have been a very small district, confined to the tract between the Ganges and Râmgangâ, of not more than 250 miles in circuit. But even with the extended limits now proposed, which would include the whole of the country lying to the east of the Ganges from Haridwâr to Kanoj as far as the bank of the Ghâgra near Khairigarh, the circuit would not be increased to more than 650 or 700 miles. This is still too small; but as some large allowance must be made on the northern mountain boundary for the difference between direct measurement on the map and the actual road distance, I think that the true circuit may be not less than 850 miles. The king of Madâwar was a *Siu-to-lo* or Sudra, who worshipped the Devas, and cared nothing for Buddhism. As Govisana and Ahichhatra were without kings, I presume that they were tributary to Madâwar, and that the circuit of the territory recorded by Hwen Thsang was the political boundary of the whole State, and not that of the district proper.

Mâyâpura, or Haridwâr.

Hwen Thsang describes the town of *Mo-yu-lo*, or *Mâyura*, as situated on the north-west frontier of Madâwar, and on the eastern bank of the Ganges.* At a short distance from the town there was a great temple called "the gate of the Ganges," that is, *Gangâ-dwâra*, with a tank inside, which was supplied by a canal with water from the holy river. The vicinity of *Gangâ-dwâra*, which was the old name of *Haridwâra*, shows that *Mayûra* must be the present ruined site of *Mâyâpura*, at the head of Ganges canal. But both of these places are now on the western bank of the Ganges, instead of on the eastern bank, as stated by Hwen Thsang. His note that they were on the north-west frontier of Madâwar seems also to point to the same position; for if they had been on the western bank of the Ganges, they would more properly be described as on the north-eastern frontier of Srughna. I examined the locality with some care, and I was satisfied that at some former period the Ganges *may* have flowed to the westward of Mâyâpura and Kankhal down to Jwâlapur. There is, however, no present trace of any old channel between the Gangâdwâra temple and the hills; but as this ground is now covered with the houses of Haridwâr, it is quite possible that a channel may once have existed, which has since been gradually filled up, and built upon. There is

---

* Julien's 'Hiouen Thsang,' ii. 230. See map No. X.

therefore no physical difficulty which could have prevented the river from taking this westerly course, and we must either accept Hwen Thsang's statement or adopt the alternative, that he has made a mistake in placing Mayûra and Gangâdwâra to the east of the Ganges.

There is a dispute between the followers of Siva and Vishnu as to which of these deities gave birth to the Ganges. In the 'Vishnu Purâna' it is stated that the Ganges has its rise "in the nail of the great toe of Vishnu's left foot;"* and the Vaishnavas point triumphantly to the *Hari-ki-charan,* or *Hari-ki-pairi* (Vishnu's foot-prints), as indisputable evidence of the truth of their belief. On the other hand, the *Saivas* argue that the proper name of the place is *Hara-dwâra,* or "Siva's Gate," and not *Hari-dwâra.* It is admitted also, in the 'Vishnu Purâna,' that the *Alakananda* (or east branch of the Ganges) "was borne by Mahadeva upon his head."† But in sipte of these authorities, I am inclined to believe that the present name of Haridwâr or Haradwâr is a modern one, and that the old town near the Gangâdwâra temple was *Mâyâpura.* Hwen Thsang, indeed, calls it *Mo-yu-lo,* or *Mâyura,* but the old ruined town between Haridwâr and Kankhal is still called *Mâyâpur,* and the people point to the old temple of *Mâyâ-Devi* as the true origin of

* Book ii. 8. Hall's edition of Wilson's translation, ii. 272.

† *Ibid.*

its name. It is quite possible, however, that the town may also have been called *Mayura-pura*, as the neighbouring woods still swarm with thousands of peacocks (*Mayûra*), whose shrill calls I heard both morning and evening.

Hwen Thsang describes the town as about 20 *li*, or 3⅓ miles, in circuit, and very populous. This account corresponds very closely with the extent of the old city of Mâyâpura, as pointed out to me by the people. These traces extend from the bed of a torrent which enters the Ganges near the modern temple of Sarvvanâth to the old fort of Raja Ben, on the bank of the canal, a distance of 7500 feet. The breadth is irregular, but it could not have been more than 3000 feet at the south end, and, at the north end, where the Siwâlik hills approach the river, it must have been contracted to 1000 feet. These dimensions give a circuit of 19,000 feet, or rather more than 3½ miles. Within these limits there are the ruins of an old fort, 750 feet square, attributed to Raja Ben, and several lofty mounds covered with broken bricks, of which the largest and most conspicuous is immediately above the canal bridge. There are also three old temples dedicated to *Nârâyana-sila*, to *Mâyâ-Devi*, and to *Bhairava*. The celebrated ghat called the *Pairi*, or "Feet Ghat," is altogether outside these limits, being upwards of 2000 feet to the north-east of the Sarvvanâth temple. The antiquity of the place is undoubted, not only from the extensive foundations of large bricks which are everywhere visible, and the numerous fragments of ancient sculpture accumulated about the temples, but from the great variety of the old coins, similar to those of Sugh, which are found here every year.

The name of *Haridwâra,* or "Vishnu's Gate," would appear to be comparatively modern, as both Abu Rihân and Rashid-ud-din mention only *Gangâdwâra.* Kâlidâs also, in his 'Meghaduta,' says nothing of Haridwâra, although he mentions Kankhal; but as his contemporary Amarasinha gives *Vishnupadi* as one of the synonyms of the Ganges, it is certain that the legend of its rise from Vishnu's foot is as old as the fifth century. I infer, however, that no temple of the Vishnupada had been erected down to the time of Abu Rihân. The first allusion to it of which I am aware is by Sharif-ud-din,* the historian of Timur, who says that the Ganges issues from the hills by the pass of *Cou-pele,* which I take to be the same as *Koh-pairi,* or the "Hill of the Feet" (of Vishnu), as the great bathing ghat at the Gangâdwâra temple is called *Pairi Ghat,* and the hill above it *Pairi Pahâr.* In the time of Akbar, the name of Haridwâr was well known, as Abul Fazl speaks of "Mâyâ, vulgo Haridwâr, on the Ganges," as being considered holy for 18 kos in length.† In the next reign the place was visited by Tom Coryat, who informed Chaplain Terry that at

* 'History of Timur,' translated by Petis de la Croix, iii. 131.

† 'Ayin Akbari,' ii. 516.

"*Haridwâra,* the capital of *Siba,* the Ganges flowed amongst large rocks with a pretty full current." In 1796 the town was visited by Hardwicke, who calls it a small place situated at the base of the hills. In 1808, Raper describes it as very inconsiderable, having only one street, about 15 feet in breadth, and a furlong and a half (or three-eighths of a mile) in length. It is now much larger, being fully three-quarters of a mile in length, but there is still only one street.

Hwen Thsang notes that the river was also called *Fo-shúi,** which M. Stanislas Julien translates as *l'eau qui porte bonheur,* and identifies with *Mahâbhadrâ,* which is one of the many well-known names of the Ganges. He mentions also that bathing in its waters was sufficient to wash away sin, and that if corpses were thrown into the river the dead would escape the punishment of being born again in an inferior state, which was due to their crimes. I should prefer reading *Subhâdra,* which has the same meaning as Mahâbhadrâ, as Ktesias mentions that the great Indian river was named ὕπαρχος, which he translates by φέρων πάντα τὰ ἀγαθά·† Pliny quoting Ktesias calls the river *Hypobarus,* which he renders by "omnia in se ferre bona."‡ A nearly similar word, *Oibares,* is rendered by Nicolas of Damascus as ἀγαθάγγελος. I infer, therefore, that the original

* Julien's 'Hiouen Thsang,' ii. 217.
† Ctesiæ Indica, Excerp. ab Photio, 19, edit. Lion.
‡ Hist. Nat. xxxvii. 11.

name obtained by Ktesias was most probably *Subhadrâ*.

5. BRAHMAPURA.

On leaving Madâwar, Hwen Thsang travelled north-ward for 300 *li*, or 50 miles, to *Po-lo-ki-mo-pu-lo*, which M. Julien correctly renders as *Brahmapura*. Another reading gives *Po-lo-hi-mo-lo*,* in which the syllable *pu* is omitted, perhaps by mistake. The northern bearing is certainly erroneous, as it would have carried the pilgrim across the Ganges and back again into Srughna. We must therefore read north-east, in which direction lie the districts of Garhwâl and Kumaon that once formed the famous kingdom of the *Katyuri* dynasty. That this is the country intended by the pilgrim is proved by the fact that it produced copper, which must refer to the well-known copper mines of Dhanpur and Pokhri in Garhwâl, which have been worked from a very early date. Now the ancient capital of the Katyuri Rajas was at *Lakhanpur* or *Vairât-pattan* on the Râmgangâ river, about 80 miles in a direct line from Madâwar. If we might take the measurement from Kot-dwâra, at the foot of the hills on the north-east frontier of Madâwar, the distance would agree with the 50 miles recorded by Hwen Thsang. It occurs to me, however, as a much more probable explanation of the discrepancy in the recorded bearing and distance that they must probably refer

* Julien's 'Hiouen Thsang,' i. 434, and ii. 231.

to *Govisana,* the next place visited by Hwen Thsang, from which *Bairât* lies exactly 50 miles due north.

According to the history of the country, *Vairât-pattan* or *Lakhanpur* was the ancient capital, as the Sombansi dynasty of Kumaon and the Surajbansi dynasty of Garhwâl date only from the *Samvat* years 742 and 745, which, even if referred to the era of Vikramaditya, are posterior to the time of Hwen Thsang. I think, therefore, that Brahmapura must be only another name for *Vairât-pattan,* as every other capital in these provinces is of much later date. *Srinagar* on the Alakananda river was founded so late as S. 1415, or A.D. 1358, by Ajaya Pala of Garhwâl, and is besides nearly as far from Madâwar as *Vairât-pattan*; while *Chândpur,* the earlier capital of Garhwâl, is still more distant, and dates only from S. 1216 or A.D 1159. The climate is said to be slightly cold, and this also agrees with the position of *Bairât,* which is only 3339 feet above the sea.

Hwen Thsang describes the kingdom of Brahmapura as 4000 *li,* or 667 miles, in circuit.* It must, therefore, have included the whole of the hill-country between the Alakananda and Karnâli rivers, which is now known as British Garhwâl and Kumaon, as the latter district, before the conquests of the Gorkhas, extended to the Karnâli river. The boundary of this tract measured on the map is

---

* Julien's 'Hiouen Thsang,' ii. 231. See Map No. X.

between 500 and 600 miles, or very nearly equal to the estimate of the Chinese pilgrim.

6. GOVISANA, OR KÂSHIPUR.

To the south-east of Madâwar, at a distance of 400 *li*, or 67 miles, Hwen Thsang places the kingdom of *Kiu-pi-shwang-na*, which M. Julien renders by *Govisana*. The capital was 15 *li*, or 2½ miles, in circuit. Its position was lofty, and of difficult access, and it was surrounded by groves, tanks, and fishponds.* According to the recorded bearing and distance from Madâwar, we must look for *Govisana* somewhere to the north of Murâdâbâd. In this direction the only place of any antiquity is the old fort near the village of *Ujain*, which is just one mile to the east of Kâshipur. According to the route which I marched, the distance is 44 kos, or 66 miles. I estimate the value of the kos by the measured distance of 59 miles between the post-offices of Bareli and Murâdâbâd, which is always called 40 kos by the natives. The true bearing of Kâshipur is east-south-east instead of south-east, but the difference is not great, and as the position of Kâshipur is just as clearly indicated by the subsequent route to *Ahichhatra*, I feel quite satisfied that the old fort near the village of *Ujain* represents the ancient city of *Govisana* which was visited by Hwen Thsang.

* Julien's 'Hiouen Thsang,' ii. 233. See Map No. X.

Bishop Heber* describes Kâshipur as a "famous place of Hindu pilgrimage which was built by a divinity named *Kâshi* 5000 years ago." But the good bishop was grossly deceived by his informant, as it is well known that the town is a modern one, it having been built about A.D. 1718 by *Kâshi-nâth*, a follower of Raja Devi-Chandra of Champâwat in Kumaon. The old fort is now called *Ujain;* but as that is the name of the nearest village, it seems probable that the true name has been lost. The place itself had been deserted for several hundred years before the occupation of Kâshipur; but as the holy tank of *Dron-sâgar* had never ceased to be visited by pilgrims, I presume that the name of the tank must have gradually superseded that of the fort. Even at the present day the name of *Dron-Sâgar* is just as well known as that of Kâshipur.

The old fort of Ujain is very peculiar in its form, which may be best compared to the body of a guitar. It is 3000 feet, in length from east to west, and 1500 feet in breadth, the whole circuit being upwards of 9000 feet, or rather less than 2 miles. Hwen Thsang describes the circuit of Goviṣana as about 12,000 feet, or nearly 2½ miles, but in this measurement he must have included the long mound of ruins on the south side, which is evidently the remains of an ancient suburb. By including this mound as an undoubted part of the old city, the

* 'Travels in India,' ii. 246.

circuit of the ruins is upwards of 11,000 feet, or very nearly the same as that given by HwenThsang. Numerous groves, tanks, and fish-ponds still surround the place. Indeed the trees are particularly luxuriant, owing to the high level of the water, which is within 5 or 6 feet of the surface. For the same reason the tanks are numerous and always full of water. The largest of these is the *Dron-sâgar*, which, as well as the fort, is said to have been constructed by the five Pandu brothers for the use of their teacher Drona. The tank is only 600 feet square, but it is esteemed very holy, and is much frequented by pilgrims on their way to the source of the Ganges. Its high banks are covered with *Sati* monuments of recent date. The walls of the fort are built of large massive bricks, 15 by 10 by 2½ inches, which are always a sure sign of antiquity. The general height of the walls is 30 feet above the fields; but the whole is now in complete ruin, and covered with dense jangal. Shallow ditches still exist on all sides except the east. Th interior is very uneven, but the mass has a mean height of about 20 feet above the country. There are two low openings in the ramparts, one to the north-west and the other to the south-west, which now serve as entrances to the jangal, and which the people say were the old gates of the fort.

The district of Govisana was 2000 *li*, or 333 miles, in circuit. No king is mentioned, and the country, as I have already noticed, was most probably subject to the Raja of Madâwar. It was confined on the north by Brahmapura, on the west by Madâwar, and on the south and east by Ahichhatra. It must, therefore, have corresponded very nearly with the modern districts of Kâshipur, Râmpur, and Pîlibhît, extending from the Râmgangâ on the west to the Sârda or Ghâgra on the east, and towards Bareli on the south. With these boundaries the circuit of the district would have been about 290 miles measured direct, or upwards of 300 miles by road distance.

7. AHICHHATRA.

From Govisana Hwen Thsang proceeded to the south-east 400 *li*, or 66 miles, to *Ahi-chi-ta-lo*, or *Ahichhatra*.* This once famous place still preserves its ancient name as *Ahichhatr*, although it has been deserted for many centuries. Its history reaches back to B.C. 1430, at which time it was the capital of northern *Pânchâla*. The name is written *Ahi-kshetra*, as well as *Ahi-chhatra*, but the local legend of Adi Raja and the Nâga, who formed a canopy over his head when asleep, shows that the latter is the correct form. This grand old fort is said to have been built by *Raja Adi*, an Ahir, whose future elevation to sovereignty was foretold by *Drona*, when he found him sleeping under the guardianship of a serpent with expanded hood. The place is mentioned by Ptolemy as Αδισάδρα, which proves that the legend attached to the name of *Adi* is at least as

* Julien's 'Hiouen Thsang,' ii. 234. See Map No. X.

old as the beginning of the Christian era. The fort is also called *Adikot*, but the more common name is *Ahichhatr*.

According to the 'Mahâbhârata,' the great kingdom of *Pânchâla* extended from the Himâlaya mountains to the Chambal river. The capital of north *Pânchâla*, or Rohilkhand, was *Ahi-chhatra*, and that of south *Pânchâla*, or the Central Gangetic Doab, was *Kâmpilya*, now *Kampil*, on the old Ganges between Budaon and Farokhabad. Just before the great war, or about 1430 B.C., the king of *Pânchâla*, named *Drupada*, was conquered by *Drona*, the preceptor of the five Pândus. *Drona* retained north *Pânchâla* for himself, but restored the southern half of the kingdom to *Drupada*. According to this account, the name of *Ahi-chhatra*, and consequently also the legend of *Adi Raja* and the serpent, are many centuries anterior to the rise of Buddhism.

It would appear, however, that the Buddists must have adopted and altered the legend to do honour to their great teacher, for Hwen Thsang records that outside the town there was a *Nâga-hrada*, or "serpent tank," near which Buddha had preached the law for seven days in favour of the serpent king, and that the spot was marked by a stupa of King Asoka.* Now, as the only existing stupa at this place is called *Chattr*, I infer that the Buddhist legend represented the *Nâga* king after his conversion as forming a canopy over Buddha with his expanded

* Julien's 'Hiouen Thsang,' ii. 235.

hood. I think, also, that the stupa erected on the spot where the conversion took place would naturally have been called *Ahi-chhatra*, or the "serpent canopy." A similar story is told at Buddha Gaya of the Nâga King *Muchalinda*, who, with his expanded hood, sheltered Buddha from the shower of rain produced by the malignant demon *Mâra*.

The account of *Ahi-chhatra* given by Hwen Thsang is unfortunately very meagre, otherwise we might most probably have identified many of the existing ruins with the Buddhist works of an early age. The capital was 17 or 18 *li*, or just three miles in circuit, and was defended by natural obstacles. It possessed 12 monasteries, containing about 1000 monks, and 9 Brahmanical temples, with about 300 worshippers of *Iswara Deva* (Siva), who smeared their bodies with ashes. The stupa near the serpent tank, outside the town, has already been mentioned. Close beside it, there were four small stupas built on the spots where the four previous Buddhas had either sat or walked. Both the size and the peculiar position of the ruined fortress of *Ahi-chhatra* agree so exactly with Hwen Thsang's description of the ancient *Ahi-chhatra*, that there can be no doubt whatever of their identity. The circuit of the walls, as they stand at present, is 19,400 feet, or upwards of 3½ miles. The shape may be described as an irregular right-angled triangle, the west side being 5600 feet in length, the north side 6400 feet, and the long side to the south-east 7400 feet. The fort is situated between the *Râm Ganga* and *Gânghan* rivers, which are both difficult to cross; the former on account of its broad sands, the latter on account of its extensive ravines. Both on the north and east the place is rendered almost inaccessible by the *Piria Nala,* a difficult ravine, with steep broken banks and numerous deep pools of water, quite impassable by wheeled vehicles. For this reason the cart road to Bareli, distant only 18 miles due east, is not less than 23 miles. Indeed the only accessible side of the position is the north-west, from the direction of *Lakhnor,* the ancient capital of the Katehria Rajputs. It therefore fully merits the description of Hwen Thsang as being defended by "natural obstacles." *Ahi-chhatra* is only seven miles to the north of *Aonla,* but the latter half of the road is rendered difficult by the ravines of the *Gânghan* river. It was in this very position, in the jangals to the north of *Aonla,* that the Katehria Rajputs withstood the Muhammadans under Firuz Tughlak.*

Ahi-chhatra was first visited by Captain Hodgson, the surveyor, who describes the place as "the ruins of an ancient fortress several miles in circumference, which appears to have had 34 bastions, and is known in the neighbourhood by the name of the "Pândus Fort." According to my survey, there are only 32 towers, but it is quite possible that one or two may have escaped my notice, as I found many parts so overgrown with thorny jangal as to be inaccessible. The towers are generallv from 28 to 30 feet in height,

* Briggs's 'Ferishta,' i. 457.

excepting on the west side, where they rise to 35 feet. A single tower near the south-west corner is 47 feet in height above the road outside. The average height of the interior mass is from 15 to 20 feet. Many of the present towers, however, are not ancient, as an attempt was made by Ali Muhammad Khan, about 200 years ago, to restore the fort with a view of making it his stronghold in case he should be pushed to extremities by the King of Delhi. The new walls are said to have been 1¼ *gaz* thick, which agrees with my measurements of the parapets on the south-eastern side, which vary from 2 feet 9 inches to 3 feet 3 inches in thickness at top. According to popular tradition, Ali Muhammad expended about a *ḳaror* of rupees, or one million pounds sterling, in this attempt, which he was finally obliged to abandon on account of its costliness. I estimate that he may perhaps have spent about one lakh of rupees, or £10,000, in repairing the ramparts and in rebuilding the parapets. There is an arched gateway on the south-east side, which must have been built by the Musalmans, but as no new bricks were made by them, the cost of their work would have been limited to the labour alone. The ramparts are 18 feet thick at the base in some places, and between 14 and 15 feet in others.

The district of *Ahichhatra* was about 3000 *li*, or 500 miles, in circuit. With these large dimensions I believe that it must have comprised the eastern half of Rohilkhand, lying between the northern hills and the Ganges, from Pîlibhît on the west to Khairabad near the Ghâgra on the east. This tract has a boundary of 450 miles measured direct, or about 500 miles by road distance.

8. PILOSHANA.

From *Ahi-chhatra* the Chinese pilgrim proceeded in a south direction a distance of from 260 to 270 *li*, from 23 to 25 miles, to the Ganges, which he crossed, and then turning to the south-west he arrived in the kingdom of *Pilo-shan-na*.* His route to the south would have taken him through Aonla and Budaon to the *Budh Ganga* (or old Ganges), somewhere near Sahâwar, a few miles below *Soron*, both of which places stood on the main stream of the Ganges so late as 400 years ago. As his subsequent route is said to have been to the south-west, I believe that he must have crossed the Ganges close to Sahâwar, which is 42 miles from Ahi-chhatra in a direct line. From all my early inquiries I was led to believe that *Soron* was the only ancient place in this vicinity; and as Hwen Thsang does not give any distance for his south-west march, I concluded that *Soron* must have been the place to which he gives the name of Pi-lo-shan-na. I accordingly visited *Soron*, which is undoubtedly a place of very great antiquity, but which cannot, I think, be the place visited by the Chinese pilgrim. I will, however, first describe *Soron* before I proceed to discuss the superior claims of the great ruined mound of *Atranji-*

* Julien's 'Hiouen Thsang,' ii. 235. See Map No. X.

Khera to be identified with the Pi-lo-shan-na of the Chinese pilgrim.

Soron is a large town on the right, or western, bank of the Ganges, on the high-road between Bareli and Mathura. The place was originally called *Ukala Kshetra;* but after the demon *Hiranyaksha* had been killed by the *Varâha Avatar,* or Boar incarnation of Vishnu, the name was changed to *Sukara* Kshetra, or "the place of the good deed." The ancient town is represented by a ruined mound called the *Kilah,* or "fort," which is one quarter of a mile in length from north to south, and somewhat less in breadth. It stands on the high bank of the old bed of the Ganges, which is said by some to have flowed immediately under it so late as 200 years ago. The modern town stands at the foot of the old mound on the west and south sides, and probably contains about 5000 inhabitants. There are no dwellings on the old mound, which is occupied only by the temple of *Sita-Râmji* and the tomb of *Shekh Jamâl;* but it is covered with broken bricks of large size, and the foundations of walls can be traced in all directions. The mound is said to be the ruins of a fort built by Raja *Somadatta* of Soron many hundred years ago. But the original settlement of the place is very much older, being attributed to the fabulous *Raja Vena Chakravartti,* who plays such a conspicuous part in all the legends of North Bihar, Oudh, and Rohilkhand.

The great mound of ruins called *Atranji-Khera* is situated on the right or west bank of the *Kâli Nadi,* four miles to the south of *Karsâna,* and eight miles to the north of *Eyta,* on the Grand Trunk Road. It is also 15 miles to the south of Soron, and 43 miles to the north-west of *Sankisa* in a direct line, the road distance being not less than 48 or 50 miles. In the 'Ayin Akbari' Atranji is recorded as one of the parganahs of Kanoj, under the name of *Sikandarpur Atreji.** *Sikandarpur,* which is now called *Sikandrâbâd,* is a village on the left bank of the *Kâli Nadi* opposite Atranji. From this it would appear that Atranji was still occupied in the reign of Akbar. The parganah was afterwards called *Karsâna,* but it is now known by the name of *Sahâwar Karsâna,* or of *Sahâwar* only. The name given by the Chinese pilgrim is *Pi-lo-shan-na,* for which M. Julien proposes to read *Virasana.* So far back as 1848 I pointed out that, as both *pil* and *kar* are Sanskrit names for an elephant, it was probable that *Pilosana* might be the same as *Karsâna,* the large village which I have already mentioned as being four miles to the north of *Atranji Khera.* The chief objection to this identification is the fact that *Karsâna* is apparently not a very old place, although it is sometimes called *Deora Karsâna,* a name which implies the possession of a temple of note at some former period. It is, however, possible that the name of *Karsâna* may once have been joined to *Atranji* in the same way that we find *Sikandarpur Atreji* in the 'Ayin Akbari.' As the identification of *Karsâna* with *Pilosana* is purely

* Gladwyn gives "Secunderpoor Aterchhy." ii. 214.

conjectural, it is useless to hazard any more speculations on this subject. The bearing and distance from *Sankisa,* as recorded by Hwen Thsang, point to the neighbourhood of *Sirpura,* near which there is a small village called *Pilkuni* or *Pilokuni,* which is the *Pilukhoni* of our maps. It is, however, a very petty place; and although it boasts of a small *khera,* or mound of ruins, it cannot, I think, have ever been more than one-fourth of the circuit of two miles which Hwen Thsang attributes to *Pi-lo-shan-na.* But there are two strong points in its favour—namely, 1st, its position, which agrees both in bearing and distance with the Chinese pilgrim's account; and 2nd, its name, which is almost identical with the old name, *sh* being very commonly pronounced as *kh,* so that Hwen Thsang's *Piloshana* would usually be pronounced *Pilokhana.*

In proposing *Atranji-Khera* as the site of the ancient *Piloshana,* I am influenced solely by the fact that this is the only large place besides *Soron* of any antiquity in this part of the country. It is true that the distance from *Sankisa* is somewhat greater than that recorded by the Chinese pilgrim,—namely, 45 miles, instead of 33 miles; but the bearing is exact; and as it is quite possible that there may be some mistake in Hwen Thsang's recorded distance, I think that *Atranji-Khera* has a better claim than any other place to be identified with the ancient *Piloshana.*

The only objection to the identification of *Atranji* with Piloshana is the difference between the distance of 200 *li*, or 33 miles, as stated by Hwen Thsang, and the actual distance of 43 miles direct, or about 48 or 50 miles by road. I have already suggested the possibility of there being some mistake in the recorded distance of Hwen Thsang, but perhaps an equally probable explanation may be found in the difference of the length of the *yojana*. Hwen Thsang states that he allowed 40 Chinese *li* to the *yojana;* but if the old *yojana* of Rohilkhand differed from that of the central Doâb as much as the kos of these districts now differ, his distances would have varied by half a mile in every kos, or by two miles in every *yojana*, as the Rohilkhand kos is only 1½ mile, while that of the Doâb is two miles; the latter being one-third greater. Now if we apply this difference to Hwen Thsang's measurement of 200 *li*, or 33 miles, we increase the distance at once to 44 miles, which agrees with the direct measured distance on the map. I confess, however, that I am rather inclined to believe in the possibility of there being a mistake in Hwen Thsang's recorded distance, as I find exactly the same measurement of 200 *li* given as the distance between *Sankisa* and *Kanoj*. Now, the two distances are precisely the same,—that is, *Sankisa* is exactly midway between *Atranji* and *Kanoj;* and as the latter disance is just 50 miles by my measurement along the high-road, the former must also be the same. I would therefore suggest the probability that both of these distances should be 300 *li*, or 50 miles, instead of 200 *li*, as recorded in the text. In favour of this proposed correction I may cite the testimony of the earlier Chinese pilgrim Fa-Hian, who makes the distance from Sankisa to Kanoj 7 *yojanas*, or 49 miles.* At Hwen Thsang's own valuation of 40 *li* to the *yojana*, this measurement would give 280 *li;* and as Fa-Hian does not record half *yojanas*, we may increase the distance by half a *yojana*, or 20 *li*, which will bring the total up to 300 *li*, or 50 miles.

But whatever may be the true explanation of the difference between the actual distances and those recorded by Hwen Thsang, there still remains the important fact that Sankisa was exactly midway between Kanoj and Piloshanna, just as it now is midway between Kanoj and Atranji. If we couple this absolute identity of position with the fact that *Atranji* is the only old place in the part of the country indicated by Hwen Thsang, we can scarcely arrive at any other conclusion than that the great ruined mound of Atranji is the site of the ancient *Piloshana*. This conclusion is strengthened by the fact that the mound of Atranji corresponds almost exactly in size with Hwen Thsang's measurement of 12 li, or 2 miles, for *Piloshana*. The mound is 3250 feet in breadth at base, or a little more than 2 miles in circuit. Its highest point is 44¾ feet above the level of the country; but there are no remains save the foundations of walls and masses of broken brick.

Piloshana is said to have been 2000 *li*, or 333 miles, in circuit; but this is certainly too great. With

* Beal's 'Fa-Hian,' chap. xviii.

reference to the surrounding districts, its limits may be defined approximately as extending from Bulandshahar to Firuzabad on the Jumna and Kâdirganj on the Ganges, which would give a circuit of not more than 250 miles.

9. SANKISA.

The position of Sankisa, which stood midway between Piloshana and Kanoj, has already been discussed. The name of the place is written *Seng-kia-she* by the Chinese pilgrims, a spelling which is well preserved in the Sankisa of the present day, and which represents with considerable faithfulness the *Sangkasya* of Sanskrit. Hwen Thsang calls it also by the name of *Kia-pi-tha,* or *Kapitha,* of which I was unable to discover any trace. Sankisa was one of the most famous places of Buddhist pilgrimage, as it was the scene of Buddha's descent from the *Trayastrinsa* heaven by a ladder of gold or gems, accompanied by the gods Indra and Brahma.* According to this curious legend, *Mâyâ,* the mother of Buddha, died seven days after his birth, and ascended at once to the *Trayastrinsa* heaven, the abode of the 33 gods, of whom Indra was the chief. But as she had no opportunity in this abode of the gods of hearing the law of Buddha, her pious son ascended to the *Trayastrinsa* heaven, and preached for three months in her behalf. He then descended to the earth with the gods Brahma

* Julien's 'Hiouen Thsang,' ii. 238.

and Indra by three staircases, one of which was formed either of crystal or precious stones, another of gold, and the third of silver. According to Fa-Hian, Buddha descended by a saircase formed of the "seven precious things," that is the precious metals and precious gems, whilst Brahma accompanied him on his right side by a silver ladder, and Indra on his left by a golden ladder. But Hwen Thsang assigns the golden staircase to Buddha himself, the silver staircase on the right to Brahma, and the crystal staircase on the left to Indra. The descent was accompanied by a multitude of Devas, who scattered flowers on all sides as they sang the praises of Buddha. Such are the main points of this curious legend, which is believed as firmly in Barma at the present day, as it was by Asoka 2100 years ago, or by the Chinese pilgrims of the fifth, sixth, and seventh centuries of our era.

The little village which still preserves the name of Sankisa is perched upon a lofty mound of ruins 41 feet in height above the fields. This mound, which is called the *Kilah*, or fort, is 1500 feet in length from east to west, and 1000 feet in breadth. On the north and west faces the sides are steep, but on the other faces the slope is much more easy. Due south from the centre of the fort, at a distance of 1600 feet, there is a mound of solid brickwork which is crowned by a modern temple dedicated to Bisâri Devi. The "fort" and the different mounds of all sizes around the temple form a mass of ruin 3000 feet in length by 2000 feet in breadth, or nearly 2 miles in circuit. But this was only the central portion of the ancient city of *Sankisa*, comprising the citadel and the religious buildings that were clustered round the three holy staircases. The city itself, which would appar to have surrounded this central mound on all sides, was enclosed with an earthen rampart 18,900 feet, or upwards of 3½ miles in circuit. The greater part of this rampart still remains, the shape being a tolerably regular dodecagon. On three sides, to the east, north-east, and south-east, there are breaks or openings in the line of rampart which are traditionally said to be the positions of the three gates of the city. In proof of the tradition, the people refer to the village of *Paor-Kheria*, or "*Gate-village*," which is just outside the south-east gap in the ramparts. But the name is pronounced *Paor*, पौर, and not *Paur*, पोर, and may therefore refer to the staircases or steps (*Paori*), and not to the gate. The Kâli, or *Kâlindri Nadi* flows past the south-west corner of the ramparts from the *Râjghât*, which is half a mile distant to the *Kakra Ghât*, which is rather more than one mile to the south of the line of ramparts.*

To the north-west, three-quarters of a mile distant, stands the large mound of *Agahat*, which is 40 feet in height, and rather more than half a mile in diameter at base. The name of the old town is said to have been *Agahat*, but the place is now called *Agahat Sarai* (Aghat of the maps) from a modern

* See Map No. X.

Sarai, which was built in A.H. 1080, or A.D. 1670, on the north-east corner of the mound, by the ancestor of the present Pathân Zamindar. The people say that before this, the place had been deserted for several centuries; but as I obtained a tolerably complete series of the copper coins of the Muhammadan kings of Delhi and Jonpur, I presume that it could not have been deserted for any very long time. The mound is covered with broken bricks of large size, which alone is a sure test of antiquity: and as it is of the same height as that of *Sankisa*, the people are most probably right in their assertion that the two places are of the same age. In both mounds are found the same old coins without any inscriptions, the more ancient being square pieces of silver covered with various punch-marks, and the others, square pieces of copper that have been cast in a mould,—all of which are, in my opinion, anterior to the invasion of Alexander the Great.

In identifying *Sankisa* with the *Sangasya* of the *Râmâyana* and the *Seng-kia-she* of the Chinese, we are supported, not only by its absolute identity of name, but likewise by its relative position with regard to three such well-known places as *Mathura, Kanoj*, and *Ahi-chhatra*. In size, also, it agrees very closely with the measurement given by Hwen Thsang; his circuit of 20 *li*, or 3½ miles, being only a little less than my measurement of 18,900 feet, or 3½ miles. There can be no doubt, therefore, that the place is actually the same. In his description of Sankisa, Hwen Thsang mentions a curious fact, that the

Brahmans who dwelt near the great monastery were "many tens of thousands" in number. As an illustration of this statement I may mention that the people have a tradition that Sankisa was deserted from 1800 to 1900 years ago; and that 1300 years ago, or about A.D. 560, the site was given by the *Kayath* proprietor to a body of Brahmans. They add also that the population of the village of *Paor-kheria* is known to have been wholly Brahman until a very recent period.

Sankisa is said to have been 2000 *li*, or 333 miles, in circuit; but with reference to the surrounding districts, this estimate must be too high. Its actual limits, as determined by the Ganges and Jumna on the north and south, and by the districts of Atranji and Kanoj on the west and east, could not have been more than 220 miles in circuit.

10. MATHURA.

In the seventh century the famous city of Mathura was the capital of a large kingdom, which is said to have been 5000 *li*, or 833 miles, in circuit.* If this estimate is correct, the province must have included not only the whole of the country lying between the districts of Bairât and Atranji, but a still larger tract beyond Agra, as far as Narwar and Seopuri on the south, and the Sindh river on the east. Within these limits the circuit of the province is 650 miles measured direct, or upwards of 750 miles by road distance. It includes the present

* Julien's 'Hiouen Thsang,' ii. 207. See Map No. X.

district of Mathura, with the small states of Bharatpur, Khiraoli, and Dholpur, and the northern half of the Gwalior territory. To the east it would have been bounded by the kingdom of *Jijhaoti*, and on the south by Malwa, both of which are described by Hwen Thsang as separate kingdoms.

In the seventh century the city was 20 *li*, or 3⅓ miles, in circuit, which agrees with its size at the present day. But the position is not exactly the same, as the houses have been gradually moving to the north and west as the Jumna encroached on the east. The old city is said to have extended from the Nabi Masjid and Fort of Raja-kansa on the north to the mounds called *Tila Kans* and *Tila Sat Rikh* on the south; but the southern half of this space is now deserted, and an equal space has been gradually built upon outside the old city to the north and west of the Nabi Masjid. The city is surrounded by numbers of high mounds; several of which are no doubt old brick kilns; but many of them are the remains of extensive buildings, which, having been dug over for ages in search of bricks, are now mere heaps of brick-dust and broken brick. I refer more especially to the great mound near the jail, 3 miles to the south of the city, which from its appearance was always supposed to be the remains of a brick and tile kiln. But this unpromising-looking mound has since yielded numbers of statues and inscribed pillars, which prove that it is the remains of at least two large Buddhist monasteries of as early a date as the beginning of the Christian era.

The holy city of Mathura is one of the most ancient places in India. It is famous in the history of Krishna, as the stronghold of his enemy Raja Kansa; and it is noticed by Arrian,* on the authority of Megasthenes, as the capital of the *Suraseni*. Now Surasena was the grandfather of Krishna, and from him Krishna and his descendants, who held Mathura after the death of Kansa, were called Surasenas. According to Arrian the Suraseni possessed two great cities, *Methoras* and *Klisoboras*, and the navigable river *Jobares* flowed through their territories. Pliny† names the river *Jomanes*, that is the Jumna, and says that it passed between the towns of *Methora* and *Clisobora*. Ptolemy mentions only Mathura, under the form of *Modura*, Μοδούρα, to which he adds ἡ τῶν θεῶν, that is "the city of the gods," or holy city.

Vrindâvana.

The city of *Klisoboras* has not yet been identified, but I feel satisfied that it must be *Vrindâvana*, 6 miles to the north of Mathura.‡ *Vrindâvana* means the "grove of basil-trees," which is famed over all India as the scene of Krishna's sports with the milkmaids. But the earlier name of the place was *Kâlikâvartta*, or "Kalika's whirlpool," because the serpent *Kâlika* was fabled to have taken up his abode just above the town, in a *Kadamb* tree, over-

* 'Indica,' viii.

† Nat. Hist., vi. 19.

‡ See Map. No. X.

hanging the Jumna. Here he was attacked by Krishna, and the rapid convolutions of his tail in his dying struggles are said to have caused the eddy, which is now known by his name. Now, the Latin name of Clisobora is also written *Carisobora* and *Cyrisoborka* in different MSS., from which I infer that the original spelling was *Kalisoborka*, or, by a slight change of two letters, *Kalikoborta* or *Kâlikâ-barta*. In the Prem Sâgar this whirlpool of the Jumna is attributed to the poison that was vomited forth by the serpent Kâli against Krishna, when he was swimming in the river. Allusion is made to the natural increase of the serpent's poison by offerings of milk, which would seem to refer to a previous state of serpent-worship. Milk offerings are still made occasionally, but only to test the divine nature of the serpent, who is supposed to possess the most miraculous powers of drinking. In the last century, Raja Chet Singh, of Benares, is said to have poured all the milk of the two cities of Mathura and Vrindâvan down the hollow *Kadamb* tree, and as the waters of the Jumna were not even tinged, the serpent Kâlika's miraculous powers of milk-drinking were established more firmly than ever.

11. KANOJ.

From *Sangkisa* Hwen Thsang proceeded to *Kanoj*, a distance of 200 *li*, or 33 miles, in a north-west direction. As the positions of both places are well known, we must correct the bearing to south-east, and the distance to 300 *li*, or 50 miles. The latter correction is supported by Fa-Hian, who makes the distance 7 *yojanas*, or 49 miles.* In the seventh century the kingdom is said to have been 4000 *li*, or 667 miles, in circuit. This estimate, as I have already observed, must certainly have included some of the petty districts to the north of the Ganges, as well as those in the Lower Gangetic Doab, otherwise the actual boundary of Kanoj proper would scarcely exceed 200 miles. Taking Hwen Thsang's estimate of 667 miles as approximately correct, the probable limits of the province of Kanoj must have included all the country between Khairabad and Tanda, on the Ghâgra, and Etâwa and Allahabad, on the Jumna, which would give a circuit of about 600 miles.

Of the great city of Kanoj, which for many hundred years was the Hindu capital of northern India, the existing remains are few and unimportant. In A.D. 1016, when Mahmud of Ghazni approached Kanoj, the historian relates that "he there saw a city which raised its head to the skies, and which in strength and structure might justly boast to have no equal."† Just one century earlier, or in A.D. 915, Kanoj is mentioned by Masudi as the capital of one of the kings of India; and about A.D. 900 Abu Zaid, on the authority of Ibn Wahab, calls "*Kaduje* a great city in the kingdom of *Gozar*." At a still earlier date, in A.D. 634, we have the account of the

---

* Beal's 'Fa-Hian,' xviii.

† Briggs's 'Ferishta,' i. 57.

Chinese pilgrim Hwen Thsang, who describes Kanoj as being 20 *li*, or 3½ miles, in length, and 4 or 5 *li*, or ¾ of a mile in breadth.* The city was surrounded by strong walls and deep ditches, and was washed by the Ganges along its eastern face. The last fact is corroborated by Fa-Hian, who states that the city touched the river *Heng*, or Ganges, when he visited it in A.D. 400. Kanoj is also mentioned by Ptolemy, about A.D. 140, as *Κανογίζα*. But the earliest notice of the place is undoubtedly the old familiar legend of the Purânas, which refers the Sanskrit name of *Kânya-ḳubja*, or the "hump-backed maiden," to the curse of the sage *Vayu* on the hundred daughters of *Kusanâba*.

At the time of Hwen Thsang's visit, Kanoj was the capital of Raja *Harsha Vardhana*, the most powerful sovereign in Northern India. The Chinese pilgrim calls him a *Fei-she*, or *Vaisya*, but it seems probable that he must have mistaken the *Vaisa*, or *Bais* Rajput for the *Vaisya*, or *Bais*, which is the name of the mercantile class of the Hindus; otherwise Harsha Vardhana's connection by marriage with the Rajput families of Malwa and Balabhi would have been quite impossible. Baiswâra, the country of the Bais Rajputs, extends from the neighbourhood of Lucknow to Khara-Mânikpur, and thus comprises nearly the whole of Southern Oudh. The Bais Rajputs claim descent from the famous *Sâlivâhan*, whose capital is said to have

* Julien's 'Hiouen Thsang,' ii. 243. See Map No. X.

been *Daundia-Khera,* on the north bank of the Ganges. Their close proximity to Kanoj is in favour of the sovereignty which they claim for their ancestors over the whole of the Gangetic Doab, from Delhi to Allahabad. But their genealogical lists are too imperfect, and most probably also too incorrect, to enable us to identify any of their recorded ancestors with the princes of Harsha Vardhana's family.

In determining the period of Harsha's reign between the years 607 and 650 A.D., I have been guided by the following evidence:—Ist, the date of his death is fixed by the positive statement of Hwen Thsang in the year 650 A.D.;* 2nd, in speaking of Harsha's career, the pilgrim records that from the time of his accesion, Harsha was engaged in continual war for 5½ years, and that afterwards for about 30 years he reigned in peace. This statement is repeated by Hwen Thsang when on his return to China, on the authority of the king himself, who informed him that he had then reigned for *upwards* of 30 years, and that the quinquennial assembly then collected was the *sixth* which he had convoked. From these different statements, it is certain that at

* In Appendix A, at the end of the Chronological Table of Hwen Thsang's route, I have brought forward strong reasons for blieving that the true date of the death of Harsha Vardhana was A.D. 648, which is the year given by Ma-twan-lin, on the authority of the Chinese ambassador, who visited India immediately after the king's death.

the date of Hwen Thsang's return to China, in A.D. 640, Harsha had reigned upwards of 30 years, and somewhat less than 35 years; his accession must, therefore, be placed between A.D. 605 and 610; 3rd, now, in the middle of this very period, in A.D. 607, as we learn from Abu Rihân, was established the Sri *Harsha* era, which was still prevalent in Mathura and Kanoj in the beginning of the eleventh century.* Considering the exact agreement of the names and dates, it is impossible to avoid coming to the conclusion that the *Harsha* who established an era in *Kanoj* in A.D. 607 was the great King *Harsha Vardhana*, who reigned at Kanoj during the first half of the seventh century.

In comparing Hwen Thsang's description of ancient Kanoj with the existing remains of the city, I am obliged to confess with regret that I have not been able to identify even one solitary site with any certainty; so completely has almost every trace of Hindu occupation been obliterated by the Musalmans. According to the traditions of the people, the ancient city extended from the shrine of *Hâji Harmâyan* on the north, near the Râj Ghât, to the neighbourhood of *Miranka Sarai* on the south, a distance of exactly 3 miles. Towards the west it is said to have reached to *Kapatya* and *Makarandnagar*, two villages on the high-road, about 3 miles from *Hâji Harmâyan*. On the east the boundary was the old bed of the Ganges, or *Chota Gangâ*, as

* Reinaud, 'Fragments,' p. 139.

the people call it, although it is recorded in our maps as the *Kâli Nadi*. Their account is that the *Kâli*, or *Kâlindri Nadi*, formerly joined the Ganges near *Sangirâmpur* or *Sangrâmpur;* but that several hundred years ago the great river took a more northerly course from that point, while the waters of the *Kâli Nadi* continued to flow down the deserted channel. As an open channel still exists between *Sangrâmpur* and the *Kâli Nadi*, I am satisfied that the popular account is correct, and that the stream which flows under Kanoj, from *Sangrâmpur* to *Mhendi Ghât*, although now chiefly filled with the waters of the *Kâli Nadi*, was originally the main channel of the Ganges. The accounts of Fa-Hian and Hwen Thsang, who place Kanoj on the Ganges, are therefore confirmed, not only by the traditions of the people, but also by the fact that the old channel still exists under the name of the *Chota Gangâ*, or Little Ganges.

The modern town of Kanoj occupies only the north end of the site of the old city, including the whole of what is now called the *Kilah*, or citadel. The boundaries are well defined by the shrine of *Hâji-Harmâyan* on the north, the tomb of *Tâj-Bâj* on the south-west, and the Masjid and tomb of *Makhdum-Jahâniya* on the south-east. The houses are much scattered, especially inside the citadel, so that though the city still covers nearly one square mile, yet the population barely exceeds 16,000 in number. The citadel, which occupies all the highest ground, is triangular in shape, its northern point being the shrine *Hâji-Harmâyan,* its south-west point the temple of *Ajay Pâl,* and its south-east point the large bastion called *Kshem Kali Bûrj.* Each of the faces is about 4000 feet in length, that to the north-west being protected by the bed of the nameless dry Nala, that to the north-east by the *Chota Gangâ,* while that to the south must have been covered by a ditch, which is now one of the main roads of the city, running along the foot of the mound from the bridge below Ajay Pâl's temple to the *Kshem Kali* bastion. On the north-east face the mound rises to 60 and 70 feet in height above the low ground on the bank of the river, and towards the Nala on the north-west it still maintains a height of from 40 to 50 feet. On the southern side, however, it is not more than 30 feet immediately below the temple of *Ajay Pâl,* but it increases to 40 feet below the tomb of *Balâ Pir.* The situation is a commanding one, and before the use of cannon the height alone must have made Kanoj a strong and important position. The people point out the sites of two gates, the first to the north, near the shrine of *Hâji Harmâyan,* and the second to the south-east, close to the *Kshem Kali Bûrj.* But as both of these gates lead to the river, it is certain that there must have been a third gate on the land side towards the south-west, and the most probable position seems to be immediately under the walls of the *Rang Mahal,* and close to the temple of *Ajay Pâl.*

According to tradition, the ancient city contained 84 wards or *Mahalas,* of which 25 are still existing within the limits of the present town. If we take the area of these 25 wards at three-quarters of a square mile, the 84 wards of the ancient city would have covered just 2½ square miles. Now, this is the very size that is assigned to the old city by Hwen Thsang, who makes its length 20 *li*, or 3½ miles, and its breadth 4 or 5 *li*, or just three-quarters of a mile, which multiplied together give just 2½ square miles. Almost the same limits may be determined from the sites of the existing ruins, which are also the chief *find-spots* of the old coins with which Kanoj abounds. According to the dealers, the old coins are found at *Bâla Pir* and *Rang Mahal*, inside the fort; at *Makhdum-Jahâniya*, to the south-east of the fort; or *Makarandnagar* on the high-road; and intermediately at the small villages of *Singh Bhawâni* and *Kûtlûpur*. The only other productive site is said to be *Râjgir*, an ancient mound covered with brick ruins on the bank of the *Chota Gangâ*, three miles to the south-east of Kanoj. Taking all these evidences into consideration, it appears to me almost certain that the ancient city of Hwen Thsang's time must have extended from *Hâji-Harmâyan* and the *Kshem-Kali Bûrj*, on the bank of the Ganges (now the *Chota Gangâ*), in a south-west direction, to *Makarand-nagar*, on the Grand Trunk Road, a length of just three miles, with a general breadth of about one mile or somewhat less. Within these limits are found all the ruins that still exist to point out the position of the once famous city of Kanoj.

12. AYUTO.

From Kanoj the two Chinese pilgrims followed different routes, Fa-Hian having proceeded direct to *Sha-chi* (the modern Ajudhya, near Fyzabad on the Ghâghra), while Hwen Thsang followed the course of the Ganges to Prayâg or Allahabad. The first stage of both pilgrims would, however, appear to be the same. Fa-Hian states that he crossed the Ganges and proceeded 3 *yojanas*, or 21 miles, to the south to the forest of *Holi*, where there were several stupas erected on spots where Buddha had "passed, or walked, or sat."*Hwen Thsang records that he marched 100 *li*, nearly 17 miles, to the town of *Nava-deva-kula*, which was on the eastern bank of the Ganges, and that at 5 *li*, or nearly 1 mile, to the south-east of the town there was a stupa of Asoka, which was till 100 feet in height, besides some other monuments dedicated to the four previous Buddhas.† I think it probable that the two places are the same, and that the site was somewhere near Nobatganj, just above the junction of the *Isan* river, and opposite *Nanamow* Ghât. But as there are no existing remains anywhere in that neighbourhood, the place has been most likely swept away by the river. This is rendered almost certain by an examination of the Ganges below the junction of the *Isan*. Formerly the river continued its course almost due south from Nanamow for many miles,

* Beal's 'Fa-Hian,' xviii. 71.

† Julien's 'Hiouen Thsang,' ii. 265.

but some centuries ago it changed its course; first to the south-east for 4 or 5 miles, and then to the south-west for about the same distance, where it rejoined its old bed, leaving an island, some 6 miles in length by 4 in breadth, between the two channels. As Hwen Thsang's account places *Nava-deva-kula* on the very site of this island, I conclude that the town as well as the Buddhist monuments must all have been swept away by the change in the river's course.

A probable source of error in all short distances was their registry in *yojanas* instead of in kos, which would have increased the distances just fourfold. If such an error should have been committed in the case of *Nava-deva-kula*, the actual distance would have been only 25 *li*, or a little more than 4 miles, instead of 17 miles. Now in this very position, 4 miles to the south-east of Kanoj there is a well-known place on the Chota Gangâ, called *Deokali*, which is the same name as that given by the pilgrim, if we omit the first two syllables *Nava*, or 'new.'

On leaving *Nava-deva-kula*, Hwen Thsang proceeded 600 *li*, or 100 miles, to the south-east, and recrossing the Ganges reached the capital city of *A-yu-to*, which was 20 *li*, or upwards of 3 miles, in circuit. Both M. Julien and M. de St. Martin have identified this place with *Ayodhya*, the once celebrated capital of Rama. I accept the probable reading of the name as Ayuda, but I differ with them altogether in looking for the capital along the line of the *Ghâghra* river, which is due east from Kanoj, whereas Hwen Thsang states that his route was to the south-east. It is of course quite possible that the pilgrim may occasionally use the generic name of Ganges as the appellation of any large river, such for instance as the *Ghâghra,* but in the present case, where the recorded bearing of south-east agrees with the course of the Ganges, I think it is almost certain that the Ganges itself was the river intended by the pilgrim. But by adopting the line of the Ganges we encounter a difficulty of a different kind in the great excess of the distance between two such well-known places as Kanoj and Prayâg. According to Hwen Thsang's route, he first made 100 *li* to *Nava-deva-kula,* then 600 *li* to *Ayuto,* then 300 *li* by water to *Hayamukha,* and lastly 700 *li* to *Prayâga.* All these distances added together make a total of 1700 *li,* or 283 miles, which is just 100 miles, or 600 *li,* in excess of the true distance. But as a part of the journey, viz. 300 *li,* or 50 miles, was performed by water, the actual excess may perhaps not be more than 85 or 90 miles; although it is doubtful whether the distance of 300 *li* may not have been the road measurement and not the river distance. It is sufficient for our purpose to know that Hwen Thsang's recorded measurement is somewhere about 100 miles in excess of the truth. The only explanation of this error that suggests itself to me is, that there may have been an accidental alteration of one set of figures, such as 60 *li* for 600 *li,* or 700 *li* for 70 *li.* Supposing that the former was the case, the distance would be shortened by 540 *li,* or 90 miles, and if the latter, by 630 *li*, or 105 miles. This mode of correction brings the pilgrim's account into fair accordance with the actual distance of 180 miles between Kanoj and Prayâg.

By adopting the first supposition, Hwen Thsang's distance from *Nava-deva-kula* to the capital of *Ayuto* will be only 60 *li*, or 10 miles, to the south-east, which would bring him to the site of an ancient city named *Kâkûpur*, just 1 mile to the north of Seorâjpoor, and 20 miles to the north-west of Cawnpore. The subsequent route would have been from *Kâkûpur* to *Daundiakhera* by boat, a distance of exactly 50 miles, or 300 *li*, and from thence to *Prayâg*, a distance of more than 100 miles, which agrees with the 700 *li*, or 116 miles, of the pilgrim. By the second supposition the subsequent route would have been from *Khara* to *Papamow* by water, about 50 miles, and thence to Prayâg, about 8 miles of land, which agrees with the 70 *li* of the proposed correction. In favour of this last supposition is the fact that the bearing from *Khara* to *Papamow* of east by south is more in accordance with Hwen Thsang's recorded east direction than the south-east bearing of Daundiakhera from Kâkûpur. I confess, however, that I am more inclined to adopt the former correction, which places the chief city of *Ayuto* at Kâkûpur, and the town of *Hayamuka* at Daundiakhera, as we know that the last was the capital of the *Bais Rajputs* for a considerable period. I am partly inclined to this opinion by a suspicion that the name of *Kâkûpur* may be connected with that of *Bâgud*, or *Vâgud*, of the Tibetan books.* According to this authority a *Sâkya*, named *Shâmpaka*, on being banished from Kapila retired to *Bâgud*, carrying with him some of Buddha's hair and nail-parings, over which he built a *chaitya*. He was made king of *Bâgud*, and the monument was named after himself (? *Shâmpaka stupa*). No clue is given as to the position of *Bâgud*, but as I know of no other name that resembles it, I am inclined to think that it is probably the same place as the *Ayuto* or *Ayuda* of Hwen Thsang. The two names have a striking resemblance; and as each of the places possessed a stupa containing some hair and nails of Buddha, I think that there are strong grounds for the identification.

Kâkûpur is well known to the people of Kanoj, who affirm that it was once a large city with a Raja of its own. It is exactly 10 miles, or 5 kos, to the north-west of Bithûr, and the land between the two places is called *Panj-kosi bhitar utpâlâranya*, or the "five kos circuit of Utpâlâranya." The ruined mound of Kâkûpur is said to be the remains of a fort named *Chhatrpur*, which was founded by Raja Chhatr Pâl Chândel 900 years ago. Kâkûpur also possesses two famous temples dedicated to *Kshireswara Mahâdeva*, and *Aswatthâma* son of Drona, near which a large annual fair is held. These details are sufficient to show that the place must

* Bengal 'Asiatic Researches,' xx. 88.

have been of some consequence in former days; while the name of Aswatthâma carries it back to the time of the Mahâbhârata.

Hwen Thsang makes Ayuto 5000 *li*, or 833 miles, in circuit,* which is so utterly beyond all possibility that I reject it without hesitation. Perhaps we should read 500 *li*, or 83 miles, which would restrict the territory to the small tract lying between Kâkûpur and Cawnpore, and thus leave room for the next district of Hayamukha.

13. HAYAMUKHA.

From Ayuto the pilgrim proceeded down the Ganges by boat for a distance of 300 *li*, or 50 miles, to *O.ye.mu.khi*, which was situated on the northern bank of the river. M. Julien† reads this name as *Hayamukha*, or "Horse-face;" but it may perhaps also be read as *Ayomukha*, or "Iron-face," which was the name of one of the ancient *Dânavas*, or Titans. Neither of these names, however, gives any clue to the site of the old city; but if I am right in my identification of *Ayuto* with Kâkûpur, it is almost certain that *Hayamukha* must be *Daundia-khera* on the northern bank of the Ganges. Hwen Thsang makes the circuit of the town 20 *li*, or upwards of 3 miles; but *Daundia-khera* presents no appearance of ever having been so large. There still exists an old ruined fort or citadel, 385 feet square, with the walls of two buildings which are

* Julien's 'Hiouen Thsang,' ii. 267. See Map No. X.
† Julien's 'Hiouen Thsang,' ii. 274.

called the palaces of the Râja and the Râni. But as *Daundia-khera* is universally allowed to have been the capital of the Bais Rajputs, who gave their name to the district of Baiswâra in Oudh, it is almost certain that the place must once have been of much greater extent. *Dondia* or *Daundia* means simply a "drum-beater," and was probably applied to some mendicant, who took up his abode on the *Khera*, or "mound," and as this name is not likely to have been imposed on the place until it was in ruins, the difference of name offers no impediment to the identification of *Daundia-khera* with *Hayamukha.*

Hwen Thsang makes *Hayamukha* 2500 *li,* or 417 miles, in circuit, which is perhaps too great; but as *Daundia-khera* was the capital of the Bais Rajputs, I conclude that the district must have comprised the whole of the present *Baiswâra,* which lies between the *Sai* river and the Ganges, from Cawnpore to Mânikpur and Salon. But as these limits would give a circuit of only 200 miles, it seems almost certain that the district must have extended to the south of the Ganges in the time of Hwen Thsang. Its probable limits were, therefore, the Ghâgra river on the north, and the Jumna on the south, a determination which derives some support from Tod,* who describes Baiswâra as an extensive district in the *Doâb* between the Ganges and Jumna.

* Julien's 'Hiouen Thsang,' ii. 276.

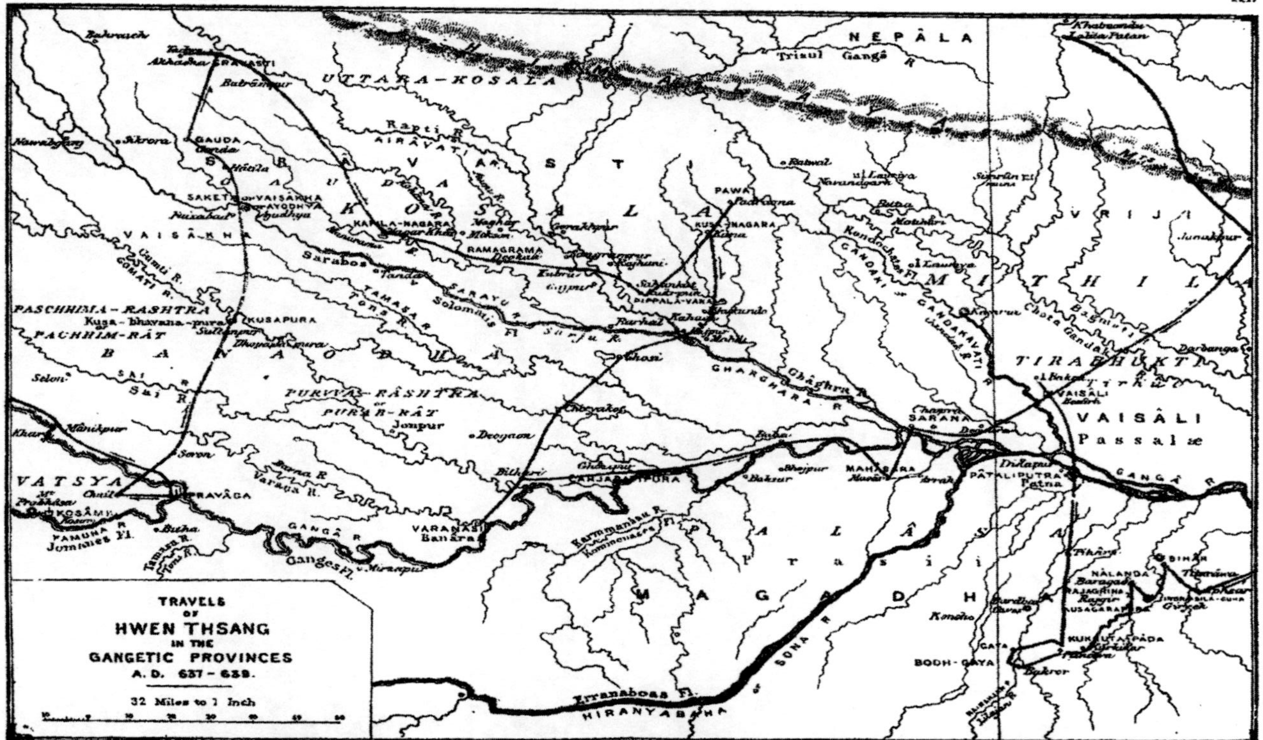
TRAVELS
OF
HWEN THSANG
IN THE
GANGETIC PROVINCES
A.D. 637 - 639.
32 Miles to 1 Inch
NEPÂLA
UTTARA-KOSALA
VAISÂKHA
PASCHHIMA-RASHTRA
PACHHIM-RÂT
PURVVA-RÂSHTRA
PURAB-RÂT
VATSYA
MITHILA
TIRABHUKTI
VAISÂLI
MAGADHA
GANGÂ R
SONA R
HIRANYABAHA
PRAYÂGA
KOSÂMBI
VARANASI
Banâra
PÂTALIPUTRA
Patna
KUSAPURA
KAPILA-NAGARA
RAMAGRAMA
KUSI-NAGARA
PAWA
NÂLANDA
RAJAGRIHA
BODH-GAYA
GAYA
SAKETA
AYODHYA
Jonpur
Ganges Fl.

14. PRAYÂGA.

From Hayamukha the pilgrim proceeded 700 *li*, or 116 miles, to the south-east to *Prayâga*, the well-known place of pilgrimage at the junction of the Ganges and Jumna, where Akbar, many centuries later, built his fort of *Ilâhabâs*, or *Allâhâbâd*, as it was afterwards called by Shah Jehân. The distance and bearing given by Hwen Thsang agree almost exactly with those of Prayâga from Daundia-khera. The distance is 104 miles by the nearest road to the south of the Ganges; but as the pilgrim followed the northern road, the distance must have been increased to 115 or 120 miles. According to him* the city was situated at the confluence of the two rivers, and to the west of a large sandy plain. In the midst of the city there was a Brahmanical temple, to which the presentation of a single piece of money procured as much merit as that of one thousand pieces elsewhere. Before the principal room of the temple there was a large tree with wide-spreading branches, which was said to be the abode of a man-eating demon. The tree was surrounded with human bones, the remains of pilgrims who had sacrified their lives before the temple, a practice which had been observd from time immemorial.

I think there can be little doubt that the famous tree here described by the pilgrim is the well-known *Akshay Bat*, or "undecaying Banian tree," which is still an object of worship at Allahabad. This

* Julien's 'Hiouen Thsang,' ii. 276.

tree is now situated underground, at one side of a pillared court, which would appear to have been open formerly, and which is, I believe, the remains of the temple described by Hwen Thsang. The temple is situated inside the fort of Allahabad, to the east of the Ellenborough Barracks, and due north from the Stone Pillar of Asoka and Samudra Gupta. Here, then, must have been the site of the city in the seventh century, and this agrees with the sunken position of the tree, for originally both tree and temple must have been on the natural ground level; but from the constant accumulation of rubbish, they have been gradually earthed up, until the whole of the lower portion of the temple has disappeared underground. The upper portion has long ago been removed, and the only access to the *Akshay Bat* now available is by a flight of steps which leads down to a square pillared courtyard. This court has apparently once been open to the sky; but it is now completely closed overhead, to secure darkness and mystery for the holy fig-tree.

The *Akshay-bat* is next mentioned by Rashid-ud-din in the *Jamiu-t-tawârikh*, where he states that the "tree of *Prâg*" is situated at the confluence of Jumna and Ganges. As most of his information was derived from Abu Rihân, the date of this notice may with great probability be referred to the time of Mahmud of Ghazni. In the seventh century a great sandy plain, 2 miles in circuit, lay between the city and the confluence of the rivers, and as the tree was in the midst of the city, it must have been at least one mile from the confluence. But nine centuries later, in the beginning of Akbar's reign, Abdul Kâdir speaks of the "tree from which people cast themselves into the river."* From this statement I infer that during the long period that intervened between the time of Hwen Thsang and that of Akbar, the two rivers had gradually carried away the whole of the great sandy plain, and had so far encroached upon the city, as to place the holy tree on the very brink of the water. Long before this time the old city had no doubt been deserted, for we know that the fort of *Ilâhâbâs* was founded on its site in the twenty-first year of Akbar's reign, that is, in A.H. 982, or A.D. 1572. Indeed the way in which Abu Rihân speaks of the "tree" instead of the city of Prâg, leads me to believe that the city itself had already been deserted before his time. As far as I am aware, it is not once mentioned in any Muhammadan history until it was refounded by Akbar.†

According to the common tradition of the people, the name of Prayâg was derived from a Brahman who lived during the reign of Akbar. The story is, that when the emperor was building the fort, the walls on the river face repeatedly fell down, in spite of all the precautions taken by the architect. On consulting some wise men, Akbar was informed that the foundations could only be secured by being

---

* Elliot's 'Muhammadan Historians of India,' p. 243.

† Reinaud, 'Fragments Arabes,' etc., p. 103. Sir H. Elliot's 'Muhammadan Historians of India,' edited by Dowson, i. 55.

laid in human blood. A proclamation was then made, when a Brahman named Prayâga voluntarily offered his life, on the condition that the fort should bear his name. This idle story, which is diligently related to the pilgrims who now visit the *Akshay Bat*, may at least serve one useful purpose in warning us not to place too much faith in these local traditions. The name of Prayâga is recorded by Hwen Thsang in the seventh century, and is in all probability as old as the reign of Asoka, who set up the stone pillar about B.C. 235, while the fort was not built until the end of the sixteenth century. Hwen Thsang makes the district of *Prayâga* about 5000 *li*, or 833 miles, in circuit; but as it was closely surrounded on all sides by other districts, I am satisfied that we should read 500 *li*, or 83 miles, and limit the district to the small tract in the fork of the Doâb, immediately above the junction of the Ganges and Jumna.

15. KOSÂMBI.

The city of *Kosâmbi* was one of the most celebrated places in ancient India, and its name was famous amongst Brahmans as well as Buddhists. The city is said to have been founded by *Kusamba*, the tenth in descent from Pururavas; but its fame begins only with the reign of Chakra, the eighth in descent from Arjun Pându, who made Kosâmbi his capital after Hastinapura had been swept away by the Ganges.

Kosâmbi is mentioned in the 'Râmâyana,' the

earliest of the Hindu poems, which is generally allowed to have been composed before the Christian era. The story of *Udâyana*, king of Kosâmbi, is referred to by the poet Kâlidâsa in his 'Megha-duta,' or 'Cloud Messenger,' where he says that "*Avanti* (or Ujain) is great with the number of those versed in the tale of Udâyana."* Now, Kâlidâsa flourished shortly after A.D. 500. In the 'Vrihat Katha,' of Somadeva, the story of Udâyana is given at full length, but the author has made a mistake in the genealogy between the two *Satânikas*. Lastly, the kingdom of *Kosâmbi*, or *Kosâmba Mandala*, is mentioned in an inscription taken from the gateway of the fort of *Khara* which is dated in *Samvat* 1092, or A.D. 1035, at which period it would appear to have been independent of Kanoj.† Kosâmbi, the capital of Vatsa Raja, is the scene of the pleasing drama of 'Ratnâvali,' or the 'Necklace,' which was composed in the reign of King Harsha Deva, who is most probably the same as Harsha Vardhana of Kanoj, as the opening prelude describes amongst the assembled audience "princes from various realms recumbent at his feet."‡ This we know from Hwen Thsang to have been true of the Kanoj prince, but which even a Brahman could

* Wilson, 'Megha-duta,' note 64; and 'Hindu Theatre,' ii. 257, note.

† 'Asiatic Researches,' ix. 433. Journ. Asiat. Soc. Bengal, v. 731.

‡ Wilson's 'Hindu Theatre.' 'Ratnâvali;' prelude, ii. 264.

scarcely have asserted of Harsha Deva of Kashmir. The date of this notice will therefore lie between 607 and 650 A.D.

But the name of Udâyana, king of Kosâmbi, was perhaps even more famous amongst the Buddhists. In the 'Mahawanso,'* which was composed in the fifth century, the venerable Yasa is said to have fled from Vaisâli to Kosâmbi just before the assembly of the second Buddhist Synod. In the 'Lalita Vistâra,'† which was translated into Chinese between 70 and 76 A.D., and which could not, therefore, have been composed later than the beginning of the Christian era, Udâyana Vatsa, son of Satânika, king of Kosâmbi, is said to have been born on the same day as Buddha. In other Ceylonese books Kosâmbi is named as one of the nineteen capital cities of ancient India. Udâyana Vatsa is also known to the Tibetans‡ as the king of Kosâmbi. In the 'Ratnâvali' he is called *Vatsa Raja*, or king of the Vatsas, and his capital *Vatsa-pattana*, which is therefore only another name for Kosâmbi. In this famous city also Buddha is said to have spent the sixth and ninth years of his Buddhahood.§ Lastly, Hwen Thsang relates that the famous statue of Buddha, in red sandal-wood, which was made by King Udâyana during the lifetime of

---

* Turnour's 'Mahawanso,' p. 16.

† Foucaux, translation of the Tibetan version of the 'Lalita-Vistâra.'

‡ Csoma de Körös, in 'Asiatic Researches,' xx. 299.

§ Hardy, 'Manual of Buddhism,' p. 356.

the Teacher, still existed under a stone dome in the ancient palace of the kings.*

The site of this great city, the capital of the later Pându princes, and the shrine of the most sacred of all the statues of Buddha, has long been sought in vain. The Brahmans generally asserted that it stood either on the Ganges or close to it, and the discovery of the name of *Kosâmbi mandala*, or "Kingdom of Kosâmbi," in an inscription over the gateway of the fort of *Khara*, seems to confirm the general belief, although the south-west bearing from Prayâga, or Allahabad, as recorded by Hwen Thsang, points unmistakably to the line of the Jumna. In January, 1861, Mr. Bayley informed me that he believed the ancient Kosâmbi would be found in the old village of Kosam, on the Jumna, about 30 miles above Allahabad. In the following month I met Babu Siva Prasâd, of the educational department, who takes a deep and intelligent interest in all archæological subjects, and from him I learned that *Kosam* is still known as *Kosâmbi-nagar*, that it is even now a great resort of the Jains, and that only one century ago it was a large and flourishing town. This information was quite sufficient to satisfy me that *Kosam* was the actual site of the once famous Kosâmbi. Still, however, there was no direct evidence to show that the city was situated on the Jumna; but this missing link in the chain of evidence I shortly afterwards found in the curious

* Julien's 'Hiouen Thsang,' ii. 283.

legend of Bakkula, which is related at length by Hardy.* The infant Bakkula was born at Kosâmbi, and while his mother was bathing in the *Jumna*, he accidentally fell into the river, and being swallowed by a fish, was carried to Benares. There the fish was caught and sold to the wife of a nobleman, who on opening it found the young child still alive inside, and at once adopted it as her own. The true mother hearing of this wonderful escape of the infant, proceeded to Benares, and demanded the return of the child, which was of course refused. The matter was then referred to the king, who decided that both of the claimants were mothers of the child,—the one by *maternity*, the other by *purchase*. The child was accordingly named *Bakula*, that is, of "two *kulas*, or races." He reached the age of 90 years without once having been ill, when he was converted by the preaching of Buddha, who declared him to be "the chief of that class of his disciples who were free from disease." After this he is said to have lived 90 years more, when he became an *arhat*, or Buddhist saint.

As this legend of Bakula is sufficient to prove that the famous city of Kausâmbi was situated on the Jumna, it now only remains to show that the distance of Kosam from Allahabad corresponds with that between Prayâg and Kosâmbi, as recorded by Hwen Thsang. Unfortunately this distance is differently stated in the life and in the travels of the

* 'Manual of Buddhism,' p. 501.

Chinese pilgrim. In the former, the distance is given as 50 *li*, and in the latter as 500 *li*, whilst in the return journey to China, the pilgrim states that between Prayâg and Kosâmbi he travelled for *seven* days through a vast forest and over bare plains.* Now, as the village of Kosam is only 31 miles from the fort of Allahabad, the last statement would seem to preclude all possibility of its identification with the ancient Kosâmbi. But strange to say, it affords the most satisfactory proof of their identity; for the subsequent route of the pilgrim to Sankissa is said to have occupied one month, and as the whole distance from Prayâg to Sankissa is only 200 miles, the average length of the pilgrim's daily march was not more than 5½ miles. This slow progress is most satisfactorily accounted for, by the fact that the march from Prayâg to Sankissa was a religious procession, headed by the great king Harsh Vardhana of Kanoj, with a train of no less than 18 tributary kings, besides many thousands of Buddhist monks, and all the crowd of an Indian camp. According to this reckoning, the distance from Prayâg to Kosâmbi would be 38 miles, which corresponds very closely with the actual road distance as I found it. By one route on going to Kosam, I made the distance 37 miles, and by the return route 35 miles. The only probable explanation of Hwen Thsang's varying distances of 50 *li* and 500

---

* Julien's 'Hiouen Thsang,' i. 121; ii. 283; and i. 260.

li that occurs to me is, that as he converted the Indian *yojanas* into Chinese *li* at the rate of 40 *li* per *yojana*, or of 10 *li* per kos, he must have written 150 *li*, the equivalent of 15 kos, which is the actual distance across the fields for foot passengers from Kosam to the fort of Allahabad, according to the reckoning of the people of Kosam itself. But whether this explanation be correct or not, it is quite certain that the present Kosam stands on the actual site of the ancient *Kosâmbi;* for not only do the people themselves put forward this claim, but it is also distinctly stated in an inscription of the time of Akbar, which is recorded on the great stone pillar, still standing in the midst of the ruins, that this is *Kausâmbi-pura*.

The present ruins of Kosâmbi consist of an immense fortress formed of earthen ramparts and bastions, with a circuit of 23,100 feet, or exactly 4 miles and 3 furlongs. The ramparts have a general height of from 30 to 35 feet above the fields; but the bastions are considerably higher, those on the north face rising to upwards of 50 feet, while those at the south-west and south-east angles are more than 60 feet. Originally there were ditches all around the fortress, but at present there are only a few shallow hollows at the foot of the rampart. The length of the north front is 4,500 feet, of the south front 6,000, of the east front 7,500 feet, and of the west front 5,100, or altogether 23,100 feet. The differnce in length between the north and south fronts is due to the original extension of the fortress on the river face; but the difference between the east and west fronts is, I believe, chiefly, if not wholly, due to the loss of the south-west angle of the ramparts by the gradual encroachment of the Jumna. There are no traces now left of the western half of the ramparts on the southern face, and the houses of the village of *Garhwâ* are standing on the very edge of the cliff overhanging the river. The reach of the river also, from the *Pakka Burj* at the south-west angle of the fortress up to the hill of *Prabhâsa,* a clear straight run of 4 miles, bears 12 degrees to the north of east, whereas in the time of Hwen Thsang there were two stupas and a cave at a distance of 1½ miles to the south-west of *Kosâmbi.* From all these concurring circumstances, I conclude that the west front of the fortress was originally as nearly as possible of the same length as the east front. This would add 2400 feet, or nearly half a mile, to the length of the west front, and would increase the whole circuit of the ramparts to 4 miles and 7 furlongs, which is within one furlong of the measurement of 5 miles, or 30 *li,* recorded by Hwen Thsang. In the three main points therefore of name, size, and position, the present Kosam corresponds most exactly with the ancient Kosâmbi as it is described by the Chinese pilgrim in the seventh century.

According to the text of Hwen Thsang, the district of Kosâmbi was 6000 *li,* or 1000 miles, in circuit, which is quite impossible, as it was closely surrounded on all sides by other districts. I would, therefore, read hundreds for thousands, and fix its circuit at 600 *li*, or 100 miles.

16. KUSAPURA.

From Kosâmbi the Chinese pilgrim travelled to the north-east, through a vast forest as far as the Ganges, after crossing which his route lay to the north for a distance of 700 *li*, or 117 miles, to the town of *Kia-she-pu-lo*, which M. Julien correctly renders by *Kasapura*.* In searching for the site of this place, the subsequent route of the pilgrim to *Visâkhâ*, a distance of 170 to 180 *li*, or from 28 to 30 miles, to the north is of equal importance with the bearing and distance from Kosâmbi. For as the Visâkhâ of Hwen Thsang, as I will presently show, is the same place as the *Shachi* of Fa-Hian, and the *Sâketa* or Ayodhya of the Hindus, we thus obtain two such well-fixed points as Kosâmbi and Ayodhya to guide us in our search. A single glance at the map will be sufficient to show that the old town of *Sultân-pur* on the *Gomati* (or Gumti) river is as nearly as possible in the position indicated. Now the Hindu name of this town was *Kusabhavanapura*, or simply *Kusapura*, which is almost the same name as that of Hwen Thsang. Remembering Mr. Bayley's note of information

* M. Julien's 'Hiouen Thsang,' ii. 287-290. In the record of the pilgrim's 'Life,' *Kusapura* is altogether omitted, and the distance from Kosâmbi to Visâkhâ is said to be 500 *li* to the east. Julien, i. 122. See Map No. XI. for its position.

derived from Raja Mân Sinh that there was "a *tope* near Sultânpur," I pitched my tent on one side of the now utterly desolate city, and searched the whole place through most carefully, but all in vain: I could neither find the trace of any tope, nor could I even hear of ancient remains of any kind. On the following day, however, after I had left Sultânpur, I heard that the village of Mahmudpur, about 5 miles to the north-west, was situated on an ancient mound of somewhat larger size than that of Sultânpur, and on my arrival at Faizabad, I learned from Lieutenant Swetenham, of the Royal Engineers, that there is an old tope to the north-west of Sultânpur, not far from this village. I conclude, therefore, that Sultânpur, the ancient Kusapura, is the same place as the Kasapura of Hwen Thsang, and this identification will be made even more certain on examination of the recorded distances.

On leaving Kosâmbi, the pilgrim proceeded first in a north-east direction to the Ganges, after crossing which he turned to the north to Kasapura, the whole distance being 117 miles. Now, the two great ghâts on the Ganges to the north-east of Kosam are at *Mau-Saraya* and *Pâpa-mau*, the former being 40 miles, and the latter 43 miles distant. But as these two ghâts are close together, and almost immediately to the north of Allahabad, the total distance to Kasapura will be the same whichever place of crossing be taken. From Pâpamau to Sultânpur the direction is due north, and the distance 66 miles; the whole line from Kosam to Sultânpur being 109 miles, which is within 8 miles of the round number of 700 *li*, or 116⅔ miles, as given by Hwen Thsang; while both of the bearings are in exact accordance with his statements. From Kasapura to *Visâkha* the direction followed by the pilgrim was to the north, and the distance was from 170 to 180 *li*, or from 28 to 30 miles. Now the present city of *Ajudhya*, the ancient *Ayodhya* or Sâketa, is almost due north from *Sultânpur*, the distance being 30 miles to the nearest point, or just six miles in excess of the distance given by Hwen Thsang. As the former of these distances is in default, while the latter is in excess, I would suggest, as a possible alternative, that our measurements should be taken from the village of *Mahmûdpur*, which would make the route from Kosam to the Buddhist establishment near Kasapura up to 114 miles, or within three miles of the number stated by Hwen Thsang, and lessen the subsequent route to Ayodhya from 36 to 31 miles, which is within one mile of the number given by the Chinese pilgrim. As all the bearings are in perfect accordance, and as the names of the two places agree almost exactly, I think that there can be little hesitation in accepting the identification of *Sultânpur* or *Kusapura* with the Kasapura of Hwen Thsang.

Kusapura, or *Kusa-bhavana-pura*, is said to have been named after Rama's son, Kusa. Shortly after the Muhammadan invasion it belonged to a *Bhar* Raja Nand Kunwar, who was expelled by Sultan Alauddin *Ghori* (read *Khilji*). The defences of the town were strengthened by the conqueror, who built a mosque and changed the name of the place to Sultânpur. The site of *Kusapura* was, no doubt, selected by its founder as a good military position on account of its being surrounded on three sides by the river Gomati or Gumti. The place is at present utterly desolate; the whole population having been removed to the new civil station on the opposite or south bank of the river. The ruined fort of Sultânpur now forms a large mound, 750 feet square, with brick towers at the four corners. On all sides it is surrounded by the huts of the ruined town, the whole together covering a space of about half a mile square, or about two miles in circuit. This etimate of the size of Sultânpur agrees very closely with that of Kusapura given by Hwen Thsang, who describes the place as being 10 *li*, or 1⅔ miles, in circuit.

Eighteen miles to the south-east of Sultânpur, or Kusapura, there is a celebrated place of Hindu pilgrimage called *Dhopâpapura*. It is situated on the right or west bank of the Gomati river, and immediately under the walls of Garhâ, or *Shir-ḳe garhi*. The site of *Dhopâp* is evidently one of considerable antiquity, as the fields for half a mile all round are covered with broken bricks and pottery.

17. VISÂKHA, SÂKETA, OR AJUDHYA.

Much difficulty has been felt regarding the position of Fa-Hian's "great kingdom of *Shachi*," and of Hwen Thsang's *Visâḳha*, with its enormous number of heretics or Brahmanists; but I hope to show in the most satisfactory manner that these two places are identical, and that they are also the same as the *Sâketa* and *Ajudhya* of the Brahmans. The difficulty has arisen chiefly from an erroneous bearing recorded by Fa-Hian, who places *She-wei*, or *Srâvasti*, to the south of *Shachi*, while Hwen Thsang locates it to the north-east, and partly from his erroneous distance of 7 + 3 + 10 = 20 *yojanas*, instead of 30, from the well-known city of Sankisa. The bearing is shown to be erroneous from the route of a Hindu pilgrim from the banks of the Godâvari to *Sewet* or *Srâvasti*, as recorded in the Ceylonese Buddhist works. This pilgrim, after passing through *Mahissati* and *Ujani*, or *Mahesmati* and *Ujain*, reaches Kosâmbi, and from thence passes through *Sâketa* to *Sewet*, that is along the very route followed by Hwen Thsang.* We have, therefore, two authorities in favour of *Sewet* being to the north of Sâket. With regard to the distance, I refer again to the Buddhist books of Ceylon, in which it is recorded that from *Sakaspura* (or *Sangkasyapura*, now Sankisa) to *Sewet* was a journey of 30 *yojanas*.† Now, Fa-Hian makes the distance from Sankisa to Kanoj 7 *yojanas*, thence to the forest of *Holi*, on the Ganges, 3 *yojanas*, and thence to *Shachi* 10 *yojanas*, or altogether only 20 *yojanas*, or 10 less than the Ceylonese books. That Fa-Hian's state-

* Hardy, 'Manual of Buddhism,' p. 334.
† *Ibid.*, p. 301.

ment is erroneous is quite clear from the fact that his distance would place Shachi in the neighbourhood of Lucknow; whereas the other distance would place it close to Ajudhya, or Faizâbâd, or in the very position indicated by Hwen Thsang's itinerary. Here, again, we have two authorities in favour of the longer distance. I have no hesitation, therefore, in declaring that Fa-Hian's recorded bearing of *She-wei* from *Sha-chi* is wrong, and that "north" should be read instead of "south."

I have now to show that Fa-Hian's *Sha-chi* is the same as Hwen Thsang's *Visâkha*, and that both are identical with *Sâketa* or *Ajudhya*. With respect to *Sha-chi*, Fa-Hian relates that "on leaving the town by the *southern gate* you find to the *east* of the road the place where Buddha bit a branch of the nettle-tree and planted it in the ground, where it grew to the height of seven feet, and never increased or diminished in size."* Now, this is precisely the same legend that is related of *Visâkha* by Hwen Thsang, who says that "to the *south* of the capital, and to the left of the road (that is, to the east as stated by Fa-Hian), there was, amongst other holy objects, an extraordinary tree 6 or 7 feet high, which always remained the same, neither growing nor decreasing.† This is the celebrated tooth-brush tree of Buddha, to which I shall have occasion to refer

* Remusat, 'Fo-kwe-ki,' c. xix.; and Beal's 'Fah-Hian,' c. xix. 27.

† Julien's 'Hiouen Thsang,' ii, 292.

presently. Here I need only notice the very precise agreement in the two descriptions of this famous tree, as to its origin, its height, and its position. The perfect correspondence of these details appears to me to leave no doubt of the identity of Fa-Hian's *Sha-chi* with the Visâkha of Hwen Thsang.

With respect to the identification of Visâkha with the Sâketa of the Hindus, I rest my proofs chiefly on the following points: 1st, that *Visâkha*, the most celebrated of all females in Buddhist history, was a resident of Sâketa before her marriage with *Purnna Varddhana*, son of *Mrigara*, the rich merchant of *Srâvasti;*—and 2nd, that Buddha is recorded by Hwen Thsang to have spent 6 years at *Visâkha*, while, by the Pali annals of Turnour, he is stated to have lived 16 years at *Sâketa*.*

The story of the noble maiden Visâkhâ is related at great length in the Ceylonese books. According to Hardy,† she erected a *Purvvârâma* at *Srâvasti*, which is also mentioned by Hwen Thsang. Now, there was also a *Purvvârâma* at Sâketa, and it can hardly be doubted that this monastery was likewise built by her. She was the daughter of *Dhananja*, a rich merchant, who had emigrated from *Râjagriha*

* I take the 6 years of the pilgrim to be a mistake for 16 years, as the whole period of Buddha's teaching is carefully accounted for in the Ceylonese annals.

† 'Manual of Buddhism,' p. 220. Julien's 'Hiouen Thsang,' i. 305. The Pubbârâmo is also mentioned in the 'Ceylonese Annals;' see Turnour, Journ. Asiat. Soc. Bengal, vii. 790.

to *Sâketa*. Now, amongst the oldest inscribed coins which have been discovered only at Ajudhya, we find some bearing the names of *Dhana Deva* and *Visâkha-Datta*. I mention this because it seems to me to show the probability that the family of *Dhananja* and *Visâkhâ* was of great eminence in Sâketa or Ayodhya; and I infer from the recurrence of their names, as well as from the great celebrity of the lady, that the city may possibly have been called *Visâkhâ* after her name.

The other proof which I derive from the years of Buddha's residence is direct and convincing. According to the Ceylonese annals, Buddha was 35 years of age when he attained Buddhahood; he then led a houseless life for 20 years, preaching in various places in Northern India, all of which are detailed; and of the remaining 25 years of his life he spent 9 in the *Jetavana* monastery at Srâvasti, and 16 in the *Pubhârâmo* monastery at Sâketapura.* Now, in the Burmese annals† these numbers are given as 19 years and 6 years, and in the last figure we have the exact number recorded by Hwen Thsang.‡ Nothing can be more complete than this proof. There were only two places at which Buddha resided for any length of time, namely, *Srâvasti*, at which he lived either 9 or 19 years, and *Sâketa*, at which he lived either 6 or 16 years; and as according to Hwen

* Turnour, Journ. Asiat. Soc. Bengal, vii. 790.

† Bigandet, 'Legend of Burmese Buddha,' p. 142.

‡ Julien's 'Hiouen Thsang,' ii. 292.

Thsang he lived for 6 years at Visâkha, which is described as being at some distance to the south of Srâvasti, it follows of necessity that Visâkha and Sâketa were one and the same place.

The identity of *Sâketa* and *Ayodhya* has, I believe, always been admitted; but I am not aware that any proof has yet been offered to establish the fact. Csoma de Körös,* in speaking of the place, merely says "*Saketana* or Ayodhya," and H. H. Wilson, in his Sanskrit Dictionary, calls *Sâketa* "the city Ayodhya." But the question would appear to be set at rest by several passages of the 'Râmâyana' and 'Raghuvansa,'† in which *Sâketanagara* is generally called the capital of Raja *Dasaratha* and his sons. But the following verse of the 'Râmâyana,' which was pointed out to me by a Brahman of Lucknow, will be sufficient to establish the identity. *Aswajita,* father of *Kaikeyi,* offers to give his daughter to Dasaratha, Raja of *Sâketanagara* :—

Sâketâm nagaram Râja nâmna Dasaratho bali.
Tâsmai deyâ mayâ kanyâ Kaikeyi nâma to janâ.

The ancient city of Ayodhya or Sâketa is described in the 'Râmâyana' as situated on the bank of the *Sarayu* or *Sarju* river. It is said to have been 12 *yojanas,* or nearly 100 miles in circumference, for which we should probably read 12 kos, or 24 miles, —an extent which the old city, with all its gardens,

---

* 'Asiatic Researches,' xx. 442.

† 'Raghuvansa,' sarg. xiii. slok. 79, and sarg. xiv. slok. 13.

might once possibly have covered. The distance from the *Guptâr* Ghât on the west, to the Râm Ghât on the east, is just 6 miles in a direct line, and if we suppose that the city with its suburbs and gardens formerly occupied the whole intervening space to a depth of two miles, its circuit would have agreed exactly with the smaller measurement of 12 kos. At the present day the people point to Râm Ghât and Guptar Ghât as the eastern and western boundaries of the old city, and the southern boundary they extend to *Bharat-Kund,* near *Bhadarsâ,* a distance of 6 kos. But as these limits include all the places of pilgrimage, it would seem that the people consider them to have been formerly inside the city, which was certainly not the case. In the 'Ayin Akbari,' the old city is said to have measured 148 kos in length by 36 kos in breadth,* or, in other words, it covered the whole of the province of Oudh to the south of the Ghâghra river. The origin of the larger number is obvious. The 12 *yojanas* of the 'Râmâyana,' which are equal to 48 kos, being considered too small for the great city of Rama, the Brahmans simply added 100 kos to make the size tally with their own extravagant notions. The present city of Ajudhya, which is confined to the north-east corner of the old site, is just two miles in length by about three quarters of a mile in breadth; but not one half of this extent is occupied by buildings, and the whole place wears a look of decay. There are no high

* Gladwyn's translation, ii. 32.

mounds of ruins, covered with broken statues and sculptured pillars, such as mark the sites of other ancient cities, but only a low irregular mass of rubbish heaps, from which all the bricks have been excavated for the houses of the neighbouring city of Faizâbâd. This Muhammadan city, which is two miles and a half in length by one mile in breadth, is built chiefly of materials extracted from the ruins of Ajudhya. The two cities together occupy an area of nearly six square miles, or just about one-half of the probable size of the ancient capital of Râma. In Faizâbâd the only building of any consequence is the stuccoed brick tomb of the old Bhao Begam, whose story was dragged before the public during the famous trial of Warren Hastings. Faizâbâd was the capital of the first Nawâbs of Oudh, but it was deserted by Asaf-ud-daolah in A.D. 1775.

In the seventh century the city of *Visâkha* was only 16 *li*, or 2⅔ miles, in circuit, or not more than one-half of its present size, although it probably contained a greater population, as not above one-third or perhaps less of the modern town is inhabited. Hwen Thsang assigns to the district a circuit of 4000 *li*, or 667 miles, which must be very much exaggerated. But, as I have alrady observed, the estimated dimensions of some of the districts in this part of the pilgrim's route are so great that it is quite impossible that all of them can be correct. I would therefore, in the present instance, read 400 *li*, or 67 miles, and restrict the territory of *Visâkha* to the small tract lying around Ajudhya, between the Ghâgra and Gomati rivers.

18. SRÂVASTI.

The ancient territory of *Ayodhya*, or Oudh, was divided by the Sarjû or Ghâgra river into two great provinces; that to the north being called *Uttara Kosala,* and that to the south *Banaodha*. Each was again subdivided into two districts. In *Banaodha* these are called *Pachham-rât* and *Purab-rât,* or the western and eastern districts; and in *Uttara Kosala* they are *Gauda* (vulgarly *Gonda*) to the south of the Rapti, and *Kosala* to the north of the Rapti, or *Râwati,* as it is universally called in Oudh. Some of these names are found in the Purânas. Thus, in the Vayu Purâna, *Lava* the son of Râma is said to have reigned in Uttara Kosala; but in the Matsya Linga and Kurma Purânas, *Srâvasti* is stated to be in *Gauda*. These apparent discrepancies are satisfactorily explained when we learn that *Gauda* is only a subdivision of *Uttara Kosala,* and that the ruins of Srâvasti have actually been discovered in the district of *Gauda,* which is the Gonda of the maps. The extent of *Gauda* is proved by the old name of Balrâmpur on the Rapti, which was formerly *Ramgarh-Gauda*. I presume, therefore, that both the *Gauda Brahmans* and the *Gauda Tagas* must originally have belonged to this district, and not to the mediæval city of *Gauda* in Bengal. Brahmans of this name are still numerous in Ajudhya and

Jahângirabad on the right bank of the Ghâgra river, in Gonda, Pakhapur, and Jaisni of the Gonda or Gauda district on the left bank, and in many parts of the neighbouring province of Gorakhpur. *Ajudhya*, therefore, was the capital of *Banaodha*, or Oudh to the south of the Ghâgra, while *Srâvasti* was the capital of *Uttara Kosala*, or Oudh to the north of the Ghâgra.

The position of the famous city of *Srâvasti*, one of the most celebrated places in the annals of Buddhism, has long puzzled our best scholars. This was owing partly to the contradictory statements of the Chinese pilgims themselves, and partly to the want of a good map of the province of Oudh. In my account of *Visâkha* or *Ajudhya*, I have compared the bearings and distances recorded by Fa-Hian and Hwen Thsang with those preserved in the Buddhist annals of Ceylon, and I have shown conclusively that Fa-Hian's distance from *Sankisa* and his bearing from *Shachi* or *Sâket* are both erroneous. We know from Hwen Thsang and the Buddhist books of Ceylon that *Srâvasti* was to the north of *Sâket* or *Ajudhya*, or in other words that it was in the district of *Gauda* or *Uttara Kosala*, which is confirmed by the statements of no less than four of the Brahmanical Purânas. And as Fa-Hian also says that *Shewei* or *Sewet* was in Kosala, there can be no doubt whatever that Srâvasti must be looked for within a few days' journey to the northward of *Sâket* or *Ayodhya*. According to Fa-Hian the distance was 8 *yojanas*, or 56 miles, which is increased by Hwen Thsang to

500 *li*, or 83 miles.* But as the latter pilgrim reduced the Indian *yojana* to Chinese measure at the rate of 40 *li* per *yojana*, we may correct his distance by the nearest round number of 350 *li*, or 58 miles, to bring it into accordance with the other. Now, as this is the exact distance from Ajudhya of the great ruined city on the south bank of the Rapti, called *Sâhet-Mâhet*, in which I discovered a colossal statue of Buddha with an inscription contatining the name of Srâvasti itself, I have no hesitation in correcting Hwen Thsang's distance from 500 *li* to 350 *li*, as proposed above.

The ruined city of Sâhet-Mâhet is situated between Akaona and Balrâmpur, at 5 miles from the former and 12 miles from the latter, and at nearly equal distances from Bahraich and Gonda.† In shape it is an almost semicircular crescent, with its diameter of one mile and a third in length curved inwards and facing the north-east, along the old bank of the Rapti river. The western front, which runs due north and south, for three-quarters of a mile, is the only straight portion of the enclosure. The ramparts vary considerably in height; those to the west being from 35 to 40 feet in height, while those on the south and east are not more than 25 or 30 feet. The highest point is the great north-west bastion, which is 50 feet above the fields. The

* Beal's 'Fah-Hian,' c. xx. 73; Julien's 'Hiouen Thsang,' ii. 292.

† See Map No. XI. for its position.

north-east face, or shorter curve of the crescent, was defended by the Rapti, which still flows down its old bed during the annual floods. The land ramparts on the longer curve of the crescent must once have been defended by a ditch, the remains of which yet exist as a swamp, nearly half a mile in length, at the south-west corner. Everywhere the ramparts are covered with fragments of brick, of the large size peculiar to very ancient cities; and though I was unable to trace any remains of walls except in one place, yet the very presence of the bricks is quite sufficient to show that the earthen ramparts must once have been crowned by brick parapets and battlements. The portion of the parapet wall, which I discovered still standing in the middle of the river face, was 10 feet thick. The whole circuit of the old earthen ramparts, according to my survey, is 17,300 feet, or upwards of 3¼ miles. Now this is the exact size of 20 *li,* or 3⅓ miles, which Hwen Thsang gives to the palace alone; but, as the city was then deserted and in ruins, he must have mistaken the city itself for the palace. It is certain at least that the suburbs outside the walls must have been very limited indeed, as the place is almost entirely surounded with the remains of large religious buildings, which would have left but little room for any private dwellings. I am therefore quite satisfied that the city has been mistaken for the palace; and this mistake is sufficient to show how utterly ruined this once famous city must have been at so distant a period as the seventh century, when the place was visited by Hwen Thasng. As Fa-Hian describes the population as already very inconsiderable in A.D. 400, while the Ceylonese annals speak of *Khira-dhâra*, king of *Sawatthipura* between A.D. 275 and 302, the great decline of Srâvasti must have taken place during the fourth century, and we may perhaps not be far wrong in connecting it with the fall of the Gupta dynasty in A.D. 319.

Srâvasti is said to have been built by Raja *Srâvasta*,* the son of *Yuvanâswa* of the Solar race, and the tenth in descent from Surya himself. Its foundation therefore reaches to the fabulous ages of Indian history, long anterior to Râma. During this early period it most probably formed part of the kingdom of Ayodhya, as the Vâyu Purana assigns it to Lava, the son of Râma. When Srâvasti next appears in history, in the time of Buddha, it was the capital of King Prasenâjit, the son of Maha Kosala. The king became a convert to the new faith, and during the rest of his life he was the firm friend and protector of Buddha. But his son Virudhaka hated the race of the Sâkyas, and his invasion of their country and subsequent massacre of 500 Sâkya maidens, who had been selected for his harem, brought forth the famous prediction of Buddha, that within seven days the king would be consumed by fire. As the story has been preserved by Buddhists, the prediction was of course fulfilled, and upwards

* Wilson, 'Vishnu Purana,' book iv. p. 2; Hall's edit., vol. iv. p. 263.

of eleven centuries afterwards, the tank in which the king had sought to avoid the flames was pointed out to the credulous Hwen Thsang.*

We hear nothing more of Srâvasti until one century after Kanishka, or five centuries after Buddha, when, according to Hwen Thsang, Vikramâditya, king of Srâvasti, became a persecutor of Buddhists, and the famous Manorhita, author of the Vibhâsha Sâstra, being worsted in argument by the Brahmans, put himself to death. During the reign of his successor, whose name is not given, the Brahmans were overcome by *Vasubandhu*, the eminent disciple of *Manorhita*. The probable date of these two kings may be set down as ranging from A.D. 79 to 120. For the next two centuries *Srâvasti* would seem to have been under the rule of its own kings, as we find *Khiradhâra* and his nephew mentioned as Rajas between A.D. 275 and 319.† But there can be little doubt that during the whole of this time Srâvasti was only a dependency of the powerful Gupta dynasty of Magadha, as the neighbouring city of Sâketa is specially said to have belonged to them. "Princes of the Gupta race," says the Vâyu Purana, "will possess all those countries; the banks of the Ganges to Prayâga, and Sâketa, and Magadha."‡ From this time Srâvasti gradually declined. In A.D. 400

* Julien's 'Hiouen Thsang,' ii. 306.

† Turnour, in Journ. Asiat. Soc. Bengal, vi. 865.

‡ Quoted in Wilson's 'Vishnu Purana,' p. 479, note ; and Hall's edition, iv. 218.

it contained only 200 families; in A.D. 632 it was completely deserted; and at the present day the whole area of the city, excepting only a few clearances near the gateways, is a mass of almost impenetrable jangal.

There is a difference in the name of the city, which Fa-Hian gives as *She-wei*, while Hwen Thsang writes it, as correctly as is possible in Chinese syllables, *She-lo-fa-si-ti* or *Srâvasti*. But this difference is more apparent than real, as there can be little doubt that *Shewei* is only a slight alteration of the abbreviated Pali form of *Sewet*, for *Sâwatthi*, which is found in most of the Ceylonese books. Similarly the modern name of *Sâhet* is evidently only a variation of the Pali *Sâwet*. The other name of *Mâhet* I am unable to explain; but it is perhaps only the usual rhyming addition of which the Hindus are so fond, as in *ulta-pulta*, or "topsy-turvy," which many people say is the true meaning of *Sâhet-mâhet*, in allusion to the utter ruin of the whole place. But some say that the name was originally *Set-met*, and as this form seems to be a corruption of *Sewet*, it is probable that *Sahet-Mahet* is only a lengthened pronunciation of *Set-met*. One man alone, a Muhammadan in charge of the tomb of Pir Barâna close to the ruined city, affirmed that the true name was *Sâvitri*, which is so close to the correct Pali form of *Sâwatthi* as to leave but little doubt that it preserves the original name of the place.

Hwen Thsang assigns to the kingdom of *Srâvasti* a circuit of 4000 *li*, or 667 miles, which is about double the actual size of the territory lying between the Ghâgra river and the foot of the mountains; but as he assigns the same dimensions to the territory of Nepâl, it is probable that in his time the two western districts of Malbhûm and Khâchi, in the hills to the north, may at that time have belonged to Srâvasti. The territory of Srâvasti would thus have comprised all the country lying between the Himâlaya mountains and the Ghâgra river, from the Karnâli river on the west to the mountain of Dhaolagiri and Faizâbâd on the east. The circuit of this tract is about 600 miles, or very nearly the same as the estimated measurement of Hwen Thsang.

19. KAPILA.

From Srâvasti both of the Chinese pilgrims proceeded direct to *Kapila,* which was famous throughout India as the birth-place of Buddha. Hwen Thsang makes the distance 500 *li,* or 83 miles, to the south-east;* but according to the earlier pilgrim Fa-Hian the distance was 13 *yojanas,* or 91 miles, in the same direction.† The difference of 1 *yojana,* or 7 miles, seems to be due to some confusion as to the relative positions of *Kapila,* and the birth-place of Krakuchanda, which were just one *yojana* apart. Fa-Hian reached the latter place first before visiting Kapila; but Hwen Thsang went first to Kapila, and afterwards to the birth-place of Krakuchanda. As

* Julien's 'Hiouen Thsang,' ii. 309.

† Beal's 'Fah-Hian,' xxi—xxii.

the site of this place may with great probability be identified with *Kakūa*, 8 miles to the west of *Nagar*, which I propose to identify with *Kapila-nagara*, I am inclined to adopt the narrative of Fa-Hian. Now the distance between *Sâhet* and *Nagar* is rather more than 81½ miles, as I found the road from Sâhet to Asokpur 42½ miles, and from Asokpur to Nagar the distance is 39 miles measured direct on the large map of the Indian Atlas. The actual distance by the winding roads of this part of the country cannot therefore be less than 85 miles, and is probably about 90 miles, as stated by Fa-Hian.

Hwen Thsang estimates the circuit of the district at 4000 *li*, or 667 miles, which agrees very well with the size of the tract lying between the Ghâgra and the Gandak from Faizâbâd to the confluence of those rivers. The direct measurement is 550 miles, which would be upwards of 600 miles in road distance.*

No trace of the name of Kapila has yet been discovered; but I believe that the position of the city can be fixed within very narrow limits by many concurring data. According to the Buddhist chronicles of Tibet, *Kapilavastu* or *Kapilanagara* was founded by some descendants of the solar hero Gotama,† on the bank of a lake near the river Rohini in Kosala. Now the town of *Nagar*, or *Nagar-khâs*,

---

* See Map No. XI.

† Csoma de Körös in Journ. Asiat. Soc. Bengal, ii. 391.

that is "the city," is situated on the eastern bank of the Chando Tâl, near a large stream named Kohâna, a tributary of the Rapti, and in the northern division of Oudh beyond the Ghâgra river, and therefore in Kosala. Its distance and bearing from Srâvasti have already been noted as agreeing most precisely with those stated by the Chinese pilgrims. To the west a small stream named *Sidh* falls into the lake. This name, which means the "perfect or the holy one," is always applied to the sages of antiquity, and in the present instance I think that it may refer to the sage Kapila, whose hermitage was also on the bank of the lake opposite the city. The Gautamas had at first established themselves near the sage's dwelling; but, as the lowing of their kine had disturbed his meditations, they founded their new city of *Kapilanagara* at some distance, that is on the opposite or eastern end of the lake.

The position of the Rohini river is more precisely indicated by the Chinese pilgrims and Ceylonese chronicles. According to Fa-Hian* the royal garden, named *Lun-ming*, or Lumbini, in which Buddha was born, was situated at 50 *li*, or 8⅓ miles, to the east of Kapila. Hwen Thsang† calls the garden *La-fa-ni*, and places it on the bank of a small stream flowing to the south-east which the people called the "River of Oil." According to the Ceylonese Chronicles,‡ the Rohini flowed

* Beal's 'Fah-Hian,' xxii. 87.

† 'Hiouen Thsang,' ii. 322.

‡ Hardy's 'Manual of Buddhism,' p. 307.

between the cities of Kapila and Koli, the latter being the birth-place of Mâyâ Devi, the mother of Buddha. It was also called *Vyâghra-pura,* or "Tiger-town."* When Mâyâ was near her confinement she went to pay a visit to her parents at Koli. "Between the two cities there was a garden of *Sâl* trees called *Lumbini,* to which the inhabitants of both cities were accustomed to resort for recreation." There she rested and gave birth to the infant Buddha. In another place it is said that during a season of drought the inhabitants of Kapila and Koli quarrelled about the distribution of the waters of the Rohini for the irrigation of their rice-fields.† From all these details I infer that the *Rohini* was most probably the *Kohâna* river of the present day, which flows in a south-easterly course about 6 miles to the eastward of Nagar. It is the *Kooana* and *Quana* of the maps, and the *Koyane* of Buchanan,‡ who describes it as "a fine little river, which, with its numerous branches, fertilizes all the south-eastern parts of the district." It therefore corresponds in all essential particulars with the Rohini of the Buddhist chronicles.

The position of *Koli* is doubtful; but it may perhaps be referred to the village of *Am Kohil,* which is exactly 11 miles to the east of *Nagar,* and rather less than 3 miles from the nearest point of the Kohâna river. The road from Nagar to *Kohil*

---

* Hardy's 'Manual of Buddhism,' p. 136.

† *Ibid.*, p. 307.

‡ 'Eastern India,' ii. 301.

crosses the Kohâna opposite the small town of *Mokson,* which may probably be the site of the once famous Lumbini garden, as it was also called *parâdi-mokṣha,** or "supreme beatitude." In later times this appellation would have been shortened to *Mokṣha* or *Mokṣhan,* to which I would refer the possible origin of Hwen Thsang's name of the "River of Oil," as *mrakṣhan* is the Sanskrit term for oil. Abul Fazl calls the place of Buddha's birth *Mokṭa,*† which is perhaps only a misreading of *Mokṣa.*

Another strong point in favour of the identification of Nagar with the ancient Kapila is the fact that the present chief of Nagar is a *Gautama Rajput,* and the districts of Nagar and Amorha are the head-quarters of the clan, as well as of the *Gautamiya Rajputs,* who are an inferior branch of the Gautamas. Now the *Sâkyas* of Kapilavastu were also *Gautama* Rajputs, and *Sâkya Muni* himself is still known amongst the people of Barma as *Gautama Buddha,* or simply *Gautama.* In the Vansalata‡ the *Gautamas* are said to be descendants of *Arkabandhu,* which is one of the names of Buddha given in the Amara Kosha of the famous Amara Sinha, who was himself a Buddhist.

I have not visited Nagar myself, but I am informed that it possesses a *khera,* or mound of brick

* '*Fo-kwe-ki,*' c. xxii., note 17, by Klaproth.
† 'Ayin Akbari,' ii. 503.
‡ Buchanan, 'Eastern India,' ii. 458.

ruins, and that there are numerous remains of brick buildings in the neighbourhood. As Fa-Hian describes Kapila in the beginning of the fifth century as "literally a vast solitude, in which there was neither king nor people," but only a few monks and some ten or twenty houses, it is scarcely possible that there would be any conspicuous traces of the city which has lain desolate for upwards of twelve centuries. In the middle of the seventh century Hwen Thsang found the place so utterly ruined that it was impossible to ascertain its original size, I am therefore quite satisfied that the absence of any extensive ruins at the present day cannot overthrow the very strong claims which *Nagar* certainly possesses to be identified with the ancient city of Kapila. But this identification is still further strengthened by the names of several places in the vicinity, which would appear to represent some of the more holy spots that were famous in the early history of Buddhism. I allude more especially to the birth-places of the two previous Buddhas, *Kraḳuchanda* and *Kanaḳa-muni*, and the *Sara-ḳupa*, or "arrow-fountain," which sprang into existence at the stroke of Buddha's arrow.

Fa-Hian names *Na-pi-ḳia* as the birthplace of Krakuchanda; but in the Buddhist chronicles* the city is called *Kshemavati* and *Khemavati*.† In the

* '*Sapta Buddha Stotra*,' quoted by Remusat in 'Fo-kwe-ki,' c. xxi. note 3.

† Turnour's 'Mahawanso,' Introduction, p. 33.

books of Ceylon, however,* *Krakuchanda* is said to have been the *Purohit*, or family priest, of Raja Kshema, of *Mekhala*. According to Fa-Hian, the city was about 1 *yojana*, or 7 miles, to the west-north-west of Kapila; but according to Hwen Thsang it was 50 *li*, or 8⅓ miles, to the south of Kapila. In the absence of other data, it is difficult to say which of these statements may be correct; but as I find a town named *Kaküa*, exactly 8 miles to the west of Nagar, I am strongly inclined to adopt the account of Fa-Hian, as *Kaku* is the Pali form of *Kraku*. According to Hwen Thsang's bearing, the city should be looked for in the neighbourhood of Kalwâri Khâs, which is 7 miles to the south of Nagar.

A similar discrepancy is found in the position of the birthplace of *Kanaka-muni*, which, according to Fa-Hian, was to the south of Krakuchanda's birthplace, but to the north-east of it according to Hwen Thsang. They agree exactly as to the distance, which the latter makes 30 *li*, or just 5 miles, while the former calls it somewhat less than 1 *yojana*, that is about 5 or 6 miles. In the Ceylonese chronicles the town is named *Sobhavati-nagara*,† which may possibly be represented by the village of *Subhay-Pursa*, at 6½ miles to the south-east of Kaküa, and the same distance to the south-west of Nagar.

The same unaccountable difference of bearing

---

* Hardy's 'Manual of Buddhism,' p. 96.

† 'Mahawanso,' Introduction, p. 34.

is found also in the position of the *Sara-Kupa*, or the "Arrow Fountain," which Fa-Hian places at 30 *li*, or 5 miles, to the south-west of Kapila, while Hwen Thsang places it at the same distance to the south-east. In this instance also I believe that Fa-Hian is right, as Hwen Thsang makes the distance from the *Sara-Kupa* to the *Lumbini* garden from 80 to 90 *li*, or 13 to 15 miles, which, as I have already shown, was on the bank of the Rohini or Kohâna river, to the east of Kapila. Now, if the Arrow Fountain was to the south-east of the capital, its distance from the *Lumbini* garden could not have been more than 6 or 7 miles, whereas if it was to the south-west, as stated by Fa-Hian, the distance would be about 12 or 13 miles. The probable position of the *Sara-Kupa*, or Arrow Fountain, may therefore be fixed near the village of *Sarwanpur*, which is exactly 5½ miles to the south-west of Nagar.

In proposing all these identifications, I have assumed that *Nagar* is the site of the ancient *Kapila*, but as I have not examined this part of the country myself, and as the information which I have been able to obtain is necessarily vague, I feel that the final settlement of this important inquiry can only be satisfactorily determined by an actual examination of Nagar itself and the surrounding localities. In the meantime I offer the results of the present disquisition as useful approximations until the true sites shall be determined by actual observation.

Râmagrâma.

From Kapila both pilgrims proceeded to *Lan-mo,* which has been identified with the *Râmagrâma* of the Buddhist chronicles of India. Fa-Hian makes the distance 5 *yojanas,* or 35 miles, to the east,* and Hwen Thsang gives 200 *li,* or 33⅓ miles, in the same direction.† But in spite of their agreement I believe that the distance is in excess of the truth. Their subsequent march to the bank of the *Anoma* river is said to be 3 *yojanas* or 21 miles by Fa-Hian, and 100 *li* or 16⅔ miles by Hwen Thsang, thus making the total distance from Kapila to the Anoma river 8 *yojanas,* or 56 miles, according to the former, and 300 *li,* or 50 miles, according to the latter. But in the Indian Buddhist scriptures, this distance is said to be only 6 *yojanas,* or 42 miles, which I believe to be correct, as the *Aumi* river of the present day, which is most probably the *Anoma* river of the Buddhist books, is just 40 miles distant from Nagar in an easterly direction. The identification of the Anoma will be discussed presently.

According to the pilgrims' statements, the position of *Râmagrâma* must be looked for at about two thirds of the distance between Nagar and the Anoma river, that is at 4 *yojanas,* or 28 miles. In this position I find the village of Deokali,‡ with a mound of ruins, which was usde as a station for the trigono-

---

* Beal's 'Fah-Hian,' c. xxii. p. 89.

† Julien's 'Hiouen Thsang,' ii. 325.

‡ See Map No. XI.

metrical survey. In the 'Mahawanso' it is stated that the stupa of Râmagâmo, which stood on the bank of the *Ganges*, was destroyed by the action of the current.* Mr. Laidlay has already pointed out that this river could not be the Ganges; but might be either the *Ghâgra*, or some other large river in the north. But I am inclined to believe that the Ganges is a simple fabrication of the Ceylonese chronicler. All the Buddhist scriptures agree in stating that the relics of Buddha were divided into eight portions, of which one fell to the lot of the Kosalas of *Râmagrâma*, over which they erected a stupa. Some years later seven portions of the relics were collected together by Ajatasatru, king of Magadha, and enshrined in a single stupa at Râjagriha; but the eighth portion still remained at Râmagrâma. According to the Ceylonese chronicler, the stupa of Râmagrâma was washed away by the Ganges, and the relic casket, having been carried down the river to the ocean, was discovered by the *Nâgas*, or water gods, and presented to their king, who built a stupa for its reception. During the reign of Dutthagâmini of Ceylon, B.C. 161 to 137, the casket was miraculously obtained from the Nâga king by the holy monk Sonuttaro, and enshrined in the *Mahathupo*, or "great stupa," in the land of Lanka.†

Now this story is completely at variance with the statements of the Chinese pilgrims, both of whom

---

*'Mahawanso,' c. xxxi. p. 185.

† 'Mahawanso,' c. xxxi.

visited Ramâgrâma many centuries after Duttha-gâmini, when they found the relic stupa intact, but no river. Fa-Hian,* in the beginning of the fifth century, saw a tank beside the stupa, in which a dragon (*Nâga*) lived, who continually watched the tower. In the middle of the seventh century, Hwen Thsang† saw the same stupa and the same tank of clear water inhabited by dragons (*Nâgas*), who daily transformed themselves into men, and paid their devotions to the stupa.‡ Both pilgrims mention the attempt of Asoka to remove these relics to his own capital, which was abandoned on the expostulation of the Nâga king. "If by thy oblations," said the Nâga, "thou canst excel this, thou mayest destroy the tower, and I shall not prevent thee." Now according to the Ceylonese chronicler, this is the very same argument that was used by the Nâga king to dissuade the priest Sonuttaro from removing the relics to Ceylon.§ I infer, therefore, that the original "tank" of Râmagrâma was adroitly changed into a river by the Ceylonese author, so that the relics which were in charge of the Nâgas of the tank, might be conveyed to the ocean-palace of the Nâga king, from whence they could as readily be transferred to Ceylon as to any other place. The river was thus a necessity in the Ceylonese legend, to convey the relics away from Râmagrâma to the

---

* Beal's 'Fa-Hian,' c. xxiii. p. 90.

† Julien's 'Hiouen Thsang,' ii. 326.

‡ *Ibid.*

§ 'Mahawanso,' c. xxxi. p. 188.

ocean. But the authority of a legend can have no weight against the united testimony of the two independent pilgrims, who many centuries later found the stupa still standing, but saw no river. I therefore dismiss the Ganges as a fabrication of the Ceylonese chriniclers, and accept in its stead the Nâga tank of the Chinese pilgrims. Having thus got rid of the river, I can see no objection to the identification of *Deokali* with the Râmagrâma of Buddhist history. The town was quite deserted at the time of Fa-Hian's visit, in the fifth century, who found only a small religious establishment; this was still kept up in the middle of the seventh century, but it must have been very near its dissolution, as there was only a single *srâmanera,* or monk, to conduct the affairs of the monastery.

River Anoma.

The river Anoma was famous in the history of Buddhism as the scene of Prince Siddhârta's assumption of the dress of an ascetic, where he cut off his hair, and dismissed his attendant and his horse. According to the Burmese* and Ceylonese† chronicles, the distance from Kapila was 30 *yojanas,* or about 210 miles,—a mistake which must have originated in an erroneous opinion that the river was

* Bigandet, 'Legend of the Burmese Buddha,' p. 41.

† Turnour, Journ. Asiat. Soc. Bengal, vii. 809. Hardy, 'Manual of Buddhism,' p. 160, says 480 miles, from which it is evident that he has adopted Turnour's erroneous valuation of the *yojana* at 16 miles.

exactly halfway between Kapila and Rajagriha, as the total distance is said to be 60 *yojanas*. In the Tibetan translation of the *Lalita Vistâra*,* the distance is stated at 6 *yojanas*, or 42 miles. This is somewhat less than the estimates of Fa-Hian and Hwen Thsang, but as the former is made up of two distances, given in whole *yojanas*, and the latter of two distances, given in round hundreds of *li*, they can only be accepted as approximations. Thus Fa-Hian's 5 *yojanas*, plus 3 *yojanas*, may have been only 4½ and 2½ *yojanas*, and Hwen Thsang's 200 *li*, plus 100 *li*, may have been actually only 180 *li*, plus 80 *li*. The former may thus be reduced to 7 *yojanas*, or 49 miles, and the latter to 260 *li*, or 43 miles. I therefore accept the 6 *yojanas*, or 42 miles, of the *Lalita Vistâra* as the nearest approach to the real distance that could be stated in whole *yojanas*.

When Prince Siddhârta left Kapila to enter upon the life of an ascetic, he took the road by Vaisâli to Rajagriha. The general direction of his route was therefore nearly east-south-east past Deokali to the bank of the *Aumi* river below Sangrâmpur, and above the point where it enters the *Aumiyar* Lake.† As the course of the Aumi is from north-west to south-east, the distance from Nagar varies from 40 to 45 miles.

* Foucaux, French translation, p. 214.

† 'Eastern India,' ii. 314. Buchanan calls it the *Nawar* Lake, but in the Atlas of India and other Government Maps it is named the *Amiyar* Tâl, and the river is called the *Ami* Nadi.

The route could not have crossed the river above Sangrâmpur, as the distance would be under 40 miles, nor below the Aumiyar Lake, which discharges itself by a very short channel into the Rapti. If the data are correct, the pint of crossing must have been just above the head of the Aumiyar Lake.

Now *Aumi*, or in Sanskrit *Avami*, means "inferior," and as the name of a river it would be descriptive of its small size as compared with other rivers in its neighbourhood. A glance at the map is sufficient to show that the *Aumi* is an old bed of the Rapti, which left the present channel near Dumariyaganj. A main branch of the Aumi, named the *Budh Nali*, or "old river," which rises in the neighbourhood of Bânsi, is still supplied from the Rapti during the rainy season by a channel called *Daldal Nala*, or "Quicksand Stream." This fact alone affords a most decisive proof that the lower course of the Aumi, below the junction of the Budh Nala near Balehar, is an old bed of the Rapti. The name of *Aumi* or *Avami Nadi*, the "inferior" or "lesser river," was therefore an appropriate appellation of the old channel to distinguish it from the larger or main stream of the Rapti.

According to the *Lalita Vistâra* the point where Buddha crossed the river was at the town of *Maneya*, in the district of *Anuvaineya*.* The name of the town is unknown, but that of the district would appear to be the same as *Anaola*, which is the name

---

* Foucaux, translation from Tibetan, p. 214.

of the division on the western bank of the lower course of the Aumi river, which includes both Sangrâmpur and the Aumiyar lake. *Anuvaineya* means the country along the *Vaineya* river, or on the lower course of the *Vaineya*. The name is probably derived from *Venu,* a "bambu," and if so it would mean "Bambu river," and would thus be equivalent to *Bânsi,* which might be appropriately applied to it, either on account of the *bambus* on its banks, or because it flows past the town of *Bânsi.*

The Buddhist legends of Barma and Ceylon are unanimous in stating that Prince Siddhârta, on reaching the bank of the stream where he dismissed his attendants and horse, inquired its name, and on being informed that it was called *Anoma,* made a remark in allusion to the name of the river, which is differently rendered by the translators. According to the Burmese legend* the name of the river was *Anauma,* on hearing which the prince remarked, "I will *not* show myself *unworthy* of the high dignity I aspire to." Then "spurring his horse, the fierce animal leaped at once to the opposite bank." Mr. Hardy states the occurrence even more briefly :† "On arriving at the river he inquired its name from the noble, and when he was told that it was *Anoma,* 'illustrious or honourable,' he received it as another omen in his favour." Turnour gives the story at

---

* 'Legend of the Burmese Buddha,' by Bishop Bigandet, p. 41.

† 'Manual of Buddhism,' p. 160.

length from the Ceylonese *Attakatha* of the Buddhawanso.* Prince Siddhârta inquired of Chhando, " 'What is the name of this river?'—'Lord, its name is *Anomâ.*' Replying, 'Nor will there be any *Anoma* (inferiority) in my ordination,' he pressed his heel to the horse and gave him the signal to leap." Turnour notes that "this remark involves a pun;" but that a pun "is by no means a matter of levity in Buddhistical literature." By some oversight, Turnour has rendered *anoma* by "inferiority," whereas its meaning is exactly the reverse, and is correctly given by Hardy and Bishop Bigandet. According to the text of the Burmese and Ceylonese chronicles, it would appear that the name of the river was *Anoma*, the "not inferior," that is the "superior," and the prince's remark must have been that so also would his ordination be *anoma*, or "superior." But as the name of the river at the present day is *Aumi*, or "inferior," and as Turnour's translation of the word as "inferiority" would seem to show that in his copy at least the name was *Oma* or *Auma*, I cannot help suspecting that this is the true reading; and that when the prince was informed that the name of the river was *Auma*, or "inferior," he remarked "My ordination shall be *anauma*," or "superior." If the original name of the stream had been *Anoma*, it is difficult to understand how it could have been changed to *Aumi*, which has the very opposite meaning. But if it was properly

* Journ. Asiat. Soc. Bengal, vii. 808.

Aumi, that is the "inferior" or lesser branch of the Rapti, and it was arbitrarily changed by the Buddhists to *Anauma*, a return to the use of the original name would have been only a natural consequence of the downfall of Buddhism.

But the identification of the Buddhistical *Anoma* with the modern Aumi is still further confirmed by the existence of three significant names on the eastern bank of the river, within a short distance of the point which I have assigned for the prince's passage of the stream. On reaching the opposite bank, the prince alighted from his horse and directed his attendant *Chandaka* to return to Kapila.* At this spot there stood a stupa called *Chandaka-nivarttana*, or "Chandaka's return," which in the spoken dialects would probably have been shortened to *Chanda-bartta*. This place may, I think, be identified with the village of *Chandaoli* on the eastern bank of the Aumi river, near the head of the Aumiyar Lake, and 10 miles to the south of Gorakhpur. With his sword the prince then cut off his long locks of hair, *chuda*, which being thrown aloft were caught by the gods, who built a stupa on the spot called *Chuda-patta-graha*, or the "heap of hair-locks." In the spoken dialects this name would have been shortened to *Chuda-gaha*, which, I think, may be identified with the village of *Chureya*, 3 miles to the north of Chandaoli. The prince next changed his royal

* 'Lalita Vistâra.' Foucaux, translation from Tibetan, p. 214.

garments, called *kâsâya*, because made of the fine fabrics of *Kâsi*, or Banâras, for the plain dress of an ascetic; and on the spot where this took place the people erected a stupa, named *Kâsâya-grahan*, or "doffed garments." This place I would identify with the village of *Kaseyar*, 3½ miles to the south-east of Chandaoli. In favour of these identifications I may mention that Hwen Thsang places the stupa of the "doffed garments" to the east of that of "Chandaka's return;" but his position of the stupa of the "cut hair" at a short distance from that of the "doffed garments" is directly opposed to the site that I have suggested at Chureya, which is 6 miles to the north of Kaseyar. It seems probable, therefore, that one of my suggested identifications must be wrong; but as the other two would appear to agree with the relative positions assigned by Hwen Thsang, I think that they are probably correct.

Pippalavana.

From the Anoma river both of the Chinese pilgrims proceeded to visit the stupa that was erected at *Pippalawano* over the charcoal ashes of the funeral pile of Buddha. The *Moriyas* of this city, having applied too late for a share of the relics of the body, were obliged to be content with the ashes. Fa-Hian places the stupa at 4 *yojanas*, or 28 miles, to the east of the Anoma; but Hwen Thsang makes the distance 180 to 190 *li*, or from 30 to 32 miles, and the bearing south-east. Fa-Hian does not mention the name of the town, but in he Burmese* and Ceylonese chronicles† it is called *Pippali-wano,* or the "Pippal-forest;" and in the Tibetan *Dulva*‡ it is called the town of the *Nyagrodha,* or Banian-trees. Hwen Thsang also speaks of the "forest of *Nyagrodha*-trees" as the site of the "charcoal stupa," and as he actually visited the place, we must accept his testimony in preference to that of the distant chroniclers of Ceylon. No place of this name is now known; but in the south-east direction indicated by Hwen Thsang, there is a large forest which completely surrounds the ruins of an ancient city called *Sahankat.* This place is described at length by Buchanan,§ who found several statues of Buddha amongst the ruins. It was therefore certainly in existence during the flourishing period of Buddhism. It is 20 miles distant from the Chandaoli Ghat, on the Aumi, measured in a direct line on the map; but by the road it is not less than 25 miles, owing to the numerous streams that intersect the route. The position therefore corresponds as nearly as possible with that assigned to the Charcoal Tower by Hwen Thsang, but I have no confirmatory evidence to offer, unless the name of the village of Srinagar *Kolua* may be connected with

* Bigandet, 'Legend of the Burmese Buddha,' p. 212.

† Turnour, Journ. Asiat. Soc. Bengal, vii. 1013.

‡ 'Asiatic Researches,' Bengal, xx.

§ 'Eastern India,' ii. 370. See Map No. XI. for its position.

Koïl, or charcoal, which is not very probable. I may add, however, that the bearing of *Kasia* from Sahankat corresponds with the north-east direction of Kusinagara from the Charcoal Stupa which is recorded by Hwen Thsang.

20. KUSINAGARA.

Fa-Hian places *Kusinagara* at 12 *yojanas,* or 84 miles, to the eastward of the Charcoal Stupa, a distance which is quite impossible when compared with its other recorded distances from Vaisâli and Banâras.* Unfortunately, Hwen Thsang, contrary to his usual custom, has omitted to note the distance, and simply states that he travelled in a north-east direction for a long time through a vast forest, full of wild bulls and wild elephants, and infested with brigands. A portion of this forest still exists to the north and east of *Sahankat,* and wild elephants still abound in the *Tarai* forests to the north of Gorakhpur. Wilson first proposed *Kasia* as the site of Kusinagara, and the suggestion has since been generally adopted. The village is situated exactly 35 miles to the east of Gorakhpur, at the crossing of two great thoroughfares.† It is 28 miles to the north-east of *Sahankat* in a direct line measured on the map, or about 35 miles by road. The distance is therefore only 5 *yojanas,* instead of 12, as noted by Fa-Hian. It cannot be placed further to the north-east without

* Beal's 'Fah-Hian,' xxiv. 93.

† See Map No. XI. for its position.

increasing its distance from Banâras, and lessening its distance from Vaisâli. Now the former is limited by Hwen Thsang to 700 *li*, or 117 miles, and the latter is fixed by Fa-Hian himself at 25 *yojanas*, or 175 miles; and as both estimates agree very closely with the actual position of *Kasia*, I am satisfied that Fa-Hian's 12 *yojanas* must be a mistake. Anrudhwa, near Kasia, is exactly 111 miles to the north-north-east of Banâras, measured in a direct line on the map, and cannot, therefore, be less than 120 miles by road. The distance between Kasia and Vaisâli, by the route which I marched, is just 140 miles; but this was along the new straight lines which have been laid out by the British authorities. By the old winding native tracks the distance would have been much greater, or certainly not less than 160 miles.

At the time of Hwen Thsang's visit the walls of *Kusinagara* were in ruins, and the place was almost deserted; but the brick foundations of the old capital occupied a circuit of about 12 *li*, or 2 miles. The existing ruins between Anrudhwa and Kasia are scattered over a much larger space; but some of these were certainly outside the city, and it is now quite impossible to ascertain its exact limits. It most probably occupied the site of the mound of ruins to the north-east of the village of Anrudhwa. The spot where Buddha obtained *Nirvâna* would then correspond with the site of the stupa and ruins now called *Mâtha-ḳuär-ḳa-ḳot*, or the "fort of the Dead Prince," and the spot where his body was burned would correspond with the site of the great stupa now called *Devisthân*. The former lies to the north-west of Anrudhwa, and to the west of the old channel of the *Chota Gandak*, or *Hiranyavati* river, which is still occasionally filled after heavy rain. The latter lies to the north-east of Anrudhwa, and to the east of the old channel of the *Hirana*, or Chota Gandak.

The only name now associated with the ruins near Kasia is that of *Mâthâ Kuär*, or the "Dead Prince." Mr. Liston gives the name as *Mâta*, but a Brahman of the neighbouring village of Bishanpur, who wrote the name for me, spelt it as I have given it, *Mâthâ*. As this spelling points to the derivation of the word from *Matha*, or Mâtha, "to kill," I have translated *Mâthâ Kuär* as the "Dead Prince," which I refer to Buddha himself after his death, or, in the language of the Buddhists, after his obtainment of *Nirvâna*. Hwen Thsang, when speaking of *Sâkya's* assumption of the mendicant's dress, calls him *Kumâra Râja*, or the "Royal Prince;" but although this title was never, I believe, applied to him by the learned after his assumption of Buddhahood, it does not seem at all improbable that it may have remained in common use amongst the people. We know from Hwen Thsang that on the spot where Buddha died there was a brick *vihâr*, or temple monastery, in which was enshrined a recumbent statue of Buddha on his death-bed, with his head towards the north. Now this statue would naturally have been the principal object of veneration at

Kusinagara, and although amongst the learned it might have been called the "statue of the *Nirvâna,*" yet I can readily believe that its more popular name amongst all classes would have been the "statue of the Dead Prince." I am therefore of opinion that the name of *Mâthâ Kuär,* which still clings to the ruins of Kasia, has a direct reference to the death of Buddha, which, according to his followers, took place at Kusinagara, on the full moon of the Vaisâkh, 543 B.C. The continuance of this name down to the present day is a strong argument in favour of the identification of *Kasia* as the "death-place" of Buddha.

Khukhundo—Kahaon.

On leaving Kusinagara, Hwen Thsang directed his steps towards Banâras, and after having travelled about 200 *li,* or 33 miles, to the south-west, he reached a large town where lived a Brahman who was devoted to Buddhism.* If we adhere rigidly to the south-west bearing, we must identify this large town with *Sahankat,* near Rudrapur. But this place has already been identified with *Pippalavana,* and is not upon the high-road to Banâras. As Hwen Thsang specially mentions the Brahman's hospitality to travellers going and coming, it is certain that the large town must have been on the high-road between Kusinagara and Banâras. Now the high-road could never have passed through Rudrapur, as it would

* Julien's 'Hiouen Thsang,' ii. 349.

have entailed the passage of the Rapti in addition to that of the Ghâgra, while Rudrapur itself is not on the direct line to Banâras. It is quite clear that the high-road must have crossed the Ghâgra somewhere below the junction of the Rapti. According to the people, the old passage of the Ghâgra was at *Mahili*, 4 miles to the south of *Kahaon*, and 7 miles below the confluence of the two rivers. From *Kasia* to the Mahili Ghât the route would have passed through the ancient towns of *Khukhundo* and *Kahaon*, both of which still possess many remains of antiquity. But the former is only 28 miles from Kasia, while the latter is 35 miles. Both are undoubtedly Brahmanical; but while the ruins at Khukhundo are nearly all of middle age, those at Kahaon are at least as old as the time of Skanda Gupta, who lived several centuries before the time of Hwen Thsang. I am inclined, therefore, to prefer the claim of Kahaon as the representative of Hwen Thsang's ancient city, partly on account of its undoubted antiquity, and partly because its distance from Kasia agrees better with the pilgrim's estimate than that of the larger town of Khukhundo.*

Pâwâ, or Padraona.

In the Ceylonese chronicles the town of *Pâwâ* is mentioned as the last halting-place of Buddha

---

* See Map No. XI. for the positions of both places.

before reaching Kusinagara, where he died. After his death it is again mentioned in the account of Kâsyapa's journey to Kusinagara to attend at the cremation of Buddha's corpse. *Pâwâ* was also famous as one of the eight cities which obtained a share of the relics of Buddha. In the Ceylonese chronicles it is noted as being only 12 miles from Kusinagara,* towards the Gandak river. Now 12 miles to the north-north-east of Kasia there is a considerable village named *Padaraona*, or *Padara-vana*, with a large mound covered with broken bricks, in which several statues of Buddha have been found. The name of *Padara-vana*, or *Padarban*, might easily be shortened to *Parban*, *Paban*, and *Pâwâ*. In the Tibetan '*Kahgyur*'† this town is called *Digpachan*, but as the meaning of the name is not given, it is impossible to say whether it is an original Indian name or a Tibetan translation. Between Pâwâ and Kusinagara there was a stream called *Kukutthâ* or *Kukukhâ*,‡ at which Buddha stopped to bathe and drink. This must be the present *Bâdhi*, or *Barhi*, or *Bandhi* Nala, which, after a course of 36 miles, joins the *Chota Gandak*, or *Hirana* river on its left bank, 8 miles below Kasia.

---

* Turnour, Journ. Asiat. Soc. Bengal, viii. 1005 ; note from Buddhaghoso.

† Csoma de Körös, Bengal 'Asiatic Researches,' xx.

‡ The first name is found in the Ceylonese chronicles, the second in the Burmese version.

21. VARÂNASI, OR BANÂRAS.

In the seventh century the kingdom of *Po.lo.-ni.sse*, or *Varânasi,* was 4000 *li,* or 667 miles, in circuit, and the capital, which was on the western bank of the Ganges, was from 18 to 19 *li,* or 3 miles, in length, and from 5 to 6 *li,* or 1 mile, in breadth. Its probable boundaries, with reference to the surrounding kingdoms, were the Gomati river on the north, a line drawn from the Gomati to Allahâbâd and up the Tons to Bilhâri on the west, a line drawn from Bilhâri to Sonhat on the south, and the Rehand Karmmnâsa and Ganges rivers on the east. With these limits the circuit is 595 miles taken direct on the map, or about 650 miles in actual road measurement.

The city of Banâras is situated on the left bank of the Ganges, between the *Barnâ Nad*i on the north-east, and the *Asi Nâla* on the south-west. The *Barnâ,* or *Varanâ,* is a considerable rivulet, which rises to the north of Allahâbâd, and has a course of about 100 miles. The *Asi* is a mere brook, of no length, and, owing to its insignificant size, it does not appear in any of our most detailed maps. It is not entered in the Indian Atlas Sheet, No. 88, which is on the scale of 4 miles to the inch, nor even in the larger lithographed map of the district of Banâras, on the double scale of 2 miles to the inch. This omission has led the learned French academician M. Vivien de Saint-Martin to doubt the existence of the *Asi* as a tributary of the

Ganges, and he conjectures that it may be only a branch of the *Barnâ,* and that the joint stream called the *Varânasi** may have communicated its name to the city. The *Asi Nâla* will, however, be found as I have described it, in James Prinsep's map of the city of Benares, published by Hullmandel, as well as in the small map which I have prepared to illustrate this account of the remains at Banâras. The position of the *Asi* is also accturately described by H. H. Wilson in his Sanskrit Dictionary, under the word *Varânasi.* I may add that the road from Banâras to *Râmnagar* crosses the *Asi* just outside the city, and only a short distance from its confluence with the river. The points of junction of both streams with the Ganges are considered particularly holy, and accordingly temples have been erected both at *Barnâ Sangam* below the city, and at *Asi Sangam* above the city. From the joint names of these two streams, which bound the city to the north and south, the Brahmans derive *Varânasi,* or *Vâranasi,* which is said to be the Sanskrit form of the name of Banâras. But the more usual derivation amongst the common people is from Râja *Banâr,* who is said to have rebuilt the city about 800 years ago.

Both of these streams are mentioned by Abul

---

* In M. Julien's 'Life and Pilgrimage of Hiouen Thsang,' i. 132, and ii. 354, it is stated that "this river is also called *Po-lo-ni-se,* or *Varânasi.*" But this is a mistake of the translator, as pointed out by Dr. Fitzedward Hall. The true name of the river is *Po-lo-nie,* or *Varanâ.*

Fazl,* who says "*Barânasi*, commonly called *Banâras*, is a large city situated between two rivers, the *Barnâ* and the *Asi*." Bishop Heber† also mentions that he was informed by the Raja of Banâras that the name "had anciently been Barânas, from two rivers, *Bara* and *Nasa*, which here fall into the Ganges." The worthy Bishop supposes that they must join the Ganges underground, as no such rivers are set down on the map; but two pages afterwards he records that his boats arrived "of the mouth of the *small river* which leads to Secrole," that is to the cantonment of Banâras. It may perhaps be objected that this was only a report from his servants, and that he had not actually seen the river; but as the Bishop lived with Mr. Brooke to the north of the Barnâ, he must have crossed that river by the large stone bridge at least twice every day during his stay at the holy city of the Hindus.

Banâras is celebrated amongst the Buddhists as the scene where the great teacher first expounded his doctrine, or as they metaphorically express it, where he first began "to turn the wheel of the law." This is one of the four great events in the life of Buddha, and the stupa which was built upon the spot was esteemed as one of the four great monuments of Buddhism. This stupa, now called *Dhamêk*, is situated about 3½ miles to the north of the city, amidst an extensive mass of ruins, which

* 'Ayin Akbari,' ii. 28.

† 'Journal,' i. 397-399.

are surrounded on three sides by large artificial lakes. The name of *Dhamêk* is most probably only an abbreviation of the Sanskrit *Dharmmopadesaka*, the "Teacher of Dharmma." This is the common term still in use to designate any religious teacher; but bearing in mind that on this spot Buddha first began to "turn the wheel of the law" (*dharmma-chakra*), the name is peculiarly appropriate for the stupa. The term is also used in the simpler form of *Dharmmadesaka*, which in familiar conversation would naturally be shortened to *Dhammadek* and *Dhamek*.

The earliest name of this city was *Kâsi*, which is still in common use, either alone or joined with the later name, as Kâsi-Banâras. It is, perhaps, the *Kassida*, or *Kassidia*, of Ptolemy. The name is referred to *Kâsi-râja* who was one of the early progenitors of the Lunar race. He was succeeded by twenty descendants, all Rajas of Kâsi, amongst whom was the celebrated *Divodâsa*.

22. GARJAPATIPURA.

From Banâras, Hwen Thsang travelled eastward for about 300 *li*, or 50 miles, to the kingdom of *Chen-chu*, which is a Chinese translation of the original name, meaning "lord-of-battles." M. Julien proposes *Yodhapati* or *Yodharâja-pura;* but as the translation alone is given, we have a choice of several terms, as *Vigrahapati, Yudhanâtha, Ranaswâmi*, etc. The capital situated on the Ganges was 10 *li*, or 1⅔ miles, in circuit. The place thus described is certainly *Ghâzipur,* which is on the Ganges just 50 miles to the east of Banâras. The present name was given by the Muhammadans, and is said to be only a slight alteration of the original Hindu name of *Garjpur.* This is most probably the name referred to by Hwen Thsang, as *Garjan,* which means primarily any roaring noise, signifies also "battle," and *Garjana-pati* is a title of the "god of war." Ghâzipur is now a large city about 2 miles in length, and 5 or 6 miles in circumference. Hwen Thsang estimates the circuit of the district at 2000 *li,* or 333 miles, which is almost exactly the size of the tract lying between the *Ghâgra* on the north and the *Gomati* on the south, from Tanda on the west to the confluence of the Ganges and Ghâgra.

At 200 *li,* or 33 miles, to the east of the capital, Hwen Thsang visited the *Aviddhakarna* monastery, which was adorned with very fine sculptures. Following the bearing and distance, this place should be looked for in the neighbourhood of *Baliya* on the bank of the Ganges. *Aviddhakarna* means the "pierced ears," and I think it possible that the name may still be preserved in *Bikapur,* a village 1 mile to the east of Baliya, as *Aviddhakarna-pura* might easily be shortened to *Bidkarnpur* and *Bikanpur.* It seems probable also that this is the same place that is mentioned by Fa-Hian under the name of the "Vast solitude,"* which he places

* *'Fo-kwe-ki,'* chap. xxxiv. The Rev. Mr. Beal in his translation calls this Vihâr simply the "Desert."

between Patna and Banâras, at 10 *yojanas,* or 70 miles, from the former, and 12 *yojanas*, or 84 miles, from the latter. The Indian name is not given, but as the literal translation of the "vast solitude" would be *Vrihadaranya* or *Bidaran,* this name might easily be altered, either by ignorance or design, to *Biddhkarn.* The two distances from Patna and Banâras agree exactly with the position of *Baliya,* which is 72 miles from the former, and 86 mlies from the latter.

From the monastery Hwen Thsang travelled to the south-east for 100 *li,* or 16 miles, to the Ganges, which he crossed, and then turning to the south for some unrecorded distance he reached the town of *Mo.ho.so.lo,* or *Mahâsâra.* This place was inhabited by Brahmans who had no respect for the faith of Buddha. It has been identified by M. Vivien de Saint-Martin with the village of *Masâr,* 6 miles to the west of *Ara* (Arrah of the maps), near which Buchanan discovered some ruined buildings, and a considerable number of Brahmanical figures.* The pilgrim then suddenly mentions his arrival at the temple of *Na-lo-yen,* or *Nârâyana,* to the north of the Ganges, without stating either its distance or bearing from the last place. But with reference to his subsequent route to Vaisâli, I feel satisfied that he must have crossed the Ganges above *Revelganj,* which is nearly due north from *Masâr* exactly 16 miles, or 100 *li.* This point,

* 'Eastern India,' i. 143.

near the confluence of the Ganges and Ghâgra, is deemed especially holy, and numerous temples have been erected on the bank of the united streams just above Revelganj. Here then I would place the site of Hwen Thsang's temple of Nârâyana or Vishnu, which he describes as being two storeys in height, and adorned with the most marvellous sculptures in stone.

At 30 *li*, or 5 miles, to the east of the temple there was a famous stupa built by Asoka on the spot where Buddha had overcome and converted certain evil Demons, who were said to live upon human flesh.* The Demons embraced Buddhism, or as it was expressed by the ancient Buddhists, sought the refuge or asylum of the Three Precious ones, that is, of the Buddhist Triad, *Buddha*, *Dharma*, and *Sangha*. Now *Sarana* is the Sanskrit term for asylum or refuge, and as this is also the true name of the district of *Sâran*, in which the conversion of the Demons was said to have taken place, I conclude that the monument erected on the spot must have been called the *Sarana Stupa*, or Asylum Tope. The stupa must therefore have been one of considerable celebrity, as there can be little doubt that its name was eventually imposed on the district in which it stood. Now 5 miles to the east of Revelganj will bring us to *Chapra*, the present capital of the *Sâran* district. Unfortunately I cannot find any information whatever about Chapra;

---

* Julien's 'Hiouen Thsang,' ii. 381. See Map No. XI.

but it is certain that it must have been a place of considerable consequence, otherwise it would not have been selected as the British head-quarters of the district.

From the *Asylum* stupa the pilgrim proceeded 100 *li*, or 16⅔ miles, to the south-east to another stupa, which was reputed to have been built by the Brahman *Drona* over the vessel with which he measured the relics of Buddha. According to the Ceylonese scriptures this stupa was built by the Brahman *Dono* (or Drona), over the *Kumbhân* or measuring-vessel, and was therefore called the *Kumbhân* stupa.* Hardy calls the Brahman *Droha*, and the vessel a "golden measure."† In the Burmese books the vessel is the same, but the Brahman is named *Dauna*.‡ In the Tibetan account the name of *Drona* is referred to the "measure" of the relics, which is certainly wrong, as the Brahman did not obtain any of the relics, but only the vessel with which he had measured them. This vessel was most probably equal to a *drona* in capacity, as each of the eight shares of the relics is said to have measured one *drona*. The stupa may therefore, have been called the *Drona* stupa, because it held the *drona* measuring-vessel with which the Brahman had divided the relics amongst the eight rival claimants. But this was not the only name

---

* Turnour, Journ. Asiat. Soc. Bengal, vii. 1013.

† 'Manual of Buddhism,' p. 351.

‡ Bigandet's 'Legend of Burmese Buddha,' p. 212.

of the monument, as the Ceylonese chronicler calls it the *Kumbha* stupa. Now a *kumbha* is a water-vessel of large size, which may be seen sculptured on many Indian pillars as a round wide-mouthed vase full of flowers. I can find no name like *Kumbha* or *Drona* in the position indicated by Hwen Thsang at 17 miles to the south of east from Chapra. But at that spot there is a village named *Deghwâra*, which, as *degh* is the common Hindi name of a large metal vessel of exactly the same shape as the *Kumbha*, may possibly be only an altered form of the original name. But *deg* is also the Persian term for a similar vessel, and I would therefore only refer to *Degwâra* as a convenient name to remember, because it has the same signification, and occupies the same position as the famous *Kumbha* stupa of Buddhist history.

23. VAISÂLI.

From the stupa of the measuring-vessel, Hwen Thsang proceeded to the north-east for 140 or 150 *li*, or 23 to 25 miles, to *Vaisâli*. He mentions having crossed the Ganges on the road; but as he was already to the north of that river, his notice must certainly refer to the *Gandak*, which flows within 12 miles of Degwâra. We must therefore look for *Vaisâli* to the east of the Gandak. Here, accordingly, we find the village of *Besârh*, with an old ruined fort which is still called *Raja-Bisal-ka-garh*, or the fort of Raja *Visala*, who was the reputed founder of the ancient Vaisâli. Hwen Thsang states that the Royal Palace was between 4 and 5 *li*, or from 3500 to 4400 feet in circuit, which agrees with the size of the old fort, according to my measurement of 1580 feet by 750 feet, or 4600 feet in circuit, along the lines of the ruined walls. The place is mentioned by Abul Fazl, as *Besâr,** and it is still a considerable village, surrounded with brick ruins. It is exactly 23 miles from *Degwâra,* but the direction is north-north-east, instead of north-east. This position also agrees with Hwen Thsang's subsequent distance and bearing to the bank of the Ganges opposite *Pâtaliputra*, or *Patna,* which was due south 120 *li,*† or 20 miles, the actual position of *Hâjipur* on the north bank of the Ganges being 20 miles almost due south. The ruined fort of *Besârh* thus presents such a perfect coincidence of name, position, and dimensions with the ancient city of *Vaisâli,* that there can be no reasonable doubt of their identity.

According to Hwen Thsang's estimate, the kingdom of *Vaisâli* was 5000 *li,* or 833 miles, in circuit,‡ which is certainly too great, unless it included the neighbouring kingdom of *Vriji,* which he described as 4000 *li,* or 667 miles, in circuit. Now the capital of Vriji is said to be only 500 *li,*

---

* 'Ayin Akbari,' ii. 198. See Map No. XI for its position.

† Julien's 'Hiouen Thsang,' ii. 399. 90 *li* to Swetapura, plus 30 *li* to the Ganges, or together 120 *li* from Vaisâli. In the pilgrim's life, the distance to Swetapura is said to be 100 *li* ; vol. i. p. 137.

‡ Julien's 'Hiouen Thsang,' ii. 384.

or 83 miles, to the north-east of Vaisâli; and as both of the districts are placed between the mountains and the Ganges, it is quite certain that there must be some mistake in the estimated dimensions of one of these. The utmost limit that can be assigned to the joint districts, with reference to the surrounding States, is not more than 750 or 800 miles in circuit, from the foot of the mountains to the Ganges on the south, and from the Gandak on the west to the Mahânadi on the east. I conclude, therefore, either that there is some mistake or exaggeration in the estimated size of one or both of the districts, or that the two districts are the same kingdom under different names. That the latter was actually the case, I will now endeavour to show.

In one of the Buddhist legends, quoted by Burnouf,* Buddha proceeds with Ananda to the *Châpâla* stupa, and seating himself under a tree, thus addresses his disciple: "How beautiful, O Ananda, is the city of *Vaisâli,* the land of the *Vrijis,*" etc. In the time of Buddha, and for many centuries afterwards, the people of Vaisâli were called *Lichhavis;* and in the *Trikandasesha,* the names of *Lichhavi, Vaideha,* and *Tirabhukti,* are given as synonymous. *Vaideha* is well known to the readers of the Râmâyana as a common name of *Mithila,* the country of Raja *Janaka,* whose daughter Sita is also named *Vaidehi.* Tirabhukti is the present *Tirahuti,* or *Tirhut.* Now, the modern town of *Janakpur,*

---

* Introduction à l'Hist. du Buddh. Ind. p. 74.

in the *Mithari* district, is acknowledged by the universal consent of the natives of the country, to be the same place as the ancient *Janakpur*, the capital of *Mithila*. It also corresponds exactly with the position assigned by Hwen Thsang to *Chen-shu-na*, the capital of Vriji. M. Vivien de Saint-Martin reads the Chinese name as *Che-thu-na,* but M. Stanislas Julien renders it by *Chha-su-na,* and points out that the second character is found in *Sukra,* and I may add also in *Sudra*. The correct rendering of the name is doubtful; but if the bearing and distance recorded by the Chinese pilgrims are correct, it is almost certain that the capital of *Vriji* in the seventh century must have been at *Janakpur*.

Hwen Thsang gives the name of the country in its Sanskrit form, as *Fo-li-shi,* or *Vriji;* but it is also stated that the people of the north called the country *San-fa-shi,* or *Samvaji*,* which is the Pali form of *Samvriji*, or the "United *Vrijis*." From this name, I infer that the *Vrijis* were a large tribe which was divided into several branches, namely, the *Lichhavis* of Vaisâli, the *Vaidehis* of Mithila, the *Tirabhuktis* of Tirhut, etc. Either of these divisions separately might therefore be called *Vrijis*, or any two together might be called *Vrijis,* as well as *Samvrijis,* or the "United *Vrijis*." We have a parallel case in the warlike tribe of the *Bâgris,* or *Sambâgris* of the Satlej, which consisted of three separate divisions.

---

* 'Hiouen Thsang,' ii. 402; note by M. Stanislas Julien.

I conclude therefore that *Vaisâli* was a single district in the territories of the United *Vrijis*, or *Wajjis*, and therefore that the estimated size of Vaisâli proper, as recorded by Hwen Thsang, is a simple mistake. Perhaps we should read 1500 *li*, or 250 miles, instead of 5000 *li*, or 833 miles. In this case the district of Vaisâli would be limited to the south-west corner of the country of the Vrijis, to the westward of the little Gandak river.

To the north-west of Vaisâli, at somewhat less than 200 *li*, or 33 miles, Hwen Thsang places the ruins of an ancient town, which had been deserted for many ages. There Buddha was said to have reigned in a previous existence, as a *Chakravartti Raja*, or supreme ruler, named Mahâdeva, and a stupa still existed to commemorate the fact. The name of the place is not given, but the bearing and distance point to *Kesariya*, an old ruined town, just 30 miles to the north-north-west of Vaisâli. The place possesses a mound of ruins with a lofty stupa on the top, which the people attribute to *Raja Vena Chakravartti*. In the *Purânas* also, Raja Vena is called a Chakravartti, or supreme monarch; and I have found his name as widely spread through northern India as that of Rama, or the five Pandus. This monument stands at the point of crossing of the two great thoroughfares of the district, namely, that from Patna northward to Bettiah, and that from Chapra across the Gandak to Nepâl. It is a curious illustration of this fact that Buddha himself, according to the Ceylonese chronicles, informed Ananda,* that "for a *Chakravartti Raja* they build the *thupo* at a spot where four principal roads meet." I have little doubt therefore that this is the identical place indicated by the Chinese pilgrim.

24. VRIJI.

From Vaisâli, Hwen Thsang proceeded to the north-east for 500 *li*, or 83 miles, to *Fo-li-shi*, or *Vriji*, which has already been identified as the territory of the powerful tribe of *Wajji*, or *Vriji*. In the time of Buddha, the *Vrijis* were divided into several clans, as the *Lichhavis*, the *Vaidehis*, the *Tirabhuktis*, and others, whose names are unknown. The exact number of their clans would appear to have been eight, as criminals were arraigned before the *atthakulaka*,† or "eight clans," which would appear to have been a jury composed of one member from each of the separate divisions of the tribe. Hwen Thsang mentions that the people of the north called them *San-fa-shi*, or *Samvajji*, that is the "United Vajjis,"—and the same name is referred to in the long and interesting account of the people of *Wajji*, which is given by Turnour from the Pâli chronicles of Ceylon.‡ The great monarch *Ajatasatru*, of Magadha, wishing to subdue the "great and powerful" people of Wajji, sent his minister to

* Turnour, Journ. Asiat. Soc. Bengal, vii. 1006.

† vii. 993, and note.

‡ *Ibid*. vii. 992.

consult Buddha as to the best means of accomplishing his object. The Raja is informed that so long as the people of Wajji remained "united," they would be invincible. The Raja, by a stratagem of his minister, "in the course of three years, so completely disunited their rulers, one from another, that no two would walk the same road together," and they were accordingly subdued without making any resistance. According to Turnour, "the union of the *Wajjian* states consisted of a *confederation* of chiefs."* The name of *Sam-vriji,* or the "United *Vrijis,"* was therefore a descriptive title of the whole nation of eight clans, who, as Buddha remarked, were accustomed to hold frequent meetings, to act in concert, and to uphold the ancient *Wajjian* institutions. No king is mentioned, but the people are stated to have respected and obeyed the orders of their elders.

According to Hwen Thsang the country of the Vrijis was long from east to west, and narrow from north to south.† This description corresponds exactly with the tract of country lying between the Gandak and Mahanadi rivers, which is 300 miles in length by 100 miles in breadth. Within these limits there are several ancient cities, some of which may possibly have been the capitals of the eight different clans of the Vrijis. Of course *Vaisâli, Kesariya,* and *Janakpur* have already been noticed; the others

* Turnour Journ. Asiat. Soc. Bengal, vii. 992, note.

† Julien's 'Hiouen Thsang,' ii. 402. See Map No. XI.

are *Navandgarh, Simrûn, Darbanga, Puraniya,* and *Motihâri.* The last three are still inhabited and are well known; but *Simrûn* has been deserted for upwards of 550 years, while *Navandgarh* has probably been abandoned for at least fifteen centuries. Simrûn has been described by Mr. Hodgson,* but its ruins still require to be carefully surveyed before we can form an opinion as to its probable antiquity. I visited *Navandgarh* myself in 1862, and found it one of the oldest and most interesting places in northern India.

Navandgarh or *Naonadgarh* is a ruined fort from 250 to 300 feet square at top and 80 feet in height. It is situated close to the large village of *Lauriya,* 15 miles to the north-north-west of Bettiah and 10 miles from the nearest point of the Gandak river.† The ancient remains consist of a handsome stone pillar, surmounted by a lion and inscribed with Asoka's edicts, and of three rows of earthen barrows or conical mounds of earth, of which two rows lie from north to south, and the third from east to west. Now the stupas usually met with are built either of stone or of brick; but the earliest stupas were mere mounds of earth, of which these are the most remarkable specimens that I have seen. I believe that they are the sepulchral monuments of the early kings of the country prior to the rise of Buddhism, and that their date may be assumed as ranging from 600 to 1500 B.C.

* See Map No. XI.

† See Map No. XI.

Every one of these barrows is called simply *bhisâ*, or "mound," but the whole are said to have been the *kots* or fortified dwellings of the ministers and nobles of Raja *Uttânpat*, while the fort of Navandgarh was the king's own residence. The word *stûpa* meant originally only a "mound of earth," and this is the meaning given to it by Colebrooke, in his translation of the 'Amara Kosha.' I believe that these earthen *stûpas* or *chaityas* of Navandgarh must form part of those alluded to by Buddha himself in his sixth question addresed to Ananda about the people of Vriji:* "Anando! hast thou heard that the *Wajjians*, whatever the number may be of the *Wajjian chetiyâni* belonging to the *Wajjian* (rulers), whether situated within or without (the city), they maintain, respect, reverence, and make offerings to them; and that they keep up without diminution the ancient offerings, the ancient observances, and the ancient sacrifices righteously made?" Now these *chetiyâni* could not have been Buddhist *stûpas*, as Buddha himself put the question during his lifetime. Accordingly, the author of the Ceylonese 'Atthakathâ' explains that they are *yakhatthânâni*, or edifices belonging to *Yakha*, or demon worship. The *Yakhas*, in Sanskrit *Yaksha* and *Jaksha*, were the attendants of *Kuvera*, the God of Riches, and the guardians of his treasures, and their chief residence was called *Alakapura*. Now somewhere in the neighbourhood of the Gandak there was a city named

---

* Turnour, Journ. Asiat. Soc. Bengal, vii. 994.

Alakappo, inhabited by a people named *Balaya* or *Buluka*, who obtained a share of Buddha's relics. It is probable, therefore, that this city of *Alakappo* may have been connected with the early *Yaksha* worship, and that the pre-Buddhistical *stûpas* of Navandgarh may be some of the ancient *chaityas* of the *Vrijis* that were referred to by Buddha. If so, the *Balayas* or *Bulukas* of *Alakappo* must have been one of the eight clans of the *Vrijis*, a conclusion which is rendered still more probable by the vicinity of Alakappo to the Gandak river.

25. NEPÂLA.

From Vriji the Chinese pilgrim visited *Ni.po.lo*, or Nepâla, which he places to the north-west at 1400 or 1500 *li*, or 233 to 250 miles.* From Janakpur there are two routes to Nepâl, one by the *Kamalâ* river, and the other by the *Bhâgmati* or *Bhâgavati* river; but the distance is not more than 150 miles by either of them. The circuit of the country is said to be 4000 *li*, or 667 miles, which is much too small, unless the estimate refers to the district of Nepâl Proper on the *Sapta Kausiki*, or seven streams of the Kosi river. But in this case the hill country on the Gandak river must have been a separate territory, which is very improbable. I would therefore assign to Nepâl the basins of both rivers, and alter Hwen Thsang's estimate to 6000 *li*, or 1000 miles, which is about the actual size of the two valleys.

* Julien's 'Hiouen Thsang,' ii. 407.

The Raja of Nepâl was a Kshatriya of the race of *Lichhavi* named *Ansu-Varmma,* who is probably the *Anghu Varmma* of the native histories, as he belonged to the *Newarit* or *Newar* dynasty of conquerors. As a Lichhavi, Ansu Varmma must also have been a foreigner, that is one of the *Vrijis* of Vaisâli. The dates likewise correspond, as *Anghu Varmma* is the fifteenth ruler prior to Râghava Deva, who established the Newar era in A.D. 880. Allowing seventeen years to each reign, the accession of Anghu Varmma will be fixed in A.D. 625, and Hwen Thsang's visit in A.D. 637 will fall towards the end of his reign.

It is curious that the kings of Tibet and Ladâk also trace their descent from the *Lichhavis.* But if their claims are well founded they must have been offshoots from the Nepâl branch of the family. Now the Lichhavi conquest of Nepâl is assigned to Newarit who preceded Anghu Varmma by 37 reigns, which at 17 years each, will give a period of 629 years, equivalent to B.C. 4 for his accession. The Tibetan history begins with the accession of *Nyahkhri-Tsanpo,* whose date is roughly fixed at 500 years prior to *Lha-Thothori* in A.D. 407, or about 93 B.C. But as Lha-Thothori's fifth successor was born in A.D. 627, there must be an error of about one century and a half in the date of 407. Applying this correction to the date of the first king, the Lichhavi conquest cannot be fixed earlier than A.D. 50, or about two generations after the conquest of Nepâl.

26. MAGADHA.

From Nepâl, Hwen Thsang returned to Vaisâli, and then proceeding to the south, crossed the Ganges and entered the capital of Magadha. He notes that the city was originally called *Kusumapura*, that it had been deserted for a long time, and was then in ruins. It was 70 *li*, or 11⅔ miles, in circuit, exclusive of the new town of *Pâtaliputra-pura*. This name the Greeks slightly altered to *Palibothra* on the authority of Megasthenes, whose account is preserved by Arrian.* "The capital city of India is Palibothra, in the confines of the *Prasii*, near the confluence of the two great rivers Erannoboas and Ganges. Erannoboas is reckoned the third river throughout all India, and is inferior to none but the Indus and the Ganges, into the last of which it discharges its waters. Megasthenes assures us that the length of this city is 80 stadia, the breadth 15, that it is surrounded with a ditch, which takes up 6 acres of ground and is 30 cubits deep; that the walls are adorned with 570 towers and 64 gates." According to this account the capital of Magadha in the time of Seleukos Nikator was 220 stadia, or 25¼ miles, in circuit. This is about the size of the modern city of Patna, which when surveyed by Buchanan was 9 miles in length by 2¼ miles in breadth,† or 22½ miles, in circumference. In the

* 'Indica,' x. Strabo, xv. 1. 36, gives exactly the same account.

† Gazetteer in *v.* Patna; he gives the area as 20 square miles.

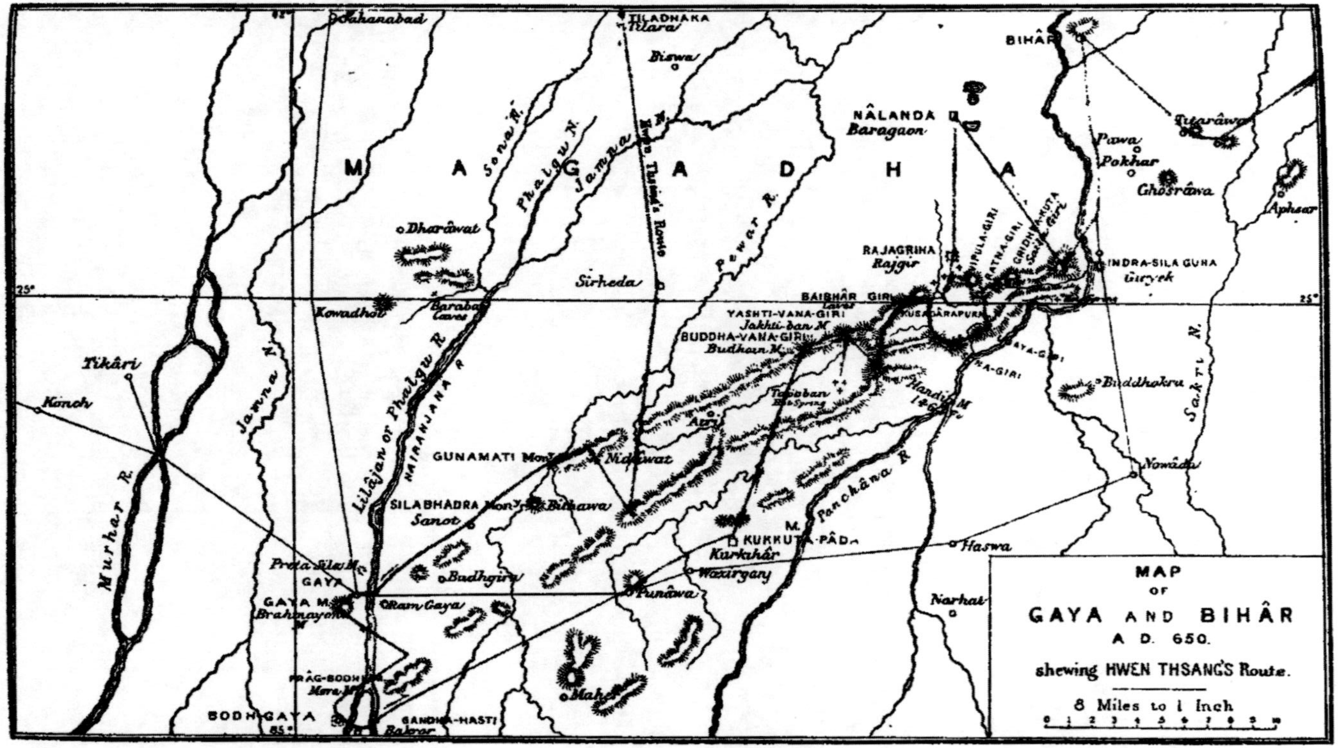

MAP OF GAYA AND BIHÂR A.D. 650.
shewing HWEN THSANG'S Route.
8 Miles to 1 Inch
M A G A D H A
Jahanabad
TILADHAKA Tilara
Biswa
BIHÂR
NÂLANDA Baragaon
Titarâwa
Pawa
Pokhar
Ghosrâwa
Aphsar
Sona N.
Phalgu N.
Jamna N.
Hwen Thsang's Route
Pewar R.
Dharâwat
Sirheda
RAJAGRIHA Rajgir
INDRA-SILA GUHA Giryek
BAIBHÂR GIRI
YASHTI-VANA-GIRI Jakhti-ban M.
BUDDHA-VANA-GIRI Budhain M.
KUSAGÂRAPURA
Kowadhol
Barabar Caves
Tikâri
Konch
Murhar R.
Lilâjan or Phalgu R.
NAIRANJANA R.
GUNAMATI Mon.y
Nidowat
SILABHADRA Mon.y
Bithawa
Sanot
Buddhakra
Sakri N.
Nowâda
Panchâna R.
KUKKUTA-PÂDA
Kurkihâr
Haswa
Waxirganj
Narhat
Preta Sila M.
GAYA
GAYA M. Brahmayoni M.
Badhgira
Ram Gaya
Punâwa
PRÂG-BODHI Mora M.
BODH-GAYA
GANDHA-HASTI Bakror
25°
85°

seventh century, therefore, we may readily admit that the old city of Kusumapura may have been about half this size, or 11 miles in circuit, as stated by Hwen Thsang.

Diodorus* attributes the foundation of the city to Herakles, by whom he may perhaps mean Bala-Râma, the brother of Krishna, but this early origin is not countenanced by the native authorities. According to the Vâyu Purâna† the city of *Kusumapura* or *Pâtaliputra* was founded by Raja Udayâswa, the grandson of Ajatasatru, who was the well-known contemporary of Buddha; but the 'Mahawanso' makes Udaya the son of Ajatsatru. According to the Buddhist accounts,‡ when Buddha crossed the Ganges, on his last journey from Râjagriha to Vaisâli, the two ministers of Ajatasatru, king of Magadha, were engaged in building a fort at the village of *Patali* as a check upon the *Wajjians*, or people of *Vriji*. Buddha then predicted that it would become a great city. From these concurring authorities I conclude that the building of the city of *Pâtaliputra* was actually begun in the reign of Ajatasatru, but was not finished until the reign of his son, or grandson, Udaya, about B.C. 450.

The position of the city at the junction of the Ganges and Erannoboas was formerly supposed to refer to the confluence of the *Gandak* or *Hiranyavati*,

---

* Hist. Univers., ii. 24.

† Wilson's 'Vishnu Purana,' p. 467. note 45.

‡ Turnour, Journ. Asiat. Soc. Bengal, vii. 998.

which joins the Ganges immediately opposite Patna. But it has been conclusively shown by Mr. Ravenshaw* that the *Son* river formerly joined the Ganges just above the city of Patna. As the *Sona,* or "golden" river, is also called the *Hiranya-bâha,* or the golden, on account of its broad yellow sands, its identification with the Erannoboas is complete both as to name and position.

Strabo and Pliny agree with Arrian in calling the people of Palibothra by the name of *Prasii,* which modern writers have unanimously referred to the Sanskrit *prâchya,* or "eastern." But it seems to me that *Prasii* is only the Greek form of *Palâsiya* or *Parâsiya,* a "man of *Palâsa* or *Parâsa,*" which is an actual and well-known name of *Magadha,* of which Palibothra was the capital. It obtained this name from the *Palâsa,* or Butea frondosa, which still grows as luxuriantly in the province as in the time of Hwen Thsang.† The common form of the name is *Parâs,* or when quickly pronounced *Prâs,* which I take to be the true original of the Greek *Prasii.* This derivation is supported by the spelling of the name given by Curtius,‡ who calls the people *Pharrasii,* which is an almost exact transcript of the Indian name *Parâsiya.* The *Proxiakos* of Ælian is only the derivative from *Palâsaka.*

---

* Journ. Asiat. Soc. Bengal, xiv. 137.

† Julien's 'Hiouen Thsang,' i. 151 : 'çà et là de beaux *kie-ni*, ou *kanaka* (Butea frondosa), laissaient pendre leurs fleurs d'un rouge éblouissant.'

‡ 'Vita Alexandri,' ix. 2.

According to Hwen Thsang's estimate the province of Magadha was about 5000 *li*, or 833 miles, in circuit.* It was bounded by the Ganges on the north, by the district of Banâras on the west, by Hiranya Parvata, or Mongir, on the east, and by Kirana Suvarna, or Singbhûm on the south. It must, therefore, have extended to the Karmnâsa river on the west, and to the sources of the Damûda river on the south. The circuit of these limits is 700 miles measured direct on the map, or about 800 miles by road-distance.

As Magadha was the scene of Buddha's early career as a religious reformer, it possesses a greater number of holy places connected with Buddhism than any other province of India. The chief places are *Buddha-Gaya, Kukkutapada, Râjagriha, Kusâgârapura, Nâlanda, Indrasilaguha,* and the *Kapotika* monastery, all of which will be described separately, whilst the smaller places will be noticed in the account of Hwen Thsang's route to the more important localities.

Bauddha Gaya.

On leaving *Pâtaliputra* the Chinese pilgrim started from the south-west corner of the city, and proceeded for 100 *li*, or 16⅔ miles, to the south-west to the monastery of *Ti-lo-shi-kia* or *Ti-lo-tse-kia,* from whence he continued his route in the same direction for 90 *li,* or 15 miles, to a lofty mountain

* Julien's 'Hiouen Thsang,' ii. 409.

from the summit of which Buddha had contemplated the kingdom of Magadha.* He then turned to the north-west for 30 *li,* or 5 miles, to visit a very large monastery on the slope of a hill, where *Gunamati* had worsted a heretic in argument. Then resuming his south-west route for 20 *li.* or 3⅓ miles, he visited an isolated hill, and the monastery of *Silabhadra,* and continuing in the same direction for 40 or 50 *li,* 7 or 8 miles, he crossed the river *Ni-lien-shen,* or *Nairanjan,* and entered the town of *Kia-ye,* or *Gaya.*†

Before attempting to identify any of the places noted in this route, I must remark that there are several errors both in the bearings and distances that require to be corrected. As the direction of Gaya is very nearly due south from Patna, the several south-west bearings should certainly be altered to south. The several distances also when added together amount to only 230 *li,* or 38 miles, while the actual distance between the cities of Patna and Gaya is 60 miles by the high-road, and must have been about 70 miles by the route followed by Hwen Thsang. The sum of his distances is, therefore, about 200 *li,* or 33 miles, short of the distance actually travelled. This amount I would divide into two even sums of 100 *li,* and add one to each of the first two distances recorded by the pilgrim.

By adopting this double correction of bearing and distance the position of the monastery of *Ti-lo-*

---

* Julien's 'Hiouen Thsang,' ii. 439, 40, 41.

† *Ibid.*, ii. 455.

tse-kia, or *Tiladaka*, will be fixed at 200 *li*, or 33 miles, to the south of the south-west corner of the city of Patna, or as nearly as possible on the site of the town of *Tillâra*, on the eastern bank of the Phalgu river. That this was nearly the true position of *Tiladaka* is proved by a later mention of the same place by the pilgrim. When leaving the Nâlanda monastery on his return to China, he went direct to *Tiladaka*, which he places at 3 *yojanas*, or 21 miles, to the west of Nâlanda.* Now the position of Nâlanda, as I will hereafter show, was at the village of Barâgaon, 6 miles to the north of Râjgir; and from Barâgaon to Tillâra the distance is 17 miles in a direct line to the north of west, or about 20 miles by road.

The next place visited by Hwen Thsang, was the lofty mountain from which Buddha had contemplated the country of Magadha. Following my proposed corrections, this mounain should be looked for at 190 *li*, or 32 miles, to the south of *Tiladaka* or Tillâra, and at 70 *li* to the north-east of Gaya. These bearings and distances fix the position of Buddha's Mountain in the lofty range of hills lying between Giryek and Gaya, somewhere about 3 miles to the north-west of Vazirganj, and about the same distance to the west of Amethi. This mention of hills is very fortunate, as it proves the necessity of applying the correction in distance to the first part of the route as the nearest hill is upwards of 50 miles from Patna.

---

* Julien's 'Hiouen Thsang,' i. 211. See Map No. XII.

From Buddha's Mountain the pilgrim proceeded 30 *li*, or 5 miles, to the north-west to the large monastery of Gunamati, which was situated on a slope in a pass of the mountains. The bearing and distance point to the low range of hills on the eastern bank of the *Pewar Nadi*, near Nidâwat. From the Gunamati monastery Hwen Thsang travelled 20 *li*, or 3⅓ miles, to the south-west to the Silabhadra monastery, which was situated on an isolated hill. This position may, I think, be identified with *Bithâwa*, an isolated hill, which is also on the eastern bank of the Pewar Nadi, 3 miles to the south-west of Nidâwat. The name of *Bithâ*, which means an artificial mound, may perhaps refer to the ruined monastery of Silabhadra.

From this place the pilgrim proceeded for about 40 or 50 *li*, about 7 or 8 miles, to the south-west, and crossing the *Nairanjan* river, entered the town of Gaya. The river is now called *Phalgu*, opposite Gaya, and the name of *Lilâjan*, or *Nilâjan*, is restricted to the western branch, which joins the *Mohâni* 5 miles above Gaya. The town was thinly peopled, but it contained about 1000 families of Brahmans. The city is still called *Brahma-Gaya*, to distinguish it from *Bauddh-Gaya*.

At 5 or 6 *li*, or 1 mile, to the south-west of the town stood the mountain of *Gayâ*, which was known amongst the people of India as the divine mountain. This hill is now called *Brahm-juīn*, or *Brahmâ-yoni*, and a small temple now occupies the site of Asoka's stupa. To the south-east of the hill there were stupas of the three Kasyapas, and to the east of them, across a great river (the Phalgu), there was a mountain named *Po.lo.ki.pu.ti*, or *Prâgbodhi*, which Buddha ascended for the purpose of dwelling in silent solitude upon its summit. He had previously spent six years in silent abstraction, but having afterwards renounced his austerities, he accepted some rice and milk, and going towards the north-east, he saw this mountain, and ascended it for the purpose of resuming his austerities ; but he was disturbed by the tremblings caused by the fright of the god of the mountain, and descended on the south-west side, from whence he reached the famous *Pippal*-tree at Bauddha Gaya, at 15 *li*, or 2½ miles, to the south-west. The last distance and bearing show that the *Prâgbodhi* mountain is the *Mora* Pahâr of the present day, as its south-west end is exactly 2½ miles to the north-east of Bauddha Gaya. Midway in the descent there was a cave, in which Buddha rested, and sat with his legs crossed. Fa-Hian* mentions this cave, which he places at half a *yojana*, or 3½ miles, to the north-east of the Bodhi-tree. It was therefore about one mile from the southern end of the mountain. I was informed that a cave still exists on the western face.

Hwen Thsang has omitted to mention the distance of this eastern mountain from that of Gayâ, or Brahmjuïn, which is about 4 miles, or 24 *li*. The account of the earlier pilgrim, Fa-Hian, is

* Beal's 'Fah-Hian,' c. xxxi. 121.

of no assistance in this place, as he makes the distance from *Kia-ye*, or Gayâ, to the neighbourhood of the Bodhi-tree only 20 *li*, or 3⅓ miles, the actual distance being upwards of 5 miles, or more than 30 *li*.

Bauddha-Gaya was famous for its possession of the holy *Pippal*-tree under which Sâkya Sinha sat for five years in mental abstraction, until he obtained Buddhahood. The celebrated *Bodhi-drûm*, or "Tree of Wisdom," still exists, but it is very much decayed. Immediately to the east of the tree there is a massive brick temple, nearly 50 feet square at base, and 160 feet in height. This is beyond all doubt the *Vihâr* that was seen by Hwen Thsang in the seventh century, as he places it to the east of the Bodhi-tree, and describes it as 20 paces square at base, and from 160 to 170 feet in height.

Kukkutapada.

From the *Bodhi-drûm* Hwen Thsang crossed the river *Nairanjan*, and visited a stupa named *Gandhahasti*, or the "Scented Elephant," near which there was a tank and a stone pillar.* The ruins of the stupa and the lower portion of the shaft of the pillar still exist at Bakror, on the eastern bank of the Lilâjan river, about 1 mile to the south-east of Bauddha-Gaya.

Travelling eastward, the pilgrim crossed the

---

* Julien's 'Hiouen Thsang,' iii. 1. See Map No. XII.

river *Mo-ho,* or *Mohana Nadi,* and entered a large forest, where he saw another stone pillar. Then proceeding to the north-east for 100 *li,* or nearly 17 miles, he reached the mountain of *Kiu-kiu-cha-po-tho,* or *Kukkutapada,* or "Cock's-foot," which was remarkable for three bold peaks. According to Fa-Hian's account, the Hill of the Cock's-foot was 3 *li,* or half a mile, to the south of the holy tree of Bauddha-Gaya. For 3 *li* we should no doubt read 3 *yojanas,* or 21 miles, which agrees very closely with Hwen Thsang's distance of 17 miles, plus about two miles for the crossings of the two rivers, or altogether 19 miles.

I have already identified this place with the present *Kurkihâr,* which, though omitted in the maps is perhaps the largest place between the cities of Gaya and Bihâr. It is situated 3 miles to the north-east of Vazirganj, 16 miles to the north-north-east of Gaya, and 20 miles to the north- east of Bauddha-Gaya.* The true name of *Kurkihâr* is said to be *Kurak-vihâr,* which I believe to be only a contracted form of *Kukkatapada-Vihâra,* or "Cock's-foot Temple," as the Sanskrit *Kûkkuta* is the same word as the Hindi *Kukkar,* or *Kurak,* a "cock." The present *Kurkihâr* therefore corresponds both in name and in position with the famous "Cock's-foot Hill" of the Buddhists. There is, however, no *three-peaked hill* in its neighbourhood; but about half a mile to the north of the village

* Julien's 'Hiouen Thsang,' iii. 6. See Map No. XII.

three rugged hills rise boldly out of the plain, which, as they stand so close together that their bases meet, may fairly be identified with the three-peaked hill of Hwen Thsang. This identification is confirmed by the presence of several ruined mounds, in which numerous Buddhist statues and votive stupas have been found.

Kusâgârapura.

From the "Cock's-foot Hill" the pilgrim proceeded to the north-east for 100 *li*, or 17 miles, to a mountain called *Fo-tho-fa-na*, or *Buddhavana*.* The bearing and distance point to the lofty hill now called *Buddhain*, which, on account of its commanding position, was made one of the stations of the great trigonometrical survey. Its distance in a direct line is not more than 10 miles, but as the whole route is hilly and winding, the actual length cannot be less than 15 or 16 miles. At 30 *li*, or 5 miles, to the east, he visited the famous *Yashtivana*, or "Bambu-forest."† This name is still well known as *Jakhti-ban*, which is only the Hindi form of the Sanskrit word. The place lies to the east of the *Buddhain* hill, on the route to the old ruined city of *Kusâgârapura*, and is still frequented by the people for the purpose of cutting Bambus. About 10 *li*, or nearly 2 miles, to the south-west of the Bambu-forest, the pilgrim visited two hot springs, to the south of a

---

* Julien's 'Hiouen Thsang,' iii. 10.

† *Ibid.*, iii. 11.

high mountain, in which Buddha was said to have bathed. These springs still exist about two miles to the south of *Jakhtiban*, at a place called *Tapoban*, which name is a common contraction of *Tapta-pâni*, or the "Hot Water." To the south-east of the Bambu-forest, at 6 or 7 *li*, upwards of 1 mile, there was a high mountain, with a stone embankment, built by King Bimbisâra. This mountain corresponds with the lofty hill of *Handia*, 1463 feet in height, which was one of the stations of the great trigonometrical survey. At 3 or 4 *li*, or upwards of half a mile, to the north, there was an isolated hill, on which still existed the ruins of a house in which the holy sage *Vyâsa* had formerly dwelt. At 4 or 5 *li*, or ¾ of a mile, to the north-east, there was a small hill with a chamber hewn out of the rock, and beside it a stone on which the gods Indra and Brahma had pounded the sandal-wood called *Gosiras* for the rubbing of Buddha's body. These two places have not been identified, but a careful search would certainly discover the sandal-wood stone, as there was close to it a very large cave, which the people called the "Palace of the Asuras." About 60 *li*, or 10 miles, to the east of this place, the pilgrim reached *Kiu-she-kie-lo-pu-lo*, or *Kusâgâra-pura*, that is the "town of the *Kusa* Grass."*

Kusâgârapura was the original capital of Magadha, which was called *Râjagriha*, or the "Royal Residence." It was also named *Girivraja*, or the

---

* Julien's 'Hiouen Thsang,' iii. 15.

"hill-surrounded," which agrees with Hwen Thsang's description of it as a town "surrounded by mountains." *Girivraja** is the name given in both the Râmâyana and the Mahâbhârata to the old capital of Jarasandha, king of Magadha, who was one of the principal actors in the Great War, about 1426 B.C. The Chinese pilgrim Fa-Hian† describes the city as situated in a valley between five hills, at 4 *li*, or two-thirds of a mile, to the south of the new town of Rajagriha. The same position and about the same distance are given by Hwen Thsang, who also mentions some hot springs, which still exist. Fa-Hian further states that the "five hills form a girdle like the walls of a town," which is an exact description of Old Râjagriha, or *Purâna Râjgir*, as it is now called by the people. A similar description is given by Turnour from the Pali annals of Ceylon, where the five hills are named *Gijjhakuto*, *Isigili*, *Webhâro*, *Wepullo*, and *Pandawo*.‡ In the Mahâbhârata the five hills are named *Vaihâra*, *Varâha*, *Vrishabha*, *Rishigiri*, and *Chaityaka*;§ but at present they are called *Baibhâr-giri*, *Vipula-giri*, *Ratna-giri*, *Udaya-giri*, and *Sona-giri*.

In the inscriptions of the Jain temples on Mount *Baibhâr*, the name is sometimes written Baibhâra, and sometimes *Vyavahâra*. It is beyond all doubt

* Lassen, Ind. Alterthum, i. 604.

† Beal's 'Fah-Hian,' c. xxviii. 112.

‡ Journ. Asiat. Soc. Bengal, 1838, p. 996.

§ Lassen, Ind. Alterthum, ii. 79. The five hills are all shown in Map No. XII.

the *Webhâro* Mountain of the Pali annals, on whose side was situated the far-famed *Sattapanni* Cave, in front of which was held the first Buddhist synod, in 543 B.C. This cave, I believe, still exists under the name of Son Bhândâr, or "Treasury of gold," in the southern face of the mountain; but following Hwen Thsang's description, it should rather be looked for in the northern face. In the Tibetan Dulva it is called the "Cave of the *Nyagrodha*," or Banian-tree.*

Ratnagiri is due east, one mile distant from the Son Bhândâr Cave. This situation corresponds exactly with Fa-Hian's position of the "Pippal-tree Cave," in which Buddha after his meals was accustomed to meditate. It was situated at 5 or 6 *li* (about one mile) to the east of the cave of the first Synod. The hill of Ratna-giri is therefore identical with the *Pandao* Mountain of the Pali annals, in which Buddha dwelt, and which in the Lalita-Vistâra is always styled the "King of Mountains." A paved zigzag road now leads from the eastern side of old Râjagriha to a small Jain temple on the top of Ratnagiri, which is frequently visited by Jains. I would identify it with the Rishigiri of the Mahâbhârata.

Mount *Vipula* is clearly identical with the *Wepullo* of the Pali annals; and as its summit is now crowned with the ruins of a lofty stupa or *chaitya*, which is noticed by Hwen Thsang, I would identify

---

* Csoma de Körös in Bengal 'Asiatic Researches,' xx 91.

it with the Chaityaka of the *Mahâbhârata*. Regarding the other two mountains, I have nothing at present to offer, but I may mention that they are also crowned with small Jain temples.

The old city between the hills is described by Fa-Hian to be 5 or 6 *li* from east to west, and 7 or 8 *li* from north to south, that is, from 24 to 28 *li* or 4⅓ miles, in circuit. Hwen Thsang makes it 30 *li*, or 5 miles, in circuit, with its greatest length from east to west. My survey of the ancient ramparts gives a circuit of 24,500 feet, or 4⅝th miles, which is between the two statements of the Chinese pilgrims. The greatest length is from north-west to south-east, so that there is no real discrepancy between the two statements as to the direction of the greatest length of the old city. Each of them must have taken his measurement from the Nekpai embankment on the east (which has been described by Major Kittoe) to some point on the north-west. If taken to the Pânch-Pandu angle of the ramparts, the direction would be west-north-west, and the length upwards of 8000 feet; but if taken to the temple of Torha Devi, the direction would be north-north-west, and the distance upwards of 9000 feet.

I have already quoted Fa-Hian's statement that the "five hills form a girdle like the walls of a town." This agrees with Hwen Thsang's description, who says that "high mountains surround it on four sides, and form its *exterior* walls, which have a circuit of 150 *li* or 25 miles." For this number I propose to read 50 *li* or 8⅓ miles, a correction which is absolutely necessary to make the statement tally with the measurements of my survey. The following are the direct distances between the hills :—

1.	From Baibhâr to Vipula	...	12,000 feet.
2.	,, Vipula to Ratna	...	4,500 ,,
3.	,, Ratna to Udaya	...	8,500 ,,
4.	,, Udaya to Sona	...	7,000 ,,
5.	,, Sona to Baribhâr	...	9,000 ,,
	TOTAL	...	41,000 feet.

This is somewhat less than 8 miles, but if the ascents and descents are taken into account, the actual length will correspond very closely with the statement of Hwen Thsang when corrected to 50 *li*. The old walls forming this exterior line of rampart are still to be seen in many places. I traced them from Vipulagiri over Ratna-giri to the Nekpai embankment, and thence onwards over Udaya-giri, and across the southern outlet of the valley to Sona-giri. Across this outlet, the walls, which are still in good order, are 13 feet thick. To obtain a circuit of 25 miles, as given in Hwen Thsang's text, it would be necessary to carry these ramparts as far as Giryek on the east. As similar ramparts exist on the Giryek Hill, it is perhaps possible that Hwen Thsang intended to include it in the circuit of his outer walls. But this immense circuit would not at all agree with his statement that "high mountains surround the city on four sides," for the distant hill of Giryek cannot in any way be said to form one of the sides of old Râjagriha.

The hot springs of Râjagriha are found on both banks of the Sarsuti rivulet; one-half of them at the eastern foot of Mount Baibhâr, and the other half at the western foot of Mount Vipula. The former are named as follows:—1. Ganga-Jumna; 2. Anant Rikhi; 3. Sapt Rikhi; 4. Brahm-kûnd; 5. Kasyapa Rikhi; 6. Byâs-kûnd; and 7. Markand-kûnd. The hottest of these are the springs of the Sapt Rikhi. The hot springs of Mount Vipula are named as follows:—1. Sita-kûnd; 2. Suraj-kûnd; 3. Ganes-kûnd; 4. Chandrama-kûnd; 5. Râm-kûnd; and 6. Sringgi-Rikhi-kûnd. The last spring has been appropriated by the Musalmâns, by whom it is called *Makhdûm-kûnd*, after a celebrated saint named *Chillah Shah*, whose tomb is close to the spring. It is said that Chilla was originally called Chilwa, and that he was an Ahîr. He must therefore have been a converted Hindu.

To the north-east of the old town, at a distance of 15 *li*, or 2½ miles, Hwen Thsang places the celebrated hill of *Gridhra-kuta*, or the "Vulture's Peak." According to Fa-Hian* it was 15 *li*, or 2½ miles, to the south-east of the new town. Both of our authorities, therefore, agree in fixing the Vulture's Peak on the lofty hill now called *Saila-giri*, or the "Rocky-Mountain;" but I could not hear of the existence of any cave in this hill. Fa-

* Beal's 'Fah-Hian,' c. xxix.

Hian calls it "Hill of the Vulture's Cave," and notes that there were also several hundreds of caves of the *Arhans* in which they sat to meditate. I presume that these were small rooms built against the cliff, and that the walls having fallen down, the names have been forgotten. The joint authority of the two pilgrims is too strong to be doubted; and future research will perhaps discover some remains of these once holy cave-dwellings.

Râjagriha.

The new town of *Râjagriha* is placed by Fa-Hian at 4 *li,* or two-thirds of a mile, to the north of the old town, which agrees exactly with the position of the ruined fortress now called *Râjgir.*

The new town of Râjagriha is said to have been built by King *Srenika,* otherwise called *Bimbisâra,* the father of *Ajâtasatru,* the contemporary of Buddha. Its foundation cannot therefore be placed later than 560 B.C. according to Buddhist chronology. In Hwen Thsang's time (A.D. 629-642), the outer walls had already become ruinous, but the inner walls were still standing and occupied a circuit of 20 *li* (3⅓ miles). This statement corresponds tolerably well with the measurements of my survey, which make the circuit of the ramparts somewhat less than 3 miles. Buchanan calls new Râjagriha an irregular pentagon of 12,000 yards in diameter. This is clearly a misprint for 1200 yards, which would give a circuit of 11,300 feet, or 2⅛ miles; but this was probably the interior measurement, which, according to my survey, is 13,000 feet. The plan of new Râjagriha I make out to be an irregular pentagon of one long side and four nearly equal sides, the whole circuit being 14,260 feet outside the ditches, or rather less than 3 miles.

On the south side towards the hills a portion of the interior, 2000 feet long and 1500 feet broad, has been cut off to form a citadel. The stone walls retaining the earthen ramparts of this work are still in good order in many places. It is possible that this work may be of later date, as suggested by Buchanan, but I am of opinion that it was simply the citadel of the new town, and that its walls have suffered less from the effects of time, owing partly to their having been more carefully and more massively built than the less important ramparts of the town, and partly to their having been occasionally repaired as a military position by the authorities, while the repairs of the town walls were neglected as being either unnecessary or too costly.

Nâlanda.

Due north from Râjgîr and 7 miles distant lies, the village of Baragaon, which is quite surrounded by ancient tanks and ruined mounds, and which possesses finer and more numerous specimens of sculpture than any other place that I visited. The ruins of Baragaon are so immense, that Dr. Buchanan was convinced it must have been the usual residence of the king; and he was informed by a Jain priest at Bihâr, that it was the residence of Raja Srenika and his ancestors. By the Brahmans these ruins are said to be the remains of *Kundilpur*, a city famed as the birthplace of Rûkmini, one of the wives of Krishna. But as Rûkmini was the daughter of Raja Bhishma, of Vidarbha, or Berâr, it seems probable that the Brahmans have mistaken Berâr for Bihâr, which is only 7 miles distant from Baragaon. I therefore doubt the truth of this Brahmanical tradition, more especially as I can show beyond all doubt that the remains at Baragaon are the ruins of Nâlanda, the most famous seat of Buddhist learning in all India.

Fa-Hian places the hamlet of Nalo at 1 *yojana*, or 7 miles, from the Hill of the Isolated Rock, that is from Giryek, and also the same distance from new Râja-griha.* This account agrees exactly with the position of Baragaon, with respect to Giryek and Râjgîr. In the Pali annals of Ceylon also, Nâlanda is stated to be 1 *yojana* distant from Râjagriha. Again, Hwen Thsang describes Nâlanda as being 7 *yojanas*, or 49 miles, distant from the holy Pipal-tree at Buddha Gaya,† which is correct if measured by the road, the direct distance measured on the map being 40 miles. He also describes it as being about 30 *li*, or 5 miles, to the north of new Râjagriha. This distance and direction also correspond with the position of Baragaon, if the distance be measured from the most northerly point of the old ramparts.

---

* Beal's 'Fah-Hian,' c. xxviii. p. 111.

† Julien's 'Hiouen Thsang,' i. 143.

Lastly, in two inscriptions, which I discovered on the spot, the place itself is called Nâlanda.

Fa-Hian makes Nâlanda the birthplace of Sâriputra, who was the right-hand disciple of Buddha; but this statement is not quite correct, as we learn from the more detailed account of Hwen Thsang that Sâriputra was born at *Kalapinâka*, about halfway between *Nâlanda* and *Indra-Sila-Guha*, or about 4 miles to the south-east of the former place. Nâlanda has also been called the birthplace of Mahâ Mogalâna, who was the lefthand disciple of Buddha; but this is not quite correct, as the great Mogalâna, according to Hwen Thsang, was born at *Kulika*, 8 or 9 *li* (less than 1½ mile) to the south-west of Nâlanda. This place I was able to identify with a ruined mound near Jagdispur, at 1¼ mile to the south-west of the ruins of Baragaon.

The remains at Baragaon consist of numerous masses of brick ruins, amongst which the most conspicuous is a row of lofty conical mounds running north and south. These high mounds are the remains of gigantic temples attached to the famous monastery of Nâlanda. The great monastery itself can be readily traced by the square patches of cultivation, amongst a long mass of brick ruins, 1600 feet by 400 feet. These open spaces show the positions of the courtyards of the six smaller monasteries which are described by Hwen Thsang as being situated within one enclosure forming altogether eight courts. Five of the six monasteries were built by five consecutive princes of the same family, and the sixth by their successor, who is called king of Central India.

To the south of the monastery there was a tank in which the dragon or *Nâga*, Nâlanda, was said to dwell, and the place was accordingly named after him, Nâlanda. There still exists to the south of the ruined monastery a small tank called *Kargidya Pokhar*, that answers exactly to the position of the *Nâlanda* tank, and which is therefore, in all probablity, the identical pool of the *Nâga*.

I cannot close this account of the ancient *Nâlanda* without mentioning the noble tanks which surrounded the ruins on all sides. To the north-east are the *Gidi Pokhar* and the *Pansokar Pokhar*, each nearly one mile in length; while to the south there is the *Indra Pokhar*, which is nearly half a mile in length. The remaining tanks are much smaller in size, and do not require any special notice.

Indra-Sila-Guha.

From the neighbourhood of Gaya two parallel ranges of hills stretch towards the north-east for about 36 miles to the bank of the Panchâna river, just opposite the village of Giryek. The eastern end of the southern range is much depressed, but the northern range maintains its height, and ends abruptly in two lofty peaks overhanging the Panchâna river. The lower peak on the east is crowned with a solid tower of brick-work, well known as *Jarasandha-ka-baithak*, or "Jarasandha's throne," while the higher peak on the west, to which the name of Giryek peculiarly belongs, bears an oblong terrace covered with the ruins of several buildings. The principal ruin would appear to have been a *vihâr,* or temple, on the highest point of the terrace, which was approached by a steep flight of steps leading through pillared rooms.

The two peaks are connected by a steep pavement, which was formerly continued down to the foot of the hill opposite the village of Giryek. At all the commanding points and bends of this road are still to be seen the stone foundations of small brick stupas from 5 and 6 feet to upwards of 12 feet in diameter. At the foot of the upper slope, and within 50 feet of Jarasandha's Tower, a tank 100 feet square has been formed, partly by excavation, and partly by building up. There is a second tank, at a short distance to the north, formed by the excavation of the rock for building materials. Both of these tanks are now dry.

At 2 miles to the south-west of the village of Giryek, and 1 mile from Jarasandha's Tower, there is a natural cavern in the southern face of the mountain, about 250 feet above the bed of the Bânganga rivulet. This cave, called Gidha-dwar, is generally believed to communicate with Jarasandha's Tower; but an examination with torches proved it to be a natural fissure running upwards in the direction of the tower, but only 98 feet in length. The mouth of the cavern is 10 feet broad and 17 feet high; but its height diminishes rapidly towards the end. The cave is filled with bats, and the air is oppressively warm and disagreeable, which alone is sufficient to prove that there is no exit to the cavern, otherwise there would be a draught of air right through it. Vultures swarm about the precipitous cliffs of pale grey horn stone, and I picked up their feathers in the mouth of the cave.

The remains at Giryek, which I have just described, appear to me to correspond exactly with the accounts given by Fa-Hian of the "Hill of the Isolated Rock," where Indra questioned Buddha on forty-two points; and with that given by Hwen Thsang of *Indra-silaguha*, which refers to the same story.

The position of Giryek corresponds so exactly, both in bearing and distance, with that of the hill of *Indrasila-guha*, that I feel quite satisfied of their identity. No etymology has yet been proposed for the name of Giryek; but it seems to me not unlikely that it is nothing more than *Giri + eḳa*, "one hill," that is, the hill of the isolated rock of Fa-Hian.

Both of the pilgrims mention the cave in the southern face of the mountain, which corresponds exactly with the natural cavern Gidha-dwar, which I have already described. *Gidha-dwar*, in Sanskrit *Gridhradwâra*, means the Vulture's pass, or opening. By Hwen Thsang the cave is called *Indra-sila-guha*, or "the cave of Indra's stone," being thus named after a stone on which were delineated the 42 points on which Indra had questioned Buddha. Fa-Hian adds that Indra himself drew the marks upon the stone with his finger.

According to Fa-Hian the hill of the "Isolated Rock" was 8 *yojanas*, or 56 miles, to the south-west of *Pâtali-putra*, the capital of Magadha, and 1 *yojana*, or 7 miles, to the east of Nâlanda. Hwen Thsang visited several places on his route from Nâlanda; but the result of his different bearings and distances places *Indra-sila-guha* at 46 *li*, or 7⅔ miles, to the east-south-east of Nâlanda. The actual distance between Baragaon and Giryek is about 9 miles, and the direction is somewhat to the west of south-west. If we read his south-east and east bearings as south-south-east and east-south-east the general direction will be south-east, and the distance will be increased to 8 miles, which is sufficiently near the truth to warrant the proposed correction.

Bihâr.

To the north-east of the isolated mountain of Giryek the Chinese pilgrim travelled from 150 to 160 *li*, or from 25 to 27 miles, to the *Kapotika*, or "Pigeon Monastery." Half a mile to the south there was a high solitary hill, on which stood a large *Vihâra* of *Avalokiteswara*, surrounded by a multitude of sculptured buildings. This place I would identify with *Bihâr*, 11 miles to the north-north-east of Giryek, by reading 60 *li*, or 10 miles, instead of the 160 *li* of the text.* In our maps the name is spelt *Behar*, but by the people it is written and pronounced *Bihâr*, which is sufficient to show that it must once have been the site of some famous Buddhist *Vihâr*. For this reason I am strongly inclined to identify the great *Vihâra* of *Avalokiteswara*, which stood on the top of a hill, with the present *Bihâr*, and its great isolated mountain covered with ruins. The hill stands to the north-west of the city of Bihâr, with a precipitously steep cliff on its northern face, and an easy slope of successive ledges of rock on the southern face. The summit is now crowned by some Muhammadan buildings; but I discovered amongst the ruins some fragments of Buddhist statues and votive stupas.

To the south-east of the Pigeon Monastery the pilgrim travelled for 40 *li*, or nearly 7 miles, to another monastery, which stood on an isolated hill. The bearing and distance point to the great ruined mound of *Titarâwa*, which is exactly 7 miles to the south-east of Bihâr. *Titarâwa* means "Partridge Mound," that is, the francolin or grey partridge. At Titarâwa there is a fine large tank, 1200 feet in length, with a considerable mound of brick ruins to the north, which from its square form has all the appearance of being the remains of a monastery.

---

* M. Vivien de Saint-Martin has already noted his suspicion that the 150 to 160 *li* of the text should be 50 or 60 *li*. 'Hiouen Thsang,' iii. 385, note. See Map No. XII.

From this place Hwen Thsang resumed his north-easterly route, and at 70 *li*, or nearly 12 miles, he reached a large village on the south bank of the Ganges. But as the nearest point of the river is 25 miles distant, we must read 170 *li*, or 29 miles, by adding the round number of 100 *li*, which was deducted from the previous journey between Giryek and the Pigeon Monastery.

I have considered these two corrections necessary, because Hwen Thsang specially notices the great height of the hill near the *Kapotika* monastery; and as I am not aware of the existence of any hills to the north or north-east of *Bihâr* and *Titarâwa*, I am obliged to shorten the one distance and lengthen the other to make Hwen Thsang's account of his route tally with the actual features of the country. There is a hill at *Shekhpura*, about 25 miles to the east-north-east of Giryek, 665 feet in height, which might perhaps be the true position of the Pigeon Monastery; but the adoption of this position would involve an alteration in the subsequent direction of the route, as well as in the distance, as *Shekhpura* is 20 miles from the Ganges. For these reasons I think that the identification with Bihâr is preferable. In either case the village on the Ganges must be looked for near Daryâpur, which is 34 miles due west from Mongir in a direct line.

The pilgrim then proceeded to the east for 100 *li*, or nearly 17 miles, to the monastery and village of *Lo-in-ni-lo*, which M. Vivien de Saint-Martin has identified with *Rohinila** or *Rohinala,* on the Ganges. The actual bearing is nearly south-east; but as the pilgrim followed the course of the river, there must be a mistake in his text.

27. HIRANYA PARVATA.

At 200 *li*, or 33 miles, to the east of Rohinala, Hwen Thsang reached the capital of the kingdom of *I-lan-na-po-fa-ta*, or *Hiranya-Parvata*, that is, the "Golden Mountain." Close to the city stood Mount *Hiranya*, "from which issued smoke and vapours that darkened the sun and moon."† The position of this hill is determined, from its proximity to the Ganges, and from its bearings and distances from Rohinala and Champa, to be *Mongir*. No smoke now issues from the hill, but the numerous hot springs in the neighbouring hills show that volcanic action still exists within a few miles of *Mongir*. These hot springs are mentioned by Hwen Thsang.

The advantageous position of this isolated hill on the bank of the Ganges, which commanded the land route between the hills and the river, as well as the water route by the Ganges, must have led to its occupation at a very early date. Accordingly it is mentioned in the Mahâbhârata as *Modâgiri*, which was the capital of a kingdom in eastern India, near *Banga* and *Tâmralipta*, or Bengal and Tamluk. At the time of Hwen Thsang's visit the king had been

---

* Julien's 'Hiouen Thsang,' iii. 385.

† *Ibid*, iii. 65—66.

lately ejected by the Raja of a neighbouring state. The kingdom was bounded by the Ganges on the north, and by great forest-clad mountains on the south; and as its circuit is estimated at 3000 *li*, or 500 miles, it must have extended to the south as far as the famous mountain of *Pârasnâth*, which has an elevation of 4478 feet. I would therefore fix its limits as extending from Lakhi Sarai to Sultanganj on the Ganges in the north, and from the western end of the Pârasnâth hill to the junction of the Barâkar and Damuda rivers in the south. The circuit of this tract is 350 miles, measured direct on the map, or upwards of 420 miles by road distance following the windings of the two rivers.*

28. CHAMPÂ.

From Mongir, Hwen Thsang travelled eastward for 300 *li*, or 50 miles, to *Chen-po*, or *Champâ*, which is an old name of the district of *Bhâgalpur*. The capital was situated on the Ganges at from 140 to 150 *li*, or 23 to 25 miles, to the west of a rocky hill that was completely surrounded by the river. On its summit there was a Brahmanical temple. From this description it is easy to recognize the picturesque rocky island opposite *Patharghâta* with its temple-crowned summit. As Patharghâta is exactly 24 miles to the east of Bhâgalpur, I conclude that the capital of Champâ must have stood either on the same site, or in its immediate vicinity. Close

* See Map No. I.

by, on the west side, there still exists a large village named Champanagar, and a smaller one named Champapur, which most probably represent the actual site of the ancient capital of Champâ*

The pilgrim estimates the circuit of Chapmâ at 4000 *li*, or 667 miles; and as it was bounded by the Ganges on the north, and by *Hiranya-Parvata*, or Mongir, on the west, it must have extended to the Bhâgirathi branch of the Ganges on the east and to the Daumda river on the south. Taking the two northern points at *Jângira* and *Teliagali* on the Ganges, and the two southern points at *Pâchît* on the Damuda and *Kalna* on the Bhâgirathi, the length of the boundary line will be 420 miles measured direct, or about 500 miles by road distance. This is so much less than the size estimated by Hwen Thsang that I think there must either be some mistake in the text or some confusion between the geographical limits of the original district of *Champâ*, and its actual political boundary at the time of the pilgrim's visit. We know from his journal that the king of Mongir, on the west of Champâ, had been dethroned by a neighbouring raja, and that the district of Kânkjol on the east of *Champâ* was then a dependency of the neighbouring kingdom. As *Champâ* lies between these two districts, I infer that the raja of *Champâ* was most probably the king who conquered them, and therefore that the large estimates of Hwen Thsang must include these two

* See Map No. 1.

states to the east and west of the original Champâ. Under this view, the political boundaries may be stated as extending from Lakhiterai to Râjmahal on the Ganges, and from the Pârasnâth Hill along the Daumda river to *Kalna* on the Bhagirathi. With these boundaries the circuit of Champâ will be about 550 miles measured direct, or 650 miles by road distance.

29. KÂNKJOL.

From Champâ the pilgrim travelled to the eastward for 400 *li*, or 67 miles, to a small district named *Kie-chu-u-khi-lo*, or *Kie-ching-kie-lo*.* The distance and bearing bring us to the district of *Râjmahal*, which was originally called *Kânkjol*, after a town of that name which still exists 18 miles to the south of Râjmahal. Following the river route viâ Kahalgaon (Colgong) and Râjmahal, the distance from Bhâgalpur is just 90 miles; but by the direct route through the hills, viâ Mângaon and Bharhat, the distance is under 70 miles. As this position agrees with that of the place indicated by Hwen Thsang, I suspect that there may have been a transposition of two syllables in the Chinese name, and that we should read *Kie-kie-chu-lo*, which is a literal transcript of *Kânkjol*. In Gladwyn's translation of the 'Ayin Akbari'† the name is read as *Gungjook*, but as all the names are given alpha-

* Julien's 'Hiouen Thsang,' iii. 73. See Map No. I.
† 'Ayin Akbari,' ii. 178.

betically in the original, it is certain that the first letter is a *k*; I conclude, therefore, that the true name is *Kânkjol*, as the final *l* might easily be misread as a *k*. In his Gazetteer, Hamilton* calls the place *Caukjole*, which is probably a misprint for *Cankjole*. He notes that the district of Râjmahal was formerly "named Akbarnagar from its capital, and in the revenue records *Caukjole*, as being the chief military division."

Hwen Thsang estimates the size of the district at 2000 *li*, or 333 miles, in circuit; but as it was a dependency of one of the neighbouring kingdoms it was probably included, as I have already noted, in the area of the dominant state. When independent, the petty state of *Kânkjol* most probably comprised the whole of the hill country to the south and west of Râjmahal, with the plains lying between the hills and the *Bhâgirathi* river as far south as Murshidâbâd. The circuit of this tract would be about 300 miles, as stated by Hwen Thsang.

30. PAUNDRA VARDDHANA.

From Kânkjol the pilgrim crossed the Ganges, and travelling eastward for 600 *li*, or 100 miles, he reached the kingdom of *Pun-na-fa-tan-na*.† This name M. Stanislas Julien renders as *Paundra-Varddhana*, and M. Vivien de Saint-Martin identifies it with Bardwân. But Bardwân is to the south of the last station, and on the same side of the Ganges,

---

* 'Gazetteer of India,' *in v.* Râjamahal.

† Julien's 'Hiouen Thsang,' iii. 74. See Map No. I.

besides which its sanskrit name is *Varddhamâna*. The difference in the direction of the route might be a mistake, as we have found in several previous instances; but the other differences are, I think, absolutely fatal to the identification of Bardwân with the place noted by Hwen Thsang. I would propose *Pubna,* which is just 100 miles from *Kânkjol,* and on the opposite bank of the Ganges, but its direction is nearly south-east instead of east. The Chinese syllables may represent either *Punya Varddhana*, or *Paundra Varddhana;* but the latter must be the true name, as it is mentioned in the native history of Kashmir* as the capital of *Jayanta,* Raja of *Gau.*, who reigned from A.D. 782 to 813. In the spoken dialects the name would be shortened from *Pon-bardhan* to *Pobadhan*, from which it is an easy step to *Pubna,* or *Pobna,* as some of the people now pronounce it. Hwen Thsang estimates the circuit of the kingdom at 4000 *li,* or 667 miles, which agrees exactly with the dimensions of the tract of country bounded by the Mahânadi on the west, the Tista and Brahmaputra on the east, and the Ganges on the south.

31. JAJHOTI.

Hwen Thsang places the kingdom of *Chi-chi-to* at 1000 *li*, or 167 miles, to the north-east of Ujain.

---

* 'Raja Tarangini,' iv. 421. See also the Quart. Orient. Mag. ii. 188, for an account of Pundra-desa, taken by H. H. Wilson from the Brâhmanda section of the Bhavishya Purâna. The greater part of the province was to the north of the Ganges, including Gauda, Pubna, etc.

As the first and second syllables of this name are represented by different Chinese characters,* it is certain that the pilgrim must have intended them to be the equivalents of two distinct Indian characters. This requirement is fully met by identifying *Chi-chi-to* with the kingdom of *Jajhoti*, or *Jajhaoti*, mentioned by Abu Rihân, who calls the capital *Kajurâhah*,† and places it at 30 parasangs, or about 90 miles, to the south-east of Kanoj. The true direction, however, is almost due south, and the distance about twice 30 parasangs, or 180 miles. This capital was actually visited by Ibn Batuta in A.D. 1335, who calls it *Kajûra*,‡ and describes it as possessing a lake about 1 mile in length, which was surrounded by idol temples. These are still standing at *Khajurâho*, and they form perhaps the most magnificent group of Hindu temples that is now to be found in northern India.

From these accounts of Abu Rihân and Ibn Batuta, it is evident that the province of *Jajhoti* corresponded with the modern district of Bundelkhand. The Chinese pilgrim estimates the circuit of *Chichito* at 4000 *li*, or 667 miles, which would form a square of about 167 miles to each side. Now, Bundelkhand in its widest extent is said to

---

* Julien's 'Hiouen Thsang,' Index, iii. 530, 408. See Map No. 1.

† Reinaud, 'Fragments Arabes,' etc., p. 106.

‡ Dr. Lee's translation, p. 162; where the name is read as *Kajwarâ*, but the original Persian characters read *Kajurâ*.

have comprised all the country to the south of the Jumna and Ganges, from the Betwa river on the west to the temple of *Vindhya-vâsini-Devi* on the east, including the districts of *Chânderi*, *Sâgar*, and *Bilhari* near the sources of the Narbada on the south. But these are also the limits of the ancient country of the Jajhotiya Brahmans, which, according to Buchanan's information,* extended from the Jumna on the north to the Narbada on the south, and from *Urcha* on the Betwa river in the west, to the Bundela Nala on the east. The last is said to be a small stream which falls into the Ganges near Banâras, and within two stages of Mirzapur. During the last twenty-five years I have traversed this tract of country repeatedly in all directions, and I have found the Jajhotiya Brahmans distributed over the whole province, but not a single family to the north of the Jumna or to the west of the Betwa. I have found them at Barwa Sâgar near Urcha on the Betwa, at Mohda near Hamirpoor on the Jumna, at Râjnagar and Khajurâho near the Kane river, and at Udaipoor, Pathâri and Eran, between Chânderi and Bhilsa. In Chânderi itself there are also Jajhotiya Baniyas, which alone is almost sufficient to show that the name is not a common family designation, but a descriptive term of more general acceptance. The Brahmans derive the name of Jajhotiya from *Yajur-hota*, an observance of the Yajur-ved; but as the name is applied to the

* 'Eastern India,' ii. 452.

Baniyas, or grain-dealers, as well as to the Brahmans, I think it almost certain that it must be a mere geographical designation derived from the name of their country, Jajhoti. This opinion is confirmed by other well-known names of the Brahmanical tribes, as *Kanojiya* from Kanoj; *Gaur* from Gaur; *Sarwariya* or *Sarjupâria* from Sarjupar, the opposite bank of the Sarju river; *Dravira* from Dravira in the the Dakhan, *Maithila* from Mithila, etc. These examples are sufficient to show the prevalence of geographical names amongst the divisions of the Brahmanical tribes, and as division is found most numerously in the province from which it derives its name, I conclude with some certainty that the country in which the Jajhotiya Brahmans preponderate must be the actual province of Jajhoti.

Khajurâho is a small village of 162 houses, containing rather less than 1000 inhabitants. Amongst these there are single houses of seven different divisions of the *Jajhotiya* Brahmans, and eleven houses of Chândel Rajputs, the chief of whom claim descent from Raja Paramâl Deo, the antagonist of the famous Prithi Raj. The village is surrounded on all sides by temples and ruins; but these are more thickly grouped in three separate spots on the west, north, and south-east. The western group, which consists entirely of Brahmanical temples, is situated on the banks of the Sibsâgar, a narrow sheet of water, about three-quarters of a mile in length from north to south in the rainy season, but not more than 600 feet square during the dry season. It is three-quarters of a mile from the village, and the same distance from the northern group of ruins, and a full mile from the south-eastern group of Jain temples. Altogether, the ruins cover about one square mile; but as there are no remains of any kind between the western group and the Khajur Sâgar, the boundary of the ancient city could not have extended beyond the west bank of the lake. On the other three sides of the lake, the ruins are all continuous, extending over an oblong space 4500 feet in length from north to south, and 2500 feet in breadth from east to west, with a circuit of 14,000 feet, or nearly 3¾ miles. This corresponds almost exactly with the size of the capital as recorded by Hwen Thsang in A.D. 641, but at some later period the city of Khajurâho was extended to the east and south as far as the *Kurar* Nala, when it had a circuit of not less than 3½ miles. As Mahoba must have been about the same size as Khajurâho, it is doubtful which of the two was the capital at the time of Hwen Thsang's visit. But as the very name of *Mahoba,* or *Mahotsava-nagara,* the "City of the great Jubilee," is specially connected with the rise of the Chândel dynasty, I think it most probable that Khajurâho must have been the capital of the earlier dynasty of Jajhotiya Brahmans; and therefore it must have been the capital of *Jajhoti* at the time of Hwen Thsang's visit. But as it is upwards of 300 miles from Ujain, or just double the distance mentioned by the pilgrim, his 1000 *li* must be increased to 2000 *li*, or 333 miles, to make it accord with the actual measurement. It is a curious fact that Abu Rihân's distance from Kanoj is also in defect in the same proportion; and this agreement suggests that the probable cause of both errors must be the same, namely, the excessive length of the kos of Bundelkhand, which is a little over 4 miles, or exactly double the ordinary *kos* of northern India.

Hwen Thsang estimates the circuit of the kingdom of Jajhoti at 4000 *li*, or 667 miles. To meet these large dimensions it must have comprised the whole tract of country lying between the Sindh and the Tons, from the Ganges on the north to Nya Sarai and Bilhari on the south. This tract includes the famous fort of Kalinjar, which became the permanent capital of the Chândel Rajas after the occupation of Mahoba by the Muhammadans, and the strong fortress of Chânderi, which became the Muhammadan capital of eastern Malwa, after the desertion of the old city of Buri Chânderi.

Mahoba.

The ancient city of Mahoba is situated at the foot of a low granite hill, 54 miles to the south of Hamîrpur, at the junction of the Betwa and Jumna, 34 miles to the north of Khajurâho. Its name is a contraction of *Mahotsava-nagara*, or the "City of the great festival," which was celebrated there by Chandra Varmma, the founder of the Chândel dynasty. It is said to have been 6 *yojanas* long and 2 broad, which is only the usual exaggeration of silly story-tellers for a large city. At its greatest extent, according to my observation, it could never have exceeded 1½ mile in length, from the small castle of Rai-kot on the west, to the Kalyân Sâgar on the east. It is about 1 mile in breadth, which would give a circuit of 5 miles, but an area of only 1 square mile, as the south-west quarter is occupied by the Madan Sâgar. Its population, therefore, at the most flourishing period, must have been under 1,00,000 persons, even allowing as high an average as one person to every 300 square feet. In 1843, when I resided at Mahoba for about six weeks, there were only 756 inhabited houses, with a population less than 4000 persons; since then the place has somewhat increased, and is now said to possess 900 houses, and about 5000 inhabitants.

Mahoba is divided into three distinct portions:—1st, *Mahoba*, or the city proper, to the north of the hill; 2nd, *Bihtari-ḳila*, or the inner fort, on the top of the hill; and 3rd, *Dariba*, or the city to the south of the hill. To the west of the city lies the great lake of *Kirat Sâgar*, about 1½ mile in circumference, which was constructed by *Kirtti-Varmma*, who reigned from A.D. 1065 to 1085. To the south is the *Madan Sâgar*, about 3 miles in circuit, which was constructed by *Madana Varmma*, who reigned from A.D. 1130 to 1165. To the east is the small lake of *Kalyân Sâgar*, and beyond it lies the large deep lake of *Vijay Sâgar*, which was constructed by *Vijaya Pâla*, who ruled from A.D. 1045 to 1065. The last is the largest of the Mahoba lakes, being not less than 4 miles in circuit; but the most picturesque of all sheets of water in the beautiful lake district of Bundelkhand is the Madan Sâgar. On the west it is bounded by the singularly rugged granite hill of Gokâr, on the north by ranges of ghâts and temples at the foot of the old fort, and on the south-east by three rocky promontories that jut boldly out into the middle of the lake. Near the north side there is a rocky island, now covered with ruined buildings; and towards the north-west corner there are two old granite temples of the Chândel princes, one altogether ruined, but the other still standing lofty and erect in the midst of the waters after the lapse of 700 years.

The traditional story of the foundation of Mahoba was originally given by the bard Chand, and has been copied by the local annalists.* According to the legend, the Chândels are sprung from *Hemâvati*, daughter of Hem-râj, the Brahman Purohit of Indrajit, Gâhirwar Raja of Banâras. Hemâvati was very beautiful, and one day when she went to bathe in the Râti Tâlâb, she was seen and embraced by *Chandramâ*, the god of the moon, as he was preparing to return to the skies. Hemâvati cursed him. "Why do you curse me?" said Chandramâ, "your son will be Lord of the Earth, and from him will spring a thousand branches."

* The portion of Chand's poem which treats of the war with the Chândel Raja Parmâl (or Paramârddi Deva), and of the origin of the Chândels, is named *Mahoba-Khand*.

Hemâvati inquired, "How shall my dishonour be effaced, when I am without a husband?" "Fear not," replied Chandramâ, "your son will be born on the bank of the *Karnavati* river: then take him to *Khajurâya*, and offer him as a gift, and perform a sacrifice. In Mahoba he will reign, and will become a great king. He will possess the philosopher's stone, and will turn iron into gold. On the hill of *Kâlinjar* he will build a fort; when your son is 16 years of age, you must perform a *Bhânda Jag* to wipe away your disgrace, and then leave Banâras to live at Kâlinjar."

According to this prophecy, Hemâvati's child, like another Chandramâ, was born on Monday the 11th of the waxing moon of *Vaisâkh* on the bank of the *Karnavati*, the modern *Kayân*, or Kane river of the maps.* Then Chandramâ, attended by all the gods, performed a "great festival" (*Mahotsava*), when Vrihaspati wrote his horoscope, and the child was named Chandra Varmma. At 16 years of age he killed a tiger, when Chandramâ appeared to him and presented him with the philosopher's stone, and taught him polity (*râjnit*). Then he built the fort of Kâlinjar, after which he went to *Kharjurpur*, where he performed a sacrifice (*Jag* or *Yajnya*) to do away with his mother's shame, and built 85 temples. Then Chandrâvati Râni and all the other queens sat

* In some of the manuscripts the name of the river is written *Kiyân*, and *Kiranavati*. The former is no doubt the original of Arrian's *Kainas*, which has perhaps been altered from *Kianas*.

at the feet of Hemâvati, and her disgrace was wiped away. Lastly he went to *Mahotsava*, or Mahoba, the place of Chandramâ's "great festival," which he made his capital.

The date of this event is variously stated by the different authorities; but according to the genealogies furnished by the inscriptions, the most probable period for the establishment of the Chândel dynasty, and the foundation of Mahoba, is about A.D. 800.

32. MAHESWARAPURA.

From Jajhoti the Chinese pilgrim proceeded to the north for 900 *li*, or 150 miles, to *Mo-hi-shi-fa-lo-pu-lo*, or *Maheswarapura*, the king of which was likewise a Brahman. As a northern direction would conduct us to the neighbourhood of Kanoj, I conclude that there is probably a mistake in the bearing. I would, therefore, propose to read 900 *li*, or 150 miles, to the south, in which position stands the old town of *Mandala*, which was also called *Maheshmatipura*.* This was the original capital of the country on the Upper Narbada, which was afterwards supplanted by *Tripuri*, or *Tewar*, 6 miles from Jabalpur. The name is old, as the 'Mahawanso' mentions that the Thero Mahadeva was sent to Mahesa-Mandala, in the time of Asoka, 240 B.C.† The products of the country are said to have resembled those of Ujain, which is a sufficient proof

* Sleeman, Journ. Asiat. Soc. Bengal, 1837, p. 622.

† Turnour's 'Mahawanso,' p. 71.

that *Maheswara* could not have been anywhere to the north of Jajhoti, as the light-coloured soils about Gwalior and in the Gangetic Doâb are quite different from the black soil around Ujain. For these reasons, I am inclined to identify Maheshmatipura on the upper Narbada, with the Maheswarapura of Hwen Thsang. The kingdom was 3000 *li*, or 500 miles, in circuit. With these dimensions, its boundaries may be fixed approximately as extending from Dumoh and Leoni on the west, to the sources of the Narbada on the east.

33. UJAIN.

Hwen Thsang describes the capital of *U-she-yen-na*, or *Ujjayini*, as 30 *li*, or 5 miles, in circuit, which is only a little less than its size at the present day. The kingdom was 6000 *li*, or 1000 miles, in circuit. To the west it was bounded by the kingdom of *Malwa*, with its capital of *Dhâra-nagar*, or *Dhâr*, within 50 miles of Ujain. The territory of Ujain could not therefore have extended westward beyond the Chambal river, but to the north it must have been bounded by the kingdoms of Mathura and Jajhoti, to the east by Maheswarapura, and to the south by the Sâtpura mountains running between the Narbada and the Tapti. Within these limits, that is from Ranthambhâwar and Burhânpur on the west, to Dumoh and Seoni on the east, the circuit of the territory assigned to Ujain is about 900 miles.*

* Julien's 'Hiouen Thsang,' iii. 167. See Map No. I.

The kingdom of Ujain was under the rule of a Brahman Raja, like the two neighbouring states of *Jajhoti* and *Maheswarapura;* but the king of Jajhoti was a Buddhist, while the other two kings were Brahmanists. To the west, the king of Malwa was a staunch Buddhist. But the *Mo-la-po,* or *Malwa,* of Hwen Thsang is limited to the western half of the ancient province, the eastern half forming the Brahmanical kingdom of Ujain. As the political divisions of the province thus correspond with its religious divisions, it may fairly be inferred that the rupture was caused by religious dissensions. And further, as the western or Buddhist half of the province still retained the ancient name of Malwa, I conclude that the Brahmanists were the seceders, and that the kingdom of *Ujain* was a recent Brahmanical offshoot from the old Buddhist kingdom of *Malwa.* Similarly, I believe that *Maheswarapura* must have been a Brahmanical offshoot from the great Buddhist kingdom of *Kosala,* or Berar, which will be described hereafter. In Ujain, there were several dozens of monasteries, but at the time of Hwen Thsang's visit, there were only three or four not in ruins, which gave shelter to about 300 monks. The temples of the gods were very numerous, and the king himself was well versed in the heretical books of the Brahmans.

34. MALWA.

The capital of *Mo-la-po,* or Malwa, is described by Hwen Thsang as situated to the south-east of the river *Mo-ho,* or *Mahi,* and at about 2000 *li,* or 333 miles, to north-west of Bharoch.* In this case both bearing and distance are erroneous, as Malwa lies to the north-east of Bhâroch, from which the source of the river Mahi is only 150 miles distant. I would therefore read 1000 *li,* or 167 miles, to the north-east, which corresponds almost exactly with the position of *Dhâranagara,* or *Dhâr,* one of the old capitals of Malwa. The present town of Dhâr is about three-quarters of a mile in length, by half a mile in breadth, or 2½ miles in circumference; but as the citadel is outside the town, the whole circuit of the place cannot be less than 3½ miles. The limits of the province are estimated at 6000 *li,* or 1000 miles. To the westward there were two dependencies of Malwa, named *Khedâ,* with a circuit of 3000 *li,* or 500 miles, and *Anandapura,* with a circuit of 2000 *li,* or 333 miles, besides an independent state, named *Vadari,* with a circuit of 6000 *li,* or 1000 miles. All these have to be squeezed into the tract of country lying between Kachh and Ujain, on the west and east, Gurjara and Bairât on the north, and Balabhi and Mahârâshtra on the south, of which the extreme boundaries are not more than 1350 miles in circuit. It seems probable, therefore, that the dependencies must have been included by the pilgrim within the limits of the ruling state. I would accordingly assign to *Malwa* and its dependencies the southern half of the tract

* Julien's 'Hiouen Thsang,' iii. 155.

just mentioned, and to *Vadari,* the northern half. The limits of Malwa would thus be defined, by Vadari on the north, Balabhi on the west, Ujain on the east, and Maharashtra on the south. The circuit of this tract, extending from the mouth of the Banâs river, in the Ran of Kachh, to the Chambal, near Mandisor, and from the Sahyâdri mountains, between Dâmân and Mâligâm, to the Tapti river, below Burhânpur, is about 850 miles measured on the map, or nearly 1000 miles by road distance. According to Abu Rihân,* the distance of the city of Dhâr from the Narabada was 7 parasangs, and thence to the boundary of *Mahrat-das,* 18 parasangs. This proves that the territory of Dhâr must have extended as far as the Tapti, on the south.

Hwen Thsang mentions that there were two kingdoms in India that were specially esteemed for the study of the Buddhist religion, namely, Magadha in the north-east, and Malwa in the south-west. In accordance with this fact he notes, that there were many hundreds of monasteries in Malwa, and no less than twenty thousand monks of the school of the Sammatiyas. He mentions, also, that 60 years previous to his visit, Malwa had been governed for 50 years by a powerful king, named *Silâditya,* who was a staunch Buddhist.

35. KHEDA.

The district of *Kie-cha,* or *Kheda,* is placed by Hwen Thsang at 300 *li,* or 50 miles to the north-west

* Reinaud, 'Fragments Arabes et-Persans,' p. 109.

of Malwa.* As both M. Stanislas Julien and M. Vivien de Saint-Martin render *Kie-cha* by *Khacha,* which they identify in the peninsula of *Kachh,* I am bound to state the ground on which I venture to propose a different reading. On looking over the other names in which the peculiar symbol *cha* is used, I find that it occurs in the well-known names of *Pâtali-putra* and *Kukkuta,* where it represents the cerebral t, and again in *O.cha-li,* which M. Julien renders by *Atali,* and M. de Saint-Martin identifies with the desert region of the *Thal,* or *Thar.* Consistently, therefore, the name of *Kie-cha* should be rendered *Khe-ta.* Now *Kheda* is the true Sanskrit form of *Kaira,* a large town of Gujarât, situated between Ahmadâbâd and Khambay; and I would therefore identify the pilgrim's *Kie-cha* with Kheda. It is true that Hwen Thsang's recorded distance is only 300 *li,* but there are so many mistakes in the bearings and distances of this part of the pilgrim's journey, that I have no hesitation in proposing a correction of the text, by reading 1300 *li,* or 217 miles, which is very nearly the exact distance between Kaira and Dhâr. When we remember that the province of Malwa was bounded on the east, within 25 miles, by the independent territory of Ujain, it is difficult to perceive how there could have been any other state within 50 miles of Dhâr, otherwise the territory of Malwa would have been compressed to a breadth of about 50 miles, between

* Julien's 'Hiouen Thsang,' iii. 161.

Ujain and *Kheda*. But this difficulty is entirely removed by adopting my proposed correction, by which the district of *Kheda* becomes the extreme western division of the kingdom of Malwa. Hwen Thsang estimates its circuit at 3000 *li*, or 500 miles, a size which agrees very well with the probable limits of the district of *Kaira*, which may be stated as extending from the bank of the Sâbarmati on the west, to the great bend of the Mahi river on the north-east, and to Baroda in the south. In shape it is a rough square.

36. ANANDAPURA.

Hwen Thsang places *O.nan.to.pu.lo*, or *Anandapura*, at 700 *li*, or 117 miles, to the north-west of *Vallabhi*.* This town has been identified by M. Viven de Saint-Martin with *Barnagar*, on the authority of the *Kalpa Sutra* of the Jains; but the bearing is to the east of north, and the distance is 150 miles, or 900 *li*. *Barnagar* has already been mentioned as the Sanskrit *Vadapura*, or *Barpur*. The district was 2000 *li*, or 333 miles, in extent, and was a dependency of Malwa. This estimate of its size will be fully met by limiting its territory to the triangular tract lying between the mouth of the Banâs river on the west, and the Sâbarmati river on the east.

37. VADARI, OR EDER.

On leaving Malwa, Hwen Thsang travelled first to the south-west to the "confluence of two

* Julien's 'Hiouen Thsang,' iii. 164.

seas," and then turning to the north-west reached *O-cha-li,* or *Vadari,** the whole distance being between 2400 and 2500 *li,* or between 400 and 417 miles. By the term "confluence of two seas," I understand the meeting of the waters of the southern and western seas in the Gulf of Khambay. The town of *Surat,* or the ancient *Surpâraka* near the mouth of the Tapti, may be considered as the entrance of the gulf; and as it lies to the south-west of *Dhâr,* it was probably this point that was first visited by Hwen Thsang. The distance is just 200 miles. From Sûrat to Eder the distance is the same, but the direction is to the east of north; I would, therefore, read north-east instead of north-west, and the position of *Eder* will then correspond sufficiently well with that of Hwen Thsang's *O-cha-li* or *Vadari.* I am ignorant of the Sanskrit name of Eder, but it seems highly probable that the city of *Vadarî* mentioned in the Basantgarh inscription† is the same place. In the middle of the eleventh century *Vadari* was the capital of a chiefship in the neighbourhood of *Vadapura* or *Barnagar,* which lies 30 miles to the westward of Eder, and on the opposite side of the Sâbarmati river. The royal family claimed descent from *Raja Bhava-Gupta,* "who was a great warrior and the illuminator of his line." This *Bhava* or *Bhaba* I believe to be the same as the *Bav* or *Bappa* of the *Sisodiya* annalists of Udaypur, whose imme-

* Julien's 'Hiouen Thsang,' iii. 160.

† Journ. Asiat. Soc. Bengal, x. 668.

diate predecessors for several generations were the Rajas of Eder. As Bappa lived in the beginning of the eighth century, the date of his predecessors, the Rajas of Eder, agrees exactly with the period of Hwen Thsang's visit. For these reasons I think that there are fair grounds for the identification of *Eder* with the *Vadari* of the inscription, as well as with the *Otali*, or *Vadari*, of the Chinese pilgrim.

The size of the province is estimated at 6000 *li*, or 1000 miles, in circuit. This large extent shows that *Atali* or Vadari must have comprised the whole of the unassigned tract of country lying between Vairât on the north, Gurjjara on the west, Ujain on the east, and Malwa on the south. Its boundaries, therefore, must have been Ajmer and Ranthambhor to the north, the Loni and Châmbal rivers on the east and west, and the Malwa frontier on the south, from the mouth of the Banâs river in the Ran of Kachh to the Châmbal near Mandisor. The circuit of these limits is about 900 miles measured on the map, or 1000 miles by road distance.

In Pliny's account of the different nations to the eastward of the Lower Indus I find the following passage, which would seem to apply to Eder and the surrounding districts.* "Next the *Nareœ*, who are bounded by *Capitalia*, the loftiest mountain of India, on the other side of which the people dig up much gold and silver. Beyond them are the *Oraturœ* (or *Oratœ*), whose king has only ten elephants, but a

* Nat. Hist., vi. c. 23.

large force of infantry, (and) the *Varetatœ* (or *Suratatatœ*), whose king has no elephants, but a strong force of horse and foot. (Then) the *Odombœrœ*" etc. The last nation has already been identified with the people of *Kachh,* and the high mountain of Capitalia can only be the holy *Arbuda,* or Mount Abu, which rises to more than 5000 feet above the sea. The Nareæ must therefore be the people of *Sarüi,* or the "country of reeds," as *nar* and *sar* are synonymous terms for a "reed." The country of Sarüi is still famous for its reed arrows.

The *Oraturœ* I would identify with the people of *Vadapura,* or *Barpur,* which is the same name as *Barnagar*. By reading π instead of τ in the Greek original of *Oratura,* the name will become *Orapura,* which is the same as *Barpur,* or *Vadapura.* The last name in Pliny's list is *Varetatœ,* which I would change to *Vataretœ,* by the transposition of two letters. This spelling is countenanced by the termination of the various reading of *Suaratarat*œ, which is found in some editions. It is quite possible however, that the *Suaratarat*œ may be intended for the Surâshtras. The famous Varâha Mihira mentions the *Surâshtras* and *Bâdaras* together, amongst the people of the south-west of India.* These *Bâdaras* must therefore be the people of *Badari,* or Vadari.

I understand the name of *Vadari* to denote a

* Dr. Kern's 'Brihat Sanhita,' xiv. 19.

district abounding in the *Badari,* or *Ber*-tree (Jujube), which is very common in southern Rajputana. For the same reason I should look to this neighbourhood for the ancient *Sauvîra,* which I take to be the true form of the famous Sophir, or Ophir, as *Sauvîra* is only another name of the *Vadari,* or *Ber*-tree, as well as of its juicy fruit. Now, Sofir is the Coptic name of India at the present day; but the name must have belonged originally to that part of the Indian coast which was frequented by the merchants of the West. There can be little doubt, I think, that this was in the Gulf of Khambay, which from time immemorial has been the chief seat of Indian trade with the West. During the whole period of Greek history this trade was almost monopolized by the famous city of Barygaza, or Bhâroch, at the mouth of the Narbada river. About the fourth century some portion of it was diverted to the new capital of Balabhi, in the peninsula of Gujarât; in the middle ages it was shared with Khambay at the head of the gulf, and in modern times with Surat, at the mouth of the Tapti.

If the name of *Sauvîra* was derived, as I suppose, from the prevalence of the Ber-tree, it is probable that it was only another appellation for the province of Badari, or Eder, at the head of the Gulf of Khambay. This, indeed, is the very position in which we should expect to find it, according to the ancient inscription of Rudra Dâma, which mentions *Sindhu-Sauvîra* immediately after *Surâshtra* and *Bhârukachha,* and just before *Kukura, Apâranta,* and *Nishada*.* According to this arrangement, *Sauvîra* must have been to the north of Surâshtra and Bhâroch, and to the south of Nishada, or just where I have placed it, in the neighbourhood of Mount Abu. Much the same locality is assigned to Sauvîra in the Vishnu Purâna: "In the extreme west are the Saurâshtras, Suras, Abhîras, Arbudas; the Kârushas and Mâlavas dwelling along the Pāripâtra mountains; the *Sauvîras*, the Saindhavas, the Hûnas, the Sâlwas, the people of Sakala, the Madras, etc."† In this enumeration we find mention of nearly every known district lying around Vadari, or Eder, on the east, west, north, and south. But there is no notice of Vadari itself, nor of Kheda, nor of Khambay, nor of Analwâra, from which I infer that Sauvîra most probably included the whole of these places. Vadari, or Sauvîra, was therefore equivalent to southern Râjputâna.

In the Septuagint translation of the Bible, the Hebrew Ophir is always rendered by Sôphir. This spelling was perhaps adopted in deference to the Egyptian or Coptic name of Sofir. The earliest mention of the name is in the Book of Job, where the "gold of Ophir" is referred to as of the finest quality.‡ At a later date the ships of Huram, king of Tyre, "went with the servants of Solomon to Ophir, and took thence 450 talents of gold, and

* Journ. Asiat. Soc. Bombay, vii. 120.

† Wilson's translation, edited by Hall, book ii. 3: vol. ii. p. 133.

‡ C. xxii. 24, and xxviii. 16.

brought them to King Solomon."* The gold of Ophir is next referred to by Isaiah, who says, "I will make a man more precious than gold, even a man than the golden wedge of Ophir."† The word here translated 'wedge' means a 'tongue, or ingot;' and I infer that the wedge of gold of 50 shekels weight that was concealed by Achan,‡ was most probably one of the ingots of Ophir.

It now remains to show that the district of Vadari, or Eder, which I have suggested as the most probable representative of Ophir, has been, and still is one of the gold producing countries of the world. The evidence on this point, though meagre, is quite clear. The only ancient testimony which I can produce is that of Pliny, who describes the people dwelling on the other side of mount Capitalia (or Abu), as possessing "extensive mines of gold and silver."§ At the present day the Aravali range is the only part of India in which silver is found in any quantity, while the beds of its torrents still produce gold, of which many fine specimens may be seen in the India museum.

But if the Gulf of Khambay was the great emporium of Indian trade with the West, it is not

---

* 2 Chron. viii. 18. In 1 Kings ix. 28, the amount is 420 talents.

† C. xii. 12.

‡ Joshua vii. 21.

§ Hist. Nat. vi. 23 "Hujus incolæ, alio latere, late auri et argenti metalla fodiunt."

necessary that the gold for which it was famous should have been produced in the district itself. At the present day, Bombay, which is on the same western coast, exports the produce of two inland districts, the opium of Mâlwa and the cotton of Berar. Wherever the emporium of commerce may have been, to that point the gold of India would have flowed naturally, in exchange for the commodities of the West.

EASTERN INDIA.

In the seventh century the division of Eastern India comprised Assam and Bengal proper, together with the Delta of the Ganges, Sambhalpur, Orissa, and Ganjam. Hwen Thsang divides the province into six kingdoms, which he calls *Kâmarupa, Samatata, Tamralipti, Kirana Suvarna, Odra,* and *Ganjam,** and under these names I will now proceed to describe them.

1. KÂMARUPA.

From *Panudra Varddhana,* or Pubna, in Middle India, the Chinese pilgrim proceeded for 900 *li,* or 150 miles, to the east, and crossing a great river, entered *Kia-mo-leu-po,* or *Kâmarupa,* which is the Sanskrit name of Assam.† The territory is estimated at 10,000 *li,* or 1667 miles, in circuit. This large extent shows that it must have comprised the

* See Map No. 1.

† Julien's 'Hiouen Thsang,' iii. 76.

whole valley of the Brahmâputra river, or modern Assam, together with Kusa-Vihâra, and Butàn. The valley of the Brahmâputra was anciently divided into three tracts, which may be described as the Eastern, Middle, and Western districts, namely, *Sadiya, Assam* proper, and *Kâmrup*. As the last was the most powerful state, and also the nearest to the rest of India, its name came into general use to denote the whole valley. *Kusa-Vihâra* was the western division of *Kamrup* proper; and as it was the richest part of the country, it became for some time the residence of the rajas, whose capital, called *Kamatipura,* gave its name to the whole province.* But the old capital of *Kâmrup* is said to have been *Gohati,* on the south bank of the Brahmâputra. Now, *Kamatipura,* the capital of *Kusa-Vihâra,* is exactly 150 miles, or 900 *li,* from Pubna,† but the direction is due north; while Gohati is about twice that distance, or say 1900 *li,* or 317 miles, from Pubna, in a north-east direction. As the position of the former agrees exactly with the distance recorded by the pilgrim, it is almost certain that it must have been the capital of *Kâmrup* in the seventh century. This would seem to be confirmed by the fact that the language of the people differed but slightly from that of Central India. It was therefore not Assamese, and consequently I infer that the

* 'Ayin Akbari,' ii. 3. "*Kamrup*, which is also called *Kamtah.*"

† See Map No. 1.

capital visited by Hwen Thsang was not *Gohati*, in the valley of the Brahmâputra, but *Kamatipura*, in the Indian district of Kusa-Vihâra. The great river crossed by the pilgrim would therefore be the *Tista*, and not the Brahmâputra.

On the east Kâmrup touched the frontiers of the south-western barbarians of the Chinese province of *Shu*; but the route was difficult, and occupied two months. On the south-east the forests were full of wild elephants, which is still the case at the present day. The king was a Brahman, named Bhâskara Varmma, who claimed descent from the god Nârâyana, or Vishnu, and his family had occupied the throne for one thousand generations. He was a staunch Buddhist, and accompanied Harsha Vardhana in his religious procession from Pataliputra to Kanoj, in A.D. 643.

2. SAMATATA.

The capital of the kingdom of *Samatata*, or *San-mo-ta-cha*, is placed at from 1200 to 1300 *li*, or from 200 to 217 miles, to the south of Kâmrup, and 900 *li*, or 150 miles, to the east of Tâmralipti, or Tamluk.* The first position corresponds almost exactly with *Jasar*, or Jessore, which is most probably the place intended. The bearing and distance from Tamluk would take us to the uninhabited part of the *Sundari-vana*, or Sundarbans, between the Huranghâta river and Bakarganj. But in a country

* Julien's 'Hiouen Thsang,' iii. 81. See Map No. 1.

so much intersected by watercourses as Lower Bengal, the road distance is about one-fourth greater than the direct distance, measured on the map. Thus, Jessore, which is 103 miles from *Dhakka*, and 77 miles from Calcutta by road, is only 82 and 62 miles distant from them by direct measurement. Accordingly, Hwen Thsang's distance of 150 miles by route will not be more than 120 miles by direct measurement on the map, which is only 20 miles in excess of the actual direct distance between Jessore and Tamluk. But as Tamluk is not approachable by land from the east, the pilgrim must have travelled at least one-half of the route by water, and his distance of 150 miles may be accepted as a fair estimate of the mixed route by land and water, which could not be actually measured. The name of *Jasar*, or "The Bridge," which has now supplanted the ancient name of *Murali*, shows the nature of the country, which is so completely intersected by deep watercourses, that before the construction of the present roads and bridges, the chief communication was by boats. *Murali*, or *Jasar*, is most probably the *Gange regia* of Ptolemy.

The country of *Samatata* is mentioned in the inscription of Samudra Gupta on the Allahabad pillar,* in which it is coupled with Kâmrup and Nepâl. It is mentioned also in the geographical list of Varâha Mihira, who lived in the beginning of the

---

* Journ. Asiat. Soc. Bengal, vi. 793; line 19 of inscription.

sixth century.* According to Professor Lassen, the name signifies "bas pays littoral," which accords exactly with Hwen Thsang's description of it as a low, moist country on the seashore. The inhabitants were short and black, as is the case at the present day with the people of Lower Bengal. From all these concurrent facts, it is certain that *Samatata* must be the Delta of the Ganges; and as the country is described as 3000 *li,* or 500 miles, in circuit, it must have included the whole of the present Delta, or triangular tract between the Bhâgirathi river and the main stream of the Ganges.

Hwen Thsang mentions several countries lying to the east of *Samatata,* but as he gives only the general bearings and not the distances, it is not easy to identify the names. The first place is *Shi-li-cha-ta-lo,* which was situated in a valley near the great sea, to the north-east of *Samatata.*† This name is probably intended for *Sri-Kshatra,* or *Sri-Kshetra,* which M. Vivien de Saint-Martin has identified with *Sri-hata,* or *Silhat,* to the north-east of the Gangetic Delta. This town is situated in the valley of the Megna river, and although it is at a considerable distance from the sea, it seems most probable that it is the place intended by the pilgrim. The second country is *Kia-mo-lang-ḳia,* which was situated beyond the first, to the east, and near a great bay. This place may, I think, be identified with the district

* Dr. Kern's 'Brihat-Sanhitâ,' xiv. 6.

† Julien's 'Hiouen Thsang,' iii. 82.

of *Komilla,* in Tipera, to the east of the Megna river, and at the head of the Bay of Bengal. The third country is *To.lo.po.ti,* which was to the east of the last. M. Julien renders the name by *Dwâravati,* but he makes no attempt to identify it. I would, however, suggest that it may be *Talaingvati,* that is, the country of the Talaings, or Pegu. *Vati* is the common termination of the names of the Burmese districts, as Hansavati, Dwayavati, Dinyavati, etc. The next name is *I-shang-na-pu-lo,* which was to the east of the last; then still further to the east was *Mo-ho-chen-po,* and beyond that to the south-west was the kingdom of *Yen-mo-na-cheu.* The first of these names I take to be the country of the *Shân* tribes, or Laos; the second is probably Cochin China or Anam; and the third, which M. Stanislas Julien renders by *Yamana-dwipa,* is almost certainly *Yava-dwipa,* or Java.

3. TÂMRALIPTI.

The kingdom of *Tan-mo-li-ti,* or *Tâmralipti,* is described as 1400 or 1500 *li,* about 250 miles, in circuit.* It was situated on the seashore, and the surface of the country was low and wet. The capital was in a bay, and was accessible both by land and water. *Tâmralipti* is the Sanskrit name of Tamluk, which is situated on a broad reach or bay of the Rupnârâyan river, 12 miles above its junction with the Hûghli. The district probably comprised the small

* Julien's 'Hiouen Thsang,' iii. 83.

but fertile tract of country lying to the westward of the Hûghli river, from Bardwân and Kalna on the north to the banks of the *Kosai* river on the south. From *Tâmalitti*, the Pâli form of the name, came the classical *Tamalites*.

4. KIRANA-SUVARNA.

Hwen Thsang places the capital of *Kie-lo-na-su-fa-la-na*, or *Kirana Suvarna*, at 700 *li*, or 117 miles, to the north-west of Tâmralipti, and the same distance to the north-east of *Odra* or Orissa.* As the capital of Orissa in the seventh century was *Jâjipur* on the Vaitarani river, the chief city of *Kirana Suvarna* must be looked for along the course of the *Suvarna-rikṣha* river, somewhere about the districts of *Singhbhûm* and *Barabhûm*. But this wild part of India is so little known that I am unable to suggest any particular place as the probable representative of the ancient capital of the country. Bara Bâzâr is the chief town in Barabhûm, and as its position corresponds very closely with that indicated by Hwen Thsang, it may be accepted as the approximate site of the capital in the seventh century. The territory was from 4400 to 4500 *li*, or from 733 to 750 miles, in circuit. It must, therefore, have comprised all the petty hill-states lying between Medinipur and Sirguja on the east and west, and between the sources of the Damuda and Vaitarani on the north and south.

This large tract of country is now occupied by a

* Julien's 'Hiouen Thsang,' iii. 84 and 88. See Map No. 1.

number of wild tribes who are best known by the collective name of *Kolhân* or *Kols*. But as the people themselves speak various dialects of two distinct languages, it would appear that they must belong to two different races, of whom the *Mûnda* and the *Uraon* may be taken as the typical representatives. According to Colonel Dalton,* "the *Mûndas* first occupied the country and had been long settled there when the *Uraons* made their appearance;" and "though these races are now found in many parts of the country occupying the same villages, cultivating the same fields, celebrating together the same festivals and enjoying the same amusements, they are of totally distinct origin, and cannot intermarry without loss of caste." This difference of race is confirmed by the decisive test of language, which shows that the *Uraons* are connected with the Tâmilian races of the south, while the *Mûndas* belong to the hill men of the north, who are spread over the Himâlayan and Vindhyan mountains from the Indus to the Bay of Bengal.

The various tribes connected with the *Mûndas* are enumerated by Colonel Dalton† as the *Kuars* of Elichpur, the *Korewas* of Sirguja and Jaspur, the *Kherias* of Chutia Nâgpur, the *Hor* of Singhbhûm, the *Bhumij* of Mânbhum and Dhalbhûm, and the

---

* Journ. Asiat. Soc. Bengal, 1866, p. 154.

† *Ibid.*, p. 158. I write *Sântal* in preference to *Sonthal*, as I believe that the short *o* is only the peculiar Bengâli pronunciation of the long *â*.

Sântals of Mânbhûm, Singhbhûm, Katak, Hazâribâgh, and the Bhâgalpur hills. To these he adds the *Juangas* or *Pattuns* (leaf-clad) of Keunjar, etc., in the Katak tributary districts, who are isolated from "all other branches of the *Mûnda* family, and have not themselves the least notion of their connection with them; but their language shows that they are of the same race, and that their nearest kinsmen are the *Kherias*." The western branches of this race are the *Bhîls* of Malwa and Kânhdes, and the *Kolis* of Gujarât. To the south of these tribes there is another division of the same race, who are called *Suras* or *Suars*. They occupy the northern end of the eastern Ghâts.

According to Colonel Dalton,* the *Ho* or *Hor* tribe of Singhbhûm is "the nucleus of the *Mûnda* nation." He calls it "the most compact, the purest, the most powerful and most interesting division of the whole race, and in appearance decidedly the best-looking. In their erect carriage and fine manly bearing the Hos look like a people that have maintained and are proud of their independence. Many have features of sufficiently good cast to entitle them to rank as Arians; high noses, large but well-formed mouths, beautiful teeth, and the facial angle as good as in the Hindu races....When the face of the *Mûnda* varies from the Arian or Caucasian type, it appears rather to merge into the Mongolian than the

* Journ. Asiat. Soc. Bengal, 1866, 168.

Negro...They are of average stature, and in colour vary from brown to tawny yellow."

In the different dialects of the *Mûnda* language *ho, hor, horo,* or *hoko* is the term for "man." The assumption of this name by the people of Singhbhûm is a strong confirmation of Colonel Dalton's description of the tribe as the most powerful division of the *Mûnda* nation. But they also call themselves *Larakas,* or the "warriors," which points to the same conclusion that they are the leading division of the Mûnda race.

Colonel Dalton gives no explanation of the name of *Mûnda;* but as I find that the head men of the villages are called *Mûnda* or *Moto* amongst the Horse of Singhbhûm and other divisions of the Mûnda race, I conclude that the *Mûndas* or *Motos* must once have been the ruling division of the nation. The name of *Mûnda* is found in the Vishnu Purâna* as the appellation of a dynasty of eleven princes who succeeded the *Tushâras* or *Tokhari.* In the Vayu Purâna, however, the name is omitted, and we have only *Marunda,* which is most probably the variant form of another name, *Murunda,* as found in two inscriptions of the second and third centuries.† Ptolemy has *Marundai* as the name of a people to the north of the Ganges; but to the south of the

---

* Wilson's translation, edited by Hall, book iv. 24, and vol. iv. p. 203.

† Samudra Gupta, about A.D. 125 ; and a copper-plate dated in 214 or A.D. 292.

river he places the *Mandali,* who may be the *Mûndas* of Chutia Nâgpur, as their language and country are called *Mundala.* This is only a suggestion; but from the position of the *Mandali* they would seem to be the same people as the *Monedes* of Pliny, who with the *Suari* occupied the inland country to the south of the Palibothri.* As this is the exact position of the country of the *Mûndas* and *Suars,* I think it quite certain that they must be the same race as the *Monedes* and *Suari* of Pliny.

In another passage Pliny mentions the *Mandei* and *Malli* as occupying the country between the *Calingæ* and the Ganges.† Amongst the *Malli* there was a mountain named *Mallus,* which would seem to be the same as the famous Mount *Maleus* of the *Monedes* and *Suari.* I think it highly probable that both names may be intended for the celebrated Mount *Mandar,* to the south of *Bhâgalpur,* which is fabled to have been used by the gods and demons at the churning of the ocean. The *Mandei* I would identify with the inhabitants of the *Mahânadi* river, which is the *Manada* of Ptolemy. The *Malli* or *Malei* would therefore be the same people as Ptolemy's *Mandalæ,* who occupied the right bank of the Ganges to the south of Palibothra. Or they

* Hist. Nat. vi. c. 22. "Ab iis (Palibothris in interiore situ Monedes et Suari, quorum mons Maleus." etc.

† Hist. Nat. vi. c. 21. "Gentes: Calingæ proximi mari, et supra Mandei Malli, quorum mons Mallus, finisque ejus tractus est Ganges."

may be the people of the *Râjmahal* hills who are called *Maler,* which would appear to be derived from the Kanarese *Male* and the Tâmil *Malei,* a "hill." It would therefore be equivalent to the Hindu *Pahâri* or *Parbatiya,* a "hill man."

The *Suari* of Pliny are the *Sabræ* of Ptolemy, and both may be identified with the aboriginal *Savaras,* or *Suars,* a wild race of wood-cutters, who live in the jangals without any fixed habitations. The country of the *Savaras* is said to begin where that of the *Khonds* ends, and to extend as far south as the Pennâr river. But these *Savaras* or *Suars* of the eastern Ghâts are only a single branch of a widely-extended tribe, which is found in large numbers to the south-west of Gwalior and Narwar, and also in southern Rajputâna. The *Savaris* or *Saharias* of the Gwalior territory occupy the jangals on the Kota frontier to the westward of Narwar and Guna. They are found along the course of the Chambal river and its branches, where they meet the Rajputâna *Surrias* of Tod. The name is preserved in the Soræ Nomades of Ptolemy, who are placed to the south of the *Kondali* and *Phyllitæ,* or the Gonds and Bhils. They must therefore be the *Suars* or *Savaras* of central India, who occupy the wild hilly country about the sources of the Wain Gangâ, and who are also found along the valley of the Kistna river. As *Kirana* means a "man of mixed race," or barbarian, it seems probable that the name of *Kirana Suvarna* may be the original appellation of the barbarian *Suvaras,* or *Suars.*

In the beginning of the seventh century the king of this country was *She-shang-kia*, or *Sasângka*, who is famed as a great persecutor of Buddhism.* I found a gold coin inscribed with the name of this prince at full length in the 'Payne Knight Collection' of the British Museum, and there are a few specimens in other collections.

5. ODRA, OR ORISSA.

The kingdom of *U-cha*, or *Oda*, corresponds exactly with the modern province of *Odra*, or *Orissa*. By a reference to the 'Biography of Hiouen Thsang,'† it would appear that the capital of Odra was 700 *li* to the south-west of Tâmralipti, and as this bearing and distance agree with the position of *Jâjipura*, I think that the pilgrim must have returned to *Tamluk* from *Kirana Suvarna* before proceeding to Odra. In the travels of the pilgrim‡ the bearing and distance are taken from Kirana Suvarna; but this is perhaps a mistake, as they are usually referred to the capital, which, whether we place it at Jâjipur or at Katak, is due south of Kirana Suvarna.

The province was 7000 *li*, or 1167 miles, in circuit, and was bounded by the great sea on the south-east, where there was a famous seaport town named *Che-li-ta-lo-ching*, or *Charitrapura*, that is, the "town of embarkation" or "departure." This

* 'Hiouen Thsang's Life,' i. 112 and 235. Also 'Travels,' ii. 349, 422, and 468.

† Julien, i. 184. See Map No. 1.

‡ Julien, iii. 88.

was probably the present town of *Puri*, or "the city," near which stands the famous temple of Jagannâth. Outside the town there were five contiguous stupas with towers and pavilions of great height. I presume that it is one of these which is now dedicated to Jagannâth. The three shapeless figures of this god and his brother and sister, Baladeva and Subhadrâ, are simple copies of the symbolical figures of the Buddhist triad, Buddha, Dharma, and Sangha, of which the second is always represented as a female. The Buddhist origin of the Jagannâth figures is proved beyond all doubt by their adoption as the representative of the Brahmanical Avatâr of Buddha in the annual almanacs of Mathura and Banâras.

The political limits of Orissa, under its most powerful kings, are said to have extended to the Hûghli and Damuda rivers on the north, and to the Godâvai on the south. But the ancient province of *Odra-desa*, or *Or-desa*, was limited to the valley of the Mahânadi and to the lower course of the Suvarnariksha river. It comprised the whole of the present districts of *Katak* (Cuttack) and Sambhalpur, and a portion of Medinipur. It was bounded on the west by Gondwâna, on the north by the wild hill-states of Jashpur and Singhbhûm, on the east by the sea, and on the south by Ganjam. These also must have been the limits in the time of Hwen Thsang, as the measured circuit agrees with his estimate.

Pliny mentions the *Oretes* as a people of India

in whose country stood Mount Maleus;* but in another passage he locates this mountain amongst the *Monedes* and *Suari;* and in a third passage he places Mount *Mallus* amongst the *Malli.* As the last people were to the north of the *Calingæ,* and as the *Monedes* and *Suari* were to the south of the Palibothri, we must look for the *Oretes* somewhere about the Mahânadi river and its tributaries. The *Monedes* and *Suari* must therefore be the *Mûndas* and *Suars,* as already noticed, and the Oretes must be the people of Orissa. *Malê* is one of the Dravidian terms for a mountain; and as the Uraons, or people of west Orissa, still speak a Dravidian dialect, it is probable that *Mallus* was not the actual name of the mountain. May not this have been the famous *Sri-Parvat* of Telingâna, which gave its name to the *Sri-Parvatiya Andhras*?

The ancient metropolis of the country was *Katak* on the Mahânadi river, but in the early part of the sixth century Raja Jajâti Kesari established a new capital at *Jajâtipura* on the Vaitarani river, which still exists under the abbreviated name of *Jâjipura.* The same king also began some of the great temples at Bhuvaneswara; but the city of that name was founded by Lalitendra Kesari. The language and pronunciation of the people is said to have differed

* Hist. Nat. ii. 75. "In Indiæ gente Oretum, mons est Maleus nomine." See also vi. 22, "Monedes et Suari, quorum mons Mallus:" and vi. 21, "Malli, quorum mons Mallus."

from those of central India, which is still true at the present day.

To the south-west there were two hills, on one of which, called *Pushpagiri*, or the "hill of flowers," there was a monastery of the same name and a stupa of stone, and on the other to the north-west only a stupa. These hills I take to be the famous *Udayagiri* and *Khandagiri*, in which many Buddhist caves and inscriptions have been discovered. These hills are situated 20 miles to the south of *Katak*, and 5 miles to the west of the grand group of temples at Bhuvaneswara. The stuaps were said to have been built by demons; from which I infer that the origin of the great caves, and other Buddhist works on these hills was quite unknown at the period of Hwen Thsang's visit.

6. GANJAM.

From the capital of Odra the pilgrim proceeded to the south-west for 1200 *li*, or 200 miles, to *Kong-yu-to*.* This name has not been identified; but M. Vivien de Saint-Martin has, I think, indicated its true position in the neighbourhood of the Chilka lake. The capital was situated near a bay, or "junction of two seas," which can only be intended for the great Chilka lake and the ocean, as there is no other great sheet of water along this surf-beaten coast. Ganjam itself must therefore be the old capital. But as Ganjam is only 130 miles from *Jâjipur* in a direct

* Julien's 'Hiouen Thsang,' iii. 91. See Map. No. I.

line measured on the map, or about 150 miles by road, I conclude that the pilgrim must have visited the hills of *Udayagiri* and *Khandagiri* and the town of *Charitrapura*, or *Puri*, on his way to Ganjam. By this route the distance would be increased to 165 miles by direct measurement, or about 190 miles by road, which agrees with the estimate of the Chinese pilgrim.

The Chinese syllables *Kong-yu-to* are rendered by M. Julien as *Konyodha;* but there is no place of this name that I am aware of. I observe that M. Pauthier* writes the name *Kiuan-yu-mo*, which would seem to be intended for a transcript of Ganjam, of which the derivation is unknown. Hamilton proposes *ganjam*, "the depot," but this term is never used alone, so far as I am aware, but always in combination, either with the founder's name or with the name of the principal article sold in the place, as *Râm-ganj*, or "Râma's market," *Thithâr-ganj*, the "brazier's market," etc. The district was only 1000 *li*, or 167 miles, in circuit, which shows that the territory was confined to the small valley of the Rasikulya river. But though the domain was small, the state would appear to have been of some consequence, as Hweng Thsang describes the soldiers as brave and bold, and their king as so powerful that

---

* 'Journal Asiatique,' 1839, p. 404. *U-cha*, or *Oda*, in eastern India, is said to be also named *Kiuan-yu-mo*, at which time, therefore, A.D. 650 to 684, it must have become dependent on Odra or Orissa.

the neighbouring states were subject to him, and no one could resist him. From this account I am led to infer that the king of Ganjam, at the time of Hwen Thsang's visit, must have been Lalitendra Kesari of the Orissa annals, who is said to have reigned for nearly sixty years, from A.D. 617 to 676. The pilgrim visited Ganjam in A.D. 639, when this prince was at the very height of his power. But only four years later, when the pilgrim revisited Magadha, he found the great King Harsha Varddhana of Kanoj* had just returned from a successful expedition against the king of Ganjam. The cause of the war is not stated, but as Harsha Varddhana was a staunch Buddhist, while Lalitendra was a devoted Brahmanist, the difference of religion would easily have furnished a sufficient pretext for war. It seems probable that Ganjam was then annexed to the dominions of the Kanoj king, and formed part of the province of Orissa.

Hwen Thsang notes that the written characters of Ganjam resembled those of central India, but that both the language and the pronunciation were different. This statement proves that the same alphabetical characters were still in use over the greater part of India at as late a date as the middle of the seventh century. It also serves to show that the intercommunications of the Buddhist fraternities throughout India were not yet broken, although they must already

* Julien's 'Hiouen Thsang,' i. 236.

have been much restricted by the steady progress of Brahmanism.

SOUTHERN INDIA.

According to Hwen Thsang's account, Southern India comprised the whole of the peninsula to the south of the *Tapti* and *Mahanadi* rivers, from Nâsik on the west, to Ganjam on the east. It was divided into nine separate kingdoms, exclusive of Ceylon, which was not considered as belonging to India. The whole of these kingdoms were visited by the pilgrim in A.D. 639 and 640. He entered *Kalinga* from the north-east, and turning to the north-west he visited the inland kingdoms of *Kosala* and *Andhra*. Then resuming his southern route, he passed through *Dhanakakata*, *Jorya*, and *Drâvida*, to *Malakuta*. At Kânchi, the capital of Drâvida, he heard of the assassination of the Raja of Ceylon, and was obliged to give up his intention of visiting that island on account of its unsettled state. Then turning to the north, he reached *Konkana* and *Mahârâshtra*, the last of the nine kingdoms of Southern India.*

1. KALINGA.

In the seventh century, the capital of the kingdom of *Kie-ling-kia*, or *Kalinga*, was situated at from 1400 to 1500 *li*, or from 233 to 250 miles, to the south-west of Ganjam.† Both bearing and

* See Map No. I.

† Julien's 'Hiouen Thsang,' iii. 92. See Maps Nos. I. and XIII.

distance point either to *Rajamahendri* on the Godâvari river, or to *Koringa* on the sea-coast, the first being 251 miles to the south-west of Ganjam, and the other 246 miles in the same direction. But as the former is known to have been the capital of the country for a long period, I presume that it must be the place that was visited by the Chinese pilgrim. The original capital of Kalinga is said to have been *Srikakola,* or Chikakol, 20 miles to the south-west of Kalinga-patam. The kingdom was 5000 *li,* or 833 miles, in circuit. Its boundaries are not stated; but as it was united to the west by Andhra, and to the south by Dhanakakata, its frontier line cannot have extended beyond the Godâvari river, on the south-west, and the Gaoliya branch of the Indrâvati river on the north-west. Within these limits, the circuit of Kalinga would be about 800 miles. The principal feature in this large tract of country is the Mahendra range of mountains, which has preserved its name unchanged from the time of the composition of the Mahâbhârata to the present day. This range is mentioned also in the Vishnu Purâna, as the source of the Rishikulya river, and as this is the well-known name of the river of Ganjam, the Mahendra mountains can at once be identified with the *Mahendra Malê* range, which divides Ganjam from the valley of the Mahânadi.

Rajamahendri was the capital of the junior, or eastern branch of the *Châlukya* princes of *Vengi,* whose authority extended to the frontiers of Orissa. The kingdom of *Vengi* was established about A.D.

540, by the capture of the old capital of *Vengipura*, the remains of which still exist at *Vegi*, 5 miles to the north of *Ellûr*, and 50 miles to the west-south-west of Rajamahendri. About A.D. 750, Kalinga was conquered by the Raja of Vengi, who shortly afterwards moved the seat of government to Raja-mahendri.

The *Calingœ* are mentioned by Pliny,* as occupying the eastern coast of India below the Mandei and Malli, and the famous Mount Maleus. This mountain may perhaps be identified with the high range at the head of the Rishikulya river, in Ganjam, which is still called *Mahendra Malê*, or the "Mahendra mountain." To the south, the territory of the *Calingœ* extended as far as the promontory of Calingon and the town of Dandaguda, or Dandagula,† which is said to be 625 Roman miles, or 574 British miles, from the mouth of the Ganges. Both the distance and the name point to the great port-town of *Coringa*, as the promontory of *Coringon*, which is situated on a projecting point of land, at the mouth of the Godâvari river. The town of *Dandaguda*, or *Dandagula*, I take to be the *Dântapura* of the Buddhist chronicles, which, as the capital of Kalinga, may with much probability be identified with Raja Mahendri, which is only 30 miles to the

* Hist. Nat. vi. 21. "Gentes: Calingæ proximo mari, supra Mandei, Malli, quorum mons Mallus, finisque ejus tractus est Ganges."

† *Ibid*. vi. 23. Philemon Holland's translation has Dandagula.

north-east of Coringa. From the great similarity of the Greek Γ and Π, I think it not improbable that the Greek name may have been *Dandapula*, which is almost the same as *Dântapura*. But in this case, the *Dânta*, or "tooth relic," of Buddha must have been enshrined in Kalinga as early as the time of Pliny, which is confirmed by the statement of the Buddhist chronicles, that the "left canine tooth" of Buddha was brought to Kalinga immediately after his death, where it was enshrined by the reigning sovereign, Brahmadatta.* Dântapura, also, is said to have been situated on the northern bank of a great river, which can only be the Godâvari, as the Kistna was not in Kalinga. This fact alone would be sufficient to fix the position of *Dântapura* at the old capital of *Raja-mahendri*, which is situated on the north-eastern bank of the Godâvari. The name of *Mahendri* is perhaps preserved in the *Pitundra Metropolis* of Ptolemy, which he places close to the *Maisôlos*, or Godâvari, that is, to the river of *Masuli-patam*.

A still earlier name for the capital of Kalinga was Sinhapura,† which was so called after its founder, *Sinha-bahu*,‡ the father of Vijaya, the first recorded sovereign of Ceylon. Its position is not

---

* Turnour, Journ. Asiat. Soc. Bengal, 1837, p. 860, quoting the Dânthâ-dhâtu-wanso, or "History of the Tooth-relic."

† Turnour, 'Mahawanso,' p. 46.

‡ *Ibid*. Appendix v. pp. 88, 89, where the Princess *Tilaka Sundari*, of *Kalinga*, is said to have come from *Sinhapura*.

indicated, but there still exists a large town of this name on the *Lalgla* river, 115 miles to the west of Ganjam, which is very probably the same place.

In the inscriptions of the Kâlachuri, or Haihaya dynasty of Chedi, the Rajas assume the titles of "Lords of *Kâlanjjarapura* and of *Tri-Kalinga.* Kâlanjar is the well-known hill-fort in Bundelkhand; and *Tri-Kalinga*, or the "Three Kalingas," must be the three kingdoms of Dhanaka, or Amaravati, on the Kistna, Andhra or Warangol, and Kalinga, or Rajâ Mahendri. The name of Tri-Kalinga is probably old, as Pliny mentions the *Macco-Calingœ* and the *Gangarides-Calingœ* as separate peoples from the *Calingœ*, while the Mahâbhârata names the Kalingas three separate times, and each time in conjunction with different peoples.* As *Tri-Kalinga* thus corresponds with the great province of *Telingâna,* it seems probable that the name of *Telingâna* may be only a slightly contracted form of *Tri-Kalingâna,* or the "Three Kalingas." I am aware that the name is usually derived from *Tri-Lingga,* or the "Three *Phalli*" of Mahadeva. But the mention of *Macco-Calingœ* and *Gangarides-Calingœ* by Pliny, would seem to show that the "Three Kalingas" were known as early as the time of Megasthenes, from whom Pliny has chiefly copied his Indian Geography. The name must therefore be older than the Phallic worship of Mahadeva in southern India. Kalinga is

* H. H. Wilson, in 'Vishnu Purâna,' pp. 185, 187 note, and 188.

three times mentioned in the Khandagiri inscription of Aira Raja,* which cannot be later than the second century B.C., and at a still earlier date, during the lifetime of Sâkya-Muni, it was noted for its manufacture of fine muslins, and at his death, the king of Kalinga is said to have obtained one of the teeth of Buddha, over which he built a magnificent stupa.†

2. KOSALA.

From Kalinga the Chinese pilgrim proceeded about 1800 or 1900 *li*, or from 300 to 317 miles,‡ to the north-west to the kingdom of *Kiao-sa-lo*, or *Kosala*. The bearing and distance take us to the ancient province of *Vidarbha*, or *Berâr*, of which the present capital is *Nâgpur*. This agrees exactly with the position of Kosala as described in the *Ratnâvali*, and in the *Vâyu Purâna*.§ In the former, the king of Kosala is surrounded in the *Vindhyan* mountains, and in the latter it is stated that *Kusa*, the son of Rama, ruled over Kosala, at his capital of *Kusasthali*, or *Kusâvati*, built upon the Vindhyan precipices. All these concurring data enable us to identify the ancient *Kosala* with the modern province of Berar, or Gondwâna. The position of the capital is more

* James Prinsep in Journ. Asiat. Soc. Bengal, vi. 1082.

† Csoma de Körös, in 'Asiatic Researches,' xx. 85 and 317.

‡ Julien's 'Hiouen Thsang,' vol. i. p. 185, gives 1800 *li*, and vol. iii. p. 94, 1900 *li*. See Map No. I.

§ H. H. Wilson, 'Vishnu Purâna,' Hall's edition, ii. 172, note.

difficult to fix, as Hwen Thsang does not mention its name; but as it was 40 *li*, or nearly 7 miles, in circuit, it is most probably represented by one of the larger cities of the present day. These are Chânda, Nâgpur, Amaravati, and Elichpur.

Chânda is a walled town, 6 miles in circuit, with a citadel. It is situated just below the junction of the Pain Ganga and Warda rivers, at a distance of 290 miles to the north-west of Rajamahendri, on the Godâvari, and of 280 miles from *Dhâranikota*, on the Kistna. Its position, therefore, corresponds almost exactly with the bearing and distance of Hwen Thsang.

Nâgpur is a large straggling town, about 7 miles in circuit; but as it is 85 miles to the north of Chânda, its distance from Rajamahendri is about 70 miles in excess of the number stated by the Chinese pilgrim.

Amaravati is about the same distance from Rajamahendri, and Elichpur is 30 miles still further to the north. *Chânda* is therefore the only place of consequence that has a strong claim to be identified with the capital of Kosala in the seventh century. The recorded distance of 1800 or 1900 *li* from Rajamahendri is further supported by the subsequent distance of 1900 *li*, or 900 plus 1000 *li*, to *Dhanakakata*, which was almost certainly the same place as *Dhârani-kota*, or Amaravati, on the Kistna river. Now, the road distance of Chânda from Dhâranikota is 280 miles, or 1680 *li*, by the direct route; but as Hwen Thsang first proceeded for 900 *li* to the south-west, and then for 1000 *li* to the south, the direct distance between the two places would not have been more than 1700 *li*.

At 300 *li*, or 50 miles, to the south-west of the kingdom, there was a high mountain named *Po.lo. mo.lo.ki-li*, which is said to mean the "black peak." M. Julien identifies this name with "*Baramula-giri* of the present day;"* but I cannot find this place in any map or book to which I have access. The mountain is described as very lofty, and without either spurs or valleys, so that it resembled a mere mass of stone. In this mountain King *So-to-po-ho*, or *Sâtavâhan*, hewed a pavilion of five storeys, which was accessible by a hollow road many dozens of *li*, that is many miles, in length. The place was not visited by Hwen Thsang, as the narrator of his journey uses the expression "on arrive," instead of "il arriva." But as the rock is said to have been excavated as a dwelling for the holy Buddhist sage *Nâgârjuna*, the pilgrim would almost certainly have visited it, if it had been only 50 miles distant from the capital; and if the south-west bearing is correct, he must have passed quite close to the place on his subsequent journey to Andhra, which is said to be either in the same direction, or towards the south. I conclude, therefore, that the curious, "au sud-ouest *du royaume*,"† which the pilgrim uses to indicate

---

* 'Hiouen Thsang,' iii. 101, note 4: "aujourd'hui Baramulaghiri;" and note 5, "en Chinois, *He-fong*, le pic noir."

† Julien's 'Hiouen Thsang,' iii. 101.

the position of this excavated rock, may possibly refer to the boundary of the *kingdom*, and consequently that the place must be looked for at 300 *li*, or 50 miles, beyond its south-west frontier. This position would agree very well with that of the great rock fortress of Deogir, near Elura, and the name of *Polomolokili*, or *Varamula-giri*, might be accepted as the original of *Varula*, or Elura. Parts of the description, such as the long galleries hewn out of the rock, and the cascade of water falling from the top of the rock, agree better with the great Buddhist establishment at Elura than with Deogir. But as the place was not actually visited by Hwen Thsang, his description must have been made up from the varying accounts of different travellers, in which the contiguous sites of Elura and Devagiri were probably treated as one place.

The same rock-hewn habitations are also described by Fa-Hian* in the beginning of the fifth century. He calls the excavation the monastery of *Pho-lo-yu*, or the "Pigeon," and places it in the kingdom of *Tathsin*, that is in *Dakshina*, or the south of India, the present *Dakhan*. His information was obtained at Banâras; and as wonders do not lose by distance, his account is even more wonderful than that of Hwen Thsang. The monastery, hewn out of the solid rock, is said to be five storeys in height, each storey in the shape of a different animal, the fifth, or uppermost, storey being in the form of a

* Beal's 'Fah-Hian,' c. xxxv.

Pigeon, from which the monastery received its name. The Chinese syllables *Pho-lo-yu* must therefore be intended for the Sanskrit *Pârâvata,* a "pigeon." A spring of water rising in the uppermost storey, descended through all the rooms of the monastery, and then passed out by the gate. In this account we have the five storeys, the spring of water falling from the top, and the name of the place, all agreeing very closely with the description of Hwen Thsang. The chief point of difference is in the meaning assigned to the name, as Hwen Thsang states that *Polomolo-ḳili* signifies the "black peak," while according to Fa-Hian, *Pholoyu* means a "pigeon." But there is still another account, of an intermediate date, which gives a third meaning to the name. In A.D. 503, the king of Southern India sent an ambassador to China, from whom it was ascertained that in his country there was a fortified city named *Pa-lai,* or "situated on a height." At 300 *li,* or 50 miles, to the eastward, there was another fortified town, named in the Chinese translation *Fu-cheu-ching,* or "ville soumise à ce qui est détesté,"* which was the birth-place of a famous saint, whose name was *Chu-san-hu,* or "Coral-beads" (grains de corail). Now, *Palâmâlâ* is the name of a "coral necklace," or "string of coral-beads;† and as it represents every syllable of Hwen Thsang's *Polomolo,* I presume that it must be the

* Pauthier, "Examen Méthodique des faits qui concernent Tien-tchu, ou l'Inde;" 'Journal Asiatique,' 1839, p. 292.

† Pauthier, 'Journal Asiatique,' Oct. 1839, p. 292.

same name. I am unable to explain Hwen Thsang's translation of the name as the "black peak" in any of the northern dialects; and I can only suggest that he may perhaps refer to one of the southern or Dravidian dialects. In Kanarese, *malê* is a "hill;" and as pârâ, or "quicksilver," and pâras, or the "touchstone," are both of black hue, it is probable that they are connected with πελός. *Pâra*, therefore, might signify "black," and *pâra-malê* would then be the black hill. One of the most venomous snakes in southern India, which is of a very dark blue or almost black colour, is called *Pâra-Gudu.* It seems probable, therefore, that Hwen Thsang's translation may be derived from one of the southern dialects. This confusion in the Chinese translations is no doubt due to the very defective power of the Chinese syllables for the transcription of Sanskrit words. Thus, *Po.lo.fa.to* might be read as *Pârâvata,* a "pigeon," according to Fa-Hian; or as *paravata,* "subject," according to the *Si-yu-ki;* while it is probable that the true reading should be *parvata,* a "mountain," as the monastery is specially stated to have been excavated in a rocky hill.

The capital itself was named *Pa-lai,** which is said to mean "qui s'appuie sur une éminence." Now the citadel of *Chânda* is called "*Bâla kila,*" or the "High Fort," which, though a Persian appella-

---

* Pauthier in 'Journal Asiatique,' 1839, p. 293.

tion given by the Muhammadans, was very probably suggested by the original appellation of *Palai.**

In all our Chinese authorities the rock-hewn monastery is connected with a holy sage; but the name in each account is different. According to Fa-Hian, it was the monastery of the earlier Buddha named Kâsyapa. In the *Si-yu-ki*, however, it is said to be the birthplace of the *Muni Parâmâlâ,* while Hwen Thsang states that the monastery was excavated by King *Sâtavâhan*, for the use of the famous Nâgârjuna. From the wonderful descriptions of Fa-Hian and Hwen Thsang I have been led to think that their accounts may possibly refer to the grand excavations of Devagiri and Elura. But if the distance given by Hwen Thsang as well as by the *Si-yu-ki* is correct, the rock-hewn monastery must be looked for about 50 miles to the west or south-west of Chânda. Now in this very position, that is about 45 miles to the west of Chânda, there is a place in the map called *Pându-kuri,* or the "Pândus' houses," which indicates an undoubted ancient site, and may possibly refer to some rock excavations, as the rock-hewn caves at Dhamnâr and Kholvi are also assigned to the Pândus, being severally named "Bhim's cave, Arjun's cave," etc. In the total absence of all information, I can only draw attention to the very curious and suggestive name of this place. There is also a series of Buddhist caves at *Patûr,*

* We have an example of such translation in Bulandshahr, which the Hindus still call Uncha-gaon.

50 miles to the south-west of Elichpur and Amaravati, and 80 miles to the east of Ajanta. As these have never been described, it is possible that the site may hereafter be found to correspond with the descriptions of the rock-hewn monastery by Fa-Hian and Hwen Thsang.

The mention of King *Sâtavâhana*, or *Sâdavâhana*, in connection with Nâgârjuna is specially interesting, as it shows that the Buddhist caves of *Parâmâlâ* must be as old as the first century of the Christian era. *Sâdavâhana* was a family name, and as such is mentioned in one of the cave inscriptions at Nâsik.* But *Sâtavâhana* is also a well-known name of the famous Sâlivâhan,† who founded the Sake era in A.D. 79, so that we have a double proof that the Buddhist caves of *Parâmâlâ* must have been excavated as early as the first century. The probable identity of *Sâtavâhan* and *Sâtakarni* will be discussed in another place. We know from the western cave inscriptions that Kosala certainly formed part of the vast southern kingdom of *Gotamiputra Sâtakarni;* and if he flourished in the first century as would appear to be the case,‡ his identity with *Sâtavâhân*,

* Bombay Journal, vii., Nasick inscriptions No. 6, by Mr. West.

† *Sâta*, or *Sâli*, was the name of a *Yaksha*, or demigod, who, being changed to a lion, was ridden by the infant prince, who thus acquired the title of *Sâtavâhan*, or *Sâlivâhan*.

‡ The greater number of the inscriptions in the caves of Kanhari, Nâsik, and Kârle belong to one period; and

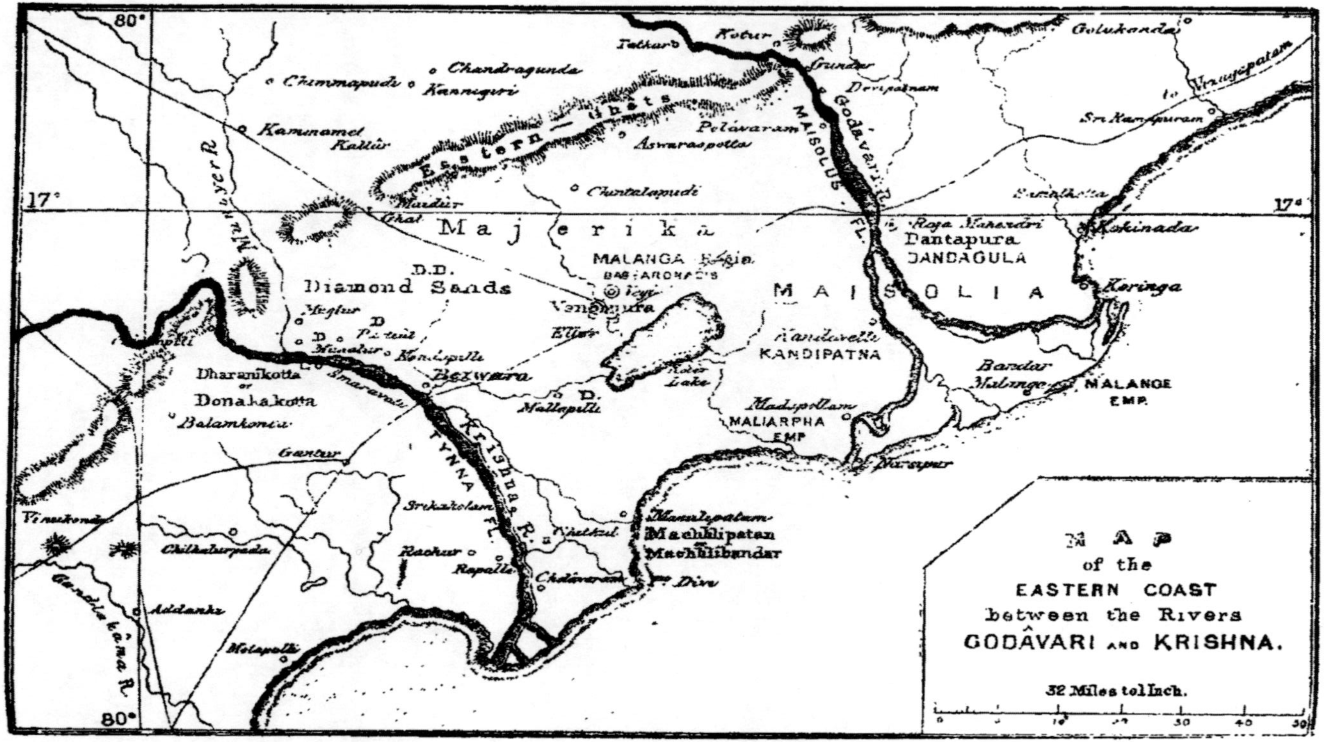
MAP
of the
EASTERN COAST
between the Rivers
GODÂVARI AND KRISHNA.
32 Miles to 1 Inch.
Chandragunda
Chimmapudi
Kannigiri
Kammamet
Kallûr
Eastern Ghats
Polâvaram
Aswaraspolla
Chuntalapudi
Godavari R.
MAISOLUS FL.
Golukonda
Sri Karapuram
Kokinada
Keringa
Roja Mahendri
Dantapura
DANDAGULA
MAISOLIA
Majerika
MALANGA
Diamond Sands
Vengipura
Ellur
KANDIPATNA
Madapollam
MALIARPHA EMP
Bandar Malinga
MALANGE EMP.
Narsapur
Dharanikotta or Donakakotta
Balamkonda
Bezwara
Kondapilli
Mallapilli
Guntur
Krishna R.
TYNNA FL.
Masulipatam
Machhlipatan
Machhlibandar
Chilakurpada
Addanki
Motapalli
Gundlakâma R.
Vinukonda
Repalle
17°
80°

or Sâlivâhan, would be undoubted. It is sufficient here to note the great probability of this interesting point in the history of Southern India.

The kingdom of Kosala is estimated by Hwen Thsang at 6000 *li*, or 1000 miles, in circuit. Its frontiers are not named; but we know from the pilgrim's itinerary that it must have been bounded by Ujain on the north, by Mahârâshtra on the west, by Orissa on the east, and by Andhra and Kalinga on the south. The limits of the kingdom may be roughly described as extending from near Bûrhânpûr on the Tâpti, and Nânder on the Godâvari, to Ratanpur in Chatisgarh, and to Nowagadha near the source of the Mahânadi. Within these limits the circuit of the large tract assigned to Kosala is rather more than 1000 miles.

3. ANDHRA.

From Kosala, Hwen Thsang proceeded to the south for 900 *li*, or 150 miles, to *An-to-lo*, or *Andhra*,* the modern *Telingâna*. The capital was named *Ping-ki-lo*, which M. Julien transcribes as *Vingkhila*, but it has not yet been identified. We know that *Warangol*, or *Varnakol*, was the capital

---

as several of them record the gifts of *Gotamiputra-Sâtakarni*, *Pudumayi*, and *Yâdnya-Sri*, the whole must be referred to the period of the Andhra sovereignty. But one of them is dated in the year 30 of the *Sakâditya-kâl*, or Sake era, that is in A.D. 108; and, therefore, the Andhras must have been reigning at that time.

* Julien's 'Hiouen Thsang,' iii. 105. See Map No. I.

of Telingâna for several centuries afterwards, but its position does not agree with the pilgrim's narrative, as it lies too far from Chânda on the Pain Ganga river, and too near to Dhâranikotta on the Kistna. The Chinese syllables also do not represent the name of Warangol, although they might perhaps be taken for *Vankol*. They may be read as *Bhimgal,* which is the name of an old town in Telingâna mentioned by Abul Fazl. But Bhimgal is only 120 miles to the south-west of Chânda, instead of 150 miles to the south or south-west, and is upwards of 200 miles to the north of Dhâranikotta instead of 167 miles. I should therefore be inclined to accept the Chinese syllables as a blundering transcription of Warangol itself, if the positions agreed more nearly. But the actual distance between *Varangol* and *Chânda* is 160 miles, and between Varangol and Dhâranikotta only 120 miles. It is, therefore, too near the latter place, and too far from the former place, according to Hwen Thsang's account. If we might adopt *Amaravati* in Berar as the capital of Kosala, then *Bhimgal* would represent the capital of Andhra beyond all doubt, as it stands rather short of midway between Chânda and Dhâranikotta; but both the distances are too great to suit Hwen Thsang's numbers of 900 *li* and 1000 *li*, or 150 miles and 167 miles. The position of *Elgandel,* which is midway between Bhimgal and Varangol, agrees better with the pilgrim's narrative, as it is about 130 miles from Chânda, and 170 miles from Dhâranikotta. I am, therefore, willing to adopt *Elgandel* as the probable representative of the capital of *Andhra* in the seventh century of the Christian era.

The province of Andhra is described as 3000 *li*, or 500 miles, in circuit. No frontier is mentioned in any direction; but it may be presumed that the Godâvari river, which is the modern boundary to the north and east, was likewise the ancient one, as it is also the limit of the Telugu language towards the north. To the west, where it met the great kingdom of Mahârâshtra, it cannot have extended beyond the *Manjhira* branch of the Godâvari. The territory may, therefore, be described as stretching from the junction of the Manjhira and Godâvari to Bhadrachelam on the south-east, a length of 250 miles, and to Haidarabad on the south, a length of 100 miles, the distance between Haidarabad and Bhadrachelam being 175 miles. These limits give a total circuit of 525 miles, or nearly the same as that stated by Hwen Thsang.

The *Andhras* are mentioned by Pliny* under the name of *Andarœ*, as a powerful nation, who possessed thirty fortified cities, and a large army of one hundred thousand infantry, two thousand cavalry, and one thousand elephants. They are also noted in the Pentingerian Tables as *Andrœ-Indi.* Wilson quotes these Tables as placing the Andhras "on the banks of the Ganges,"† but the extremely elongated form of the Petingerian Map has squeezed

---

* Hist. Nat., vi. 22.

† 'Vishnu Purana,' Hall's edition, iv. 203, note.

many of the peoples and nations far out of their true places. A much safer conclusion may be inferred from a comparison of the neighbouring names. Thus the *Andrœ-Indi* are placed near *Damirice*, which I would identify with Ptolemy's *Limyrike* by simply changing the initial *Δ* to *Λ*, as the original authorities used for the construction of the Tables must have been Greek. But the people of Limyrike occupied the south-west coast of the peninsula, consequently their neighbours the Andræ-Indi must be the well-known Andhras of Telingana, and not the mythical Andhras of the Ganges, who are mentioned only in the *Purânas*. Pliny's knowledge of the Andaræ must have been derived either from the Alexandrian merchants of his own times, or from the writings of Megasthenes and Dionysius, the ambassadors of Seleukus Nikator and Ptolemy Philadelphus to the court of Palibothra. But whether the Andaræ were contemporary with Pliny or not, it is certain that they did not rule over Magadha at the period to which he alludes, as immediately afterwards he mentions the Prasii of Palibothra as the most powerful nation in India, who possessed 600,000 infantry, 30,000 horses, and 9000 elephants, or more than six times the strength of the Andaræ-Indi.

The Chinese pilgrim notices that though the language of the people of Andhra was very different from that of Central India, yet the forms of the written characters were for the most part the same. This statement is specially interesting, as it shows that the old Nâgari alphabet introduced from Northern India was still in use, and that the peculiar twisted forms of the Telugu characters, which are found in inscriptions of the tenth century, had not yet been adopted in the south.

4. DONAKAKOTTA.

On leaving Andhra, Hwen Thsang proceeded to the south through forests and over desert plains for 1000 *li*, or 167 miles, to *To.na.ḳie.tse.ḳia,* which M. Julien renders by *Dhanaḳacheḳa.* But I have already pointed out in my account of *Tse-ḳia,* or *Taḳi,* in the Panjâb, that the Chinese syllable *tse* is used to represent the Indian cerebral *t,* which would make the name *Dhanaḳataḳa.* I have also referred to the inscriptions in the caves of Kânhari and Kârle with the name of *Dhanaḳaḳata,* which I have suggested as the true reading of the Chinese word, by the transposition of the last two syllables.* The name of *Dhanaḳaḳata* is found in no less than four of the cave inscriptions, in all of which it has been read by Dr. Stevenson as the name of a man, whom he calls *Xenoḳrates,* a Greek. But according to my reading of these inscriptions, the name is undoubtedly that of

* See Maps Nos. I. and XIII. My correction was printed in my Archæological Report to the Government of India in 1864, but it was made several years previously. Dr. Bhau Dâji has also identified the Chinese name with the Dhanakakata of the inscriptions, but he has not noticed the true reading of the Chinese syllable *tse.* (Bombay Journ., vol. vii. p. 68.)

the city or country to which the recorders of the inscriptions belonged. As these inscriptions are short, I will, in justice to Dr. Stevenson, here quote them.

The inscription on which Dr. Stevenson founds his opinion of the Greek origin of the recorder is thus read by himself :*—

Dhanukâkadha Yavanasa Sihadhayânam thabha dânam.

"A gift of lion-supporting pillar by the Greek Xenocrates."

My rendering is somewhat different,—

"Lion-bearing pillar-gift of *Yavana* of *Dhanukakata*."

Dr. Stevenson translates *Yavana* as "Greek;" but the following inscription† shows most distinctly that *Dhanukakata* is the name of a place, and consequently *Yavana* must be the name of a man.

Dhenukakata Usabhadata-putasa
Mita Deva nakasa thabha dânam.

This is translated by Dr. Stevenson as :—

"The gift of a pillar by the chief Mitra Deva, son of Dhenukakata (surnamed) Rishabadatta."

To explain this translation he supposes Dhenukakata to be a Greek, with a Greek name, and to have also a Hindu name which he "probably assumed when he embraced Buddhism, or on adoption into some Hindu family, when names also are changed." But by taking *Dhanukaka* as the name of a place,

* Journ. Asiat, Soc. Bombay, v. 156. Kârle inscription No. 14.

† *Ibid.*, v. 156. Kârle inscription No. 11.

this inscription may be rendered without any forced assumption of a second name. My rendering is,—

"Pillar-gift of the chief *Mitra-Deva*, son of *Rishabadatta* of *Dhanukakata*."

The third Kârle inscription is unfortunately slightly imperfect in the donor's name, and the concluding word is unintelligible, but the opening of the inscription as read by Dr. Stevenson is :*—

Dhanukakata (su) bhavikasa, etc.

which he translates, "The gift of a pleasant abode by Dhanukakata," etc. Here the word which has been restored and translated as "a pleasant abode" is the recorder's name, which I feel strongly inclined to read as *Bhoviveka*, as Hwen Thsang mentions a famous saint of *Donakakatta* named *Po-pi-fei-kia*, that is literally *Bhoviveka* in Pali, or in Sanskrit *Bhâvaviveka*.

The fourth inscription, which is found at Kânhari, consists of nine lines, and is one of the most important of the western cave records, as it is dated in the well-known era of Sâlivâhana. Dr. Stevenson† reads the opening as follows :—

Upâsakasa Dhenukakatinasa kalapa (naka) manakasa, etc.

and refers the record to "*Dhenukakata* the architect." But a more perfect copy of this inscription, published

---

* Journ. Asiat. Soc. Bombay, v. 155. Kârle inscription No. 10.

† *Ibid*., v. 20. Kânhari inscription No. 8.

by Mr. West,* gives the true reading of the first line as :—

Upâsakasa Dhanukakateyasa Kulapiyasa.

of which the literal translation is, "(Gift) of *Kulapiya*, an Upâsika of *Dhanukakata.*"

The date of the inscription, which is at the end of the last line, is erroneously transcribed by Dr. Stevenson thus :—

data va salâ sâka datya lena.

and by adding the previous word *chivarika* he translates it as follows :—

"Here is a hall established for Buddhist-priests; here the Buddha-tooth cave."

In his transcript of this record I notice that Dr. Stevenson altogether omits the letter *k* which occurs between *datya* and *lena* in both copies of the inscription, in that made by Lieut. Brett, which was published by Dr. Stevenson himself,† as well as in that made by Mr. West. With this correction I read the concluding words of the inscription as follows :—

data vase 30 Sakâditya kâla,

of which the literal translation is :—

"Given in the year 30 of the era of *Sakâditya*," that is in A.D. 78 + 30 = 108. *Sakâditya* is one of the common titles of *Sâlivâhana;* and the Sake era, which was established by him, is usually called in

---

* Journ. Asiat. Soc. Bombay, vi. Inscription No. 39.

† *Ibid.*, v. No. 10 of Lieut. Brett's plates of Kânhari inscriptions, which accompany Dr. Stevenson's Memoir, No. 8, p. 20.

ancient inscriptions *Saka-bhûpa kâla*, or *Saka-nripa kâla*, both terms being mere synonyms of *Sakâditya kâla*. Dhanukakata must, therefore, have possessed a Buddhist establishment as early as the beginning of the second century of the Christian era; and if my suggested reading of the name of *Bhâvaviveka* in the Kârle inscription be admitted, Buddhism must have been equally flourishing during the first century, as *Bhâvaviveka* would appear to have been a disciple of Nâgârjuna.*

In fixing the position of *Dhanakakata*, at *Dhâranikotta*, or Amaravti, on the Kistna, I have been guided not only by the bearing and distance from Andhra and Kosala, but by several other concurring reasons, which I will now detail.

Amongst the Buddhist traditions of Ceylon and Siam, we have an account of a country lying between the mouth of the Ganges and the Island of Ceylon, which was inhabited by *Nâgas*. These *Nâgas* possessed either one or two *Drona* measures of the relics of Buddha, which were enshrined in a beautiful and costly stupa, near the "Diamond Sands." Originally, this portion of relics had belonged to Râmagrâma, near Kapilavastu; but when the Râmagrâma stupa was washed away by the river, the relic casket containing one of the original eight divisions of Buddha's remains was carried down the Ganges to the sea, where it was picked up by the

* Burnouf, 'Introduction à l'Histoire du Buddhisme Indien,' p. 560.

Nâgas, and conveyed to their own country, called *Majerika.* Now this country was to the south of *Dantapura,* because Prince *Danta Kumâra* and the Princess *Hemamâla,* when flying from Dantapura to Ceylon with the tooth of Buddha, were wrecked on the coast near the "Diamond Sands." The name itself also helps to fix the position of the Diamond Sands, at or near *Dhâranikotta,* on the Kistna, as the diamond mines of this part of the country are restricted to the small district of *Partiâl,* lying immediately to the north of Dhâranikotta. The flight from Dantapura took place in A.D. 310, at which time, according to the Siamese version, the two Drona measures of relics were still preserved in the Nâga country.* But three years later, or in A.D. 313, the Raja of Ceylon sent a holy priest to bring away these relics from *Majerika.* which was miraculously effected, in spite of the opposition of the Nâgas. The Nâga king then solicited a few relics from the Raja of Ceylon, "which were bestowed upon him accordingly."

There are several minor variations in the Ceylonese account, but the chief difference is in the date. According to the 'Mahâwanso,'† the relics at Râmagrâma consisted of only one *Drona* measure, which, after being enshrined by the Nâgas at Majerika, were carried off to Ceylon in the fifth year of the reign of *Dutthagâmini,* B.C. 157, by whom

* Colonel Low, in Journ. Asiat. Soc. Bengal, 1848; part ii. p. 87. See Map No. XIII.

† Turnour's 'Mahawanso,' p. 185.

they were enshrined in the *Mahâ-thupo*, or great stupa, at Ruanwelli.

The author of the 'Mahâwanso' gives a glowing account of the magnificence of this great stupa of Ceylon; but he admits that the *Chaitya* at Majerika, "was so exquisitely constructed, and so superbly ornamented in various ways . . . that all the accumulated treasures in Lanka would fall short of the value of the last step of its stair."* According to our present knowledge of the antiquities of Southern India, this description can apply only to the magnificent stupa of *Dharanikotta*, on the Kistna, which was literally encased in a profusion of sculptured bas-reliefs.

It is difficult to reconcile the discrepancy between the dates of the Siamese and Ceylonese chronicles; but I think it is highly improbable that these Nâga relics could have been carried to Ceylon at so early a date as 157 B.C., at which time it is more than doubtful whether Buddhism had penetrated to any part of Southern India. I would suggest, as a possible explanation of the discrepancy, that the relics may have been carried off to Ceylon in A.D. 313, as stated in the Siamese chronicles, and there enshrined in the great stupa of Ruanwelli; and that in after times their acquisition was erroneously assigned to *Duttha-gâmini*, the original founder of the stupa. The famous tooth itself, which was taken from *Kalinga* to Ceylon, in A.D. 310, was enshrined in the

* Turnour's 'Mahawanso,' p. 188.

Dharmmachakra, an edifice erected by *Dewânanpiyatisso*, the contemporary of Asoka, about 240 B.C., and was afterwards transferred to the Abhayagiri Vihâra, which was erected in B.C. 89.*

But whether this explanation be accepted or not, we know from the general consent of all the Buddhist chroniclers and pilgrims, as well as of the 'Mahâwanso' itself, that the Râmagrâma relics were still enshrined in their original receptacle, at Râmagrâma, in the middle of the third century, B.C., when Asoka was building stupas over all the relics of Buddha that were divided after his death. If, therefore, the relics were removed to Ceylon in B.C. 157, as stated in the 'Mahâwanso,' we must crowd into a period of little more than 80 years the destruction of the original stupa at Râmagrâma, the enshrinement of the relics at Majerika in the most magnificent stupa in all India, and their subsequent removal to Ceylon. But according to the very competent authority of Mr. Fergusson,† the erection of the Dharanikotta stupa, "judging from its elaboration, may have taken fifty years to complete." We have, therefore, only about thirty years left for the stay of the relics at Râmagrâma, after the time of Asoka, and for their subsequent stay amongst the Nâgas of Majerika. For this reason, I prefer the account of the Siamese chronicles; and I would accordingly fix the date of the removal of the *Drona*

* Turnour's 'Mahawanso,' p. 241.

† Journ. Royal Asiat. Soc., new series, iii. 155.

measure of relics, from Dharanikotta to Ceylon, in the year 313 A.D.

It must be noted, however, that the people of Northern India were happily unaware that the *Drona* of relics enshrined at Râmagrâma had been carried off by the Nâgas to Majerika, as both Fa-Hian and Hwen Thsang, who actually visited the place in the fifth and seventh centuries, mention that the stupa was still standing. It is curious, however, to learn from the journals of both pilgrims, that even in their days the Râmagrâma relics were believed to be watched over by the *Nâgas* of a tank close by the stupa.* According to the original Buddhist legend, these Nâgas had prevented Asoka from removing the relics from Râmagrâma. In the lapse of time, when Râmagrâma had become deserted, as it was found by both pilgrims, this legend might easily have assumed the slightly altered form that the Nâgas had carried off the relics to prevent their removal by Asoka. This form of the legend would have been eagerly seized upon by the *Nâgas* of Southern India, and the transfer of the relics to their own country of *Majeriḳa*, would at once have commanded the easy belief of a credulous people.

In mentioning the relics that were removed from Râmagrâma, the Ceylonese chronicles call them one *Drona* measure, and the Siamese two *Dronas*. I presume, therefore, that they were generally known

---

* Beal's 'Fah-Hian,' c. xxiii.; and M. Julien's 'Hiouen Thsang,' ii. 326.

as the *Drona-dhâtu,* or "*Drona* of relics." In Pali this name would be *Dona,* which may probably be the true original of Hwen Thsang's *To.na.kie.* The full name would have been *Donakadhâtu,* or simply *Donaka,* which with *kot a* added would make *Donaka-kotta,* corresponding with the Chinese syllables *To.na-kie-kia-tse,* as well as with the *Dhanakakata* of the inscriptions. Now I have already shown from the dated inscription of *Kânhari* that the name of *Dhanakukata* is as old as A.D. 108, but as it is spelt in all the inscriptions with *dh* and not with *d,* I infer that the legend about the *Drona* of relics is later than that date. We know that it was a common practice amongst the Buddhists to alter the spelling of the local names so as to obtain meanings which might be adapted to legends of their Teacher. Thus *Takshasila,* the "hewn stone," became *Taksha-sira,* or the "cut-off head," and *Adi-chhatra,* or "King Adi's canopy," became *Ahi-chhatra,* or the "serpent canopy," over the head of Buddha. With reference, therefore, to the Nâga guardianship of the *Drona* of relics at Râmagrâma, I think it highly probable that the old name of *Dhanaka* was changed to *Donaka* by the Buddhists, for the special purpose of adapting it to their legend regarding the disposal of the Râmagrâma *Drona* of relics.

The present name of the place is *Dhârani-kotta,* which I take to be derived from the later legend regarding *Bhâvaviveka,* which is preserved by Hwen Thsang. This holy priest, wishing to behold the future Buddha, Maitreya, fasted for three years, while he continually repeated the mystical verses called *dhâranis*. At the end of that time *Avalokiteswara* appeared to him and instructed him to return to his native country of *Dhanakakata*, and in front of a cavern to the south of the town to recite with perfect faith the *dhâranis*, or mystical verses, addressed to *Vajra-pâni*, when his wish would be accomplished. At the end of three years more *Vajra-pâni* appeared to him, and taught him a secret formula which had power to open the cavern in the palace of the *Asuras*, where the future Buddha was dwelling. After three years spent in the recitation of these secret *dhâranis*, the rock opened, and *Bhâvaviveka* bidding farewell to the multitude, who were afraid to follow him, entered the cavern, which immediately closed upon him and he was no more seen. As this miraculous legend of the *dhâranis* was the popular belief of *Dhanakakata* in the seventh century, the place would naturally have been known amongst the people as *Dhârani-kotta*, or the "Cavern of the *Dhârani* Miracle."

From the mention of *Dhanakakata* in the cave inscriptions of the first and second centuries of the Christian era, we might expect to find some trace of the name in the Geography of Ptolemy. But instead of this we find a people named *Aruarni*, or *Avarni*, occupying the country below the *Maisôlus*, or Godâvari river, with a capital called *Malanga*, the residence of King *Bassaronaga*. As *Malanga* is placed between the two rivers *Maisôlus* and *Tyna*, its position corresponds with that of *Ellûr*, close to which are the remains of the old capital named *Vengi*, which are still known as *Pedda* and *Chinna Vegi*, or Great and Little *Vegi*.* That *Malanga* was in this neighbourhood is proved by the existence of the name at the present day in *Bandar-malanga*, or the "port of *Malanga*," a small town on the coast 54 miles to the east-north-east of Masulipatam. I conclude, therefore, that *Dhanakakata* was only the seat of a great religious establishment, while *Vengi* was the political capital of the country.

With regard to the king's name, I think that the Greek *Bassaro-naga* may be identified with the Pali *Majeri-ka-Nâga* of the 'Mahâwanso.'† Remembering the frequent interchange of the labials *m* and *b*, and that *ka* is an optional affix, the Greek *Bassaro* may be accepted as a tolerably close rendering of the Pali *Majeri;* and thus Ptolemy's *Malanga* would become the capital of the Nâgas of *Majerika*.

On a general review of all the evidence in favour of the identification of *Dhâranikotta* with the *Dhanakakata* of Hwen Thsang and with the *Majerika Stûpa* of the Nâgas, the most striking point is the exceeding beauty of the relic stupa, which is common to all of them. I have already quoted the account of the 'Mahâwanso' as to the gorgeous magnificence of the *Nâga Stûpa of Majerika*, the last step of which was

---

* See Map No. XIII.

† Turnour's 'Mahawanso,' p 185, *Manjerika-nâga-bhawanau*, "the land of the Nâgas of Majeri."

beyond the power of all the riches of Ceylon to equal. Similarly the Chinese pilgrim was struck with the unusual beauty of the religious edifices of *Dhanakakata,* which he describes as possessing all the magnificence of the palaces of Bactria.* We have also the evidence of our own eyes as to the exceeding beauty and lavish ornament of its sculptures, many of which now grace the India Office Museum, in London. And lastly, we have the tradition of the people that *Dhâranikotta* was once the capital of this part of India.†

The age of the stupa can only be determined approximately, as the twenty inscriptions on the sculptures in London give no dates, and make no certain mention of any kings or persons whose age is known. But from the style of the alphabetical characters, I am satisfied that the inscriptions belong to the same period as those of the famous caves of Kânhari, Nâsik, and Kârle, which record the gifts of Gotamiputra—Sâtakarni, Pudumâyi, and Yâdyna Sri, of the Andhra dynasty. They agree also with those of the Sâtakarni inscription on the gateway of the Bhilsa tope,‡ as well as with those of Rudra

* M. Julien's 'Hiouen Thsang,' i. 188.

† Hamilton's 'Gazetteer of India,' *in voce* "Amravatty."

‡ 'Bhilsa Topes,' p. 264. Mr. Fergusson refers to this inscription as being in the same characters as the *Lât* inscriptions of Asoka ; but he is undoubtedly mistaken, as the gateway inscriptions of the Bhilsa tope are in a very different character, as may be seen by a reference to my work.

Dama's inscription on the rock of Girnar. I have already noted that one of the Kânhari inscriptions is dated in the year 30 of the Sakâditya Kâl, or era of Sake, equivalent to A.D. 108; and I may now add that Rudra Dama's inscription is dated in the year 72, which, if referred to the Vikramâditya era, will be A.D. 15, or if to the Sake era, A.D. 150, both dates being within the period of the first two centuries of the Christian era, to which I refer the Amaravati inscriptions. Colonel Mackenzie also obtained some leaden coins of Gotamiputra* and of other princes of the Sâtakarni dynasty of Andhras, when excavating the ruins at Dharanikotta—a discovery which alone is sufficient to establish the existence of some important buildings at this very spot during their reigns. I have already suggested that *Gotamiputra Sâtakarni* was probably the same person as the great *Sâlivâhan*, or *Sâdavâhan*, who established the Sake era; and I am inclined to assign the foundation of the Amaravati stupa to him, in about A.D. 90, and its completion to *Yâdrya Sri Sâtakarni*, one of his successors, who ascended the throne in A.D. 142. This date corresponds very well with the only facts that we possess regarding the age of the stupa, namely, that it cannot be earlier than the Christian era or later than A.D. 313, when its relics were carried away to Ceylon.

* Sir Walter Elliot, in 'Madras Literary Journal,' 1858, vol. iii. new series: "I am responsible for the readings." See Plate XI. No. 105, *Rajnya Gotamiputa Satakanisa*; also Nos. 92 and 101. No. 96 has *Satakanisa*, and No. 100 *Pudumâvisa*.

At a much later date, in the beginning of the eleventh century, *Danaka* is mentioned by Abu Rihân, who describes it as "the plains of the *Konkan.*" Now, the Konkan is the valley of the Kistna river, and this description of the country of *Danaka* adds another proof to the correctness of my identification of Hwen Thsang's *Dhanakakata* with the ruined city of *Dhâranikotta* on the Kistna. According to Abu Rihân,* Danaka was the native country of the *Karkadan,* or rhinoceros. Now the same statement is made by the merchant Sulimân† of a country in the south of India, named *Ruhmi,* رهمي, which was famous also for extremely fine muslins, that could be passed through a ring. The same country is noticed by Masudi‡ as *Rahma,* and by Idrisi as *Dumi.* Masudi, also, notes that it extended along the seacoast. Now Marco Polo mentions the town of *Mutafili,* in the province of Masulipatam and to the north of Malabar, as famous for diamonds and for the thinnest and most delicate cotton cloths resembling spiders' webs. Mutafili has generally been identified with Masulipatam itself; but a considerable town named Mutapili still exists near the seacoast at 65 miles to the south of *Dhâranikotta,* and 70 miles to the south-west of Masulipatam. In either case, however, Marco's notice determines the

* Reinaud, 'Fragments Arabes,' etc., p. 109.

† Sir Henry Elliot's 'Muhammadan Historians of India,' by Professor Dowson, i. 5.

‡ *Ibid.,* i. 25.

fact that the country about the mouths of the Godâvari was famous for diamonds and for delicately fine muslins. It must, therefore, have included the diamond district of *Partyâl*, immediately to the north of *Dhâraniḳo ta*, as well as the muslin district of Masulipatam; and, accordingly, it may be identified with the *Rahmi* or *Dumi* of the Arab geographers. By a very slight change in the characters رهمى *Rahmi* might become دهنك *Dhanaḳ*, which would agree with the *Danaḳa* of Abu Rihân.

According to the chronicles of Orissa,* the present town of Amaravati was founded, or established as a subordinate seat of government, by Surya Deva, Raja of Orissa in the twelfth century. The name is connected with the worship of Siva as *Amaranâtha*, or *Amareswara;* and one of the twelve great *Lingas* of this god, which is assigned to Ujain, almost certainly, belonged to the holy city on the Kistna, as we know that Ujain possessed its own famous temple of Mahâkâla, and that all the other ten shrines of Siva belong to different places.

I cannot close this account without noting that M. Vivien de Saint-Martin has stated his suspicion that the name of Dandaka is connected with *Dhanaḳaḳata.*† The Dandakâranya, or forest of Dandaka, is celebrated in Indian story. *Varâha*

* Stirling in Journ. Asiat. Soc. Bengal, 1837, p. 760.

† M. Julien's 'Hiouen Thsang,' iii. 396. 'Mémoire Analytique sur la Carte de l'Asie Centrale et de l'Inde.'

*Mihira,** the great astronomer, mentions *Dandaka* along with other places in the South of India as follows: *Kerala, Karnâta, Kânchipura, Konkana, Chinna-pattana* (or *Madras*), etc. In this list Dandaka is distinct from Konkana, or the Upper Kistna; and may, therefore, perhaps be identified with the lower valley of the Kistna of which *Dhanaka-kata* was the capital. But as the latter name is found in the early inscriptions of the western caves, it is probable that the mere verbal resemblance of *Dandaka* may be quite accidental.

Hwen Thsang describes the province of *Dhanakakata* as 6000 *li*, or 1000 miles, in circuit. These large dimensions are corroborated by its other name of *Ta-an-ta-lo,* that is *Mahâ Andhra,* or the great Andhra, which is noted by the Chinese editor,† as the other districts of *Telingâna,* namely *Kalinga* and *Andhra* proper are smaller than *Dhanakakata.* No frontier is mentioned in any direction; but it is most probable that the boundaries of the province corresponded as nearly as possible with the limits of the Telugu language, which extended to Kulbarga and Pennakonda on the west, and to Tripati and the Pulikat lake on the south. On the north it was bounded by Andhra and Kalinga, and on the east by the sea. The circuit of these boundaries is, as nearly as possible, 1000 miles; and I am, therefore, inclined to believe that the large tract of country thus

* Kern's 'Brihat-Sanhita,' c. xiv.; v. 12, 13, 14.

† M. Julien's 'Hiouen Thsang,' iii. 110, note 2.

described is the famous Dhanakakata of Hwen Thsang.

5. CHOLIYA, OR JORIYA.

From Dhanakakata, Hwen Thsang travelled to the south-west for 1000 *li*, or 167 miles, to *Chu-li-ye*, or *Jho-li-ye*, which he describes as a small district only 2400 *li*, or 400 miles, in circuit.* To enable us to fix the position of this unknown territory it is necessary to note the pilgrim's subsequent route to the south for 1500 or 1600 *li*, or about 260 miles, to *Kânchipura* or Conjeveram, the well-known capital of Drâvida. Now, the distance of Kânchipura from the Kistna is from 240 to 260 miles, so that *Chuliya* must be looked for somewhere along the south bank of that river, at 167 miles to the south-west of *Dhâranikotta*. This position corresponds almost exactly with *Karnûl*, which is 230 miles in a direct line to the north-north-west of Kânchipura, and 160 miles to the west-south-west of Dhâranikotta. M. Julien has identified *Choliya* with *Chola*, which gives its name to *Chola-mandala*, or Coromandel. But *Chola* was to the south of Drâvida, whereas the Choliya of Hwen Thsang lies to the north of it. If we accept the pilgrim's bearings and distances as approximately correct, the position of Choliya must certainly be looked for in the neighbourhood of Karnûl.

Professor Lassen has suggested that the names

* Julien's 'Hiouen Thsang,' iii. 116. See Map No. I.

of *Choliya* and *Drâvida* may have been transposed by the Chinese editor of the pilgrim's travels. The same suggestion occurred to me when I first examined the travels some years ago; and if it was quite certain that the Chinese syllables *Chu-li-ye* represented *Chola,* there would be a very strong temptation to adopt the suggestion. But I agree with M. Vivien de Saint-Martin* that it is difficult to admit the possibility of such a transposition, although an adherence to the text of Hwen Thsang involves the total omission of any mention of the famous kingdom of *Chola.* M. de Saint-Martin points to the present use of the name of Coromandel, which is applied to the whole of the Madras coast, as far north as the mouths of the Godâvari, as a possible explanation of the extension of the name of *Chola* to the country immediately to the south of the Kistna. But I believe that this extension of the name is solely due to European sailors, who adopted it for the sake of convenience. This name besides applies only to the sea-coast, whereas *Chuliya* is described by Hwen Thsang as a small district lying to the south-west of *Dharanikotta,* so that if we accept the pilgrim's account as it stands, it is scarcely possible that Choliya could have extended so far to the east as the sea-coast.

It is admitted that the identification of Choliya is difficult; but I am of opinion that we must either accept the pilgrim's account as it now stands, or

* M. Julien's 'Hiouen Thsang,' iii. 398.

adopt the transposition suggested by Professor Lassen. In the former case, we must look for Choliya in the neighbourhood of Karnûl; in the latter case, it may be at once identified with the famous province of *Chola*, and its well-known capital Tanjor.

In the Chino-Japanese map of India, constructed to illustrate the pilgrim's travels, the district of *Choliya* is named *Chu-ey-no*, and is placed to the north of Drâvida, and to the south-west of Dhanaka, as in the text of Hwen Thsang. These Chinese syllables may perhaps represent *Kandanûr*, which, according to Buchanan, is the correct form of the name of *Karnûl*.

Immediately under the walls of Karnûl, lies the old town of *Zora*, or *Jora*, the *Jorampur* of the maps, which answers exactly to the *Choliya* or *Joriya* of the pilgrim. The initial Chinese syllable seems to be very rarely used, but a similar letter is found in *Kajugira*, *Jutinga*, and *Jyotishka*, and I am satisfied that M. Julien's reading of the character as *ju*, or *jo*, is correct. I am also inclined to identify *Jora* with Ptolemy's *Sora regia Arcati*. In some editions the words are transposed, as *Arcati regia Sora*. But though the cart may be put before the horse, it is still the cart, and therefore, I take *Sora* to be the capital of King *Arkatos*, whether it be placed before or after his name. *Arkatou* has been usually identified with *Arcot*, near Madras; but the name of this city is believed to be quite modern, and the position of *Sora* must be far to the north of Arcot.

The *Soræ Nomades* of Ptolemy may therefore be a branch of the *Sauras,* who are still located on the banks of the Kistna river. One hundred miles to the west-north-west of Karnûl, there is also a large town, named *Sorapur,* the Raja of which "still holds his patrimonial appanage, surrounded by his faithful tribe (*Bêdars*), claiming a descent of more than thirty centuries."*

As *Chuliya* is described as being only 2400 *li,* or 400 miles, in circuit, its small size offers no help towards its identification. If it is placed in the Karnul district, it will cut off the north-western corner of the province of *Dhanakakata,* but will not lessen its circuit, although it will diminish its area. If, however, *Chuliya* is to be identified with *Chola,* I would assign to it the modern district of *Tanjor,* extending from *Sankeri-Drûg,* near Salem on the north-west, to the mouth of the *Kâveri* or *Kolrûn* river, on the north-east, and from Dindigal, on the south-west, to Point Calimere on the south-east. This tract is about 120 miles in length, by 80 miles, or just 400 miles, in circuit.

6. DRÂVIDA.

In the seventh century the province of *Ta-lo-pi-cha,* or *Drâvida,* was 6000 *li,* or 1000 miles, in circuit, and its capital, named *Kien-chi-pu-lo,* or *Kânchi-pura,* was 30 *li,* or 5 miles, in circuit.† *Kânchipura*

* General Briggs in Journ. Royal Asiat. Soc., xiii. 294.

† Julien's 'Hiouen Thsang,' iii. 118. See Map No. 1.

is the true Sanskrit name of *Conjeveram*, on the Palâr river, a large straggling town of great antiquity. As *Drâvida* was bounded by *Konkana* and *Dhanakakata* on the north, and by *Malakuta* on the south, while no district is mentioned to the west, it seems certain that it must have extended right across the peninsula, from sea to sea. Its northern boundary may therefore be approximately defined as running from *Kundapur*, on the western coast, viâ Kadur and Tripati, to the Pulikat Lake, and its southern boundary from Calicut to the mouth of the Kâveri. As the circuit of these limits is very nearly 1000 miles, the boundaries suggested may be accepted as very nearly correct.

During the pilgrim's stay at Kânchipura, about 300 Buddhist monks arrived from Ceylon, which they had quitted on account of political disturbances, consequent on the death of the king. By my reckoning, Hwen Thsang must have arrived in Kânchipura, about the 30th of July, A.D. 639, and, according to Turnour's list of the kings of Ceylon, Raja Buna Mugalân was put to death in A.D. 639. From the information furnished by these monks, the pilgrim drew up his account of *Seng.kia.lo*, or Ceylon, which he was prevented from visiting by the disturbed state of the country.

7. MALAKUTA, OR MADURA.

From Kânchipura, Hwen Thsang proceeded to the south for 3000 *li*, or 500 miles, to *Mo-lo-kiu-cha*,*

* Julien's 'Hiouen Thsang,' iii. 121. See Map No. I.

which M. Julien renders by *Malakuta*. In the southern part of the territory, towards the sea-coast, stood the mountain named *Mo-la-ye*, or *Malaya*, which produced sandal-wood. The country thus described is therefore the southern end of the peninsula, part of which is still called *Malayâlam* and *Malayawâra*, or *Malabâr;* I would accordingly read the Chinese syllables as an abbreviated form of *Malayakuta*. The circuit of the kingdom was 5000 *li*, or 833 miles, being bounded by the sea to the south, and by the province of Drâvida to the north. As this estimate agrees almost exactly with the measurement of the end of the peninsula, to the south of the Kâveri river, the province of Malaya-kuta must have included the modern districts of Tanjor and Madura, on the east, with Coimbator, Cochin, and Travancore, on the west.

The position of the capital is difficult to fix, as a distance of 500 miles, to the south of Conjeveram, would take us out to sea beyond Cape *Kumâri*, (Comorin). If we might read 1300 *li*, or 217 miles, instead of 3000 *li*, both bearing and distance would agree exactly with the position of the ancient city of Madura, which was the capital of the southern end of the peninsula in the time of Ptolemy. It is possible that *Kaulam* (Quilon) may have been the capital at the time of Hwen Thsang's visit; but neither the distance nor the bearing agrees with the pilgrim's statement, as the place is not more than 400 miles to the south-west of Conjeveram. To the north-east of the capital there was a town named *Charitra-pura*, or "Departure-town," which was the port of embarkation for Ceylon. If *Madura* was the capital, the "port-city" was probably Negapatam; but, if *Kaulam* was the capital, the "port-city" must have been Râmnâd (*Râmanâthapura*). From this port, Ceylon was distant 3000 *li*, or 500 miles, to the south-east.

According to the writer of the 'Life of Hwen Thsang,'* Malayakuta was not visited by the pilgrim, but described by hearsay, and the distance of 3000 *li* is said to be from the frontiers of Drâvida. But this would only increase the difficulty by placing the capital of Malayakuta still further to the south. In a note to this passage,† M. Julien quotes the *Si-yu-ki* as fixing the distance at 300 *li*, instead of 3000 *li*, as given in his translation of the Memoirs of Hwen Thsang. If this number is not a misprint, these different readings may show that there is some uncertainty as to the distance, as well as to the point of departure. I am inclined, therefore, to think that the original distances given in the memoirs and life of the pilgrim may perhaps have been 300 *li*, or 50 miles, from the frontiers of Drâvida in the latter, and 1300 *li*, or 217 miles, from the capital of Drâvida in the former. In either case, the capital of *Malayakuta* would be fixed at *Madura*, which has always been one of the principal cities of Southern India.

---

* Julien, i. 193: "Il entendit dire qu'à trois mille *li* des frontières de ce pays [Drâvida] il y avait un royaume appelé *Mo.lo.kiu.cha.*"

† 'Hiouen Thsang,' i. 193; and iii. 121.

According to Abu Rihân, and his copyist, Rashid-ud-din, *Mâlya* and *Kûtal* (or *Kunak*) were two distinct provinces, the latter being to the south of the former, and the last, or most southerly district of India. It seems probable therefore, that *Malyakuta* is a compound name, formed by joining the names of two contiguous districts. Thus, *Mâlya* would answer to the district of *Pândya,* with its capital of Madura, and *Kûta,* or *Kûtal,* to Travancore, with its capital of *Kochin,* the *Kottiara* of Ptolemy.

Hwen Thsang's omission of any mention of *Chola* may be explained by the fact that at the time of his visit the *Chola-desa* formed part of the great kingdom of the *Cheras.* Chola is, however, duly noticed by Ptolemy, whose *Orthura regia Sornati* must be *Uriûr* the capital of *Soranâtha,* or the king of the *Soringœ,* that is the *Soras, Choras* or *Cholas.* Uriûr is a few miles to the south-south-east of Trichinopoli. The Soringæ are most probably the *Syrieni* of Pliny with their three hundred cities, as they occupied the coast between the *Pandœ* and the *Derangœ* or Dravidians.

According to M. Julien* *Malyakuta* was also called *Chi-mo-lo,* which I read as *Jhi-mu-ra,* because the initial syllable is the same as the second syllable of *Chi-chi-to,* or *Jajhoti. Jhimura* is perhaps only a variant form of the Limurike of Strabo, Ptolemy, and Arrian, and of the *Damirice* of the Pentingerian Tables. It would also appear to be the same name as

* 'Hiouen Thsang,' iii. 121.

Pliny's *Charmæ,* a people who occupied the western coast immediately above the Pandæ.

In the Chino-Japanese map of India the alternative name of *Malyakuta* is *Hai-an-men,* which suggests a connection with Ptolemy's *Aioi.*

8. KONKANA.

From *Malayakuta* the pilgrim returned to *Drâvida* (Conjeveram), and then proceeded to the north-west for 2000 *li,* or 333 miles, to *Kong-kien-na-pu-lo,* or *Konkanapura.** Both the bearing and distance point to *Annagundi* on the northern bank of the *Tûngabhadra* river, which was the ancient capital of the country before the Muhammadan invasion. M. Vivien de Saint-Martin has suggested the old town of *Banawâsi,* which is mentioned by Ptolemy as *Banauasei.* But the distance is rather too great, and the subsequent bearing to the capital of *Mahârâshtra* would be almost due north instead of north-west as stated by the pilgrim. *Annagundi* is a remarkable old site, and was the capital of a *Yâdava* dynasty of princes before the foundation of the modern city of *Vijayanagar* on the southern bank of the river.†

According to Hamilton, the name of *Konkana* amongst the natives includes "much country lying to the east of the western ghâts." This extension agrees with Abu Rihân's description of *Danaka* as the "plains of the *Konkan,*" which can only apply to

---

* Julien's 'Hiouen Thsang,' iii. 146. See Map No. I.

† Wilks' 'Mysore,' i. 14; note, quoting from the Mackenzie MSS.

the table-land above the ghâts. Such also may have been its application in the time of Hwen Thsang, as he describes the kingdom as being 5000 *li*, or 833 miles, in circuit, which, if limited to the narrow strip of land between the ghâts and the sea, would include the whole line of coast from Bombay to Mangalûr. But in the seventh century the northern half of this tract belonged to the powerful *Châlukya* kingdom of Mahârâshtra; and consequently, if the pilgrim's estimate of its size is correct, the kingdom of *Konkana* must have extended inland far beyond the line of the western ghâts. Its actual limits are not mentioned, but as it was bounded by Drâvida on the south, by Dhanakakata on the east, by Mahârâshtra on the north, and by the sea on the west, it may be described as extending along the coast from Vingorla to Kundapûr, near Bednûr, and inland from the neighbourhood of Kulbarga to the ancient fortress of *Madgiri*, which would give a circuit of about 800 miles. This was the ancient kingdom of the *Kâdambas*, which for a time rivalled that of the *Châlukyas* of Mahârâshtra. Hamilton states that the name of the country is pronounced *Kokan* by the natives, which suggests its identification with the people called *Cocondœ* by Pliny, who occupied a middle position in the route from the south of India towards the mouth of the Indus.

9. MAHÂRÂSHTRA.

From Konkana the pilgrim proceeded to the north-west for 2400 to 2500 *li*, or upwards of 400 miles, to *Mo-ho-la-cha,* or *Mahârâshtra.* The capital was 30 *li,* or 5 miles, in circuit, and on the west side touched a large river.* From this description alone I should be inclined to adopt *Paithan,* or *Pratishthâna,* on the Godâvari as the capital of Mahârâshtra in the seventh century. It is mentioned by Ptolemy as *Baithana,* and by the author of the 'Periplus' as *Plithâna,* which should no doubt be corrected to *Paithana.* But the subsequent distance of 1000 *li,* or 167 miles, westward or north-westward† to Bhâroch is much too small, as the actual distance between *Paithan* and *Bhâroch* is not less than 250 miles. M. Vivien de Saint-Martin thinks that Devagiri accords better with the position indicated: but Devagiri is not situated on any river, and its distance from Bhâroch is about 200 miles. I think it more probable that Kalyâni is the place intended, as we know that it was the ancient capital of the *Châlukya* dynasty. Its position also agrees better with both of Hwen Thsang's distances, as it is about 400 miles to the north-west of Annagundi, and 180 or 190 miles to the south of Bhâroch. To the west of the city also flows the Kailâs river, which at this point is a large stream. *Kalyân* or *Kalyâni* is mentioned by Kosmas Indikopleustes in the sixth century as the

* Julien's 'Hiouen Thsang,' iii. 149. See Map No. I.

† M. Julien's 'Hiouen Thsang,' iii. 401. In the life of the pilgrim, i. 203, the direction is said to be north-east, but as this would place the capital of Mâhârâshtra in the midst of the Indian Ocean, the correction to north-west is absolutely necessary.

seat of a Christian bishopric, under the name of *Kalliana,* and by the author of the 'Periplus' in the second century as *Kalliena,* which had been a famous emporium in the time of *Saraganos* the elder.* The name of Kaliyana also occurs several times in the Kânhari cave inscriptions, which date from the first and second centuries of the Christian era.

The circuit of the province is said to be 6000 *li,* or 1000 miles, which agrees with the dimensions of the tract remaining unassigned between Malwa on the north, Kosala and Andhra on the east, Konkana on the south, and the sea on the west. The limiting points of this tract are Dâmân and Vingorla on the sea-coast, and Idalâbâd and Haidarâbâd inland, which give a circuit of rather more than 1000 miles.

On the eastern frontier of the kingdom there was a great mountain with ridges rising one over another, and scarped crests. In former days the Arhat Achâra had built a monastery, with rooms excavated in the rock, and a front of two storeys in height facing a "sombre" valley. The *Vihâr* attached to it was 100 feet in height; and in the midst of the monastery there was a stone statue of Buddha about 70 feet high, which was surmounted by seven stone caps suspended in the air without any apparent support. The walls of the *Vihâr* were divided all round into panels in which were sculptured with minute detail all the great events of Buddha's life. Outside the north and

* Hudson, Geogr. Vet. i. 30: καλλίενα πολίς, ἡ ἐπὶ τῶν Σαραγάνου τοῦ πρεσβυτέρου χρόνων ἐμπόριον ἔνθεσμον γενόμενον.

south gates of the monastery there were stone elephants, both on the right-hand and on the left, which according to the belief of the people occasionally roared so loudly as to make the earth quake. The description of the hill is too vague to be of much use in identifying its position; but if the easterly bearing is correct, the hill of *Ajayanti* is most probably the place intended, as its bluff ridges appear to answer better to the pilgrim's account than the smoother slopes of Elura. But with the exception of the stone elephants, the account is too vague to enable us to identify the place with any certainty. There are two stone elephants outside the Kailâs excavation at Elura, but that is a Brahmanical temple, and not a Buddhist *vihâr*. There is also an elephant close to the *Indrasabha* at Elura, but the animal is inside the courtyard, instead of outside the gate as described by the pilgrim. Scenes from Buddha's life formed the common subjects of Buddhist sculpture, and would therefore offer no special assistance towards the identification of the monastery. But though the pilgrim's account is vague, it is so minute as to the positions of the elephants and the arrangement of the sculptures that I am inclined to think he must have seen the place himself. In this case I would read "western" frontier of the kingdom, and identify his cave monastery with the well-known excavations of Kânhari in the island of Salsette. Indeed, if I am correct in the identification of Kalyâni as the capital of Mahârâshtra in the seventh century, it is almost certain that the pilgrim must have visited the Buddhist establishments at *Kânhari,* which are not more than 25 miles distant from Kalyâni. The numerous inscriptions at Kânhari show that some of its excavations must date as early as the first century before Christ, and the bulk of them during the first and second centuries after Chirist. One of the inscriptions is dated in the year 30 of the *Sakâdityakâl,* or A.D. 108. No remains of stone elephants have yet been found at *Kânhari,* but as the structural *facades* in front of the excavated *vihârs* have all fallen down, some elephant torsos may yet be discovered amongst the ruins along the foot of the scarped rock. Mr. E. West has already disinterred the remains of a stone stupa with all its sculptured friezes from amongst these ruins, and further research will no doubt bring to light many other interesting remains.

CEYLON.

The famous island of Ceylon is not reckoned amongst the kingdoms of India, and it was not visited by the pilgrim on account of political disturbances. But as he gives a description of it from the account of the monks whom he met at *Kânchipura,* and as it is closely connected with India both religiously and politically, my work would not be complete without some notice of this interesting island.

In the seventh century of our era Ceylon was known by the name of *Seng-kia-lo,* or *Sinhala,* which was said to be derived from the lion-descended *Sinhala,* whose son Vijaya is fabled to have conquered the island on the very day of Buddha's death, in B.C. 543. Its original name was *Pao-chu,* or "Isle of Gems," in Sanskrit *Ratna-dwîpa.* Its existence was first made known to the European world by the expedition of Alexander, under the name of *Taprobane.* The popular Pâli form is *Tâmba-panni,* or "red-handed," in allusion to the "red palms" of the hands of Vijaya's sick companions, who, on landing from their vessel, touched the red ground with their hands. The true form, however, would appear to be *Tâmba-panni,** or "red-leaved," from the Sanskrit *Tâmra-parni.* Lassen also gives *Tambra-pani,* or the "great pond," or "pond covered with the red lotus," as a probable derivation. In later times it was known to the western world as *Simundu,* or *Palai-Simundu,* which Lassen thinks may have been derived from *Pali-Simanta,* or "head of the holy law." As Pliny applies the latter name to the city containing the royal palace, it has been supposed to be only another appellation for the capital *Anarajapura,* or *Anuragrammon,* of Ptolemy. No explanation is offered of *Andrasimundu,* which Ptolemy gives as the name of a promontory on the western coast of Ceylon, opposite Anarajapura. From its position it may be only another name for *Palaisimundu.*

Ptolemy calls the island *Salike,* which, as Lassen suggests, would appear to be only a sailor's corrupt form of *Sinhalaka,* or *Sihalaka,* shortened to *Silaka.* Ammianus calls it *Serendivus,* which is the same as

---

* Turnour's 'Mahawanso,' p. 50.

the *Sieladiba* of Kosmas, both being derived from *Sihala-dîpa*, which is the Pâli form of *Sinhala-dwîpa*, or "Sinhala's island." Abu Rihân gives the form of *Singal-dib*, or *Sirindib*, which is the *Serendib* of European sailors. From the same source came the Arabic *Zilan*, and our own Ceylon. Amongst the Hindus the most familiar name is *Langka-dwîpa*, which is also mentioned in the 'Mahâwanso' under the Pâli form of *Lanka-dipa*.*

According to Hwen Thsang, the circuit of the island was 7000 *li*, or 1167 miles,† which is nearly double the truth,—its actual size, according to Sir Emerson Tennent, being 271½ miles in length from north to south, and 137½ miles from east to west, or about 650 miles in circuit. Its dimensions are so uniformly exaggerated by the classical authors that I cannot help suspecting some misconception as to the value of a local measure. Kosmas, on the authority of Sopater, who had actually visited the island, gives its size as 300 *gaudia*, γαυδία, in length, and the same in breadth. This name Sir Emerson Tennent identifies with that of a local measure, named *gaou*,‡ which he estimates at about 3 miles,

---

* Turnour's 'Mahawanso,' pp. 2, 3, 49.

† Julien's 'Hiouen Thsang,' iii. 125. See Map No. I.

‡ 'Ceylon,' i. 567. He indentifies the γαυδία with the *gaou* now in use, which is "the distance that a man can walk in an hour." But how about the word *hour*, which has a strong European smack about it? Was not the original *gaou* the distance that a man could walk in 1 *ghari*, or 24 minutes, the well-known Indian division of

thus making the island 900 miles long, and as many broad. But the *gaudia* may just as likely be the well-known *gao-kos* of India. This was the distance at which the lowing of a cow could be heard, that is 1000 *dhanus*, or bows, equal to 6000 feet, or 1.136 of a mile. The 300 *gaudia* would thus be equal to 340 miles, which is only 70 miles in excess of the real length of the island. Pliny makes the length 10,000 stadia, or 1149 English miles. Ptolemy assigns nearly 15 degrees of latitude, or about 1000 miles, which is slightly reduced by Marcianus to 9500 stadia, or 1091½ English miles. Now the earlier Chinese pilgrim, Fa-Hian, who visited Ceylon in A.D. 412, or about one century before Sopater, states the size of the island at 50 *yojanas* in length by 30 in breadth,* or about 350 miles by 210 miles. If, as we may fairly suppose, both travellers derived their dimensions from the statements of the people of the country, the 300 *gaudia* of Sopater may be taken as the equivalent of 50 *yojanas*, which gives 6 *gaudia* to the *yojana*, and makes the native measure rather more than one English mile, or exactly equal to the *gao-kos* of India.

---

time? If so, the length of the *gaou*, at 3 miles to the hour, would be 1·2 miles, which agrees very closely with the actual length of the *gao-kos*, as noted above. The *gaou* is valued by Wilson at 4 kos ; *vide* his Glossary *in voce*.

* Beal's 'Fah-Hian,' c. xxxvii. p. 148. But he makes the length from east to west, instead of from north to south.

In his interesting and valuable work on Ceylon, Sir Emerson Tennent has suggested that the port of Galle may be the *Tarshish** of the Bible, "which lay in the track between the Arabian Gulf and *Ophir,*" and that *Ophir* itself is Malacca, or the Aurea Chersonesus, because "*Ophir,* in the language of the Malays, is the generic name for any gold mine." But this view seems to me to be quite untenable, as the names of all the articles brought back by Solomon's fleet are pure Sanskrit. Sir Emerson states that they are "identical with the Tâmil names by which *some* of them are called in Ceylon to the present day." These names are *sen-habim,* or "teeth of elephants," *kophim,* or "apes," and *tukïm,* or "parrots." But these are the pure Sanskrit words *ibha, kapi,* and *suka,* with the mere addition of the Hebrew plural termination. It is true that these Sanskrit names have been naturalized in the south of India, but they have not displaced the original Tâmil appellations, which still remain the terms in common use, namely, *yânê* for elephant, *kuranga* for monkey, and *mayil* for peacock, or *kilip-pillai* for parrot. Now, if the fleet of Solomon obtained these Sanskrit names in Ceylon, then we must admit that the Aryan race had pushed their conquests to the extreme south of India some centuries before the time of Solomon, that is about 1200 or 1500 B.C. But at this very time, as we learn from their own records, the Aryas had not yet

* 'Ceylon,' ii. 101.

crossed the Narbada, nor even penetrated to the mouth of the Ganges. It does not therefore seem possible that any of their names could have been obtained either in Ceylon or in the south of India so early as the time of Solomon. Even according to their own annals,* the Ceylonese were barbarians until the landing of Vijaya, in B.C. 543; and there is no satisfactory evidence of any Aryan connection or intercourse before the time of Mahendra, the son of Asoka, in B.C. 242.

The writer of the article *Ophir* in Smith's 'Dictionary of the Bible' argues in favour of Arabia, by assuming that "ivory, apes, and peacocks" were not imported from Ophir, but from Tarshish, and that gold and *algum* trees only were imported from Ophir. By this assumption he gets rid of the Indian names for the elephant, monkey, and parrot; but there still remains the name of *algum* wood, which Professor Lassen derives from the Sanskrit *valgu,* or sandal-wood. He admits that Arabia does not now produce gold, but thinks that it may once have done so, or if not, that it at least possessed gold by importation, as the Queen of Sheba presented much gold to Solomon.

This subject has already been discussed in my account of Vadari, or Eder, in Western India; but I may here again state my opinion that the Ophir of the Bible, which is rendered *Σώφειρ* and *Σουφίρ*

* 'Fo-kwe-ki,' c. xxxviii. 'Mahawanso,' p. 48. 'Hiouen Thsang,' iii. 132.

by Josephus and the Septuagint,* is most probably the *Sauvîra* of Hindu geography, or south-western Râjputana, which amongst the people of the west would have been pronounced *Hobir*, just as *Sindhu* became Indus, and as *sapta* became *haft* and ἕπτα. According to Pliny the country to the north of the Gulf of Khambay formerly produced both gold and silver, which it does even at the present day. Specimens of gold from the Aravali mountains may be seen in the India Museum, and the same range is the only part of India in which silver is found in any quantity. Western India also was colonized by the Aryan race at least two thousand years before Christ, and the Aryan language had become the common speech of the country long before the time of Solomon. I would therefore identify the *Ophir* or *Sophir* of Scripture with the Indian *Sauvîra* of the Hindus, where the captains of Solomon's fleet could have obtained the fine pure gold for which Ophir was famed, and where they would have obtained ivory, apes, and peacocks (or parrots) called by the very names which they have preserved to us in the Bible.

---

* Josephus, Antiq., i. 6, 4. 1 Kings x. 11; and 2 Chron. viii. 18. *Sofir* is the Coptic name of India.

APPENDIX A.

APPROXIMATE CHRONOLOGY OF HWEN THSANG'S TRAVELS.

A.D.		References. Julien's 'Hiouen Thsang.'
629, Aug. 1	Left *Liang-cheu,* in 8th month of 3rd year of *Ching-kwang,* on horseback	Vol. i. 14.
Dec. 1	*Akini,* about 1200 miles, including 2 months' detention on the way	Vol. i. 15, 39.
Dec. 28	*Baluka,* about 500 miles.	
630, Jan. 10	*Issikul,* about 250 miles.	
Feb. 10	*Talas,* about 600 miles.	
Mar. 5	SAMARKAND, about 500 miles.	
,, 20	*Khulm* (Hu-o), halt for 1 month	Vol. i. 62.
Apr. 20	BALKH.	
,, 30	*Bamian.* Snowstorm on road to *Kapisa*	Vol. i. 71.
May 10	KAPISA. Halt till end of summer	Vol. i. 75.
Aug. 15	*Lamghân.* Halt 3 days . . .	Vol. i. 75.
,, 20	*Nagarahâra.* Halt 2 months (?) to visit holy places.	
Nov. 1	*Gândhâra.* Visits holy spots.	
Dec. 1	*Utakhanda.*	
631, Jan. 1	*Udyâna.* Visits holy places.	
Mar. 1	Source of *Subhavastu* river; frost and ice.	
Apr. 1	Returns to *Utakhanda.*	
,, 10	TAXILA. Halt 1 month (?) to visit holy places.	
May 25	*Sinhapura.*	
June 15	Returns to *Taxila.*	
July 10	*Urasa.*	
Aug. 10	KASHMIR. Halt 2 entire years.	Vol. i. 96.
633, Oct. 1	Leaves Kashmir.	
,, 10	*Punach.*	
,, 20	*Rajaori.*	

A.D.		'Hiouen Thsang.'
633, Nov. 10	*Tseka* or *Taka*.	
,, 15	*Sâkala* or *Sangala*.	
,, 25	Large town (? Kusâwar or Kasûr). Halt 1 month . . .	Vol. i. 101.
634, Jan. 1	*Chinapati*. Halt 14 months. .	Vol. i. 101.
635, Mar. 15	*Jâlandhara*. Halt 4 months .	Vol. i. 102.
Aug. 1	*Kuluta*.	
Sep. 10	*Satadru*.	
,, 25	*Pâriyâtra*, or *Bairât*.	
Oct. 5	*Mathura*.	
,, 25	*Thânesar* or *Sthâneswara*.	
Nov. 1	SRUGHNA. Halt 4½ months, for whole winter and half spring	Vol. i. 106.
636, Mar. 15	MADAWAR. Halt 4½ months, for half spring and whole summer.	Vol. i. 109.
Aug. 1	*Brahmapura*.	
,, 5	Returns to *Madâwar*.	
,, 10	*Govisana*.	
,, 15	*Ahichhatra*.	
,, 20	*Pilosana*.	
,, 25	*Sankisa*.	
Sep. 1	KANOJ. Halt 3 months . . .	Vol. i. 113.
Dec. 1	*Ayuto*.	
,, 4	*Hayamukha*.	
,, 7	*Prayâga*.	
,, 10	*Kausâmbi*.	
,, 13	*Kusapura*.	
,, 16	*Vaisâkha*, or *Sâketa*, or *Ajudhya*.	
,, 20	SRAVASTI.	
,, 25	*Kapilavastu*.	
Dec. 28	Râmagrâma.	
637, Jan. 1	*Kusinagara*.	
,, 3	Large Brahmanical town (? *Khukhundo*).	
,, 12	BANARAS, or VARANASI.	
,, 20	*Garjapatipura*.	
,, 25	VAISALI.	
,, 30	*Vriji*.	
Feb. 5	*Nepâla*.	
,, 15	Returns to *Vaisâli*.	
,, 20	MAGADHA. Capital, *Pâtaliputra*.	

A.D.		'Hiouen Thsang.'
637, Mar. 1	*Rajagriha*, NALANDA. Long stay. Visits all the holy places ; returns to *Nâlanda* for 15 months.	Vol. i. 152. Vol. i 164.
	Study of language—say altogether 22 months.	
639, Jan. 1	*Hiranya-parvata.*	
,, 5	*Champa.*	
,, 10	*Kânkjol.*	
,, 15	*Paundra Varddhana.*	
Feb. 20	*Kâmarupa.*	
Mar. 20	*Samatata.*	
Apr. 10	*Tâmralipti.*	
,, 20	*Kirana Suvarna.*	
May 5	*Odra*, or *Orissa.*	
,, 15	*Ganjam.*	
,, 30	*Kalinga.*	
June 20	*Kosala.*	
July 20	*Andhra.*	
,, 30	*Dhanakakata.* Halt "many months," say 6	Vol. i. 189.
640, Feb. 1	*Jorya.*	
,, 20	*Drâvida.* Capital *Kânchipura*, or Conjeveram	Vol. i. 190.
Apr. 1	*Malyakuta.*	
May 10	Returns to *Drâvida.*	
June 20	*Konkanapura.*	
July 20	*Mahârâshtra.*	
Aug. 10	*Bhâroch.*	
Sep. 1	*Malwa.*	
Oct. 10	*Vadari*, or *Eder.*	
,, 15	*Kheda*, or *Khaira.*	
Nov. 1	*Vallabhi.*	
,, 16	*Anandapura.*	
,, 26	*Surashtra.*	
641, Jan. 1	*Gurjara.*	
Feb. 20	UJAIN.	
Mar. 20	*Jajhoti.*	
Apr. 5	*Maheswarapura.*	
May 15	Returns to *Surashtra.*	
June 20	*Udumbara*, or *Kachh.*	
July 30	*Lângala*, or *Biluchistan.*	

A.D.		'Hiouen Thsang.'
641, Aug. 13	*Pitasila*, or *Patala*.	
,, 20	*Avanda*, or *Brahmanabad*.	
Sep. 1	SINDH. Capital *Alor*. Halt 20 days.	
Oct. 10	MULTAN.	
,, 20	*Polofato* (? Solofato), or Shorkot. Halt 2 months.	
642, Apr. 1	Returns to Magadha. Halts 2 months, to resolve doubts .	Vol. i. 211.
Aug. 5	Revisits *Kâmarupa*. Halts one month ; messengers sent to different kingdoms. . . .	Vol. i. 236.
Nov. 1	Starts for *Kânyakubja*, or *Kanoj*, "in beginning of winter," in company with King Silâditya.	Vol. i. 242.
Dec. 25	Arrives in last month of the year.	Do.
	Religious assembly at Kanoj ; discussions for 18 days . .	Vol. i. 246.
643, Mar. 1	*Prayâga*. Grand religious assembly held in 2nd month of spring	Vol. ii. 257.
	Lasts for 75 days	Vol. i. 252.
May 25	*Kausâmbi*. 7 days' march . .	Vol. i. 260.
July 1	*Pilosana*. March 1 month, halt 2 months	Vol. i. 261.
Sep. 20	JALANDHARA. Halt 1 month .	Do.
Nov. 15	*Sinhapura*.	
Dec. 15	TAXILA. Halt 7 days . . .	Vol. i. 264.
,, 25	Fords the Indus on an eleplant ; therefore in midwinter to	
	Utakhanda. Halt 1 month and 20 days	Do.
644, Mar. 15	Reaches *Lamghân* with the king in 1 month	Vol. i. 265.
June 15	*Falana*, or *Banu*. 15 days' march	Do.
,, 20	*Opokien*, or *Afghan*.	
,, 25	*Tsaokiuto*, or *Ghazni*.	
July 1	*Urddhasthâna*, or *Ortospana*, or *Kabul*.	

A.D.		'Hiouen Thsang.'
644, July 5	KAPISA. Halt. Religious assembly 7 days	Vol. i. 266.
,, 20	*Andarâb*. Cross snowy mountains, and frozen streams.	
Aug. 1	*Tukhâra*. Halt 1 month.	
Sep. 1	*Munkan*.	
,, 3	*Himatala*.	
,, 8	*Badakshân*.	
,, 10	*Kiepokian*.	
,, 12	*Kuilangnu*.	
,, 25	*Pamer*.	
,, 26	*Kopanto*. Halt 20 days.	
Oct. 10	Great rock.	
,, 12	*Ush*.	
,, 15	*Kâshgâr*.	
,, 22	*Yârkand*.	
Nov. 2	*Kotan*. Halt 7 days.	
,, 13	*Khima*. Sandy desert.	
,, 16	*Nijang*. Great desert.	
,, 21	*Tukhâra*.	
Nov. 29	*Chemotana*.	
Dec. 13	*Nafopo*.	
Jan. 1	Frontier of China, after some détours.	
Apr. 1	Enters the capital of Western China, in spring of 645 (first moon of spring, nineteenth year of Ching-kwang) . .	Vol. i. 292.

The above chronology gives the approximate dates as nearly as I can determine them, partly from the facts stated, and partly from my own lengthened experience of travelling in India. The estimated dates are well supported by facts noted in the histories of Ceylon, Sindh, and Kashmir; but I may here repeat, that on Hwen Thsang's arrival at *Kânchi*, in February, 640, he heard of the assassination of the King of Ceylon. This must have been

Raja Buna Mugalan, who was put to death in A.D. 639.

Another proof of the general accuracy of my estimate of the pilgrim's rate of travelling is afforded by his statement made to the Great Abbot of the Nâlanda Monastery that his travels had occupied three years.* This period must refer to the actual time spent in travelling, as his recorded halts at various places for the purpose of study, before he reached Nâlanda, amount to four years and seven months. These halts, as stated in his life, are as follows :—

	Years.	Months.
At Kapisa, one whole summer	0	3
,, Kashmir, two entire years	2	0
,, a large town (Kasur ?)	0	1
,, Chinapati	1	2
,, Jâlandhar	0	4
,, Srughna, whole winter and half spring	0	4½
,, Madâwar, half spring and whole summer	0	4½
Years	4	7

Adding to these recorded halts the three years said to have been spent in travelling, the whole period elapsed, between the pilgrim's departure from Liang-cheu in August, 629, and the date of his conversation with the Great Abbot, is seven years and seven months, which fixes his arrival at Nâlanda in February, 637 A.D., the date according to my estimate being 1st March, 637.

* Julien's 'Hiouen Thsang,' i. 147.

The chronology here detailed follows the route indicated in the *Life* of Hwen Thsang, which differs from that given in the *Memoirs* after the departure of the pilgrim from *Maheswarapura* in April, A.D. 641. According to the Memoirs, the route was as follows :—

A.D.

641, Apr. 5, *Maheswarapura.*
June 1, SINDH.
July 10, MULTAN.
,, 20, *Polofato* or *Shorkot.* Halt 2 months.
Oct. 20, *Udumbara.*
Nov. 30, *Lângala.*
Dec. 13, *Pitasila,* or *Patala.*
,, 20, *Avanda,* or *Bahmana.*
642, Feb. 10, *Falana,* or *Banu.*
Mar. 1, *Tsaokiuto,* or *Ghazni.*

By this route the pilgrim would have reached *Tsaokiuto* just two years and two months earlier than by the other route, and as the date of his return to China is fixed with certainty, this long period of upwards of two years is wholly unaccounted for in the record of the pilgrim's travels. It seems almost certain, therefore, that it must have been spent in revisiting Magadha, as stated in the 'Life.'

In the 'Life' it is recorded that at the end of his second visit to Magadha, after two years' study, the pilgrim had a dream, in which the Bodhisatwa *Mânju Sri* appeared to him, and foretold the death of King Silâditya in ten years.* The king's death is then noted to have taken place at the end of the

* Julien's 'Hiouen Thsang,' i. 215.

period *Yong-hoei*, or in A.D. 650. According to this date, the pilgrim's two years' residence in Magadha must have been from A.D. 638 to 640. But I find it quite impossible to reconcile this date with the detailed statements of his travels. If, however, we might refer the dream to the end of his *first* visit to Magadha, in November A.D. 638, which would seem to have also extended to about two years, then the date of Silâditya's death would be fixed to A.D. 648, which is the very year assigned for it in the Chinese account of India by *Ma-twan-lin*.* In the 22nd of the years Ching-kwan (A.D. 668), the Emperor of China sent an ambassador to Magadha, but before his arrival Silâditya was dead. The information obtained by this ambassador is, I think, more trustworthy than the account of Hoeï-li, the biographer of Hwen Thsang, as the former had no object to serve in making an erroneous statement, while the latter was obliged to support the prophetic announcement of Hwen Thsang's dream. I am, therefore, inclined to adopt A.D. 648 as the true date of Silâditya's death, and to refer the period of the pilgrim's dream to the close of his first visit to Magadha in A.D. 638.

According to this view, the greater part of his two years' study at Nâlanda must be referred to his first visit in A.D. 637—638, to which I have assigned a period of twenty-two months, which, added to his

* Journ. Asiat. Soc. Bengal, 1837, p. 69 ; anonymous English translation. See also Journ. Asiatique, 1839, 398 ; French translation by M. Pauthier.

subsequent two months' study for the resolution of doubts* at his second visit, makes up the total period of two years' study at Nâlanda. The longer period of five years' study of all the works of both Buddhists and Brahmans, which is mentioned in another place,† I understand to refer to the whole duration of his three principal halts, namely, at Kashmir for two years, at Chinapati for fourteen months, and at Nâlanda for two years, which, taken in round numbers, amount to just five years.

---

* Julien's 'Hiouen Thsang,' i. 211.

† *Ibid.* i. 171.

APPENDIX B.

MEASURES OF DISTANCE.

Yojana, Li, Krosa.

THE measures of distance noted by the Chinese pilgrims are the Indian *yojana* and the Chinese *li.* The first is generally used by the elder traveller, Fa-Hian, and the other by the later travellers, Sung-Yun and Hwen Thsang. The *krosa* or kos, which is the common Indian measure of length at the present day, is not used by any of them. Hwen Thsang mentions that the *yojana,* according to tradition, was equivalent to 40 Chinese *li,* but that the measure then in use was equal to only 30 *li.** From a comparison of the different pilgrims' recorded distances between well-known places, it appears that Hwen Thsang adopted the traditional measure of the *yojana* as equal to 40 *li.* I give four distances as an example :—

			Fa-Hian.		Hw. Thsang.
I.	Srâvasti to Kapila	...	13	*yojanas* or	500 *li.*
II.	Kapila to Kusinagara	...	12	,,	485 ,,
III.	Nâlanda to Giryek	...	1	,,	58 ,,
IV.	Vaisâli to the Ganges	...	4	,,	135 ,,
		Total	30	*yojanas* =	1178 *li.*
		Or	1	,, =	39¼ ,,

Hwen Thsang describes the *yojana* as equal to

---

* Julien's 'Hiouen Thsang,' ii. 60.

8 *krosas,* or kos, of 500 *dhanus,* or "bow lengths" of 4 cubits each. The *yojana* would therefore be only 24,000 feet, or a little more than 4½ miles. But in all the Hindu books the *yojana* is reckoned at 4 *krosas,* either of 1000 or of 2000 *dhanus* or bow lengths. The former value agrees with the length of the *yojana* as stated by Hwen Thsang, and the latter is the double measure of about 9 miles, which gives the common kos of 2¼ miles that is in use in many parts of India at the present day.

The smaller kos of upwards of 6000 feet is certainly an old Indian measure, as Strabo mentions, on the authority of Megasthenes, that along the royal road to Palibothra there were pillars set up at every 10 stadia,* or 6067½ feet apart, to mark the distance. Taking this valuation of the kos, the *yajana* would be little more than 24,000 feet, or 4½ miles, while the actual Chinese *li* of 30 to the *yojana* would be only 800 feet, and the traditional *li* of 40 to the yojana not more than 600 feet. There would consequently be 6½ of the former, and 8½ of the latter to the British mile. But from a comparison of the recorded distances of the Chinese pilgrims with the actual measured road distances between well-ascertained places, it would appear that there must be some mistake in the value of 30 *li,* assigned to the Indian *yojana* by Hwen Thsang.

---

* Strabo, Geogr. xv. i. 50. This statement is confirmed by the 'Lalita Vistara,' in which the *krosa* of Magadha is valued at 4000 cubits. (Foucaux, p. 142.)

The following distances recorded by Fa-Hian show that the value of the *yojana* in British road distance was about 6¾ miles, but as the old native cart-tracks generally followed a zigzag route from village to village, the actual length of the *yojana* may be taken at 7½ or 8 miles.

		Fa-Hian.	British roads.
I. Bheda to Mathura	...	80 *yojanas*, or	536 miles.
II. Mathura to Sankisa	...	18 ,,	115¾ ,,
III. Sankisa to Kanoj	...	7 ,,	50 ,,
IV. Banâras to Patna	...	22 ,,	152 ,,
V. Patna to Champa	...	18 ,,	136½ ,,
VI. Champa to Tamluk	...	50 ,,	316 ,,
VII. Nâlanḍa to Giryek	...	1 ,,	9 ,,
		196 *yojanas*, or	779¼ miles.

These distances make the *yojana* of Fa-Hian equal to 6.71 miles of British road measurement.

A similar comparison of Hwen Thsang's measurements establishes the value of his *li* at one-sixth of a mile in road distance; but it is probable that it was not less than one-fifth of a mile in actual length, as the old zigzag cart-tracks were considerably longer than the straight British roads.

		Hw. Thsang.	British roads.
I. Madâwar to Govisana	...	400 *li*, or	66 miles.
II. Kosâmbi to Kusapura	...	700 ,,	114 ,,
III. Srâvasti to Kapila	...	500 ,,	85 ,,
IV. Kusinagara to Banâras	...	700 ,,	120 ,,
V. Banâras to Ghazipur	...	300 ,,	48 ,,
VI. Ghazipur to Vaisâli	...	580 ,,	103 ,,
		3360 *li*, or	567 miles.

The average of these distances gives 5.925, or nearly 6 *li* to the mile, which is the value that I have used throughout this work for reducing the numbers of Hwen Thsang to road distance in British miles.

These independent values of the *yojana* and *li* mutually corroborate each other; for as Hwen Thsang states that the *yojana* was traditionally said to be equal to 40 *li*, the value of the *yojana*, according to his recorded distances, was 40 divided by 5.925, or 6.75 miles, which is practically the same result as 6.71 miles, the value already deduced from Fa-Hian's distances between well-known places.

M. Vivien de Saint-Martin, quoting Le Père Gaubil,* shows that the Chinese *li*, shortly after the time of Hwen Thsang, was equal to 329 mètres, or 1079.12 English feet. As this agrees very nearly with the value of one-fifth of an English mile, or 1056 feet, which I have deduced for the *li* from the recorded distances of Hwen Thsang, I think that it must have been the actual *li* which the pilgrim used in estimating the length of his marches in India. Accepting it as the true value of the Chinese *li* of the seventh century, the length of the *yojana* would have been 43,164.8 feet, or nearly $8\frac{3}{16}$ miles,

* 'Histoire de l'Astronomie Chinoise,' i. 77, quoted in Julien's 'Hiouen Thsang,' iii. 258. The value of the *li* is determined from the mean measurement of three different degrees by the Chinese astronomer Y-hang, between 713 and 756 A.D., or just one century after the date of Hwen Thsang's travels.

which agrees very closely with the popular valuation at from 8 to 9 miles.

The *actual* value of the Chinese *li* in the seventh century was, therefore, 1079.12 feet, or rather more than one-fifth of an English mile; but for the reasons which I have assigned, and the proofs which I have adduced, its value in British *road distance* was not more than one-sixth of an English mile.

The variations in the length of the Indian kos must have puzzled the Chinese pilgrims. It is on this account perhaps that Fa-Hian uses the greater measure of the *yojana*, while Hwen Thsang records all distances in his native *li*. At the present day the length of the kos varies in almost every district; but practically there are only three absolutely distinct values of the kos now in use in Northern India.

1. The short kos, generally known as the *Pâdshâhi* or *Panjâbi* kos, which is in common use in North-west India and the Panjâb, is about 1¼ mile in length.

2. The kos of the Gangetic provinces, which is in use throughout the districts on both banks of the Ganges, was about 2¼ miles in length, but for the sake of convenience it is now generally considered as equal to 2 British miles.

3. The Bundela kos, which is in use throughout Bundelkhand, and other Hindu provinces to the south of the Jumna, is about 4 miles in length. The same long kos is also in use in Mysore, in Southern India.

I take the first of these kos to have been

originally just one-half of the second, so that the two measures were parts of the same system. Thus Wilson states the value of the *krosa,* or kos, as either 4000 or 8000 cubits. The smaller kos must have been in use in Magadha in the time of Megasthenes,* as he records that pillars were set up at every ten stadia along the royal road to mark the distances. Now 10 stadia are equal to 6066.72 feet, or just 4000 *hastas,* or cubits, which, according to the 'Lalita Vistara,' was the actual value of the *krosa* of Magadha. The longer measure of 8000 *hastas,* or cubits, is given by Bhâskara in the 'Lilâvati,' and by other native authorities.

To determine the exact value of these measures we must have recourse to the unit from which they were raised. This is the *angula,* or 'finger,' which in India is somewhat under three-quarters of an inch. By my measurement of 42 copper coins of Sikandar Ludi, which we know to have been adjusted to fingers' breadths, the *angula* is .72976 of an inch. Mr. Thomas makes it slightly less, or .72289. The mean of our measurements is .72632 of an inch, which may be adopted as the real value of the Indian finger, or *angula,* as I found the actual measure of many native fingers to be invariably under three-quarters of an inch. According to this value the *hasta,* or cubit, of 24 *angulas* would be equal to 17.43168 inches, and the *dhanu,* or "bow," of 96 *angulas* would be 5.81 feet. But as 100 *dhanus*

* Strabo, Geogr., xv. i. 50.

make one *nalwa,* and 100 *nalwas* make one *krosa* or kos, it seems probable that the *dhanu* must have contained 100 *angulas* to preserve the centenary scale.* According to this view the *hasta,* or cubit, would have contained 25 fingers instead of 24, and its value would have been 18.158 inches, which is still below the value of many of the existing *hastas,* or cubits of the Indian Bâzârs. Adopting this value of the *hasta,* the higher measures would be:—

			Feet.	
4	*hastas,* or	100 *angulas*	= 6·052	= 1 *dhanu.*
400	,,	100 *dhanus*	= 605·2	= 1 *nalwa.*
4000	,,	100 *nalwas*	= 6052	= 1 *krosa.*

As this value of the *krosa* or kos is within 15 feet of that derived from the statement of Megasthenes, I think that it may be accepted as a very near approximation to the actual value of the ancient *krosa* of Magadha.

The larger kos of the Gangetic provinces, which measured 8000 *hastas,* would be just double the above, or 12104 feet, or rather more than 2¼ miles.

In later times several of the Muhammadan kings established other values of the kos, founded on various multiples of different *gaz,* which they had called after their own names. Our information on this subject is chiefly derived from Abul Fazl, the minister of Akbar.† According to him, Shir Khan

* The same confusion of the numbers 96 and 100 exists in the monetary scale, in which we have 2 *bâraganis,* or 'twelvers,' equal to 1 *panchi,* or 'twenty-fiver.'

† 'Ayin Akbari,' i. 171.

fixed the *kroh*, or kos, at 60 *jarîbs*, each containing 60 Sikandari *gaz*, of 41½ Sikandaris, which was still in use about Delhi when Abul Fazl wrote. This kos would be equal to 9042.66 feet, or rather less than 1¾ mile. Another kos was established by Akbar, composed of 5000 Ilâhi *gaz*, the value of which is said to be equal to 41 Sikandaris. But this is certainly a mistake, as the existing Ilâhi *gaz* measures vary from 32 to 33 inches, and are therefore equal to 44 or 45 Sikandaris. Sir Henry Elliot has attempted to ascertain the value of this kos from the measurements of distances between the existing kos *minârs* on the royal road "from Agra to Lahor of Great Mogul." But as the people generally attribute the erection of the present kos *minârs* to Shah Jahân, who had established another *gaz* of his own, no dependence can be placed on his value of the Akbari kos. Sir Henry has also given undue prominence to this kos, as if it had superseded all others. That this was not the case is quite certain, as Akbar's own minister, Abul Fazl, uses the short kos throughout his descriptions of the provinces of his master's empire. Even Akabar's son, Jahângîr, has discarded the Akbari kos in his autobiography, where he mentions that he ordered a Sarai to be built at every 8 kos between Lahor and Agra.*

---

* 'Memoirs of Jahângir,' p. 90. The distances between the Sarais vary from 9 to 13 miles.

APPENDIX C.

CORRECTION OF PTOLEMY'S EASTERN LONGITUDES.

PTOLEMY'S longitudes are so manifestly in excess of the truth that various methods of rectification have been suggested by different geographers. That of M. Gossellin was to take five-sevenths of Ptolemy's measures, but his system was based upon the assumption that Ptolemy had made an erroneous estimate of the value of the degree both of the equinoctial and Rhodian diaphragms, as detailed by Eratosthenes. But for the geography of Asia, Ptolemy seems to have depended altogether upon the authority of Marinus, the Tyrian geographer, and of Titianus or Maës, a Macedonian merchant. M. Gossellin's method was probably founded upon the average of Ptolemy's errors, deduced from the longitudinal excess of many well-known places. It is in fact an empirical correction of Ptolemy's errors, of the cause of which his theory offers nothing more than a mere guess. The true sources of Ptolemy's errors of longitude have been pointed out so clearly by Sir Henry Rawlinson that I cannot do better than repeat his explanation of them.*

1st. Upon a line drawn from Hierapolis on the Euphrates to the stone tower he converted road distance into measurement upon the map at a

---

* 'On the Site of the Atropatenian Ecbatana,' p. 122.

uniform reduction of 1 in 11½ instead of 1 in 8, or perhaps, which would be more accurate upon so long a line, of 1 in 7.

2nd. He computed an equatorial degree at 500 instead of 600 Olympic stadia, and thus upon the line of the Itinerary, which he assumed to be about the parallel of Rhodes, he allowed only 400 stadia to a degree, while the true measurement was 480.

3rd. In converting the *schœni* of the Itinerary into Olympic stadia, he assumed their uniform identity with the Persian parasang of 3¾ Roman miles, whereas Sir Henry believes the *schœnus* to have been the natural measure of one hour employed by all caravans, both in ancient and modern times, to regulate their daily march, and to have averaged as nearly as possible a distance of 3 British miles.

The different corrections to be applied to Ptolemy's eastern longitudes on account of these three errors have been calculated by Sir Henry Rawlinson to amount to *three-tenths*, which is within one-seventieth part of the empirical correction used by M. Gossellin.

To show the accuracy of the correction here proposed, I need only refer to the difference of longitude between Taxila and Palibothra, which has been given at p. 10 of this work.

NOTES

Pp. 1-17 (1-15) *General Description of India.*

A. Its Shape :

(*i*) as described by Eratosthenes (a rhomboid), (*ii*) as described in the Mahâbhârata (an equilateral triangle), (*iii*) as described by Ptolemy and (*iv*) by Hwen Thsang or Yüan Chwang (a half-moon).

B. Its Divisions :

(*i*) as described in the *Kûrma-vibhâga* of the *Brihat Samhitâ* on the authority of the *Parâsara-tantra* which has been quoted by *Utpala* in his commentary on the *Brihat Samhitâ.* (Vizianagram Sanskrit Series, Benares). This *Nava-khanda* (नव-खण्ड) (or nine divisions) of India has also been stated in detail in the *Mârkandeya Purâna,* Chap. LVIII. (*ii*) as described in Chinese records (the five Indies, N., W., Central, E., and S.). This system differs very little from that stated in the (*iii*) Kâvya-Mîmâmsâ (p. 93):

तत्र वाराणस्याः परतः पूर्व्वदेशः। माहिष्मत्याः परतः दक्षिणापथः। देवसभाया परतः पश्चाद्देशः। पृथूदकात् परतः उत्तरापथः। विनशनप्रयागयोः गङ्गा-यमुनयोश्च अन्तरम् अन्तर्व्वेदी॥

Thus the Chinese system was borrowed from the then current Indian system with this difference that the "Middle Country" of the Buddhist Literature was substituted for अन्तर्वेदी and that it included the western portion of the *Pûrvadesa* or Eastern India.

Note also that the *Purânas* mention, in their (*iv*) *Bhuvana-kosha* section, the countries and nations of India under the following heads:—(1) *Madhyadesa* (Central), (2) *Udîchya* (N.), (3) *Prâchya* (E.), (4) *Dakshinâpatha* (S.), (5) *Aparânta* (W.). Thus the Puranic system is also the same as (*ii*) and (*iii*). But the *Purânas* add (6) the

Vindhyavâsinah (those who dwell on the Vindhyas), (7) the *Parvatâsrayinah* (nations dwelling on the Himalayas) and (8) the North-Westerners (mentioned in the *Mârkandeya*).

(*v*) As for the Nine Divisions—*Indra, Kaserumat, etc.* see Appendix I, dealing with the divisions of Greater India.

C. PHYSICAL FEATURES.

As for Mountains, Rivers, changes in their course, read M'Crindle's Ptolemy, pp. 75-104, Pargiter's *Mârkandeya Purâna*, LVII., 11-32 ; J. A. S. B., 1886, Part II, pp. 332-340 ; 1892, Part I.

Pp. 17-19 (15-17) *Northern India.*

The Skr. name is *Uttarâpatha* ; पृथूदकात् परत: उत्तरापथ: (*Northern India* is on the other side of *Prithûdaka* or Pehoa, about 14 miles W. of Thaneswar) [Kâvya Mîmâmsâ, p. 93]. Bâna Bhatta also has used the word in this narrower sense. (Harsha Charita). [The word means, in its later and wider sense, the whole of *Aryâvarta*].

Historical Sketch.—It was the first settlement of the Vedic Aryans. [Mr. Pargiter has controverted this view in his Ancient Indian Historical Traditions, London, 1922.] The Rigveda mentions *Gândhâra*, the *Suvâstu* (Swat), *Kubhâ* (Greek Kophen, mod. Kabul river), *Gomatî* (Gomal) and *Krumu* (Kurrum)—the western tributaries of the *Sindhu* (*Sindhus* in nominative singular, *Hindus* in Iranian, 'Ινδός in Greek which had no H) During the epic age it was stigmatized as impure. Its N. W. was included within the Persian Empire (500-331 B. C.). Alexander the Great conquered the greater portion of it from various princelings. Chandragupta Maurya re-conquered it from the Greeks. The weak successors of

Asoka could not retain it and so we hear of a series of foreign inroads—Greek, Parthian, Saka, Kushan and Hun. The descendants of Kaniska, the Great Buddhist Emperor, ruled its N. W. portion for many centuries (Alberuni). The last king of that family was deposed and the throne was usurped by his Brâhman Minister, who founded the Brâhman Shâhi family of Kabul and Ohind, defeated and driven away by Mahmud of Ghazni.

Ancient Routes and States.—Though our author has discussed the geography of Alexander's March and the routes resorted to by F. H. and Y. Ch. in the body of the book, the following lists have been added to help students to form a clear idea of the subject.

(i) *Alexander's Invasion.*—The whole of North-western India was parcelled out into innumerable kingdoms and republics at the time of the Macedonian invasion. The more important among them are :—

1. *The Aspasian Territory.*—(Aspasioi=Skr. Asvaka अश्वक through the Iranian form of *Aspa* meaning horse). It lay in the difficult hill country north of the Kabul river. Its capital was on or near the river Euaspla (supposed to be identical with the Kunar, a tributary of the Kabul).

2. The country of the *Guraeans* washed by the R. Guraeus Skr. Gaurî, mod. Panjkora).

3. The kingdom of *Assakenus*—Asmaka अश्मक (Pâṇini, IV. 1. 173). It had its capital at Massaga situated E. of the Guraeus—a formidable fortress probably situated not very far to the north of the Malakand Pass but not yet precisely identified.

4. *Peukelaotis* (Pushkalâvatî).

5. *Nysa.*—It was a small hill-state with a republican constitution. It was alleged to have been founded by Greek colonists long before the invasion of Alexander. Arrian says that the Nysaeans are not an Indian race, but descended from the men who came into India with Dionysus. Curiously enough a *Yona* or Greek state is

mentioned along with *Kamboja* in the *Majjhima Nikâya* (II. 149) as flourishing in the time of Gotama Buddha and Assalâyana.

According to Holdich (Gates of India, p. 122) the lower spurs and valleys of Koh-i-Mor are where the ancient city of Nysa once stood.

6. *Taxila* (Takshasilâ).

7. *Abisares* (Abhisâra, lower and middle hills between the Jhelum and Chenab).

8. *Arsakes* (Urasâ, उरशा; modern Hazara).

9. The kingdom of the Elder Poros (between the Jhelum and the Chenab).

10. The country of the *Glauganicians* (Aristobulus) or Glausians (Ptolemy) to the west of the Chenab.

11. *Gandaris* (between the Chenab and the Ravi). The name seems to be connected with Gândhâra, the easternmost part of which it once might have been. It was ruled by the Younger Poros.

12. The *Adraistoi* on the eastern side of the Hydraotes or the Râvi. The name stands for Skr. *Adri-stha* अद्रि स्थ or mountain-dwellers. [Camb. H. I., p. 371 gives Adhrishtas, अधृष्ट]. Their main stronghold was Pimprama.

13. *Kathaioi* or Cathaeans (Probably Skr. Kantha [Pânini II. 4. 20] or Kratha [M. Bh. VIII. 85. 16.] : Camb. H. I., p. 371 takes the word to be identical with *Kshatriyas*).

Some writers locate their country in the tract between the Hydaspes and the Acesines. (Jhelum and Chenab) ; some on the other side of the Acesines and of the Hydraotes (Ravi).

14. The kingdom of *Sophytes* "lord of the fastness of the Salt Range stretching from the Jhelum to the Indus." (V. Smith ; but there is difficulty in accepting the identi-

fication, for "our sources all agree in placing the principality E. of the Jhelum"—Camb. H. I., p. 372).

15. The kingdom of *Phegelis* or Phegeus [probably Skr. "Bhagala," a royal race of Kshatriyas mentioned in Pâninian Ganapâtha] lying between the Hydraotes (Ravi) and the Hyphasis (Bias).

16. The *Siboi*.

They were probably identical with the Siva (शिव) people of the Rigveda VII, 18, 7. The Jâtakas (No. 527 ; 547) mention a *Sivi* country. A place called *Siva-pura* is mentioned by the scholiast on Pânini as situated in the northern country. It is, doubtless, identical with Sibipura mentioned in a Shorkot inscription edited by Dr. Vogel who takes the mound of Shorkot to be the site of the city of the Sibis (E. I., 1921, p. 16). The local tradition also connects Shorkot with *Siva* ; *Sivapura*=Siaura=Shór. [C. A. S. R., V. pp. 97-103]. The *Sivis* migrated (probably 300 B. C.) to the territory round Nagri, a small town near Chitor where have been discovered seven coins with the legend *Majhamikâya Sivijanapadasa* which thus locates Sivi and Madhyamika [C.A.S.R., VI. pp. 196, 202.] near Chitor.

17. The *Agalassoi*.

18. The *Sudracae* or *Oxudrakai* dwelling on the banks of the Hyphasis (Bias). The Skr. form of their name is *Kshudraka or Kshaudraka* [M. Bh. VII. 68.9.]

19. The Malloi [or *Mâlavas* who seem to have migrated (300-200 B. C.) to the tract about Nâgar or Karkota Nâgara about 30 miles N. of Bundi where have been discovered more than 500 coins with the legend Mâlavâna—C. A. S. R., VI. pp. 162-195] between the lower Hydraotes (Ravi) and the Acesines.

20. The *Abastanoi* on the lower Akesines. So named by Arrian. Diodorus calls them Sambastai, Curtius Sabarcæ and Orosius Sabagræ. They seem to be the Ambashthas (अम्बष्ठ) mentioned in the Mahâbhârata

(II. 52. 14-15), along with the Sivis (शिबि), Kshudrakas, Mâlavas and other north-western tribes. The Bârhaspatya Arthasâstra (Ed. by Dr. Thomas, p. 21) mentions their country with Kashmîra, Hûna and Sindhu. An Ambashtha king is mentioned in the Aitareya Brâhmana (VIII. 21).

They migrated, in a later period, to the neighbourhood of Maikal hill (मेकल)—the source of the Narmadâ (Kûrmavibhâga of the Brihat Samhitâ and Mârkandeya Purâna). Thence they have dispersed themselves to Bengal where they can still be traced.

Dialogues of the Buddha (Part I, p. 109) state an Ambastha to be a Brâhmana. It seems that they were a tribe of *Brahma-Kshatriyas* (i.e. Brahmins by descent but warriors by profession), but some of them took to other occupations, viz. those of farmers (Jâtaka, No. 363) and physicians (Manu, X. 47).

21. The *Xathroi* (Kshatri) and the *Ossadioi* (Vasâti बसाति of the M. Bh. VII, 19. 11 ; 89. 37 ; VIII. 44. 46).

22. The *Sodrai* (Sogdoi) and the *Massanoi* (occupying N. Sindh).

23. The Kingdom of *Mousikanos*.

24. The Principality of *Oxykanos*. (Portikanos).

25. The principality of *Sambos* with Sindimana as capital.

26. *Patalene*.

[22-26 are in W. India. But they have been mentioned here to make the list a complete one.] (Raychowdhuri's P.H.A.I., p. 125 *ff*).

Fahian's Route.—Udyâna (Swat valley), Soo-ho-to (Bunir-valley), *Gândhâra, Takshasilâ, Purushapura, He-lo, Bannu, Pe-to* (Bhida) ; [Mathura].

Yuanchwang's Route :—1. Ka-pi-shih, 2. Lan-po, 3. Na-ki-lo-ho, 4. Gândhâra, (*a*) Pushkalâvatî, (*b*) Purushapura, (*c*) Udabhândapura (उदभाण्डपुर), 5. Udyâna, 6. Takshasilâ, 7. Sinhapura, 8. Urasâ उरसा, 9. Kashmir,

10. Parnotsa, 11. Rajapurî, 12. Takka टक्क (capital-Sâkala शाकल), 13. Chînabhûkti, 14. Jâlandhara, 15. Kulûta, 16. Satadru [Pâryâtra, Mathura].

Alberuni's account of the route from Kanoj to Ghazni. From Kanoj *via* Mirat (W. 10+10+10+10 farsakhs), Panipat (10 far.), Mandahukur, the capital of Lauhawur (Lahore district), east of the R. Irawa (Ravi) (10+10+N.W. 9+6+8 far.), Waihand (Ohind) the capital of Kandhar (Gandhar) (12+8+20 far.), Purshawar (Peshawar 14 far.) and Kabul (15+12 far.) to Ghazna (17 far.) [Alberuni's India, chap. 18.]

1. KAO-FU OR AFGHANISTAN.

P. 19 (17).—Kao-fu was in Y. Ch.'s time the border land of the Barbarians—Indian in religion and culture but not in race. It seems to have derived its name from *Kao-fu* (the *Kuhakas*, a northern nation mentioned in Mar. LVII. 42). It was then divided into ten districts of which Kâpisî कापिशी was the chief. The king of Kâpisî—a benevolent Buddhist Kshatriya—was the overlord of the 10 districts, 8 of which were directly under his rule and two (Kabul and Ghazni) had their separate Buddhist kings—that of Kabul being of Turkish descent. Buddhism was not the only religion, there were numerous Digambaras (Jains), Pâsupatas (पाशुपत) and Kâpâlikas ; the Non-Buddhists were the most numerous in Gândhâra. [Y. Ch.].

P. 21 (18). *Kapisene*.—The Skr. name is not Kapisâ which is being used since the days of Cunningham but *Kâpisî* कापिशी mentioned in Pânini IV. 2. 99 as famous for its grape-wine, कापिशायनी सुरा, referred to in Kautilya's Arthasâstra, Book II, Chap. XXV. Y. Ch.'s *Ka-pi-shih* (Watters, I, p. 122) also gives the same sound and is nearer to the original than the classical forms of *Capisa* or *Kapisa*.

P. 22 (19). *Mount Aparasin*.—Upairi-saena of Avesta

[Skr. Upari-syena उपरि-श्येन 'higher than eagles' (can fly). Dr. Stein in a paper communicated to the 7th Oriental Congress held at Vienna].

P. 23 (*20*). *Opiân.*—The name may be connected with the *Aupadhas* (Pkr. *Opaha*), a northern nation. (Mar. LVII, 40).

For other sites proposed for Alexandria under the Caucasus, read V. Smith's E. H. I., p. 49.

P. 23 (*20*). *Begram* : it means, in the local language, *the city*.

P. 30. *Si-pi-to-fa-la-sse* : Watters (I. p. 126) transcribes it as *Svetavatâlaya* and spells the last syllable (sse) as tzu.

Aruna : Y. Ch.'s *A-lu-no* ; referred to by Alberuni (II., p. 143).

Kiu-lu-sa-pang : Watters (Vol. II, p. 269) transcribes it as Gulsafan.

Milindu : printing mistake for Milinda identified with Menander.

The names Karisi, Kalasi and Ku-la-sa-pang suggest that the Rigvedic river Kulisî (कुलिशी) is to be located here and I identify it with the united Panjshir and Ghorband.

P. 40 (*33*).—Our author thinks that Y. Ch. interchanged the names between the province and the capital ; that *Hu-phi-na*=*Kipin* and *Fo-li-shi-sa-tang-na*=Portosthâna, Urddhasthâna or Kabul. But Y. Ch. does not transcribe initial *K* with *H*. Again, "the Chinese texts distinguish *Kipin* from *Kao-fu* or Kabul. In the 7th century, Kipin generally meant Kapisâ. In the time of the Han and Wei dynasties the term ordinarily meant Kashmir." [V. Smith's E. H. I. p. 251. Read also Sten Konow's remarks on the location of Kipin in E. I., XIV, p. 291].

Fo-li-shi-sa-tang-na sounds more like Skr. *Pratishthâna* प्रतिष्ठान (settlement, colony). We know of two other Pratishthânas, one on the Jumna and the other on the Godâvarî.

P. 42 (36). *Nikaia.*—Sir Thomas Holdich supported Cunningham's identification. Dr. V. Smith located it at Jalâlâbâd. But their discussions "are invalidated by the fact that Nicaea (Nikaia), if we follow Arrian, was not on the river Kabul at all. Alexander from Nicaea advances towards the Kabul." [Prof. Bevan in Camb. H. I., p. 348].

P. 44 (38). *Vaekereta.*—Its identification with Kabul supported by Prof. Jackson. [Camb. H. I., p. 327].

P. 46 (40). *Ozola.*—Spelt Axola in M'Crindle's Ptolemy (P. 316). Watters (II. 226) takes *Tsau-ku-to* as Skr. Jâguda (ज). (Juguda or Jaguda)—a northern nation (Mar. LVII, 40 ; Vâyu XLV. 199 ;) through whose country flows the Indus (Matsya CXX. 46-48). Cunningham derived it from *'Αραχωτός* (Arachosia ; Arokhaj or Rokhaj of the Arabs). The Arachosia of the Greeks comprised a considerable portion of Eastern Afghanistan. It extended westward beyond the meridian of Kandahar and its eastern frontier was skirted by the Indus. This name is usually derived from *Haraqiati*. Prof. Jackson informs us that the true Avestic form of the name is Harahvaiti and that Arachosia was known in later Parthian times as "White India"—'Ινδικήλευκή. [Camb. H. I., p. 326] Harahvaiti is the Persian form of Skr. *Sarasvatî* (the original Saras-vatî having a *saras* or lake, Arakhotos Krênê of Ptolemy, Hâmûn Lake or Zirrah, through which it flows). [When the Vedic Aryans migrated to Kurukshetra, they named the local sacred river after this original Sarasvati. Sir R. G. Bhandarkar prefers to derive it from the Arkshodas, the people of Mt. Rikshoda referred to in Pânini IV. 3. 91. (I. A. 1872, p. 21)].

P. 45.—Amongst the most remarkable relics of a bygone age in the Kabul district are the colossal figures carved in the cliff at Bamian, N. of the Koh-i-Baba, and the adjacent caves. The largest of these figures is 180 ft. high. Authorities differ as to their origin, but it seems most probable that they are Buddhist. The surrounding caves answer to the requirements of a Buddhist monastery, and close to the foot of the cliff is a mound resembling a Buddhist stupa, the exploration of which may some day put the question at rest. [Imp. Gaz. Ind. XIV, p. 242 ; read also I. A., VIII, pp. 82, 198, 227, 225].

P. 46 (39). *Ho-si-na identified with Ghazni.*—Dr. Stein supports it in his Report of Arch. Surv. in N. W. F. Province, Peshawar, 1905. *River Helmand* is Haêtumant of Avesta, Etumandros and Hermandus of classical authors. (I. A., 1886, p. 22).

P. 49 (42). *Lan-po.*—[Y. Ch.'s description in Watters, Vol. I, pp. 180-81 ; M'Crindle's Ptolemy, pp. 104, 106]; its Skr. form is *Lampâka* [M. Bh., Drona-p cxxi, 4846-7 ; Mar. LVII, 40, etc.].

The *Abhidhâna-chintâmaní* of Hemachandra (IV. 26. लम्पाकास्तु मुरुण्डाः स्युः) gives *Murunda* (mentioned in the Allahabad Pillar Inscription of Samudra-Gupta) as another name of the same people. Dr. Sten Konow has pointed out that *Murunda* is a later form of a Saka word meaning lord, master. Lampâka was thus the capital of the Sakas.

P. 51 (43). *Nagarahâra.*—Fa-Hian (Chap. XIII) saw at *Nagara* various objects of Buddhist interest, a tooth-relic etc. Y. Ch.'s Records locate *Na-ki-lo-ho* 100 *li* south-east of Lan-po ; but his Life gives a southern direction. Mr. Watters transcribes the name as Nagarakot (Vol. I, pp. 182-7), which has been mentioned by Alberuni. (II, p. 11). For Ptolemy's Nagar see M'Crindle, pp. 112-13. The Skr. name of Nagarahâra occurs in the *Parâsara-Tantra* (quoted by Utpala in his commentary on the Brihat Samhitâ, Vizianagram Skr. series, Benares). Baber refers to it as Nungnehar (Erskine's Translation of his Memoirs, p. 141).

As regards the site of the capital, Cunningham located it at Begram 2 miles W. of Jalâlâbâd. But Mr. William Simpson (who investigated the local antiquities during the Afghan War) proposes to identify it with the numerous remains (called *Balar Hissar* of a *Purâna Sherh* i.e. citadel of an old city) of an old town of importance on the right bank of the Surkhab at its junction with the Kabul river (about 4 miles E. of Jalâlâbâd). [J. R. A. S. 1881, p. 183]. The correctness of the identification he could not doubt, since Nagrak, 'Nagarat' or 'Nagara' was still applied to the ruins by the natives on the spot, since the site answers the description of Y. Ch. and since there is no other place in the vicinity where he could discover the ruins of a city.

P. 52 (44). *Hi-lo,* or *Fo-ting-ko-ching.*—It was 30 *li* S.E. (Watters I. 184) or 1 yojana S. of Nagara and was 16 yojanas to the W. of Purushapura. (F. H. Chap. XIII). It was famous for the skull-bone relic of Buddha. It has been identified with Hidda 5 miles S. of Jalâlâbâd. The vicinity of Hidda is covered with *Stûpas,* tumuli and caves. (Masson's Travels, II, 164 ; Ariana Antiqua, plate VIII and the plate opposite to p. 262 ; Simpson in J.R.A.S. 1882, p. 328 ; Rev. C. Swinnerton's discovery of a Buddhist tope, I. A., 1879, p. 198).

P. 54 (47). *Gândhâra.*—*Gândhâra* is a name of high antiquity occurring in the Rigveda. It is mentioned frequently in the Mahâbhârata and other Skr. works as containing the two royal cities of Takshasilâ and Pushkalâvatî, the former situated to the E. and the latter to the W. of the Indus which flows through it (Vâyupurâna). It would therefore, appear that in early times the Gândhâric territory lay on both sides of that river, though in subsequent times it was confined to the western side. The old Persian form of the name was Ga(n)dâra. (Camb. H. I., p. 327). [Strabo, Bohn's Library Ed. III, p. 89 ; Ptolemy (p. 115), F.-H. Chap. X., Y. Ch. (I. 198)].

Capitals of Gândhâra.—The oldest capital was Pushkalâvatî. Kaniska's city was Purushapura (in Y. Ch.'s time also). Alberuni mentions Waihand (Ohind) as the capital of 'Qandhar.'

Pushkalâvatî ("abounding in lotuses"?).—It is said to be named after Pushkara, a son of Bharata. [Râmâyana VII. 100, 10; the com. states that the city was in Gândhâradesa]. M'Crindle's Ptolemy, pp. 115-17. Schoff's Periplus (pp. 41-42) informs us of its trade. Y. Ch. (I. 214) locates *Pu-se-kia-lo-fa-ti,* famous for the stûpa of eye-offering, at a distance of 100 *li* (Life; 50 *li*—Records). N.E. of Purushapura.

P. 58 (50). *Charsada.*—Its ruins described in C. A. S. R. Vol. II, p. 90; Vol. XIX, pp. 96-110. The site has been excavated and the identification is certain [Annual Rep. A. S. I. for 1902-3, pp. 140-154].

P. 60 (51). *Po-lu-sha.*—Famous as the scene of the *Vessantara* (विश्वंतर) Jâtaka, was about 100 *li* S.E. of Pushkalâvatî. (Y. Ch. I. 217). Y. Ch. describes a double-chambered cave in which Prince Sudâna and his wife took refuge (20 *li* N.E. of the town).

Cunningham's identification of the site as stated in the text has been discarded. The town has now been identified with Shahbazgarhi (famous for its Kharosthi version of the Rock Inscriptions of Asoka). The name Shahbazgarhi is not older than Baber. It is built on the actual ruins of an ancient stone-built town. About 1¾ mile N.E. of the Asokan Inscriptions is a double-chambered cave which answers exactly to the Chinese description of Sudâna's cave.

Arrian's description of Bazaria as situated upon an eminence and surrounded by a stout wall agrees so closely with it, as well as with the account of Sudâna's city, that the three seem to be identical. [C. A. S. R., Vol. V, pp. 9—18].

Takht-i-Bahai.

100 *li* N.W. of the city of Sudâna, Y. Ch locates a great mountain with a Mahâyâna monastery and an Asoka stupa marking the scene of *Ekasringa* (एकशृङ्ग) *Avadâna*. Cunningham identified it with Takht-i-Bahai (where an inscription of Gondophornes, गर्दभिल्ल of the Purânas, was discovered) [C. A. S. R., V., p. 23 ; excavation report in An. R. A. S. I. 1907-8, p. 132 ff ; 1910-11, p. 33 ff.]. Sir A. Stein locates the scene at Butan, a large important Buddhist site, in the Palai valley, not far from the S. foot of the Shahkot Pass leading into Swat. [An. R. A. S. I., 1911-12, Part I, p. 12].

P. 61 (52). *Utakhanda.*—The real form is Udakabhânda. (उदकभाण्ड). The Râjataranginî mentions Udabhândapura and its kings, Lâlliya Sâhi, Kamaluka and Trilochanapâla who was conquered by Hâmmîra (Amir-ul-Mumin Mahmud of Ghazni). In Alberuni's account of Mahmud of Ghazni's conquest we find mention of the Hindu Shahis—Lalliya, Kamaluka—who were Brahmins by caste. He also states that their city was "Waihand the capital of Qandhar."

Thus *Wu-to-ka-han-cha = Udakabhânda = Udabhânda* (भण्ड) (pura) = Pkr. Uahanda = Waihand = Mod. Ohind on the N. bank of the Indus. [Dr. Stein on Râjataranginî, II, 337 ; C. A. S. R., V, 83]. उदकभाण्ड or उदभाण्ड means a pitcher full of water.

P. 66 (56). *Ohind.*—Cunningham's location of Alexander's bridge at this place has been supported by Prof. Bevan. [Camb. H. I., p. 357]; its ruins etc. described in C. A. S. R., II, p. 95 ff.

Pp. 66-7 (57). *Sâlâtura* (शालातुर): Watters' Y. Ch., I, p. 221 ; C. A. S. R., II, p. 95.

P. 67 (58). *Aornos.*—Read V. Smith's E. H. I., 2nd Edn., Appendix D ; it was not far from modern Amb. [Camb. H. I., p. 356]. Dr. Stein explored (in 1904-5) the hitherto inaccessible mountain tract of the Mahaban range. His survey proved beyond all question that the natural features of that mountain are totally dissimilar from those of Mount Aornos as described by the historians of Alexander, and demolished consequently, at a sweep, the arguments in favour of their identity. [Annual Rep. A. S. I. for 1904-5, p. 42].

P. 76 (66).—Bâzâr or Bazaria : read notes on Po-lu-sha. [P. 673-74].

P. 90 (78). *Purusha-pura* (Peshâwar).—F.-H., Chap. XII ; Watters' Y. Ch., I, 198-202 ; C. A. S. R., II, p. 87 ; Annual Rep. A. S. I. for 1908-9, p. 38 ff ; 1909-10, p. 135 ff ; 1910-11, p. 25 ff.

Its identification with Peshâwar (capital of N.-W. F. Province ; 30° 1′ N. and 71° 35′ E.) referred to by Alberuni as Purshawar (through the Prakrit form of *Purisaura*) is now certain. The site has been excavated and Buddha's relic casket has been discovered in the ruins of the great *Kaniṣka stupa* now known as *Shah-ji-ki-dheri*.

P. 93 (81). *Udyâna*.—F.-H., Chap. VII ; Y. Ch., I, pp. 225-6.

Y. Ch.'s statement that there were 1400 old *Sanghârâmas* on the banks of the river Su-po-fa-su-tu [शुभवास्तु, Suvâstu, or Swat] was no exaggeration, as ruins are now found all through the country. [Mr. Deane, the Chief Political Officer with the Chitral Relief Force, in J. R. A. S., 1896, p. 653].

P. 95 (82). The identification of the capital of *Udyâna* with Mangora or Monglora has been supported by Dr. Stein who made an archæological tour with the Buner Field Force. [I. A., 1889, p. 44].

As for *A-po-lo-lo*, the source of the Subha-vâstu (Swat), Mr. Deane writes : "The distance and direction given by the Pilgrim bring us exactly to Kalâm, the point at which the Utrot and Laspur (Ushu of Maps) streams meet. The junction of these is the present head of the Swat river." [J. R. A. S., 1896, p. 656].

P. 97 (84). *Banu* or *Varnnu* (वर्णु).—*Poh-na,* 13 days' journey to S. of Nagara and three days' journey to W. of the Indus. (F. H. Chap. XIV). *Fa-la-na,* 15 days' journey to the S. of Lampâka ; above 900 *li* N.E. of A-fan-tu ; 4000 *li* in circuit ; mountainous (Y. Ch. II. 262).

"General Cunningham's identification of Fa-la-na with the territory of which Bannu was the natural and political centre must appear convincing to any student who is familiar with the actual geography of this part of the N. W. Frontier." (Stein's Report of Arch. Survey in N. W. F. Province, Peshawar 1905, p. 5.)

The Skr. is not *Varana* or *Barna,* but *Varnnu* ref. to in *Pânini* [IV. 2. 103 ; IV. 3. 93]. The district is watered by the Kuram (Vedic *Krumu*) and the Gomal (Vedic *Gomatî*) rivers. Mod. Bannu is one of the four trans-Indus districts of the N. W. F. Province and lies between 32° 16′ and 32° 5′ N. and 70° 23′ and 71° 16′ E.

P. 99 (86). Ki-kiang-na (Skr. Kokankana of the *Kûrmavibhâga)* district, on the W. frontier of Fa-la-na ; situated in a valley under a high mountain (Y. Ch. II. p. 262). Identified by Stein with Waziristan (Arch. Surv. in N. W. F. Province, Peshawar 1905, p. 6.)

P. 100 (87). *Opokien* or *A-po-kan.*—It was N.W. of Fa-la-na and S.E. of Tsau-ku-ta ; mentioned, not in the *Records,* but in the *Life* of Y. Ch. (II. p. 265).

Cunningham thinks that it stands for Afghan and locates it near the source of the Tochi branch of the Kurram river. It may be the भापगा: a northern nation ref. to in the *Vâyupurâna* (*Bhuvana-kosha* section).

P. 103 (89). *Kashmîr.*—The ancient geography of *Kashmîr* has been fully treated by Dr. Stein in the second volume of his English translation of the Râjataranginî. He has shown that Ptolemy's *Kaspeira, Kaspeiroi* of

Dionysios and Nonus and *Kaspatyros* of Herodotos refer to Kashmir, though located wrongly on the lower course of the Rhuadis or Ravi. It was called Ki-pi-n by the Chinese in the time of the Han and Wei dynasties. (Notes on p. 40). In Yuan Chwang's time its king (*Durlabha-vardhana Prajnâditya*) was the overlord of Wu-la-shi (उरशा ; modern district of Hazara ; ref. to by Alexander's Historians as Arsakes), Puan-nu-tso (पर्णोत्स mod. Punach or Prunts), Ko-lo-she-pu-lo (राजपुरी. mod. Rajaori), Seng-ha-pu-lo (सिंहपुर, Salt Range) and Ta-cha-shi-lo (तक्षशिला). The last mentioned district was then a newly conquered one, being formerly included with the dominion of Kâpisî (कापिशी).

Other adjoining hill-states mentioned in the Râja-taranginî are :—Kâshthavâta (काष्ठवाट, mod. Kishtwar), Champâ (चम्पा, mod. Chamba) and Vallâpura (Ballâwar) to the S.E. of Kashmîra proper and Lohara (लोहर, mod. Loharin) to the S.W.

The ancient capital of Kashmîr was (old) *Srînagara*, now known as Pândrethân (from पुराणाधिष्ठान or old capital) about 3 miles to the S.E. of Modern *Srinagara* the real name of which was Pravarapura.

P. 120 (104). *Takshasilâ* (तक्षशिला):—The name is generally connected with *Takshaka*, King of the Nâgas, who killed *Parikshit* ; *Janamejaya* invaded Takshasilâ and conquered it. (Mahâ Bh. Adi-P. III. 682-3 and 832-4 ; XL-XLIV ; XLIX. 1954, L. 1991). Takshaka's descendants are the *Takkas* who held all the country around. (C. A. S. R., II. p. 6). The name may also mean "Hewn rock"—it having been built of that material instead of brick or mud. Skr. Siras शिरस्=Pkr. Sila (head) ; hence it="Severed Head" ; and a legend originated of the alms-gift of the head of Buddha at this place. It was a great Buddhist *tîrtha* and University.

Taxila—60 Roman miles (=55 Eng. m.) from Peucolaites ; situated on a low but level plain in a district called Amanda. (Pliny, IV. 23). The greatest of all the cities between the Indus and the Hydaspes. (Arrian, M'Crindle's Alexander p. 83). Thickly peopled and extremely fertile (Strabo, p. 34 of M'Crindle). Taxila in the Arsa Skr. Urasâ) territory. (Ptolemy p 118). Chu-sha-she-lo ("Severed Head") 7 days' journey to E. of Gândhâra (F. H., X.). 3 days' journey to the E. of the Sintu (Indus, Sung-yun). The city, 10 *li* in circuit, 12 or 13 *li* N. of it was the *stûpa* marking the spot of Buddha's alms-gift of his head, or 1000 heads in so many births ; the country had a very fertile soil with flowing streams and luxuriant vegetation ; then a dependency of Kashmir ; circuit 2000 *li* ; (Y. Ch. I. 240). After this we lose sight altogether of Taxila, and do not even know how and when its ruin was accomplished. Muhammadan writers do not refer to it. Alberuni, in his notes on the *Kûrma-vibhâga* (Chap. 29) remarks Takshasilâ *i.e.* Mârikala.

Boundaries of the country—N. Urasâ ; E. the Jhelum ; S. Sinhapura ; W. the Indus.

The city has been identified by Cunningham with the ruins near *Shah-dheri* (=Royal Residence) 12 m. N.W. of Rawalpindi. Here have been found colossal statues, thousands of coins, traces of at least 55 stupas, 28 monasteries, 9 temples, a copper plate containing the name of Takshasila and a vase with Kharosthi inscription "the tope was erected at Taxila—", [C. A. R. S., II pp. 111-35 ; III. 135 ; V. 66-75 ; XIV.] The ruins cover several miles and stretch up to Hassan Abdal (Attock district, Punjab). It has been recently excavated. [Annual Report, A. S. I. 1912-13, pp. 1-5 ; *ibid* part I. pp. 8-16 · 1915-16 ; Part I, pp. 10-12.] Sir John Marshall's Guide to Taxila describes the remains of three distinct cities located in the same valley watered by the Haro river. These are situated immediately to the E. and N.E. of

Saraikala, a junction on the railway, 20 miles N.W. of Rawalpindi.

P. 139 (121). *Mânikyala.*—(The spot where Buddha gave his body to feed a starving tigress—2 days' journey to the S.E. of Taxila (F. H. XI,), 8 days' journey to the S.E. of the capital of *Udyâna* (and not of Gândhâra as Cunningham wrongly states). [Sung-yun] 200 *li* S.E. from the north of the country of Taxila. [Y. Ch. I. 255.]

Cunningham fancied that all these accounts suit exactly with the identification of this spot with Mânikyala (15 m. S.E. of Rawalpindi, 33° 27′ and 73° 13′ E.) where are the ruins of a monument built, according to an inscription found inside, during the reign of Kanishka. Everybody is now agreed that Cunningham was mistaken. Dr. Stein shows strong, if not absolutely conclusive, reason for believing that the buildings on Mount Banj, (Gadun territory in N. W. F. Province) a spur of Mahaban, represent the scene of body-offering. [But Stein's identification involves an awkard correction of a bearing given by Y. Ch. from S.E. to N.E. Stein's Rep. Arch. Sur. N. W. F. Province. Peshawar, 1905, pp. 41-45.]

P. 142 (124). *Sinhapura.*—*Seng-ho-pu-lo,* 700 *li* S.E. of Takshasilâ ; rested on hills and was a natural fortress : circuit of the district with the Indus on its W. frontier was 3500 *li*. [Watters' Y. Ch., I. p. 248.]

Khetas or *Katas* : On the north side of the Salt range, Jhelum district, Punjab ; 32° 43′ N. and 72° 59′ E.; 2000 ft. above sea-level. It is visited every year by thousands of pilgrims. Next to Jwâlâmukhi, it is the most frequented place of pilgrimage in the Punjab : Katas (कटाक्ष) and Pushkara lakes have their origin from the tears of Siva. [C. A. S. R., II., p. 188 ; Imp. Gaz. Ind.]

P. 145 (126). *Kotera.*—At its foot are the remains of twelve temples (of Kashmir architecture of 800-1300 A.D.) clustered in a corner of an old fort. These are attributed to the Pândavas. Facing them to the east is the basement of a great structure—probably a Buddhist stupa. (C. A. S. R. II., pp. 188-90). At a short distance lies the hill of Murti on which are the ruins of a Jain temple marking the spot where Mahávîra was supposed to have obtained his enlightenment. [Stein in Vienna Oriental Journal, 1890, p. 80 ; p. 260.]

P. 148 (129). *Ko-lo-she-pu-lo* : राजपुर (mod. Rajaori) repeatedly mentioned in the Râjataranginî. As a passage of the Mahâbhârata (VII, 4, 5 ; *Karna, Râjapuram gatvâ Kâmbojâ Nirjitâs-tvayâ*) states that Râjapura was the home of the Kâmbojas and as Kâmboja is constantly associated with Gândhâra (M. Bh., XII, 207, 43 ; Asoka's R. E., V.), Dr. Hemchandra Roy Chowdhury locates *Kâmboja* here. [P. H. A. I., p. 77.]

P. 150 (130). *Dogra.*—The Skr. form is Durgara (दुर्गर).

P. 156 (136). *Jâlandhara.*—She-lan-ta-lo ; E. to W.—1000 *li* ; N. to S.—800 *li*. (Y. Ch. I. 296). जालन्धरास्त्रिगर्ताःस्युः (Hemachandra's अभिधानचिन्तामणि IV. 24). *Trigarta* is the land watered by three rivers—the Râvi, the Bias, and the Sutlej (C. A. S. R., V. p. 148). It formerly comprised the whole of the upper Doâb between the Ravi and the Sutlej. Its cities were Jâlandhar and Kot Kangra. (*Ibid.* p. 145).

P. 157 (137). *Kulindrine of Ptolemy* is Kulûta. (M'Crindle's Ptolemy, p. 110 ; spelt as Kylindrine).

P. 161 (141). *Chamba.*—Champâ (चम्पा) of the Râjataranginî. (*Kâstwar* is Kâsthavâta काष्ठवाट).

A remarkable series of inscriptions authenticate its history. It was founded probably in the 6th century A.D. by Marut, a *Sûryavamsiya* Rajput, who built *Brahmapura*, mod. Barmawar, on the Budhil river, the southern affluent of the Ravi. (C. A. S. R., XIV, pp. 109-119 ; a separate vol. (Chamba) published by the Arch. Department treats of its antiquities).

P. 162 (142). *Kullu*.—Watters' Y. Ch., I. p. 298. It is the *Kulûta* or Kaulûta of the Râmâyana, Mahâbhârata, Purânas, Brihatsamhitâ, Mudrârâkshasa, and Kâdambari, which refers to its princess Patralekhâ. (An. R. A. S. I. 1907-8, p. 261 ff.)

P. 164 (142). *Lo-hu-lo* district (N.E. of Ku-lu-to) is *Lho-yal* of the Tibetans and *Lâhul* of the people of Kullu. Still further to the N., Y. Ch. (I. 299) places Mo-lo-so (=Tibetan Mar-sa, a synonym of Mar-yul "Low-land" —the old as well as the present name of) Ladakh. [Francke (J. R. A. S. 1908, pp. 188-9) has pointed out that there is no necessity of correcting it into *Mo-lo-po* as Cunningham has done].

P. 164 (143). *Mandi*.—Read C. A. S. R., XIV, p. 119.

P. 165 (144). *Satadru*.—Y. Ch.'s *Sha-to-tu-lo* has been transcribed as *Satadru*. Watters proposes *Satadûra*. (Y. Ch. I, p. 300). Both the words begin with श.

P. 170 (148). *Taḳi*.—Tse-kia (Cheh-ka) above 10,000 *li* in circuit ; lying between the Indus (W) and Pi-po-she (Bias) (E) ; ancient capital—She-kie-lo (=Sâkala शाकल) (Y. Ch. I, 287).

Sâkala, the capital of the *Madras*, *Arattas* (Skr. A-râshtra, अराष्ट्र or kingless ; Arattii of Periplus, p. 41), *Jârtiḳas* or *Bâhîḳas* (Mahâ Bh. Sabhâ—P. XXXI. 1197, Karna—P. VII. 6, 32, 80) who are पञ्चानां सिन्धुषष्ठानां नदीनाम् अन्तराश्रिताः ; वाहीकाः टक्कनामानः (Hemachandra's Abhidhâna-Chintâmani, IV, 25).

P. 177 (155). *Old Bhira* or Jobnath-nagar.—Extensive mound of ruins on the W. bank of the Jhelum. It may be identical with *Pi-cha* or *Pe-too* through which F. H. (Chap. XV.) passed on his way from Bannu to Mathurâ. (C. A. S. R. XIV. 35-36). As for the kingdom of Sophytes ("lord of the fastness of the Salt-Range stretching from the Jhelum to the Indus," V. Smith), there is difficulty in locating it, for "our sources all agree in placing the principality E. of the Jhelum." [Camb. H. I., p. 372].

Hence Cunningham may not be right in placing the capital to the W. of the Jhelum. As for modern Bhira on the eastern bank, it is not an ancient city being founded by Sher Shah in A. D. 1540. (C. A. S. R., XIV., p. 36).

P. 192 (159). *Boukephala*.—Cunningham located it at Dilawar opposite to Jalâlpur. (C. A. S. R., II. p. 173-186) Jalâlpur has also been identified with *Râjagriha* or *Girivraja, the capital of the Kekayas* (C. A. S. R., II., p. 14) whose country has been located, in the Râmâyana (II, 68, 19-22) on the other side of the Vipâsâ (Bias) and stretching up to Gândhâra.

V. Smith located *Boukephala* at Jhelum. Here have been discovered many old coins, but not earlier than the Indo-Scythian period, three iron tripods of Greek form, two brass bowls and portions of some 24 later stone pillars. (C. A. S. R. II, pp. 174-5 ; XIV, pp. 41-2). A point in its favour is that it is higher up and Alexander seems to have kept close to the hills. But it is not possible to decide the question with our defective documents. (Camb. H. I. p. 361).

P. 204 (177). *Nikœa*.—As for the site of Mong read C. A. S. R., II. p. 186-7. Dr. V. Smith has located it at Sukhcainpur. [E. H. I.]

P. 205 (179). *Gujarât*.—The name of this city indicates that the *Gurjaras* once dwelt in the Punjab. They were found, by Yuan Chwang, to occupy a portion of Râjaputana. Then they migrated to what is now known as the peninsula of Guzerat.

P. 206 (179). *Ali Khan*.—Alakhâna defeated by Sankaravarman, king of Kashmîra (883-902 A.D.) ; he was ruler of the upper portion of the flat Doab between the Jhelum and the Chenab rivers south of the Dvârvâbhisâra, together with a part of the Punjab plain further east. He had to cede *Takkadesa* (टक्कदेश) or the tract adjoining the lower hills to the E. of the Chenab to his victor. (Stein's Râjataranginî, V.).

P. 206 (179). *Sangala and Sâkala.*—(शाकल) Cunningham (A. S. R. II. pp. 192-200) identified *Sangala* with *Sâkala* and located them at Sângalawâla-tîba (Jhang district ; 31°43′ N. and 73°27′ E).

But they are not identical: *Sangala* (Sânkala of Pânini, IV. 2.75) was to the E. of the Hydraotes or the Râvi (Arrian and Curtius) ; whereas *Sâkala* was, as the following passage clearly states, to the W. of the Râvi.

शाकलं नाम नगरमापगा नाम निम्नगा। जार्तिका नाम बाहीकास्तेषां वृत्तं सुनिन्दितम्॥ ......शतद्रुकं नदीं तीर्त्वा तां च रम्यामिरावतीम्। गत्वा स्वदेशम् ....॥ पञ्च नद्यो वहन्त्येता यत्र पीलु-वनाबहिः। शतद्रुश्च विपाशा च तृतीयेरावती तथा॥ चन्द्रभागा वितस्ता च सिन्धुषष्ठा बहिर्गिरेः। आरट्टा नाम ते देशाः नष्टधर्माः न तान् व्रजेत्॥

(M. Bh. Karna-p VII.) Skr. Sâkala=Pkr. Sâgala "the capital of Milinda" and of Mihirakula.

Recent authorities place Sangala in Gurdaspur district (Lahore Division) [Imp. Gaz. Ind. XII. p. 393]. Prof. Bevan notes that the site is uncertain and that Anspach conjectures Jandiâla. (Camb. H. I., p. 371).

Sâkala is Sial-kot (Fleet in 14th Oriental Congress). A Brahmin informed Cunningham (C. A. S. R., xiv, pp. 44-6) that Sial-kot was originally called *Sâkala*, the capital of *Bâhîka* country. The name Sial-kot is said to have been originated from the fact that it was the fort (kot) of Raja Sâla (शल्य, the brother of Queen Mâdrî, the princess of *Madra* identical with Bâhîka) the maternal uncle of the Pândavas. (Note that the modern name of the Madras Presidency has nothing to do with ancient मद्र).

The passage from the Mahâ Bhârata quoted above states that the *Bâhîkas* were also called *Jârtikas* (Jat) and Arattas (Arattai of Schoff's Periplus, p. 41 ;=Skr. Arâshtra अराष्ट्र, Kingless). The word *Bâhîka* has been derived by Kâtyâyana, in his Vârttikas on Pânini, from बहिस् 'outside'. Thus the word means those who live outside the land of the Aryans. These Bâhîkas were held in so much disrepute that we find the following description in the Mahâbhârata:

बहि नाम ह्रीकस्च विपाशयां पिशाचकौ ।
तयोरपत्यं बाह्रीकाः नैषा सृष्टिः प्रजापतेः ॥

(Karna p., VII.)

P. 219 (191). *Asarur*:—in Gujranwala district; 31° 47′ N and 73° 43′ E; the ruins (described in C. A. S. R., II, pp. 200-202.) consist of an extensive mound 15000 ft. in circuit.

As Cunningham's location of *Sâkala* has been rejected and it has been identified with Sialkot, so we shall have to locate Tse-kia, the capital described by Y. Ch. (I. p. 288) about two miles N.E. of Sialkot.

P. 221—223 (193). *Ransi and Ambakapi*:—ruins described in C. A. S. R., II. pp. 202-205, XIV. p. 48

P. 228 (199). *Kasûr*:—31° 8′ N; 74° 24′ E.

P. 230 (200). Chi-na-puh-ti:—

The winter residence of the Chinese hostages in the time of Kanishka (Y. Ch. I. 292). Julien and Cunningham transcribe it as Chîna*pati*. Cunningham identified it with *Patti*, a very old town 27m. N.E. of Kasur. Watters has shown that the real Skr. form is "*Chîna-Bhukti*" i.e. Chîna-allotment—the district assigned by Kanishka to the Chinese hostages. So it cannot be identified with Patti.

Mirza Muhammad Beg places *Chiniyari* on the road from Amritsar to Parsarur. (Mod.) Chine is exactly 11 miles from Amritsar on the high road to Sialkot (=Sâkala) (C. A. S. R. XIV. p. 54). It may be identified with Chînabhukti. V. Smith (Appendix, Watters' Y. Ch. Vol. II) located it at Ferozpur.

P. 233 (203). *Po-fa-to*:—(Skr. *Parvata* ref. to in Pânini iv. 2. 143), circuit 5000 *li*; 700 *li* N.E. of Mou-lo-san-pu-lo (Multan?) [Y. Ch., II, p. 255]. Cunningham wrongly corrected the name into *So-lo-fa-to* and identified the capital with Shorkot. But he afterwards abandoned the identification and located it at Harapa (Montgomery district) where are most extensive ruins (prehistoric stone-implements ; three "Harapa seals" with strange inscriptions ; a chain of mounds 3500 ft. long ; C. A. S. R., V, pp. 105-8). Dr. Fleet has accepted this location. (J. R. A. S., 1907. p. 650).

[V. Smith (Y. Ch., II appendix) identified it with Jammu included within the state of Kashmir. But as Jammu is about 250 miles away from Multan, the identification cannot be accepted.]

P. 235 (205). *Shorkot* :—the old fort of Shorkot is the loftiest of all the mounds in the Punjab, being 100 ft. above the surrounding fields. The local Brahmins derive the name from Skr. शिवपुर, Pkr. Siaura. Here have been found some bricks inscribed in early Gupta characters. (C. A. S. R., V. pp. 97-103 ; plate XXX.). Dr. Vogel takes it to be the city of the Sibis. (E. I., 1921, p. 16).

P. 238 (208). *Kot Kamâlia* :—Cunningham's derivation of the word from *Malli* cannot be accepted.

P. 246 (216). *As for the futility of identifications of the sites mentioned in connection with Alexander's march, Read V. Smith. p. 92-93.*

P. 257 (224) *Tulamba* :—the name was originally Kulamba. (C. A. S. R., V. pp. 111-112).

P. 264 (230) *Multan* :—Cunningham believes that it has been referred to by classical writers as *Kaspapuros, Kaspeira* &c. But Dr. Stein has shown (Translation of Râjataranginî, vol. II, topography of Kashmir) that these names refer to Kashmir, though located wrongly.

Yuan-chwang visited *Mou-lo-san-pu-lo* (Skr. Mûlasthâna) which he located 900 li to the *east* of Sindh.

(Watters, II, p. 254). This Mûlasthâna has been identified by Cunningham with Multan. Mr. Watters (vol. II, p. 254) objected to this identification, for Multan is to the N., *and not to the E.*, of Sindh. V. Smith (Appendix, Watters, vol. II) supports Cunningham evidently on the ground that we know of no other Mûlasthâna and as such the eastern direction is a slip of the pen. But a ninth century A. D. record of Indrarâja, (uncle to the Râshtra-kûta ruler Amoghavarsha I), the ruler of Lâta (लाट (mentions a Mûlasthâna on the Narmadâ in the Province of Bhrigukachchha (Bharoch—श्रीभृगुकच्छे नर्मदायां मूलस्थानतीर्थे स्नात्वा I. A.). This can be identified with Y. Ch.'s *Mou-lo-san-pu-lo* to the *E*. of Sindh.

Some authorities connect the name of Multan with that of the *Malloi*. But it was never a *Mâlava* city, for it is to the south of the confluence of the Hydraotes and Akesines. (Camb. H. I., p. 375).

The idol of the Sun-god of Multan has been referred to by Alberuni. (Chap. XI.)

P. 277 (241) *Kahror*: Alberuni is our authority to locate here the scene of the great battle between *Vikramâditya* and the *Sakas*.

P. 281 (245). *Johiya*:—Prakrit form of *Yaudheya* (यौधेय) . The Yaudheyas have been mentioned in the Pâninian system with the *Saubhreyas* (probably identical with *Sabracoe* of Curtius) as war-like tribes in the Punjab. They are mentioned in the inscriptions of Rûdradâman and Samudra-Gupta. The find-spots of their coins indicate that the extensive territories of the tribe comprised the southern portion of the Punjab, including the Sikh states and the northern part of Rajputana. Either the Bias or the Râvi was probably the N.W. boundary of the tribal country which abutted on the territory of the *Madras* or *Mâdrakas* in the Central Punjab. The

44

cities of Lahore, Bahawalpur, Bikanir, Ludiana and Delhi roughly indicate the limits of the tribal territory.

WESTERN INDIA.

P. 284 (248). देवसभायाः परतः पश्चाद्देशः। तत्र देवसभ-सुराष्ट्र-दशेरक-त्रवण-भृगुकच्छ-कच्छीय आनर्त-अर्बुद-ब्राह्मणवाह-यवन-प्रभृतयो जनपदाः॥ (Kâvyamîmâmsâ p. 93). *Devasabhâ* is a city on a mt. (not identified) referred to in Arthasâstra (Skr. text p. 78) as producing red sandal (पद्मगन्धि चन्दन).

It comprised Sindh, Western Rajputana, Cutch, Gujarât and a portion of the adjoining coast on the lower course of the Narmadâ, 3 states—Sindh, Gurjara and Valabhi (Y. Ch.)

1. SINDHUDESA.

P. 285 (248). 'The country along the Indus'; denoted lower portion only of it, *i.e.* Sindh. The *Saindhavas* identified, or closely connected with the *Sauvîras* (? M. Bh. Vana—P. cclxiii, 15576-81 ; cclxvi, 15618 and 15635-7 etc.). Alberuni (chap. 29) notes 'सौवीर *i.e.* Multan and Jahrâwar'. *Vrachada* (व्र) (Pischel's Gram. Prakrit, §. 28.) seems to be a name of it.

Places and nations mentioned in connection with Alexander's invasion :—Sodrœ or Sogdi, Massanœ, Musikani, Prœsti, Sindimana, Patala.

It is identical with the *Indo-Scythia* through which flows the *Sindhus* (Indus) with its seven mouths on the middle of which is the market-town of *Barbaricum* and the capital of which is Minnagara subject to Parthian princes ; (Gulfs of Eirinon and Baraca are the Rann and Gulf of Cutch). (Schoff's Periplus, pp. 37-8).

P. 286 (249) *Vichavapura* :—Lieut. Col. Branfill has suggested its identification with Vijnot (Vijnor, Vijnaur, Vijnavapur), a ruined town in Upper Sindh in the Ubauro taluk of the Rohri division. It was, according to tradition, one of the five ancient sites of Sindh. (I.A., 1882, p. I ; p. 5.)

P. 294 (257).—*Alor*: Its identification with the city of *Mousikanos* (which may be the *Mushika*, of Sanskrit Literature, occupying Sindh in this period and afterwards migrating to the South) is probable but not certain. (V. Smith, E. H. I., p. 100 ; Camb. H. I., p. 377).

P. 300 (262). *Middle Sindh* :—O-fan-cha (as it has been spelt by Watters) or A-fan-tu. It was above 300 *li* N.E. of Pi-to-shih-lo, 2400 *li* in circuit. (Y. Ch. II. 259). The name has been transcribed as *Avanda* (वण्ड) (Julien) or Avanta (वट) (Watters.)

P. 302 (263) *Sehwan* :—It has been identified with *Sindimana* for no better reason than that both names begin with S. (V. Smith, E. H. I., p. 101.) It is in Karachi district, about 192 miles from Karachi. Here are the remains of a fort said to have been built by Alexander. (A. S. I., N. I. S., vol. xvi, p. 213.)

P. 306 (267). *Brâhmanâbâd* :—25° 56′ N. and 68° 54′ E. ; ब्राह्मणवाह of *Kâvyamîmâmsâ* (p. 93). It was probably one of the oldest cities in India. The historian Bilâdhûra writing a thousand years ago calls it *Brahmana-bad-al-atiqah* or Brâhmanâbâd, the ancient. Here is one vast mass of ruins forming irregular mounds within a circumference of four miles. (J. B. B. R. A S., vol. v., p. 413 ; A. S. I., N. I. S., xvi., pp. 215-216.) It has been excavated recently (Annual Rep. A. S., 1903-4, pp. 132-144 ; 1908-9, p. 79 ff.) and various prehistoric remains have been discovered. The correct spelling of the name is said to be Bahmanâbâd (said to be named after Bahman, an Iranian King in the fifth century B. C.)

V. Smith (E. H. I. pp. 102-3) identified it with *Pattala* which was located by Cunningham at Hyderabad and about 30 miles S.E. of the latter by Holdich. (Camb. H. I., p. 378).

P. 318 (281). *Pi-to-shih-lo*:—It was 700 *li* N. of Atien-po-chih-lo and 300 *li* S.W. of O-fan-cha (Y. Ch. II, p. 258); 3000 *li* in circuit.

Julien sanskritized the name as *Pîta-silâ* (पीतशिला) or Yellow Rock; Cunningham as *Pâtasilâ* or "Flat Rock" and identified it with Lower Sindh the important town in which is Haidarabad, formerly called Patalpur, situated on a *flat-topped* hill.

Mr. Watters transcribes it as *Bheda-Sira* (भेदशिरः) or "Cleft Head" and remarks that the name may have reference to the Jâtaka of which the Pilgrim makes mention and that he may have used a Buddhist designation unknown to ordinary Indian Literature.

As *A-tien-po-chih-lo* has been identified, with better reasons, with Lower Sindh, Bhedasira is to be located somewhere to the N.W. of the Lower and to the S.W. of the Middle Sindh or O-fan-cha.

P. 330 (288). *Min-nagar*:—probably the 'city of Min' (a saka name); the capital of *Indo-Scythia*. (Schoff's Periplus, pp. 37-8); =Binagar of Ptolemy. (C. A. S. R.; II., p. 46).

Alexander's Haven and Barbaricum.

P. 337 (294). "No Indian author, Hindu, Buddhist or Jain, makes even the faintest allusion to Alexander or his deeds." These are the words with which Dr. Vincent Smith concludes his account of Alexander's Indian campaign. Though there is no allusion to the deeds of Alexander, is there not a reference to the cities founded by him in India? A careful search ought to be made for them. The hypothetical Sanskrit forms for *Αλέξανδρος* and *Αλέξαδρεια* are, according to the rules of Sanskrit phonetics, Alakshandrah and Alakshandrâ. In the vernacular Alakkhandâ or Alashandâ'* are the forms expected. The second form is very nearly identical with Alasanda or Alasadda, the birth place of Milinda, which has been identified with Alexandria Opiane at the foot of Mount Caucasus.† But this Alasadda was not in India proper. Is there any reference to Alexander's Haven which certainly bore his name and which was in India proper? Now the Haven must have been famous on account of its commercial importance. Hence we ought to search for it in works like Kautilya's *Arthasâstra,* the Sabhâparvan of the *Mahâbhârata, Ratna-Sâstras* and *Vaidyakâ Nighantus* which mention the products and articles of commerce of the various parts of India. And it is actually referred to in Kautilya's *Arthasâstra* in the expression 'Alakandaka coral' (=Coral of Alakanda).‡ Where was this Alakanda? Kautilya is silent. The commentator remarks that at the mouth of the river of Barbara, a river falling in the Sea of Barbara was, according to the same authority, the River Srotasî mentioned as a source of pearls. A lake named Srighanta श्रीघण्ट in a corner of the Sea of Barbara has also been mentioned by him.§ The Epics and Purânas mention the Barbaras (or Varvaras) as a northern or north-western people.|| Now by combining these bits of information we find that the country of the Barbaras was in the W. or N.-W. frontier of India and that it stretched up to the [Arabian] sea. Through it flowed

---

* As *sh* was preserved in the Shahbazgarhi, Mansera and Kalsi versions of Asoka's Inscriptions, we expect to find *sh* in the early vernaculars of N.W. frontier. As a school of the White Yajurveda pronounced *sha* as *kha,* we expect *kh* for Skr. *ksh.* This *sh* was changed, in the later period, to *s.*

† *Ind. Ant.,* vol. ii, p. 146; Cunningham, *A. G.,* pp. 26-30.

‡ Sanskrit Text, p. 78; English Translation, p. 90.

§ *Arthasâstra,* Eng. trans., p. 86, ftn. 7, 8; p. ftn. 1.

|| Pargiter's note on the word in his *Mârkandeya Purâna.*

a river named Srotasì. In it was a lake not far from the sea. And Alakanda stood at the mouth of a river.

The above description of Alakanda fits well with that of Alexander's Haven. Dr. Smith has shown, on the authority of Major Raverty, that the large lake at the mouth of the river where stood Alexander's Haven still exists and is called Samârâh.*

Identity of name and the above facts lead me to take Alexander's Haven as the Alakanda of Kautilya.

The Haven must have been a very flourishing city making a good trade in coral and pearl which were brought thither from various countries. But why is it that the author of the Periplus who evidently sailed round the western and southern coasts of India did not mention it? Had it changed its name or was it deserted on account of the silting up of the river? The great emporium of coral trade (for which Alakanda was famous in Kautilya's time) was then Barbaricum—the Barbari of Ptolemy. This name is, in the opinion of Mr. Schoff, the Hellenised form of some Hindu word. We have seen that Barbara was the name of the country in which was situated Alexander's Haven. Barbaricum is thus connected with Barbara. Barbàrika or '(the port) of Barbara country' was probably an epithet of Alexandria itself and it came to be used instead of the name of the port because of the confusion caused by the use of the word Alakanda which was probably used to designate the other Alexandrias also. 'Barbarika' as the name of a place is not a theoretical word formed by sanskritising Barbaricum. It actually occurs in the *Dhanvantarîya Nighantu*, an Ayurvedic work. "White (*svete*) and scentless (*nirgandha*) is the *Barbarikachandana*. It is *pittâsrik-*

* Smith, *Early History of India* (2nd ed.), pp. 101-3 and specially the foot-notes.

kapha-dâhaghnam krimighnam guru rukshanam."* This is the description which the *Dhanvantariya Nighantu* gives of a kind of sandal called *Barbarika-chandana.* The *Râjanighantu* also mentions *Barbara-chandana.* Thus Barbara or Barbarika must be the name of a country after which the sandal produced there or imported therefrom was called. Kautilya† mentions Daivasabheya, Jongaka, Sâkala and other varieties of *chandana* and these are epithets derived from place-names. The *Râjanighantu* mentions the वैट्टचन्दन and remarks मलयाद्रिसमीपस्थाः पर्व्वताः वैट्टसंज्ञकाः । तज्जातं चन्दनं यत्तु वैट्टाख्यं कथितं । This remark clearly shows that one kind of sandal was named after its place of origin—वैट्टपर्व्वत, which I take to be the Sanskrit (or sanskritised Dravidian) form of Mt. Bêttigô mentioned in Ptolemy's geography.‡ It may be objected that the sandal-producing Barbarika cannot be identified with Barbaricum, for sandal grows in Southern India only. But such a great authority as Kautilya has mentioned sandals of Devasabhâ (a city and a hill in Western India),§ Jonga (in Assam).|| Sâkala (a part of the Punjab) etc. Thus there is no difficulty in identifying *Barbarika* with *Barbaricum.*

P. 345 (297). *Debal* :—It has now disappeared ; its site was near the existing shrine of Pir Patho. (Camb. H. I., p. 378 ; V. Smith ; E. H. I. p. 104.)

P. 347 (302). *O-(or A-)tien-po-chi-lo* : It was 1500 or 1600 *li* S.W. of Sindh (Y. Ch. II. 256) ; 5000 *li* in circulit; its capital *Kie-chi-ssu-fa-lo was away in the W. on the Sin-tu* (Indus) river and near the sea.

---

* *Vanaushadhidarpana* by Kaviraj B. C. Gupta, Vol. I, pp. 283-4.

† Text, p. 78, translation, p. 90.

‡ Pp. 75, 105.

§ Ftn., 5, 7, p. 90 of the English translation of Kautilya.

|| देवसभायाः परतः पश्चाद्देशः । तत्र देवसभ सुराष्ट्र......प्रभृतयो जानपदः ......देवसभ......अर्बुदादयः च पर्व्वताः । *Kâvyamimâmsâ,* p. 93.

The name of the country was sanskritized as *Adhyavakila* by Julien ; as *Audumbara* (the Odombœræ of Pliny) by Cunningham who identified it with Cutch ; as *Adinavachila* by Watters. The name of the capital is Kachchhesvara कच्छेश्वर according to Lassen and Watters. (vol. II. p. 256-7).

As the capital was on the *Sin-tu* river, the country cannot be identified with Cutch as Cunningham has done. It was the Lower Sindh. The name *Kachchesvara* here does not refer to Cutch ; it is to be derived from Skr. *Kachchha* which means simply "Sea-Coast Land."

P. 349 (305). Lang-kie-lo :—Langala or Lankara. It was 2000 *li* W. of A-ti-en-po-chih-lo ; its language differed little from that of India proper. (Y. Ch. II. 257-8).

The country is the E. part of Makran ; a branch of the Langga tribe still exists in the N. of Biluchistan (St. Martin). The name of their capital was according to Watters, *Strîsvara*) स्त्रीश्वर or "Women Paramount".

P. 350 (305). *Arabitœ* :—a people of Dravidian stock, Arava. (Camb. H. I., p. 380).

P. 352 (307). *Oritœ* :—of Dravidian stock ; from Tamil *ur*, village. (Camb. H. I. p. 380).

P. 353 (309). *Rambacia* :—identified with Sonmiâni by Tomaschek. (Camb. H. I. p. 380).

P. 354 (309). *Hingulâj* :—*Hingulâdevî*, one of the 51 *Pîthasthânas* sacred to the devotees of Goddess Kâlî, nine days' journey from Tatha by Karachi and about nine miles from the sea-shore.

P. 357 (312). *Gurjjara* :—Name of a nation who once dwelt in the Punjab and migrated to the Peninsula of Kathiawad which is now called Guzarat after them. Y. Ch. (Watters, II, pp. 249-50) locates *Kiu-cho-lo* (Gurjara) 1800 *li* N. of *Valabhî* (Records) or N.E. of *Surâshtra* (Life) and 2800 *li* N.W. of Ujjain. The inscriptions of the 9th century also applied the name *Gurjara*-

râshtra गुर्जरराष्ट्र to the country N. of Ajmer and Sambhar Lake. [Imp. Gaz. Ind., xii, p. 350]. Its capital *Pi-lo-mi-lo* is modern Bhinmâl, 25° N. and 76° 16′ E. a town in the Jaswantpur district of Jodhpur. (Imp. Gaz. Ind. VIII, p. 111). Bhinmâl, भिल्लमाल or Plateau of the Bhils, was the original capital of the *Gurjara-Pratihâras* who transferred their headquarters to Kanauj (early part of the ninth century). For the history of the Pratihâras, read V. Smith, E. H. I., p. 378 ff.

VALABHI.

P. 363 (316). *Kathiawad*, so called from the Kathis who settled here from Cutch. The name Gujarat is connected with the *Gurjaras* who came here in the 10th Century. Marco Polo calls the Peninsula Sumenat. (Somanâtha). The old name was Surâshtra सुराष्ट्र (Mahâ Bh.; Syrastrene of Ptolemy and Periplus, Sarastos of Strabo); but it now means a part and not the whole. In Y. Ch.'s time (J. R. A. S., 1906, pp. 96-97) the Northern part was Surâshtra and S. part Lâta लाट (the district between the Lower Mâhî and Tâpî); the Cambay plates of Govinda (E. I. VII.) shows that sometimes it extended to the N. beyond Mâhî as far as the Sheri. *Fa-la-pi=Skr.* Valabhi (mentioned in Pânini's Ganapâtha on iv. 2.82). This Kingdom included the whole of the peninsula and the districts of Bharoch and Surat (Y. Ch.). Valabhî city is represented by the ruins at Wala 18 m. N.E. of Bhaonagar (A. S. W. I. vol. ii.).

1. SURÂSHTRA (सुराष्ट्र).

P. 372 (324). *Su-la-cha.*—above 500 *li* W. (Records) or N.W. (Life) from Valabhî; circuit 4000 *li*; touched the river Mo-hi (Mâhî) on the W. Its capital at the foot of Mt. *Yuh-shan-ta* (Pkr. Ujjanta, Skr. *Urjayat* of Rudradâman's and Skandagupta's inscriptions) is Junâgad (Jîrnagad or Old Fort), ancient Girinagara (Girnâr) [Y. Ch. ii. 248].

Girnâr is a sacred hill (3500 ft. high) with ruined temples. It is about 10 miles E. of Junagarh which was sanskritized by Lassen (Ind. Alter, p. 105 ftn), followed by Cunningham, as Yavana-garh but which I take to be Jîrna (जीर्ण) garh or Old Fort. It is famous for its inscriptions of Asoka (covering over 100 sq. ft. of rock), Rudradâman, and Skanda-gupta (and various later ones. Burgess, A. S. W. I, II. pp. 18-33). There are however, no remains of any ancient city, temples or ruins of a corresponding age to the inscriptions and but for their dates the place (21° 30′ N. and 70° 42′ E) would have seemed to be not older than the 10th century A. D. (Imp. Gaz. Ind., xii, p. 248). To the E. of Junagarh there is a number of Buddhist caves arranged in three lines. (A. S.W.I., Kathiawad and Kachh, p. 139).

The inscriptions of Rudradâman (E. I., vol. viii) and Skandagupta (Fleet, G. I.) inform us that here lived the Provincial Governors of Chandragupta and Asoka, and of the Imperial Guptas.

The *Girnâramâhâtmya* (in 30 chapters) of the Prabhâsa Khanda (खण्ड) describes Girnâr and the adjoining holy places, *Vastrâpathakshetra, Raivataka* etc. (I.A., 1875, pp. 238-244).

To the south of the Peninsula of Guzarat was *Prabhâsa* or *Somanâtha* ; to the W. was Dvârakâ. Dvârâvatî, Abdhinagarî (Trikândasesha, II, 1, 15) or Kusasthalî (कुशस्थली), the capital of Anarta (Vâyu). The Jaina sacred place of Satrunjaya (शत्रुंजय) is on the isolated mountain to the south of Palitana.

Hathab, in the Gogha Tâkulâ of the Bhaunagar territory has been identified with *Hastakavapra,* a territorial sub-division mentioned in three Grants of Dhruvasena I. of Valabhi. This Hastakavapra is to be identified with

Astakampron or Astakapra, a city mentioned by Ptolemy and the author of the Periplus. Hathab is now not on the sea, but it was once a port. (I. A., 1876, p. 204 ; p. 314 ; 1878, p. 54.)

Historical Sketch :—The peninsula of Surâshtra was included in the Empire of the *Mauryas*. Then we find it included in the dominions of the *Western Kshatrapas*. It then passed to the Gupta Empire. From the last quarter of the 5th century A. D. we find the *Maitrakas of Valabhi* who were at first subordinate to the Guptas and then to the Hûnas and later became independent. Y. Ch. attests to their grandeur and notes that the reigning king obtained as dowry the countries of Anandapura, *Ki-cha* and Surâshtra (in the narrower sense) from his father-in-law, Emperor *Harshavardhana*. The dynasty was overthrown (third quarter of the 8th century A.D.) by a Moslem expedition from Sindh. The *Châpotkatas* (चापोत्कट) of Anahilapattan were lords of the Peninsula for some two centuries (from 750 A.D.), sometimes as feudatories of the Pratihâras. They were overthrown by Mûlarâja, the founder of the *Châlukya* family (975 A.D. to the 12th Century) of Anahilapattan. It was during the rule of this family that Somanâtha was destroyed. In the middle of the 13th Century we find the *Bâghela Châlukyas* the last important Hindu family of the Peninsula before its absorption to the Moslem Empire.

P. 374 (326). *Bharoch or Bhrigukachchha* :—Probably not mentioned in the Epics ; mentioned in the *Kûrmavibhâga and Bhuvanakosha* ; the great port of Bharukachchha of Buddhist Literature ; Barygaza of Ptolemy (p. 38 ; p. 152) and Periplus (p. 40 ; p. 287)—modern Bharoch (20° 42′ N. and 72° 59′ E.).

It was the capital of the Lâta (लाट) country=Larike of Ptolemy (p. 38).

The district of Po-lu-kie-che-po, 2400 or 2500 *li* in

circuit; Chief city—on the bank of the Nai-mo-te (Narmadâ); 1000 *li* from Mahârâshtra (इ) [Y. Ch. II, 241].

Bhrigu-Kachchha means *high coast land* and so the district really is. But the Hindus account for the name by remarking that it is so called because it was originally founded by (sage) Bhrigu. (Imp. Gaz. Ind., IX, p. 30). In the *Divyâvadâna* of the *Mahâyâna* Buddhists pp. 544-586), we find a story which accounts for the name of Bhirukachchha. It runs thus: *Rudrâyana, king* of Roruka (probably Alor, the old city of Sindh) in Sauvîra was killed by his son Sikhandin (शिखण्डी). For this sin of Sikhandin the whole of his realm was destroyed by a fatal rain of sands. Only three good men—two ministers and a Buddhist Monk—were alive and they left the place in search of a new land. Bhiru, one of the two good ministers founded *Bhiruka* or *Bhirukachchha*.

CENTRAL INDIA.

P. 375 (327). Its Skr. name is मध्यदेश (*Madhyadesa*). It has been defined in the *Manusamhitâ* (II) as the land between the Himalayas (N) and the Vindhyas (S) and between the Sarasvatî (W) and Prayâga or Allahabad (E). The *Kûrmavibhâga* also follows this system. Its eastern boundary changed gradually. The *Kâvya-mîmâmsâ* (p. 93) giving Benares as the W. limit of Eastern India extends Madhyadesa up to that. The "Middle Country" of the Buddhist Literature (see Introduction) has been described here as the Central India of Y. Ch. Its eastern boundary was Pundravardhana (पुण्ड्रवर्धन). Y. Ch. described it as divided into 37 states. He refers to *Harshavardhana* as its emperor. Other kings mentioned by him are those of Pâryâtra (a Vaisya), Matipura (a non-Buddhist Sûdra), Nepal (Amsuvarman), Magadha (Pûrnavarman, the last descendant of Asoka), Ujjayini, Mahesvarapura and Chi-chi-to. The rulers of the last three states had been described as Brahmanas.

1. STHÂNESWARA.

P. 376 (328). The Skr. name is *Sthânvîsvara* from *Sthânu* (Siva) and *Isvara* (ईश्वर Lord). It was the capital of the state named *Srikantha-janapada* (श्रीकण्ठजनपद) [Bâna's Harsha Charita]. The founder of its royal family was *Pushyabhûti* whose illustrious descendant was *Harshavardhana* who transferred the capital to Kanauj. For Y. Ch.'s description of this state read Watters, Vol. I, p. 314. For its identification with *Sthuna*, the W. boundary of the Middle country, read Introduction.

The country immediately around Thaneswar between the *Sarasvatî* (mod. Sarsuti) of Rigvedic fame and the *Drishadvatî* or Rigvedic *Asmanvatî* (अश्मन्वती) (mod. *Râkshî* ; C. A. S. R. XIV, p. 88) is *Brahmâvarta* (Manu, II. 17-18) or *Kurukshetra* or the Holy land of the Kurus.

The famous battle-field of Kurukshetra is situated on the S. side of Thaneswar, about 30 miles to the S. of Ambala and 40 miles N. of Panipat. (C. A. S. R., XIV, p. 86 ; this Report pp. 86-88, C. A. S. R. II, p. 212 and I. A., 1904, pp. 298-300 describe some three hundred places of pilgrimage connected with the Kuru-Pândava war).

The kingdom of Kuru extended from the Sarasvatî to the Ganges, and was divided into three parts, Kurukshetra, the Kurus (*i.e.*, the country of the Kurus) and Kurujângala (the forest tract included in the kingdom) (M. Bh. Adi—p. 109, 1). Its southern boundary was Khândava खाण्डव (Taittirîya Aranyaka) so famous in Epic lore. Its capital in the Vedic age was *Asandîvant* which was probably identical with *Hastinâpur* or *Gajasâhvaya* repeatedly referred to in the Mahâbhârata. (Ray

Chowdhuri's P. H. A. I. pp. 5-6) and traditionally identified with an old town in Mawâna tahsil, 22m. N. E. of Merat. (Fürher's Monts. Antiq. p. 10).

P. 385 (336). *Prithûdaka.*—Referred to in the Kâvyamîmâmsa (p. 93) as the boundary between Northern and Central India.

2. BAIRÂT.

P. 387 (337). *Po-li-ye-to-lo* (Pâryâtra); 3000 *li* in circuit, above 500 *li* W. of Mathurâ; over 800 *li* from Satadru (Y. Ch. I. 300-1). Cunningham takes it to be Bairât. But it is double of 800 *li* from Satadru. It is said to be so called because it was the capital of Virâta, King of the Matsyas. (Its antiquities described in C. A. S. R., II, 242-9; vi. p. 98). The country of the Matsyas (R(i)gveda VII. 18. 6; Gopatha Br. I. 2. 9) lay to the S. or S.W. of *Indra-prastha* (Sabhâ-P. XXX. 1105-6) and to the S. of Sûrasena शूरसेन or *Mathurâ* (Virâta-p. v. 141-5); it thus corresponds to mod. Alwar state and the land around that (portions of Jaypur and Bharatpur). Pargiter thinks that its capital was Upaplavya, 2 days' journey by chariot from Hastinâpura (M. Bh. Udyoga-p. lxxxiii, 3010-17). But according to *Nîlakantha* (ण्ठ) (M. Bh. IV. 72, 14) Upaplavya was "Virâta (ट)-nagara-samîpastha-nagarântaram" (Rai Chaudhury, p. 29).

3. SRUGHNA.

P. 395 (345). The position of this country is fixed unmistakably by the specification that it was bounded on the N. by high mountains and on the E. by the Ganges, while the Jumna flowed through the midst of it. (Y. Ch. I. 318).

It thus corresponds to the Dehra district with probably a part of the Saharanpur district and some of the hill-states abutting on the Dehra (Watters Y. Ch. II., p. 338).

C. A. S. R., I. p. 245 ; II. 226-31 ; xiv. p. 134 describe the antiquity of Sugh which is not far from *Kâlsi* (30° 32′ N. and 77° 53′ E.) where exist fourteen Rock Edicts of Asoka.

4. MADÂWAR.

P. 399 (348). *Matipura.*—Mo-ti-pu-lo, 6000 *li* in circuit ; from *Su-lu-ḳin-na* Y. Ch. proceeded to it by crossing to the E. bank of the river (Ganges). [Y. Ch. I. 322]. Watters transcribed it as *Matipura.* It is represented by the Bijnor district or the Eastern part of it. Mr. Watters rejects St. Martin's identification of the capital with Mandawar (29° 29′ N, 78° 8′ E ; extensive Buddhist ruins) 8 m. N. of Bijnor ; for it is to the S. E. of Srughna and to the S. of *Gangâdvâra* whereas Matipura was to the E. of them (Watters I., 322.)

The first considerable affluent of the Ganges in the Bijnor district is the Malin (Imp. Gaz. Ind. VIII., p. 193) —the *Mâlinî* of Kâlidâsa's *Saḳuntalâ*.

P. 402 (351). *Mo-yu-lo* : *Mâyâpura.*—Mo-yu-lo (Mayûra) was in the N. W. of this district and on the East bank of the Ganges. Near the city and close to the Ganges was a large Deva-temple of many miracles and within its enclosure was a tank fed by an artificial passage from the Ganges. This was called the *Ganges-Gate*, a place of pilgrimage (Y. Ch. I. 328).

Watters objects to Cunningham's identification of *Mo-yu-lo* with Mâyâpura or Hardwar on the ground that Mâyâpura cannot be the transcript of the Chinese name and that it is on the W. bank of the river, whereas Mo-yu-lo was on the E. side (Y. Ch. I., p. 329). But Cunningham has (anticipating this criticism) remarked that the town may have also been called *Mayûra-pura* as thousands of peacocks are to be found in the neighbourhood and the river may have changed its course. However it may be *Mo-yu-lo* was close to Hardwar (29° 58′ N. and 78° 10′ E.)

5. BRAHMAPURA

P. 407 (355). *Brahmapura.—Po-lo-ki-mo-pu-lo* 4000 *li* in circuit, 300 *li* N. "from this" (Mayûra or Matipura ?) [Y. Ch. I. 329.]

Cunningham (supported by V. Smith) treats the *N.* as a mistake for *N.E.* (for N. will take Y. Ch. back again to Srughna) and finds Brahmapura (located in the N.E. division of the *Kûrmavibhâga*) in the districts of Gharwal and Kumaon. In these districts reigned the Katur or Katuria Râjâs connected with *Kortripura* of Samudra-Gupta's Allahabad Pillar Inscription (J. R. A. S., 1898, p. 199).

6. GOVISANA.

P. 409 (357). *Watters* (I, 331) transcribes it as Govisanna. Dr. Führer identified its capital with Vairatpattan (29° 28′ N. and 79° 11′ E), the Brahmapura of Cunningham (Mons. Antiq. p. 49).

7. AHICHCHHATRA.

P. 412 (359). *Epic Panchâla.*—Bounded by Sub-Himalayan tribes (N. and N.E.), Kosala कोसल (E), *Sûrasena* शूरसेन, the junction of the Jumna and the Chambal and *Kânyakubja* (S) (Adi-P. CXXXVIII. 5512-3 ; Virâta-P. V. 144) ; and by *Sûrasena* and the *Kurus* (W) (Sabhâ-P. XXVIII. 1061 ; Bhîshma-P. IX. 346). Divided into two kingdoms by the Ganges ; Ahichchhatra was the capital of *North* Panchâla and *Kâmpilya* (Mod. Kampil in Farokhabad dist. U. P.; C.A.S.R., XI, pp. 11-13) was the capital of *South* Panchâla.

Pratyagrathâs-tu-Ahichchhatrâh (Hemachandra's Abhidhânachintâmani, IV. 26 'Ahichchhatra was also called *Pratyagratha*'). Panchâla roughly corresponds to the

Budaon, Furrukhabad and the adjoining districts of U.P. Vedic texts refer to an eastern and western division of the country. (Vedic Index, I. 469. In Epic Age it was divided into northern and southern Panchâlas as has already been stated).

The *Panchâlas* were also called *Krivi* in the Saptapatha Brâhmana. The *Krivis* appear in the Rig Veda as settled on the *Sindhu* (Indus) and *Asikni* (Chenab). The Panchâlas also included *Turvasas, Kesins,* and *Srinjayas.* Thus Panchâla seems to mean *'a combination of five'* (Camb. H. I., p. 118 ; Raichaudhuri, P.H.A.I., pp. 31-2).

The old name of *Ahi-chhatra* (Serpent-umbrella) is *Adhichchhatra* (preserved in an inscription ; Lüder's List of Brâhmî Inscriptions, Index) which is nearer to the Greek form of Adisdara (Adisadra ?) of Ptolemy (p. 133). At *Râmanagar* (which has been identified with *Ahichchhatra*) has been found a large number of Sunga (?) Coins. (C.A.S.R., I. pp. 255-65 ; J.A.S.B., 1880, p. 21).

8. PI-LO-SHAN-NA.

P. 417 (364).—About 260 *li* S ('E', one MS.) of *Ahichchhatra* and then crossing the Ganges and then S. ("S.W.", one MS.) (Y. Ch. I. 332). Watters transcribes it as *Bhilasana.*

The city is Bilsar or Bilsand (Etah district, U. P.) where were discovered the inscribed pillars of Kumâragupta (415-6 A.D. Fleet's G. I. p. 42). (C.A.S.R. xi. pp. 13-22 ; Cunningham himself rejected the site of *Atranjikhera*).

9. SÂNKÂSYA (साङ्काश्य) KAPITHIKÂ.

P. 423 (369).—*Sânkâsya* on the *Ikshumatî* was the capital of Kusadhvaja, the brother of Janaka. (Râmâyana, Bâlakânda, LXX). A sacred Buddhist place ; Buddha descended here from the *Trayastrinsa* heaven (F. H., xvii ; 18 yojanas S.E. of Mathurâ). Some 200 *li* S.E. of *Pi-lo-shan-na* was *Kah-pi-ta* (Skr. *Kapitthikâ* of the Madhuvan plate of Harshavardhana ; E.I., vii, p. 157 ; Kâpitthaka of Varâhamihira ; J.R.A.S., 1897, p. 422) the old name of which was (according to a note added to the text of Y. Ch.) Seng-ka-she. (Sânkâsya ; Y. Ch. I. 333).

Cunningham (C.A.S.R. I, p. 271 ; xi. p. 22) identifies it with *Sankisa* or *Sankisa-Basantapur* (27° 20′ N. and 79° 16′ E.) on the Ikshumatî (Furrukhabad district, U.P.), —a village on a mound of ruins. V. Smith does not believe in this identification. "The Elephant pillar at Sankisa cannot be the Lion-pillar seen by Y. Ch." He would look for it in the N.E. corner of the Ita district. (Watters, II, p. 338 ; I. A. 1909, p. 153-154 ; J.R.A.S., 1898, p. 508 F. N.).

10. MATHURÂ.

P. 427 (373).—It was the capital of *Sûrasena* शूरसेन, which was to the S. of *Indraprastha* (Sabhâ-P. XXX. 1105-6) and *E.* of *Matsya* (Virâta-P., V. 144-5) ; it extended from the Chambal to about 50 miles *N.* of Mathurâ. *Madhu,* king of the Daityas, and his son Lavana reigned here ; Satrughna, the brother to Râma, killed Lavana and built *Madhurâ* or *Mathurâ* which is its *Paisâchî* form. (Hari-V. LV. 3061-3 ; 3083-96 ; XCV 5243-7). A son of Satrughna was *Sûrasena* after whom the country is so called (Vâyu-Purâna). It subsequently passed into the hands of the Yâdavas. (Hari-V., XCV—5247-8).

Mod. Mathurâ (27° 30′ N. and 77° 41′ E.), is not on the ancient spot ; it has moved to the N. owing to the encroachment of the river. Its antiquities—inscriptions of the Kushanas, Saka Saptras, Guptas, pillars, sculptures, Kanishka's statue, Jaina stupas at Kankâli etc.

(C.A.S.R., III, plates I-XVI. A.S.I., N.I.S., Vol. XX; An. R.A.S.I., 1911-12, part I, p. 14 &c.)

P. 429 (375). *Clisobora or Klisoboras.*—Cunningham here transcribed it as *Kâlikâvarta* (identified with वृन्दावन 27° 33′ N. and 77° 42′ E.). But it is philologically impossible. Lassen transcribed it as *Kr(i)shnapura* (Ind. Alt., I., p. 127, n.3.) and that is the correct form. As for its location, Gokul, on the left bank of the Jumna and 5 miles S.S.E. of Mathurâ, has better claim. (Lassen located it at Agra. Cunningham identified it, in C.A.S.R., XX, p. 45, with *Kesavapura* Mahalla of Mathurâ.)

11. KÂNYAKUBJA (Crooked maiden).

P. 430 (376). It is so called because the Wind-God transformed, here, the 99 *Kanyâs* of its King, Kusanâbha, to *Kubjas* for scorning him. (Râmâyana). Mentioned in the Mahâ Bh. and the Mahâbhâshya. Ptolemy's Kanogiza? (Probably not; J.R.A.S., 1908, p. 760). 200 *li* N.W. (correct "S.E." with text D., F.H., Cunningham and Watters) of Sânkâsya was *Ka-no-ku-she* or the "city of flowers" (Y. Ch. I. 35). The site of *Kânyakubja* is a fixed one. The correction of the direction shows that *Sânkâsya* has not been properly located.

Kânyakubja was also called *Gâdhipura, Mahodaya* and *Kusasthala.* It was the capital of the (Guptas ?) *Maukharis,* Harsha Vardhana, Yasovarman (the patron of *Bhavabhûti*), *Pratihâras* and *Gâhadavâlas.* Mahmud of Ghazni plundered and destroyed it (1016-7 A.D.); the capital was then transferred to Bâri, 3 or 4 days march from Kanouj. (Alberuni, XVIII.)

12. A-YU-TE.

P. 438 (382).—5000 *li* in circuit; from the neighbourhood of Navadevakula city ("Records"; from Kanouj—"Life"), Y. Ch. travelled 600 *li* to the S.E., crossed the

Ganges to the S. and reached *A-yu-te*. (Y. Ch. I. 354). *Navadevakula* has been identified with Newal (an ancient site where Dr. Hoey found Kushan coins) a little N. of Bangarman in Unao district, U. P. (C.A.S.R., XI., p. vi and J.A.S.B., 1900, p. 74).

The name sounds like *Ayodhyâ* (1 m. from Fyzabad, U. P.), the capital of Kosala bounded by *Panchâla* (W), the *Sarpikâ* or Syandikâ (Sai) River (S), the Sadânîrâ (E) and Nepal hills (N). (Raichaudhuri, P.H.A.I., p. 48).

But in making this identification Watters has to take Ganges to be a mistake for its affluent Ghograâ. Other sites proposed: (1) Kakupur (C.A.S.R., I., p. 295); (2) Patanvihar (C.A.S.R., XI., pp. 54-6); (3) Asnî in Fatepur (Führer's Mons., Antiq., pp. 157-8); (4) Aphuni 29 m. S.E. of Fatepur, on the old road from Kanauj to Prayâga along which the pilgrim is travelling (V. Smith in Watters, Y. Ch. Vol. II.)

13. AYOMUKHÎ (अयोमुखी)

P. 443 (387).—This Skr. form is mentioned in the Kâsikâ commentary on Pânini (Section dealing with feminine suffixes). The state was Partabgarh and Rai Bareilly districts. (V. Smith in Watters, vol. II.). The city identified by Cunningham (C.A.S.R., XI., p. 68) with Tusaran Bihar (30 m. S.W. of Partabgarh).

14. PRYÂGA (प्रयाग)

P. 445 (388).—The holy place of *Gangâ-Yamunâ-sangama*; a clearing in a forest, probably the *Kâlaka-vana*, the E. boundary of the land of the Aryans (Râmâ-yana, Ayodhyâ, LIV., LV.; my Introduction).

In the midst of the city was a Deva temple in front of which was a large tree where the Hindus sacrificed their lives. (Y. Ch.) Cunningham (C.A.S.R., I., p. 297) takes the tree to be the Akshaya or Syâmavata, अक्षय or

अक्षयवट, (of Râmâyana) which is now situated within a dark subterranean chamber in the fort due N. from the Asoka pillar. In Y. Ch.'s time it was in the midst of the city, but now on the very brink of the river.

15. KAUSÂMBÎ (कौशाम्बी)

P. 448 (391).—About 500 *li* S.W. from Prayâga (through a forest infested by wild elephants and other fierce animals) was Kiao-shang-mi : 6000 *li* in circuit. (Y. Ch. I., 365.)

F. H. (who did not visit it) locates it 13 *yojanas* N.W. of the Deer Park (mod. Sarnath), (F. H. Chap. XXXIV). In Buddhist Literature it is sometimes mentioned with Srâvastî and Kosala. Hence Watters was inclined to place it to the *N.* of Prayâga. But the Epics indicate that the Jumnâ flowed through *Vatsa* (c. Kausâmbî—the capital of the descendants of Parîkshit after the destruction of Hastinâpura). Certain Buddhist texts also give the same indication. (Hardy's Manual of Buddhism, 2nd edn., p. 520).

Cunningham located the capital at Kosam (an old village on the Jumnâ, 30 m. S. W. of Allahabad) which is still called Kausâmbî by the Jainas (C.A.S.R., I., 303 ; Führer's Mons., Antiq., p. 142, I.A., II., p. 244) and where are extensive ruins.

As 30 m. is too short for 500 *li*, the location has been doubted ; the country taken to be (1) Rewah (Major Vost, J.R.A.S., 1904, p. 249 ; Smith's objection, *ibid*, p. 545) ; (2) the district round the Buddhist ruins at Bharhut (V. Smith in J.R.A.S., 1898, p. 511) ; (3) the city to be searched for at the extremity of the Banda district to the N.E. of Ajaigarh (Watters II., 339).

VATSA is referred to in Pâli literature as Vamsa (Rhys David's Buddhist India, p. 23), one of the sixteen countries. As Skr. TSA is changed into Pâli CHCHHA (cf. Matsya and Machchha), there is some difficulty in deriving Vamsa from Vatsa, though there is no doubt about their identity. So Vamsa seems to be derived from Vasa वश, which I take to be the old Vedic form of Vatsa. The *Vasas* of Vedic literature have been mentioned together with the *Usînaras, Kuru-Panchâlas* and *Matsyas* and as such they can be identified with the *Vamsas* (वशादित्वात् शुम्) or *Vatsas*, a "t" being introduced on the analogy of *Matsya.*

16. KUSAPURA.

P. 456 (398).—Read C.A.S.R., I., p. 313 and Mons. Antiq., p. 329. Sites proposed: (1) Jhûsî (Vost in J.R.A.S., 1903, p. 543); (2) ruins near Mohanlâlganj, S. of Lucknow (V. Smith in J.R.A.S., 1898, p. 510).

17. PI-SHO-KA.

P. 459 (401).—Cunningham (C.A.S.R., I., p. 318), Dr. Hoey (J.A.S.R., 1900, p. 75), and Dr. Führer (Mons., Antiq., p. 274; but his location is different, *viz.*, Sanchânkot in Unao) identify *Pi-sho-ka* (Skr. *Visâkha*—Cunningham; *Visoka*—Watters) with *Sha-che* where F. H. (Chap. XIX) located a similar "tooth-stick-tree". *Sha-che*=*Sâketa* or *Ayodhyâ.* (Note that Cunningham, in his Bhilsa Tope, p. 180, wrongly identified Sânchi with the capital of Sha-che).

Watters objects to the identification of *Pi-so-ka* with *Sa-che*; for *Sa-che* was 3 *yojanas* S. then 3 *yojanas* S.E. of *Kanauj* and 8 *yojanas* N. of *Srâvastî* (F. H. XVIII—XX), while *Pi-so-ka* was 500 *li* E. of *Kausâmbî* and 500 *li* S.W. of *Srâvastî* (Y. Ch., I., p. 373-4). As for the *tooth-brush tree,* similar trees have been located by Y. Ch. at two other places also.

V. Smith (Watters, II., p. 339) takes *Pi-so-ka* to the ancient site of *Nimkhar* (20 m. S. of Sitapur) or *Naimishâranya* नैमिषारण्य on the Gomatî, the famous place of pilgrimage (27° 20′ N. and 80° 35′ E.)

18. SRÂVASTÎ (श्रावस्ती)

P. 467 (407). Founded by Sravasta, an ancestor of Râma ; it is in the Gauda-desa गौड़-देश (Matsya Purâna, XII., 30).

Cunningham (C.A.S.R., I., pp. 330-337 ; XI., pp. 84-98) located the capital at *Sahet-Mahet* on the borders of the Bahraich and Gonda (= गौड़ "Gauda") districts of the Fyzabad division, U. P. This identification is based on topographical evidence and on the discoveries of (i) a colossal Bodhisattva image in a shrine at *Sahet* with an inscription that it was set up at *Srâvastî* (C.A.S.R., I., pp. 330-7) ; (ii) the inscribed parasol-post of the above image ; (iii) a copper-plate grant discovered in a cell of the large ruined monastery at *Sahet* recording the grant by Govindachandra, the king of Kanauj, to the community of Buddhist friars residing in the great convent of Holy Jetavana (Vogel in J.R.A.S., 1908) ; (iv) another statue of Kushana date bearing the name of the Jetavana at Srâvastî (Annual Report A.S.I., 1907-8, p. 38, p. 81 ff ; 1910-11, pp. 1-24 ; for V. Smith's attempt to disprove this identification, Read his articles in J.R.A.S., 1898, 1900).

19. KAPILAVÂSTU.

P. 475 (414). Read F. H. Chap. XXI-XXII ; Y. Ch. II., p. 1. It was above 500 *li* S.E. from the neighbourhood of Srâvastî ; Y. Ch. (who found it in ruins) visited *Kapilavâstu, Krakuchandra's Town, Konâgamana's Town,* and *La-fa-ni* (Lumbini) the birthplace of Lord Buddha.

The *Rummin*-dei pillar of Asoka (Approx. E. long. 80° 20′ ; N. lat. 27° 29′) locates, beyond doubt the *Lumbini*-grove. The inscription on the Nigliva pillar (now situated 38 m. N.W. of the Uska Bazar station of B. N.

W. Railway) shows that it was erected near the stûpa of Konâgamana ; but it is not in situ. The village of Piprâwâ (Birdpur Estate, Basti District)—the findspot of the famous Piprâwâ Vase—marks, according to Dr. Fleet, the site of *Kapilavâstu*. (J. R. A. S., 1906, p. 180).

As there are differences between the "Life" and "Records" of Y. Ch. and F. H., V. Smith thinks that the remains at Piprâwâ were shown to F. H. as those of Kapilavâstu, while the guides of Y. Ch. identified the town with Tilaura Kot. But when he admits that the two pilgrims must have seen the same towns of *Krakuchandra* and *Konâgamana* or *Kanakamuni*, his theory that they saw two different *Kapilavâstus* is thin. (Dr. Hoey, J. R. A. S. 1906, 454). Dr. Rhys Davids takes Tilaura Kot to be the old *Kapilavâstu* and Piprâwâ to be the new city built after the destruction of the old city by Vidudaha. Vost (J.R.A.S. 1906) tries to establish that (*i*) the pilgrims knew one city only, *viz*. Tilaura Kot and the ruins S. of it ; (*ii*) Krakuchandra's town is mod. Sisanihava ; Konâgamana's is Gutanihava ; and (*iii*) the Arrow Well is now in the Basti District.

It is to be noted in this connection that Dr. Führer, in his Monograph on Buddha Sâkyamuni's birth, fabricated evidence and described ruins which existed in his imagination only. The Government had to withdraw his Report from circulation. [V. Smith's note (p. 4) added to A.S.I., N.I.S., XXVI, part I.]

20. KUSINAGARA. (कुशीनगर).

P. 493 (430). As for the scene of Buddha's Mahâparinirvâna, the Chinese pilgrims gave three distinct bearings with distances :—

(*i*) *Lumbini* to Râmagrâma, E. 5 *yojanas* (F. H.), 200 *li* (Y. Ch.). Râmagrâma to Chhandaka's Return, E. 3 *yojanas* (F. H.), 100 *li* (Y. Ch.), Chhandaka's

Return to Ashes Stupa, E. (F.H.) or S.E. (Y. Ch.). 4 *yojanas* (F. H.) 180 *li* (Y. Ch.) ; Ashes Stupa to *Kusinagara*, E. (F. H.) or N.E. (Y. Ch.) 12 *yojanas* (F. H.).

(*ii*) Kusinagara to the Scene of Lichhavi-farewell, S.E. (F. H.) 12 *yojanas* (F. H.) ; Lichhavi-farewell to *Vaisâli*, E. (F. H.), S.E. (Y. Ch.) 5 *yojanas* (F.H.), 60 *li* (Y. Ch.).

(*iii*) From the vicinity of Kusinagara 200 *li* or so S.W., then 500 *li* away was the kingdom of Benares (Y. Ch.).

200 *li* or 5 *yojanas*, E. from Lumbini will be E. of the Little Gandak and W. of the Gandak. Hence, Lan-po or *Râmagrâma* (F. H. XXIII, Y. Ch. II. p. 20) may be Dharmauli (Dharmapurî) where Dr. Hoey discovered a stupa and other remains. [Vost located it at Bhuilâ-dih J. R. A. S., 1903, p. 367.].

3 *yojanas* or 100 *li* further E. was the place where Siddhârtha (Buddha) sent back his Charioteer Chhandaka (F. H. XXIV.). 17 or 18 m. S.E. from Dharmauli is the village of Bihar in the Champâran District.

4 *yojanas* E. or 180 or 190 *li* S.E. from it was the Ashes or Charcoal stupa—Nyagrodha or *Pippalavana* ; here was a ruined stupa of Asoka. (Y. Ch. II. pp. 20—23).

It may be identified with the remarkable remains at Lauriyâ-Nandangarh. (Asoka's inscribed pillar, a score of stupas &c. prove its antiquity).

Thence 12 *yojanas* E. or N.E. was *Kusinagara*. As 12 *yojanas* on the map-line extends far beyond Kâthmandu, we must take the *yojanas* in the hilly country to be shorter ones. The kingdom was the valley of the little Rapti (Achiravatî). H. H. Prince Khadga Shamsher Jung Bahadur has located the city at the confluence of the little Rapti with the Gandak (Hiranyavatî), near Bhavasâr Ghat. On the route from Nandangarh is the Rampurwa pillar of Asoka. [V. Smith in J. R. A. S.,

1902, p. 140 ff.; I. A. 1909, p. 155 ; Vost's locations in J. R. A. S., 1903, pp. 367-8.]

Cunningham located Kusinagara at *Kasia* ; the site has been excavated (An. R. A. S. I., '04-5, pp. 43-58 ; '05-6, pp. 61-85 ; '06-7, pp. 44-85) ; ruins of monasteries, ancient coins, 464 clay-seals with the legend *"Srî-Mahâparinirvâna-Vihâre Bhikshusamghasya"* and a seal-die *"Srî-Vishnudvîpa-Vihâre Bhikshusamghasya"* ; so probably Kasia is Vishnudvîpa or Vethadîpa which received a portion of the relics of Buddha. [Dr. Vogel.] Fresh excavation (An. R. A. S. I. for 1910-11, p. 63 *ff* ; p. 73 ; 1911-12, Part I. pp. 17-18) ; a number of clay seals with "Buddha's Coffin" and the legend *Srî-Mahâparinirvâna-Vihâra* in "Gupta Characters" and a copper-plate inscribed in ink ending with *"Nirvâna-Chaitye tâmrapatta iti"* निर्वाण-चैत्ये ताम्रपट्ट इति (recovered from the central stupa at Kasia). These discoveries support Cunningham. [Dr. Vogel, however, thinks that a Nirvâna-Chaitya may be erected at other places also.]

P. 496 (433). *Kahaon.*—Skr. *Kakubha* mentioned in Skanda-Gupta's inscription on a pillar discovered here. [Fleet's G. I.; C.A.S.R., I., pp. 85-95]. Carlleyle has identified the great city, where Y. Ch. was hospitably treated, with Rudrapur in Gorakhpur district. (C.A.S.R., XVIII, p. 41).

P. 497 (434). *Pâwâ.*—Between it and Kusinagara was a stream called the *Kukuttha* where Buddha bathed himself. Mr. Carlleyle has pointed out that there exists a river now known as Kuku. To its S. W. are the ruins at Fazilpur (Gorakhpur district ; 10 miles S. E. of Kasia) with which he proposes to identify Pâwâ. (C.A.S.R., XVIII, p. 106).

21. BENARES (काशि).

P. 499 (435). The kingdom of Kâsi was 300 leagues in extent (Jâtaka No. 391). It had its capital at Bârânasî also called Surundhana, Sudassana, Brahmavaddhana, Pupphavatî, Ramma City and Molini (Prof. D. R. Bhandarkar, Carmichæl Lectures, 1918, pp. 50-51).

The Kâsis first appear in the Paippalâda recension of the Atharvaveda. [Roychowdhuri, P.H.A.I., pp. 33-34.]. In the Brâhmanas we hear of the city of Kâsi on the *Varanâvatî* river (Camb. H. I. p. 117) which is evidently identical with the modern Varunâ. This mention of *Varanâvatî* in Brâhmana literature indicates that *Vâranâvata* of the Mahâ Bhârata was either identical with Benares or was a village on the Varunâ. According to the Râmâyana Kâsi was a kingdom while *Prayâga* and the country around was still forest. (Adi-K.-XII. 20). Krishna burnt it for a succession of years (Udyoga-P. XLVII. 1883 ; Hari-V. CLXI. 9142-3 ; see also Hari-V. XXIX. and XXXII.). The वायु पुराण states that the kingdom of Benares stretched up to the Gomatî or Goomti. It is the *Kassida* of Ptolemy (p. 228).

Mod. Benares and Sarnath. (An. R. A. S. for '04-5 ; pp. 59-104 ; '07-8, p. 43 *ff.*). Monograph on Sarnath published by the Archæological department gives its full account.

22. CHEN-CHU (GAZIPUR).

P. 502 (438). Y. Ch. II, p. 59 ; Watters objected to Cunningham's identification which has been supported by V. Smith. (Y. Ch. II, Appendix).

The most important place in Gazipur is Bhitari where have been discovered various ruins including bricks inscribed with the name of Kumâra-Gupta and the famous inscription of Skanda-Gupta on a pillar 15 ft. high. (C.A.S.R., I, pp. 97-100 ; Fleet's G. I.).

P. 503 (439). *Baliya.*—Read C.A.S.R., XXII., pp. 76-87 ; Führer's Mons. Antiq., pp. 190-1.

Mr. Carlleyle believed that close to it was Dharmâranya or the Vast Solitude of F. H.

P. 504 (440). *Mo-ho-so-lo.*—Its identification with Masâr in Shahabad district (Bihar & Orissa) is confirmed by an inscription in which the place has been called *Mahâsâra*. Another modern local inscription calls the territory *Karûshadesa*. (C.A.S.R., III., pp. 66-71). Mr. Pargiter has shown that the *Râmâyana* (Bâla, XXVII, 8-23) suggests that the *Karushas* or *Kârushas* once dwelt in the Shahabad district ; but they migrated towards the S.W. and according to the Mahâ Bhârata (Bhîshma, LVI, 2415 ; Drona, XI, 396 ; Sabhâ, XIII, 575-7 &c.) they occupied the hilly country to the S. of Kâsi and Vatsa, W. of Chedi, E. of Magadha and enclosing the Kaimur hills—*i.e.* the hilly tract of which Rewah is the centre, from the Ken (W.) to the confines of Bihar (E.).

Two other important sites in Shahabad are Sahasram, famous for its inscription of Asoka (C.A.S.R., XI, p. 132) and Arrah which is, according to the local tradition, the *Ekachakrâ* of the Mahâbhârata. Close by it (Arrah) is the village of Bakri where बकासुर dwelt. As Yuan Chwang also has alluded to the Demon of the desert, this identification may be accepted. [C.A.S.R., III., p. 12 ; p. 73]. *Ekachakrâ* is mentioned, in the Mahâvamsa, as one of the ancient capital cities of India in the time of Buddha. [*Ibid*, p. 77. F. N.].

Temple of Nârâyana.—Carlleyle (C.A.S.R., XXII., pp. 76-77) identifies it with Narayan, a small village where is the usual ferry for travellers going north from Masâr. About 8 miles N.E. (and not E. as stated by Y. Ch.) of Narayan is Godena with which he proposes to identify Asylum tope. (*Ibid*, p. 78).

P. 507 (442). *Deghwâra.*—As the true name is Dighwara (and not *Degh*) and as there are no ruins here so Carlleyle objected to this identification and proposed

Cheran or Cherand (in Saran district) which is said to be the site of Chyavana's hermitage. (C.A.S.R., XXII, pp. 78-79 ; for the hermitage of Chyavana, Read J.A.S.B., 1903, p. 89).

23. VAISÂLÎ (वैशाली).

P. 507 (443). The city of Vaisâlî, famous in Buddhist literature, has been identified by St. Martin and Cunningham (C.A.S.R., I., 55 ; XVI., 6, 34, 89-91) with the ruins at and near Besârh or Basâr (Muzaffarpur district, Bihar ; 25° 58′ N. and 85° 11′ E.) [For objection against this location and other identifications proposed, Read J.A.S.B. 1900 ; J.R.A.S., 1902, p. 267 ; J.R.A.S., 1903, p. 583 &c.].

Basâr was excavated by Dr. Bloch ; he writes :—

Tîrabhuktau Vaisâlî-Târâ of a 12th century MS. points out that Vaisâlî was in Tîrabhûkti or Tirhut ; its position with regard to other places fits exactly with the description of the Chinese ; here are two groups of ruins which correspond with two similar groups seen by Y. Ch. at Vaisâli in a striking way—'Râjâ *Bisâl kâ* garh' [1580 ft. × 750 ft.; C.A.S.R., I. p. 56] and the "Lion-pillar" stupa and tank E. of Bakhra, 2 m. N. of Besâr. [Here have been found seals of Gatotkacha-Gupta, Dhruvasvâminî and many other Gupta Princes. An. R. A. S. I. for 1903-4, p. 81.]. An inscription in early Brâhmi (200 or 300 B.C.) "Vesâli anusamyânaka Takâre" discovered here (An. R. A. S. I. 1911-12, part I., pp. 18-19 ; 1913-14, p. 98 *ff*.).

This identification has also been supported by the following facts (Pargiter): *Visvâmitra,* when taking Râma from the scene of the slaughter of Tâdakâ in the Shahabad district to Mithilâ, stopped at Visâla on the way. Their route was—crossing the river Sona from the Shahabad district and travelling N.E., they reached the Ganges near the site of Patna (Adi XXXVII, 1-7); and then crossing the Ganges by boat, and travelling N. towards Mithilâ the whole of one day, they reached *Visâla* at evening. (*Ibid.* XLVI, 5-11; XLVIII, 21-5; XLIX, 1-8). This agrees with the situation of Basâr, 27 m. N. N. E. of Patna.

Tirhut or *Tîrabhukti* is *Videha* (Trikândasesha); so named after Mâthava the *Videgha* who colonized it. [Satapatha Br. I. IV. 1.] It is bounded by the *Kausikî* (Kosi) (E.), the Ganges (S), the *Sadânîrâ* ["Gandak"—Muir; "Rapti"—Pargiter; "Little Gandak"—Fleet in J.R.A.S., 1907, p. 644.] (W), and the Himâlayas (N.).

Mithilâ (मिथिला) was the name of both the country and the capital. (Adikânda XLIX, 9—16; Sânti-P. CCCXXVII, 12233-8). Cunningham (C.A.S.R. XVI. 34) identifies the city with Janakapura, a small town within the Nepal border, north of which the Muzaffarpur and Darbhanga districts meet.

24. VRIJI.

P. 512 (447). This country seems to be roughly equivalent to the N. part of Darbhanga and the adjacent Nepal Terai. As for Y. Ch.'s Chen-shu-na, the capital of the country, V. Smith proposes the ruins at Bâligarh about 16 m. N. of Madhuvâni. (Watters, II. App.)

25. MAGADHA.

P. 518 (452). "Kîkata कीकट a district of the Non-Aryans whose Chief was Pra-*Maganda*" (Rigveda III, 53, 14) is said to be identical with Magadha. [Kîkatâh Magadhâhvayâh; Abhidhânachintâmani, IV. 26]. Its name might have some connection with *Maganda*. Atharva Veda V. 22. 14. and Gopatha Brâhmana II, 9. mention the Magadhas. The Vagadha of the Aitareya Aranyaka [Keith's Ed. 200] may be a mistake for it or it may refer to the *Bâgdi* caste of Bengal. (H. P. Sastri).

The Kingdom (C. Girivraja) established by Vasu son of Kusa (Visvâmitra to Râma, Adikânda XXXV. 1-10 ; 35). The Mahâ Bhârata informs us that Vasu Uparichara of Chedi conquered it and established his son, Vrihadratha, as king over it. It is the scene of Buddha's early career. Its history is the history of the whole of N. India.

The districts of Patna and Gayâ formed this territory proper.

PÂTALIPUTRA.

(For *putra* cf. Satiya*puta* and Ketala*puta* of Asoka's R. E. II.; legend of the name in Kathâsaritsâgara and Y. Ch.).

Erannaboas.—Skr. Hiranyavâha (Son river) occurs in Bâna's Harshacharita.

F. H. (XXVI-XXVII) travelled 4 *yojanas* E. from Vaisâli to "the confluence of the five rivers," crossed a river (Ganges) 1 *yojana* to the S. of which was *Pâtaliputra.* [There can never have been in historical times any actual meeting of five rivers near Pâtaliputra ; hence F. H. means the place where the fifth of the five rivers (Gangâ, Yamunâ, Achiravatî, Sarabhu (Sarabos of Ptolemy) *i.e.* Sarayu or Ghogra, and Mahî (or Mhye in Saran district, Bihar) famous in Buddhist literature (Vinaya Culla., 9, 1, 3 and 4 ; Milinda., 4, 1, 35) flows into the already united stream of the other four. Dr. Hoey in J.R.A.S., 1907, p. 41.].

Lt. Col. Waddel (Report on the excavations at Pâtaliputra, Calcutta, 1903) has shown that nearly the whole of the site of the city is intact ; much lies below Patna, Bankipore and the E. I. Railway ; buried at a depth of from 10 to 20 feet. The old city was on the north bank of the old Sona, but it was several miles distant from the Ganges which shifted later to the south. Dr. Spooner's excavation (1912-13) has resulted in the discovery of traces of the Maurya "Hall of a Hundred Columns." [Annual Report A. S. I. 1912-13, Part I. pp. 24-27 ; 1912-13, pp. 53-86.]

P. 521 (455). *From Patnâ to Bodh Gayâ.*—Cunningham has remarked that both distance and direction supplied by Yuan Chwang are wrong. But if that Chinese pilgrim's record be so corrupt as to require such manipulation in so short a distance, it is no use going further with it, for no satisfactory conclusion can possibly be arrived at from it. [Fergusson, J.R.A.S., 1872-73, pp. 222-223]. Here I point out certain identifications which can be accepted.

Ti-lo-shi-kia.—(Watters, II, p. 105) : Its identification with *Telâra* is supported by the discovery of two inscriptions containing its Skr. name—*Telâdhaka* तैलाढ्क [C.A.S.R. VIII, p. vii.; XI, Plate XLII]. 90 *li* S.W. from it was a lofty mountain from the summit of which Buddha had contemplated the kingdom of Magadha. [Watters, II, p. 107]. It has been identified by Beglar with Barâbar hill (Skr. *Pravaragiri*), famous for its cave inscriptions of Asoka (16 miles to the N. of Gayâ. C.A.S.R., VIII., p. 36) 30 *li* N.W. of it was Gunamati's monastery (Y. Ch., II., p. 108). Beglar's location of it in the village of Dharawal or Dharmapura (in Kunwa) where were discovered Punch-marked coins, a colossal statue of Padmapâni *in situ* with an inscription in *Kutila* characters (C.A.S.R., VIII., pp. 37-39 ; XVI, pp. 39-48) has been accepted by Cunningham. (*Ibid.*, XV., p. iv.).

Buddha-Gayâ.—About six miles S. of Gayâ ; hamlet "Urel" represents the name of *Uruvilva* (C.A.S.R., XI., p. vi.; p. 147). Its ruins described in Cunningham's Mahâbodhi ; Annual Rep. A.S.I., 1908-1909, p. 139 *ff.*

P. 526 (459). *Kukkuta-pâda* कुक्कुटपाद or *Gurupâda-Giri* (the mt. of the venerable teacher Mahâkâsyapa) F. H. XXXIII ; Y. Ch. II. p. 140-3). Cunningham (C.A.S.R.I., pp. 14-16) identified it with the three *insignificant* rugged *hills* (which rise boldly and touch each other at their bases) near the village of Kurkihar (16 m. N.E. of Gayâ).

Dr. Stein (I. A., 1901, p. 88) and Keith [Bengal, Past and Present, 1910] identify it with Sabhnath (15 miles E. N. E. of Bodhgayâ). Mr. R. D. Banerjee's (J.A.S.B., 1906) identification with Gurpâ Hill 20 m. E. S. E. of Bodhgayâ is probable, for it has preserved the name of *Gurupâda*.

P. 528 (461). *Buddhavana.*—It cannot be identified with Buddhain [C.A.S.R., III., p. 139] for Jeshtivan is not to the E. but S.W. of it. [Stein, I.A., 1901, p. 62].

Yashtivana.—Stein (*Ibid*) confirms its identification with Jeshtiban (and not Jakhtiban).

The House of Vyâsa.—Stein identifies it with Pansabda recess in the hill which forms the S.W. end of the Handia range. (*Ibid*, p. 82).

P. 535 (467). *Râjagriha.*—Girivraja, the ancient capital of Magadha. [Mahâ Bhârata, Sabhâ, XX., 798-80 ; Râmâyana, Adi, XXXV, 1-9]; also called Râjagriha [Adi, CXIII, 4451-2 ; Asvamedha, LXXXII, 2435-63]. It is to be distinguished from the old capital of Kekaya which has been located at Jalalpur.

For the Chinese account, Read F. H., XXVIII ; Y. Ch., II., pp. 146-153.

For an excellent map and topography of Râjagriha (mod. Râjgir) *vide* Annual Rep. A.S.I., 1905-6, pp. 84-106 ; 1913-14, p. 265 *ff*.

NÂLANDÂ (नालन्दा)

P. 536 (468). Cunningham's identification with Baragâon [or Badgaon (बटगाम) as spelt by Dr. Bloch in J.R.A.S., 1908, p. 440] was based on the discovery of two acute-angled inscriptions (found on the spot) naming the place Nâlandâ. [C.A.S.R., I., plate XIII.; ruins described in *Ibid*, pp. 28-35 ; An. Rep. A.S.I., 1915-16, part I, pp. 12-13.]

P. 539 (471).—*Indra-silâ-guhâ.*—The rugged hill rising immediately to the W. of the village can be shown beyond all doubt to be identical with it. (Stein, I.A., 1901, p. 54.)

27. I-LAN-NA-PO-FA-TA.

P. 545 (476). Watters (II., p. 178 *ff*.) correctly transcribes it as Irinaparvata (इरिण पर्व्वत) or Barren Hill. Y. Ch. (II., p. 178 *ff*.) mentioned that on the W. frontier of this country to the S. of the Ganges was a solitary mt. where Buddha subdued the Yaksha Vakula. Dr. Waddel (J.A.S.B., 1892, p. 1) identifies it with Mt. Uren [=I-lan-na ; about 20 m. S.W. from Mungir City and 7 m. S. of the present course of the Ganges] where are ruins, statues, old inscriptions and a foot-print of Buddha.

Mungir is the Mudgagiri of Pâla inscriptions and it is said to be the Modâgiri (the capital of an eastern kingdom near Vanga ; Mahâ Bhârata). Madgurakas of E. India [Matsya CXIII. 44] seem to be connected with it.

28. ANGA, CHAMPÂ.

P. 546 (477). *Anga.*—The easternmost country named in the Atharva-Veda (V. 22, 14) ; so called after its king Anga (Mahâ Bhârata, Adi-p. CIV., 4179-*ff*) who seems to be identical with Anga Vairochani mentioned in Aitareya Br. (VIII., 4, 22) ; [Anga (body) of the Love-god Kâma was consumed here and so it is so called (Râmâyana, Adi-k. XXIII). It became an appendage of Magadha in Jarâsandha's time. (Sabhâ—P. XXIX. 1090-3.)]

Its capital—Mâlini or Mâlina ; this name was superseded by Champâ [after king Champa, great-grandson of Loma-pâda ; Sânti—P. V.] ; it was on the Ganges. [Vana—P. LXXXV., 8156]. Anga proper of the Epics comprised the modern districts of Bhagalpur and Monghyr and extended northwards up to the Kosi river (Pargiter). The *Anga* dominions at one time included Magadha and extended to the shores of the sea. The Vidura Pandita Jâtaka (No. 545) describes Râjagriha as a city of Anga. The Sânti Parvan of the Mahâ Bhârata (29, 35) refers to an Anga king who sacrificed on Mount Vishnupada at Gayâ. The Sabhâ Parvan (44, 9) mentions Anga and Vanga as forming one kingdom. The Kathâ-sarit-sâgara says that Vitanka-pura, a city of the Angas, was situated on the shore of the sea.

Champâ, the famous capital of Anga, stood on the river of the same name (Jâtaka 506 ; Modern Chândan) and the Ganges (Y. Ch. II., 181). (Raychowdhuri, P.H.A.I., p. 23.)

29. KAJANGALA.

P. 548 (478). Above 400 *li* E. from Champâ ; Ka-chu-wen-ki-lo ; 2000 *li* in circuit. (Y. Ch. II., 182).

Julien and Cunningham sanskritized it as Kajughara ; but the real form is Kajangala—the E. boundary of the Middle Country (Vinaya II., 38). Jâtaka, IV., 310 tells us that Kajangala was, even in Buddha's time, an ancient place famous for its *kusa* grass. *(J. R. A. S.,* 1904, pp. 86-88 ; 538). It is mentioned as *Kayangala* in the Com. on the Râmapâlacharita. C. A. S. R., XV., pp. 37-9 locates its capital at Rajmahal.

30. PUNDRAVARDDHANA. (पुण्ड्रवर्द्धन)

P. 549 (480). The *Pundras*—outcasted descendants of Visvâmitra (Aitareya Br. VII. 18) ; various spellings—*Pundraka, Paundra, Paundrika*—in the Mahâ Bhârata ; these names sometimes used as equivalents (Sabhâ—P. XIII, 584) ; but sometimes a distinction is made between the *Pundras* and *Paundras* (Bhîsma—P. IX., 358 ; 365 ;

Sabhâ—P. LI., 1872-4) ; the *Pundras* (पुण्ड्र) are linked with the Vangas and Kirâtas (hilly tribes of Mongolian affinity from the Punjab to Assam) [Sabhâ—P. XIII, 584], with Angas and Vangas [Sabhâ—P. IV., 119]. Thus the Pundras occupied some intermediate position between the Angas, Vangas and the Himâlayas. So their country is to be identified with Mâldah, portions of Purnea east of the Kosi, part of Dinajpur and Rajshahi.

The *Paundras* (पौण्ड्र) are linked with the Udras, Utkalas, Mekalas, Kalingas and Andhras. [Vana—P., Li., 1988 ; Bhîsma—P., IX., 365 ; Drona—P., IV., 122.] Thus the *Paundras* dwelt in and to the W. and S.W. of Bengal Proper, *i.e.* the modern districts of Santal Parganas and Birbhum and the N. portion of Hazaribag. (Pargiter).

Pundravarddhana was the E. boundary of the "Middle Country." [Divyâvadâna ; J.R.A.S., 1904, p. 86] ; capital of a district in Bengal (Râjatarangini IV.) ; Pun-na-fa-tan-na above 600 *li* E. from Kajangala ; circuit 4000 *li*. (Y. Ch. II., p. 184). Mentioned in Pâla and Sena inscriptions. (E. I. IV. 247 ; J.A.S.B., 1900, p. 71 ; I.A. XII., 251 etc.). It included Varendra—one of the 4 divisions of Bengal—bounded by the Mahânandâ (W.), Brahmaputra (E.), Ganges (S.), and Kuch Bihar (N.). [C.A.S.R., XV. 145-6.]

Sites proposed for the capital:—(1) Gauda, Lakshmanâvatî or Lakhnauti (ruined city in Maldah district, 24° 54′ N.; 88° 8′ E.)—the capital of the Hindus and the Mussalmans down to 1350. (J.A.S.B. '08).

(2) Pândua, Hazrat Pândua or Firozabad (deserted town, 25° 8′ N.; 88° 10′ E.) built of Hindu ruins (An. R.A.S.I., 1902-3, pp. 51-3 ; I. A., 1874, p. (63): [Objections against 1 and 2:—their distances from Kajangala would be less than 600 *li*.]

(3) Mahâsthâna, on the W. bank of the Karatoyâ, 7 m. N. of Bogra ; the remains at Bhâsu Bihar, 4 m. W.

of it, answer to Y.Ch.'s description of Po-shi-po monastery 20 *li* W. of Pundravarddhana. [Y. Ch. II., 184 ; C.A.S.R., XV., pp. 104-11.]

31. CHIH-CHI-TO.

P. 550 (480). Above 1000 *li* N.E. of Ujjayinî ; 4000 *li* in circuit. (Y. Ch. II., 251).

Cunningham took it to be the Jajhoti of Abu Rihân, Skr. *Jejâkabhukti* or Bundelkhand with *Kharjjûravâhaka* or Khajuraho [24° 51′ N. and 79° 56′ E.] as capital (of the Chandellas). But as its distance from Ujain (300 miles) is almost double of that recorded by Y. Ch., Watters rejects it and locates it at Chitor.

32. MA-HI-SSU-FA-LO-PU-LO.

P. 559 (488). Above 900 *li* N. (Records) or N.E. (Life) from Chih-chi-to ; 3000 *li* in circuit (Y. Ch. II., p. 251-2).

Mahesvarapura was probably Gwalior. [Smith in Y. Ch. II., App.] Cunningham took it to be Mâhishmatîpura, the capital of the Chedis.

The Chedis.—Mentioned in the Rigveda (VIII., 5, 37-39). Their country has been located by Pargiter along the S. bank of the Jumna from the Chambal (*Charmanvatî*) on the N.W., to Karwi (N.E. of Chitrakûta) on the S.E. Its limit southwards seems to be the plateau of Malwa and the hills of Bundelkhand. Its capital in the Epic age is said to be Suktimatî or Suktisâhvayâ (Vanaparvan, XXII., 898 ; Asvamedha—P. LXXXIII., 2466-7) on the river of the same name identified by Pargiter with Ken. The same city has been referred to in Pali Literature (Chetiya Jâtaka, No. 422) as *Sotthivati-nagara* which is to be located somewhere near Banda.

The other *Chedi* cities referred to in Skr. literature are *Tripurî* or *Chedi-nagarî* (Hemachandra), mod. Tewar about six miles from Jabbalpur and Mâhishmatîpura which has been described in Buddhist Literature as one of the regular stages (the others being Ujjain, Gonarda, Bhilsa, Kausâmbî and Sâketa) on the route from Paithan to Srâvastî. (Imp. Gaz. Ind., XVII., p. 9). Pargiter has identified it with Mandhata on the *Narmadâ* (also called Mekalasutâ, Revâ, Somodbhavâ, Muralâ—Trikândasesha, 1, 2, 31).

Hemachandra's Abhidhâna-Chintâmani, IV, 22 gives Dâhala (डाहल), [the older form of which is Dabhâlâ (डभाला) occurring in inscriptions] and Chedi as synonymous terms.

33. UJJAYINÎ OR UJAIN.

P. 560 (489). Capital of Mâlava or Avanti ; on the Siprâ (शिप्रा) ; (23° 11′ N. and 75° 47′ E.; in Gwalior state) ; one of the seven sacred Hindu cities ; famous for its celebrated temple of Mahâkâla or Kâlapriyanâtha. (Cambay Plates, E. I. VII). The first meridian of Indian astronomers. Capital of Pradyota, and of the viceroys of the Mauryas. 'Ozênê,' formerly a royal capital ; from this place is brought to Barygaza every commodity for local consumption or export. (Periplus, Schoff's Ed. p. 42). Ptolemy (p. 152) informs us that it was the capital of Tiastanes (Chastana). These Saka Satraps were conquered by Chandra-Gupta II. Vikramâditya. In Y. Ch.'s time it was the Katachchuri capital. Then we find the Paramâras.

The country around Ujjayinî is full of *ancient sites* :— Bhilsa, Besnagar [An. R. A. S. I., '08-9, p. 126 ; 1913-14, p. 186], Sanchi, Andher, Mandasore, [Dasapura], Narwar (Nalapura, Padmâvatî). The most magnificent of the ruins discovered here is the great stupa of Sanchi [Marshall, Guide to Sanchi]. Narwar or Nalapura was the capital of Nala and Damayanti [Beglar in C. A. S. R., VII, pp. 95-102 records their romantic legend heard locally there which differs slightly from the Epic version].

Its suburb is Padampawaya or *Padmâvatî*, the scene of Bhavabhûti's Mâlatî-Mâdhava which describes four rivers, *Pârâ*, (mod. Pârbati or Pârâ), *Sindhu* (Sindh on which stands Narwar), *Lavana* (Lun) and *Madhumatî* (Mohwar). (C. A. S. R., II., p. 307-9 ; XXI, 58 &c.).

34—37. MO-LA-PO, KI-TA, ÂNANDAPURA, A-TA-CHI.

Pp. 561—565 (490-494). 2000 *li* N. W. from *Bhrigukachchha* was *Mo-la-po* or (as a note added to the text tells us) *South Lo* (or *Lo-lo*) ; circuit 6000 *li* ; capital situated on the S. E. side of the *Mo-ha* or *Mo-hi* (Mahi) river ; *Mo-la-po* and *Magadha* were the two countries in India where learning was much prized. (Y. Ch. II. pp. 242-3).

S. W. from it was an estuary ; thence 2400 or 2500 *li* N.W. was *A-ta-*(or *Cha*)*-li* country (Eder, Cunningham ; Middle Sindh—V. Smith) ; above 6000 *li* in circuit. (*Ibid.* p. 243).

300 *li* N.W. from *Mo-la-po* was *Ki-ta* or *Ki-cha* ; subject to *Mo-la-po* ; 3000 *li* in circuit. (*Ibid.* p. 245).

Fa-la-pi or North *Lo-lo* was above 1000 *li* N. from *Ki-cha*. (*Ibid*, p. 246).

A-nan-to-pu-lo (*Anandapura*) was 700 *li* N.W. from *Fa-la-pi* (*Valabhi*) ; circuit 2000 *li* (*Ibid.* p. 247).

V. Smith remarks "Cunningham being convinced of the identity of *Mo-la-po* with *Mâlava*, disregards both the bearing and distance given by Y.Ch. and identifies it with Western Malwa with Dhar (धारा) as Capital. Taking this to be correct, he identifies *Ki-ta* with *Kheda* (Khetaka-pura खेटकपुर mentioned in the *Dasakumâracharita*, mod. Kaira, a large town in Gujrat, situated between Ahmedabad and Cambay). *Anandapura*, he identifies with the triangular tract lying between the mouth of the *Banâs* river on the W. and the *Sâbarmatî* on the E." Thus criticizing Cunningham, Dr. Smith identifies *Mo-la-po* with the tract lying between *Bhrigukachchha, Kachchha* (=Ki-cha), *Valabhi* and Vadnagar (=Anandapura ; St. Martin and Prof. D. R. Bhandarkar), and corresponding roughly to the modern districts of Kaira and Ahmedabad together with parts of the Baroda state and some adjoining territory. (Watters II., p. 341). But in making this identification Dr. Smith has really altered 2000 *li* of Y. Ch. to 200 and his 2800 *li* to about half ; he has altogether ignored Y. Ch.'s account of the size of *Mo-la-po.* (J. R. A. S., 1906, p. 90). M. Sylvain Levi states that *Mo-la-po* may stand for nothing except *Mâlava* and *Kie-cha* for *Kheta* खेट (Jour. des Savants, 1905, Oct. p. 534-48). And as we know of no district in Gujrat proper that ever bore a name at all resembling *Mâlava,* it is absolutely impossible to place *Mo-la-po* as Dr. Smith has done. (Burgess in J. R. A. S., 1906, p. 220). Dr. Grierson also takes *Mo-la-po* to be Mâlava, or Mâlwa. (*Ibid.* p. 95).

Thus did Levi, Burgess, and Grierson demolish the theory of Dr. V. Smith. But a 7th Century A. D. *Valabhi* record (E. I., VIII., No. 20) actually mentions a *Mâlavaka* in Valabhi dominion and as such proves the thesis of Smith. It was included within the territory of Valabhi and as such this *Mâlavaka* cannot be identical with Mâlwa. The diminutive suffix *Ka* also indicates that it was then known as *Lesser Mâlava* to distinguish it from *Mâlava* proper. It is rather curious that attention of scholars has not been directed towards it. It is dated 320 Valabhi Era—639 A. D.

EASTERN INDIA.

P. 572 (500). It is to the E. of *Madhyadesa ;* but as *Madhyadesa* extended to the E., its western extent diminished. *It is to the E. of* (i) Prayâga (*Manu ; Kûrma-vibhâga*), (ii) *Vârânasyâh paratah Pûrvadesah* (*Kâvya-*

mîmâmsâ, p. 93), (iii) to the E. of Anga (Com. on *Vâtsyâyanasûtra*), (iv.) to the E. of *Kajangala or Pundravarddhana* पुण्ड्रवर्धन (Buddhist Lit.; Y. Ch.) *i.e.* Bengal proper and Assam together with Orissa and Ganjam.

It was divided into six states in Y. Ch.'s time :— *Kâmarûpa* ruled by Bhâskaravarman, a Hindu ; and 5 other states probably included in the Dominions of Sasânka शशाङ्क of Karnasuvarna.

1. KÂMARÛPA. (कामरूप)

P. 572 (500). *Prâgjyotishâh Kâmarûpâh* (*Abhidhânachintâmani* IV. 22) ; but in the Raghuvamsa (IV. 83-4) they are described as two different nations ; the name *Kâmarûpa* is later. The M. Bh. mentions *Kâmâkhyâ*, near Gauhati, famous in ancient times. Kâmarûpa included, according to the *Yoginî Tantra*, the whole of the *Brahmaputra* (*Lauhitya*) Valley, with Rangpore and Kooch Behar (Imp. Gaz. Ind. XIV. p. 331.).

Above 900 *li* E. from *Pundravarddhana* was *Kia-mo-len-po* ; circuit 10,000 *li* (Y. Ch. II., p. 185). He crossed the R. Ka-lo-tu (करतोया) to reach it. (*Ibid.* p. 187).

There is no difficulty in taking Gauhati to be the old capital, for Pubna is not (as has already been shown) the *Pundravarddhana* of Y. Ch.

2. SAMATATA. (समतट)

P. 574 (501). "The country of which the rivers have flat and level *banks* of *equal* height on both sides" ; mentioned in *Samudra-Gupta's* Allahabad Pillar Inscription (Fleet's G. I., No. 1) and in the *Kûrmavibhâga* (E.).

1200 or 1300 *li* S. of Kâmarupa and 900 *li* E. of Tâmalipta was *San-mo-ta-ta* ; low, moist and on the Sea-side. (Y. Ch. II. 187-9.).

It is the Delta of the Ganges or Bâgdî (बागड़ी), one of the four traditional divisions of Bengal :—

(1) Banga, (2) Râdha (राढ़), (3) Varendra and (4) Bâgdî. *Banga* is bounded by the Brahmaputra (W.), the Ganges (S.), the Meghna (E.) and the Khasi hills (N.). *Varendra* is the tract lying between the Mahânandâ (W.) and the Brahmaputra (E.) and between the Ganges (S.) and Cooch Bihar (N.). The traditional boundaries of *Râdha* are the Rajmahal hills, the Ganges and the Jalinghi branch of the Delta. *Bâgdî* comprises the Delta of the Ganges and the Brahmaputra.*

Banga or Vanga† seems to be mentioned in the *Aitareya Aranyaka*‡. The Epics and other Sanskrit works refer to it repeatedly. It was also called, at a later period, Harikela.§ Râdha occurs in its Prâkrit from of Lâdha in the *Achârânga Sutra* of the Jainas. It is identical, as Nîlakantha has remarked, with the *Suhma* of the Epics.|| Varendra or Varendrî occurs in the *Râma [pâla]-charita*. Thus we have Sanskrit (or Sanskritised) names of the first three of the four divisions of Bengal and their early uses show the antiquity of those names. But what is the Sanskrit form of the name of Bâgdî and when was it first used? Though Bâgdî was formerly the least important of the four divisions on account of its swampy jungle (the remnant of which is now called the Sundarban), it is now the most important division wherein is situated Calcutta, the second city of the British empire. In order to find out the old name of Bâgdî I began to examine the land grants of the kings of Bengal

---

* Cunningham, *A.S.R.*, Vol. XV., p. 145-6.

† *b* and *v* are not distinguished in Bengali Script and pronunciation. Skr. works generally spell it with *v*.

‡ Keith's *Aitareya Aranyaka*, p. 200.

§ *I-Tsing*, p. xlvi; Hemachandra's *Abhidhânachintâmani* iv, 23; etc.

|| *S.B.E.*, xxii, pp. 84-5; Nilakantha's commentary on the *Sabhâparvan* of the *Mahâbhârata*.

and strangely enough it is mentioned in the earliest inscription of the Pâlas. The Khalimpur grant of Dharmapâla records that the king granted the village of Krauncha-svabhra in the Mahantâprakâsa *vishaya* (district) of Vyâghratatî (व्याघ्रतटी) *mandala* (division) of Pundravarddhana *bhukti* (province.)* The inscriptions of the Pâlas mention three *bhuktis* (provinces) of the Pâla Kingdom—Srînagarabhukti (Behar), Tîrabhukti (Tîrbhut) and Pundravarddhanabhukti. Though Pundravarddhana was identical with Varendra, the *bhukti* of Pundravarddhana seems to have included the whole of Bengal, for we know of no other *bhukti* which might have included the other divisions of Bengal.† Thus Vyâghratatî was one of the divisions of Bengal. A village of Vyâghratatî is mentioned in a grant of Lakshmanasena also.‡ The usual Prâkrit form of Vyâghratatî व्याघ्रतटी is Vagghaädi or Vagghadî (वग्घअड़ी or वग्घड़ी) from which the regular Bengali form expected is Bâgdî, or Bâghdî. Thus there is no difficulty in taking Bâgdî as the modern equivalent of ancient Vyâghratatî. The Delta of the Ganges and the Brahmaputra was called Vyâghratatî ("Tiger Coast"), evidently because it was then, as was in very recent times, infested by the 'Royal Bengal' tigers. [My article in Sir Ashutosh Jubilee Vol. III, Part II, Pp. 423-24].

Other locations for the capital of *Samatata*:—Sonârgaon in Dacca (Fergusson), in Faridpur district (Watters), Comilla (R. D. Banerjee's Bânglâr Itihâsa, Vol. I. p. 48.)

---

* *Epigraphica Indica*, Vol. iv, pp. 243 ff.; *Gaudalekhamâlâ*, Inscription No. 1.

† The expression 'Varendra *mandala*' in Paundravarddhana-*bhukti* in Tarpandighi grant also supports it.

‡ Anulia grant of Lakshmanasena.

3. TÂMALIPTI.

P. 577 (504). *Dâmalipta, Tâmralipta* etc ; connected with the *Tamils.*

Mentioned in the Mahâ Bh. (Sabhâ-P. XXIX, 1094-1100) ; *Tamalites* on the River Ganges (Ptolemy, p. 169) ; Taluctœ (Pliny). F. H. describes it as being "at the sea-mouth", 50 yojanas E. from Champâ ; here he shipped himself for Ceylon. (F. H. XXXVII). 900 li W. of *Samatata ;* above 1400 li in circuit ; situated on sea-side ; low and wet ; the capital was on a bay. (Y. Ch. II. pp, 189-90).

The capital is mod. Tamluk, near the mouth of the Rupnârâyan, in Midnapur district. (22°18′ N. and 87° 56′ E.)

Dâmalipta was the capital of the *Suhma* country (story of Mitragupta in *Dasakumâracharita*). But the Mahâ Bh. (Adi-P. Chap. CLXXXVI, 6993 ; *Sabhâ*-P. Chap. XXIX, 1094-1100, &c.) informs us that (in the earlier period) *Tâmralipta and Suhma* were two distinct countries. *Suhmâh Râdhâh* राढ़ाः (Nîlakantha's Com. on the *Sabhâ*-P.). The *Bhâgîrathî* flows through Suhma (*Pavanadûta,* v. 36) ; the Ganges passes through the country of the ताम्रलिप्ताः (वायुपुराण) *Râdha* राढ़ *and Suhma* are the *Lâdha* लाढ and *Subbhabhûmi* of *Ayârângasûtta.* (S. B. E. XXII, pp. 84-5.) *Suhma* or *Râdha* must have comprised the mod. districts of Hooghly, Howrah, Bankura, Burdwan and the E. portions of Midnapore. Râdha was divided into Uttara and Dakshina Râdha by the R. Ajaya.

4. KIE-LO-NA-SU-FA-LA-NA.

P. 578 (504). Its king was Sasânka शशाङ्क, the murderer of the elder brother of Harshavardhana ; it was above 700 li N. W. of *Tâmralipta,* about the same distance N. E. of *Odra* औड्र and 900 li S. E. of *Pundra varddhana* (Y. Ch. II, 191-3 ; the directions are conflicting) ; near the capital was a magnificent monastery "*Lo-to-mo-chih*" (=Red Clay).

The city has been identified with *Rângâmâti* राङ्गामाटि (12m. S. of Murshidabad). The identification rests on the similarity of name, and of an alleged older name of it, *Kânsonâgar* (Karna-suvarna) and on its remains—mounds, images, old coins, etc. (J. A. S. B., 1893, pp. 315-28) ; other identifications proposed :—(i) Sufaran in Chutia Nagpur (Beglar in C. A. S. R., VIII, p. 191) ; (ii) Rohtâsagarh (24°37′N. and 83° 55′ E.) in Shahabad district, Bihar. Here is a rock-cut seal-matrix of Sasânka. So Dr. Fleet proposed this identification.

5. ODRA औड्र AND UTKALA.

P. 584 (510). Orissa is named after *Udras, Odras* or *Audras,* the Oretes of Pliny ; but their country could not have been the whole of it, for *Utkala* and *Kalinga* occupied portions of it.

Hence Epic Udra उड्र = Western Midnapur (E. part was in *Suhma*) and probably Manbhum, E. Singbhum and S. Bankura. Probably the *Udras* drove away the *Kalingas* and overran the whole of Orissa in a later period.

The *Utkalas* are linked with the *Mekalas* (Bhîshma-P. IX, 348 ; Drona-P. IV. 122), and with the *Kalingas* (Karna-P. XXII, 882). They were to the S. of R. Kapisâ कपिशा (=Kâsâi ; Raghu IV). Hence the *Utkala* country was the tract from Balasore to Lohârdâgâ and Sarguja (Pargiter.)

U-cha (Odra), 700 li S. W. of *Tâmralipti* (Life) or *Karnasuvarna* (Records) ; 7000 li in circuit. (Y. Ch. II, 193.).

To the S. E. of the province was a famous port, *Che-li-ta-lo,* outside which were five monasteries. (Y. Ch. II. 194).

As to the site of the city and port, Lt. Col. Dr. Waddel (Proceedings of A. S. B., 1892, p. 185) has pointed out that the tradition of the port of *Chitratola* is still current at the village of Nendra (about 15 m. below Cuttack) on an 'older channel of the Mahânadî' (still called *Chitrotola* river). [It is to be added that *Chitrotpalâ*, as a poetic name of the Mahânadî is still current (E. I., XII, p. 218)]; it is now 50 miles inland from the present coast line.

6. KONGODA. (कोङ्गोद)

P. 587 (513). Over 1200 li S. W. from the capital of *Odra* was *Kong-yu-to ;* capital bordering on a bay. (Y. Ch. II. 196.).

Its Skr. form is *Kongoda-(mandala)* mentioned in inscriptions (E. I., VI. 136) ; its overlord was Sasânka शशाङ्क (*Ibid*), and as such its inhabitants defied Harsha-vardhana (Y. Ch.).

SOUTHERN INDIA.

P. 590 (515). It is the *Dakshinâpatha* दक्षिणापथ in the wider sense, the land to the S. of the *Narmadâ ; "Mâhishmatyah Paratah Dakshinâpathah"* (*Kâvya-mimâmsâ*) ; *Mâhîshmatî* has been identified with *Mandhata* on the Narmadâ. *Dachinabades* of Periplus. (Schoff, p. 43). *Ta-thsin* of F. H. (Ch. XXXV.).

It was divided into 9 kingdoms in the time of Y. Ch.

1. KALINGA.

P. 590 (515). *Raghuvamsa* (IV. 38-43) shows that it was to the S. of *Vanga* beyond the R. *Kapisâ* कपिशा (mod. *Kâsâi on* which stands Midnapore) and that it stretched southwards so far as to include Mt. *Mahendra* (=portions of the Eastern Ghats above the Godâvarî). Mahâ Bh. (Vana-P. CXIV. 10096-10107) informs that the

Pândavas, travelling from the *Gangâsâgara* reached the *Kalingas* and the *Vaitaranî* वैतरणी about the same time (i.e. the N. boundary was the *Vaitaranî*). Thus the ancient *Kalinga* comprised modern Orissa to the S. of the Vaitarnî, and the seacoast southward as far as Vizagapatam. According to the Kûrma Purâna, II, XXXIX, 19 it included the *Amarakantaka* अमरकण्टक *hills* (in which the Narmadâ and the Sona rise). Its capital in the Epic period was *Râjapura* (Sânti-P. IV.) on the sea-coast. (Raghu, IV. 56) [Pargiter].

1400 or 1500 *li* (through jungle and dense forests) S.W. from *Kongoda* was *Ka-ling-ka*. (Y. Ch. II. 198).

The capital of this period, *Kalinganagara*, is mod. Mukhalingam and the adjacent ruins in Ganjam district. (E. I., IV. 187).

P. 592 (517). *Dantapura* दन्तपुर. the city of *tooth-relic*, existed ages before Buddha (*Jâtaka*, II, 367 ; Mahâvastu III, 361, etc. mention it as the capital) ; probably it is the *Dantakura* where *Krishna* crushed the *Kalingas* (Udyoga-P. XLVII, 1883) ; *Dandagula* or *Dandaguda*, the capital of *Calingoe*, mentioned by Pliny shows that the original form was Dantakura and not Dantapura. The latter form was evidently due to the common Prakrit form of *Danta-ura* and when the name of *Danta-pura* was coined, it was accounted for by explaining as 'the city of tooth (relic).' *Dantakura* seems to be of *Dravidian* origin, *Kura* standing for *Kurram*, a division. It is mod. Dantan (दँतन) on the Kâsâi.

2. (DAKSHINA) KOSALA. (कोसल)

P. 595 (519). It comprised the whole of the Upper Valley of the *Mahânadî* and its tributaries, from the source of the Narmadâ on the N. to the source of the Mahânadî itself on the S. and from the valley of the Wenganga (W.) to the Hasda and Jonk rivers (E.). Under some of the earlier rulers, the supremacy of the king of *Mahâ-kosala* was acknowledged by the Râjâs of Orissa. The ancient capital was *Sripura* श्रीपुर (Sirpur) on the Mahânadî (Raipur dist.); from this place *Tîvaradeva* issued a grant in or about 800 A.D. (Fleet's G.I., No. 81 : C.A.S.R., XVII., p. 68 ; A.S.I., N.I.S., XIX., p. 55 &c.) Other cities :—*Ratnapura,* the *Chedi* capital (C.A.S.R., VII., p. 214). Chanda (C.A.S.R., IX., p. 136, A.S.I., N.I.S., XIX., p. 12).

3. ANDHRA. (अन्ध्र)

P. 603 (527). Above 900 *li* (through a forest) S. (*Records*), or S. E. (*Life*) from *Kosala* was *An-to-lo* ; capital named *Ping-ki-lo* ; circuit 3000 *li*. (Y. Ch. II., 209).

Andhras, a rude race in early times (Mahâ Bh. Sabhâ-P. IV. 119 ; XXX. 1175 ; Vana-P. LI., 1988 etc.). Referred to by Megasthenes and in Asoka's inscriptions ; Andar of Pliny.

Warangol is the Muhammadan spelling of Orungallu (Skr. Ekasilâ एकशिला-nagarî). It became the capital of the *Kâkatîyas* since the days of *Rudradeva* (12th century A.D.). Before its foundation the *Kâkatîya* capital was *Anumakonda* or Hanumakonda (18° 1′ N.; 79° 34′ E.).

Inscriptions speak of it as a great city and as an ornament of the Andhra country. It contains some very interesting buildings of which the '1,000 pillared temple' was built in 1162 A.D. in the *Châlukyan* style. The places surrounding it were, in the earlier period, under the sway of the *Andhrabhrityas.* It was a part of the *Châlukya* kingdom. When Râjendra Chola II., the Eastern Châlukya king (1070) seized the *Chola* throne of his maternal grandfather, he was forced to leave the paternal kingdom in the hands of his viceroys in order to proceed to the South. Taking the advantage of the time we find the rise of an independent family, the *Kâkatîyas,* defeated by Malik Kafur (1310 A.D.) (Subrahmanya Aiyer's Ancient Dekhan, pp. 267-272).

The *Eastern Châlukya* capital (700 A.D. to 1100 A.D.) was *Vengi* [mod. villages of *Pedda* (Greater) *Vegi* and *Chinna* (Lesser) *Vegi* situated at a short distance from Lake Colair. (Sewell's Lists, I., 36 ; II., 239)] which sounds, according to Fergusson, supported by Rev. Beal, very like *Ping-ki-lo.* (J.R.A.S., Vol. VI., p. 261).

4. DHANAKATAKA. (धनकटक)

P. 607 (530). Cunningham identified the capital with Dharanikot (a mile W. of *Amarâvatî* on the *Krishnâ* famous for its marble scriptured stûpa ; Guntur District, Madras). Though the discovery of *Mauryan* and other inscriptions and ruins shows that it was *Dhanakataka,* one of the capitals of the *Andhras,* Y. Ch.'s description of the city and its hilly surroundings does not suit it. Hence Fergusson, Burgess and Sewell locate his city at Bezwada (J.R.A.S., 1873, p. 263 ; Vol. XII., pp. 98-109.) the Skr. form of which is Vijayavâdi ढि (Aiyangar's Anc. Ind. p. 48).

5. CHU-LI-YE.

P. 624 (545). Above 1000 *li* S. (*Life*) or S. W. (*Records*) from *Dhanakataka* was *Chu-li-ye* or *Jho-li-ye,* a wild jungle region ; it was 1500 or 1600 *li* N. of *Kânchîpuram.* (Y. Ch. II., 224 ; 226).

The name sounds like Skr. *Chola, Telugu* Chola, *Tamil* Sora (the Sora Regia Arcati of Ptolemy).

The Cholas are mentioned in the *Vârtikas* of *Kâtyâyana,* the inscriptions of Asoka and the Epics.

Their country was, in the early period, the east coast from the mouth of the *Krishnâ* to the S. of Tondi (Ramnad Zamindari, 10° N., 79° E.). (Aiyangar's Beg. S. I. H., p. 126-8). Their traditional capital was Uraiyur (Sanskritized as *Uragapura*, *Argaru* of Periplus ; also known as Koli ; mod. Trichinopoly) ; an alternative capital and port was *Puhar* or *Pugar—Kâveripattana*—which was a great emporium during the reign of *Kârikâla* ; *Kânchi* was also an important town, being the seat of a viceroy. (2nd century A. D.).

The *Pallavas*, who probably came from the west, made themselves lord of the country round *Kânchi* driving the *Cholas* to the S. of the *Palaru*. The Pândyas (पाण्ड्य) of Madurâ then began to molest the Cholas and, in the early part of the 7th century, made themselves lord of the *Chola* kingdom (Tanjore and Trichinopoly). The Cholas thereafter confined themselves to Cuddapah, Kurnool and Bellary districts where they were feudatories to the *Pallavas*. Y. Ch. saw them in this locality and 8th or 9th century A. D. inscriptions of local Chola chiefs have been discovered in the Cuddapah district. With the decline of the *Pallava* power (from the last quarter of the 8th century A. D. to the beginning of the 9th century) on account of their incessant struggles with the *Kadambas*, कादम्ब, *Châlukyas*, and *Pândyas*, the *Cholas* sought for supreme power. Internal dissension in the *Pândya* family at this period was also for their great advantage. And for nearly two centuries and a half (2nd quarter of the 9th century to 1070) the *Chola* kingdom became very powerful. Their empire comprised, in its palmy days, the whole of the Madras Presidency with Ceylon and a good portion of Mysore ; Pudukkottai, Cochin and Travancore states were also comprised in it. And the *Chola* inscriptions state that even the rulers of parts of central provinces, Bombay and Bengal were made feudatories to the *Cholas*. In 1070 Râjendra-Chola of the Eastern Châlukya family made himself master of the *Chola* throne of his maternal grandfather, and his family maintained the *Chola* glory up to 1278. Then *Chola* princes began to sink into a position of insignificance. It is to be noted that the name of *Coromondal* coast roughly indicates the *Chola* kingdom (Chodamandala चोड़मण्डल). (Subrahmanya Aiyer's Ancient Dekhan, pp. 183-262).

6. DRÂVIDA. (द्राविड़)

P. 627 (548). The word *Drâvida* is a Skr. form for Tamil. *Tamilakam* or Tamil country—Damirica of Periplus, Damirike of Ptolemy and the Peutingerian Tables. It is the southern part of the Peninsula bounded on the N. by the *Krishnâ* and the *Tungabhadrâ*. It traditionally contained the three dominions of *Chola, Chera* and *Pândya*. But Y. Ch. uses it in the narrower sense of the *Pallava* kingdom of *Kânchi*—one of the seven sacred cities of India.

Kânchîpuram is the sanskritized form of *Kachchippedu*. It was the chief town of *Eyil-kottam*, one of the 24 *Kottas* or districts of *Tondai-mandalam* or *Tundâkavishaya*. It is situated on the *Kambai* or *Vegavatî* river.

It was, in the early period, the seat of the *Chola* viceroys (2nd century A.D.). Then it became the capital of the *Pallavas* (mentioned, in the Purânas, with the Sakas and Yavanas) who probably came from the W. being driven by Gotamiputra Sâtakarni. They made themselves lord of the country round *Kânchi* driving away the *Kalingas* to the N. and the *Cholas* to the S. They had to fight continually for their existence. Their ruler *Vishnugopa* had to fight against the army of *Samudra-Gupta* who invaded their territory.

In the zenith of *Pallava* power, their territory included Bellary and a part of the present Mysore state, the mod. districts of N. Arcot, S. Arkot and Chingleput with a portion of Tanjore. In N., their arms were carried as far as Orissa.

Their incessant struggle with the *Kadambas*, W.

Châlukyas, Gangas, Pândyas, Cholas, and *Râshtrakûtas* (राष्ट्रकूट) caused their downfall. From the 10th to the 13th century *Kânchi* was the *Chola* capital. The *Kâkatîyas* of Warangol and the Telugu-Cholas from N. Arcot then took the country, but found competent rivals in the rising *Pândya* kings of Madurâ. After the invasion of Malik Kafur (1310 A.D.), several feudatory families asserted their independence. The *Vijayanagara* kings finally took possession of it (14th century) and retained it till the beginning of the 17th century (Subrahmanya Aiyer's Ancient Dekhan, pp. 1-65).

The *Pallava* rulers claimed descent from Asvathâman अश्वत्थामा, son of Drona. *Dharma-Mahârâjâdhirâja* was their usual epithet. Their surname was generally Varman. But *Gopa* also occurs. It is to be noted that many *Pallava-Gopas* dwell in the S. W. part of Bengal. Most probably they are the descendants of the *Pallavas* who migrated thither.

7. MO-LO-KU-TA.

P. 628 (548). 3000 *li* S. from Kânchi ; 5000 *li* in circuit ; towards the sea-coast ; in the S. of the country stood the sandal-producing Mo-la-ye mt. (Y. Ch. II. 228).

Malai is the Tamil for "hills"; *Ku-ta* stands for *Kotta* (=district) or *Kurram* (=division) (Hultzsch in I.A., 1889, p. 239).

Julien and Cunningham sanskritized it as *Malayakûta* (ट) . A Skr. name making the nearest approach to it is "*Malayakoti* टि)," mentioned in the com. on Arthasâstra, as a mt. in *Pândya* country and as a synonym of Pândya-kavâta पाण्ड्यकवाट mentioned by Kautilya as a source of pearls and referred to in the Râmâyana. It is the *Kavâta-puram* of Tamil literature. It was a mt., a door of the *Pândya* country, and a source of pearls ; hence it is to be identified with the promontory where the W. Ghats dip into the sea.

But 3000 *li* S. of *Kânchi* will not take so much to the S. The ancient road to the S. of *Kânchi* passed through Tirukkoilur, Trichinopoly (Uraiyur, Skr. उरगपुर, Argaru of Periplus), Tanjore district, and Kodumbai (in Pudukotta state), to Madurâ the capital of the *Pândyas*; and this route makes up the distance of 3000 *li*; hence the capital of *Mo-lo-ku-ta* is to be located somewhere near Madurâ. One of the most important territorial divisions of the *Pândya* country in ancient times was *Milalai-Kurram* (a division covering a large area surrounding Madurâ) and this may be Y. Ch.'s *Mo-lo-ku-ta* (deleting the intermediary *la*).

The pilgrim takes us from somewhere near *Madurâ* southwards to *Tinnevelly* (Tiru-Nelveli) district where he refers to the Sandal-producing *Malaya* mt.; then he speaks of *Potalika* i.e. the *Podiyamalai* hill giving us, as shown by Prof. Hultzsch, a distorted version regarding the sage Agastya who is frequently mentioned in Tamil literature as the family priest of the *Pândyas* (पाण्ड्य).

The *Pândyas* are mentioned in the Epics, the Vârttikas of *Kâtyâyana* and the inscriptions of Asoka. Megasthenes refers to *Pandœ*, the only Indian race ruled by women. The author of Periplus, Ptolemy and Pliny also mention them.

Their country corresponds to Madurâ and Tinnevelly (Tiru-Nelveli) districts, Travancore and parts of Coimbatore and Cochin. It included the chieftaincies of (1) *Aay* (*Aioi* of Ptolemy) round *Podyil* hill in W. Ghats S. of Palghat gap and W. of Tinnevelly, (2) *Evvi* round about the port of Korkai in Tinnevelly, and (3) *Pehan* round the Palnis. (Aiyangar's Beg. S.I.H., pp. 126-8.)

The capital was Madurâ (मथुरा). It was evidently so called after *Madhurâ* or *Mathurâ* (Muttra), the original city of *Pandœ*, the daughter of Herakles who ruled over the region round Muttra (Megasthenes). It was famous, according to *Kautilya,* for its cotton fabric. There was a viceroyalty at the port of Korkai (Colchi) the pearl-fisheries of which were worked by condemned criminals (Periplus). *Korkei* or *Kolkei* (=an army ; a camp) was the cradle of S. Indian Civilization—the place where, according to tradition, the three eponymous brothers *Cheran, Cholan* and *Pândyan* were said to have been born and brought up, and whence they set forth to form kingdoms. The insignificant village of *Kayal* (=a lagoon ; an opening into the sea) on the *Tâmraparnî,* some 3 miles below *Korkei,* was to be identified with the "*Cael*" *of Marco Polo,* the most important city and seaport on the eastern coast of India during the middle ages.

The Periplus mentions the ports of *Nelcynda* (mod. *Nîrkunram* and its outer port *Vaikkarai,* some 12 miles down the river) and *Bacare* and the harbour and the cape of *Comari* (Cape Comorin).

During the 2nd quarter of the 7th century A.D., Seliyan Sendan expanded the *Pândya* power far beyond its traditional limit by conquering the *Chola* and *Chera* territories and this expansion lasted for nearly two centuries. In the continued struggle between the *Cholas* and the *Pândyas,* the *Cholas* became successful in the end (middle of 9th century). But the *Pândyas* did not meekly bear the *Chola* yoke and there took place a series of chronic revolts from the 10th to the early part of the 13th century. During the middle of the 13th century, the *Cholas* were forced to yield back to the *Pândyas* the territory they had taken years to obtain from them. *Madurâ* was taken and looted by Malik Kafur in 1314. The kingdom of *Vijayanagara* finally extinguished the energy of the *Pândyas* by reducing them as vassals.

We have inscriptions of the *Pândyas* up to the 17th century. (Subrahmanya Aiyer's Ancient Dekhan, pp. 76-173.)

Megasthenes's account makes the *Pândyas* an Aryan tribe migrated from Muttra. But Tamil records connect them with the *Cholas* and *Cheras*. If the name be a *Drâvidian word* it means "the ancient inhabitants" (from *Pandu* "old times".)

CHERA OR KERALA.

The country of the *Cheras*, the *Keralaputras* of Asoka's Inscriptions, the Cerobothra of the Periplus, was to the N. of the *Pândya* country. It stretched right across the *Palghat* gap through Salem and Coimbatore. It contained (in the second century A.D.) the four feudatory chieftaincies of :—(a) Arayam in Mysore proper to the W. of the Western *Ganga* Kingdom of *Talakkâd* and to the N. of Kongu country (Coimbatore and S. part of Salem), (b) Parambunâdu, (c) Anji (southern half of Mysore and part of Salem) having for its chief city Togadûr (= Dharmapuri) and (d) Kollimalai in Salem. (Aiyanger's Beg. S. I. H., pp. 126-8.)

It is needless to add that the boundary varied from time to time ; thus Travancore and Cochin were sometimes in *Kerala* and sometimes in *Pândya*.

It was connected with *Pândya* by a high road from Madurâ which kept close to the banks of the R. *Vaigai* up to the *Palnis* and from there went up the hills and down again along the banks of the *Periyâr* to the town of *Vanji* or *Tiru-vanjaikkalam*, (=mod. Cranganore 10 miles E. of Ponnâni in Cochin state), the capital of the *Cheras*, situated near its mouth. Thence the road proceeded to Karûr (another city of the Cheras) on the *Kâveri*.

The Periplus mentions their ports of Naura (Cannanore), Tyndis (mod. Ponnâni) and Muziris (=Tamil Muyiri or Musiri=Cranganore.)

Y. Ch. does not mention them, because, their country was included, in his time, in the dominion of the *Pândyas*.

BANAVÂSI.

14° 32′ N., 75° 1′ E.; on the banks of the Varadâ (Wurda) river; in Sirsi Taluk, North Kânârâ district, (कर्णाट is a sanskritized form of *Kan-nadu=black country*).

It is referred to as a place where Asoka sent his missionaries. It was one of the capitals of the *Kadambas* (कदम्ब) (300—1200 A.D.) whose territory comprised the N. W. parts of Mysore and portions of N. Kanara. It was also called Vaijayantî (Buzantion).

GANGAVÂDI OR W. GANGA COUNTRY.

It comprised the greater portion of Mysore; boundaries—(N.) probably the *Krishnâ* and *Tungabhadrâ;* (N. E.) *Nolambavâdi* (first under *Pallava* and then under *Chola* overlordship); (S.) *Kongu;* (W.) *Banavâsi* and *Punnâda* (S. W. of Mysore.).

It is through this country the *Bhadrabâhu* led a Jaina migration from N. India (300 B. C.). Asoka's Siddâpur inscription is located within it. It probably became a new state after the fall of the *Andhras*.

Capitals:—the earliest *Ganga* capital was *Kuvalâla* (mod. Kolar in E. Mysore). In the 3rd century the capital was removed to Talekâd (Skr. *Talavanapura*) which is encircled by the Kâvery on three sides. A later royal residence was Mânyapura (mod. Manne a few miles from Bangalore). [Rice in Bhandarkar commemoration volume]. It was feudatory to the lords of *Mahârâshtra*.

In Y. Ch.'s time it acknowledged the overlordships of the *Châlukyas*. In the tenth century it was at the zenith of its power and prosperity well testified by the colossal 70 ft. high monolithic Jaina image standing on the summit of a granite hill 400 ft. high at *Sravan Belgola* (Hassan district, Mysore) of which Mr. Fergusson says

"Nothing grander or more imposing exists anywhere out of Egypt."

Gangavâdi was conquered by the *Cholas* (1004) from whose hands it passed, along with *Nolambavâdi,* (1116 A. D.) to the Hoysâla Ballâlas of *Dvârasamudra* (mod. Halebid in Hassan district ; 13° 13′ N., 76° E ; *Halebidu* means 'old capital') defeated by Malik Kafur in 1310. Out of the ruins of the *Yâdavas* of *Dvârasamudra* and of *Devagiri* sprang up the Empire of *Vijayanagara* (mod. Hampi, Bellary district, Madras.).

8. KONKANA. (कोङ्कण)

P. 632 (552). It is the country between the Western Ghats and the sea, from about Bombay southward to Goa ; in the wider sense it included the *Keralas, Tulangas, Saurâshtras, Karahâtakas, Karanâtas, Varvaras* and the *Konkanas proper.* (*Sahyâdrikhanda,* II, VI, 47-8). It was reclaimed by Parasu-Râma from the ocean. (I. A., 1874, p. 248).

In Konkana reigned the Mauryas (6th and 7th century A. D.) and the शीलाहार's.

2000 *li* N. (*Records*) or N.W. (*Life*) from *Kânchi* was *Kung*-ku-na-pu-lo (*Konkana-pura*) ; v. l. *Tu* for *Kung* i.e. *Dakhanapura ; 5000 li* in circuit. (Y. Ch. II. 237.)

The capital is Kopal or Kôkanur, still remarkable for some very old temples of about 700 A.D., 310 miles from Kânchi and 335 miles from Nasik. (Burgess, I.A., 1894, p. 28).

9. MAHÂRÂSTRA. (महाराष्ट्र)

P. 633 (553). '*Maharathi* ठ (mentioned in early inscriptions) is to be derived from the *Râshtrikas, Rattis* or Ratthas (of Asoka's Edicts) who appear to have added later, the word "Mahâ" (great) to glorify themselves. Their country is *Dakshina* or *Dekkan* in the narrowest sense. (R. G. Bhandarkar's E. H. D., Chap. I). It is said to be the *Ariake* (=Aparânta?) of Ptolemy (p. 39).

2400 or 2500 *li* (through a great forest-wilderness ravaged by wild beasts and harried by banded robbers) N. W. from *Kung-kun-na-pu-lo* was *Mo-ha-la-cha* (*or ta*) ; circuit 6000 *li* ; the *capital* was on the west of a great river, having 4 or 5 *stûpas* and a *Sanghârâma* to its south ; the reigning king was *Pu-lo-ki-she* (Pulakesin II). (Y. Ch. II, 239.).

Ancient capitals :—(1) *Pratisthâna* प्रतिष्ठान Paithan, on the Godâvarî ; the 'Baithana of Siro Polomaios' of Ptolemy (p. 176.) ; capital of the *Andhras* whose grandeur is referred to in Pilny IV. XXII, 4 ; 'Pœthana' of Periplus, (p. 43.). (2) *Kalyâna* of the Kshatrapas (19° 14′ N., 73° 14′ E.) on the eastern shore of the harbour of Bombay ; the Calliena of Periplus, (p. 43) ; (3) *Vâtâpi* (Badami in Bijapur district) of the early *Châlukyas.* (4) The real capital in Y. Ch.'s time was Badami ; but his description of the unnamed capital and its distance from Broach etc. show that it was *Nâsik*—the Nasika of Ptolemy (p. 156) and the *Nâsikya* of the *Mahâbhâshya.* (I. A. 1893, p. 113 ; 1894, p. 28). (5) *Mânyakhetaka* मान्यखेटक (Malkhed) of the *Râshtrakûtas.* (6) *Kalyâni* of the Later Châlukyas (near Bidar, in Nizam's dominion). (7) *Etagiri* (mod. Yatagiri, 80 m. S.E. of Kalyan), the capital of Vikramâditya Tribhuvanamalla. (8) Devagiri (Daulatabad) of the *Yâdavas.*

This country was a part of the Empire of Asoka as his *Soupara* and *Maski* inscriptions indicate. Asoka mentions the *Râshtrikas.* The *Andhras* coming from *Dhanakataka* on the E. coast occupied the whole of it and ruled from their Western Capital of *Pratisthâna.* During the time of *Samudra-Gupta's* conquest it was divided, according to Dr. V. Smith, into Devarâshtra देवराष्ट्र (Mahratta country) and *Erandapalla* एरण्डपल्ल

(Khandas). But J. Dubreuil (A. H. D., pp. 58-60) has shown that Samudra-Gupta had nothing to do with *Mahârâshtra* and that *Devarâshtra* and *Erandapalla* are to be located in the Madras Presidency. Then we find the *Vâkâtakas* [वाकाटक] (Raychaudhuri, P. H. A. I., pp. 276-7) and then the Early *Châlukya* Empire ; Pulakesin II was the lord of the whole of the Dekkan—defeating in battle the rulers of *Vanavâsi, Alupa, Konkana, Mahâkosala, Kalinga, Pithâpuram,* the country round *Colair* and *Kânchi*. The empire passed, with some loss, to the *Râshtrakûtas* and then to the Later *Châlukyas* of Kalyani. Now began struggle with the *Cholas* for the lordship of their borderlands. The *Karnâtaka* कर्णाटक or *Kuntala* empire of Vikramâditya Tribhuvanamalla (1076-1126) stretched southwards from the Satpura range to the end of the Dekkan plateau ; it contained the whole of *Rattappâdi* (Bombay Presidency to the S. of Vindhya), major portion of Nizam's dominions and portions of C. P. It contained some 12 important feudatory kings :—

(1) *Yâdavas of Seuna-Desa* सेउणदेश with capital first at *Sinnar* (near Nasik) and then at *Devagiri* (Daulatabad). (2) Sîlâhâras शीलाहार of N. and S. Konkan, and of (3) Kolhapur. (4) *Kadambas* कादम्ब of Goa and (5) of Hangal or Virâta's city in Dharwar. To their E. were (6) the *Sindas* of Yelburga. (7) The *Guttas* of *Guttal* in Dharwar. (8) *Rattas* of Saundatti in Belgaum. (9) Banavâsi (often under the *Kadambas*). (10)Nolambavâdi, then under *Pândya chiefs,* (11) Hoysâlas of Gangavâdi. (12) *Târdavâdi* round Vijayapura (Bijapur).

The dominions under the head quarters included (1) all the Nizam's dominion except the most E. part—the Khamamet division—and (2) the neighbouring parts of C. P.

After the overthrow of the *Châlukyas* the main portion of the empire was divided by the *Yâdavas* of

Devagiri and the *Hoysâlas* of *Dvâra-Samudra*—the *Malaprabhâ* and the *Krishnâ* rivers being the boundary line. This was the political geography up to the time of the inroad of Malik Kafur. (S. Krishnaswami Aiyangar's Ancient India, p. 141.)

OTHER IMPORTANT SITES :—

Souppara (Sûrpâraka शूर्पारक said to be founded by Parasu-Râma), where have been discovered fragments of the Rock edicts of Asoka. *Tagara* (Mod. Ter, in Nizam's dominion, J. R. A. S., 1901, pp. 537-52), Junnar (*Jîrnanagara* or "old town"; probably of Nahapâna), Karhad (करहाटक) Kolhapur, Elora or Elurâ (Skr. एलापुर of *Râshtrakûta* inscriptions wrongly identified by our author with Erâwal, p. 365) and Ajanta (which rose in importance under the Vâkâtakas and the early Châlukyas). (For the Ancient Geography of Mahârâshtra, vide J. Bombay Branch R. A. S., 1917.)

APPENDIX I

PURANIC NINE DIVISIONS OF GREATER INDIA.

Sir Alexander Cunningham has pointed out, in his Ancient Geography of India (p. 7), that the *Mahâbhârata*, the *Purânas and Bhâskarâchârya*, the astronomer, have given names of a *Nine-Division* of India and that the names are *Indra, Kaserumat, Tâmraparna, Gabhastimat, Kumârika, Nâga, Saumya, Vâruna* and *Gândharva.* No clue has been given, remarks he, to their identification. But he has suggested that Indra was the eastern division, Vâruna the western and Kumârika the middle, while Kaseru must have been the northern one.

Alberuni also has quoted this Purânic account and has added the following description :—(1) *Indradvîpa*—the middle, (2) *Kaserumat*—eastern, (3) *Tâmraparna*—south-eastern, (4) *Gabhastimat*—southern, (5) *Nâga*—south-western, (6) *Saumya*—western, (7) *Gândharva*—north-western, (8)————————, (9) *Nagarasamvritta*—north-eastern.

Thus the two authorities differ not only as to the location of the divisions, but as to one name also—the *Kumârika* of Cunningham appearing as *Nagarasamvritta* in the list of Alberuni who has not mentioned the 8th name.

Let us now refer to the original sources. The majority of the Purânas* agree in reading, in the

* भारतस्यास्य वर्षस्य नव भेदान् निबोध मे।
समुद्रान्तरिता ज्ञेयास्ते त्वगम्याः परस्परम्॥
इन्द्रद्वीपः कशेरुमान् ताम्रपर्णी गभस्तिमान्।
नागद्वीपस्तथा सौम्यो गान्धर्व्वो वारुणस्तथा॥
अयं तु नवमस्तेषां द्वीपः सागरसंवृतः।
योजनानां सहस्रं वै द्वीपोऽयं दक्षिणो त्तरात्॥
पूर्व्वे किराता यस्यान्ते पश्चिमे यवनास्तथा।

Bhuvanakosha section [*Mârkandeya* LVII; *Matsya* CXIV; *Vâyu* XLV, etc.], the first seven names of Alberuni but without giving any direction. Their eighth name is *Vâruna*. As for the ninth, they read

"अयं तु नवमस्तेषां द्वीपः सागरसंवृतः ।" "And this sea-girt isle is the ninth of them." Alberuni's *Nagarasamvritta* is thus a corruption of *Sâgarasamvrita* meaning 'Sea-girt'. The Purânas do not give any name to it and refer to it as a *dvîpa* too well-known to require the mention of its name. Râjasekhara, however, in his *Kâvyamîmâmsâ* (Gaekwad Oriental Series No. 1.) named it *Kumârî* and has supplied a clear clue to locate it by stating:—

"तत्रेदं भारतवर्षम् । अस्य च नव भेदाः । इन्द्रद्वीपः [etc.] .... कुमारीद्वीपश्चायं नवमः । ......अत्र च कुमारीद्वीपे

विन्ध्यश्च पारियात्रश्च शुक्तिमानृक्षपर्वतः ।
महेन्द्रसह्यमलयाः सप्तैते कुलपर्वताः ॥ Page 92

And the "Sea-girt ninth *dvîpa*" has also been thus described in the Purānas: "This *dvîpa* is a thousand yojanas from S. to N. At its east end are the Kirātas and at the west end are the Yavanas." [*Mārkandeya*, LVII, vv. 5-11.]

By combining these two accounts we find that the "Sea-girt ninth *dvîpa*" called *Kumārî* was the tract peopled by the Yavanas (Greeks) at its west end and by the Kirâtas (Mongoloid tribes) at its east end and having the mountain-chains now known as the Vindhyas, Western and Eastern Ghats and the Nilgiris in it. It is thus the whole of India, or almost the whole of it. And it has been described as one of the nine divisions of *Bhāratavarsha*. But it is absurd to take the whole as equal to its part. Hence either *Kumārî-dvîpa* cannot be the whole of India or the term '*Bhāratavarsha*' has been used here in a wider sense. But as the description of *Kumāri* is very clear, we cannot but take it as equal to almost the whole of India. So '*Bhāratavarsha*' is used here in a wider sense, in the *sense of Greater India, i.e.*

India proper and her colonies, eight *dvîpas* not far from it. That the *dvîpas* were separated from the main land of India by water is clear from the following Purānic account: "Hear from me the nine divisions of this country of *Bhārata* ; they must be known as extending to the ocean, but as being *mutually inaccessible.*" [*Mārkandeya*, LVII, 5.]. It is also to be added in this connection that the word *dvîpa* has been derived by *Pānini* as *dvi+ap*. It thus means land having water on two of its sides. Thus *dvîpa* is not identical with 'island'. It includes peninsulas and sometimes *doabs* also.

As for the identification of the other *dvîpas*, it requires no comment to take *Tāmraparna* as Ceylon. It is to the south of India. *Indradvîpa* is to be located to the east. For India is the eastern *Dikpāla*. The Purânas also corroborate it in a passage which describes the courses of seven rivers rising from बिन्दुसरस् in the Himalayas—the three western rivers, *Sîtâ, Chakshu* and *Sindhu*, the Gangâ, and the three eastern rivers, *Nalinî*, *Hlādinî* and *Pāvanî*. One of these eastern rivers is described as rising from बिन्दुसरस् in the Himalayas, flowing to the east and then to the south and then emptying its water into the Ocean near *Indradvîpa* [इन्द्र-द्वीप-समीपे तु प्रविष्टा लवणोदधिम् *Matsya*, CXXI. 57.] Thus *Indradvîpa* was Burma. And this conjecture seems to be supported by so great an authority as Ptolemy. While describing *India beyond the Ganges*, Ptolemy (M'Crindle, p. 219) mentions the country of *Kirrhadia* [=the किराताः placed, in the Purânas, to the east end of the *ninth 'dvîpa'*—the 'Sea-girt' Kumārî] producing *Malabathrum* ; then he locates the Silver country [Arakan] and then the "Gold country" [the *Suvarnabhûmi* of Buddhist literature and the Sonâparânta of Burmese documents]. And again he remarks (M'Crindle, p. 221), between the ranges of Bepyrrhos and Damassa the country furthest north is inhabited by the Aninakhai [occupying the mountain region to the north of the Brahmaputra, corresponding to a portion of Lower Assam—M'Crindle's note, p. 222] ; to the south of these Ptolemy places the *Indaprathai*. Thus in the *dvîpa* or peninsula of Burma and just to the south of Lower Assam we hear the name of *Inda* or *Indra*. *Prathai* is to be connected with *Prastha* meaning a plain level country.

Indra-dvîpa was, thus, Burma and it was to the east and *Tāmraparna* (Ceylon) to the south of India. Hence *Kaserumat* which is mentioned, in the Purānas, between them is to be located to the S.-E. of India. The word means 'abounding in excellent *Kaserus*' (called Kesur in Bengali and Kaseru in Hindi) for which Singapur is famous. So I propose to identify *Kaserumat* with the Malay Peninsula in the Wellesley district of which was discovered a fourth century A. D. Pillar inscription of the Buddhist Sea-Captain Mahānāvika Budha-gupta of Raktamr(i)ttikā (in Murshidabad district) showing that the Hindus were acquainted with it.*

The only other *dvîpa* which I can identify with certainty is *Gândharva*. It is identical with *Gândhâra*, the valley of the Kabul with a small tract of land to the east of the Indus. Its position in the Puranic list of eight *dvîpas* [*Indra* (E.), *Kaserumat* (S.E.), *Tāmraparna* (S), *Gabhastimat* (S.W.), *Nāga* (W.), *Saumya* (N.W.), *Gândharva* (N.) and *Vâruna* (N.E.)†] would suggest that it is the northern *dvîpa* (=doab) and Indian geographers placed *Gândhâra* to the N. (and not N.W.) of India.‡

---

* Kern's *Verspreide Geschriften*, III (1915), p. 255.

† Varuna is the lord of West and so Varuna ought to be located to the west. But the order of the *dvîpas* as mentioned in the Purânas would suggest that it is in the N.-E.

‡ See the Bhuvanakosha of the Purânas—मार्कण्डेय, LVII; मत्स्य CXIV; वायु, XLV—and the कूर्मविभाग of the बृहत्संहिता.

That the country of *Gândhâra* was also known as the Land of the *Gandharvas* is clear from the following verses of the *Rāmāyana* :—

अयं गन्धर्वविषयः फलमूलोपशोभितः ॥
सिन्धोरुभयतः पार्श्वे देशः परमशोभनः ।
तं च रक्षन्ति गन्धर्वाः सायुधाः युद्धकोविदाः ॥
[Rāmāyana, Uttarakānda, CXIII, 10-11.]

तक्षं तक्षशिलायां तु पुष्कलं पुष्कलावते ।
गन्धर्वदेशे रुचिरे गान्धारविषये च सः ॥
[Uttarakānda, CXIV, 11.]

These verses mean: This exceedingly charming *country on both the banks of the Sindhu* [*Indus*] decorated with fruits and roots *is the land* [विषय] *of the Gandharvas.* It is protected by the Gandharvas who are expert in fighting. [They were defeated by Bharata, the brother of Rāma ; their country was divided into two provinces, each of which was governed by a son of Bharata.] He (Bharata) installed his son Taksha at Takshasilâ and [his other son] Pushkala at Pushkalâvatî [identified with modern Charsada ; Peucelaotis of classical writers] in the charming *Gandharva*-country (also called) *Gândhâra-vishaya* (district). We thus see that *Gândharva* was Gândhâra. It was, as Yuan Chwang has aptly remarked, the border-land of the Barbarians who were Indians in culture and religion (*i.e.* Buddhism). So it was considered as a separate *dvîpa* included within Greater India and not as a part of India proper.

As for the four other *dvîpas*, a search is to be made for them keeping in view their directions as suggested by the order of their names in the Purânic list. *Gabhastimat*, *Nâga*, and *Saumya* are to be located in S.-W., W. and N.-W. respectively. And we have Laccadive, Maldive or Ernaculam in the S.-W., Salsette, Elephanta (meaning the same as *Nâga* or Elephant), and Kathiawar in the W., and Cutch in the N.-W. (according to the direction of

Kûrmavibhâga and Bhuvanakosha). Vâruna of N.-E. seems to be the Indian colony in Central Asia the exploration and research in connection with which by Sir A. Stein and a host of Russian, French, German, English and Japanese scholars are supplying new light on Indian culture.

The above are my suggestions for the location of the eight *dvîpas* of the Purânas. As for the location of *Indra, Tâmraparna* and *Gândharva* there cannot be any doubt. Tâmraparna has long ago been correctly identified. The two others I identify—*Indra* on the authority of the Purānas and Ptolemy and *Gândharva* on the authority of the Râmâyana. As for the location of others I offer suggestions only. But what I have pointed out is enough to show that the Purânic nine divisions of Bhâratvarsha are not so many provinces of India but of *Greater India.*

[Reprinted from my article in the Journal of the Bihar and Orissa Research Society 1922, March.]

APPENDIX II

ABBREVIATIONS USED IN THE NOTES.

Alberuni.—Sachau's English translation of Alberuni's India (Trübner's Oriental Series ; original edition in two volumes).

Aiyangar's Beg. S. I. H.—Aiyangar's Beginnings of South Indian History. (Madras University Lectures).

Ann(ual) R(ep.) A. S. I.—Annual Report Archœological Survey of India. (Director General's Report).

A. S. I., N. I. S.—(Reports of the) Archœological Survey of India, New Imperial Series.

A. S. W. I.—Archœological Survey of Western India.

Bhuvanakosha—मार्कण्डेयपुराण LVII.; मत्स्य, CXIV.; वायु XLV.

Camb. H. I.—Rapson's Cambridge History of India, vol. I.

C. A. S. R. ; Cunningham (A. S. R.)—Cunningham's Reports on the Archœlogical Survey of India in 23 volumes.

E. H. D.—Sir R. G. Bhandarkar's Early History of Dekkan.

E. H. I.—V. Smith's Early History of India (3rd Edition).

E. I.—Epigraphica Indica.

F. H.—Fa Hian. (All references are to Chapters).

Fleet's G. I.—Fleet's Gupta Inscriptions (Corpus vol. III).

(Führer's) Mons Antiq.—Führer's List of Monuments and Antiquities in N. W. Province (=U. P.), Archœological Survey of India.

I. A.—Indian Antiquary.

Ind. Alter.—Lassen's Indische Altertumskunde.

Imp. Gaz. Ind.—Imperial Gazetteer of India. New Edition.

J. A. S. B.—Journal of the Asiatic Society of Bengal.

J. B. B. R. A. S.—Journal of the Bombay Branch of the Royal Asiatic Society.

J. R. A. S.—Journal of the Royal Asiatic Society.
Kûrmavibhâga—बृहत्संहिता XIV.; Utpala's Com. on it gives quotations from पराशर; मार्कण्डेय LVIII.

M. Bh.
Mahâ Bh. } —Mahâ Bhârata.

Matsya—Matsya Purâna. (Bangabâsî Press, Calcutta, Original Edition in Devanâgarî).

Mâr—Mârkndeya Purâna (Pargiter's), Asiatic Society of Bengal's publication.

Periplus.—Schoff's translation.

Ptolemy—M'Crindle's translation of Ptolemy's Geography.

Raichowdhury's P.H.A.I.—Political History of Ancient India by Hem Chandra Raichowdhury. (Calcutta University Publication).

Sewell's List—Sewell's List of antiquities in Madras Presidency. (Arch. Surv.).

Vâyu—Vâyu Purâna (Asiatic Society of Bengal).

Y. Ch.—Yuan Chwang (Houen Tsiang); Watters' translation of his travels has been referred to

INDEX

N.B.—*An asterisk indicates that the word has been treated in the notes.*

INDEX TO NOTES.

N.B.—Words marked with an asterisk in the "Index to the Text" have, as a rule, not been repeated here.